For Kyung-Ae

With warm regards,

BC

7-20-07

BETWEEN
DISCORD AND COOPERATION
JAPAN AND THE TWO KOREAS

Byung Chul Koh

Yonsei University Press

Acknowledgments

While working on this project intermittently since 1989 I have incurred tons of debt to numerous institutions and individuals in both Japan and South Korea. To mention the institutions that have supported my project with fellowships, grants, and visiting faculty or research appointments, I am most grateful to the Japan–Korea Cultural Foundation (Nikkan Bunka Koryu Kikin), the Committee on the International Exchange of Scholars (Fulbright), the University of Tsukuba, Daito Bunka University (Tokyo), Temple University Japan (Tokyo), Seoul National University, the Institute of Social Sciences (Seoul), and Yonsei University (Seoul).

Of the numerous individuals in Japan who gave generously of their time, shared their experience in dealing with North and South Korea, and kindly made available to me documents and materials that were otherwise inaccessible to a foreign researcher, the following members, either retired or active, of the Japanese Foreign Ministry merit special mention: Sunobe Ryozo (former administrative vice-minister), Tanino Sakutaro (director-general of the Asian Affairs Bureau), Tanaka Hitoshi (director of the Northeast Asia Division), Nakamura Shigeru (director of the Northeast Asia Division), Abe Takaya (area coordinator of the same division), Yamamoto Eiji (deputy director of the same division), Soma Hirohisa (deputy director of the same division), Matsui Sadao (assistant director of the same division), Iwamoto Takuya (Intelligence and Analysis Bureau), Shibuya Haruhiko (consul-general in Chicago), and Terasawa Genichi (consul in Chicago). I must also mention the late Fujii Arata (director of the Northeast Asia Division, 2003-2004), whose untimely death in January 2004 was a great loss not only to the Japanese Foreign Ministry but to the small community of exceptionally competent Korea specialists in Japan. Fluent in Korean, Fujii was both a source of valuable information and insight and a dear friend to me.

Members of other Japanese government or government-affiliated organizations that gave me the benefit of their expertise and insights include Sakai Takashi (Public Security Investigation Agency), Satoh Hirotake (Cabinet Information Research Office), Komaki Teruo (Institute of Developing Economies), and Hirota Takao (Japan Foundation).

I was most fortunate to have the opportunity to interview the Hon. Ishii Hajime, member of the House of Representatives (Shugiin), who played a pivotal role in Kanemaru Shin's visit to the Democratic People's Republic of Korea in 1990. For introducing me to Representative Ishii and helping me secure a visiting professorship at Temple University Japan for two consecutive summers, I express my heartfelt thanks to Dr. Higashi Chikara, former Shugiin member and chancellor of the university.

Numerous scholars in Japan have enriched my understanding of Japan—Korea relations and helped me in countless other ways. They include Ichikawa Masaaki (Aomori University), Izumi Hajime (University of Shizuoka), Ijiri Hidenori (University of Tsukuba), Okonogi Masao (Keio University), Hanai Hitoshi (University of Tsukuba), Suzuki Masayuki (Seigakuin University), Sakata Yasuyo (Kanda University of International Studies), Hiraiwa Shunji (University of Shizuoka), Hattori Tamio (Tokyo Keizai University), Nagano Shinichiro (Daito Bunka University), Whang Soon Hee (University of Tsukuba), Wada Haruki (University of Tokyo) and Takesada Hideshi (National Institute for Defense Analysis).

In the Republic of Korea I had the good fortune of having friends—

most of whom are former classmates or seniors (sonbae) from high school or college days—in key government positions, who provided invaluable assistance by sharing their expert knowledge with me and by introducing me to working-level officials who in turn gave me most useful information and materials related to my project. I wish to express my profound thanks to them as well as to the diplomats to whom they introduced me: Lee Hong Koo (prime minister), Yoo Chong Ha (foreign minister), Han Sungjoo (foreign minister),Lee Joung Binn (foreign minister), Lee See Young (vice foreign minister), Lee Ki-Joo (vice foreign minister), Park Sang seek (chancellor of the Foreign Ministry's Institute of Foreign Affairs and National Security), Lee Chang Ho (ambassador to Israel), Kim Chung Gi (ambassador to Saudi Arabia), Choi Sang Yong (ambassador to Japan), Yoon Hyung Kyu (consul–general in Osaka), Yu Byung Woo (director-general of the Foreign Ministry's Asian Affairs Bureau), Shim Yoon Jae (director of its Northeast Asia Division I), Cho Jung-Pyo (director of its Northeast Asia Division I), Shin Kak-Soo (director of its Northeast Asia Division I), and Park Joon Woo (director of its Northeast Asia Division I).

Of the many friends in academia who have helped me both substantively and logistically during my long sojourns in and frequent visits to Seoul, I am most indebted to Kim Kyung Won (president of the Institute of Social Sciences), Youn Jung Suk (Joong-Ang University), Chey Myung (Seoul National University), Kil Soong Hoom (Seoul National University), Moon Chung-In (Yonsei University), Lee Jung Hoon (Yonsei University),Gong Yooshik (Ajou University) and Choi Eunbong (Ewha Womans University).

I would also like to acknowledge the able research assistance of Korean graduate students in Japan in the various stages of my research, of whom four merit special recognition: Bae Chung Nam (University of Tsukuba), Kim Woong Hee (University of Tsukuba), Cho Jin Gu (University of Tokyo) and Lee Won Duk (University of Tokyo). I am deeply appreciative of the friendship and support of Tsutsui Tetsuro, a former classmate of my brother-in-law at the University of Tokyo (mechanical engineering), who has kindly sent me books, magazines, and other materials related to my research for over two decades. I also express my heartfelt thanks to Hasegawa Toshihiro, my former high school classmate, for his warm friendship and boundless hospitality. Finally, I am greatly indebted to the East Asia Foundation for kindly sponsoring this book. Its secretary general, Hong Hyung Taek, moreover, oversaw every phase of the book's production with an extraordinary degree of dedication and professionalism. I express my heartfelt thanks to him and his staff, particularly, Assistant Program Officer Che Sohee.

B.C. Koh

Note on Romanization of Japanese and Korean Terms

For the Romanization of Japanese words and names, I use the Hepburn system without diacritical marks.

For the Romanization of Korean words and names, I adopt the McCune-Reischauer system without diacritical marks. Exceptions are made, however, for the names of South Korean newspapers and well-known persons whose idiosyncratic spellings are known. This applies to the names of North Korean leaders and officials as well.

Finally, for all Japanese and Korean names, I follow the custom of putting the family name first, even though Japan's English-language newspapers follow the Western custom.

Table of Contents

Acknowledgments | 5
Note on Romanization of Japanese and Korean Terms | 9
Introduction | 13

Part I Japan and North Korea

Chapter 1 From *Seikei Bunri* to Diplomatic Negotiations ········ 37

Chapter 2 Normalization Talks, 1991-1992 ···························· 77

Chapter 3 Nuclear and Humanitarian Issues ····················· 115

Chapter 4 The Persistence of Discord and the Limits
 of Cooperation ··· 191

Part II Japan and South Korea

Chapter 5 Between Discord and Cooperation:
Japan-ROK Normalization and Its Aftermath ········· 265

Chapter 6 Japan-ROK Summit Diplomacy, 1990-1995 ············ 301

Chapter 7 The Resilience of Conflict in Japan-ROK Relations ··· 343

Chapter 8 Forging a Future-oriented Japan-ROK Relationship:
A Long Road Ahead ·· 437

Chapter 9 Conclusion ··· 499

Appendix 1 Treaty of Basic Relations between Japan and The Republic of Korea | 511
Appendix 2 Japan-DPRK Pyongyang Declaration | 515
Bibliography | 519
Index | 545
About the Author | 551

Introduction

Why do states cooperate with each other? What accounts for their failure to do so? Under what conditions does non-cooperation escalate to conflict? These are among the most important questions in the study of international relations and foreign policy. Amid a dizzying array of ideas, approaches, and propositions, one can nonetheless find consensus on the definition of cooperation. As far as the key variables that help explain its occurrence, intensity, scope, and duration are concerned, however, scholarly opinion is more divided.

According to Robert D. Putnam and Nicholas Bayne, interstate cooperation occurs when "the policies of one or more states are modified to reduce the costs (or increase the benefits) that those policies entail for the welfare of other states, so that national policies differ from those that would have been expected from purely unilateral or autarkic policy-making."[1] Robert O. Keohane argues that cooperation needs to be distinguished from harmony, which "refers to a situation in which actors'

---

1 Robert D. Putnam and Nicholas Bayne, *Hanging Together: Cooperation and Conflict in the Seven-Power Summits*, revised and enlarged ed. (Cambridge, MA: Harvard University Press, 1987), 2.

policies (pursued in their own self-interest without regard to others) *automatically* facilitate the attainment of others' goals." Unlike harmony, however, cooperation "requires active attempts to adjust policies to meet the demands of others."[2]

Conflict or "discord" refers to "a situation in which governments regard each other's policies as hindering the attainment of their goals, and hold each other responsible for these constraints." "Cooperation," Keohane stresses, "should not be viewed as the absence of conflict or potential conflict. Without the specter of conflict, there is no need to cooperate."[3]

Depending on one's theoretical or methodological orientation, ideas on how to explain cooperation diverge to a considerable degree. Methodologically, game theory has provided core concepts and propositions. The dominance of game theoretic-approach becomes apparent when one reviews the literature on cooperation. A preponderance of books, not to mention journal articles, on cooperation utilizes game theory, and Prisoner's Dilemma (PD) is a metaphor that is familiar to non-game theorists as well.[4]

---

2 Robert O. Keohane, *After Hegemony: Cooperation and Discord in the World Political Economy* (Princeton: Princeton University Press, 1984), 51.
3 Ibid., 52 and 54.
4 To mention some of the books that rely heavily on game theory: Robert Axelrod, *The Evolution of Cooperation* (New York: Basic Books, 1964), Kenneth A. Oye, ed., *Cooperation Under Anarchy* (Princeton, NJ: Princeton University Press, 1985), Michael Taylor, *The Possibility of Cooperation* (Cambridge, England: Cambridge University Press, 1987), Joseph M. Grieco, *Cooperation Among Nations: Europe, America, and Non-tariff Barriers to Trade* (Ithaca, NY: Cornell University Press, 1990), Arthur A. Stein, *Why Nations Cooperate: Circumstance and Choice in International Relations* (Ithaca: Cornell University Press, 1990), and Helen V. Milner, *Interests, Institutions, and Information: Domestic Politics and International Relations* (Princeton: Princeton University Press, 1997). Two books that are not explicitly game-theoretic in orientation are Thomas Risse-Kappen, *Cooperation among Democracies: the European Influence on U.S. Foreign Policy* (Princeton: Princeton University Press, 1995) and Benjamin Miller, *When Opponents Cooperate: Great Power Conflict and Collaboration in World Politics* (Ann

The key explanatory variables in the study of international cooperation include the following:
1. National interests
2. National power
3. Number of actors
4. Iteration or the "shadow of the future"
5. International regimes
6. Epistemic community
7. Ideas, learning, and other cognitive factors
8. Domestic politics

Of the preceding, number of actors and iteration have the unmistakable imprint of game theory,[5] and domestic politics has been encapsulated in its vocabulary as well, namely as "two-level games."[6] The remaining variables emanate from the contending "schools of thought" in International Relations (IR)—neorealism or structural realism and neoliberalism or liberal institutionalism.[7] Whereas the former privileges national interests and national power, the latter underscores international regimes, epistemic community, and ideas. Such ideational factors as

---

Arbor, MI: University of Michigan Press, 1995).

5 "Number of actors" refers to the hypothesis that "the prospects for cooperation diminish as the number of players increases" due in large part to the problem of defection. Iteration or the shadow of the future refers to the hypothesis focusing on the player's expectations about the future. "Their willingness to cooperate is influenced by whether they believe they will continue to interact indefinitely." Helen Milner, "International Theories of Cooperation among Nations: Strengths and Weaknesses," *World Politics* 44, no. 3 (April 1992): 473-75; Oye, ed., *Cooperation under Anarchy*, 12-14.

6 Robert D. Putnam, "Diplomacy and Domestic Politics: The Logic of Two-level Games" in *Double-Edged Diplomacy: International Bargaining and Domestic Politics*, ed. Peter B. Evans et al. (Berkeley: University of California Press, 1993), 431-68 (Appendix).

7 As Robert Jervis reminds us, "they are better labeled schools of thought or approaches than theories." See his "Realism, Neoliberalism, and Cooperation: Understanding the Debate," *International Security* 24, no. 1 (Summer 1999): 43, footnote 3.

ideas, identity, and culture play a pivotal role in the research programs of scholars who embrace constructivism.[8]

Neorealism and International Cooperation

Tracing its lineage from classical realism, neorealism or structural realism is most closely identified with Kenneth N. Waltz.[9] To the core assumptions of the classical realists—such as the primacy of states as actors in world politics, the salience of power as the main goal and determinant of state behavior, and the assumption of rationality in state behavior[10]—, the neorealists have added a structural explanation of politics, that is, how the attributes of the international system condition the behavior of states. The foremost "ordering principle" of the international system, the realists argue, is anarchy, the absence of any central authority to regulate the sovereign states. Also important are the distribution of power and the placement of states in the pecking order. Small states will behave differently from bigger and more powerful ones;

---

8 Constructivism has many versions. For widely varying explanations of its key tenets and approaches, see Ronald L. Jepperson et al., "Norms, Identity, and Culture in National Security" in *The Culture of National Security: Norms and Identity in World Politics*, ed. Peter J. Katzenstein (New York: Columbia University Press, 1996), 33-75; Alexander Wendt, *Social Theory of International Politics* (Cambridge, England: Cambridge University Press, 1999); Vendulka Kubalkova et al., eds., *International Relations in a Constructed World* (Armonk, NY: M.E. Sharpe, 1998); Ralph Pettman, *Commonsense Constructivism or the Making of World Affairs* (Armonk, NY: M.E. Sharpe, 2000).
9 Kenneth N. Waltz, *Man, the State and War: A Theoretical Analysis* (New York: Columbia University Press, 1964) and idem, *Theory of International Politics* (New York: Random House, 1979).
10 Among the best known works of classical realists are Thucydides(c. 400 B.C.), *History of the Peloponnesian War*, translated by John H. Finley, Jr. (New York: Modern Library, 1951); Edward H. Carr, *The Twenty Years' Crisis, 1919-1939* (New York: Harper & Row, 1964); Hans J. Morgenthau, *Politics Among Nations: The Struggle for Power and Peace*, 4th ed. (New York: Knopf, 1967).

alliances will shift in response to changes in the distribution of power in a balance of power system.[11]

Neorealists' belief that states seek "relative gains from international cooperation" leads them to be pessimistic about its feasibility. According to Waltz:

> When faced with the possibility of cooperation for mutual gains, states that feel insecure must ask how the gain will be divided. They are compelled to ask not "Will both of us gain?" but "Who will gain more?" If an expected gain is to be divided, say, in the ratio of two to one, one state may use its disproportionate gain to implement a policy intended to damage or destroy the other. Even the prospect of large absolute gain for both parties does not elicit their cooperation so long as each fears how the other will use its increased capabilities.[12]

Additionally, realists, both classical and structural, assert that preoccupation with security and power predisposes states toward conflict and competition. Nor do realists share the neoliberal view that international regimes can mitigate the adverse effects of anarchy on the willingness of states to cooperate.[13]

Neoliberalism and International Cooperation

Neoliberalism or the "modified structural research program," as Keohane puts it, differs from neorealism in several aspects:

First, while acknowledging the pivotal role of states, neoliberalism also stresses the influence of nonstate actors, intergovernmental organizations, and transnational and transgovernmental relations.[14]

---

11 Waltz, *Theory of International Politics*, especially chap. 5 and 6.
12 Ibid., 105.
13 Grieco, *Cooperation among Nations*, 4.

Second, although neoliberalism retains the "rationality assumption," it notes that the postulate "does not assume perfect information, consideration of all possible alternatives, or unchanging actor preferences."[15]

Third, while regarding power and influence as "important state interests," the modified structural approach would reject the realist "implication that the search for power constitutes an overriding interest in all cases, or that it always takes the same form."[16]

Fourth, the modified structural approach revises the neorealist assumption of fungibility, arguing that the "value of power resources for influencing behavior in world politics depends on the goals sought" and that "power resources are differently effective across issue-areas."[17]

Finally, the modified structural approach "would pay much more attention to the roles of institutions and rules than does Structural Realism."[18] One should note the liberal institutionalists' reliance on "regime theory," which posits that international regimes—the set of norms, rules, and procedures that structure actors' expectations—can help foster cooperation by monitoring compliance and by increasing the costs of noncompliance.[19]

A few additional differences between neorealism and neoliberalism should be noted. First, the neoliberals take issue with the neorealist idea on the primacy of *relative* gains, leaning toward the proposition that "actors with common interests try to maximize their *absolute gains*."[20]

---

14 Koehane, ed., *Neorealism and Its Critics*, 193.
15 Ibid., 194.
16 Ibid., "Over the long run," Keohane writes, "whether an environment is malign or benign can alter the standard operating procedures and sense of identity of the actors themselves."
17 Ibid.
18 Ibid.
19 Stephen D. Krasner, ed., *International Regimes* (Ithaca, NY: Cornell University Press, 1983); Keohane, *After Hegemony*, 85-109.
20 David A. Baldwin, ed., *Neorealism and Neoliberalism: The Contemporary Debate* (New York: Columbia University Press, 1993), 6 (emphasis added).

Second, neoliberals tend to stress economic welfare more than national security, and neorealists exhibit the opposite predilection. Their differing estimates of the ease and probability of international cooperation may be related to this phenomenon.[21]

Third, neorealists and neoliberals disagree on the relative importance of capabilities and intentions. According to Joseph M. Grieco, "uncertainties about the future intentions and interests of other states lead statesmen to pay close attention to capabilities," which he labels "the ultimate basis for their security and independence." In Keohane's view, however, the "sensitivity of states to the relative gains of other states is significantly influenced by perceptions of the intentions of such states. Thus states worry more about relative gains of enemies than of allies."[22]

Constructivism and International Cooperation

If neoliberalism represents a "moderate critique" of neorealism, then "constructivism" poses a more "radical challenge" to the neorealist logic.[23] Just as both neorealism and neoliberalism display some diversity among their respective adherents, so constructivism encompasses varying degrees of commitment to its central postulates and even disagreement on what the latter should be. Alexander Wendt calls his own approach a "thin" variant of constructivism, a "moderate" version. Two "basic tenets" of constructivism, according to Wendt, are the following: (1) "the structures of human association are determined primarily by shared ideas rather than material forces" and (2) "the identities and interests of purposive actors are constructed by these shared ideas rather than given by nature."[24]

Constructivists' emphasis on the cultural-institutional context of state

---

21 Ibid., 7.
22 Ibid.
23 Muthiah Alagappa, ed., *Asian Security Practice: Material and Ideational Influences* (Stanford, CA: Stanford University Press, 1998), 59-60.
24 Wendt, *Social Theory of International Politics*, 1-2.

behavior, it must be noted, is shared by the neoliberals; what set the former apart from the latter, however, is the insistence that "cultural environments affect not only the incentives for different kinds of state behavior but also the basic character of states—what we call state 'identity.'"[25] This concept, which functions as a "crucial link between environmental structures and interests," is borrowed from social psychology, "where it refers to the images of individuality and distinctiveness ("selfhood") held and projected by an actor and formed (and modified over time) through relations with significant 'others.' Thus the term (by convention) references mutually constructed and evolving images of self and others."[26]

External cultural environments affect state identities, and their interests and policies, in at least three ways. "First, they may affect states' prospects for survival as entities in the first place." "Second, environments may change the modal character of statehood in the system over time." Change in "international norms and domestic factors," for example, "has 'tamed' the aggressive impulses of many states, especially in the West, thus creating a disposition to see war as at best a necessary evil." "Finally, cultural environments may cause variation in the character of statehood within a given international system. The aftermath of World War II, for example, initiated a period of identity politics in both Germany and Japan, which generated 'trading state' identities."[27]

In sum, from a constructivist perspective, ideational factors eclipse material ones in shaping state behavior in the international arena, including international cooperation. Of particular importance is state identity, which is constructed through dynamic interaction between states, their leaders and people on the one hand and their cultural and social environments on the other.[28]

---

25 Jepperson et al., "Norms, Identity, and Culture in National Security," 33.
26 Ibid., 5.
27 Ibid., 35-36.
28 For useful ideas on "national identity" by scholars who do not identify themselves with constructivism, see Lowell Dittmer and Samuel S. Kim, "In

Japan and the two Koreas

The two sets of bilateral relationships between Japan and Korea—Japan-the Republic of Korea (ROK) and Japan-the Democratic People's Republic of Korea (DPRK)—are marked by a cycle of cooperation and conflict, large and small. Cooperation between Japan and the ROK has ranged from inter-governmental negotiations on diplomatic normalization, fisheries, and other issues to the forging of a quasi-alliance against a common threat. Inter-governmental negotiations, however, not only exemplify a form of cooperation but also entail conflicts of varying intensity. The historical legacy of Japanese colonial rule in Korea, a territorial dispute, fishing, and perennial trade imbalance—these have remained the principal sources of conflict.

Japan-DPRK relations, by contrast, have been notable more for instances of conflict than for episodes of cooperation. Cooperation, nonetheless, has taken the form of negotiations, both governmental and quasi-governmental; a repatriation of thousands of Korean residents in Japan to the North; personnel exchanges; and humanitarian assistance from Japan to the DPRK. Conflicts have flared up over alleged abductions, terrorist incidents aimed at the ROK, the firing of ballistic missiles over Japan, and the North's suspected nuclear weapons program. Even inter-governmental negotiations have been so contentious on many occasions that one hesitates to cite them as an example of cooperation.

All this makes the two dyads an ideal laboratory in which to test the ideas and propositions about international cooperation adumbrated in the preceding pages. Not only can the major episodes of cooperation and conflict be analyzed through the prism of neorealism, neoliberalism, and constructivism, but comparison can be made between the two dyads as well as longitudinally within each of the three states. That is, how do the

Search of a Theory of National Identity" in *China's Quest for National Identity*, eds. Lowell Dittmer and Samuel S. Kim (Ithaca, NY: Cornell University Press, 1993), 1-31 and Samuel S. Kim and Lowell Dittmer, "Whether China's Quest for National Identity?" in ibid, 237-290.

patterns differ, both empirically and theoretically, between Japan-ROK and Japan-DPRK relations? Did North Korean policy manifest any notable change after Kim Il Sung's 46-year rule ended in 1994? Did South Korea's democratic transition in 1987 make any difference in its relations with Japan? Finally, in what ways, if any, is Japan's policy toward the two Korean states different in the post-hegemonic era—that is, after the 38-year hegemonic rule by the Liberal-Democratic party ended in 1993?

From a practical standpoint, an understanding of what kinds of bilateral relations Japan and the two Koreas have had over the years and, especially, of whether cooperation has eclipsed conflict or vice versa can be useful. For one thing, the relative importance of all three players makes

<Table 1> Japan, South Korea, and North Korea:
A Comparison of Selected Attributes/Indicators

Attribute or Indicator	Japan	South Korea	North Korea
Area (in km^2)	377,899	99,268	121,608
Population (2004) (in thousands)	127,690	48,082	22,522
Nominal GDP (2004) (in billion US$)	4,920	680.1	20.8
Per capita GDP (in current US$)	38,533	14,162	914
External trade (2004) (in million US$)	1,019.700	478,307	2,860
Total armed forces	148,000	690,000	1,100,000
Tanks	980	2,330	3,500
Armored vehicles	970	2,250	2,300
Naval vessels number	150	190	730
total weight (in 1000 tons)	426	148	103
Tactical aircraft	480	600	580

SOURCES: Boeicho (ed.), *Nihon no boei, Heisei 17-nenban* (Tokyo: K.K. Gyosei, 2005); Taehan Minguk Kukbangbu, *Kukbang paekso*, 2004(Seoul,2004); Somusho, Tokei-kyoku, *Nihon no Tokei, 2005* (Tokyo: Kokuritsu Insatsu-kyoku, 2005); Ministry of Internal Affairs and Communication, *Statistical Handbook of Japan, 2005*(Tokyo, 2005); Hanguk Unhaeng, *Kyongje t'onggye yonbo, 2005* (Seoul, 2005); Kukbang-bu, *Kukbang paekso, 2004* (Seoul, 2004).

it worthwhile to know how they have dealt with each other.

Japan is the world's second largest economy and one of the leading trading nations. Although the United States eclipses Japan in terms of the value of total trade, Japan is unsurpassed in terms of trade balance; no other nation has compiled such a strong record of consecutive trade surpluses for so many years on such a large scale as Japan has.[29] What is more, Japan's scintillating performance in global trade has been unaffected by its prolonged recession at home. Japan's military alliance with the US is also noteworthy, a factor that adds a special dimension to Japan's interactions with the two Korean states.

South Korea also commands attention because it is a powerhouse in the world marketplace.[30] Until recently, it boasted one of the fastest growing economies in the world and appeared to have made a transition from a newly industrializing country (NIC) to an advanced industrialized nation, as its admission to the Organization of Economic Cooperation and Development (OECD) in 1996 signaled.[31] In late 1997, however, a

---

29 In 2004 the value of the global merchandise trade of the U.S. exceeded $2,287 billion, more than twice that of Japan. The U.S., nonetheless, had a deficit of $652 billion, while Japan had a surplus of $110 billion. For U.S. trade data, see the Web site of the U.S. Department of Commerce, Office of Trade and Industry Information at http://tse.export.gov. For Japanese data, see Ministry of Internal Affairs and Communication, *Statistical Handbook of Japan 2005* (Tokyo, 2005). In 2004 China surpassed Japan in both exports and imports in merchandise trade. See World Trade Organization, *International Trade Statistics 2005* (Geneva, Switzerland, 2005).
30 In 2004 South Korea ranked 11th in the world in GDP and 7th in the value of merchandise exports ($253,840 million). It registered a surplus of nearly $30 billion. Ibid.
31 According to the World Bank, South Korea ranked third in the world in terms of the growth rate of per capita Gross National Product (GNP) during the 1985-1995 periods. South Korea, with the average annual growth rate of 7.6 percent during the 11-year period, trailed Thailand (8.4 percent) and China (8.0 percent). *Chosun ilbo* [Chosun Daily] (Seoul), May 2, 1997. Meanwhile, in a report released in April 1997, the International Monetary Fund (IMF) placed South Korea in the category of "advanced economies," a new category

currency crisis pushed Seoul to the brink of a default. Thanks to a combination of an emergency rescue plan crafted by the International Monetary Fund (IMF) and the efforts of the South Korean government, businesses, and labor, however, Seoul succeeded in overcoming the crisis within two years.[32] An additional factor that serves to enhance the importance of South Korea is its military alliance with the US. As is the case with Japan, there is a sizable U.S. military presence in South Korea—29,500 US troops as compared to 47,000 in Japan.[33]

Unlike Japan and South Korea, North Korea is neither a major trading nation nor a US ally. Since the mid-1990s, moreover, the DPRK has not been able to produce a sufficient quantity of food or earn enough foreign exchange with which to purchase food to feed its people. Notwithstanding its dire economic situation, however, the North has maintained a formidable military capability. Its ballistic missile program, in particular, is a major source of concern to South Korea, Japan, and their common ally, the US. Not only does Pyongyang possess ballistic missiles capable of reaching all of South Korea and Japan but it also exports missiles, missile parts and technology to Iraq, Iran, Syria and other nations. Increasing the North's leverage further is its nuclear weapons capability. If its official claims are to be believed, it may already possess a

---

that replaces "industrialized countries." Only 28 countries were so classified, and in addition to South Korea, Taiwan, Singapore, Hong Kong, and Israel were upgraded. *Joongang ilbo* [Joongang Daily] (Seoul), April 25, 1997.

32 "Kim Says '97 Economic Crisis 'Completely' Over," *Korea Herald* (Seoul), November 19, 1999. By November 1999, South Korea's foreign exchange reserve had grown from $3.8 billion in November 1997 to $68 billion. In June 2000 the figure surpassed $90 billion. An advance repayment of loans to the IMF and other lenders, moreover, helped to turn South Korea into a net creditor nation: Seoul's total external credits at the end of 1999 ($145.7 billion) exceeded its total external liabilities ($136.4 billion) by $9.3 billion. *Korea Times* (Seoul), February 19, 2000.

33 Anthony Faiola, "Japan Plans to Press U.S. on Troops," *Washington Post*, October 6, 2004; "U.S., S. Korea Reaffirm Military Alliance," *Associated Press*, February 2, 2006, Seoul, http://www.navytimes.com/print.php?f=1-292925-1508185.php.

few atomic bombs.[34]

If all three countries are forces to be reckoned with in their own right, then, why should one be concerned with how they interact among themselves? What difference does the Japan-ROK relationship make for other countries? What does it matter whether Japan and the DPRK cooperate with each other or not? In an increasingly interdependent world no one can afford to be indifferent to the possibility of peace and stability being disturbed in other parts of the world, especially if economic heavyweights are involved either directly or indirectly.

What makes the situation in Japan and the two Korean states more critical to the rest of the world than would be the case otherwise is the strategic importance of the Korean Peninsula, where the interests of major powers intersect. In addition to Japan, in other words, the United States, China, and Russia have a huge stake in what happens on and around the peninsula. International security, in other words, is the major reason why the two dyads take on importance.

If Japan and the ROK can forge a genuinely cooperative relationship, it will greatly strengthen their "quasi-alliance," while simultaneously bolstering the trilateral security cooperation among Tokyo, Seoul, and Washington.[35] Cooperation between Japan and South Korea also has the

---

34 "DPRK FM on Its [Decision] to Suspend Its Participation in Six-party Talks for Indefinite Period," *Korean Central News Agency* (KCNA), February 10, 2005, Pyongyang, http://www.kcna.co.jp /item/2005/200502/news02/11.htm. In February 2006 the highest-ranking intelligence official in the U.S. government stated in a Congressional testimony that the North Korean claim, in his assessment, "is probably true." John D. Negroponte, *Annual Threat Assessment of the Director of the National Intelligence for the Senate Select Committee on Intelligence* (Washington, DC, February 2, 2006), 13.

35 Since both have bilateral military alliances with the United States, Japan and South Korea may have become "quasi allies." See Victor D. Cha, *Alignment Despite Antagonism: The United States-Korea-Japan Security Triangle* (Stanford, CA: Stanford University Press, 1999). Trilateral consultations among the U.S., the ROK, and Japan began in the 1990s to deal with the nuclear and missile issues related to North Korea and were institutionalized in the form of the Trilateral Coordination and Oversight Group (TCOG) in 1999. More on this

potential to make contributions to the solution of regional and global issues, which obviously would benefit a large number of other states and peoples.

Cooperation between Japan and the DPRK, of which diplomatic normalization is a pivotal element, will vastly improve the security situation. A network of interdependence that is most likely to follow in its wake will measurably abate North Korean threat, both perceived and real, to Japan's security. For neighbors that are deeply enmeshed in multifaceted exchanges may find it either impractical or counterproductive to fight each other. If, as expected, diplomatic normalization paves the way for the infusion of sizable Japanese funds and technology into the North, then it will surely go a long way toward reinvigorating the latter's economy, thereby sharply reducing the probability of hostile military action being triggered by Pyongyang.

Given all this, one may be justified in exploring a set of intellectual puzzles. The largest of them all, of course, is why do states cooperate and why do they fail to do so? Under this general rubric, one may ask why have Japan and the two Koreas found it so hard to forge friendly, cooperative relationships? Why has the Japan-ROK relationship fared markedly better than has the Japan-DPRK relationship? What accounts for success or failure in bilateral negotiations between Japan and the ROK and between Japan and the DPRK? In what ways have ideational factors helped to compensate for or eclipse material ones in the two sets of bilateral relationships?

Although the literature on Japan-Korea relations does provide some clues to these questions, it is far from adequate. The number of scholarly books in English dealing solely with contemporary Japan-Korea relations, actually, can be counted on one hand. The first comprehensive study of the topic appeared in 1985, when Chong-Sik Lee published *Japan and Korea: The Political Dimension*.[36] Based on primary and secondary sources

---

later.
36 Chong-Sik Lee, *Japan and Korea: The Political Dimension* (Stanford, CA: Hoover Institution Press, Stanford University, 1985).

in Korean and Japanese, Lee's study provides both an excellent overview of the bilateral relationship and an in-depth analysis of the principal issues Japan and South Korea dealt with up to 1984.

Particularly insightful are the chapters dealing with loan negotiations and the textbook controversy. Lee's account of the loan negotiations provides fascinating glimpses into the dynamics of bargaining: the clash of perceptions and bargaining styles, the blending of rigidity and flexibility, the constraints of domestic politics, the effects of leadership changes, and the role of a third party (the United States). In the end, the two sides reached a compromise settlement in which Japan agreed to provide a $4 billion loan not tied to any explicit recognition of South Korea's contribution to Japan's security.[37]

Lee's analysis of the textbook controversy that erupted in the summer of 1982 is most illuminating, not only because he presents all sides of the controversy with remarkable impartiality, but also because he places it in the larger context of the interplay of historiography and Japanese colonial policy. Although the news stories that had triggered the controversy later proved to be erroneous—for Japanese textbook publishers had failed to implement the instructions of the Ministry of Education to gloss over accounts of Japanese aggression and atrocities—, Lee argues that the controversy nonetheless performed the salutary function of focusing the Japanese people's attention on the pain and suffering to which their neighbors had been subjected.[38]

Although he does not utilize any theoretical framework or explanatory variable in any explicit fashion, Lee nonetheless makes it clear that national interests, national power, domestic politics, and ideational factors played an important role in shaping the postures and policies of Japan and Korea toward each other.

The second comprehensive study of Japan-Korea relations is *Japan and Korea in the 1990s: From Antagonism to Adjustment* by Brian Bridges.[39]

---

37 Ibid., 105-41.
38 Ibid., 141-64.
39 Brian Bridges, *Japan and Korea in the 1990s: From Antagonism to Adjustment*

The author provides not only an overview of how Japan has interacted with the two Korean states but also how the latter two have dealt with each other and how the United States, Russia, and China have affected the triangular relationship. Of the factors that help shape Japan-Korea relations, Bridges singles out for detailed discussion historical legacy, policymaking processes, mutual perceptions, and domestic politics.

His analysis of the security, political, economic, and cultural dimensions of Japan-Korea interactions, then, is informed by insights from all the contending schools of thought in IR, even though none is explicitly mentioned. He displays a keen sensitivity to ideational factors, without neglecting material considerations. His book covers events up to mid-1992, including the first seven rounds of Japan-DPRK normalization talks.

The third and latest monograph on Japan-Korea relations is *Alignment Despite Antagonism: The United States-Korea-Japan Security Triangle* by Victor Cha.[40] It is the first theoretically-oriented book-length study in the literature. The puzzle Cha attempts to solve is the seeming anomaly of two states, Japan and South Korea, that have a common ally and a common enemy, being unable to forge a close cooperative relationship, expressed, for example, in a defensive alliance, but engaging in friction more frequently than Realist theory would predict.

Drawing on the literature of alliance theory, Cha proposes a "quasi-alliance" model, which posits that a key determinant of state behavior is the fear of being "abandoned" or "entrapped" by an ally. He argues that the "normal state of relations between Japan and the ROK," which "is characterized by friction," is attributable not only to "historical animosity" but also to "a fundamental disparity in each other's perceptions of the surrounding security environment and expectations of support from the other." He asserts that "variations from this baseline of contentious behavior are a function of the United States defensive commitment to the region."[41]

(Aldershot, Hants, England: Edward Elgar Publishing, Ltd., 1993).
40 Victor Cha, *Alignment despite Antagonism: The United States-Korea-Japan Security Triangle* (Stanford, CA: Stanford University Press, 1999).

Cha demonstrates that his model can explain variance in Japan-ROK relations during some periods to a large degree. "In the 1969-71 and 1975-79 periods," he asserts, "anxieties about U.S. retrenchment caused Seoul and Tokyo to agree on containment policies vis-à-vis Pyongyang." When "fears of U.S. abandonment" declined in the 1980s, however, friction occurred between Tokyo and Seoul regarding, for example, policy toward Pyongyang.[42]

Cha concedes, however, that it is "difficult to draw direct causal inferences between the model's predictions and contention over specific incidents such as the Kim Dae-jung controversy or the general resurgence of historical animosity" during the 1980s. He contends, nonetheless, that "decreased fears of U.S. abandonment provided, not the specific, but the *permissive* conditions for such friction to arise." Nor, as he acknowledges, is the model capable of explaining "instances of Japan-ROK cooperation during the 1980s." "The reduced fears of U.S. abandonment and the lack of compelling reasons to move to higher levels of cooperation," Cha argues, may nonetheless have served as "plausible contributing factors," along with other circumstantial ones, in explaining why cooperation did not become more salient than was actually the case.[43]

Two other weaknesses of Cha's otherwise scintillating study are its omission of the post-Cold War developments and its focus on Japan-ROK relations to the neglect of Japan-DPRK relations. His quasi-alliance model, actually, would not be able to explain the developments in the 1990s. Nor can it be applied to analysis of Tokyo-Pyongyang relations for the simple reason that they could not be further from anything resembling a quasi-alliance.

If we turn from monographs to anthologies, we find numerous chapters that deal either directly or tangentially with aspects of Japan-ROK and Japan-DPRK relations. *North Korean Foreign Relations in the Post-Cold War Era* edited by Samuel S. Kim, for example, contains an excellent

---

41 Ibid., 2-3.
42 Ibid., 197.
43 Ibid., 198.

theoretical chapter and a substantive chapter on North Korea-Japan relations that is most informative but largely atheoretical. In his introductory chapter, the editor presents a critique of major theoretical approaches, including structural realism, proposing an outline of what he calls a "synthetic theory" that, he hopes, "would help us better describe, explain, and predict DPRK foreign policy behavior in various issue areas, towards major international actors, and across time."[44]

The core concept of the synthetic theory is national identity, which is postulated to play a pivotal role in North Korea's foreign policy behavior. The delineation of North Korea's identity, however, remains a key task for future research. Kim underscores the importance of ascertaining "North Korea's current national identity—its content as well as its boundaries— compared with its past national identity." No less pressing, in his view, is the task of gauging the "relative weight of domestic/societal and external/systemic factors in the formulation of North Korea's national identity."[45]

Another anthology worth noting is *Asian Security Practice: Material and Ideational Influences* edited by Muthiah Alagappa, which contains three chapters, all of them theoretically-oriented, dealing with the security policies of Japan, North Korea, and South Korea, respectively. In his chapter, "Japan: Normative Constraints Versus Structural Imperatives," Yoshihide Soeya argues that "both realism and constructivism are relevant in explaining Japan's security behavior." He shows that Japan's failure to "reassert its identity as an independent military power" is attributable in large measure to the "tension between Japan's security needs and the normative constraints within which it operates."[46]

In his chapter, "North Korea: Deterrence through Danger," David

---

44 Samuel S. Kim, *North Korean Foreign Relations in the Post-Cold War Era* (Hong Kong: Oxford University Press, 1998). See Samuel S. Kim, "In Search of a Theory of North Korean Foreign Policy," 3-31 and Hong Nack Kim "Japan in North Korean Foreign Policy," 116-39.
45 Kim, ed., *North Korean Foreign Relations*, 24-26.
46 Allagapa, ed., *Asian Security Practice*, 199.

Kang tests hypotheses derived from structural realism against North Korean behavior—such as "preponderant capabilities make a state appear threatening to weaker nations regardless of intentions" and "intentions are not fixed, but follow changes in capabilities." He finds that the realist theories "do in fact explain the North Korean conception of security fairly accurately."[47]

In his chapter, "South Korea: Recasting Security Paradigms," Chung-in Moon applies to Seoul's security policy an innovative conceptual framework, grounded in both realism and constructivism, consisting of (1) metastructure, (2) institutional foundation, (3) external management, and (4) security agenda. The metastructural foundation of South Korea's security practice, Moon shows, can be understood by examining the "dynamic interplay of perception, ideology, and identity." South Korea's on-going democratization is the most salient aspect of its institutional foundation impinging on security policy. Seoul's "alliance management" and its "recent policy tilt toward regional and multilateral security cooperation regimes" are the major external variables. Finally, the changing internal and external environments, Moon argues, have triggered a reassessment of Seoul's security agenda to expand the scope of security to economic, ecological, and social security.[48]

A noteworthy addition to the literature is a monograph on Japanese foreign policy, *Japan's Reluctant Realism*, by Michael J. Green. In a 34-page-long chapter on "Japan and the Korean Peninsula," Green presents an excellent overview of Japan's policy toward the two Koreas, focusing on "(1) management of the North Korean problem; (2) bilateral disputes on fisheries, territorial claims, and history; and (3) bilateral response to the economic crisis." Identifying the key "variables" that are likely to shape Japan-ROK relations as (1) leadership, (2) the Japanese economy, (3) China, (4) the US commitment, and (5) unification of the Korean peninsula, Green concludes his analysis by suggesting the steps the US should take to enhance trilateral cooperation among Washington, Tokyo,

---

47 Ibid., 234-263. The quotations are from 238 and 263.
48 Ibid., 264-287. The quotation is from 265.

and Seoul.⁴⁹

Finally, a 65-page-long chapter on "North Korea Confronts Japan: Politics of Normalization and Rice" by Young C. Kim in a recent anthology I edited, *North Korea and the World: Explaining Pyongyang's Foreign Policy*, presents an in-depth analysis of selected major developments in Japan-DPRK relations. Based in part on interviews with an impressive array of leading players in the Japanese political arena, including three former prime ministers and five former foreign ministers, Kim's account of the dynamics of policy-making in Tokyo is particularly insightful. He also had the benefit of conversations with "senior government and party leaders in Pyongyang," which he had "intermittently over the years" during numerous visits to North Korea.⁵⁰

Kim's scrutiny of several high-powered missions to Pyongyang led by heavy-weight Japanese politicians, including two visits by Prime Minister Koizumi Junichiro, leads him to identify four factors that, in his view, "go a long way toward explaining the failure of the two countries to establish diplomatic relations." They are (1) the "rigidity of ideological beliefs that fundamentally conditioned North Korea's policy choices," (2) the "issue of abduction [that] emerged in 1996, with all its potential for politicization," (3) the nuclear issue, and (4) "a distorted view of Japanese politics on the part of the North Korean leadership."⁵¹

Objectives of This Study

The puzzle of why Japan and the two Korean states cooperate on some issues some of the time but engage in conflict on other issues on other occasions cannot be solved on the basis of the extant literature

---

49 Michael J. Green, *Japan's Reluctant Realism: Foreign Policy Challenges in an Era of Uncertain Power* (New York: Palgrave, 2001), 111-44.
50 Byung Chul Koh, ed., *North Korea and the World: Explaining Pyongyang's Foreign Policy* (Seoul: Kyungnam University Press, 2004), 133-98.
51 Ibid, 183-88.

alone. The latter either is not up-to-date or does not provide plausible explanations for all the key dimensions of the puzzle, including, especially, Japan-DPRK interactions.

Empirically, a detailed examination of the dynamics of cooperation and conflict between Japan on the one hand and the two Korean states on the other focusing on the period since the mid-1980s can make a contribution to the literature. Theoretically, analysis of the key events through the prism of the insights, ideas, and propositions of the contending schools of thought in IR has the potential to enhance our understanding of the sources of interstate cooperation and conflict.

Notwithstanding the claims or perceptions of some of the scholars, the archives of Tokyo, Seoul, and Pyongyang bearing on the developments covered in this study are not yet open to outsiders.[52] This necessitates a nearly exhaustive review of all publicly available material from all three countries concerned in their original languages. Being "publicly available," however, is not the same thing as being "available to the public." Most government documents in Tokyo and Seoul, in fact, are inaccessible to the general public, even though the situation has begun to improve markedly with the arrival of the Internet age. The ability to obtain unpublished, though not classified, material from government officials in Japan and South Korea, therefore, can be most useful in conducting research. No less valuable are the opportunities to talk with people who have either first-hand knowledge or inside information—to the extent that they can be shared with a researcher without breaching any laws or regulations—about the various issues and events under study.

In sum, I hope to present in the following pages both an account of the most important developments in Japan-ROK and Japan-DPRK

---

52 The library of the Institute of Foreign Affairs and National Security (IFAN) of the ROK Foreign Ministry, for example, is not really an archive, for it does not contain any original documents, whether previously classified or not. As a former visiting professor at IFAN, I have personal knowledge of its library resources. Some of the authors cited above, however, erroneously refer to it as an archive. The same is true of the National Diet Library in Tokyo.

relations, with emphasis on those since 1985, that is as reliable as the available evidence permits and theoretically-informed knowledge—an explanation of what has happened, why cooperation has occurred in some cases, and why it has failed to occur in others in light of the relevant concepts and ideas culled from the theoretically-oriented literature.

PART I

Japan and North Korea

CHAPTER 1

From *Seikei Bunri* to Diplomatic Negotiations

During the first four decades of Tokyo-Pyongyang relations Japan's North Korea policy was characterized for the most part by *seikei bunri* (separation of politics from economy). Security loomed large in Tokyo's policy calculus but until the 1990s the linkage between security and Japan's North Korea policy was mediated by the United States.

As the principal guarantor of Japan's security, the United States has provided the general framework within which Japan's policy toward the Korean Peninsula can be set. That is to say, Japanese policy could not deviate too far from American policy. As long as the integrity of its common strategic interests with the United States could be preserved, however, Japan could and did go its own way in dealing with North Korea. That was the background against which it applied the principle of *seikei bunri* for four decades.

It is therefore not coincidental that both Tokyo and Washington changed their respective policies toward Pyongyang almost simultaneously. Thanks to the transformation of the US-ROK relationship from that of patron and client to that of equal partners, however, the principal impetus for change emanated not from Washington but from Seoul. It was ROK President Roh Tae Woo's statement on July 7, 1988 enunciating a policy of accommodation with all Communist states, including the DPRK, that prompted both the US and Japan to adopt a markedly conciliatory posture toward Pyongyang.

Overall, conflict or discord was the dominant pattern of Japan-DPRK relations during this period. There were, however, two notable instances of cooperation—an ostensibly non-governmental agreement in 1959 on the repatriation of thousands of Korean residents in Japan to the North and another agreement concluded among three political parties in 1990 that paved the way for inter-governmental negotiations for diplomatic normalization.

Both material and ideational factors help explain the persistence of conflict and the occurrence of cooperation. National interests, domestic politics, and state identity were salient factors shaping the behavior of policymakers in Japan and North Korea.

Japan-DPRK Relations before the Japan-ROK Normalization

When the DPRK came into being in September 1948, Japan was formally under the Allied (actually US) occupation, which lasted until 1952. Hence the need for bilateral relations did not arise for several years. During the Korean War, moreover, Japan served as a major logistical base for the United Nations forces, thereby reaping huge economic rewards. That meant that Japan was virtually a belligerent in the war allied de facto with North Korea's enemies.

It was a year and a half after the Korean Armistice that North Korea made its first overtures toward Japan, which had regained its sovereignty and was theoretically in a posistion to formulate its own foreign policy. In February 1955, DPRK Foreign Minister Nam Il indicated his country's desire to normalize relations with Japan. After expressing "profound sympathy for the Japanese people in their plight as a semi-occupied nation," Nam Il said that North Korea "is ready to establish normal relations with any nation which seeks to do so, based on the conviction that all nations of different social systems can coexist in peace." He added that North Korea was ready to "undertake concrete discusssion of various problems to establish and further trade, cultural, and other relations with Japan."[1]

Although the Japanese government did not respond directly to North Korean overtures, it did permit a number of developments that would facilitate private economic transactions. They included the signing of an agreement between Tokyo Bussan, a private trading company, and a North Korean trading corporation in October 1955 and the establishment of a Japan-DPRK Trade Association in March 1956. The Japanese government, however, did not permit direct trade between Japanese firms and North Korea; hence all trade was routed first through Dalian, China and later through Hong Kong.[2]

These developments did not sit well in Seoul, which did not hesitate to lodge protest with Tokyo. The absence of formal diplomatic relations between the ROK and Japan—and the fact that negotiations for diplomatic normalization between them were not going well—meant, however, that Seoul had but limited leverage over Tokyo. Expelling Japanese journalists was one of the few weapons in Seoul's arsenal.[3]

In a sense, then, there was more discord in Tokyo-Seoul relations than in Tokyo-Pyongyang relations. This became all the more apparent in 1959, when the Japanese government made an important decision

---

1 Okonogi Masao, "The Political Dynamics of Japan-North Korea Relations: The Basic Framework," an unpublished paper, March 1990, 5-6. The main ideas and arguments of this paper are also found in Okonogi Masao, *Nihon to Kita Chosen: korekarano 5-nen* [Japan and North Korea: The Next Five Years] (Tokyo: PHP Kenkyujo, 1991), chap. 3.
2 Okonogi, "The Political Dynamics of Japan-North Korea Relations," 7.
3 Nikkan Kankei Kenkyukai, ed., *Nikkan kankei no kiso chishiki: deta to bunseki* [Basic Information on Japan-Republic of Korea Relations: Data and Analysis] (Tokyo: Tabata Shoten, 1975), 145.

affecting both of the rival states on the Korean Peninsula: it decided to permit the repatriation of Korean residents in Japan to North Korea. The decision was formalized in an agreement signed on August 13 in Calcutta, India between the representatives of the Japanese and North Korean Red Cross organizations. The first group of 957 repatriates from 238 families left Niigata aboard a North Korean ship on December 14, and by the end of 1967 some 88,000 Korean residents in Japan had repatriated themselves to the DPRK. All this occurred amid the vehement protest of the ROK government, which first suspended all trade with Japan and then threatened to take the case to the International Court of Justice.[4]

The behavior of both Japan and North Korea regarding the repatriation issue lends support to the assumption of rationality shared by neorealism and neoliberalism. Both countries gained much from their transaction. Japan succeeded in reducing substantially the number of Korean residents who imposed a heavy burden on Japan financially and otherwise. North Korea scored a major propaganda victory in its contest for legitimacy with South Korea, a victory that had implications for North Korea's sense of identity. More on this below. In the medium to long term, moreover, the North gained economically as well, for the repatriates would become an important source of foreign exchange earnings thanks to gifts and remittances from their relatives in Japan.

Although the Japan-ROK normalization talks entered a new phase in 1961, especially after the military coup in Seoul that brought to power Park Chung Hee, Japan continued to take measures aimed at facilitating its trade with North Korea. In April 1961 the Japanese government permitted direct trade between Japanese firms and North Korea for the first time. In January 1962 a Ministry of International Trade and Industry (MITI) regulation concerning the settling of trade accounts was revised,

---

4 Ibid., 147; Okonogi, "The Political Dynamics of Japan-North Korea Relations," 7; "88,000 Koreans Returned to North Korea from Japan," *Korea Herald* (Seoul), April 13, 1998. South Korea's suspension of its trade with Japan was short-lived; in April 1960 Seoul lifted the temporary ban. Seoul's threat to take its dispute with Tokyo to the world court lacked credibility, for, under the court's statute, no country can be sued unless it gives consent, either in advance or in each case.

effectively lifting a ban on direct settlement with North Korea. Discriminatory treatment of North Korea, however, continued. For one thing, unlike their South Korean counterparts North Korean engineers and technicians were not allowed to visit Japan in connection with purchases of plants. Nor were the funds of the Japan Export-Import Bank available for transactions with North Korea. It was, moreover, not until February 1964 that permission for deferred payment—one-year deferral—was granted to Japanese exports to North Korea.[5]

As far as North Korean visitors to Japan were concerned, the only type of visitors to whom the Japanese government issued visas was athletes. First to enter Japan were ten North Korean athletes and support personnel who were allowed to participate in a world speed skating championship event held in Karuizawa in February 1963. In the following year a North Korean team consisting of over 60 athletes and support personnel entered Japan to compete in the Tokyo summer Olympic games.[6]

In sum, on the eve of the Japan-ROK normalization, Japan's relations with North Korea displayed cooperation that, albeit limited, was far from negligible. Japan's national interests and identity as a "trading state" undergirded its North Korea policy.

The Japan-ROK Normalization and North Korea

The normalization of diplomatic relations between Japan and the ROK in 1965 was a historic milestone in Japan's policy toward the Korean Peninsula. It had profound implications not only for the ROK but for the DPRK as well. To probe its implications for the DPRK, we need to

---

5 Yamamoto Tsuyoshi, "Nitcho kankei to Nihon no sentaku" [Japan-North Korea Relations and Japan's Options] in *Sengo Nihon gaikoshi, VII: Nihon gaiko no kadai* [History of Japan's Postwar Diplomacy, vol. 7: The Tasks of Japanese Diplomacy], Yamamoto Susumu et al. (Tokyo: Sanseito, 1985), 192-94.
6 Ibid., 192.

examine a key provision in the Treaty on Basic Relations Between Japan and the Republic of Korea. Article 3 of the treaty states:

> It is confirmed that the Government of the Republic of Korea is the only lawful Government of Korea as specified in Resolution 195 (III) of the United Nations General Assembly.[7]

Does this mean that Japan has accepted the ROK government's consistent claim that it is not only the exclusive repository of legitimacy on the Korean Peninsula but also has jurisdiction over all of Korea, including the northern half? Why did Japan insist on adding the qualifying phrase, "as specified in Resolution 195 (III) of the United Nations General Assembly"? In that resolution, which was adopted in December 1948, the UN General Assembly declared:

> ......that there has been established a lawful government (the Government of the Republic of Korea) having effective control and jurisdiction over that part of Korea where the Temporary Commission was able to observe and consult and in which the great majority of the people of all Korea reside; that this Government is based on elections which were a valid expression of the free will of the electorate of that part of Korea and which were observed by the Temporary Commission; and that this is the only such Government in Korea.[8]

Given its lack of clarity, the preceding UN resolution lends itself to

---

[7] Kagoshima Heiwa Kenkyujo. ed., *Nihon gaiko shuyo bunsho, nenpyo, dai-2-ken, 1961-1970* [Basic Documents on Japanese Foreign Relations, vol. 2, 1961-1970] (Tokyo: Hara Shobo, 1984), 570-71. The English translation of the title is the editor's.

[8] U.S. Department of State, *The Record on Korean Unification, 1943-1960: Narrative Summary with Principal Documents*, Department of State Publication, No. 7084, Far Eastern Series, no. 101 (Washington, DC: Government Printing Office, 1961), 10-11 and 76.

divergent interpretations. One, preferred by the successive governments in Seoul, is that the UN General Assembly has recognized only one government in Korea as meeting the criteria of a lawful government, namely, the ROK government; hence the latter is the "only lawful government" on the Korean Peninsula as a whole.

Another interpretation, which is viewed as more plausible by disinterested parties, is that the UN General Assembly has recognized the ROK government as the only "lawful government" that meets two key conditions: (1) "having effective control and jurisdiction over that part of Korea where the [UN] Temporary Commission was able to observe [elections] and consult [with the people concerned]," that is to say, the US occupation zone in the south and (2) being "based on elections which were a valid expression of the free will of the electorate of [the same part of Korea]. It is this latter interpretation that Japan has embraced, and that is precisely why Japan wanted to add an explicit reference to that resolution in Article 3 of the Japan-ROK basic treaty.

In the Japanese view, then, Article 3 inferentially restricts the ROK's jurisdiction to that part of the peninsula which it actually controls, i.e., the southern half. Foreign Minister Shiina Seisaburo made that plain in his testimony to the Special Committee on Japan and the ROK of the House of Representatives of the Japanese Diet on October 29, 1965. Both Shiina and Prime Minister Sato Eisaku told the committee that they acknowledged the existence of a de facto government that controlled the northern half of the Korean Peninsula. They both stressed that the Japan-ROK basic treaty does not deal with North Korea at all; in other words, the treaty leaves open Japan's relations with North Korea.[9]

The preceding position of the Japanese government was reaffirmed several times in the 1970s. In their statements before the Foreign Affairs Committee of the House of Representatives, two successive directors-

---

9 Yamamoto Tsuyoshi, "Nitcho fuchosei kankeishi" [The History of Abnormal Relations Between Japan and North Korea], *Sekai, rinji zokan: Nitcho kankei: sono rekishi to genzai* [The World, temporary, extra issue: Japan-North Korea Relations: Their History and Current Situation], April 1992, 153.

general of the Foreign Ministry's treaty bureau and the director-general of its Asian affairs bureau confirmed Tokyo's official view that the ROK government is not the only lawful government on the entire Korean Peninsula, that the ROK government's jurisdiction extends only to the southern half which it actually controls, and that the question of property claims arising from the northern part of the Korean Peninsula is wide open (or "blank"). In short, the Japan-ROK basic treaty, as far as Tokyo was concerned, would not in and of itself pose a barrier to diplomatic normalization between Japan and the DPRK.[10]

Interestingly, however, Pyongyang's interpretation of Article 3 of the Japan-ROK basic treaty was identical to Seoul's. The DPRK government lost no time in condemning both the basic treaty and related agreements, declaring them null and void. Premier Kim Il Sung told Minobe Ryokichi, governor of Tokyo, in October 1971 that Article 3, by declaring that the ROK "is the only lawful government on the Korean Peninsula," implies that "the DPRK must be obliterated." Kim therefore called for the nullification of the basic treaty.[11]

The Japan-ROK normalization had direct implications for the contest for legitimacy that was being waged between the two rival Korean states. The stakes in the contest were high, not because of any material considerations but because of its ideational dimension—namely, the identity of each state. Neither was willing to accept the identity of a half state—a state representing only a half of the Korean Peninsula. Each proclaimed loudly that it was the sole representative of all the people and territory of the peninsula, labeling the other side an imposter, a puppet of its great power master, be it the Soviet Union or the United States.

---

10 Ibid., 153-54.
11 Ibid., 164.

Japan-North Korea Relations in the 1970s

Before noting a change in Pyongyang's interpretation of the Japan-ROK basic treaty, we need to discuss briefly how Japan-DPRK relations evolved in the years following the Tokyo-Seoul diplomatic normalization.

Japan did not alter its previous policy of allowing non-political—primarily economic—contacts between its citizens and North Korea. The value of trade did decline by 11.3 percent during the year immediately following the normalization—from $31,228,000 to $27,708,000. Beginning in 1967, however, the bilateral trade was back on the growth track, increasing by 23 percent that year and 34.3 percent the following year.[12]

<Table 2> Japan-North Korea Trade

(in millions of dollars; custom clearance basis)

Year	Exports	Imports	Total	Balance
1965	16.5	14.7	31.2	1.8
1966	5.0	22.7	27.7	-17.7
1967	6.4	29.6	36.0	-23.2
1968	20.7	34.0	54.8	-13.3
1969	24.2	32.2	56.3	-8.0
1970	23.3	34.4	57.8	-11.1
1971	28.9	30.1	59.0	-1.2
1972	93.4	38.3	131.7	55.1
1973	100.2	72.3	172.4	27.8
1974	251.9	108.8	360.7	143.1
1975	180.6	64.8	245.5	115.8
1976	96.1	71.6	167.7	24.4
1977	125.1	66.6	191.7	58.5
1978	183.3	106.9	290.2	76.5
1979	283.8	152.0	435.9	131.8
1980	374.3	180.0	554.4	194.3
1981	291.0	139.5	430.5	151.5
1982	313.2	152.0	465.2	161.1

12 Ibid., 181.

1983	327.1	126.1	453.2	200.9
1984	254.7	145.2	399.9	109.5
1985	247.0	179.2	426.3	67.7
1986	183.9	173.2	357.2	10.7
1987	213.7	241.7	455.4	-28.0
1988	238.8	324.6	563.5	-85.7
1989	197.0	298.7	495.7	-101.7
1990	175.9	300.3	476.2	-124.4
1991	224.0	283.6	507.6	-59.6
1992	223.0	258.6	481.6	-35.6
1993	219.7	252.4	472.1	-32.7
1994	170.8	322.7	493.5	-151.9
1995	254.9	339.7	594.6	-84.8
1996	250.8	266.1	516.9	-15.3
1997	179.1	302.0	481.1	-122.9
1998	175.0	219.4	394.4	-44.4
1999	147.6	202.2	349.8	-54.6
2000	206.8	251.0	473.8	-50.2
2001	1,065.4	226.8	1,292.2	838.6
2002	132.2	235.3	367.5	-103.1
2003	91.1	173.6	264.7	-82.5
2004	88.5	164.0	252.5	-75.5
2005	62.8	133.0	195.8	-70.2

SOURCES: Gaimusho, Hokuto Ajia-ka, *Kita Chosen gaikyo*, June 20, 1990; *Saikin no Kita Chosen josei*, April 1993; *1995-nen no Nitcho boeki*, June 1996; Japan External Trade Organization, "JETRO Releases Estimates on International Trade with North Korea in 1996," August 29, 1997; Tsusho Sangyosho (ed.), *Tsusho hakusho*, 1998, 1999, 2000, 2001 (Tokyo: Okurasho Insatsu-kyoku,1998,1999, 2000, 2001); Nihon Boeki Shinko Kiko, *Boeki, toshi, kokusai shushi tokei* (Tokyo: JETRO, 2006) on line at http://www.jetro.go.jp

Meanwhile, political relations, which didn't exist in a strict sense, took a turn for the worse. That is to say, Pyongyang's denunciation of Tokyo steadily escalated. In his report to the representatives' conference of the Workers Party of Korea in October 1966, Kim Il Sung underscored the danger of "Japanese militarism," which he charged the US had helped to restore and was using as an instrument of its expansionist policy. While condoning economic relations between socialist countries and Japan,

Kim warned that to have political dealings with the Sato government in Japan would be tantamount to encouraging the expansion of Japanese domination overseas and strengthening the position of American imperialism in Asia."[13]

The adoption of the "security clause" in the Sato-Nixon joint communique in November 1969 served further to inflame North Korea's anti-Japanese rhetoric. In that communique the two leaders had agreed that "the security of the Republic of Korea is essential to the security of the Far East and therefore to the security of Japan itself."[14]

Since the preceding marked the first time that Japan had explicitly linked its own security to that of South Korea, it appeared to confirm North Korea's perception that a de facto strategic alliance had been formed among Washington, Seoul, and Tokyo whose goal was not only to contain but ultimately to destroy Pyongyang.

In less than two years, however, the strategic environment of the world as a whole and that of Northeast Asia in particular changed dramatically. Detente had replaced conflict, both verbal and other, between the US on the one hand and its arch adversaries, the USSR and the PRC, on the other. Rapprochement between their respective allies and patron states compelled the two Korean states to jettison their erstwhile posture of unremitting hostility toward each other and to begin a dialogue for the first time in the annals of inter-Korean relations. Such

---

13 Kim Il Sung, "Hyon chongse wa uri tang ui kwaop" [The Current Situation and the Tasks of Our Party], in *Kim Il Sung chojak sonjip* [Selected Works of Kim Il Sung], vol. 4 (Pyongyang: Choson Nodongdang Ch'ulp'ansa, 1968), 323-26.

14 Gong Yooshik, "Hanbando t'ong'il kwa Ilbon ui yokhal: Ilbon ui tae Hanbando chongch'aek ui pyonhwa wa ap'uro ui chonmang" [The Reunification of the Korean Peninsula and the Role of Japan: Change in Japan's Policy toward the Korean Peninsula and Future Prospects], a paper presented to the Fall Conference of the Korean Sociological Association, December 13-14, 1990, Seoul, p. 17, table 1. Gong provides a useful compilation of policy statements on Korea embodied in U.S.-Japan joint communiques between 1969 and 1990.

change in the policies of the two Koreas, it could be argued, was consistent with the neorealist postulate on the potency of systemic attributes on state behavior.

North Korea adopted a conciliatory posture toward Japan as well, expressing its wish that the latter adopt an equidistance policy toward the two Korean states. Pyongyang also dropped its previous demand for the nullification of the Japan-ROK normalization treaty (the basic treaty) as a precondition for the establishment of diplomatic relations between the DPRK and Japan. Kim Il Sung told *Yomiuri shinbun* in January 1972:

> The ROK-Japan treaty, which recognizes the Park regime in the South as the only lawful government, poses a barrier to the diplomatic normalization of our two countries. That treaty is an interference in the internal affairs of our country. I do not think, however, that a repudiation of the ROK-Japan treaty is a sine qua non for the normalization of relations between the DPRK and Japan. Should diplomatic relations [between our countries] be normalized, the ROK-Japan treaty would be repudiated automatically.[15]

In the preceding quotation, Kim Il Sung still adhered to the position that the Japan-ROK basic treaty posed a barrier to the Japan-DPRK normalization; the only concession he made was to drop the insistence that Japan formally repudiate the treaty. Six months later, however, Kim unveiled a more substantive change. He told *Jiji* News Agency that the treaty was "not as big a barrier to the Japan-DPRK normalization as Japan thinks."[16]

If the detente helped to produce new overtures from Pyongyang toward Tokyo, it also induced Tokyo to ease restrictions on personnel and other exchanges between Japan and North Korea. The Japanese government issued visas to a large number of North Korean groups such

---

15 Yamamoto, "Nitcho fuseijo kankeishi," 166.
16 Ibid., 166-67.

as the DPRK International Trade Promotion Committee, broadcasting engineers, journalists (led by Chong Jun Gi, the editor-in-chief of *Nodong sinmun*, the daily organ of the Workers Party of Korea), and the Mansudae performing arts troupe (led by Yun Gi Bok, the chairman of the DPRK Committee for Cultural Relations With Other Countries).[17]

In the realm of economic relations, the Japanese government permitted the formation of a number of organizations, notably the DPRK-Japan export-import company (*Cho-Nichi Yushutsuyunyu Shosha*; founded by Korean businessmen in Japan loyal to North Korea) and, *Kyoa Bussan*, a front for Japanese trading firms. As a result, the total value of the Japan-North Korea trade jumped from $58,966,000 in 1971 to $131,754,000 in 1972, an increase of 123 percent. In 1973 the Japanese government allowed Japanese firms to export plants to North Korea on a deferred-payment basis and to utilize the funds of the Japan Export-Import Bank.[18]

There was no change, however, in Japan's policy of *seikei bunri* vis-a-vis North Korea. Not only did Tokyo ignore Pyongyang's repeated overtures, but Japan also took actions on the international stage that were supportive of the ROK at the expense of the DPRK. In May 1973, for example, Japan joined the US and other Western countries in co-sponsoring a resolution aimed at blocking the DPRK's entry to the World Health Organization (WHO).[19] The attempt nonetheless failed, and the DPRK gained a foothold in the UN system for the first time, promptly using it as a springboard to gain an observer status at the UN.

Shortly thereafter, Japan's relations with South Korea began to deteriorate, which paradoxically hurt the chances for an early normalization of relations between Japan and North Korea. The events that helped to aggravate Tokyo-Seoul relations included the kidnapping of Kim Dae Jung, the most prominent opposition leader, by agents of the South Korean Central Intelligence Agency (KCIA) from a Tokyo hotel in

---

17 Okonogi, "The Political Dynamics of Japan-North Korea Relations," 14.
18 Ibid.; Yamamoto, "Nitcho fujosei kankei-shi," 181.
19 Okonogi, "The Political Dynamics of Japan-North Korea Relations," 14-15.

August 1973; the Mun Se Gwang incident of August 1974 in which a Korean resident in Japan killed President Park Chung Hee's wife while trying to assassinate him; and the Kimura affair of August 1974 in which Japanese Foreign Minister Kimura Toshio told the Foreign Affairs Committee of the House of Councillors that the Japanese government did not think that North Korea posed a military threat to South Korea. As Tokyo-Seoul relations plummeted to an all-time low, they received top priority in the Japanese Foreign Ministry, then led by Miyazawa Kiichi, thus eclipsing Prime Minister Miki's "strong wish for a breakthrough in Tokyo-Pyongyang relations."[20]

Miki took the unusual step of dispatching Utsunomiya Tokuma, an LDP member of the House of Representatives with close ties to North Korea, to Pyongyang before embarking on a visit to the US for a summit meeting with President Ford. Miki reportedly took into account a message Utsunomiya had brought from Kim Il Sung. A talking paper Miki took to the US reportedly contained the statement that while Japan would for the time being emphasize an expansion of cultural, economic, and sports exchanges with North Korea, it would nonetheless make an effort ultimately to establish diplomatic relations. The Japanese draft of the Ford-Miki joint statement, reportedly omitted any reference to the "Republic of Korea," saying instead that "the maintenance of peace on the Korean Peninsula is essential to the peace and stability of Asia. The final version of the joint statement, issued in December 1974, however, did mention the Republic of Korea.[21]

It is worth noting in this connection the unusual statement in the 1974 edition of Japan's "Diplomatic Bluebook" (*Gaiko seisho*) to the effect that Japan would "actively seek" exchanges with North Korea in the cultural, sports, and economic fields, noting that such exchanges had

---

20 Ibid., 16.
21 Yamamoto, "Nitcho fujosei kankei-shi," p. 161. Foreign Minister Miyazawa confirmed in a news conference in Washington after the joint statement was issued that the so-called "Kankoku joko" (The Republic of Korea clause) was not in the Japanese draft but was added at the insistence of the US side. Ibid.

greatly increased in 1974.[22] The bottom line, nonetheless, is that political relations between Japan and North Korea remained unchanged, i.e., non-existent.

Fukuda Takeo, who succeeded Miki as prime minister in December 1976, lacked any interest in changing Japan's policy toward the Korean Peninsula. His posture, in fact, was more conservative than that of his American ally. President Jimmy Carter had elevated human rights to a key foreign policy goal and was intent on implementing his campaign pledge to withdraw US ground troops from South Korea. This latter policy apparently caused concern in the Fukuda administration, which urged the US to proceed with caution, stressing that the threat to the security of the Korean Peninsula had by no means evaporated.[23]

One marginal change the Fukuda administration did make in its North Korea policy was to allow the entry of an unmistakably political delegation from North Korea. A group of North Korean parliamentarians led by Hyon Jun Guk, a member of the DPRK Supreme People's Assembly, a former ambassador to the PRC, and a vice-chairman of the DPRK Committee on Cultural Relations With Other Countries, entered Japan on May 11, 1977 for a ten-day visit. Invited by the Dietmen's League for the Promotion of Friendship Between Japan and the DPRK, the seven-person delegation was to engage in negotiations for the conclusion of a non-governmental fisheries agreement. The Japanese government justified its policy on the ground that notwithstanding the political credentials of the North Korean visitors, the purpose of their visit was non-political.[24]

The North Korean delegation, however, simply ignored the restrictions imposed by the Japanese government, repeatedly engaging in political activities—notably criticizing Japan's policy toward the Korean Peninsula, raising doubts about the sincerity of President Carter's announced policy of partial withdrawal of US troops from South Korea,

---

22 Gong Yooshik, "Hanbando t'ong'il kwa Ilbon ui yokhal," 17.
23 Yamamoto, "Nitcho fujosei kankeishi," 162.
24 Ibid., 162.

and quoting extensively from the statements of their "great leader," Kim Il Sung. Despite repeated warnings by the Japanese government about their violation of the conditions of their entry permits, the North Korean delegation managed to meet with Hori Shigeru, the speaker of the House of Representatives; Kimura Toshio, the former foreign minister; Narita Satoshi, the chairman of the Japan Socialist party; Miyamoto Kenji, the chairman of the Japan Communist party; and Kono Yohei, the head of the New Liberal Club.[25]

Japan-North Korea Relations in the 1980s

During the decade of the 1980s Japan's policy toward North Korea manifested two extremes: the temporary suspension of the principle of *seikei bunri* and the enunciation of a willingness to engage in political contacts with the DPRK. On two separate occasions Japan joined many Western countries in imposing sanctions on North Korea in the wake of terrorist acts resulting in the death of over a hundred innocent people. Change in Japan's policy unveiled in the latter part of the decade, on the other hand, was prompted by a significant change in South Korean policy. A covert adjustment in Japanese policy, however, preceded the enunciation of a new policy in 1988; the temporary adjustment had been necessitated for purely tactical reasons—the need to secure the release of Japanese citizens in North Korean custody.

As the decade dawned, Japan continued the policy of allowing non-political exchanges with North Korea. Hyon Jun Guk, who had visited Japan as the head of a North Korean delegation in 1977, made his second visit in June 1981, again leading a group of North Korean lawmakers. Once again Hyon received a warning from the Japanese government concerning his political activities. In an interview with *Asahi shinbun*, Hyon had described ROK President Chun Doo Hwan as a "criminal" who was unworthy of being a dialogue partner with North Korea. ROK

---

25 Ibid., 163.

Ambassador to Japan Choi Kyung Rok reportedly asked the Japanese Foreign Ministry to expel the North Korean delegation for engaging in political activities in violation of the conditions of their entry permits.[26]

The number of North Korean visitors to Japan increased sharply between 1982 and 1983—from 246 to 434. In 1984, however, it plummeted to 167 due to sanctions imposed by the Japanese government.[27] The sanctions, as noted, were in retaliation against North Korea's involvement in a terrorist bombing incident in Rangoon, Burma in October 1983. The Burmese authorities obtained irrefutable evidence that the bombing, which killed 16 persons, including four South Korean cabinet ministers and two top presidential aides, had been carried out by North Korean agents, of whom one was killed and two were captured by the Burmese authorities. Their mission, as one of the captured agents confessed, had been to assassinate ROK President Chun Doo Hwan, who narrowly escaped injury by arriving late on the scene.

On November 7, 1983 the Japanese government announced through its chief cabinet secretary that it would take the following measures vis-a-vis North Korea:

First, Japan will restrict contacts between its diplomats and North Korean officials in a third country.

Second, visits by Japanese public employees to North Korea will be postponed in principle.

Third, North Korean officials will not be allowed to enter Japan, and the applications by other North Koreans for Japanese visas will be subject to a strict evaluation.[28]

On November 18, the DPRK government announced counter-measures against the preceding; North Korea would bar its own diplomats from meeting their Japanese counterparts in a third country

---

26 Ibid., 163-64.
27 Ibid., 159.
28 Komazawa Kazuo et al., "Gaiko rongi no shoten" [Focal Points of Foreign Policy Debate], *Rippo to chosa* [Legislation and Investigation], no. 224, October 1984, 11.

and would restrict the visit of Japanese citizens to the DPRK.[29] Foreign Minister Abe, however, made it plain in his policy speech to the Diet in January 1984 that the imposition of sanctions on North Korea did not signal any change in the "basic framework" (*kihonteki wakugumi*) of Japan's North Korea policy, namely, maintaining economic, cultural, and other non-political exchanges. In other words, the sanctions were designed as temporary measures.[30] Nonetheless, they remained in effect for over a year.[31]

Japan's decision to cooperate with South Korea and the US in imposing sanctions on North Korea reflected the combined effects of national interests, international regimes, and state identity. In terms of national interests, cooperation with its only military ally, the US, which in turn was allied with South Korea, served Japan's security and, indirectly, economic interests. Just as individuals possess multiple identities—for example, a patriotic citizen, a father, a husband, a professional, a member of an ethnic group, etc.—, so do states have more than one identity. Japan therefore could be conceptualized not only as a trading state but also as a law-abiding state strongly opposed to international terrorism. Finally, an international regime on anti-terrorism—a collection of norms, rules, procedures, and institutions—may have emerged, thus influencing Japanese policy.

Meanwhile, a serious incident erupted that would have important consequences for Japan-North Korea relations. On November 4, 1983 a North Korean soldier named Min Hong-gu entered Japan illegally as a stowaway on board the Japanese cargo ship, *Dai-18 Fujisan Maru*. Although the Japanese government rejected his request for political asylum, it nonetheless kept him in a detention center, instead of turning

---

29 *Nodong sinmun* (Pyongyang), November 19, 1983.
30 Komazawa et al., "Gaiko rongi no shoten," 11.
31 The chief cabinet secretary announced on October 31, 1984 the Japanese government's intention to lift the sanctions; the decision took effect on January 1, 1985. Gaimusho, Ajia-kyoku, Hokuto Ajia-ka, *Kita Chosen gaikyo* [An Overview of North Korea], January 1988, an unpublished document, 24.

him over to North Korea as the latter demanded. When the Dai-18 Fujisan Maru went to North Korea again on November 15 to pick up fresh cargo, all of its five crew members were detained by the North Korean authorities. North Korea, after trying unsuccessfully to barter the Japanese crewmen for Min Hong-gu, charged the captain and the engineer of the ship with espionage, releasing the remaining crew.[32]

Citing humanitarian grounds—for the North Korean defector would most probably face a severe penalty, perhaps execution, should he be repatriated to his country —, the Japanese government continued to reject the North Korean demand for Min's immediate return. Eager to obtain the release of the two Japanese citizens, however, Japan conducted covert negotiations with North Korea on the issue. Diplomats from the two countries met in secret in Vienna in January and April, 1986 and in Beijing in January and October, 1987.[33] Both Japan's identity as a law-abiding state and national interests, reinforced by domestic political considerations, were on display in the evolution of the incident.

While the details regarding the secret negotiations are not available, one can safely surmise that Japan did not retreat from its previous position that it would not exchange Min Hong-gu for the two Fujisan Maru crew members. Shortly after the last covert contact with North Korea in Beijing, the Japanese government in November 1987 released Min from custody and in December 1988 gave him a special residence permit. A week later a North Korean court sentenced the two Japanese crewmen to 15 years of "reform with labor."[34]

---

32 Suzuki Masayuki, "Nitcho kankei: Chosen Minshushugi Jinmin Kyowakoku no tainich seisaku o chushin ni" [Japan-North Korea Relations: With Focus On the DPRK'S Policy Toward Japan," an unpublished paper, 1990, 3-4. For a detailed account of the Fujisan Maru incident, with a focus on the ordeals of the two crew members who were incarcerated in North Korea, see Nishimura Hideki, *Kita Chosen: yami karano seikan: Fujisan Maru supai jiken no shinso* [North Korea: Returning Alive from Darkness: The Truth About the Fujisan Maru Spy Incident] (Tokyo: Kobunsha, 1997).
33 Suzuki, "Nitcho Kankei···," 3-4; Yamamoto, "Nitcho fujosei kankei-shi," 176.
34 Ibid., 176-77; Nishimura, Kita Chosen, 108.

Meanwhile, two more incidents occurred that would further strain Tokyo-Pyongyang relations. In January 1987 a crippled North Korean ship carrying 11 North Korean would-be defectors reached Japanese shores. The "captain" of the ship, Kim Man-ch'ol, told the Japanese authorities that the ship's engine had broken down while he and his passengers, all of whom were either his family members or relatives, were trying to reach a "warm country." The Japanese government's initial decision was to escort the ship along with its crew and passengers to the high seas after repairing its engine and replenishing its supplies; however, the ROK government protested that such action would place the lives of the eleven North Koreans in jeopardy, thus violating humanitarian principles and straining Tokyo-Seoul relations.[35]

The Japanese government then allowed South Korean diplomats based in Nagoya to interview the Kim Man-ch'ol family in the presence of its own Foreign Ministry officials. On the basis of the interview, the ROK Foreign Ministry announced that the Kim family was seeking political asylum in a country other than Japan and South Korea. On February 8, two and a half weeks after their arrival in Japan, the eleven North Koreans were flown to Taiwan in a Maritime Security Agency plane, accompanied by Japanese Foreign Ministry officials. The Taiwan authorities then allowed South Korean officials to talk with the asylum-seekers, which led to their decision to accept South Korea's offer of asylum and assistance. Within 20 hours of their arrival in Taipei, the North Koreans flew to Seoul.[36]

Predictably, North Korea, which had demanded the immediate return of the ship and the would-be defectors, was enraged. Fueling their anger was the fact that Kim Man-ch'ol had stolen the ship, which belonged to the North Korean government. Dismissing Japan's explanation that it had nothing to do with the North Koreans' decision to go to South Korea, Pyongyang accused Tokyo of "international terrorism."[37]

---

35 Yamamoto, "Nitcho fujosei kankei-shi," 177.
36 Ibid., 177.

From Seikei Bunri to Diplomatic Negotiations   57

While few would agree with North Korea's characterization of Japanese behavior as "terrorist," terrorism did indeed play a role in their bilateral relations. For, in November 1987, North Korea was implicated in another serious terrorist incident, and Japan joined other nations in imposing sanctions on North Korea for the second time in four years.

On November 29, 1987 a Korean Air passenger plane (Flight 858) carrying 115 crew members and passengers was blown up in mid-air near Burma; all 115 persons were killed. One of the two North Korean agents who had planted a bomb on the plane was subsequently arrested in Bahrain—her accomplice committed suicide while being questioned at the airport—and extradited to South Korea, where she made a full confession. She confessed that she had received a lengthy training as an agent and that her and her accomplice's mission had been to blow up the Korean Air plane in order to disrupt the Seoul summer Olympic games that were scheduled to be held in 1988 by proving the danger of flying to Seoul. The 26-year-old North Korean woman named Kim Hyon-hui was later tried, convicted, and sentenced to death; she was later pardoned by President Roh Tae Woo. She would play a role, albeit indirectly, in the Japan-North Korea negotiations for diplomatic normalization in the early 1990s.

The world community reacted to the Korean Air 858 incident with shock and grief. Not only was the loss of 115 lives lamentable, but a state sponsorship of international terrorism was abominable. That North Korea would commit such an act for the second time in four years was as horrifying as it was mystifying. The Japanese government had little choice but to join other states in imposing sanctions on North Korea. Unlike the Rangoon incident, the Korean Air bombing had a Japanese connection: the two North Korean agents had used forged Japanese passports.

On January 26, 1988 the chief cabinet secretary announced the rationale for and contents of sanctions. He stated that the Japanese government, having cooperated closely with the ROK and other

---

37 Ibid., 178.

governments in collecting information on the incident, had become convinced that it was an "act of organized terrorism by North Korea." Recalling that Japan had always taken the position that the international community should strongly condemn and take measures to prevent terrorist acts aimed at airplanes and expressing "profound regret" that forged Japanese passports had been used by the terrorists, the Japanese government would take several temporary measures against North Korea.[38]

The measures were all but identical to those taken in 1983 except for the addition of a clause banning all special flights, including those using the airplanes of third states, between Japan and North Korea. The chief cabinet secretary's statement also mentioned the intention of the Japanese government to cooperate fully with the ROK government to ensure the security of the Seoul Olympics, to make a special effort to prevent forgery of Japanese passports, and to cooperate closely with other countries in international organizations to prevent the recurrence of similar terroristic acts in the future. Finally, the Japanese government urged all the countries concerned to engage in a dialogue to reduce tensions and ensure a lasting peace on the Korean Peninsula.[39] The effects of the Japanese sanctions can be seen in Table 3, which shows a precipitous decline in the number of both Japanese visitors to North Korea and North Korean visitors to Japan in 1988.

North Korea, which denied any responsibility for the Korean Air bombing, claiming that it was South Korea that had "enacted the drama," escalated its already vehement denunciation of Japan. As far as North Korea was concerned, Japan's "hostile policy" toward it had become more pernicious than ever before, and it could only respond in kind.[40] The shrillness of North Korea's anti-Japanese rhetoric, however, belied its need

---

38 Gaimusho, Ajia-kyoku, Hokuto Ajia-ka, *Chosen hanto to Nihon* [The Korean Peninsula and Japan], an unpublished document, August 1, 1988, 2-3 (the text of the January 26, 1988 statement by the chief cabinet secretary).
39 Ibid., 2-3 and 2-4.
40 Suzuki, "Nitcho kankei," 2-3.

<Table 3> Visitors between Japan and North Korea

Year	Japanese Nationals Visiting North Korea	DPRK Nationals Visiting Japan	Re-entry Permits Issued to Korean Residents in Japan Visiting N.Korea
1972	924	32	145
1973	770	316	462
1974	877	157	—[a]
1975	615	84	—
1976	587	94	—
1977	408	124	—
1978	639	262	—
1979	818	191	—
1980	746	258	4,245
1981	844	270	4,101
1982	755	246	4,215
1983	876	434	4,133
1984	798	167	5,645
1985	1,291	403	7,819
1986	1,482	464	8,607
1987	2,055	403	11,224
1988	654	27	11,246
1989	1,746	180	14,478
1990	1,943	444	14,369
1991[b]	2,347	1,132	14,003
1997	1,068	252	
1998	672	207	
1999	640	150	
2000	1,616	332	
2001		254	
2002		162	
2003		73	
2004		120	

SOURCES: Gaimusho, *Waga gaiko no kinkyo*, 1973 through 1985; Gaimusho, Hokuto Ajia-ka, *Kita Chosen gaikyo*, June 20,1990 and *Saikin no Kita Chosen josei*, April 1993; Gaimusho, "Kita Chosen(Chosen Minshushugi Jinmin Kyowakoku), *"Kakkoku chieki josei (2005-nen genzai)*, on line at http://www.mofa.go.jp/mofaj/area/n_korea/data.html

a Not available
b The data for the ensuing years are incomplete, because the Japanese Foreign Ministry stopped the practice of making them available on a regular basis in 1992.

and desire for improved relations. The North Korean economy was in such a dire condition that it could not generate enough hard currency with which to service trade debts. In October 1986 MITI paid out 3 billion yen in export insurance claims to Japanese firms to whom North Korea owed trade debts. This meant that, technically, North Korea was in default.[41]

It was, therefore, understandable that North Korea would send signals to Japan through unofficial channels that were patently conciliatory. As early as June 1984 North Korea reportedly conveyed to Prime Minister Nakasone through Prince Sihanouk of Cambodia its desire for improved relations. In September of the same year, Kim Il Sung told Chairman Ishihara of the Japan Socialist Party that since he wished to have friendly relations with Japan, he had never personally criticized the Nakasone administration. In September 1985 Kim Il Sung told a visiting Japanese businessman that North Korea would need the cooperation of Japanese business in securing technology and capital in order to implement its Third Five-Year Plan that was scheduled to begin in 1987; Kim underscored his desire for strengthening economic, trade, cultural, and other ties with Japan in such a way as to obviate the criticism of the US and South Korea.[42] Japan lifted the sanctions on North Korea on September 16, 1988, on the eve of the Seoul Olympic Games. In announcing the decision on September 13, the chief cabinet secretary pointed to new encouraging moves toward reducing tensions on the Korean Peninsula, particularly President Roh Tae Woo's special statement on July 7, 1988; noting that preparations for the games with respect to security had proceeded smoothly, he stated that the lifting of sanctions would help ease tensions and promote a climate of friendship and tolerance.[43]

---

41 Ibid.
42 Ibid., 5. It should be noted that Nihon Shakaito did not change its official English name to the Social Democratic Party of Japan (SDPJ) until after the collapse of socialism in Eastern Europe. In 1984 it used the name the Japan Socialist Party (JSP).
43 Ibid., 2-1.

President Roh's July 7, 1988 statement, which was specifically cited by the Japanese government, was in fact a very important, if not a decisive, factor in the unfolding of a new Japanese policy toward North Korea. In his statement Roh gave a green light to the countries allied with or friendly toward Seoul to improve their relations with Pyongyang. The first clearcut sign of change in Japanese policy appeared in January 1989. In a statement issued on January 20, the Japanese Foreign Ministry outlined Japan's policy toward the Korean Peninsula as follows:

First, Japan takes the position that the Korean question should be resolved primarily through dialogue between the North and the South. Japan does not support the division of the peninsula but hopes that "a peaceful unification will be achieved." "Japan does not maintain hostile policy toward North Korea, and we recognize that it will be appropriate...for us to move positively toward improved relations between Japan and North Korea, with all due regard for maintaining the international political balance as it affects the Korean Peninsula, if North Korea so desires." "Japan hopes that a solution can be found soon to the Dai-18 Fujisan Maru problem. ...we are prepared to enter into discussions of any type with North Korea on the entire range of pending issues with no preconditions whatever."

Second, both the government and people of Japan regret that Japan has in the past "inflicted great suffering on the people of nearby lands. To ensure that the past will not repeat itself, Japan has been pursuing a peace-oriented policy, which applies to both South and North of the Korean Peninsula. "Article 3 of the Treaty on Basic Relations between Japan and the Republic of Korea only quotes a Resolution of the United Nations General Assembly in defining the basic nature of the Republic of Korea government and does not touch in any way on relations between Japan and North Korea." The Japanese government "has been making every possible effort" to stabilize the status of Koreans in Japan, and notwithstanding the absence of a treaty governing their status, is trying to ensure that "non-ROK Koreans" are "treated basically the same way" as ROK citizens.

Third, Japan is "convinced that the captain and [the] engineer [of the

Dai-18 Fujisan Maru] are innocent of the charges against them" and hopes that North Korea will release and allow them to return to Japan as soon as possible based on "humanitarian considerations." The Japanese government made the decision to give Min Hong-gu, the North Korean who had illegally entered Japan as a stowaway, a special residence permit "entirely [on] humanitarian grounds, in accordance with international practice," and it followed the "most objective procedures...to determine his own wishes."

Finally, "it is important for Japan and North Korea to achieve better understanding of each other's positions and approaches through direct contacts and dialogue. Japan takes note of a recent North Korean statement that indicates an interest in improved relations between Japan and North Korea. "If North Korea is sincerely interested in building better relations, this would be a good time to move ahead with steady and meaningful dialogue."[44]

Not only was the preceding the most conciliatory statement toward North Korea by the Japanese government, it was also an unmistakable signal that Japan was prepared to drop the erstwhile policy of *seikei bunri* and begin gradually to restore a semblance of balance in its posture toward the two Korean states. If Pyongyang failed to get the message, then it must surely have grasped the significance of Prime Minister Takeshita's remarks two months later.

In a Budget Committee hearing in the House of Representatives on March 30, 1989, Takeshita expressed his "remorse and regret" (*hansei to ikan no i*) to "all the people" of the Korean Peninsula for the past Japanese actions inflicting great suffering and damage on them. He expressed the hope that Japan and the Democratic People's Republic of Korea would be able to improve their relations, reiterating Japan's previously expressed desire for unconditional talks with North Korea on all bilateral issues.[45]

---

44 Gaimusho, Ajia-kyoku, Hokuto Ajia-ka, *Chosen hanto to Nihon*, 5-1 through 5-4. The quoted passages are from the Foreign Ministry's own translation on 5-3 and 5-4.
45 Ibid., appendix. Takeshita said: "Based on the basic position that the problems

This was the first time that a Japanese prime minister or any government official had referred to the DPRK by its official name. By using the phrase "all the people" of the Korean Peninsula, moreover, Takeshita had left no doubt that his "remorse and regret" were extended to the North Korean people. This set the stage for the opening of a new chapter in Japan-North Korea relations. An important part of the backdrop against which all this unfolded, however, was Takeshita's political calculus. With the popularity of his government at a dangerously low level but facing a House of Councilors election in a few months, Takeshita needed a "major diplomatic achievement." The timing of his statement, which amounted to an olive branch to Pyongyang, therefore, was most probably dictated by his political needs.[46]

Kanemaru's Visit to North Korea

Shortly after Takeshita's statement in the Diet, the Japanese Foreign Ministry began exploring the possibility of secret contacts with North Korea, which materialized in Paris in March 1990. A second round of secret contacts occurred in Tokyo four months later.[47] When North Korea expressed an interest in receiving an LDP delegation headed by a "man of real influence, Tanabe Makoto, vice-chairman of the Social Democratic Party of Japan (SDPJ) recommended Kanemaru.[48]

---

of the Korean Peninsula should be resolved through dialogue between the authorities of South and North, the [Japanese] government hopes to pursue diplomacy toward the Korean Peninsula with a new determination."

46 Young C. Kim, "North Korea Confronts Japan: Politics of Normalization and Rice," in *North Korea and the World: Explaining Pyongyang's Foreign Policy*, ed. B. C. Koh (Seoul: Kyungnam University Press, 2004), 142-43.

47 Kobayashi Kenji, "Kanemaru bocho eno michiwa Paride hajimatta" [The Road to Kanemaru's North Korea Visit Began in Paris], *AERA* (Asahi shinbun weekly), December 11, 1990, 24-28.

48 Kanemaru Shin and Tanabe Makoto, "Taidan: ima issono hakusha o" [Conversation: Now, More Efforts Than Ever], *Sekai*, temporary, extra issue,

Much preparatory work, however, remained to be completed before the Kanemaru visit could materialize. First, there were nogotiations among the LDP, the SDPJ, and the Foreign Ministry, which proved to be rocky at times. Basically, the Foreign Ministry argued strongly for a cautious approach; in order to achieve the intended results and avoid embarrassment for Kanemaru, the Foreign Ministry wanted to formulate a concrete plan based on consultations with other ministries and agencies within the government. That, effectively, meant that the Kanemaru visit would be postponed for a week; the possibility that it might even be canceled altogether arose. All the uncertainty, however, was removed when Kanemaru made a "political judgment on the spot" and announced to the press that the visit would take place on schedule. At one point during the pre-visit consultations, Kanemaru allegedly called the director-general of the MFA's Asian Affairs Bureau, Tanino Sakutaro, "stone head" (*ishi atama*).[49]

Another important preparatory step was a visit to North Korea by advance teams representing the LDP and the SDPJ. The consultations among the three groups noted above took place both before and after such a visit. Given Kanemaru's stature at the time—as leader of the largest LDP faction (the Takeshita faction)—, the LDP advance team headed by Ishii Hajime, a seven-term member of the House of Representatives, had to secure a reasonable assurance that Kanemaru would accomplish his

---

April 1992, 44. It is noteworthy that Tanabe acknowledges that ROK President Roh Tae Woo's July 7, 1988 statement had provided a turning point in Japan-North Korea relations. Although its Japanese name remained unchanged (Nihon Shakaido), the Japan Socialist Party began calling itself the Social Democratic Party of Japan in English in the wake of the collapse of socialism in the former Soviet Union and in Eastern Europe. In January 1996, however, the party shortened its English name to the Social Democratic Party (SDP). See "History of Japanese Political Parties," *Daily Yomiuri* (Tokyo), January 30, 1997.

49 Ishii Hajime, *Chikazuite kita toi kuni* [A Distant Country Getting Closer] (Tokyo: Nihon Seisanhonbu, 1991), 63-71. The English translation of the book's title is Ishii's own.

principal goal—namely, winning the release of the two Fujisan Maru crew members.[50]

A most interesting aspect of the preliminary negotiations, as recounted by Ishii, pertained to the issue of compensation. Ishii explained to Kim Yong Sun, the secretary of the Workers' Party of Korea (WPK) in charge of international affairs, that diplomatic practice calls not only for the conduct of negotiations over the compensation issue by governments, not political parties, but also for the normalization of diplomatic relations as a precondition for payment of any compensation. Kim Yong Sun countered by pointing out that inasmuch as custom and treaties are mere instruments, they cannot be a barrier to improvement of inter-state relations as long as there is a political will. He used the analogy of two families trying to mend their strained relations: unless one side first returns "the watch and pen" it has stolen from the other side, its sincerity remains suspect and no trust will emerge. Kim argued that for North Korea to normalize relations with a country that has already established diplomatic relations with South Korea is tantamount to recognition of "two Koreas," which will lead to the perpetuation of the division of the Korean Peninsula. North Korea, he insisted, would not normalize relations with Japan before the reunification of the North and the South. Ishii found the DPRK's position on that issue unyielding.[51]

North Korea apparently had not yet abandoned that position when the Japan Air Lines charter plane carrying Kanemaru and his compatriots touched down in Pyongyang's Sunan Airport on September 24, 1990 at approximately 3 p.m. Kanemaru was accompanied by Tanabe Makoto, and the two led separate delegations—the LDP and the SDPJ delegations, respectively. There were, in fact, two other groups—one consisting of 13 government officials, including four from the Foreign Ministry, and

---

50 Ibid., 14-33. I had a chance to interview Ishii in his Diet office in August 1990, several days before his departure for Pyongyang. He told me that Kanemaru would not visit North Korea unless there was a good chance that the two Fujisan Maru crew members might be released from North Korean captivity.
51 Ibid., 34-37.

another comprising 36 journalists from 16 news organizations.⁵² The first negotiating session among the three political parties—the LDP, the SDPJ, and the WPK—on September 25 revealed that North Korea was interested in one overriding issue: that of compensation by Japan. The WPK delegation headed by Kim Yong Sun insisted that Japan should pay some form of compensation ahead of everything else as a token of sincerity. It also stated its opposition to diplomatic normalization on the ground that such a step would imply North Korea's acceptance of the division of the Korean Peninsula.⁵³

Although North Korea abandoned its opposition to diplomatic normalization by September 27, it tried very hard until the last minute to secure the Japanese side's commitment to the idea of partial payment of compensation in advance. Change in North Korea's position on diplomatic normalization was unveiled at a meeting between Kawashima Yutaka, a counselor in the Asian Affairs Bureau of the Japanese Foreign Ministry, and Ch'on Yong-bok, a deputy director of the Asia Bureau of the DPRK Foreign Ministry, on September 27. Ch'on proposed government-to-government negotiations for that purpose, suggesting that preliminary talks be held in November. Kawashima was so stunned and excited by the proposal that he traveled some distance to the guest house where Kanemaru was staying and barged into Kanemaru's room, where he was having a private talk with Tanabe, to break the news.⁵⁴

Meanwhile, an extraordinary thing happened at the resort of the scenic Myohyang Mountain where the Japanese visitors had gone to meet President Kim Il Sung on September 25. After a "summit" meeting among Kim, Kanemaru, and Tanabe, there was an audience between Kim and the rest of the Japanese delegations, complete with picture-taking and

---

52 The LDP delegation consisted of 13 Diet members and 12 support personnel, while the SDPJ delegation consisted of ten members (of whom nine were Diet members) and five support personnel. For a complete roster of all four groups, see ibid., 236-42.
53 Ibid., 103-5.
54 Ibid., 138-39; 151-54.

a luncheon hosted by Kim. Then, as the Japanese visitors were preparing to return to Pyongyang, Kanemaru was suddenly asked to stay on for another day for one-on-one meeting with Kim Il Sung. Notwithstanding the traditional friendship between the WPK and the SDPJ and notwithstanding the fact that Tanabe had played a pivotal role in paving the way for the Kanemaru visit, Kim Il Sung or his advisors had decided that the presumed influence of Kanemaru in Japanese politics mattered more than Tanabe's feelings. It was, in fact, Kanemaru who worried about the latter, for being left out in the cold was bound to be upsetting, perhaps humiliating, for Tanabe. Although Kanemaru instructed his top lieutenant, Ishii, to explain to Tanabe what was happening, Tanabe could not be found.[55]

What was happening was proof positive that pragmatism can and does triumph over ideology in North Korean behavior. In this case pragmatic calculations had eclipsed not only ideological solidarity but human feelings as well. North Koreans had asked Kanemaru to keep his secretaries and bodyguards only, which meant that he had to rely on a North Korean interpreter in his tete-a-tete with Kim Il Sung. While neither Kanemaru nor Kim Il Sung has disclosed the details of what transpired during the five hours they spent together, what Ishii has been able to piece together suggests that Kanemaru was immensely impressed by Kim Il Sung. It was during these encounters that Kanemaru asked Kim for the release of the two Fujisan Maru crew members; Kim is said to have told Kanemaru that since the responsible authorities were examining how to release them, "good results" might come out of it.[56]

In short, the release of the two Japanese citizens, which occurred in October, could be viewed as Kanemaru's biggest achievement from his talks with Kim Il Sung. But what Kim gained in return was deep gratitude by an influential politician who would play a decisive role in breaking an impasse over the wording of the three-party declaration. For it was Kanemaru who instructed the Japanese negotiators to accede to North

---

55 Ibid., 113-25.
56 Ibid., 130-33.

Korea's insistence that Japan had an obligation to pay compensation not only for 36 years of colonial rule but also for 45 years of hostility toward North Korea during the postwar period.[57]

The three-party declaration, which was signed on September 28, just before Kanemaru and his entourage departed Pyongyang, also contained the following items:

- The three parties agreed that they would strongly urge their respective governments to start negotiations in November with the aim of establishing diplomatic relations between the DPRK and Japan and resolving other bilateral issues.
- The three parties agreed that in order to improve their bilateral relations the DPRK and Japan should develop political, economic, cultural, and other exchanges; utilize communication satellite;, and establish direct flights.
- The three parties agreed that all discrimination against Korean residents in Japan who profess allegiance to the DPRK should cease, that their human rights and legal status should be respected, and that the Japanese government should provide legal guarantees for the foregoing. In this connection, the three parties recognize the need for the Japanese government to delete the clause in Japanese passports that make them invalid for travel to the DPRK.
- The three parties recognize that Korea is one and that it is in the common interest of the Korean people for North and South to attain a peaceful unification through dialogue.
- The three parties agreed that they should make joint efforts to build a peaceful and free Asia and to remove the threat of nuclear weapons from all areas of the earth.[58]

It is plain that North Korea initially greeted the three-party declaration with a great deal of satisfaction, viewing it as a real breakthrough as well as a harbinger of a new era in DPRK-Japan relations.

---

57 Ibid., 159-66.
58 For the Japanese-language text of the three-party declaration, see ibid., 163-165; for a Korean version, see *Nodong sinmun* (Pyongyang), September 29, 1990.

What North Korea had failed to appreciate sufficiently, however, was that in the Japanese political system political parties and the government are not interchangeable and that even the ruling party lacks the power to dictate foreign policy. North Korea, moreover, had overestimated Kanemaru's personal influence and underestimated the ability of the foreign policy bureaucracy to circumvent political pressure. Nor had North Korea made adequate allowance for the weights of South Korea and the United States in Japan's policy calculus.

Prelude to Normalization Talks

To no one's surprise, the three-party declaration set off a storm of controversy in Japan and South Korea alike. The foremost source of adverse reaction was its reference to Japan's obligation to "make an official apology and ample compensation to the Democratic People's Republic of Korea" not merely for 36 years of colonial rule but also for "having inflicted damages on the Korean people during the 45-year postwar period."

To allay South Korean concerns Kanemaru went to Seoul on October 8, ten days after he returned from Pyongyang; he explained the background and meaning of the three-party declaration to President Roh Tae Woo. Roh in turn set forth five principles that, in Seoul's view, should guide Japan-DPRK negotiations:

(1) Japan should consult with South Korea in advance.

(2) Japan should link progress in its negotiations with North Korea to significant progress in the dialogue and exchanges between North and South Korea.

(3) Japan should insist on North Korea's acceptance of inspections of nuclear facilities by the International Atomic Energy Agency (IAEA).

(4) Japan should neither pay any compensation nor provide any economic cooperation to North Korea prior to diplomatic normalization.

(5) Japan should encourage North Korea to adopt a policy of openness and cooperate with the world community.[59]

Kanemaru promised Roh that there would be ample consultations between Tokyo and Seoul regarding North Korea. When Prime Minister Kaifu Toshiki visited Seoul in January 1991, he assured Roh that Japan would take heed of the five principles. In addition to the five principles, South Korea asked Japan to persuade North Korea to support the admission of both Korean states to the UN and to show sincerity regarding the reunion of separated family members and home visits of Japanese wives of North Korean men. South Korea also asked Japan not to give Pyongyang more money than what it had given Seoul in the form of economic cooperation on the heels of the Japan-ROK normalization.[60]

The United States was most concerned about the nuclear issue. US Ambassador to Japan Michael H. Armacost conveyed his government's concern to Kanemaru on October 9, 1990 and just before the preliminary talks between Japan and North Korea began, US officials were dispatched to Tokyo with data, including satellite photographs of suspected North Korean nuclear facilities, with the aim of convincing Japan to insist on North Korea's acceptance of IAEA inspections as a precondition for diplomatic normalization.[61]

Even though North Korea pressed Japan to act expeditiously so as to start normalization talks in November 1990 in accordance with what it construed as the commitment embodied in the three-party declaration, the political calendar in Japan, coupled with the need for consultations with South Korea and the US, precluded such a possibility. Actually, even the preliminary talks aimed at laying the groundwork for the main talks turned out to be contentious. It took three rounds of negotiations spanning six weeks to agree on the venues, dates, and agenda of the main normalization talks.

The first round of the preliminary talks occurred on November 3 and

---

59 Yamamoto Tsuyoshi, "Nitcho kokko seijoka kosho no shoten" [The Focal Points of the Japan-North Korea Negotiations on Diplomatic Normalization], *Sekai*, temporary, extra issue, April 1992, 81.
60 Ibid.
61 Ibid., 82.

4 in Beijing. The Japanese negotiating team was headed by Tanino Sakutaro, the director-general of the MFA's Asian Affairs Bureau, while the North Korean team was led by Chu Chin-guk, the director of the first bureau of the DPRK Foreign Ministry. A basic difference between the two sides became manifest during the first round: whereas North Korea was eager to establish diplomatic relations with Japan based on the principles enunciated in the three-party declaration, Japan displayed a cautious posture, insisting that normalization must enhance the prospects of peace and stability on the Korean Peninsula and that the understanding and support of all the countries concerned need to be secured.[62]

Faced with the North Korean side's repeated references to the three-party declaration and citation of Kanemaru's name and statements, the Japanese side explained that the Japanese government was not legally bound by the three-party declaration. Tanino even went so far as to hand to his North Korean counterpart a Foreign Ministry pamphlet explaining Japan's political system and government structure. The first round of the preliminary talks, however, ended without any agreement, thus necessitating at least another round of negotiations.[63]

It actually required two more rounds, which took place in Beijing on November 17 and December 15-17, to reach an agreement on the framework of the normalization talks:

- The talks will start in the latter part of January in 1991.
- The first round will be held in Pyongyang, the second round in Tokyo, and the remainder in Beijing.
- Each delegation will be led by a vice-minister-level negotiator.
- Agenda of the talks will be (1) the basic issues relating to diplomatic normalization, (2) economic issues related to normalization, (3) international issues related to normalization, and (4) other issues of mutual concern, such as the legal status of DPRK-oriented Korean residents in Japan and the problem of Japanese wives of North Korean men.[64]

---

62 *Asahi shinbun* (Tokyo), November 4, 1990.
63 Ibid., November 6, 1993. See also the editorial on the talks in the same issue.

Before the first round of the normalization talks began in Pyongyang in January 1991, the Japanese government formulated a four-point guideline:

(1) Japan shall conduct negotiations with a view toward enhancing the peace and stability of the entire Korean Peninsula.

(2) Japan-North Korea diplomatic normalization shall not occur at the expense of the friendly relations between Japan and South Korea.

(3) While Japan shall respond positively to property claims arising out of Japan's 36-year colonial rule in Korea, it will not agree to compensate North Korea for what happened during the postwar period.

(4) North Korea's acceptance of IAEA inspections of nuclear facilities is important to Japan's national security.[65]

Conclusion

As already noted, the behavior of both Japan and North Korea in their bilateral relationship is broadly consistent with the assumption of rational state behavior common to neorealism and neoliberalism. Rationality, however, must be understood as subjectively constructed by each state, and identity, another ideational construct, plays a key role in the process. Japan's postwar identity as a trading state goes a long way toward explaining its policy of *seikei bunri* vis-a-vis North Korea. The DPRK's quest for legitimacy, an important component of its identity, largely dictated its response to the Japan-ROK normalization.

Such episodes of cooperation as the conclusion and implementation of the 1959 agreement on the repatriation of Korean residents in Japan to the North and the 1990 agreement to enter into negotiations for diplomatic normalization exemplified the rational dimension of both sides, who derived benefits, material or ideational or both, from their transactions.

---

64 Ibid., November 18, December 16-18, 1990.
65 Yamamoto, "Nitcho kokko seijoka kosho no shoten," 81.

In the 1990 agreement Japan's most important gain was not explicitly stated in the document signed, for it was a tacit understanding that the North would release the two Japanese crew members of the ill-fated Fujisan Maru, who were in their seventh year of captivity, before the commencement of normalization talks. The North subsequently honored that commitment.

Since North Korea secured not only a joint commitment by Japan's ruling and main opposition parties to urge the Japanese government to enter into negotiations with the North but also an acknowledgment that Japan owed the North compensation for both colonial rule and Japan's policy toward the North during the postwar period, it could be argued that North Korea gained more than Japan did.

If that is the case, it lends support to the neoliberal position in the debate over relative versus absolute gains. For Japan clearly went for the latter rather than the former. What the episode demonstrates, however, is not the superiority of absolute gain over relative gain as an explanatory variable but the difficulty of measuring them in specific cases. The yardstick one must use can only be subjective—that is, the calculations of the parties concerned. Trying to ascertain the latter is an enormously difficult task, perhaps beyond the capacity of most researchers.

Another difficulty has to do with the temporal dimension. Should gains and losses be measured in the short term or the long term? In the long term the commitment embodied in the three-party declaration of September 1990 was not as costly to Japan as it appeared initially. The controversial reference to Japan's obligation to pay compensation to North Korea for both Japan's colonial rule and postwar actions was not legally binding, for it was contained in a non-governmental agreement. Nor did the commitment to hold inter-governmental negotiations really entail exorbitant costs for Japan, for it left open a wide range of options, including that of suspending negotiations at any time.

Change in Japan-DPRK relations examined above was clearly triggered by notable change in their respective environments. In Japan's case South Korea's *nordpolitik* (northern policy), which gave the green light to Tokyo to improve relations with Pyongyang, and the eruption of the Fujisan Maru incident were catalytic events. Just as North Korea's jettisoning of efforts to improve relations with Japan in the mid-1960s was prompted, if not dictated, by a dramatic change in its external milieu, namely, the Japan-ROK normalization, so was Pyongyang's abrupt change of direction in 1990 to seek diplomatic normalization with Tokyo triggered by a need to compensate for an adverse development in its external setting—the ROK-USSR normalization. Even though North Korea's reversal of its policy toward Japan preceded the announcement of the ROK-USSR normalization, which took effect immediately, by three days, Pyongyang had been given an advance notice by Moscow; hence it is reasonable to assume that the impending development may have figured as a key factor in Pyongyang's decision-making.

In both cases, then, South Korea played a pivotal role. What is more, neither Tokyo nor Pyongyang had any control over what Seoul did and, especially, their timing. Creating its capacity to act and actually availing itself of the opportunities that materialized, however, reflected autonomous decisions on the part of North Korea. While the North clearly did not create the Min Hong-gu incident, its decision to detain the captain and the engineer of Fujisan Maru Number 18 was a deliberate act designed to create a bargaining chip. Pyongyang's abortive attempts to trade the two Japanese citizens for Min Hong-gu and delaying a trial for them until the Japanese government granted the North Korean defector a temporary residency permit bespoke its calculus.

All this illustrates how serendipity can play a part in opening windows of opportunity in international relations. Min Hong-gu's illegal entry into Japan as a stowaway proved to be a blessing in disguise for North Korea. The failure of Pyongyang's attempt to strike a deal with Tokyo using two Fujisan Maru crew members as a bargaining chip, too, turned out to be beneficial to Pyongyang. For the repatriation of a single defector pales in comparison to the initiation of normalization talks.

The gap between the operational environment and how it is perceived by decision-making elites—the psychological environment— can be detected in North Korea's perception of the three-party talks and, especially, of their final product, the three-party declaration. Blinded by its own domestic structure in which the principle of party supremacy is firmly embedded, North Korea failed to appreciate that the ruling party in Japan, the LDP, did not speak for, let alone control, the Japanese government. Having succeeded in getting its principal demands adopted in the three-party declaration, North Korea erroneously believed that it had extracted a legally binding commitment from Japan. To be fair, the presence of over a dozen government officials, including four from the Foreign Ministry, among the Japanese visitors, coupled with the de facto participation of some of them in negotiations, could have reinforced North Korea's belief that what was being negotiated was a binding agreement between the two countries in a substantive sense, albeit not in form. Moreover, the three-party declaration did serve as the catalyst and basis for the initiation of inter-governmental negotiations for diplomatic normalization.

Internal political dynamics plainly affected the Kanemaru visit to North Korea in September 1990 in more ways than one. Had it not been for his political clout, the visit might have been either delayed or canceled due to the Foreign Ministry's reservations. Once in North Korea, Kanemaru appeared to succumb to Kim Il Sung's charisma and power of persuasion. It was Kanemaru who once again overruled the objections of Foreign Ministry officials, allowing the insertion in the three-party declaration of such a controversial clause as one enunciating Japan's obligation to pay compensation to North Korea for having harmed North Korea during the 45-year postwar period.

Kim Il Sung's decision to exclude Tanabe, who was technically on a par with Kanemaru, from the crucial negotiations at Myohyang Mountain underscored the limits of ideology in shaping North Korean foreign policy. It also turned out to be a brilliant tactic on Kim's part. It should not be overlooked, of course, that there was a quid-pro-quo at Myohyang Mountain: in exchange for his pledge of cooperation to Kim, Kanemaru must have received Kim's commitment to have the two Japanese crewmen released, albeit not immediately.

CHAPTER 2

Normalization Talks, 1991-1992

The eight rounds of inter-governmental negotiations Japan and the DPRK held between January 1991 and November 1992 provided both countries with an unprecedented opportunity. Never before had they conducted such protracted negotiations with each other on such a wide range of issues with the manifest goal of finding common ground, a mutually satisfactory formula for beginning a new relationship as friendly neighboring states.

Apart from such manifest goal, however, the two sides diverged sharply in terms of their respective latent objectives, their perceptions of the operational environment, and their negotiating styles. Nor did they possess a deep understanding of each other's political institutions, modus operandi, and constraints. Last but not least, the level of mutual trust was appallingly low.

All this seemed virtually to ensure that the negotiations would be long, arduous, and contentious. What transpired during the two years of intermittent negotiations may actually have widened the chasm separating Japan and the DPRK rather than narrowing it.

In other words, what turned out to be the first phase of the normalization talks—for the second phase would begin in 2000—displayed both cooperation and discord between Tokyo and Pyongyang. The talks themselves symbolized mutual adjustment, that is, attempts by the two sides to adjust their policies to forge a compromise between their initially divergent positions. But not only did the process prove to be strikingly discordant but it ended in an impasse that served only to raise the level of discord. Of the various explanatory variables that can be deployed, the most potent appears to be state identity. This, of course, is not to overlook the other variables, both ideational and material.

The First Round, January 1991

The arrival of the Japanese delegation to the first round of the Japan-DPRK normalization talks in Pyongyang on January 29, 1991 was a milestone in Tokyo-Pyongyang relations. Never before had an official delegation representing the Japanese government set foot in North Korea. Chon In-ch'ol, head of the DPRK delegation to the talks, told the Japanese visitors that "you are the first Japanese delegation to visit Korea with honorable intentions and goodwill in the history of Korea-Japan relations."[1]

The Japanese delegation was led by Nakahira Noboru, who had previously served as Japanese ambassador to Malaysia. Although his North Korean counterpart, Chon In-ch'ol, held the position of vice-minister in the DPRK Foreign Ministry, Chon was one of 13 vice-ministers, albeit the third-ranking one.[2] A comparison of the speeches made by the leaders of

---

1 *Nodong sinmun* (Pyongyang), January 30, 1991. Chon made the remark in a speech at a banquet welcoming the Japanese delegation on January 29. Chon was either exaggerating or intentionally overlooking the numerous visits made to South Korea by Japanese government delegations. For a balanced analysis of the Japan-DPRK normalization talks up to their seventh round in May 1992, see Brian Bridges, *Japan and Korea in the 1990s: From Antagonism to Adjustment* (Aldershot, Hants, England: Edward Elgar Publishing, Ltd., 1993), 143-62.

the two delegations at the first session of the first round on January 30 reveals the differences between their respective perceptions and positions.[3]

Chon In-ch'ol began by underlining the historical significance of the meeting, which, in his words, was "the first inter-governmental meeting in the 100-odd year history of Korea-Japan relations that was based on complete equality and mutual respect." Chon, then, noted the necessity for both an official apology and compensation to the Korean people by Japan, with the apology being given by the "highest responsible person" of the Japanese government.[4]

Chon stated that compensation should take two forms: (1) reparations between former belligerents and (2) compensation based on property claims. Regarding the former, he argued that both historically and legally, Japan and Korea were not merely a colonial master and a colony but also belligerents; from the 1930s the "Korean People's Revolutionary Army, under the leadership of the Great Leader, General Kim Il Sung, formally established an anti-Japanese front; fought the Japanese army for 15 years; and won a victory."

The Japanese side, Chon insisted, has absolutely no basis for making

---

2 The observation by a Japanese scholar that Nakahira was not really a "vice-minister-level" person, as required by the previous agreement, therefore, seems unwarranted. In terms of seniority in the Japanese Foreign Ministry, Nakahira was comparable to Chon In-ch'ol. See Yamamoto, "Nitcho kokko seijoka kosho no shoten," 78.

3 Information on the first round of the normalization talks was gleaned from Gaimusho, Ajia-kyoku, Hokuto Ajia-ka, "Nitcho kokko seijoka kosho dai-1-kai hon kaidan" [The First Regular Meeting of the Japan-North Korea Negotiations on Diplomatic Normalization], an unpublished document; *Asahi shinbun* (Tokyo), *Yomiuri shinbun* (Tokyo) and *Nodong sinmun,* January 30 and 31, 1991.

4 Here Chon was clearing ignoring the history of Japan–ROK relations, even though he was referring to the annals of relations between Japan and the Korean Peninsula as a whole. By the expression, "the highest responsible person" representing the Japanese government, he meant the prime minister, for he specifically mentioned the apology by Prime Minister Kaifu in his letter to President Kim Il Sung, which Kanemaru had personally delivered to Kim in September 1990. It is worth noting that Kaifu wrote the letter in his capacity as the president of the LDP rather than as prime minister.

property claims. Any Japanese property that may have been left in Korea was totally destroyed by the indiscriminate bombing by the US forces, who received Japanese support, during the Korean War, he said. Only the North Korean side has the right to demand both war reparations and compensation for property losses. Japan, he added, should return the cultural treasures it took from Korea in the past.

Chon then gave the following basis for North Korea's demand for compensation from Japan for the latter's acts during the 45-year postwar period: (1) Japan bears a measure of responsibility for the division of the Korean Peninsula; (2) Japan also has some responsibility relating to the Korean War; (3) By pursuing a hostile policy toward North Korea in the period following the Korean armistice, Japan has inflicted damages on North Korea in the political and economic fields; (4) Finally, since Japan has not paid what it owes to North Korea in the form of compensation, an enormous amount of interest has accrued.

As for an official apology, Chon explained that the documents that establish diplomatic relations between the two countries should include an explicit apology. Finally, he indicated that his country was working on how to calculate the amount of compensation it would demand from Japan.

Nakahira's opening speech, on the other hand, showed how far apart the two sides were on key issues. He, too, began by noting the "historical significance" of the Japan-DPRK negotiations on diplomatic normalization, stating that Japan was embarking on the course with "seriousness and sincerity." He hastened to add, however, that the negotiations should be conducted in such a way as not only to improve the bilateral relations between Japan and North Korea but also to contribute to the peace and security of the Northeast Asian region as a whole. Japan, therefore, expects North Korea to pursue a policy of openness and play a more responsible role in the world, taking into account the relaxation of tensions between East and West in recent years.

Nakahira expressed regret that "in the past there was a period in which unfortunate relations prevailed between Japan and the Korean Peninsula." He recalled that former Prime Minister Takeshita had expressed his "remorse and regret" regarding this matter in March 1989

<Table 4> Japan-DPRK Normalization Talks, 1991-1992

Round	Date	Place	Outcome
1	Jan.30-31 1991	Pyongyang	Both sides spell out their positions, revealing a wide gap.
2	March 11-12 1991	Tokyo	Japan's assertion that Kim Il Sung's guerrilla force was not autonomous but under Chinese command stuns N.Korea.
3	May 20-22 1991	Beijing	N.Korea tries in vain to separate the issue of diplomatic normalization. N.Korea lashes out against Japan when the latter raises the issue of "Yi Un-hye," a Japanese woman allegedly abducted by N.Korea.
4	Aug.31-Sep.2 1991	Beijing	N.Korea refuses to honor a previous agreement on how to deal with the "Yi Un-hye" issue. Both sides argue over the issue of compensation.
5	Nov. 18-20 1991	Beijing	N.Korea calls on Japan to make public documentary proof related to property claims. N. Korea provides some information on 32 Japanese wives of North Korean nationals.
6	Jan.30-Feb.1 1992	Beijing	The two sides disagree on whether N.Korea has fulfilled conditions Japan had set. N. Korea condemns Japan on the "comfort women" issue.
7	May 13-15 1992	Beijing	N.Korea raises the "comfort women" issue again. Japan urges N.Korea to implement agreements with IAEA and S.Korea.
8	Nov. 5-6 1992	Beijing	A N.Korean walkout over the "Yi Un-hye" issue leads to collapse of talks.

and that Prime Minister Kaifu had done the same in the Japanese Diet.

Nakahira, then, made it clear that Japan would never allow diplomatic normalization between Japan and the DPRK to have any adverse effect on Japan-ROK relations. For, he said, any deterioration in the latter would benefit neither the peace and security of Northeast Asia nor North Korea. Japan-DPRK negotiations must, therefore, leave intact the legal framework of Japan-ROK relations delineated in the Japan-ROK basic treaty.

As for economic issues, Nakahira said that the Japanese side would not accept the ideas of compensation and reparations, for Japan and North Korea were never in a state of war. The Japanese government, he stressed, is not bound by the three-party declaration, which mentions compensation.

Nakahira, then, raised a number of "international issues." One pertained to North Korea's obligation, under the provisions of the Nuclear Non-proliferation Treaty (NPT), to conclude a safeguards agreement with the IAEA. North Korea's failure to do so, he pointed out, has created the suspicion both in Japan and elsewhere that North Korea is trying to develop nuclear weapons. Should that really happen, it would pose a grave threat to Japan's security as well as to the peace and security of Northeast Asia as a whole.

Another "international issue" Nakahira mentioned concerned inter-Korean relations. While Japan believes that the problems of the Korean Peninsula should be resolved by the parties directly concerned, it nonetheless intends to conduct its negotiations with North Korea in such a way as not to hamper progress in the North-South dialogue.

By way of conclusion, Nakahira emphasized the need for the two sides to work with sincerity and patience toward finding common ground, given the great disparity in their ideologies, social systems, and positions on the various issues.

Discussions following the opening speeches failed to bridge the gap in the perceptions and positions of the two sides. North Korea used both moral and legal arguments to bolster its position. From a moral or ethical standpoint, in the North Korean view, Japan, as the aggressor and perpetrator of wrongs (*kahaeja*), has an obligation to compensate its victim (*p'ihaeja*) so as to alleviate the latter's sense of outrage and to induce a conciliatory posture.[5] North Korea further argued that under international

---

5 This account is based on Chon In-ch'ol's statements during a news conference on January 30, 1991, as reported in *Nodong sinmun*, January 31, 1991.

law a war can be waged not merely between regular armies but also between a regular army and an irregular army such as guerrillas, noting that there are many types of wars such as wars between states, colonial wars, and national liberation wars. International law, North Korea pointed out, does not stipulate that reparations should apply only to wars between states and not to wars of national liberation. North Korea also insisted that in addition to a formal apology, Japan should declare that the 1910 treaty of annexation between Japan and Korea and "all other treaties Japan imposed on the old Korean regime were illegal and thus null and void."

In response to the Japanese demand that North Korea promptly conclude a safeguards agreement with the IAEA, North Korea stated that since it and the IAEA had already reached an agreement in principle, the real hurdle remained the refusal of the United States to "remove the threat of nuclear attack against us." In view of all this, North Korea asked rhetorically, "wouldn't it be better for the Japanese government to make a friendly suggestion [to the US] so that negotiations can occur as soon as possible between the DPRK and US governments?"

Other issues discussed in the three sessions of the first round included North Korea's trade debts to Japanese firms, the status of DPRK-oriented Korean residents in Japan, and Japanese wives of North Korean nationals. Japan pressed North Korea to settle the issue of the debt, estimated to exceed 70 billion yen, as soon as possible. Regarding the North Korean residents in Japan, the Japanese side conveyed to the North Korean side its government's decision to confer on them the same legal status as South Korean residents in Japan—such as giving them the right of permanent residency and abolishing the requirement for finger-printing within two years. The Japanese side made it clear that it hoped North Korea to reciprocate by locating Japanese wives of North Korean men and allowing them to visit Japan on humanitarian grounds. The Japanese government puts the number of Japanese women who accompanied their Korean husbands to the North at 1,831. Information, however, is available in Japan, through correspondence and other means, on less than a third of them.[6]

Even though the first round merely saw an exchange of the two sides' basic positions, one could nonetheless detect state identity and national interests at work. Of the multiple dimensions of North Korea's state identity, none is more important than *chuch'e* (roughly translatable as "self-reliance." It extols independence, sovereignty, national pride and dignity. Kim Il Sung, who ruled the DPRK from its inception in 1948 to his death in 1994, is said to have authored *chuch'e* while leading anti-guerrilla struggle in the 1930s and 1940s; hence it constituted a pillar of his legitimacy and the North Korean state identity alike.[7]

All this can help explain North Korea's demand for both an apology and a compensation for Japanese colonial rule and its insistence that North Korea had been a belligerent in a war against Japan under Kim Il Sung's leadership. North Korean position also reflected material considerations: its need for Japanese funds, technology, and other forms of economic cooperation. Obtaining all of these in the form of compensation and reparation would have the distinct advantage of not compromising its national pride. For, in Pyongyang's view as articulated by its chief delegate, the DPRK was fully entitled, both morally and legally, to Japanese compensation. His argument about the illegality of all the treaties Japan had concluded with the Korean kingdom before annexation was driven by both ideational and material motives. For, not only was it designed to bolster North Korea's moral position vis-à-vis Japan but it would, if accepted by Japan, also serve to expand the basis for calculating the amount of what Japan owed to the North.

Which of Japan's multiple state identities can help explain its positions? Its identity as a peace-loving state, noted in the preceding chapter, is critically dependent on a military alliance with the US, which in turn

---

6 *Chosun ilbo* (Seoul), October 30, 1997; *Daily Yomiuri*, October 31, 1997.
7 Byung Chul Koh, *The Foreign Policy Systems of North and South Korea* (Berkeley: University of California Press, 1984), 71-74; Koh, "Chuch'e sasang ui hyongsong kwa sasang ch'egye punsok" [Analysis of *chuch'e* Ideology's Formation and Structure] in *Pukhan kaeron* [An Overview of North Korea], ed. Chey Myung (Seoul: Uryu Munhwa-sa, 1990), 87-111.

has spawned a quasi-alliance with the ROK. Supporting the core interests of Washington and Seoul, many of which Tokyo shared, therefore, was *de rigueur*. Japan's unequivocal support for the integrity of the legal framework of its relations with the ROK also served Tokyo's economic interests, for Seoul's value to Tokyo as a trading partner was far greater than Pyongyang's (in 1991 the total value of Japan-ROK merchandise trade was 65 times that of Japan-DPRK merchandise trade). Japan's identity as a trading state, in short, was by no means dormant.

Finally, Japan's insistence that North Korea conclude a safeguards agreement with the IAEA could be construed as evidence of an international regime—i.e., the nonproliferation regime—in operation.

The Second Round, March 1991

At the second round of the talks, held in Tokyo on March 11 and 12, 1991, North Korea took the position that since it had spelled out its views and demands at the first round in Pyongyang, its principal goal in the second round was to hear Japan's response to the North Korean arguments.[8] If North Korea had expected any change in or softening of Japan's stance, however, it could only have become deeply disappointed.

One Japanese response was something of a shocker. Japan's chief delegate, Ambassador Nakahira, pointed out in his opening speech that a state of war did not exist between Japan and Korea during World War II, because there was no independent state on the Korean Peninsula at the time. He added that the anti-Japanese guerrillas Kim Il Sung led were but a "unit of the Northeast People's Revolutionary Army under the Chinese Communist Party;" hence, he argued, they did not provide a basis for belligerency under international law. Ambassador Chon In-ch'ol, the chief North Korean delegate, dismissed the Japanese argument as unworthy of dicussion on the ground that it was based on flimsy evidence.[9]

---

8 *Nodong sinmun*, March 12, 1991.

Nakahira had clearly raised a sensitive issue, for, as previously noted, Kim Il Sung's leadership of anti-Japanese struggles is a corner stone of North Korea's state identity as well as the centerpiece of the cult of personality centered on him; any suggestion, therefore, that Kim had not been *the* leader of an autonomous *Korean* revolutionary army but had fought as part of a CCP-affiliated force under Chinese command cast a shadow on the legitimacy of the Kim Il Sung regime itself, thus posing a challenge to North Korea's self-identity. *Nodong sinmun* omitted any reference to the preceding exchange in its coverage of the second round of the talks.[10]

Regarding the North Korean argument that the 1910 annexation treaty and other related treaties were illegal and hence invalid *ab initio*, because they had been forcibly imposed on the Korean kingdom, Japan maintained that they were consistent with the law in effect at the time. Japan conceded, however, that they were no longer valid.[11]

Japan asked North Korea to state unequivocally that the latter's jurisdiction is limited to the northern half of the Korean Peninsula, thereby withdrawing its claim to be the only lawful government on the entire Peninsula. North Korea, however, refused to go along.

Japan not only raised the issue of Japanese wives again but also

---

9 *Nihon keizai shinbun* (Tokyo), March 12, 1991; *Asahi shinbun* (Tokyo), March 12, 1991.

10 *Nodong sinmun* (Pyongyang), March 12 and 13, 1991. The daily organ of the Workers' Party of Korea devoted a much smaller space to the second round than it did to the first. Nakahira's statement was actually consistent with the available evidence. See Dae-Sook Suh, *Kim Il Sung: The North Korean Leader* (New York: Columbia University Press, 1988); Wada Haruki, *Kita Chosen: yugekitai kokka no genzai* [North Korea: Portrait of a Guerrilla State] (Tokyo: Iwanami Shoten, 1998), chap. 2.

11 Gaimusho, Ajia-kyoku, Hokuto Ajia-ka, "Nitcho kokko seijoka kosho dai-2-kai hon kaidan (3-gatsu 11-nichi, 12-nichi) no gaiyo" [A Summary of the Second Regular Meeting of the Japan-North Korea Negotiatiions on Diplomatic Normalization (March 11 & 12)], March 14, 1991, a mimeographed document, 1.

added a new one: the return of the seven former Japanese Red Army members who hijacked a Japan Air Lines passenger plane (*Yodo-go*) to North Korea in March 1970. North Korea dismissed the Yodo issue as irrelevant to diplomatic normalization but showed some flexibility on the other issue: although a full resolution of the issue is contingent upon diplomatic normalization, North Korea stated, some relief can be provided on a case-by-case basis depending on the progress of the normalization talks.[12]

On international issues, North Korea reiterated its argument that the main barrier to its conclusion of a nuclear safeguards agreement with the IAEA was the refusal by the US to give assurance that it would not launch a nuclear attack against North Korea; North Korea also told Japan that the issue concerned Pyongyang and Washington only and was therefore irrelevant to diplomatic normalization between Pyongyang and Tokyo. North Korea also criticized Japan's linking their bilateral negotiations to progress in the inter-Korean dialogue on the ground that the two were fundamentally different: whereas both Japan and North Korea shared a common interest in normalizing their relations, North and South Korea were pursuing sharply divergent goals, North Korea claimed. While North Korea was pursuing the reunification of the Peninsula, North Korea asserted, South Korea was intent on maintaining the status quo of divided Korea.[13]

Notwithstanding the lack of progress, North Korea sounded a note of optimism. Chon In-ch'ol said in a news conference on March 11 that the talks were "proceeding in a general climate of mutual respect and friendship," expressing his "conviction" that the third round of the talks would witness the beginning of real forward movement.[14]

---

12 Ibid., 2; *Asahi shinbun*, March 11, 1991 (evening edition) and March 12, 1991 (evening edition).
13 *Nodong sinmun*, March 12, 1991.
14 Ibid.

The Third Round, May 1991

Chon's optimistic prognosis, however, proved to be way off the mark. For the third round of the talks, held in Beijing from May 20 to 22, 1991, turned out to be the most contentious encounter between the two sides since they embarked on negotiations six months ago (counting their preliminary contacts prior to the initiation of the main negotiations). Unlike the first two rounds, each of which featured three negotiating sessions in two days, the third round lasted three days, during which five negotiating sessions occurred.

The Japanese side was apparently caught off guard by North Korea's new tactical maneuver: Chon In-ch'ol proposed that the first item on the agenda (the basic issue) be separated from the remaining items with the aim of establishing diplomatic relations before resolving the other issues. He argued that the "new proposal" was designed to break the deadlock in the negotiations. Diplomatic normalization, he said, will enable the two countries to deepen their mutual understanding and trust, thereby facilitating the solution of the other issues. Chon stressed that all the issues need to be tackled sequentially, rather than simultaneously.[15]

For its part, the Japanese delegation had come to Beijing to prod North Korea to meet three preconditions and to raise a sensitive issue anew. The three preconditions were: (1) North Korea's acceptance of inspections of its nuclear facilities by the IAEA, (2) an early resumption of the high-level or prime ministerial talks between North and South Korea, and (3) North Korea's acceptance of South Korea's proposal for their simultaneous admission to the United Nations. The sensitive issue pertained to "Yi Un-hye," the Japanese woman who had allegedly been kidnapped by North Korea and served as a tutor to Kim Hyon-hui, the North Korean agent who blew up a Korean Air passenger plane in November 1987.[16]

---

15 *Nodong sinmun*, May 21, 1991.
16 Gaimusho, Ajia-kyoku, Hokuto Ajia-ka, "Nitcho kokko seijoka kosho dai-3-kai hon kaidan" [The Third Regular Meeting of the Japan-North Korea

Regarding the nuclear issue, North Korea stuck to its previously-enunciated position that the principal hurdle to its signing a safeguards agreement with the IAEA was the United States. North Korea once again urged Japan to persuade the US to conduct negotiations with North Korea on the issue. North Korea's response to the other two preconditions was equally negative. Arguing that the responsibility for the suspension of the inter-Korean dialogue lay exclusively with the US and South Korea, which, in the North Korean view, are jointly manuevering to provoke a new war on the Korean Peninsula, North Korea accused Japan of pursuing a "policy biased in favor of South Korea (*Nam Choson e taehan ilbyondo chongch'aek*)." The UN issue, North Korea insisted, constitutes an "internal problem of the Korean people," in which Japan has no right to interfere. North Korea also accused South Korea of taking such an internal problem to the international arena to drum up support for its own position.[17]

When Japan rejected on the last day of the third round the North Korean proposal for the separation of the four items on the agenda with a view toward resolving the diplomatic normalization issue first, North Korea reacted angrily. The need to consult Tokyo on the matter had led to a delay in the Japanese response. Nakahira stated that Japan preferred to deal with all the issues prior to diplomatic normalization. North Korea's failure to perform its international obligations, notably the conclusion of a nuclear safeguards agreement with the IAEA, moreover, led Japan to question the trustworthiness of North Korea, he said.[18]

Chon In-ch'ol, recalling the three-party declaration's provision on the issue, asked rhetorically: "[If the Japanese government believes that our

---

Negotiations on Diplomatic Normalization], May 23, 1991, a mimeographed document; *Asahi shinbun,* May 20, 1991 (evening edition); *Yomiuri shinbun,* May 20, 1991 (evening edition). On the Korean Air incident that spwaned the Yi Un-hye issue, see B. C. Koh, "North Korea in 1988: The Fortieth Anniversary," *Asian Survey* 29, no. 1 (Jan. 1989), 43.

17 *Nodong sinmun,* May 21, 1991.
18 Ibid, May 23, 1991; *Yomiuri shinbun,* May 23, 1991.

Republic is unqualified to establish diplomatic relations with it,] then why has it started the negotiations on diplomatic normalization?" Denouncing the Japanese government's behavior as an "insult" to North Korea, Chon told the Japanese side that "we can survive without normalizing diplomatic relations with Japan" and that "since we have lived freely and well for the past 45 years, we shall live in our own way in the future, too."[19]

It was, however, the Yi Un-hye issue that irked North Korea the most. When Nakahira raised the issue during the fifth and final session of the third round, asking North Korea to investigate whether she is alive, Chon In-ch'ol interrupted Nakahira. Due to North Korean manuevers, the Japanese side had been unable to obtain North Korea's prior consent to that particular agenda item. Referring to the absence of consent, Chon accused the Japanese side of disrupting the orderly conduct of the negotiations. "If your side behaves this way, then we see no need to sit face to face at the conference table," he said. Chon then demanded that Nakahira immediately withdraw his statement on Yi Un-hye and apologize. Chon even questioned the "sanity" of the Japanese action, calling it "an intolerable insult and challenge to us" and "behavior calculated to torpedo the normalization talks."[20]

North Korea's reaction described above stems from its consistent position that it had nothing to do with the Korean Air bombing incident, that the latter had been a "self-enacted drama" (*chajakguk*) by South Korea, and that Kim Hyon-hui, the confessed North Korean agent, was a "phony culprit" (*katja pomin*) totally alien to North Korea. If Kim Hyon-hui is phony, then her alleged tutor, Yi Un-hye, cannot be a real person, either.[21] To even agree to look into the matter, therefore, would be tantamount to an indirect admission by North Korea that it had been less than truthful regarding the Korean Air incident. To admit responsibility for the

---

19 *Nodong sinmun*, May 23, 1991.
20 Ibid.
21 Chon In-ch'ol repeated all these points about the Korean Air bombing incident in his angry response to the Japanese request. Ibid.

incident, on the other hand, would be to acknowledge that it does indeed engage in international terrorism, which North Korea's celebrated *chuch'e* ideology, with its accent on national pride and dignity, would not condone. At stake, in other words, was none other than its identity as a proud, sovereign state pursuing independence and national dignity in the world arena.

The harsh language used and the pugnacity displayed by North Korea during the third round of the normalization talks stunned the Japanese negotiators; the North Korean rhetoric and behavior probably had few or no precedent in the annals of Japan's diplomatic negotiations. The third round ended without any agreement on the date of the next round, even though both sides did agree that it should be held.

The Fourth Round, August-September 1991

The Yi Un-hye issue would become a major impediment to the conduct of future negotiations. It was, in fact, only after a compromise was reached on how to deal with the issue that the fourth round of the normalization talks convened in Beijing on August 31. In July two Japanese emissaries and the North Korean side reached an agreement in Pyongyang under which the issue would be handled in a "working-level" meeting that would be held in conjunction with the main meeting. When such a working-level meeting convened on August 31 between the second-ranking members of both delegations, however, North Korea reneged on its promise and refused Japan's request for an investigation of the Yi Un-hye matter. North Korea claimed that it had never agreed to such an arrangement; all it had accepted, it asserted, was to acknowledge Japanese request without necessarily agreeing to take any action.[22]

---

22 Gaimusho, Ajia-kyoku, Hokuto Ajia-ka, "Dai-4-kai Nitcho kokko seijoka kosho no gaiyo" [A Summary of the Fourth Round of the Japan-North Korea Negotiations on Diplomatic Normalization," August 1991, an unpublished document; *Asahi shinbun*, September 1, 1991; *Nodong sinmun*, September 1,

The Japanese delegation responded by refusing to hold a regular meeting. The impasse was finally broken with another compromise under which North Korea acquiesced to Japan's right to raise the issue whenever it so desired in working-level meetings. Since that was not really a compromise but equivalent to a Japanese concession, there was speculation that the decision to hold a regular meeting, after a one-and-a-half-day delay, was made by Prime Minister Kaifu who had to take into account the pressure from Kanemaru and Tanabe, the latter of whom by then had become the chairman of the SDPJ.[23]

In his opening speech at the first session of the fourth round, Nakahira noted that at least two of the conditions Japan had previously set were close to being met. In May, within a few days of the stormy conclusion of the third round of the normalization talks, North Korea announced a reversal of its policy on the UN membership issue, and by the time the fourth round of the talks began, had already submitted an application to the UN for membership. A key factor in the DPRK's reversal of its UN policy appeared to be China's decision not to veto the ROK's application for UN membership.[24] North Korea also announced that it and the IAEA had resolved their differences regarding the wording of a safeguards agreement. Welcoming that development, Nakahira urged North Korea not only to sign the agreement promptly but also to allow the IAEA actually to conduct inspections of nuclear facilities. With respect to the third condition, however, Nakahira expressed regret that North Korea had unilaterally postponed the convening of the inter-Korean prime ministerial talks.[25]

North Korea denounced Nakahira's remarks as constituting an interference in its internal affairs. It also repeated its previous charge that Japan

---

1991.
23 *Asahi shinbun*, September 1, 1991.
24 B. C. Koh, "North Korea's Policy toward the United Nations," in *The United Nations and Keeping Peace in Northeast Asia*, ed. Sung-Hack Kang (Seoul: Institute for Peace Studies, Korea University, 1995), 43-72.
25 *Yomiuri shinbun*, September 1, 1991.

was being partial to South Korea and excessively hostile toward North Korea on all these issues. North Korea even suggested that if Japan is really interested in seeing progress made in the inter-Korean dialogue, it should advice South Korea to show sincerity in the dialogue.[26]

It was on the issue of compensation or, according to the official agenda, economic issues that North Korea made the strongest pitch. Japan had stated that the term "property claims" would be broadly construed to encompass claims for "human" damages provided they could be proven with "objective" documentary and other material. Upon hearing Japan's explanation that conscription of Koreans for either military service or work in mines and factories had not created any liability for the Japanese government, because it was consistent with the law in effect at the time, however, North Korea expressed its anger. If practically everything the Japanese did during the colonial period was consistent with the laws Japan had enacted, North Korea asked, then is Japan really interested in making any compensatory payments? Japan's position that it would only pay for losses that can be verified with bank passbooks, pension certificates, and other documents, North Korea charged, was a total sham. How many people, North Korea asked, can be reasonably expected to have saved such documents for 50 years or more?[27]

North Korea argued that the damage Japan had inflicted on the Korean people was criminal in nature, citing the death of "several million" Koreans in Japanese prisons, in combat, and in forced labor camps as well as the conscription of "hundreds of thousands" of Korean women to serve as "comfort women" for Japanese soldiers. Given all this, North Korea said, Japan can never evade its responsibility to pay compensation to the Korean people, whether it be called "war reparations," "compensation for damages," or whatever.[28]

If there was any forward movement during the fourth round, it was on the issue of jurisdiction. North Korea agreed that it would seriously

---

26 *Nodong sinmun*, September 3, 1991.
27 Ibid., September 2, 1991.
28 Ibid.

consider Japan's proposal that the North Korean statement, "the DPRK's jurisdiction extends to the northern part of the Korean Peninsula," be replaced by the statement, "the DPRK's jurisdiction extends to the north of the armistice line." With respect to the issue of Japanese wives, North Korea repeated its previous position that while a complete resolution of the problem hinged on diplomatic normalization, it would nonetheless take action on a case-by-case basis depending on the progress of the normalization talks.[29]

The Fifth Round, November 1991

By the time the fifth round of the normalization talks opened in Beijing on November 18, the issue of the UN admission had been settled, with both North and South Korea having been admitted to the world organization as full-fledged members in September. What is more, the inter-Korean prime ministerial talks had resumed, even though no real progress had been registered. The only international issue on which Japan found it necessary to express concern, therefore, was the nuclear issue. Japan urged North Korea to sign a safeguards agreement with the IAEA without further delay, stressing in particular that if North Korea does indeed possess a nuclear reprocessing facility, that would pose a serious threat to Japan's security. Japan expressed hope that the DPRK would respond positively to ROK President Roh Tae Woo's call for the denuclearization of the Korean Peninsula.[30]

Predictably, North Korea did not take Japan's demand kindly. Accusing Japan of having created "artificial barriers" to the talks, North Korea repeated its previous argument that the root cause of the nuclear

---

29 *Yomiuri shinbun*, September 2, 1991 (evening edition).
30 Gaimusho, Ajia-kyoku, Hokuto Ajia-ka, "Nitcho kokko seijoka dai-5-kai hon kaidan no gaiyo (11-gatsu 18-20-nichi)" [A Summary of the Main Meeting of the Japan-North Korea Normalization Talks (November 18-20)], November 21, 1991, an unpublished document.

problem was the United States, not North Korea. North Korea belittled Roh Tae Woo's "denuclearization declaration" as "barely worth 50 percent" of the proposal it had unveiled on July 30. Since the Roh declaration does not mention the nuclear weapons deployed by the US in South Korea, North Korea asserted, it fails to deal with the crux of the problem. North Korea reiterated the charge that Japan was being too partial to South Korea, behaving as the latter's spokesman; North Korea pointed an accusing finger to Japan's co-sponsorship of a "resolution aimed at exerting pressure on us" at the September meeting of the IAEA executive board.[31]

On the economic issue, North Korea presented a lengthy argument on why it thought Japan's demand for "objective material" (i.e., proof) relating to damages suffered by the Korean people was unreasonable. Pointing to some "international precedents"—notably, Germany's compensation of Jews and the compensation by the US and Canada of their nationals of Japanese descent—, North Korea argued that international practice does not require legal basis for compensation. North Korea called on Japan to show sincerity by making public "legal proof" Japan itself possesses. Japan rejected the North Korean argument about "international practice," repeating its previous position that North Korea must provide basis for any property claims it wishes to make.[32]

The jurisdictional issue, on which North Korea had hinted the possibility of concession at the fourth round of the talks, failed to get resolved, although there was useful exchange of views. Something new, however, did happen with respect to the issue of Japanese wives. North Korea brought some information on 32 Japanese wives: Of the 12 women on whom Japan had previously requested information, North Korea informed the Japanese delegation that six were alive and well, five had died of illness, and one could not be located. Regarding 20 other women whom Japan had asked North Korea to allow to visit their relatives in Japan, North Korea said that they were all alive and well, even though it

---

31 *Nodong sinmun*, November 20, 1991.
32 Ibid.; *Yomiuri shinbun*, November 20, 1991.

would not comply with the Japanese request. Japan requested North Korea to ascertain the status of 20 other Japanese wives.[33]

As for the Yi Un-hye issue, there was absolutely no change in the picture. While Japan offered in a "working-level meeting" to give North Korea material Japan had gathered on Yi Un-hye, asking North Korea to verify it, North Korea flatly turned down both the offer and the request on the ground that Yi was a fictional character from South Korea's "self-enacted drama." Claiming that its own version of the Korean Air incident was "internationally accepted" as true, North Korea urged Japan to make its request to South Korea's Agency for National Security Planning, the alleged "producer" of the "South Korean drama."[34] As noted, this issue was directly linked to North Korea's state identity, thus prompting Pyongyang to cling to a hard line.

The Sixth Round, January-February 1992

The sixth round of the normalization talks convened in Beijing on January 30, 1992, exactly one year after the talks began in Pyongyang. Several developments that had either preceded or were happening concurrently with the sixth round made North Korea very cocky and go on the offensive. The relevant developments included the following: In December 1991 North and South Korea signed two major agreements—one on reconciliation, non-aggression, and mutual exchanges (known as the basic agreement) and another on the denuclearization of the Korean Peninsula. On January 22, 1992 North Korea attained its long-sought goal of upgrading its diplomatic contacts with the US, when Kim Yong Sun, the WPK secretary in charge of international affairs—who incidentally had been a key figure in the political negotiations between Japan and the DPRK that produced the three-party declaration in September 1990—

---

33 Ibid., November 21, 1991.
34 *Nodong sinmun*, November 19, 1991.

held a meeting in New York with Arnold Kanter, the Under Secretary of State for Political Affairs. Finally, on January 30, 1992, the very same day when the sixth round of the Japan-DPRK talks opened, North Korea signed a full-scope safeguards agreement with the IAEA.[35]

As far as North Korea was concerned, all this meant that the three preconditions Japan had previously set—namely, (1) acceptance of inspections of its nuclear facilities by the IAEA, (2) progress in the inter-Korean dialogue, and (3) the admission of both Korean states to the UN—had been fulfilled; hence North Korea challenged Japan to move expeditiously toward diplomatic normalization.[36] The Japanese perception, however, was different. In its view, the mere signing of the nuclear safeguards agreement by North Korea had not settled the nuclear issue. Actual inspections by the IAEA need to occur, and the suspicions about North Korea's nuclear weapons development program need to be cleared.[37]

Subsequent developments showed that Japan's cautious approach had been most prudent. Nonetheless, at the sixth round of the talks, North Korea staked out a moral high ground. It even exaggerated the global response to its new pragmatism, saying that the IAEA, the US, and South Korea had all expressed their satisfaction with North Korea's signing of the safeguards agreement. Why, it asked, does Japan persist in raising doubts? It then turned the table, accusing Japan of scheming to pro-

---

35 For the texts of the two inter-Korean agreements, which entered into force in February, 1992, see Republic of Korea, Unification Board, *Nambuk taehwa* [South-North Dialogue], no. 54 (Seoul: T'ong'il-won, Nambuk Taehwa Samuguk, 1992); for articles on the Kim-Kanter meeting and North Korea's signing of the nuclear safeguards agreement, *see New York Times*, January 23 and 31, 1992.

36 *Nodong sinmun*, January 31, 1992.

37 Gaimusho, Ajia-kyoku, Hokuto Ajia-ka, "Dai-6-kai Nitcho kokko seijoka kosho no gaiyo" [A Summary of the Sixth Round of Japan-North Korea Negotiations on Diplomatic Normalization], February 6, 1992, an unpublished document; *Yomiuri shinbun and Asahi shinbun*, January 30 (evening edition) and 31, 1992.

duce nuclear weapons, citing Japan's import of huge amounts of plutonium. North Korea also argued that "even the United States has embarked on the path of normalizing relations with us and the countries of the European Community are showing interest in establishing diplomatic relations" with it. North Korea warned that Japan might become the only major country without diplomatic relations with it.[38]

North Korea pounded repeatedly on the question of Japan's responsibility for "crimes committed against the Korean people," concentrating on the issue of "comfort women." Recalling that Japan had previously argued that the conscription of Korean men for work in war-related projects had been consistent with the laws that were in force at the time, North Korea asked: "Which specific law provided the basis for the heinous act of forcing 200,000 Korean women, including adolescents between the ages of 12 and 16, to serve as 'comfort women' for Japanese soldiers in the battle zones?"[39]

North Korea also quoted from an article in a French newspaper saying that it had taken a half century for the tragedy of Korean comfort women to be revealed to the world and for the Japanese government to apologize for it. North Korea then asked: "How many centuries will be required before Japan will admit all of its crimes [against the Korean people]?" North Korea also challenged the Japanese side to clarify the discrepancy between Prime Minister Miyazawa's apology for the harm done to Korean comfort women on one hand and Japan's insistence at the normalization talks on the other hand that nearly everything that had happened during the colonial period, inflicting damage beyond repair, had been consistent with Japanese laws then in force.[40]

Another issue on which North Korea made an impassioned argument was the legality or, in its view, illegality of the 1910 annexation treaty and other related treaties. North Korea cited the Vienna Convention on the Law of Treaties to the effect that treaties that are concluded under

---

38 *Nodong sinmun*, January 31, 1992.
39 Ibid.
40 Ibid.

duress are void *ab initio*; hence, it asserted, none of the coerced treaties had been valid under international law. In response to the North Korean contention, Japan drew a distinction between legality and morality or justifiability, arguing that while the treaties in question might have been immoral or unjustifiable, they were nonetheless legal, given the laws in force at the time.[41]

Japan argued that in order to ensure that the treaty that is to be concluded between the two sides not disturb the basic legal framework of Japan-ROK relations, it should affirm the provision of the San Francisco peace treaty that mentions Korea. North Korea rejected the Japanese view, saying that since the DPRK came into being in 1948 as an independent state on the basis of "the struggle of our own people," the San Francisco peace treaty, which was signed three years later in 1951, had no relevance whatsoever for the DPRK. North Korea charged that Japan's covert aim was to induce North Korea to accept the claim that Korea had become independent after being separated from Japan, which was diametrically opposed to North Korea's position.[42]

North Korea made a proposal of its own regarding what the treaty between the two countries should contain: it wanted an anti-domination clause. That is, North Korea wanted both parties to renounce any intention to dominate other states. Japan responded by saying that such a clause would be superfluous if both sides would respect the principles of the UN Charter, as they are legally obligated to do as UN members. North Korea countered by arguing that given the history of Japan-Korea relations, it believed that such a clause was essential.[43]

On the issue of compensation, North Korea mentioned the Potsdam declaration, the Cairo declaration, and the charter of the International Military Tribunal for the Far East. All of these documents, in the North Korean view, prove that what Japan did to the Korean people during the colonial period—such as forcing them to serve in the armed services, in

---

41 Ibid., February 1, 1992; Gaimusho, "Dai-6-kai······."
42 *Nodong sinmun* (Pyongyang), February 1, 1993.
43 Ibid.; Gaimusho, "Dai-6-kai······."

war-related projects, as comfort women and imprisoning and killing them as "thought criminals"—created criminal responsibility under international law and thereby imposed an obligation on Japan to make compensatory payments.[44]

North Korea provided information on the status of 20 Japanese women in response to a specific request Japan had made at the fifth round of the talks: nine were alive, seven were dead, and the remaining four could not be located. Once again North Korea reminded Japan that the entire problem could be resolved when and if normalization should materialize. North Korea complained that Japan had not fully implemented its earlier commitment to treat DPRK-oriented Korean residents in Japan fairly, citing what it called incidents of harassment against such people; North Korea wanted Japan to stop not only harassment but also discriminatory treatment of North Korea-oriented schools.[45]

Finally, both sides sounded like a broken record when they held "working-level consultations" on the Yi Un-hye issue, with Japan demanding that North Korea investigate the case and North Korea reiterating its position that since no such person ever existed, there was absolutely no need to do anything about it. On the whole, the most striking aspect of the sixth round was the self-confidence and self-righteousness displayed by North Korea. Apparently convinced that it had a stronger case to make than Japan, North Korea courted the press with unparalleled vigor, handing out press releases and holding press conferences more frequently than had been the case during the previous rounds of the talks. North Korea allowed South Korean journalists to attend its press briefings for the first time; in addition to its eagerness to publicize its views, the improvement in inter-Korean relations in the wake of the signing of the two inter-Korean agreements helped to explain North Korean behavior.

---

44 *Nodong sinmun*, February 2, 1992.
45 Ibid.

The Seventh Round, May 1992

The seventh round of the normalization talks was held in Beijing from May 13 to 15, 1992. While both sides adhered doggedly to their previously articulated positions, there were nonetheless some notable developments. First of all, the head of the North Korean delegation had changed. Due to the death of Chon In-ch'ol, Yi Sam-no, who had been second in command, had been promoted to take charge of the North Korean team. Second, North Korea tried in vain to persuade Japan that it was in Japan's best interests to accede to North Korean demands regarding compensation. Third, North Korea made a veiled threat about "serious consequences," should Japan persist in raising the Yi Un-hye issue. In view of what happened at the next round of the talks, the North Korean threat seemed prophetic.[46]

North Korea asserted that since the compensation issue was linked to human rights, human conscience, and reason, Japan's handling of it would reflect upon the moral values of the Japanese government and would affect Japan's international standing. To underscore the point that forcing Korean women to serve as "comfort women" for Japanese soldiers during World War II had been a "heinous and anti-human crime of unparalleled magnitude," North Korea introduced a testimony of a 74-year-old "former comfort woman." North Korea insisted that whether Japan is willing to "admit its responsibility before history" for all of its "past crimes" will provide a test of whether Japan is determined not to repeat its mistakes in the future. North Korea also accused Japan of practicing discrimination against other national groups by paying compensation to its own citizens only.[47]

---

46 Gaimusho, Ajia Kyoku, Hokuto Ajia-ka, "Nitcho kokko seijoka dai-7-kai hon kaidan no gaiyo (5-gatsu 13-nichi-15-nichi) [A Summary of the Seventh Regular Meeting of Japan-North Korea Negotiations on Diplomatic Normalization (May 13-15), May 15, 1992, an unpublished document; *Asahi shinbun* and *Yomiuri shinbun*, May 13 through 16, 1992 (including evening editions); *Nodong sinmun*, May 14-16, 1992.

Japan stressed once again that unless all the doubts about North Korea's nuclear weapons program are removed through effective implementation of its safeguards agreement with the IAEA and the inter-Korean declaration on denuclearization, Japan would find it difficult to establish diplomatic relations with North Korea. North Korea responded by saying that the nuclear issue was on the verge of resolution, citing its preliminary report to the IAEA and the visit of IAEA director-general Hans Blix to North Korea. In the North Korea view, Japan was simply trying to create a new impediment to block progress in the normalization talks; North Korea reiterated its earlier assertion that it was Japan that posed a nuclear threat in Northeast Asia, not North Korea.[48]

As noted, in "working-level consultations" on the Yi Un-hye issue, North Korea not only stuck to its previous position but also sounded an ominously harsh note. Accusing the Japanese side of "damaging the honor of our Republic," North Korea warned that should the Japanese side attempt to use the issue as a bargaining tool, that would "greatly escalate the anti-Japanese feelings of our people, creating severe consequences on the relations between our two countries."[49]

The Eighth Round, November 1992

The Yi Un-hye issue did indeed prove to be the rock on which the normalization talks came very close to foundering. The eighth round of the talks, which opened in Beijing on November 5, 1992 after a six-month hiatus, closed on the same day due to North Korean intransigence on the issue. The eighth round, which lasted only half a day, thus became the shortest ever.[50]

---

47 *Nodong sinmun*, May 15, 1992.
48 Ibid.
49 Ibid., May 14, 1992.
50 Gaimusho, Ajia-kyoku, Hokuto Ajia-ka, "Dai-8-kai Nitcho kokko seijoka kosho hon kaidan ni tsuite (11-gatsu 5-6-nichi)" [On the Eighth Main

During the first and only session of the main meeting on the morning of November 5, the heads of both delegations, Nakahira Noboru and Yi Sam-no, delivered their opening speeches. Nakahira repeated Japan's consistent demand that North Korea promptly dispel all suspicions about its nuclear weapons program by agreeing to mutual inspections of nuclear facilities with South Korea and by fulfilling all of its obligations under the nuclear safeguards agreement with the IAEA. Nakahira also expressed the hope that both sides can engage in "constructive" negotiations on economic issues. Additionally, he asked North Korea to allow Japanese wives to visit their relatives in Japan on humanitarian grounds.[51]

Yi Sam-no stressed that a core problem in the Japan-North Korean negotiations was to "settle the past," during which Japan was the aggressor and Korea the victim. North Korea repeated its argument about the invalidity of the treaties the old Korean kingdom had concluded with Japan; in addition to their coerced nature, North Korea pointed to their failure to observe the domestic laws of old Korea. According to North Korea, the latter stipulated that treaties with other countries should have both the prior approval and the seal of the king, neither of which appeared on some of the treaties, notably the 1905 and 1907 treaties; hence these were invalid, North Korea contended.[52]

In view of the invalidity of the various treaties, North Korea argued, the compensation issue should be handled not on the basis of property claims but on the basis of the relationship between the aggressor and the aggressed, between the inflictor of harm and the victim. Yi Sam-no called on Japan to stop raising "artificial barriers that have nothing to do with the talks such as the nuclear issue." In response to Japan's reiteration of its demand for removal of doubts about North Korea's alleged nuclear

---

Meeting of the Japan-North Korea Negotiations on Diplomatic Normalization (November 5-6)], November 9, 1992, an unpublished document; *Asahi shinbun* and *Yomiuri shinbun*, November 5 (evening edition) and 6, 1992; *Nodong sinmun*, November 6, 1992.

51 Gaimusho, "Dai-8-kai······"
52 *Nodong sinmun*, November 6, 1992.

weapons program, North Korea reminded Japan that IAEA inspections had occurred and were continuing; it challenged Japan to produce specific evidence regarding North Korea's alleged nuclear weapons program. North Korea also chided Japan for raising the issue of Japanese wives, while ignoring the tragedy of "200,000 Korean women who had been forced to serve as sex slaves for the [Japanese] 'imperial army.'"[53]

The most stunning development occurred, however, in the working-level contacts—between the deputy heads of both delegations—after the morning session. Ch'on Yong-bok, the North Korean delegate, asked for the right to speak first. Reading from a prepared text, Ch'on repeated the North Korean claim that North Korea had absolutely nothing to do with the Korean Air bombing incident, the source of the Yi Un-hye issue. He then denounced Japan for raising the issue of a "nonexistent [Japanese] woman," while refusing to apologize for the "atrocities committed against [Korean] comfort women." Accusing Japan of having harmed the "dignity of our Republic," Ch'on declared that there was no need to listen to what the Japanese side had to say on the issue. He and his three colleagues then walked out.[54]

As far as the Japanese side was concerned, the North Korean action was in breach of an understanding that had been reached between the two sides during the fourth round of the talks; North Korea had agreed to hold working-level consultations with Japan at any time when Japan wishes to discuss the Yi Un-hye issue. When North Korea refused to heed Japan's call for the resumption of the working-level consultations, Japan decided not to proceed with the remainder of the talks. The talks thus adjourned without any agreement on the dates of the next round.

---

53 Ibid.
54 *Asahi shinbun*, November 6, 1992; *Nodong sinmun*, November 7, 1992.

Conclusion

State identity, a core concept in constructivism, may help us understand the behavior of North Korea and Japan alike during the first phase of their bilateral negotiations for diplomatic normalization. To begin with North Korea, the high moral ground the North staked out for itself, the persistence with which it sought to maximize the scope of Japan's liability to the Korean people, and the shrillness, not to mention the shrewdness, with which it reacted to Japan's raising of the Yi Un-hye issue—all these can be understood in terms of North Korea's state identity.

As Scott Snyder points out, the charismatic experience of a national founder and ruler "has played a major role in the construction of both state and national identity in many postcolonial societies of Asia and Africa." In North Korea, it was the guerrilla experience of Kim Il Sung that provided the material with which to "weave a new history, a mythic identity that would erase the past humiliations and failures, replacing historical reality with national mythology."[55] Themes that Kim Il Sung chose to stress included (1) the "will to persevere despite tremendous odds for the sake of redeeming the nation," (2) "defiance of fate and assertion as the actor, or subject, as the creator of history rather than as the passive object shaped by historical experience,"[56] (3) independence in thought, economic self-reliance, and self-defense, and (4) national pride and dignity. These are the essence of his *chuch'e* idea, which became North Korea's reigning ideology.[57]

To the above should be added "commitment, solidarity, and unconventional tactics," which Snyder identifies as the "core resources of a guerrilla fighter who has nothing to lose and yet faces the prospect of losing

---

55 Scott Snyder, *Negotiating on the Edge: North Korean Negotiating Behavior* (Washington, DC: United States Institute of Peace Press, 1999), 21-22.
56 Ibid., 22.
57 Robert A. Scalapino and Chong-Sik Lee, *Communism in Korea, Part II: The Society* (Berkeley: University of California Press, 1972), 863-70.

everything." "There is," Snyder adds, "little benefit to be gained and much danger to be faced if one plays strictly by the opponent's rules."[58]

North Korea's state identity affects its negotiating behavior in a number of ways. One can see its effects in Pyongyang's "'stubbornness' (or resolve accompanied by guerrilla tactics), 'self-reliance,' and a strong defense of sovereignty." So, too, can North Korean negotiators' obsession with "equivalency" and "reciprocity" in negotiations with the United States be construed as a manifestation of North Korea's *chuch'e*-centered identity.[59]

Given all this, North Koreans could not but react angrily to Japanese statements that, wittingly or unwittingly, detracted from the legend of Kim Il Sung's "heroic anti-Japanese struggle" as leader of a putatively independent Korean revolutionary army.[60] Nor could North Korea budge from its contention that as the aggressor Japan is both legally and morally obligated to compensate its victims. Any challenge to the sovereignty and dignity of the DPRK must be met with stubborn resistance, and the Yi Un-hye issue represented precisely such a challenge.

The guerrilla tradition in North Korea's state identity may help explain its lack of sincerity, that is, its repeated reneging of agreements hammered out in laborious negotiations. It is also possible that *chuch'e* may give rise to self-righteousness and a mindset that is prone to justify any means, no matter how devious, for a higher cause. If that is indeed the case, the need to defend perceived national interest can easily justify a breach of promise.

In what ways did state identity also help shape Japan's negotiating behavior vis-a-vis North Korea? Japan's "trading state" identity was not as

---

58 Snyder, *Negotiating on the Edge*, 22.
59 Ibid., 9.
60 For authoritative scholarly accounts of Kim Il Sung's background, see Dae-Sook Suh, *The Korean Communist Movement 1918-1948* (Princeton: Princeton University Press, 1967), Part V: The Rise of Kim Il-song, chap. 9 and 10; Scalapino and Lee, *Communism in Korea, Part I: The Movement*, 202-230; Wada Haruki, *Kita Chosen: yugekitai kokka no genzai* [North Korea: The Current Condition of a Guerrilla State], 23-84.

salient in the first phase of the normalization talks as a "peace-loving state" and a leading industrialized democracy, a member of the Group of Seven (G-7).

Although Japan embraced "antimilitarism" in the postwar period,[61] its identity as a "peace-loving state" in the essentially anarchic world could be sustained only with the aid of a military alliance with the United States. That in turn brought Japan into a de facto alliance or a quasi-alliance with South Korea. This meant that Japan could not deviate from the positions of the US and South Korea on North Korea's perceived nuclear threat, the need for inter-Korean dialogue, and other issues relating to the Korean peninsula. Japan thus steadfastly adhered to what North Korea saw as the policy of championing the cause of South Korea and the US on issues not directly related to normalization.

Japan's self-identity as a leading industrialized democracy, the sole non-Western member of G-7, dictated that it adhere scrupulously to all of the internationally-accepted norms of inter-state behavior, including *pacta sunt servanda*. Commitments made therefore were not only to be honored by Japan but expected to be honored by North Korea as well. What actually transpired, then, was a clash of norms and identities—those of what Wada calls a "guerrilla state" and those of a "peace-loving state" dependent on an alliance with a superpower and an advanced industrialized nation boasting a G-7 membership.

The concept of "two-level games" may help illuminate the behavior of the two negotiating parties. As postulated by Robert D. Putnam, the process of international bargaining consists of two stages (or levels): (1) Level I in which the negotiators representing their states bargain with the aim of reaching a tentative agreement and (2) Level II in which separate discussions take place "within each group of constituents about whether to ratify the agreement." The need to obtain ratification in each state's domestic political arena generates what Putnam calls the "win-set"—"the set of all possible Level I agreements that would 'win'······when simply

---

61 Berger, "Norms, Identity, and National Security in Germany and Japan," 318.

voted up or down."[62] In North Korea, the win-set is delimited by its governing elite's need to safeguard the DPRK's systemic integrity, reigning ideology, and state legitimacy. In Japan, which, unlike North Korea, is a pluralist democracy, political rivalry and competition among various groups, be they bureaucratic agencies, political or civic organizations, or interest groups, define the boundaries of the win-set.

A case in point is the way in which the Yi Un-hye issue emerged as a major stumbling block. The revelation by Japan's police authorities about Yi Un-hye was made while the normalization talks were under way apparently without prior consultation with the Foreign Ministry.[63] Such a lack of inter-agency coordination is not unusual in the modus operandi of Japanese government bureaucracy.[64] The possibility cannot be ruled out that the conservative elements in the Japanese government, who are well represented in the police leadership, may have released the information on Yi Un-hye in order to impede Japan-DPRK negotiations. Once the issue had become salient in Japan, the Foreign Ministry had little choice but to raise it in the normalization talks.

Another way in which internal political dynamics may have affected Japanese behavior pertains to the compromise reached at the fourth round of the talks on how to deal with the Yi Un-hye issue. As already noted, by merely accepting North Korea's offer to recognize Japan's right to raise the issue in working-level meetings, Japan made a concession to North Korea. For the right to raise the issue, as experience had already shown, was not the same as the right to have a discussion on the issue.

---

62 Putnam, "Diplomacy and Domestic Politics: The Logic of Two-level Games," 438-39.
63 Information on Yi Un-hye supplied by the South Korean authorities matched Taguchi Yaeko, a Tokyo resident who had been missing since June 1978. She was 22 at the time. In 1991 the Japanese authorities concluded that Yi and Taguchi were the same person. See Hasegawa Hiroshi, "Tsuiseki Nihonjin rachi giwaku" [Pursuit: Suspected Kidnaping of Japanese Nationals], *AERA* (Asahi Shimbun Weekly), no. 27, July 5, 1997, 21-22.
64 See B. C. Koh, *Japan's Administrative Elite* (Berkeley: University of California Press, 1989), 27-28; 40-41; 255-56; 262.

Reservations by Japanese negotiators on the scene, it was speculated, may have been simply overruled by their superiors in Tokyo, who in turn may have been under pressure from influential politicians.

The operational environment, of which domestic structure is a component, affected the conduct of the normalization talks in other ways as well. Japan made an explicit linkage between progress in the talks and the occurrence of certain external events—tangible progress in inter-Korean dialogue, the conclusion of a nuclear safeguards agreement between the DPRK and the IAEA, the implementation of such an agreement, the admission of the two Korean states to the UN as separate members. All of these were conditions over which North Korea exercised control.

North Korea's perception that it had fulfilled them by early 1992 when the sixth round of the talks convened, however, did not jibe with Japan's understanding of what had happened. The discrepancy between the operational and psychological environments was on display. Subsequent developments proved that Japan's cautious approach, which in effect drew a distinction between outcome (agreement) and effect (implementation), was most prudent. The fate of interim procedural agreements on how to handle the Yi Un-hye issue also underscores the utility of differentiating between outcome and effect.

From a substantive standpoint, what did two years of intermittent negotiations accomplish? At a minimum, the two sides gained a better understanding of the goals and tactics of each other. North Korea left no doubt whatever that its overriding objective was to extract maximum compensation from Japan. North Korea's assertion that since there was a state of belligerency between Japan and Kim Il Sung-led "Korean revolutionary army," Japan owed North Korea "reparations," in addition to "compensation" for human and material damages, bespoke such motive. North Korea's tenacious attempts to prove that the treaties concluded between Japan and Korea in the early 20th century, including the annexation treaty of 1910, were null and void *ab initio* can be construed in the same vein.

North Korea's tireless recitation of crimes committed by the Japanese against the Korean people, particularly, those connected with "comfort women" reflected not only its genuine sense of outrage but also its wish to maximize the size of Japan's ultimate compensation, even though it may be called economic cooperation.

Tactical behavior displayed by North Korea during the talks may have been an eye-opening experience for Japan, which previously had only limited experience in negotiating with the North. The occasional shouting matches, the intemperate language used, and the cavalier attitude shown toward previous commitments—all these left strong impressions on the Japanese participants in the talks.

If North Korea learned anything from the talks, it must have been that Japan was a tough negotiator. Even though the North tried very hard to sway Japan, there was very little to show for the effort. At the end of the two-year negotiations, the two sides adhered to the same positions they had when the talks began. The bargaining power of the two sides was clearly asymmetric. What North Korea sought from Japan was compensation of substantial magnitude accompanied by a formal apology embodied in a written agreement. What North Korea could offer to Japan in return, however, was quite modest. Japan would be able to settle one of the two issues left over from the Pacific war, the other being the territorial dispute with Russia. Japan's sense of security might be enhanced by having normal inter-state relations with the DPRK. The plight of Japanese wives of North Korean nationals would be alleviated. Finally, there was a remote possibility that North Korea might turn out to have some economic value for Japanese businesses.

Of these, the issue of Japanese wives was probably the only one about which there was any sense of urgency in Japan. Realistically, notwithstanding their vastly greater number, the Japanese women did not carry as much weight as did the two Japanese crew members of Fujisan Maru in Japan's policymaking vis-a-vis North Korea. The latter, as discussed in the preceding chapter, proved to be a potent bargaining chip for North Korea in its quest for diplomatic normalization with Japan.

It is possible that notwithstanding all this, North Korea may not have fully grasped the reality that moral and legal arguments do not go very far in inter-governmental negotiations and that when all is said and done, it is a state's capacity to offer tangible inducements that are greater than the costs involved that will make the difference.

What transpired between Japan and the DPRK in the early 1990s, then, were asymmetrical negotiations. The asymmetry, however, was more pronounced in the realm of aggregate structural power than in the arena of issue-specific structural power. Drawing on a conceptual framework proposed by Mark Habeeb, let us examine the three components of issue power balance—alternatives, commitment, and control.[65]

Alternatives, the first variable in the equation, "denote each actor's ability to gain its preferred outcomes from a relationship other than that with the opposing actor." Since diplomatic normalization by definition is a bilateral process, neither Japan nor the DPRK had any alternative but to conduct negotiations to hammer out mutually acceptable terms of normalization. There was, in short, no discernible difference between the two sides as far as this variable was concerned.

What of commitment, the second variable—namely, "the extent and degree to which an actor desires and/or needs its preferred outcomes?" Here the source of commitment—whether it stems from need or aspiration—is germane. Whereas the DPRK's commitment to diplomatic normalization with Japan was rooted primarily in the former's *need* for the latter's compensation or economic cooperation, Japan's commitment to the establishment of diplomatic relations with the DPRK was based primarily on aspiration, "a self-contained motivation." The expected benefits of normalization for the two states, therefore, were unequal, which may help explain why Japan's commitment appeared to be somewhat lower than the DPRK's.[66]

---

65 Whereas "aggregate structural power refers to an actor's resources, capabilities and position vis-a-vis the external world as a whole," "issue-specific power is concerned with an actor's capabilities and position vis-a-vis another actor in terms of a specific mutual issue." William Mark Habeeb, *Power and Tactics in International Negotiation: How Weak Nations Bargain with Strong Nations* (Baltimore: Johns Hopkins University Press, 1988), 17-23.

66 Ibid. The quotations are from 17 and 19.

The third variable, control, refers to "the degree to which one side can unilaterally achieve its preferred outcome despite the costs involved in doing so." It can encompass "one side's ability to gain a greater share of its preferred outcome than its opponent……"[67] If diplomatic normalization is equated with the preferred outcome of both sides, then neither side is in a position "unilaterally to achieve it." Depending on the terms of normalizaton, however, its costs and benefits will necessarily vary between Japan and the DPRK. Under no circumstances will either side have control.

The balance of issue-specific power, then, did not favor either side in any overwhelming fashion. The both sides' "security points"—"the point[s] at which [they] would prefer stalemate over negotiation"[68]—were coterminous, as the abruptness with which the talks broke down demonstrated.

No less important than structural power, both at the aggregate level and the issue-specific level, is "behavioral power"—the ways in which the actors use their structural power in negotiations to achieve preferred outcomes. This is revealed by the "actors' tactics"—"threats, warnings, promises, predictions, rewards and side payments, punishments, concessions, coalition building, stalling, and so on."[69] To judge from results, neither Japan nor the DPRK succeeded in displaying behavioral power during their two-year-long negotiations that was potent enough to sway the other side.

Finally, if one were to apply the "formula-detail approach," which "presents negotiation as a three-stage process: the diagnostic phase, the formula phase, and the detail phase," then one could argue that Japan and the DPRK merely passed the diagnostic phase by recognizing that a "negotiated solution to their conflict is possible" but found that impediments to negotiation were far more formidable than either had anticipated. They became enmeshed in an impasse in the formula phase—a phase "charac-

---

67 Ibid., 22.
68 For a discussion of the concept of "security point," see ibid., 21-22.
69 Ibid., 23.

terized by a search for general principles, or a formula," of which the single most important element is a "shared perception of the problem."[70]

As the preceding review shows, such a shared perception failed to materialize, which helps to explain why stalemate soon developed. The third and final phase, the detail phase that "consists of a long, tense search for an agreement on details to implement the general framework set out in the [formula] phase," thus proved to be out of the reach for both sides.[71]

---

70 Ibid., 28-33.
71 Ibid., 31.

CHAPTER 3

Nuclear and Humanitarian Issues

The balance of issue-specific power during the eight rounds of Japan-DPRK negotiations spanning nearly two years, as we concluded in the preceding chapter, did not favor North Korea because it possessed neither alternatives nor control, while its level of commitment was somewhat higher than that of Japan. If we construe alternatives broadly, however, we can argue that the DPRK-US high-level talks that were conducted between June 1993 and October 1994 presented an alternative of sorts.

If, as a result of the bilateral inter-governmental negotiations, DPRK-US relations were to improve measurably, that would give Japan a strong incentive to seek ways of resuming normalization talks with North Korea. Since there was little or no chance that the US would agree to provide Pyongyang with the kind of economic assistance Japan was expected to provide in conjunction with diplomatic normalization—such as sizable grants-in-aid, low-interest, long-term loans, and technical assistance—, however, a breakthrough in DPRK-US relations would not amount to a realistic alternative to DPRK-Japan normalization.

The DPRK-US high-level talks over nuclear issues, therefore, could not have totally eclipsed Pyongyang's goal of establishing full diplomatic relations with Tokyo. They were nonetheless linked, albeit indirectly, to that goal. There was another sense in which the DPRK-US negotiations affected Japan's national interests. The persistence with which Japan had raised the nuclear issue during the normalization talks was not related exclusively to Japan's identity as a peace-loving state dependent on an alliance with the US. It also bespoke Japan's high stakes in issues related to nuclear nonproliferation on the Korean peninsula, which paralleled those of the US and South Korea.

Given such a dual linkage, we need to examine how the DPRK-US high-level talks unfolded and their effects on Japan and Japan-DPRK relations. In a sense, DPRK-US negotiations approximated an indirect form of cooperation between the DPRK and Japan. For the close consultations the US held with its two allies, Japan and the ROK, had the effect of elevating the latter two from interested bystanders to indirect participants in the negotiations.

We shall also examine instances of direct cooperation between Japan and North Korea, notably Japan's humanitarian assistance to the North, the realization of homecoming visits by Japanese wives of North Korean men, economic relations, and the resumption of normalization talks after a seven-and-a-half-year hiatus.

Of the events that spawned discord, the most noteworthy are (1) the controversy surrounding the alleged kidnapping of Japanese citizens by North Korean agents, (2) Japan's suspension of humanitarian assistance to the North, and, most serious of all, (3) the missile/satellite incident of August 1998. The episodes of cooperation and conflict to be examined below will allow us to test, albeit in a rudimentary way, such a diverse array of concepts as the rationality of state behavior, relative and absolute gains, capabilities versus intentions, the nonfungibility of power, the role of international regimes, and state identity.

North Korea's Nuclear Card

North Korea's suspected nuclear weapons development program emerged as a high-priority item on the policy agendas of Washington, Seoul, and Tokyo in the early 1990s. Not only would North Korea's possession of nuclear weapons, regardless of their level of sophistication and number, pose a tangible threat to the security of South Korea and Japan and to the safety of US troops stationed in both of these countries but it would also seriously undermine the global nuclear nonproliferation regime. There was a danger that North Korea might even sell nuclear weapons to what the US viewed as "rogue states" in the Middle East and elsewhere.[1]

As long as North Korea adhered to the Treaty on the Nonproliferation of Nuclear Weapons (NPT) and allowed the International Atomic Energy Agency (IAEA) to conduct inspections of its nuclear facilities, however, there was hope that Pyongyang's nuclear weapons program might be contained or held in abeyance. All this changed when Pyongyang announced on March 12, 1993 that it would withdraw from the NPT. That decision in turn had been triggered by an IAEA request for "special inspection" of two undeclared sites in Yongbyon, a nuclear complex located 60 miles north of Pyongyang. Claiming that they were military facilities unrelated to its nuclear program, North Korea had turned down

---

1 For analysis of the crisis precipitated by North Korea's suspected nuclear weapons development program and the manner in which it was defused, see Leon V. Sigal, *Disarming Strangers: Nuclear Diplomacy with North Korea* (Princeton: Princeton University Press, 1998); Don Oberdorfer, *The Two Koreas: A Contemporary History* (Reading, MA: Addison-Wesley, 1997), 249-368; Bruce Cumings, *Korea's Place in the Sun: A Modern History* (New York: W. W. Norton & Co., 1997), 465-487; Scott Snyder, *Neogotiating on the Edge: North Korean Negotiating Behavior* (Washington, DC: United States Institute of Peace Press, 1999); Chung Oknim, *Pukhaek 588 il! Kulinton haengjongbu ui tae'ung kwa chollyak* [588 Days of North's Nuclear Problem: The Clinton Administration's Response and Strategy] (Seoul: Seoul Press, 1995); B. C. Koh, "Confrontation and Cooperation on the Korean Peninsula: The Politics of Nuclear Nonproliferation," *Korean Journal of Defense Analysis* 6, no. 2 (Winter 1994), 53-83.

the request. North Korea stated that its decision to withdraw from the NPT was dictated by the need "to safeguard our supreme national interests."[2]

Since the NPT calls for a three-month notice before withdrawal, however, North Korean withdrawal would take effect on June 12, 1993. Significantly, North Korea left open the possibility that its decision might be reversed, saying that its "self-defensive measure" would remain in effect until "the United States ceases its nuclear threat against us and the Secretariat of the International Atomic Energy Agency restores the principles of independence and impartiality."[3]

Given the danger North Korea's withdrawal from the NPT would pose not only to the peace and security on the Korean Peninsula but also to the nonproliferation regime, the Clinton administration decided to accept a North Korean proposal for "high-level talks," which materialized in New York on June 2. The North Korean delegation was led by Kang Sok Ju, the First Vice Minister of Foreign Affairs, while the US delegation was led by Robert L. Gallucci, the Assistant Secretary of State for Political and Military Affairs. This marked only the second time since the initiation of diplomatic contacts in 1988 that officials above the rank of embassy political counselor engaged in direct negotiations between the two countries.

On June 11, nine days after the talks began and one day before North Korean withdrawal from the NPT was to take effect, the two sides reached a dramatic agreement. Both sides pledged to accept the principles of (1) "assurances against the threat and use of force, including nuclear weapons," (2) "peace and security in a nuclear-free Korean peninsula, including impartial application of full-scope safeguards, mutual respect for each other's sovereignty, and non-interference in each other's internal affairs," and (3) "support for the peaceful reunification of Korea." They also agreed

---

2 *Nodong sinmun* (Pyongyang), March 13, 1993.
3 Ibid. Pyongyang's accusation that the IAEA Secretariat lacks independence and impartiality is based on evidence of informal cooperation between US intelligence and the IAEA, namely the US's sharing of satellite reconnaissance data with the IAEA.

"to continue dialogue on an equal and unprejudiced basis." In connection with all this, the DPRK government "has decided unilaterally to suspend as long as it considers necessary the effectuation of its withdrawal from the Treaty on the Non-Proliferation of Nuclear Weapons."[4]

Pursuant to their agreement "to continue dialogue on an equal and unprejudiced basis," the two sides held the second round of their high-level talks in Geneva from July 14 to 19. Perhaps the most noteworthy development during the second round was a startling request by North Korea for US assistance in replacing its graphite moderated reactors with light water moderated reactors (LWRs). The US gave a conditional pledge of assistance, saying that it "is prepared to support the introduction of LWRs and to explore with the DPRK ways in which LWRs could be obtained."[5] Since it is more difficult to extract weapon-grade plutonium from LWRs than from graphite-moderated reactors and since North Korea would have to rely on imported enriched uranium to operate them, the conversion would be in the interest of the US, South Korea, and Japan, all of which fear Pyongyang's acquisition of nuclear capability.

All of these three countries would need to lend a helping hand to North Korea if LWRs are to be installed in that country. The probability of its happening appeared to increase markedly in August 1994 when the third round of the US-DPRK high-level talks held in Geneva produced a tentative agreement.[6] North Korea and the US also agreed in principle to exchange liaison offices as a first step toward full diplomatic normalization. For its part, the DPRK pledged to remain in the NPT, not to reprocess the 8,000 fuel rods it had removed from a five-megawatt experimental reactor in Yongbyon in May, and to refuel the reactor. In a word, by August 1994, within a month after the death of Kim Il Sung, the chances of a genuine reconciliation between the DPRK and the US appeared to improve sharply.[7]

---

4 *Korea Times* (Seoul), June 14, 1992, 5.
5 *Japan Times* (Tokyo), July 21, 1993, 6.
6 *New York Times*, August 13-15, 1994; editorial, "A Breakthrough on Korean Arms?" Aug.15, 1994.

Although the subsequent negotiations, which included two sets of meetings by experts in Pyongyang and Berlin, proved to be contentious, the two sides finally hammered out an "agreed framework" by mid-October. The last hurdle was North Korea's refusal to accept two provisions in the US draft pertaining to inter-Korean relations: (1) implementation of the denuclearization declaration and (2) the resumption of inter-Korean dialogue. North Korea relented at the very last minute after receiving an ultimatum from the US.

Before signing the agreed framework, however, North Korea demanded a letter of assurance from President Clinton. Addressed to "His Excellency Kim Jong Il, Supreme Leader of the Democratic People's Republic of Korea," Clinton's letter, dated October 20, "confirm[ed]" that Clinton would use "the full powers of my office to facilitate arrangements for the financing and construction of a light water nuclear power reactor project within the DPRK and the funding and implementation of interim energy alternatives for [the DPRK] pending completion of the first reactor unit of the light water reactor project."[8]

The key components of the Agreed Framework, which was signed by Gallucci and Kang Sok Ju on October 21 and entered into force immediately, were as follows:[9]

First, the US would organize an international consortium to finance and supply LWRs to the DPRK with "a total generating capacity of approximately 2,000 MW (e) by a target date of 2003."

---

7 For the English text of the "agreed statement," see *Korean Report*, no. 289 (August 1994), 2-3; for the Korean text, see *T'ongil sinbo* (Pyongyang), August 20, 1994, 3. The *Korean Report* is a monthly publication of the International Affairs Bureau of the Central Standing Committee of Ch'ongnyon (Chosoren in Japanese), the federation of Korean residents in Japan who profess allegiance to the DPRK.

8 For the text of the Clinton letter, see *Korean Report*, no. 291 (October 1994), 5.

9 Since the Agreed Framework was de facto nullified in January 2006, the past tense will be used in discussing its contents. Annie I. Bang, "KEDO's Reactor Project in North Korea Closes, Workers Return to South," *Korea Herald* (Seoul), January 8, 2006.

Second, the US would provide heavy fuel oil (HFO) to the DPRK, which "will reach a rate of 500,000 tons annually" in compensation for "the energy foregone due to the freeze of the DPRK's graphite-moderated reactors, pending completion of the first LWR unit."

Third, "the DPRK will freeze its graphite-moderated reactors and related facilities and will eventually dismantle these reactors and related facilities." The "IAEA will be allowed to monitor this freeze, and the DPRK will provide cooperation to the IAEA for this purpose."

Fourth, the "US and the DPRK will cooperate in finding a method to store safely spent fuel from the 5MW(e) experimental reactor during the construction of the LWR project, and to dispose of the fuel in a safe manner that does not involve reprocessing in the DPRK."

Fifth, the "two sides will move toward full normalization of political and economic relations." To that end, they would "reduce barriers to trade and investment, including restrictions on telecommunications service and financial transactions," open liaison offices in each other's capital, and eventually "upgrade bilateral relations to the Ambassadorial level."

Sixth, "[b]oth sides will work together for peace and security on a nuclear-free Korean peninsula." "The US will provide formal assurance to the DPRK against the threat or use of nuclear weapons by the US." "The DPRK will consistently take steps to implement the North-South Joint Declaration on the Denuclearization of the Korean Peninsula. The DPRK will engage in North-South dialogue, as this agreed framework will help create an atmosphere that promotes such a dialogue."

Seventh, the "DPRK will remain a party" to the NPT and "will allow implementation of its safeguards agreement under the Treaty." "When a significant portion of the LWR project is completed, but before delivery of key nuclear components, the DPRK will come into full compliance with its safeguards agreement with the IAEA," including inspection of the two undeclared sites in Yongbyon."[10]

The Geneva Accords had something to offer to all parties directly

---

10 *Korea Report*, no. 291 (October 1994), 2-5.

concerned: the US, the DPRK, and the ROK. Japan, also a high stakes holder, stood to benefit from it as well. All of these states would, however, also incur risks and costs. To mention the benefits that were expected to be shared by the US, the ROK, and Japan first, the threat of nuclear proliferation on the Korean peninsula—that is, the danger that North Korea might acquire nuclear weapons—appeared to have been either averted or abated. The freezing of North Korea's nuclear program would mean that it would not be able to extract weapons-grade plutonium from the 8,000 fuel rods it had removed from the five-megawatt experimental reactor in Yongbyon.[11]

When all of North Korea's graphite-moderated reactors and related facilities were dismantled, the threat of future proliferation would be alleviated. If all this could help preserve the NPT regime, by facilitating the extension of the NPT for an indefinite period, all three states could breathe a sigh of relief. The indefinite extension of the NPT did materialize in 1995.

The alleviation of the danger of nuclear proliferation would be conducive to Japan's security both in a substantive and a psychological sense. Since, unlike the situation in the early 1950s, Japan would not be able to profit from renewed hostilities on the peninsula, stability and peace on the peninsula, to which the Geneva accords are designed to contribute, would be in the best interests of Japan. It was for these reasons that Japan was prepared to incur the costs of the agreement. Not only did Japan agree to become a core member of the Korean Peninsula Energy Development Organization (KEDO), the international consortium that would manage the LWR project, but Japan would become the second largest financial contributor to KEDO. Overcoming reservations fueled by North Korea's launching of a rocket across it in August 1998, Japan agreed in October 1998 to contribute $1 billion to the LWR project. South Korea

---

11 This assessment of the gains and losses incurred by the parties concerned from the Geneva accords draws on my article, "Confrontation and Cooperation on the Korean Peninsula: The Politics of Nuclear Nonproliferation," *Korean Journal of Defense Analysis* 6, no. 2 (Winter 1994): 53-83.

agreed to shoulder 70 percent of the project's cost, estimated at $4.6 billion.

Additionally, the US agreed to supply HFO to the North to the tune of 500,000 metric tons a year for at least five years. The deferral of "special inspection" of the two undeclared sites in Yongbyon for approximately five years would mean that the US would not be able to verify North Korea's past nuclear activity for a long time. The US, along with the ROK and Japan, moreover, had to live with the risk that the DPRK might change its mind and decide to reprocess the 8,000 spent fuel rods that would remain under its control, albeit under IAEA safeguards, for five years or so.

What North Korea expected to gain from the Geneva accords was quite extensive. If the LWR project was to be completed without a hitch, the North's electricity generating capacity would increase markedly. The generating capacity of two 1,000 MW(e) LWRs would be nearly eight times the combined generating capacity of the three graphite-moderated reactors the North had agreed to forego. Even though the LWRs would not be free, the North, in an agreement signed with KEDO in December 1995, obtained most favorable terms of financing—the loan would be interest-free and repayable over 17 years following a three-year grace period, with the repayment clock beginning to tick after the provision of the first LWR unit.[12] What is more, the LWRs the North would get would feature state-of-the-art technology and will be much safer than the graphite-moderated reactors they would replace.

As noted, the DPRK would also get HFO, free of charge, for at least five years—until the first LWR unit becomes operational. The inflow of 500,000 tons of HFO a year would help alleviate the North's serious shortage of energy and hard currency. The HFO was intended for use in

---

12 See "Agreement on Supply of a Light-Water Reactor Project to the Democratic People's Republic of Korea Between the Korean Peninsula Energy Development Organization And the Government of the Democratic People's Republic of Korea," signed in New York on December 15, 1995. http://www.koreasociety.org/kedo/agreementon.htm.

electricity-generation and heating; since it could not easily be refined into either aviation fuel or diesel, its value for North Korea's armed forces would be limited.

The negative security guarantee the DPRK received from the US in the Geneva accords, which actually reaffirms an identical guarantee contained in two earlier statements jointly issued by the two sides—the June 11, 1993 joint statement and the August 12, 1994 agreed statement—, could also be counted as an important gain for Pyongyang. The negative security guarantee, in which the US provided the DPRK "assurances against the threat and use of force, including nuclear weapons," seems to enhance Pyongyang's sense of security.

The agreement to "move toward full normalization of political and economic relations" was a major gain for the DPRK. The opening of liaison offices in each other's capitals would mark a significant milestone in North Korean diplomacy, and the reduction of "barriers to trade and investment, including restrictions on telecommunications service and financial transactions," would pave the way for mutually advantageous economic intercourse.

The very fact that high-level talks were held between the US and the DPRK represented a huge symbolic gain for Pyongyang. In the perennial legitimacy war between the two rival Korean states, being able to exclude the other side from such a high-stakes negotiating table was fraught with symbolism. Given its zero-sum nature, Pyongyang's gain spelled Seoul's loss, which became plain in President Kim Young Sam's public criticism of US negotiating tactics on October 7, 1994, at a time when the US and North Korean negotiators were trying strenuously to hammer out a compromise agreement.[13]

---

13 To the surprise of observers and to the chagrin of Washington, Kim Young Sam openly criticized the Clinton administration for failing to understand the North Koreans and for "an overeagerness to compromise." In an interview with James Sterngold of the *New York Times* on October 7, 1994, Kim "expressed deep doubts about whether the North Koreans could be trusted to live up to any agreements and whether the American negotiators understood that possibility." *New York Times*, October 8, 1994.

Another ideational gain emanated from President Clinton's "letter of assurance," which had addressed Kim Jong Il as "your excellency, the Supreme Leader of the DPRK."[14] Although this had been done at the specific request of the North Korean negotiators in Geneva, it nonetheless signified, in North Korean view, recognition of Kim Jong Il's lofty status by the chief executive of the world's only superpower. Coming as it did within four months of Kim Il Sung's death, when Kim Jong Il's consolidation of power was still under way, such "recognition" must have been most welcome to the North Korean leader.

These gains for the North, of course, would not be cost-free. The most obvious cost would be the freezing and eventual dismantling of its graphite-moderated reactors and related facilities, including a reprocessing plant (or a "radio-chemical laboratory" in North Korean terminology). Coupled with its commitment not to reprocess the 8,000 spent fuel rods and to allow their eventual transfer to a third country, this meant that the North would be compelled to abandon any plan it might have had to develop nuclear weapons in the near future.

That the fuel rods would remain under the North's de facto control for five years or so implied, however, that the North had not given up its nuclear option altogether. The postponement of "special inspection" of the two undeclared facilities in Yongbyon and, more important, the fact that what would happen would not be called special inspections, which the DPRK regards as an infringement of its sovereignty, would make the North Korean concession on the issue palatable to Pyongyang.

The North's grudging acceptance of the two provisions regarding inter-Korean relations must obviously be counted as a cost to Pyongyang. Potentially more troublesome to the North, however, was its acquiescence

---

14 C. Kenneth Quinnones, *Kita Chosen—Beikokumusho tantokan no kosho hiroku* [North Korea: A Memoir of a U.S. State Department Official], translated by Yamaoka Kunihiko and Yamaguchi Mizuhiko under the supervision of Izumi Hajime (Tokyo: Chuo Koronsha, 2000), 355-56. The English translation of the book's title given by the translators is "North Korea's Nuclear Threat: 'Off the Record' Memories."

to the South's central role in the financing and, especially, construction of LWRs. After trying very hard to minimize the South's central role in the LWR project in the months following the signing of the Geneva accords, however, the North tacitly agreed to accept South Korean-model LWRs and allow hundreds of South Korean engineers, technicians, and managers to work on the project on its territory—in Sinp'o, South Hamgyong province where the LWRs was to be installed.

Insofar as Japan-DPRK relations were concerned, all this appeared to have affected Pyongyang's tactical calculus. Pyongyang would play a waiting game vis-a-vis Tokyo, for a breakthrough in Pyongyang-Washington relations, in North Korean view, would most likely make Tokyo eager to resuscitate normalization talks with Pyongyang.

Domestic political developments in Japan were also a factor in the equation. The end of the 38-year monopoly of power by the LDP in the summer of 1993 and the emergence of a coalition government in which the SDPJ was a major player, appeared to raise hopes in Pyongyang that Japan's North Korea policy might change. As things turned out, Japan's coalition partners had neither the incentive nor the capacity to change the direction of foreign policy. That did not mean, however, that the Socialists, who had long maintained close relations with the North, did not make any difference at all.

When Pyongyang's refusal to cooperate with the IAEA and abrupt removal of 8,000 spent fuel rods from its five-megawatt nuclear reactor in Yongbyon spawned moves to impose sanctions on the DPRK in June 1994, for example, the Socialists argued strenuously against sanctions. Although the coalition government eventually decided to go along with sanctions, should diplomacy fail, it nonetheless conveyed to the US the practical difficulty of blocking the flow of Japanese money to the North through pro-DPRK Korean residents in Japan.[15] Since such money transfer constituted a major source of funds for the North, blocking or

---

15 *Asahi shinbun* (Tokyo), June 7, 1994, 3. On June 4, 1994, representatives of the US, Japan, and the ROK published a "joint press release" following tripartitie consultations, which had become routinized since the DPRK's declaration of its intention to withdraw from the NPT in March 1993. According to the press

significantly decreasing it would have hurt Pyongyang. Inability to do so, on the other hand, would have measurably diluted the efficacy of sanctions.

A combination of circumstances, of which the most noteworthy were the opposition by China, which has veto power in the UN Security Council, to sanctions and the visit of former US President Jimmy Carter to North Korea in June 1994, however, led the US and its allies to abandon efforts to impose sanctions on North Korea. In the following month, the US-DPRK high-level talks resumed in Geneva, producing an agreement three and a half months later.

In what ways did North Korea enjoy an edge in the power balance over the nuclear issue? Although the US had explored such alternatives to negotiation as sanctions and the use of force, neither proved to be viable.[16] By contrast, North Korea did have a real alternative to negotiation, namely the resumption of its nuclear weapons development program, and its decision to defuel its five-megawatt experimental nuclear reactor in Yongbyon in May bespoke not only its commitment to embrace that alternative but also its control over the nuclear option—an

---

release, "all sides expressed their support for the IAEA and agreed that North Korea's actions created a serious situation on the Korean peninsula and a threat to the peace and stability of the Northeast Asian region as well as to international non-proliferation efforts. They shared the view that the international community, through the U.N. Security Council, urgently consider an appropriate response, including sanctions." Gaimusho, Ajia Kyoku, Hokuto Ajia-ka, *Kita Chosen kaku heiki kaihatsu mondaini kansuru Nichi-Bei-Kan sansha kyogino kyodo puresu ririsu* [Joint Press Release on the Tripartite Consultations Among Japan, the US, and the ROK Concerning the Issue of North Korea's Nuclear Weapons Development], June 4, 1994 (emphasis added).

16 For a sobering account of how close the US had come to igniting a new war by contemplating a massive reinforcement of troops and wepons deployed on or near the Korean peninsula, a move that the North might well have equated with an act of war, see Oberdorfer, *The Two Koreas*, 311-36; "Mi, 94-nyon e puk e sonje konggyok chunbi······habod-dae pogoso ch'ulgan" [In 1994 US Prepared Preemptive Strike Against North······Harvard Report Published], *Dong-A ilbo* (Seoul), December 7, 1998.

ability unilaterally to achieve its preferred outcome despite the heavy costs involved in doing so.

Having discovered the sterility of "coercive diplomacy" vis-a-vis the North, which, as Leon V. Sigal shows, had been fueled by a number of "shared images" on the part of policymakers and other members of the "foreign policy establishment" in the US regarding North Korean behavior, nuclear proliferation, and the efficacy of the "crime-and-punishment approach," the US finally embraced the strategy of "cooperative threat reduction."[17]

The road to the actual implementation of the Geneva accords proved to be bumpy. When the US trade embargo and other long-standing restrictions on economic transactions between the US and the DPRK were not lifted—except for the establishment of telephone and postal links— and the refusal by the Republican-controlled Congress to appropriate sufficient amounts of funds hampered the delivery of HFO to the North in 1998, the DPRK threatened to suspend the implementation of the Geneva accords. The discovery by US satellite reconnaissance of a huge underground construction project near Yongbyon in October 1998, which the US suspected might indicate the North's resumption of its nuclear weapons development program, increased the danger that the Geneva accords might fall apart.[18]

What did all this mean to Japan? Given its high stakes, Japan was kept informed of progress of the Geneva talks and consulted on key issues by the US. Trilateral consultations among the US, South Korea, and Japan were institutionalized in connection with the nuclear issue. As already noted, moreover, Japan became a founding member of KEDO, along with the US and the ROK, and Japan's financial contribution to the LWR project was second only to South Korea's. Due to difficulties in

---

17 Sigal, *Disarming Strangers*, 3-14, 131-67.
18 U.S. Department of State, Office of the Spokesman, "U.S.-D.P.R.K. Talks," press statement by James P. Rubin (Washington: September 10, 1998); "Pukhan, jeneba habuimun 'p'agi haedo jot'a" [North Korea: "Terminating the Geneva Accords is OK with Us"], *Joongang ilbo* (Seoul), October 24, 1998.

obtaining funds from Congress, the US turned to Japan for assistance in providing HFO to North Korea in 1996, and Japan provided $19 million.[19]

The Four-Party Agreement

To return to Japan-DPRK relations of a more direct kind, it was not until March 1995 that there was a notable movement in the direction of resuscitating their normalization talks. In that month, representatives of the three parties participating in Japan's coalition government—the LDP, the SDPJ, and the New Party *Sakigake* (Forerunner)—visited Pyongyang and signed a four-party agreement with the Workers' Party of Korea.[20] The agreement, signed on March 30 by Watanabe Michio of the LDP, Kubo Wataru of the SDPJ, Hatoyama Yukio of the New Party *Sakigake*, and Kim Yong Sun of the WPK, contained four main provisions:

First, the four parties "shall make positive efforts to settle the

---

19 Although it costs $60-70 million to provide 500,000 metric tons of heavy fuel oil to the North each year, the US Congress appropriated only $22 million in 1996 and $25 million in 1997. On October 19, 1998, Congress appropriated $35 million but attached conditions that might make it difficult for the US government to use the money. They were (1) certification by the US government that North Korea had not resumed its nuclear weapons development program and (2) cessation of missile exports by North Korea. In September 1997 the European Union joined the KEDO as the fourth member of its executive board and pledged to contribute 15 million European Currency Unit (ECU or approximately $17 million) toward the supply of HFO to North Korea each year. *Joongang ilbo* (Seoul), July 21, 1997; *Chosun ilbo* (Seoul), September 21, 1998; Tom Raum, "Budget Bill Includes Weapons Treaty," *Associated Press*, Washington, October 19, 1998.

20 Japan's decision to dispatch the three-party delegation to the North, in which party politicians played a dominant role, was facilitated by the signing of the Agreed Framework in Geneva in October 1994. What was then perceived as a breakthrough in resolving the North Korean nuclear issue had removed a major hurdle in the path of improving Tokyo-Pyongyang relations. Young C.

unhappy past between the two countries and establish diplomatic relations at an early date."

Second, "the four parties acknowledge that there shall be no precondition for the resumption of dialogue and the talks for the normalization of diplomatic relations between the two countries and that such talks shall be strictly for the purpose of improving relations."

Third, "the four parties confirm that the talks between the two countries should be held strictly from an independent and autonomous position [*jishutekide katsu tokujino tachiba*].

Fourth, "the four parties, acting with a sense of responsibility as ruling parties, shall make efforts so that their respective governments will actively pursue the talks for normalizing diplomatic relations as soon as possible."[21]

The reference to preconditions and independence were concessions to the North's demands, which wanted to prevent a recurrence of what it regarded as bitter experience during the 1991-1992 negotiations. As noted in the preceding chapter, Japan had attached preconditions that for the most part reflected the policies of the US and the ROK. The North's attempt to include a clause affirming the validity and binding effects of the 1990 three-party declaration, however, failed due to staunch Japanese opposition. As a compromise, the preamble noted that the "historic three-party joint declaration" adopted in September 1990 had become the basis for the initiation of normalization talks in January 1991, of which there were eight rounds.[22] Had the North succeeded in its attempt to have the four-party agreement affirm the validity and binding effects of

---

Kim, "North Korea Confronts Japan: Politics of Normalization and Rice," in *North Korea and the World: Explaining Pyongyang's Foreign Policy*, ed. B. C. Koh (Seoul: Kyungnam University Press, 2004), 148-51.
21 Gaimusho, Ajia Kyoku, Hokuto Ajia-ka, *Nitcho kaidan saikaino tameno goisho* [Agreement for the Resumption of Japan-DPRK Talks], March 30, 1995.
22 Ibid. See also *Wolgan pukhan tonghyang* [Monthly Summary of Developments Pertaining to North Korea], March 1995 (Seoul: T'ongil-won, Chongbo Punsok-sil), 216-17.

the 1990 declaration, it would undoubtedly have tried to underscore the controversial reference to Japan's need to compensate North Korea for post-World War deeds with the aim of maximizing the amount of compensation.

Ignoring all this, Kim Yong Sun, the WPK secretary who signed the 1995 agreement on his party's behalf, insisted that the principles embodied in the 1990 declaration would form the basis for the normalization talks should they resume. The agreement not to attach any preconditions, he explained, meant that such issues as the "nuclear issue" and the "Yi Un-hye" issue would not be raised. The principle of independence, Kim said, would preclude Japan from behaving as a "spokesman for the positions of the US and other external forces." Finally, Kim argued that the four-party agreement was binding on their respective governments.[23] By contrast, Kubo Wataru, one of the three Japanese signatories, asserted that the 1990 declaration "existed in history only" but had "in fact been nullified." He added that the expression in the 1995 agreement, "without any preconditions," means simply that both sides would be free to say whatever they wished to say."[24]

Japan's Rice Aid to North Korea

Unlike the three-party declaration of September 1990, which really paved the way for normalization talks, however, the four-party agreement of March 1995 failed to jump-start the stalled talks. Nonetheless, dialogue did occur between Japan and North Korea concerning a novel issue—namely, rice aid to the North. In May 1995 North Korea made a surprising request to Japan for emergency assistance of rice.[25] The

---

23 See the text of Kim Yong Sun's press conference on April 5, 1995 (in Japanese translation) in *Gekkan Chosen shiryo* [Monthly Materials on Korea], no. 409 (June 1995), 23-25. This is published by Chosen Mondai Kenkyujo (Korean Affairs Institute), a pro-DPRK organization in Japan.
24 *Dong-A ilbo*, April 6, 1995.

coalition government in Tokyo headed by Socialist Prime Minister Murayama Tomiichi, however, found it necessary to seek South Korea's understanding, which meant that, deferring to Seoul's wishes, Tokyo would comply with Pyongyang's request only on condition that Pyongyang receives Seoul's aid first.[26]

After North and South Korea reached an agreement in vice-minister-level talks in Beijing on Seoul's provision of 150,000 metric tons of rice to Pyongyang free of charge, Japan and North Korea held talks in Tokyo from June 24 to 30. Japan agreed to provide 150,000 metric tons of rice to the North free of charge through Red Cross channels and to sell an additional 150,000 metric tons on deferred payment basis. There would be a grace period of not more than ten years after which the North will pay the cost of rice over 20 years. During the first ten years interest rate on the loan will be 2 percent per annum, and afterward it will be 3 percent per annum. The agreement called for a "guarantee" by the North that the rice supplied by Japan would be consumed by civilians only.[27]

Significantly, Japan sought to underline the humanitarian character of its rice assistance to North Korea. In a statement released on the day when the preceding agreement was announced, Foreign Minister Kono Yohei expressed the hope that North Korea's unprecedented actions—frank admission of "its food shortage for the first time" and request for "assistance from the international community"—will be "a step toward the opening of North Korea and its participation in the international

---

25 Young C. Kim raises the possibility that the North may actually have begun its quest for rice aid from Japan in November 1994. He states that rice aid was an important topic of discussion during the March 1995 visit of Japan's three-party delegation to Pyongyang, even though it was not made public. Kim, "North Korea Confronts Japan," 150-51.
26 "Tai Kita Chosen kome enjono hoshin kakunin, seifu.yoto 'Kankokuno rikai ete'" [Plan to Provide Rice Aid to North Korea Confirmed; Government and the Ruling Parties To "Seek the ROK's Understanding"], *Asahi shinbun*, May 30, 1995.
27 Gaimusho, Ajia Kyoku, Hokuto Ajia-ka, *Kita Chosen eno kome shien ni tsuite* [On Rice Aid to North Korea], June 30, 1995.

community." Kono then added:

> Japan has not extended state recognition to North Korea, and there is no change in the position of the Government of Japan that any economic cooperation with [i.e. aid to] North Korea has to be preceded by the successful conclusion of the negotiations for the normalization of relations between Japan and North Korea. However······Japan has decided to accept the request by North Korea and to provide this assistance as a special and exceptional measure.[28]

The June 30 agreement left room for additional "export" of rice by Japan to North Korea if it should become necessary. After North Korea suffered severe flooding in the ensuing two months, which exacerbated the already serious shortage of food, Pyongyang turned to Tokyo again for help. Although Tokyo had donated $500,000 to UN relief organizations for aid to the North following the flood, a complication arose before Japan could seriously consider North Korea's request. A high-ranking North Korean official had been quoted in a magazine article as having said that Japan's earlier rice aid had not been motivated by humanitarian considerations. The official was none other than Kim Yong Sun, who had signed both the 1990 three-party declaration and the 1995 four-party agreement. He had allegedly told the South Korean monthly magazine *Mal* (Speech) that Japan's motives included both an expression of an apology and a desire to expedite the resumption of the stalled normalization talks.[29] After being asked to clarify the statement attributed to Kim Yong Sun, the North assured Japan that it did view Japan's rice aid

---

28 Foreign Press Center Japan, *Statement by Foreign Minister Kono on Japan's Rice Assistance to North Korea*, F.P.C. Press Release, no. 0368-09, June 30, 1995, F.P.C. Translation of Foreign Ministry Release. For the Japanese text of the statement, see Gaimusho, *Kita Chosen eno kome shienni kansuru gaimu daijin danwa* [Foreign Minister's Statement on Rice Assistance to North Korea], June 30, 1995.

as a humanitarian measure. This opened the way for negotiations between Japan and North Korea in Beijing from September 30 to October 3, producing an agreement on Japan's sale of an additional 200,000 metric tons of rice to North Korea on deferred payment basis, the terms of which were identical to those embodied in the June 30 agreement.[30]

All told, Japan provided 500,000 metric tons of rice to North Korea in 1995, more than three times South Korea's aid. In terms of *gratis* aid, however, Japan and South Korea were even, with both providing 150,000 metric tons each. North Korea reacted differently to the two aid donors. Whereas it expressed gratitude to Japan, it conspicuously withheld any word of appreciation to South Korea. On the contrary, the North in effect slapped the hands of the South that was spending $232 million for the rice aid: on June 28 North Koreans forcibly hoisted a DPRK flag on a South Korean ship that was about to enter Ch'ongjin harbor with the first shipment of rice. Then on August 2 the North detained the entire crew of a South Korean ship, along with the ship itself, that had just unloaded rice in Ch'ongjin. The North accused one of the South Korean crew members of espionage for having taken unauthorized photographs of the harbor. While the North apologized for the first incident and released the ship and crew after extracting an apology from Seoul in the second, these episodes antagonized South Korean public opinion, adversely affecting the already strained inter-Korean relations.[31]

---

29 For a description of the incident, see *Gendai Koria* [Modern Korea], no. 355, Tokyo (October 1995), 14. The Japanese magazine quoted from *Mal*, which had published Kim Yong Sun's comments in its August 1995 issue. A dissident magazine in South Korea, *Mal* is not readily available to the general public.

30 Gaimusho, Ajia Kyoku, Hokuto Ajia-ka, *Kono gaimu daijin danwa: Kita Chosenno kosui higaini taisuru kinkyu enjo oyobi kome shien mondaini tsuite* [Foreign Minister Kono's Statement: On Emergency Aid and Rice Assistance to North Korea Related to Flood Damage], September 19, 1995; idem, *Kita Chosen eno kome tsuika shien ni tsuite* [On Additional Rice Assistance to North Korea], October 3, 1995.

31 For a discussion of these incidents, see B. C. Koh, "South Korea in 1995: Tremors of Transition," *Asian Survey* 36, no. 1 (Jan. 1996): 58-59. A failure of

Meanwhile, the Murayama government showed no sign of changing Japan's Korea policy. As he told the Japanese Diet in a policy speech on September 29, 1995, "the strengthening of friendly, cooperative relations with the Republic of Korea" continued to be the fundamental goal of his government's policy toward the Korean peninsula. Murayama added that he would "tackle negotiations for diplomatic normalization between Japan and the DPRK" under two conditions: (1) such negotiations must "contribute to the peace and stability of the Korean peninsula" and (2) there will be close consultations with the Republic of Korea.[32]

In 1996 North Korea experienced massive flooding again, prompting the United Nations to make an appeal for international aid with a target sum of $43.6 million. The Japanese government, now headed by an LDP prime minister, Hashimoto Ryutaro, decided to contribute $6 million, of which all but $750,000 was channeled through the UN World Food Program (WFP). The remainder was channeled through the World Health Organization (WHO) and the UN Children's Fund (UNICEF).[33]

The persistence of food shortages in North Korea in 1997 led the UN to make a third annual appeal for international humanitarian assistance. The US, which gave the North a total of $8.4 million through UN agencies in 1995 and 1996, became the largest doner in 1997 by pledging

---

communication played a role in the first incident. Unaware that a previous agreement between Seoul and Pyongyang prohibited the hoisting a national flag, the captain of the South Korean cargoship had hoised an ROK flag, which North Koreans replaced with their own national flag before allowing the ship to dock in Wonsan port. The cost of providing 150,000 metric tons of rice to the North in 1995 was published by the ROK Ministry of Agriculture and Forestry. See *Joongang ilbo* (Seoul), July 19, 1997.

32 "Dai 134-kai kokkai ni okeru Murayama naikaku soridaijin shoshin hyomei enzetsu" [Prime Minister Murayama's Speech Expressing His Opinions at the 134th Diet] in Gaimusho, Gaiko seisho 1996, *Dai 1-bu* [Diplomatic Blue Book Part I] (Tokyo: Okurasho Insatsu-kyoku, 1996), 164.

33 Gaimusho, Ajia Kyoku, Hokuto Ajia-ka, *Kita Chosen ni taisuru kosui kanren kinkyu jindo shien apiru eno waga kunino kyoshutsu ni tsuite* [On Our Country's Donation Relating to the Appeal for Flood-related Emergency Humanitarian Assistance to North Korea], July 1996.

$52 million.³⁴ South Korea, which, as already noted, gave rice valued (with shipping costs added) at $232 million in 1995 and contributed a total of $3 million to the WFP and UNICEF in 1996, gave $16 million in 1997. In addition to government aid, non-governmental organizations (NGOs) in South Korea entrusted the ROK Red Cross to deliver relief goods, mostly food, worth $4.6 million, to the North on 17 occasions between January 1996 and May 1997.³⁵

The surge of anti-North Korea sentiment in Japan sparked by revelations of alleged kidnappings of Japanese nationals by North Korean agents, however, led the Hashimoto government, which had earned a new lease on life after the LDP had come very close to capturing a majority in the October 1996 general election, not to join the US and South Korea in responding to the UN appeal in 1997. On January 23 an opposition member of the Diet, Nishimura Shinso of the New Frontier party (*Shinshinto*) submitted a written question to the House of Representatives in which he introduced a report quoting a North Korean defector to the South as saying that he had heard from a North Korean agent about the latter's involvement in a kidnapping incident. The agent had allegedly told the defector that he and his colleagues kidnapped a middle school girl from Japan's west coast in November 1977. The agent's account matched the description of a 13-year-old middle school girl named Yokota Megumi who vanished in November 1977 while walking home from her school in Niigata.³⁶

---

34 U.S. Department of State, *Daily Press Briefing, Monday*, July 14, 1997, Briefer: Nicholas Burns, 5.

35 "Taebuk nongsanmul chiwon'aek ch'ong 2-ok 5-ch'on 6-baekman talla - Nongrimbu chipgye" [The Amount of Food Aid to the North Totals $256 Million - Ministry of Agriculture and Forestry Calculation], *Joongang ilbo*, July 19, 1997.

36 "Deta: Nishimura Shinso gi'in no teishutsu shita 'Kita Chosen kosaku soshiki ni yoru Nihonjin yukai rachi ni kansuru shitsumon shuisho" [Data: "Statement of Questions Regarding the Abduction of Japanese Nationals by North Korean Agents" Submitted by Dietman Nishimura Shinso], (1-gatsu 23-nichi teishutsu) [Submitted on January 23], *Gendai Koria* [Modern Korea]

In response to Nishimura's questions, which included whether the governments of Japan and South Korea were working together to verify the facts of the case and what measures the Japanese government might take vis-a-vis North Korea, the Japanese government disclosed that it was investigating the Yokota case in light of the new information and that there had been six incidents in the past, involving nine individuals, in which North Korea was suspected of having engaged in abductions. In addition, there was one failed attempt at kidnapping by suspected North Korean agents involving two Japanese nationals. The government response mentioned the case of Yi Un-hye, the alleged tutor of the former North Korean terrorist Kim Hyon-hui, noting that there was a "high" probability of North Korean involvement in that case.[37]

This turn of events spurred the parents of the suspected kidnap victims to step up their efforts to get their cases resolved, and scores of Diet members who belong to the New Frontier party and the LDP formed a group to "ascertain the facts concerning the kidnapping of Japanese citizens by North Korean agents."[38] The Japanese press reported that there were actually eleven Japanese nationals, two more than had been admitted by the government, who were believed to be victims of kidnapping by North Korean agents. In one of the cases, the mother of the Japanese victim had visited North Korea to see her son four times. She was reportedly told by her son, who was a factory worker in the North, not to question Pyongyang's official version of what had happened, which was that he had voluntarily settled in North Korea.[39]

(Tokyo), no. 369, (March 1997), 51-53.

37 "Nishimura Shinso gi'in no shitsumon ni taisuru seifu no tobensho" [Government's Response to the Questions Raised by Dietman Nishimura Shinso], ibid, 53-54.

38 *Dong-A ilbo*, March 9, 1997.

39 "Tsuiseki Nihonjin rachi giwaku" [Pursuit: Suspected Kidnaping of Japanese Nationals], AERA (Asahi Shimbun Weekly), no. 27, July 5, 1997, 19-23. The case of Teraoshi Takeshi who, after being kidnaped to North Korea by its agents in 1963, along with his two uncles, was finally reunited with his mother in Pyongyang in 1987, is also recounted in Irene M. Kunii/Kanazawa,

The notoriety of the kidnapping incidents led the Japanese press to focus its attention on other alleged misdeeds of the North Korean regime, of which the most prominent was the plight of Japanese women married to Korean men who were living in North Korea. The Japanese government estimates that about "1,800 Japanese women left [Japan] for North Korea between 1959 and 1982 with their North Korean husbands."[40] Letters written by some of the women that were smuggled out of the North and addressed to their relatives and, in some cases, to total strangers, were excerpted in the *Asahi shinbun* weekly AERA in April. All of them included pleas for help—for Japanese money with which to purchase food in North Korean black markets. One letter gave some statistics: whereas the average monthly salary was 80-90 won in the North, one kilogram (2.2 lbs) of pork costs 40 won, a single egg 2.5 won, one kilogram of rice 30 won, and a chicken 100 won in the black market. "You can well imagine how one ekes out living in North Korea," the unnamed North Korean wrote.[41]

North Korea's already tarnished image in Japan received another blow in April when Japanese police found 70 kilograms (154 lbs) of amphetamines with a street value estimated at 11.9 billion yen ($95 million) hidden in cargo from a North Korean freighter that was labeled honey. The North Korean ship had left Nampo port on April 5 and docked at the port of Hososhima in Kyushu on April 9. The ship's captain, a North Korean citizen, was arrested along with two Korean residents of Japan.[42]

"Plea for the Missing: Stories of Kidnapped Japanese Living in North Korea Stir Demands for Their Return," *Time*, June 2, 1977 (available from the Internet).

40 "Japan, N. Korea to Hold Talks On Resuming Ties," *The Daily Yomiuri*, August 16, 1997.

41 "Kita Chosen Nihonjin tsuma no taibo seigatsu 'Kusuri mo kaenai'" [Austere Life of Japanese Wives in North Korea: "We Cannot Even Afford to Buy Medicine"], *AERA*, April 7, 1997 (from the internet).

42 "Japan Police Seize Stimulants," *Associated Press* (Tokyo), April 19, 1997; Teruaki Ueno, "Japan Drug Haul Seen Showing Dark Side of N. Korea,"

Nuclear and Humanitarian Issues 139

When the leaders of the US and Japanese governments held a summit meeting in Washington in late April, Clinton tried in vain to persuade Hashimoto to take part in the international humanitarian aid to North Korea. Hashimoto's remarks at a press conference on April 25 are worth quoting at length:

> We certainly are aware of the situation in North Korea that requires humanitarian food aid. At the same time, if we speak of humanitarian circumstances, there are certain things we would like the North Koreans to do for us. And one of them relates to Japanese nationals—Japanese women who got married to North Koreans. And those people who went to North Korea have not been able to send letters to Japan, whereas North Koreans visiting Japan could always go, you know, back and forth between Japan and North Korea. These Japanese women who married North Koreans have not even been allowed to return to their families for temporary visits. So speaking of humanitarian issues, we would like the North Koreans to allow these Japanese wives to write letters back home or, you know, [make] temporary visits to their families in Japan.
> And also, according to information that we have gleaned, there [have] been several mysterious incidents that took place, one after another, in a rather limited time period, where some [people]······ suddenly disappeared from Japanese shores. And North Korean spies, who later have confessed in South Korea······have said these people were abducted. So there is a high [probability] that these Japanese, who disappeared from Japanese shores, were abducted by the North Koreans······.[43]

Reuter, Tokyo, April 21, 1997 (both from the Internet). See also "Il, mayak milbanip hyomui puksonjang ch'ep'o" [Japan Arrests North Korean Captain on Suspicion of Drug Smuggling], *Chosun ilbo* (Seoul), April 20, 1997.

43 "Excerpts from the Clinton-Hashimoto News Conference," *Washington Post*, April 26, 1997, A16. Following Hashimoto's remarks quoted here, Clinton thanked Hashimoto "for Japan's support for the program to end the North

How did North Korea respond to the escalation of demands for an accounting of kidnapping cases and for humanitarian treatment of Japanese wives of North Koreans? Frustrated by Japan's linkage of the resumption of normalization talks to an improvement of inter-Korean relations—i.e., the resumption of dialogue—and, beginning in April 1995, to the North's acceptance of the proposal for a four-party peace talks—involving the two Koreas, the US, and China—jointly proposed by Presidents Clinton and Kim Young Sam, the North repeatedly called upon Japan to jettison all preconditions and "come to a conference table to *settle the past [kwago rul ch'ongsan]* without delay." To "settle the past," as Pyongyang sees it, requires two things as a bare minimum: (1) Japan must apologize for its actions during colonial rule and (2) Japan must pay adequate compensation to the North.[44]

To increase pressure on Japan to "settle the past" on North Korean terms, the DPRK openly opposed not only the deletion of "enemy state" clauses in the UN Charter but also Japan's elevation to permanent membership in the UN Security Council. When the UN General Assembly discussed the issue of deleting the provisions mentioning

---

Korean nuclear efforts, to freeze it and dismantle it, and for Japan's generosity in so many areas around the world where Japan spends a higher percentage of its income than the United States on humanitarian efforts. We have devoted a significant amount of money, and have pledged more, to feed the people of North Korea." Clinton added that the "world will find a way to keep the people of North Korea from starving and from······malnutrition, but they need to lift the burden of a system that is failing them in food and other ways off their back, resolve their differences with the South. That will permit them the freedom to reconcile the problems they have still with Japan······"

44 See the statement by the spokesman for the DPRK Foreign Ministry issued on January 10, 1997 in *Nodong sinmun*, January 11, 1997, 4 and his response to questions submitted by reporters for the *Korean Central News Agency*, North Korea's official press agency, on January 30, 1997 in *Nodong sinmun*, January 31, 1997, 6. See also Ch'oe Hak-ch'ol, "Ilbon tangguk un chongch'ijok kyoldan ul naeryoya handa" [The Japanese Authorities Must Take Decisive Political Measure], ibid., February 26, 1997, 6.

"enemy states" in the UN Charter, which appear in Articles 53, 77, and 107, the DPRK proposed a revision, not a deletion, of the provisions so as to make them applicable solely to Japan. The North's reasoning was that as the only former enemy state that has failed to "settle the past," Japan does not deserve to be rid of the stigma.[45] A DPRK delegate reiterated the preceding argument at a meeting of a working group for the reform of the UN Security Council held in New York in March 1997.[46]

North Korea used the same argument to oppose UN Security Council permanent membership for Japan. As the spokesman for the DPRK Foreign Ministry put it on February 13, 1997, to allow Japan to become a permanent member of the UN Security Council "would be tantamount not only to tacitly condoning its past crimes but also to encouraging it to repeat such crimes." He asserted that Japan was not in the same league with Germany, for the latter has already settled its past with apology and compensation to its former victims. Seats in the UN Security Council, he argued, should never be "sold and bought with money," adding that the level of a member's development or its financial contributions to the UN should not be used as criteria in expanding the permanent membership of the UN Security Council.[47]

As for the furor over alleged kidnapping of a Japanese middle school girl, North Korea flatly denied any responsibility, claiming that it "has

---

45 *Wolgan pukhan tonghyan*, December 1995, 67-68, 164-65.46 "Japan Cannot Escape 'Enemy State' Clause," *Pyongyang Times*, April 5, 1997, 8 and Ch'oe Hak-ch'ol, "Ilbon un 'chokguk' chohang sakje taesang uro toelsu opda" [Japan Cannot Be the Beneficiary of the Deletion of the 'Enemy State' Clauses], *Nodong sinmun*, April 4, 1997, 6.
46 "Japan Cannot Escape 'Enemy State' Clause," *Pyongyang Times*, April 5, 1997, 8 and Ch'oe Hak-ch'ol, "Ilbon un 'chokguk' chohang sakje taesang uro toelsu opda" [Japan Cannot Be the Beneficiary of the Deletion of the 'Enemy State' Clauses], *Nodong sinmun*, April 4, 1997, 6.
47 "UNSC's Permanent Seat Cannot Be Taken for Money," *Pyongyang Times*, February 22, 1997, 8; *Nodong sinmun* (Pyongyang), February 14, 1997, 6; Ch'oe Hak-ch'ol, "Ouliji annun taeguk haengse" [An Awakward Playing of a Great Nation Role], ibid., July 19, 1997, 6.

nothing to do with us." Noting that the Japanese authorities are using the word "suspicion"—*uihok* in Korean or *giwaku* in Japanese—, the spokesman for the DPRK Foreign Ministry questioned the credibility of the source of information about the alleged kidnapping—South Korea's Agency for National Security Planning (ANSP). He argued that South Korea's motive for "fabricating" the story was to apply brakes on moves toward improvement of DPRK-Japan relations in tandem with improvement in DPRK-US relations. He warned that the only real loser will be Japan.[48] The spokesman for the Korean Central News Agency also called the case a fabrication by the "South Korean puppets" aimed at fueling anti-DPRK sentiment and escalating confrontation. "Right-wing reactionary forces in Japan," he charged, joined hands with South Korea to defame the North. He underscored the ANSP's—actually, its predecessor, the Korean Central Intelligence Agency's—track record of kidnapping South Korean citizens from abroad, implying that it was the South, not the North, that engages in such dubious practices.[49]

Although there was virtually no chance that the North would change its stance regarding the kidnapping issue, there clearly was room for compromise on the issue of Japanese wives of North Korean nationals. With the food crisis showing no signs of abating, Pyongyang apparently decided that concessions on the issue would be tactically prudent. In an unofficial working-level meeting held in Beijing in mid-May, of which there had been several since April 1995, North Korean diplomats told their Japanese counterparts that their government may allow Japanese wives of North Korean nationals to visit their relatives in Japan. "During the meeting, the Japanese side sought a gesture from the North to placate

---

48 See the statement by the DPRK Foreign Ministry spokesman issued on April 28 in *Nodong sinmun* (Pyongyang), April 29, 1997, 5.
49 "Ilbon uik pandong seryoktul un pan konghwaguk sodong ui taekarul ch'onbaekbaero ch'iruge toel kosida-Choson Chungagn T'ongsin taebyonin tamhwa" [Japan's Right-wing Reactionary Forces Will Pay for their Anti-DPRK Uproar Hundred-fold and Thousand-fold-Statement by the Spokesman for the Korean Central News Agency], ibid, June 10, 1997, 6.

the Japanese public, pointing out increasing hostility among Japanese citizens toward the North's human rights record, according to [Japanese government] sources." "Although North Korean officials continued to deny the allegations [about kidnapping], they proposed that Japanese wives return temporarily to Japan."[50]

Such North Korean gesture, coupled with increasing pressure from the US, set the stage for change in Japan's policy. The Japanese government decided in principle that it would provide additional humanitarian aid to the North. The Hashimoto government, however, delayed the planned visit to the North by Diet members belonging to the LDP, the SDP, and the New Party *Sakigake*, pending progress in the working-level Japan-DPRK contacts in Beijing. Inter-governmental negotiations, in other words, would take precedence over negotiations involving party representatives.[51]

Negotiation soon materialized in Beijing at the deputy director-general level, which was the highest-level negotiation between Japan and North Korea since the breakdown of the normalization talks in

---

50 "N. Korean Government May Let Japanese Wives Visit Home," *The Daily Yomiuri* (Tokyo), May 16, 1997.
51 "Kita Chosen shokuryo shien meguri seifu yoto ashinami ni midare" [Government and Ruling Parties out of Step Regarding Food Aid to North Korea], *Asahi shinbun*, July 9, 1997. An article by North Korea's supreme leader Kim Jong Il dampened the enthusiasm of some Japanese politicians for the resumption of aid to the North. On June 21, *Nodong sinmun* published a lengthy article by Kim in which he characterized reliance on aid as "foolish and dangerous." "'Aid' by the imperialists," he wrote, "is the noose of plunder and subordination with which to give one but take ten and hendred." "Nothing is more foolish and dangerous," he warned his compatriots, "than pinning one's hopes on 'aid' by the imperialists······." Kim Jong Il, "Hyongmyong kwa konsol eso chuch'e-song kwa minjok-song ul kosu halte taehayo" [On Safeguarding *chuch'e* Character and National Character in Revolution and Construction], *Nodong sinmun*, June 21, 1997, 1-3. For reaction in Japan, see "Kita Chosen no Kim ronbun ni fukaigan, Jiminto no Kato kanjicho" [LDP Secretary-General Kato Expresses Displeasure with Article by North Korea's Kim], *Asahi shinbun*, June 22, 1997.

November 1992. After two days of talks, the two sides on August 22 reached an agreement on the resumption of normalization talks "as soon as possible," with the understanding that details would be worked out "through close contact between the embassies of the two countries in Beijing."[52] The Japanese Embassy in Beijing disclosed that the two sides had agreed to realize the home visit of some Japanese wives of North Koreans within a month and to hold Red Cross talks for that purpose.[53] It is noteworthy that even after the normalization talks had entered into an impasse Japan has always kept the position of chief delegate to the normalization talks filled. On July 30 Foreign Minister Ikeda appointed Takahashi Masaji, a 60-year-old career diplomat who was serving as Japan's representative to the Organization for Economic Cooperation and Development (OECD)—ambassadorial rank—as Japan's chief delegate to the talks; Takahashi's predecessor, Seki Hiroki, had been appointed as Japan's ambassador to Italy.[54]

Japanese Wives' Homecoming

It would take nearly three months to implement the agreement on the home visit of Japanese women married to North Korean nationals. The Hashimoto government's decision to provide 70,000 tons of rice

---

52 "Japan, North Korea Praise Accord to Push Normalization Talks," *AFP* (Agence France Presse), Tokyo, August 23, 1997.

53 "Il-buk sugyo hoedam habui" [Japan and North Agree on Normalization Talks], *Chosun ilbo* (Seoul), August 23, 1997, p 1. A dispatch by Kyodo News Agency quoted "Japanese officials" as saying that North Korea had agreed to allow a dozen Japanese wives of North Koreans to visit their relatives in Japan in September and that "the Red Cross societies of the two countries will now form a task force to oversee arrangements for the trips." See "Pyongyang, Tokyo Strike Deal," *Japan Times*, Weekly International Edition, September 1-7, 1997, 1 and 6.

54 "Nitcho kokko seijoka seifu taihyo ni Takahashi OECD taishi o kiyo e" [OECD Ambassador Takahashi Appointed Government Representative to Japan–DPRK Normalization Talks], *Asahi shinbun*, July 31, 1997.

valued at $23 million to North Korea through the UN World Food Program in late September helped to nudge Pyongyang to action.[55] An agreement on the implementation of home visits had actually been signed between the two countries' Red Cross organizations in Beijing on September 9 but the North had been stalling.[56] In mid-October, the DPRK Red Cross handed its Japanese counterpart a list of 15 Japanese wives ranging in age from 55 to 84 who would constitute the first group of home visitors. After confirming that all of them had relatives in Japan who would be willing to receive them, the Japanese government approved the list. It was then made public on October 30.[57]

The Japanese women finally arrived in their homeland for a weeklong visit on November 8. Accompanied by five North Korean Red Cross officials, their prearranged itinerary called for only a few days of visit to their relatives. During the remainder of their visit, the women stayed together in the Yoyogi Olympic Memorial Center in Tokyo's Shibuya Ward.[58]

At a press conference held at Narita International Airport upon their arrival, in which only four of the 15 women participated, the home visitors said that they were happy living in North Korea. As a 64-year-old woman, Arai Yoshie, put it, "I am so happy that I am not sure how to express it. I have been in North Korea nearly 40 years, but there has been no discrimination against me and I have been very happy."[59] When asked

---

55 "Government to Send Food Aid to N. Korea," *Daily Yomiuri*, September 27, 1997.
56 See the Japanese-language text of the agreement in *Chosen sinpo* (Tokyo), April 3, 1998. The agreement stipulated that the Japanese side would "make an effort" to pay all the expenses of visitors, including their roundtrip travel, lodging, transportation, and medical costs incurred during their visit.
57 "Nihonjin tsuma satogaeri, dai ichijin 15-nin kyo happyo" [The First Group of 15 Homecoming Japanese Wives Announced Today], *Asahi shinbun*, October 30, 1997.
58 "Kita Chosen kara Nihonjin tsuma 15-nin ga satogaeri" [15 Japanese Wives Return Home from North Korea], ibid., November 8, 1997; Nicholas D. Kristof, "After North Korean Isolation, Japanese Wives Visit Homes," *New York Times*, November 9, 1997, A5.

by a Japanese reporter whether they still believed that North Korea was a "paradise on earth," all four women either said yes or nodded their heads.[60]

It is noteworthy that only a half of the Japanese women disclosed their Japanese names; the remaining half failed to do so at the request of their relatives in Japan. At a farewell press conference on November 14, one of the women whose Japanese name had been withheld said in Korean: "Before arriving in Japan, I was looking forward to seeing my relatives. But now, it seems that people here think we committed some kind of sin by marrying North Koreans and moving to our husbands' country." Another woman agreed: "I regret that some of our relatives refused to allow us to make our Japanese names public."[61]

On the whole, however, the home visit by the first group of Japanese wives in North Korea went smoothly. To underscore the linkage between the wives issue and normalization of diplomatic relations, a North Korean Red Cross official accompanying the women pointed out that "Japanese-born spouses will be free to visit their homelands if diplomatic relations [between the DPRK and Japan] are established.[62] Japan's Foreign Ministry assessed the visit as "the first step toward the amelioration of the climate for Japan-DPRK normalization," adding that Japan would hasten negotiations with North Korea for the dates and scales of the second and third groups of Japanese wives who would visit their homeland.[63]

On January 27, 1998, the second group of 12 Japanese wives living in North Korea arrived in Tokyo for a week-long visit. The Japanese

---

59 "Japanese Wives Arrive for Visit from N. Korea," *Daily Yomiuri*, November 9, 1997.
60 "Ilbonin ch'o 1-jin 15-myong Ilbon toch'ak" [The 1st Group of 15 Japanese Wives Arrive in Japan], *Chosun ilbo*, November 9, 1997.
61 "Wives Reveal Discrimination Regrets," *Daily Yomiuri*, November 14, 1997.
62 Ibid.
63 "Ilbonin ch'o kohyang pangmun i namginkot, puk il sugyo kyosop hanbal chopgun" [What Has the Japanese Wives' Home Accomplished: One Step Closer to North-Japan Negotiations on Normalization], *Joongang ilbo*, November 15, 1997.

government had released their Japanese names, ages, and hometowns on January 16. Reflecting the importance the Japanese government attached to the continuation of the home visit program, Chief Cabinet Secretary Muraoka Kanezo made the announcement of the impending visit. Faced with the criticism that the withholding of the Japanese names, ages, and former addresses of seven of the 15 members of the first group betrayed discrimination, the Japanese government decided to release all relevant information on the second group, overriding the objections of the women's relatives.[64]

The itinerary of the second group was identical to that of the first group. Upon arrival at Narita Airport, only two of the twelve women talked with reporters. Accompanied by three North Korean Red Cross officials, the Japanese wives, aged between 59 and 70, were taken to the Yoyogi Olympic Memorial Center in Tokyo. Relatives and friends visited the women on the following day. On the third day the women headed for their hometowns for two-day visits. After spending their last day in Tokyo together, the women returned to Pyongyang on February 1.[65]

Of the comments made by the visitors, the only thing that could be construed as remotely negative pertained to the food situation in the North. One of the two women who spoke on behalf of the group, Murakami Tamao, 69, said that food shortages had made her life "very difficult" during the past three years. In her words, "I tried to manage by eating only twice a day, and then once." Asked about the alleged kidnappings of Japanese nationals by North Korean agents, the other spokesperson, Arai Yoshiko, 61, said that she was not aware of the issue.

---

64 "Nihonjin tsuma sato kaeri dai 2 jin meibo happyo" [The List of the Second Group of Homecoming Japanese Wives Released], *Yomiuri shinbun*, January 17, 1998; "Government Releases List of 2nd Group of Japanese Spouses to Visit," *Daily Yomiuri*, January 17, 1998.
65 "Japanese Wives in North Korea Arrive in Tokyo for Homecoming Visit," AFP (Agence France Presse), Tokyo, January 27, 1998; "Wives Begin Hometown Visits," *Daily Yomiuri*, January 29, 1998; "Nihonjin haigusha dai 2 jin ga kokyo homon oeru" [The Second Group of Japanese Spouses Ends Home Visits], *Asahi shinbun*, February 1, 1998.

"Things should have been examined by those in authority. I myself have never heard of that," she said.[66]

Although the smoothness with which the home visit program had proceeded raised the hope that it would continue in the months ahead, the subsequent deterioration of Tokyo-Pyongyang relations dashed such hope. More on this later.

Visit to North Korea by a Delegation of Japan's Ruling Parties

The home visit by the first group of Japanese wives coincided with a visit to North Korea by a delegation of the three ruling coalition parties. The nine-member delegation technically consisted of three separate delegations representing the Liberal-Democratic Party (LDP), the Social Democratic Party (SDP), and the New Party *Sakigake*, respectively. Leaders of the three delegations were Mori Yoshiro, the chairman of the LDP Executive Committee; Ito Shigeru, the Secretary-General of the SDP; and Domoto Akiko, the chairwoman of the *Sakigake* Diet members' organization.[67]

It was the second visit by representatives of Japan's three ruling coalition parties to North Korea in nearly three years. A main difference

---

66 "2nd Group of Japanese Wives Arrive From North Korea," *Daily Yomiuri*, January 28, 1998.

67 Mori, whose LDP delegation eclipsed the other two with five members, served as the leader of the combined delegation as well. Ito's group consisted of three members, while Domoto was the lone representative of Sakigake. See "Nitcho seijoka kosho no soki saikai de itchi" [Early Resumption of Negotiations for Japan-DPRK Normalization Agreed Upon], *Yomiuri shinbun*, November 12, 1997; "Nitcho no kokkyo kosho soki saikaide itchi, rachi giwaku wa heikosen" [Agreement on Early Resumption of Negotiations for Japan-DPRK Diplomatic Relations, Parallel Lines on Suspected Abductions], *Asahi shinbun*, November 12, 1997. Effective January 1996 Nihon Shakaito changed its name to Shakai Minshuto and its official English name became the Social

between the March 1995 visit and this one was that the SDP and *Sakigake* had stopped participating in the cabinet but were merely cooperating with the LDP in an informal coalition. During their four-day visit, the Japanese lawmakers met with North Korean leaders and held talks with a delegation of the Workers' Party of Korea (WPK). North Korea signaled its conciliatory mood within hours of the Japanese delegation's arrival. In a welcoming banquet for the visitors on the evening of November 11, Kim Yang Gon, the chairman of the WPK International Department, proposed a toast for "Prime Minister of Japan, President of the Liberal-Democratic Party, His Respected Excellency Hashimoto Ryutaro." Never before had North Korea used such an honorific expression for a Japanese prime minister, a fact that did not escape the attention of both the Japanese visitors and journalists who accompanied them.[68]

During negotiations on substantive issues, however, the North adhered to its previous positions. Most important, the North refused to acknowledge even the allegations implicating its agents in the suspected abductions of Japanese youths. Calling on Japan to "stop resurrecting the [abduction] issue," Kim Yang Gon said: "[The suspected abductions] are a fabrication, and this issue just irritates us······If Japan wants to discuss humanitarian issues, if any, we have more to say in that area."[69]

The North presented a three-point proposal to the Japanese delegation, which would commit both sides to (1) "work······actively for the resumption of normalization talks," (2) "resolve······humanitarian issues even before the normalization of diplomatic ties," and (3) "realize······a wide range of exchanges beyond the political field." Given

---

Democratic Party (SDP). "History of Japanese Political Parties," *Daily Yomiuri* (Tokyo), January 30, 1997; "Words & Phrases," *Japan Times International*, January 1-5, 1999, 22.

68 "'Chonggyong hanun Hashimoto kakha'······puk kukje bujang iryejok chonch'ing sayong" ["His Respected Excellency Hashimoto"······North's International Department Head Uses an Unusual Honorific], *Dong-A ilbo*, November 12, 1997.

69 "N. Korea Rejects Talks on Alleged Abductions," *Daily Yomiuri*, November 14, 1997.

the lack of agreement on the meaning of "humanitarian issues," the Japanese side rejected the North Korean proposal for a written agreement incorporating these points.[70]

Faced with the Japanese delegation's firm stand, the North made a tactical retreat, offering to investigate the alleged abductions as a case of "missing persons." In return for this concession, the Japanese delegation gave the green light to the release of a "press communique" before returning to Tokyo. The communique said that the two sides had noted that "since 1990 when the visits and contacts between the ruling parties of the two countries began, there has been cooperation in satellite communications service and airline service, thanks to the efforts of the ruling parties and governments of the two countries." The communique also listed such positive developments as Pyongyang's expression of sympathy for and provision of "financial support" to the Japanese people at the time of the great Hanshin earthquake in January 1995, the realization of the home visit by the first group of Japanese wives, and Japan's provision of humanitarian aid to the North. It then stated:

> 1. The two sides······agreed to use [their] influence to realize the convening of the ninth round of the full-fledged intergovernmental talks [on diplomatic normalization] as soon as possible. The [North] Korean side stressed that the talks should be aimed at improving relations between the two countries, that it is necessary to refrain from hurting the other side and doing things not conducive to the improvement of bilateral ties, and that [both sides should] pursue mutually fair policies with an independent stand.
> 2. The two sides shared the view that it is necessary to solve humanitarian issues and those relating to cooperation between the two countries even before the normalization of diplomatic relations. The [North] Korean side expressed its willingness to continue to permit Japanese wives······to visit their hometowns.

---

70 "Mission Rejects N. Korean Proposal," ibid.

The chairman of the [North] Korea-Japan friendship association said that though the alleged disappearance of a Japanese girl is a fabrication that has nothing to do with the DPRK, the DPRK side may [nonetheless] make an investigation into the case along with the investigation into the issues of other missing persons. While in [North] Korea, the Japanese delegation toured disaster-striken areas and concurred in the urgency of food aid. It expressed its willingness to ask the Japanese government to continue providing food to the DPRK through international organizations.

3. Both sides considered that it is desirable for the ruling parties of the two countries to visit each other frequently and promote mutual understanding with a view to creating an atmosphere conducive to inter-governmental talks and successful solution of humanitarian issues and issues relating to cooperation······.[71]

In sum, the November 1997 visit to North Korea by representatives of Japan's three ruling coalition parties demonstrated that while both countries were eager to resume negotiations for diplomatic normalization, there still remained some hurdles to be cleared. It also appeared that the North's positions on key issues and tactics had not become any more flexible than they were during the 1991-1992 negotiations.

The main stumbling block to the resumption of normalization talks proved to be the issue of alleged abductions. While denying categorically that its agents had ever engaged in abductions in Japan, North Korea agreed nonetheless to conduct an investigation into "missing persons" from Japan. Japan, however, refused to accept Pyongyang's claim that not

---

71 "Chosen Rodoto to Nihon 3-yoto taihyodan no hotobun" [Press Communique by the Workers' Party of Korea and the Delegation of Japan's Three Ruling Parties], *Chosen sinpo*, November 14, 1997; "WPK, Japanese Coalition Issue Communique," *People's Korea* (Tokyo), November 14, 1997. Both of these papers are published by *Ch'ongnyon* or *Chosoren*, the federation of pro-DPRK Korean residents in Japan.

152 Between Discord and Cooperation

a single person from Japan had been found in the North. North Korea then accused Japan of having defamed its honor and engaged in an "unpardonable" hostile act [that was] without precedent in history."[72]

North Korea asserted that Japan had reneged on its commitment to resume normalization talks without any preconditions. Such a commitment, Pyongyang said, was made not once but twice—in the four-party agreement unveiled in Pyongyang in March 1995 and in the agreement reached at a high-level (foreign ministry deputy bureau chief level) talks held in Beijing in August 1997. North Korea then went on the offensive, charging that Japan lacked any moral authority to accuse anyone of having abducted its citizens, for it was guilty of the "most heinous crimes" involving kidnapping, torturing, raping, and killing millions of Koreans during the colonial era. North Korea underscored the "unspeakable inhuman crimes" Japan had allegedly committed against "200,000 Korean girls and women who were forced to serve as sex slaves for the Japanese Imperial Army."[73]

Growing pressure within Japan, where the family members of the alleged kidnap victims collected a million signatures on a petition urging their government to take prompt and effective measures to "rescue" the victims, left the Japanese government little choice but to take a hard line on the issue vis-a-vis North Korea.[74] This issue, combined with the

---

72 "Uri konghwaguk ul simhi modokhan Ilbon tangguk ui chondae mimun ui chokdae haengwi nun choltaero yongin toelsu opta" [The Unprecedented Hostile Act That Has Seriously Defamed Our Republic Will Never Be Tolerated], *Nodong sinmun*, June 11, 1998, 6. This is a statement issued by the spokesman for the DPRK Foreign Ministry.

73 Nonp'yongwon, "Ilbon ui tae Choson chase rul nonham" [On Japan's Posture toward Korea], ibid., May 8, 1998, 6. Articles signed by nonp'yongwon (commentator) represent the most authoritative views of the DPRK. They usually deal with issues of utmost importance to North Korea.

74 "Pukhan ui Irin napch'i uihok haemuyong ch'okku somyong 1-baengmanmyong tolp'a" [Signatories Calling for Clarification of Suspected Abductions of Japanese Citizens by North Korea Surpass One Million], *Joongang ilbo* (Seoul), April 18, 1998. On April 2, 1998 the Association of the

Japanese government's decision to exclude those who had renounced Japanese citizenship at the time of their repatriation to North Korea from the pool of Japanese wives who would be eligible to visit Japan under the "home visit" program, had the effect of virtually suspending the program. The spokesman for the Central committee of the DPRK Red Cross Society announced on June 5 that Japanese wives themselves had withdrawn their applications for home visits in view of Tokyo's "hostile acts."[75]

The rapidly cooling climate in Tokyo-Pyongyang relations, however, worsened precipitously in August and September, when the missile/satellite incident erupted. We now turn to analysis of that incident.

The Missile/Satellite Incident

Shortly after noon on August 31, 1998 North Korea launched a three-stage rocket from its east coast that flew over Japan and landed off the coast of the Sanriku in the Pacific Ocean. Its first stage had crashed in the Sea of Japan (or the East Sea), and a third stage may have tried but failed to propel a satellite into orbit from the Pacific Ocean. After corroborating the information from various sources, of which the single

---

Families of Victims Kidnapped by North Korea and the National Association for the Rescue of Japanese Kidnapped by North Korea published a full-page advertisement in The *New York Times* detailing the North Korean government's "heinous crimes," urging "the U.S. government to take appropriate measures toward the North Korean government," and appealing readers to "join [them] in asking the United Nations to set up a commission for the express purpose of investigating these violations of human rights and to send a mission to North Korea to investigate these horrific crimes." See "We Appeal to All the Freedom-loving American People, Justice to Our children and Fellow Citizens," *New York Times*, April 2, 1998, A27.

75 "Uri e taehan choktaesi onhaeng i kyesok toenunhan Ilbon i odulgosiran amugotto opta" [Japan Has Nothing to Gain by Continuing Hostile Acts and Statements toward Us], *Nodong sinmun*, June 25, 1998, 6.

most important was the US military, the Japanese government on September 1 "lodged a strong protest against North Korea" through its diplomatic channels at the United Nations.[76]

On the same day Chief Cabinet Secretary Nonaka Hiromu, the principal spokesman for the Japanese government, issued a statement calling the North Korean action "deeply regrettable." Saying that "this action directly affects Japan's security and······presents a very serious situation of concern······from the viewpoint of the peace and stability of Northeast Asia and of the non-proliferation of weapons of mass destruction," Nonaka stated that "Japan must reconsider its policy toward

---

76 Ministry of Foreign Affairs of Japan, *Press Conference by the Press Secretary* (Tokyo: September 1, 1998). Although the US government analysts concluded that "North Korea tried but failed to launch a small satellite into orbit when it fired a multistage rocket in an arc over Japan" on August 31, 1998, the Japanese Defense Agency (JDA) dissented from the US view. In a report released on October 30, the JDA said that "the rocket was a three-stage missile, based on the Taepodong-1 missile, with a range of more than 1,500 kilometers." The JDA report added that the "first stage of the missile, which had a range of 1,300 kilometers, fell into the Sea of Japan." "The second stage of the missile," the report continued, "fell into the Pacific Ocean about 520 kilometers off the [Sanriku] coast." The "third stage of the rocket," the report confirmed, "was equipped with a propulsion mechanism." "Although it flew for a short time, it failed to achieve a speed sufficient to attain orbit," the report concluded. For the US view, see Steven Lee Myers, "U.S. Calls North Korean Rocket a Failed Satellite," *New York Times*, September 15, 1998; Bradley Graham, "N. Korean Missile Threat Is Reassessed," *Washington Post*, September 25, 1998, A31. For the Japanese view, see Boeicho, Jieitai, "Oshirase: Kita Chosen no misairu hassha no bunseki kekka ni tsuite" [Report: On the Results of Analysis of North Korea's Missile Launch], October 30, 1998, Tokyo; "Agency: N.Korean Rocket Probably Missile," *Daily Yomiuri* (Tokyo), October 31, 1998. The Boeicho (Japan Defense Agency) report noted that the trajectory of the North Korean rocket was comparatively flat and that the "apex of the trajectory was lower than that usually attained by a ballistic missile." It did not, however, rule out the possibility that the third stage of the rocket, which contained a propulsion mechanism, may have attempted unsuccessfully to place a satellite into orbit as US government analysts had concluded.

North Korea······and take stringent responses in a firm manner."[77]

The "concrete measures" Nonaka announced Japan would take included (1) consultations among Japan, the US, and the ROK; (2) pursuing the option of raising the issue in the General Assembly and the Security Council of the UN; (3) not entering into any negotiations with North Korea on diplomatic normalization "for the time being"; (4) not extending "food and other assistance" to North Korea for the time being; and (5) suspension of "progress on KEDO······for the time being." The last-mentioned measure referred to Japan's withholding of its signature on a cost-sharing agreement on the LWR project. Under the agreement, Japan's share of the estimated $4.6 billion cost of the project would be $1 billion, while South Korea would contribute "about 70% of the cost."[78]

On September 2 the Japanese government took additional measures consisting of "canceling permission for charter flights between Japan and North Korea scheduled from 3 to 15 September" and deciding "not to accept the applications [for] 14 further flights." On September 3 Foreign Minister Komura Masahiko held a meeting with ROK Foreign Minister Hong Soon Yung in Tokyo, during which, according to the Japanese Foreign Ministry, Hong expressed full support for the way in which Japan was dealing with the missile incident. Hong reportedly told Komura that the citizens of his country shared the sense of "indignation and shock" on the part of the Japanese and that it was not necessary for Japan to hasten to sign the cost-sharing agreement for the LWR project. Hong "also agreed to the holding of [the meeting of the foreign ministers of the US, Japan, and the ROK] on the occasion of the opening of the United Nations General Assembly in New York," pledging that his country would cooperate with Japan at the UN.[79]

On September 4 Japan's permanent representative to the UN, Owada

---

77 Ministry of Foreign Affairs of Japan, *Announcement by the Chief Cabinet Secretary on Japan's Immediate Response to North Korea's Missile Launch* (Tokyo: September 1, 1998).
78 Ministry of Foreign Affairs of Japan, *Press Conference by the Press Secretary* (Tokyo: September 1, 1998), 4.

Hisashi, sent a letter to the president of the Security Council, Hans Dahlgren of Sweden, asking that it be circulated among the members of the council. After describing the facts as understood by Japan, the letter "points out that this launch took place without prior warning and that the missile landed in the vicinity of frequently used sea lanes." Japan, therefore, considered "this action as being in disregard of the norms of international law relating to the use of the high seas." "In launching this missile without prior warning," the letter continued, "North Korea ignored the fundamental principles of the Convention on International Civil Aviation and······ the Convention of the International Maritime Organization to which North Korea is a party."[80]

When the president of the UN Security Council, after conducting informal consultations with council members, issued a "press statement" on September 15, expressing "concern" and "regret" over the DPRK's launching of the rocket, North Korea charged that "the UN Security Council is being inveigled [by Japan] into applying double standards, having already lost impartiality." Recalling that the Council had never questioned satellite launchings before, North Korea declared that the Council "has no reason to call our satellite launch [into] question." "It is not the DPRK but the Japanese militarist forces," North Korea said, "that should be warned and called to task." In North Korean words, "the Japanese government's malicious slander at the DPRK over the satellite launch is chiefly aimed at inventing a pretext and reason to cover up their crimes as the sworn enemy of the Korean people and turn Japan into a military power for aggression and war."[81]

Prime Minister Obuchi Keizo's reference to the missile/satellite launch in his address to the UN General Assembly on September 21 prompted more harsh rhetoric from Pyongyang. Obuchi said that the

---

79 Ibid. (Tokyo: September 4, 1998), 2-3.
80 Ibid. (Tokyo: September 8, 1998), 1-2.
81 "Biased Behavior," *Korean Central News Agency* (KCNA) (Pyongyang), September 22, 1998. The KCNA dispatch quoted from *Nodong sinmun*, September 22, 1998.

"missile launch by North Korea, even if it was an attempt to orbit a satellite, poses a serious problem which directly concerns both Japan's security and peace and stability in Northeast Asia." He called on Pyongyang to "consider seriously the September 15 statement by the president of the U.N. Security Council as a message reflecting the views of the entire international community and never to repeat such an act.[82]

In a commentary published on September 26, *Nodong sinmun* called Obuchi's remarks "arrogant." Having launched satellites dozens of times itself, the daily organ of the Workers' Party of Korea argued, Japan was in no position to protest the DPRK's first ever satellite launch. Japan, the paper said, permits its territory to be used as a "forward military base of the US on which numerous nuclear missiles are deployed, constantly threatening the peace and security" of the region. Only the "brazen-faced" dare to take issue with Pyongyang's satellite launch under these circumstances, *Nodong sinmun* argued. The North Korean paper also castigated Japan for failing to recognize or acknowledge that North Korea had launched a satellite, not a missile. "For Japan's highest authority to denigrate our satellite launch as 'missile firing' on the sacred UN stage," *Nodong sinmun* asserted, "betrays the deeply-entrenched hostile policy of Japan's reactionary ruling clique toward the DPRK and is an intolerable act of provocation against our people." Should Japan fail to jettison its "anti-DPRK mania," the paper warned, "we would have no choice but to treat Japan as our eternal enemy and respond in a forceful manner."[83]

On October 21 Japan partially lifted its sanctions on North Korea by signing a "KEDO Executive Board resolution concerning the cost-sharing

---

82 "Obuchi Condemns North Korea in U.N. Speech," *Japan Times* (Tokyo), Weekly International Edition, September 28-October 4, 1998, 3; Watanabe Shinya, "Obuchi Blasts N.Korea at U.N. over Test-firing," *Daily Yomiuri*, September 23, 1998.

83 "'*Nodong sinmun*, Ilbon ch'ongni ui yu'en ch'onghoe ilban yonsul kwa kwallyon hayo nonp'yong" [*Nodong sinmun* Comments on Japanese Prime Minister's Speech during UN General Assembly's General Debate], *Choson sinbo*, October 1, 1998.

of the light water reactor project." Chief Cabinet Secretary Nonaka cited three reasons for Japan's decision to "resume cooperation" with KEDO. First, Japan saw "no realistic alternatives" to KEDO and the Agreed Framework in pursuing the goal of trying "to prevent North Korea from developing nuclear weapons." Second, "Japan's response to the missile launch by North Korea is having certain effects." Japan has sent "a clear message to North Korea" and "Japan's position has gained broad understanding and support in the international community." Third, since Japan believes that "cooperation among Japan, the Republic of Korea, and the United States remains extremely important in dealing with North Korea," it has decided to heed the appeal of Washington and Seoul for the resumption of Tokyo's cooperation with KEDO and, particularly, the LWR project.[84]

North Korea, meanwhile, continued to take a hard line against Japan, issuing statements critical of, even derogatory toward, the Tokyo government with an unprecedented frequency and vigor. To cite but two examples, on November 30, the DPRK Foreign Ministry spokesman strongly criticized Prime Minister Obuchi for mentioning not only the North's "missile launch" but also the issue of "secret underground nuclear facility" in a policy speech to the Diet three days earlier. Expressing concern over the latter, Obuchi had underscored the need to maintain close cooperation with the US and South Korea. Claiming that the allegations about a "secret underground nuclear facility" in the North "are nothing but a provocation concocted by the hard-line conservative forces in the US who are bent on increasing tensions on the Korean peninsula and······crushing us militarily," the spokesman accused Japan of following US instructions. "We are both contemptuous of and disillusioned by Japan's foreign policy that is utterly devoid of autonomous thinking and contents but dancing to other people's tunes," he said.[85]

On December 7 *Nodong sinmun* published an article signed by

---

84 Ministry of Foreign Affairs of Japan, *Press Conference by the Press Secretary*, October 23, 1998, 2-3.

"commentator" accusing Japan of plotting to "realize its old dream of establishing 'Greater East Asia Co-prosperity Sphere" by piggybacking on American policy of aggression against Asia and committing aggression against Korea anew." "Should Japan, in league with the US and South Korean authorities, embark on the path of aggression in the end," the article warned, the Japanese, "along with the US, would not be able to salvage even their bones." As long as "Japan persists in refusing to atone for its past crimes but in adhering to its hostile policy toward our Republic in subservience to the US, our Republic does not expect to engage in negotiations with Japan relating not only to such strategic issues as diplomacy and security but also to economic issues," the article said. Noting that international cooperation in exploring crude oil and other natural resources had a good prospect of materializing in the North, the article concluded that the DPRK "will never engage in transactions of any kind" with Japan unless the latter jettisons its "bad behavior" that "betrays its jealousy about our Republic's becoming rich and powerful."[86]

In sum, the missile/satellite incident helped to plunge Japan-DPRK relations to a new low, sharply reducing the probability of an early resumption of normalization talks. Pyongyang does not seem to have anticipated the unusually strong response from Tokyo. Pyongyang may have had multiple goals in mind when it launched the rocket on August 31. Internally, the launch may have been designed to enhance the legitimacy of Kim Jong Il, who was scheduled to be reconfirmed as the DPRK's supreme leader on September 5. Even though, contrary to expectations, Kim did not assume the position of the DPRK president (*chusok*), North Korea made it clear that as the chairman of the DPRK

---

85 "Konghwaguk oemusong taebyonin, Ilbon ch'ongni ui 'pimil chiha haek sisol' mangon ul tanjoe" [Our Republic's Foreign Ministry Spokesman Condemns Japanese Prime Minister's Reckless Remarks on "Secret Underground Nuclear Facility"], *Choson sinbo*, December 2, 1998.
86 "'Ilbon kwa to isang sangjong hal saenggak i opta' *Nodong sinmun* nonp'yong" ["We Have No Thought of Dealing With Japan Any Longer" Comments *Nodong Sinmun*], ibid., December 9, 1998.

National Defense Commission, Kim was the country's paramount leader. The post of *chusok* was abolished and the president of the Presidium of the Supreme People's Assembly, North Korea's nominal parliament, became the ceremonial head of state under the newly revised "Socialist Constitution."[87]

A related internal goal may have been to boost the sagging morale of the North Korean people. By flaunting its rocket technology, the Kim Jong Il regime may have hoped to drive home both its determination and ability to turn the DPRK into a *kangsong taeguk* (a great country that is powerful and prosperous), a phrase one encounters with increasing frequency in the North Korean media. Although US government experts concluded that the North's attempt to put a small satellite into orbit had failed, Pyongyang insisted that a satellite named *Kwangmyongsong 1-ho* (Bright Star Number 1) had been successfully launched and was orbiting the earth beaming patriotic songs. Pyongyang claimed that the rocket's third stage had used solid fuel, which, if true, would indicate a level of sophistication that is higher than had been previously estimated by outside observers. Pyongyang even held a "grand banquet" on September 26 "in honour of the scientists, technicians, and workers who had contributed to successfully launching the first artificial satellite."[88]

---

87 For an unofficial English translation of the revised DPRK Socialist Constitution adopted by the first session of the 10th Supreme People's Assembly on September 5, see *People's Korea*, September 17, 1998.

88 "Kwangmyongsong 1-ho nun chigurul tonda, ch'ot ingong wisong palsajadul ul manna pogo" [Kwangmyonsong Number 1 Circles the Earth, Meeting the People Who Launched the First Artificial Satellite], *Nodong sinmun*, September 8, 1998; "Banquet for Those Related to Launch of Satellite," *Korean Central News Agency*, September 27, 1998; Brandley Graham, "N.Korean Missile Threat Is Reassessed: 3-Stage Rocket Was Not Foreseen by U.S.," *Washington Post*, September 25, 1998, A31. See also "olhae rul kangsong taeguk konsol ui widaehan chonhwan ui haero pinnae ija" [Let Us Make This Year Shine as the Year of Turning Point for the Construction of a Great Nation That Is Both Strong and Prosperous], *Nodong sinmun*, January 1, 1999, 1. This is a joint editorial by the daily organs of North Korea's three most important institutions—the Workers' Party of Korea, the Korean People's Army, and the

Externally, Pyongyang's goals may have included (1) prodding Japan to seek an early resumption of normalization talks and (2) showing to its clients in the global arms market what it has to offer. Acutely aware of the need to bolster its bargaining power—or issue-specific structural power—vis-a-vis Japan, North Korea may have calculated that a demonstration of its missile capability, which now placed all of Japan within range, might serve to jump-start the stalled negotiations for diplomatic normalization.

As for a possible advertising function the launch may have performed, one must take note of the role of missile sales as a key source of North Korea's foreign exchange earnings. According to data collected by the ROK Ministry of Unification, the DPRK exported some 250 Scud missiles to Iran, Syria, the United Arab Emirates, and other countries between 1987 and 1992, earning an estimated $580 million. In 1993, however, North Korea began exporting missile components for assembly in client countries such as Iran, Iraq, Pakistan, and Syria. North Korea also began providing "technical cooperation" to these countries. Both the "Ghauri" missile launched by Pakistan in April 1998 and the "Shehab" missile launched by Iran in July 1998 were products of North Korean technology. In its negotiations with the US on the missile issue, North Korea has offered to cease exporting missile equipment and technology in exchange for $1 billion a year, an amount it claims to earn in missile exports each year. The US, which estimates Pyongyang's actual earnings from missile exports at $100 million a year, has rejected the offer.[89]

Whether any or all of the North Korean aims were attained is uncertain. Internal goals probably fared better than external ones. Japan's strong response showed that if the DPRK had in fact entertained any hope of inducing Japan to a conference table, such hope was rudely

---

Kim Il Sung Youth League. The organs of the latter two are called *Choson inmingun* and *Ch'ongnyon chonwi*, respectively.

[89] "US, N.Korea Missile Talks End," *Associated Press*, Kuala Lumpur, Malaysia, July 12, 2000; "Kita Chosen no misairu yushutsu wa nenkan 1-oku doru soto, Bei ga suitei" [North Korea's Missile Exports Around $100 Million, America Estimates], *Asahi shinbun*, July 11, 2000.

dashed. From Japan's perspective, what the North did not only exposed Japan's vulnerability to possible North Korean attack but infringed Japan's territorial integrity as well. It was the greatest tangible threat Japan had ever experienced from North Korea, to which Japan had no choice but to respond in a forceful and resolute way.[90]

Economic Relations

North Korea's continuing inability to service, let alone repay, its trade debt to Japan, estimated at 90 billion yen, is a major factor in the bilateral economic relations. As Table 2(pp. 45-46) shows, however, North Korea has maintained a surplus continuously since 1987, with a notable exception of 2001. Because the bulk of the trade is conducted by firms owned by Korean residents of Japan who are loyal to the DPRK and affiliated with *Chosoren* (called *Ch'ongnyon* in Korean), it is commonly labeled *Cho-Cho boeki* [*Chosoren-Chosen* (North Korea) trade].

What is more, most of "foreign direct investment," which Pyongyang has been courting assiduously since enacting a joint venture law in 1984, is traceable to *Chosoren*-affiliated Korean residents in Japan. They actually began donating "patriotic factories" (*aeguk kongjang*) to their fatherland long before the joint venture law took effect, a practice that has continued unabated to date. About 70 percent of such factories, estimated to number about 50, produce daily necessities and other light industrial goods.[91]

The dramatic increase in Japan's exports to North Korea in 1995—49

---

90 Even though in its Fiscal Year 1999 budget Japan's defense spending will most likely decline by 0.2 percent for the second year in a row, the government's final proposal to the Diet contained expenditures for launching a reconnaissance satellite, fortifying radar facilities, and joint Japan-US R&D for theater missile defense (TMD)—all related to the perceived need to cope with North Korean threat. "99 nendo seifu yosan'an 12-gatsu 25-nichi, boei reda kyoka hobo yokyu tori" [Fiscal Year 1999 Government Budget Proposal, December 25—Request for Strengthening Defensive Radars Approved for the Most Part], *Yomiuri shinbun*, December 26, 1998.

percent increase over the previous year—reflects Japan's rice exports to the North. (See Table 2 in Chapter I) In 1995 the top five Japanese exports to the North were textiles (32.7 percent), rice (20.6 percent), machinery (9.1 percent), electric goods (7.7 percent), and transportation equipment (7.3 percent). Japan's top five imports from the North in the same year were textile goods (37.9 percent), vegetable goods, primarily Matsutake mushrooms (20.4 percent), animal goods, primarily fish (18.6 percent), base metal (9.6 percent), and mineral goods (7.2 percent).[92]

That textiles and textile goods are at the top of Japan's exports to and import from North Korea reflects the practice of having clothes made in the North with material and design provided by Japan and then importing them to Japan. Men's suits, blazers, trousers, and coats as well as women's suits and skirts worth 12.2 billion yen were processed in this manner in 1995. That marked 30 percent increase in men's clothes and 50 percent increase in women's that underwent such "processing on commission." Although Japan remained North Korea's second largest trading partner in 1995, the gap between Japan and China was less than $6 million. What is more, Japan imported five times as much goods ($305.7 million) from the North as China did ($57.2 million). It was plain that Japan's importance to North Korea had grown markedly, accounting for 25 percent of Pyongyang's global trade and 36 percent of its exports. By contrast, trade with North Korea constituted a miniscule 0.076 percent of Japan's global trade.[93]

---

91 Yun Tok-min, "Ilbon ui tae-Pukhan chongch'i kyongje kwangye" [Japan's Political and Economic Relations With North Korea] in *Hanbando chubyon 4-guk ui tae-Pukhan chongch'aek* [The North Korea Policies of the Four Countries Surrounding the Korean Peninsula], ed. Yu Chang-hui (Seoul: Taeoe Kyongje Chongch'aek Yonguwon, 1996), 92-94.
92 Gaimusho, Ajia Kyoku, Hokuto Ajia-ka, *1995-nen no Nitcho boeki* [Japan-North Korea Tade in 1995], May 1996. Reproduced from *Higashi Ajia keizai joho* [Economic Information on East Asia].
93 Ibid., 1; Nihon Boeki Shinkokai, *Kita Chosen no keizai to boeki no tenbo* [Prospects for North Korea's Economy and Trade] (Tokyo: JETRO Kaigai Keizai Joho Senta, 1996), 166-67.

These patterns continued basically unchanged in 1996. Although the value of bilateral trade declined 13.1 percent from the preceding year, Japan still retained its position as North Korea's second largest trading partner behind China. Aside from the disappearance of rice from the list of Japan's top export items, the export picture did not change much, with textiles accounting for 32.9 percent, followed by mineral products (11.8 percent), transportation equipment (11.4 percent), electric goods (7.3 percent), and machinery (6.9 percent). Leading the list of Japan's imports from North Korea was once again textile goods (42.3 percent). They were followed by animal goods, primarily fish (19.2 percent), vegetable goods, primarily Matsutake mushrooms (13.9 percent), and mineral goods (10.4 percent).[94] Whereas Japan accounted for 24.2 percent of North Korea's global trade and 33.6 percent of its exports, North Korea's share of Japan's global trade was only 0.068 percent.[95]

There was a precipitous decline in Japan's exports to North Korea in 1997, a decline of 28.6 percent over the previous year, a record surpassed only once in the past—in 1976. The value of total trade turnover, however, declined only 6.9 percent. North Korea continued to have a surplus in its trade balance with Japan for the eleventh year in a row. The top five categories of Japan's export goods were textiles (35 percent), transportation equipment (18.1 percent), electric equipment (14 percent), machinery (8.5 percent), and mineral products, mainly fuels (8 percent). Japan's top five imports were textile goods (31.6 percent), vegetable products (24.5 percent), fish (17.6 percent), base metals and products (10.2 percent), anthracite coal (5.9 percent0. All of the textile imports were clothes made in the North on a "processing on commission" basis, of which 81 percent were men's suits, blazers, trousers, and coats, while 31 percent of the vegetable products were

---

94 *Hankook ilbo* (Seoul), October 31, 1997.
95 These were calculated from statistics in Japan External Trade Organization, *White Paper on International Trade 1997* (Tokyo: JETRO, 1997) and idem, *JETRO Releases Estimates on International Trade with North Korea in 1996*, August 29, 1997.

matsudake mushrooms.[96]

Although Japan's position as North Korea's number two trading partner remained intact, the gap between Japan and China, North Korea's top trading partner, visibly widened—from $93.2 million in 1996 to $225 million in 1997. South Korea continued to be North Korea's third largest trading partner. The asymmetrical pattern in Japan-DPRK trade also persisted. Whereas Japan accounted for 19.2 percent of North Korea's global trade and 29.3 percent of the latter's exports to the world, North Korea's share of Japan's global trade was a mere 0.063 percent.[97]

In 1998 Japan was still North Korea's number two trading partner but only $18.6 million behind China in terms of the total value of trade. Most notable, however, was the continuing decline in Japan-North Korea trade, a trend that continued in 1999.[98] The total value of Japan-North Korea trade in 1999, at $349.8 million, was still $20.6 million less than that of China-North Korea trade. Japan's major export goods to North Korea in 1999 were textiles (28.9 percent), transportation equipment (20.1 percent), electric equipment (15.1 percent), other machinery (8.5 percent) and mineral products (3.3 percent). Japan imported from North Korea marine products (mainly fish) (43.9 percent), textiles (29.6 percent), base metals and products (4.5 percent), vegetables (3.3 percent), and magnesium clinker (2.5 percent). The asymmetric pattern of trade remained unchanged: whereas Japan accounted for 23.6 percent of North Korea's global trade, North Korea accounted for a miniscule 0.048 percent of Japan's global trade.[99]

---

96 Tsuhso Sangyosho, ed., *Tsusho hakusho, Heisei 10-nenban* [Trade and Commerce White Paper, 1998] (Tokyo: Okurasho, Insatsu-kyoku, 1998), 319-320; "Statistics of DPRK-Japan Trade in 1997," *People's Korea*, April 16, 1998.

97 Nihon Boeki Shinko-kai, *97-nen no kita Chosen taigai boeki* [North Korea's External Trade in 1997] (Tokyo, August 18, 1998).

98 Tsusho Sangyosho, ed., *Tsusho hakusho Heisei 11-nenban* [White Paper on International Trade 1999], (Tokyo: Okurasho Insatsu-kyoku, 1999), 269-270; Taehan Muyok T'uja Chinhung Kongsa [Korea Trade-Investment Promotion Agency (KOTRA)], *1999-nyon Pukhan-Chungguk kan kyoyok* [Trade Between North Korea and China in 1999] (Seoul: March 6, 2000).

In 2000 Japan's trade with North Korea increased for the first time in five years. The total value of merchandise trade, $463.8 million, represented a 32.6-percent increase over the preceding year, and Japan's exports to the North, $206.8 million, was 40.1 percent greater than in 1999. For the 14th year in a row, moreover, Japan incurred a deficit in its balance of trade: its imports from the DPRK exceeded its exports to that country by $50.2 million. The composition of items traded remained unchanged, even though their relative weights varied slightly. Machinery (23.9 percent), textiles (21.7 percent), and transportation equipment (19.3 percent) were Japan's leading export items, while fish (35.8 percent), textiles (26.7 percent), and base metals and products (6.9 percent) led the list of Japan's imports from the North.[100]

The sharp decline in the total value of Tokyo-Pyongyang trade beginning in 2003 coincided with a deterioration of their bilateral relations in the wake of the Koizumi-Kim Jong Il summit in September 2002. We shall examine this, along with Japan's options relating to possible economic sanctions against the North in the next chapter.

Resumption of Normalization Talks

The path to the resumption of normalization talks between Japan and the DPRK proved to be unusually long, for the ninth round of the talks would not materialize until April 2000—seven and a half years after

---

99 Tsusho Sangyosho, ed., *Tsusho hakusho 2000* (International Trade White Paper 2000) (Tokyo: Okurasho Insatsu-kyoku, 2000), 218. For statistics on Japan's global trade, see ibid., 5; for statistics on North Korea's trade, see Taehan Muyok T'uja Chinhung Kongsa, *1999-nyondo Pukhan ui taeoe muyok tonghyang* [North Korea's External Trade in 1999] (Seoul: Taehan Muyok T'uja Chinhung Kongsa, 2000), 1.

100 Keizai Sangyosho, ed., *Tsusho hakusho 2001: 21 seiki ni okeru taigai keizai seisaku no chosen, kakuron* [White Paper on Trade and Commerce 2001: The Challenge of External Economic Policy in the 21st Century, Details] (Tokyo: K.K. Gyosei, 2001), 194-95.

the eighth round abruptly ended before any substantive discussion could begin. As noted, the missile/satellite incident of August 1998 generated discord of unprecedented magnitude in the annals of Tokyo-Pyongyang interactions. In March 1999 an incident involving an intrusion into Japanese territorial waters by two unidentified ships that the Japanese government suspected of being North Korean spy ships further strained the bilateral relationship.

In that incident, after Japan's Maritime Self-Defense Force patrol plane first detected two "suspicious ships" within Japanese territorial waters on Honshu's west coast on March 23, patrol boats and aircraft pursued them. Ignoring both orders to stop and warning shots, the two ships managed to cross the line beyond which Japan's Self Defense Forces stops hot pursuit. After concluding that, in view of their final destination, the two ships were North Korean, the Japanese government lodged a protest with Pyongyang.[101]

As the perceived threat from North Korea continued, Japan became increasingly interested in breaking the impasse in its relations with the North. With trilateral cooperation among the US, South Korea, and Japan gaining momentum and the search for a new strategy toward the North in full gear under the direction of former US Secretary of Defense William Perry, Japan began cautiously to seek ways of resuscitating the long-stalled normalization talks with North Korea. The pace accelerated after the publication of the Perry report in October 1999. The report, based on Perry's visit to the North and on close trilateral consultations among Washington, Seoul, and Tokyo, proposed a "two-path strategy"—one aimed at persuading the North to cease efforts to test, produce, and deploy nuclear weapons and medium- and long-range missiles, and the alternative strategy of containing North Korea with unspecified but presumably forcible means should diplomacy fail.[102]

Against this background a "supra-partisan" delegation of Japanese

---

101 For a detailed account of the incident, see Boeicho, ed., *Heisei 11-nenban Boei hakusho* ['99 Defense of Japan] (Tokyo: Okurasho Insatsu-kyoku, 1999), 335-45.

Diet members led by former Prime Minister Murayama Tomiichi visited Pyongyang in December 1999. Even though it did not officially represent the Japanese government, the delegation did in fact have the full support of the Obuchi government. Obuchi even entrusted to Murayama a letter addressed to General Secretary Kim Jong Il of the Workers' Party of Korea (WPK).[103] A joint press statement issued on December 3 by Murayama on behalf of the Japanese delegation and Kim Yong Sun on behalf of the WPK delegation indicated that the two sides had agreed to urge their respective governments to resume normalization talks as soon as possible, noting the urgent need to "liquidate the unfortunate past" and to improve bilateral relations in accordance with the interests of the peoples of both countries. The two sides, according to the statement, had also agreed to recommend to their respective Red Cross organizations to "cooperate with each other with the help of their governments" in order to resolve the "humanitarian issues" of concern to both countries.[104]

On December 14 Chief Cabinet Secretary Aoki Mikio issued a statement officially "welcoming" the results of the Murayama delegation's visit to the North, saying that the Japanese government "takes seriously the joint announcement issued with the North Korean side." Aoki noted that "Japan, the U.S., and the R.O.K., in close contact with each other, have been exploring ways of reducing 'threats' that the three countries and

---

102 U.S. Department of State, *Review of U.S. Policy Toward North Korea: Findings and Recommendations*, unclassified report by Dr. William J. Perry, North Korea Policy Coordinator and Special Advisor to the President and the Secretary of State (Washington, DC), October 12, 1999. Available from the U.S. Department of State's web site, http://www.state.gov.

103 "Shusho Kim Jong Il shoki ate shinsho o Murayama hochodan ni takusu" [Premier Entrusts Murayama Delegation Visiting North Korea with Letter Addressed to General Secretary Kim Jong Il], *Asahi shinbun* (Tokyo), November 30, 1999.

104 "Choson Nodongdang taep'yodan kwa Ilbon chongdang taep'yodan i kongdong podomun palp'yo" [The Delegations of the Workers Party of Korea and Japanese Political Parties Publish a Joint Press Communique], *Nodong sinmun* (Pyongyang), December 3, 1999, 2; "Delegation Urges Resumption of Talks with Pyongyang," *Japan Times* (Tokyo), December 4, 1999.

North Korea perceive in each other" along the lines "jointly elaborated" in the Perry report. Aoki singled out Pyongyang's announcement of a moratorium on missile launching made in the wake of US-DPRK missle talks in Berlin in September. The Japanese government, he added, "deems that establishing a full-fledged forum for overall dialogue between the authorities of Japan and North Korea will contribute not only to redressing the anomalous Japan-North Korea relations after World War II but also to easing the tension on the Korean Peninsula and promoting Japan's security." The Japanese government, he said, "has decided to seize [the] opportunity [created by the Murayma mission] and start coordination toward the holding in the course of this year of preliminary talks for resuming normalization talks and talks on humanitarian issues between the Red Cross societies of the two countries."[105]

Within a week of Aoki's statement Japan and North Korea held two separate talks in Beijing back to back—one between representatives of Red Cross organizations and another between foreign ministry officials. Only the former, however, produced an agreement, after, in a reversal of roles, the Japanese side resorted to brinkmanship, having walked out of a negotiating session and left for the airport. There were four points in the agreement. First, the homecoming visits of Japanese wives of North Korean men would resume in the spring of 2000. Second, the North Korean Red Cross Society would ask the "relevant agencies" of the DPRK government to investigate the status of "missing persons" from Japan. Third, the Japan National Red Cross would ask the Japanese government to consider providing food assistance to the North. Finally, the Japanese government would also be asked to investigate the status of Koreans who disappeared from Japan before 1945.[106]

---

[105] Ministry of Foreign Affairs of Japan, *Announcement by Chief Cabinet Secretary Mikio Aoki on Policies vis-a-vis North Korea* (Tokyo, December 14, 1999), http://www.mofa.go.jp/announce/announce/1999/12/1214.html.

[106] "Rachi chosa, satogaeri saikai no kyodo bunsho ni shomei" [Joint Document on Kidnap Investigation and Homecoming Signed], *Yomiuri shinbun*, December 22, 1999; "Tests of Diplomacy," an editorial, *Mainichi*

In the preparatory talks for the resumption of normalization talks, in which directors-general of foreign ministry bureaus headed their respective delegations, the only agreement reached was to meet again in January 2000. On the issue of suspected Japanese abductees and North Korean missiles, the two sides merely articulated their divergent positions. The North Korean side strongly objected to the use of the word *rachi* (or *napch'i* in Korean) [abduction], arguing that it should be replaced by "missing persons." As for the missile issue, the North Korean side asserted that just as Japan did not feel threatened by US missiles, so it would not find North Korean missiles threatening once the two countries establish friendly neighborly relations based on diplomatic normalization.[107]

On March 7, 2000 the Japanese government announced its decision to donate 100,000 tons of rice to North Korea through the World Food Program. It would be the first shipment of food aid from Japan to the North since November 1997. Japan and North Korea simultaneously announced on the same day that they would resume normalization talks in April, meeting first in Pyongyang, then in Tokyo, and in Beijing or another third country thereafter. They also announced that Red Cross talks would be convened in Beijing on March 13.[108]

Daily News, December 25, 1999; Ministry of Foreign Affairs of Japan, "Press Conference by the Press Secretary, 17 December 1999," *Archives on Press Conferences* (Tokyo), 1; idem, "Press Conference by the Press Secretary, 21 December 1999," ibid, 2-3.

107 "Nitcho yobi kaidan toshi akeni sai kyogi e" [Japan-North Korea Preparatory Talks to Resume in the New Year], *Asahi shinbun*, December 23, 1999. The Japanese delegation was headed by Anami Koreshige, the director-general of the Foreign Ministry's Asian Affairs Bureau, while the North Korean delegation was led by O Ul Rok, the director of the 14th Bureau [in charge of North Korean affairs] of the DPRK Foreign Ministry.

108 "Kita chosen shien: 10-man tonno shokuryo enjo o happyo, Nihon seifu" [Aid to North Korea: Japanese Government Announces Food Aid of 100,000 Tons], *Mainichi shinbun*, March 8, 2000; "Cho-il chongbu-gan pon hoedam, choksipja hoedam i chinhaeng toenun kotgwa kwallyon han podo" [Report Concerning the Holding of Regular Meeting Between Korean and Japanese Governments and Red Cross Meeting], *Choson chungang t'ongsin* [Korean

In the Red Cross talks both sides agreed to realize the third homecoming of Japanese wives of North Korean men "sometime in the spring—April or May" and to continue the program thereafter. The North Korean side reported that "investigations to locate missing Japanese" had already started with the participation of local government and Ministry of Public Safety (police) officials and Red Cross personnel. The Japanese side informed the North Korean side that Japan would do its best to "locate the whereabouts of North Koreans missing in Japan before 1945." Finally, the North Koreans expressed thanks for the Japanese government's March 7 decision to donate 100,000 tons of food to the North through the WFP.[109]

The Ninth Round of Normalization Talks

The ninth round of the Japan-DPRK talks for diplomatic normalization took place in Pyongyang from April 4 to 7, 2000. Two sessions were held on April 4 and the third and final session was held on April 7, with April 6 reserved for sightseeing and hiking on Myohyang Mountain, the site where in September 1990 the crucial one-on-one meeting between Kim Il Sung and Kanemaru Shin had occurred. The Japanese delegation to the talks was headed by Ambassador Takano Kojiro, while the North Korean team was led by Jong Thae Hwa, a "roving ambassador" (*sunhoe taesa*) in the DPRK Foreign Ministry.

Given the lapse of seven and a half years since the eighth round, the ninth round was less a continuation of dialogue than the beginning of a new phase of negotiations. Both sides therefore laid on the table their respective priorities. Jong Thae Hwa stressed that in order not to repeat

---

Central News Agency (KCNA)] (Pyongyang), March 7, 2000, Http://www.kcna.co.jp/contents2/07.htm.
109 Ministry of Foreign Affairs of Japan, "Press Conference by the Press Secretary, 14 March 2000," *Archives on Press Conferences* (Tokyo), 1, Http://www.mofa.go.jp/announce/press/2000/3/314.html.

the past record of "endless arguments and breakdown" of negotiations, both sides must come to grips with the "special nature" of the Korea-Japan relationship, namely, that between *p'ihaeja* (victim) and *kahaeja* (wrong-doer), and concentrate on the "main agenda" of the talks. The latter, he said, was none other than the "settlement of the past by Japan."[110]

Jong listed four items under the heading of "settling the past:" (1) an apology, (2) compensation, (3) the issue of Korean cultural treasures, and (4) the legal status of Korean residents in Japan. Of these, only the third was really new. Regarding apology, Jong insisted that an apology by Japan's highest authority embodying "genuine remorse for crimes committed against the Korean people" as well as an unmistakable political will not to repeat them in the future must be included in the final document formalizing normalization. Such apology, he added, is so important that his government would not even consider receiving compensation without it. "Material compensation not accompanied by an apology," he said, "would be tantamount to an economic transaction or a deal-making between merchants."[111]

As for compensation, Jong pointed to the "widely recognized historical fact that in the past Japan inflicted spiritual, moral, human, and material wrongs on our people." As "wrong-doer," therefore, Japan was morally and legally obligated to compensate its "victims," he said. Such compensation must be convincing to the victims, prompt, and effective, he added.[112]

Conceding that North Korea had not raised the issue of cultural treasures before, Jong indicated that it was "most sensitive" and had "serious national dimension." The "countless cultural treasures Japan destroyed in our country in the past and took away," he said, were the

---

110 "Cho-il kwangye munje t'agyol ul wihan chongdanghan ipjang" [The Just Position for Resolving Problems in Korea -Japan Relations], *Nodong sinmun*, April 7, 2000, 6.
111 Ibid.
112 Ibid.

"repositories of our national tradition, patriotic spirit, national wisdom and talents, the soul of our nation, and our national feelings and customs." "In a word," he said, "the issue of Korean cultural treasures is an important issue related to our people's identity, dignity, and development." Jong called on Japan to provide an official apology, compensate for items destroyed, and return those that are still intact.[113]

Finally, Jong explained why Pyongyang considers the Korean residents' legal status as part of the problem of settling Japan's past. Most of them, he said, either had been forcibly taken to Japan during wartime to work in mines and other hazardous places or were their descendants. Yet, he said, they were subject not only to humiliation and discrimination but also to threats, blackmails, and terrorism. Jong accused the Japanese government of pursuing a policy of encouraging naturalization by Korean residents and of trying to dissolve or destroy *Ch'ongnyon*, the pro-DPRK federation of Korean residents. Improving the legal status of Korean residents, therefore, must be treated as an essential component of settling the past, he argued.[114]

Japan's priorities were far removed from those articulated by the North Korean chief delegate. Takano Kojiro responded to some of Jong's assertions. Takano pointed out that the then Prime Minister Murayama had already expressed an apology in 1995, which remained the Japanese government's position on the issue. Jong, however, rejected the Murayama apology as insufficient on the ground that it was addressed not to the DPRK specifically but to Asia in general. Takano also reiterated Japan's position, which had been communicated to North Korea during the first phase of the normalization talks, that Japan would consider neither reparations nor compensation but property claims only.[115]

Japan placed its highest priority on the abduction issue and North

---

113 Ibid.
114 Ibid.
115 "7-nenhan buri Nitcho kokkyo joseika kosho hajimaru" [Japan-North Korea Talks for Diplomatic Normalization Begin After Seven and a Half Years], *Yomiuri shinbun* (Tokyo), April 5, 2000, evening edition; "Kita Chosen,

Korea's missile program. Takano also expressed Japan's interest in inter-Korean dialogue and progress in US-DPRK negotiations. Jong objected to the word "abduction," insisting that only "missing persons" was the appropriate expression. On the issues of concern to both sides, then, their positions remained divergent, and no hint of middle ground could be detected. Despite the lack of progress, the Japanese delegation put a positive spin on what had happened, saying that both sides had shown "strong political will" to keep the talks going and to bring them to a successful conclusion. The North's proposal to establish subcommittees to deal with different issues was cited as a sign of its "positive stance" toward the talks.[116]

Actually, it was the Japanese side that was eager to keep the talks going. This was reflected in the joint press release issued at the end of the ninth round on April 7. It conspicuously omitted any reference to the issues Japan had raised but mentioned the "problem of how to settle the past." Japan's priorities were simply lumped together under the category of "other issues." The joint press communique noted that "both sides have confirmed anew" the need to continue the normalization talks, agreeing to hold the tenth round in Tokyo in the latter part of May.[117] The Japanese side was reported to have made the concession in order to avert the danger of the talks' premature collapse. In Tokyo's view, as long as the

---

    shazai hosho o, Murayama danwa dewa fujubun, Nitcho kosho" [Japan-North Korea Talks: North Korea, "Apology, Compensation," "Murayama Statement Insufficient."] *Asahi shinbun* (Tokyo), April 6, 2000.

116 "Nitcho kokkyo seijoka kosho, shucho no hedatari senmei ni" [Japan-North Korea Talks: Gap Between Positions Becomes Clear], *Yomiuri shinbun*, April 8, 2000.

117 "Cho-il chongbugan che 9-ch'a pon hoedam e kwanhan kongdong podo" [Joint Report on the Ninth Regular Meeting Between the Korean and Japanese Governments], *Nodong sinmun*, April 8, 2000, 4; Gaimusho, *Nitcho kokkyo seijoka kosho dai 9-kai honkaidan ni tsuiteno kyodo puresu happyo* [Joint Press Release on the Ninth Regular Meeting Between Japan and the DPRK for Diplomatic Normalization] (Tokyo, April 7, 2000); Yuzuru Endo, "Japan, North Korea Skirt Abduction Issue," *Daily Yomiuri*, April 8, 2000.

channel of dialogue remained open, Pyongyang would be less inclined to precipitate such provocative incidents as launching a missile again.[118]

At North Korea's request, however, the tenth round of the talks was postponed indefinitely. There were unexpected developments in Japan as well. On May 14, three days after Prime Minister Obuchi was hospitalized due to serious illness, Mori Yoshiro became his successor. Obuchi died on May 14. As a consequence, elections for the House of Representatives (HR) were called earlier than had been contemplated. They took place on June 25. Although the LDP suffered a stinging setback with its share of HR seats plunging from 54.2 to 48.5 percent, it retained control of the government with the support of two coalition partners, New *Komeito* and *Hoshuto* (New Conservative Party).[119]

The historic inter-Korean summit and marked improvement in Seoul-Pyongyang relations in its wake served only to increase Tokyo's desire to make headway in its relations with North Korea. Prime Minister Mori had in fact asked President Kim Dae Jung to convey to Chairman Kim Jong Il Japan's wish for an early normalization. Kim Jong Il reportedly responded favorably to the message. Against this backdrop, a meeting between the foreign ministers of Japan and the DPRK materialized on July 26 in Bangkok, where both were attending the ASEAN Regional Forum (ARF), to which North Korea was admitted as a new member. The meeting between Kono Yohei and Paek Nam Sun marked the highest-level contact between the two governments thus far.[120]

---

118 "Nitcho kokkyo seijoka kosho, shocho no hedatari senmei," *Yomiuri shinbun*, April 8, 2000.
119 "Yoto 2-to gekigen, Minshu ga yakushin" [Three Ruling Parties Decline Sharply, Democratic Party Gains Big], *Asahi shinbun*, June 26, 2000.
120 Gaimusho, *Nitcho gaisho kaidan (kaiyo)* [Foreign Ministers' Meeting Between Japan and the DPRK (Summary)] (Tokyo, July 26, 2000); "Hatsu no Nitcho gaisho kaidan, kokkyo seijoka kosho no saikai nittei nado goi" [First Japan-North Korea Foreign Ministers' Meeting, Agreement on Schedule for Resuming Normalization Talks and Other Matters], *Asahi shinbun*, July 27, 2000; "Talks Held Between Foreign Ministers of DPRK and Japan," *Korean Central News Agency* (KCNA), July 27, 2000.

The joint press announcement issued after the meeting indicated, however, that North Korea had once again extracted a concession from Japan. The only issue that was specifically mentioned in the announcement was that of settling the past. "Bearing in mind the recent positive development of the situation on the Korean peninsula," it said, "both sides expressed their intention to settle the past and establish new friendly neighborly relations." The two foreign ministers agreed to "strive in all sincerity to resolve the various issues that exist between Japan and the DPRK." They further agreed to "increase exchanges in various fields with the aim of developing mutual understanding and amity." Finally, they agreed to hold the tenth round of normalization talks in Tokyo from August 21 to 25.[121]

The Tenth Round of Normalization Talks

The tenth round of the Japan-DPRK normalization talks did finally take place from August 21 to 24. Its first session, held in a Japanese Foreign Ministry guest house in Tokyo on August 22, lasted a little over an hour. The chief delegates of both sides, Ambassador Jong Thae Hwa of the DPRK and Ambassador Takano Kojiro of Japan, made statements reiterating their respective positions they had unveiled during the ninth round of the talks in Pyongyang in March. Jong argued that the issue of settling the past must take precedence over all other issues, while Takano asserted that all issues, including those relating to abductions and missiles, must be tackled simultaneously.[122]

---

121 *Gaimusho, Nitcho gaisho kaidan ni kansuru kyodo happyo* [Joint Communique on the Foreign Ministers' Meeting between Japan and the DPRK] (Tokyo: July 26, 2000); "Cho-il oemu hoedam chinhaeng" [Korea—Japan Foreign Ministers' Meeting Held], *Choson chungang t'ongsin* [KCNA], (Pyongyang), July 27, 2000.
122 "Nitcho kokko kosho: Nihon 'rachi nado ikkatsu kyocho" [Japan-DPRK Normalization Talks: Japan Stresses Concurrent Discussion of Abduction and Other Issues], *Nihon keizai shinbun* (Tokyo), American edition, August

Takano underscored the importance of finding a satisfactory solution of the abduction issue by explaining its linkage to Japan's domestic politics. Any treaty that may emanate from the talks, he said, must receive the approval of the Diet before it can be ratified. He went on to point out that Diet approval would not be forthcoming without support from public opinion, which in turn would hinge on whether the abduction issue can be resolved. When the North Korean delegation paid a courtesy call on Foreign Minister Kono prior to the start of the first session, it received a similar message. Telling the North Korean visitors that the crowd gathered outside the Foreign Ministry building consisted of family members of kidnap victims, Kono requested that the North conduct a thorough-going investigation into the matter of missing persons. Although Jong objected to Kono's reference to kidnap victims, asserting that no such persons existed in the North, he said that he had noticed the crowd and that in order to prevent that kind of problem from arising, the two countries must forge a friendly relationship.[123] The logic of "two-level games" was clearly on display.

Following the precedent set in Pyongyang five months earlier, the second session was preceded by a day of sightseeing. The North Korean delegation, however, canceled its previously scheduled tour of the Diet and NHK facilities at the last minute, opting instead to visit the headquarters of *Ch'ongnyon* (or *Chosoren*), the federation of pro-DPRK Korean residents in Japan. What happened that evening, however, was worth noting. Accompanied only by their interpreters, Takano and Jong got together at a restaurant in Kisarazu, Chiba Prefecture for unofficial talks over drinks. During their four-hour tete-a-tete, the two chief

---

23, 2000, 2; "Cho-il chongbugan che 10-ch'a pon hoedam chinhaeng" [The Tenth Regular Meeting between the Governments of the DPRK and Japan Under Way], *Nodong sinmun*, August 23, 2000, 4.

123 *Nihon keizai shinbun*, American edition, August 23, 2000, p.2; "Itsudemo dokodemo Nitcho gaisho kaidan o Kono gaisho ga iyoku" [Foreign Minister Kono Willing to Meet DPRK Counterpart Any Time Any Place], *Asahi shinbun*, August 22, 2000, evening edition.

delegates reportedly showed some flexibility in their respective positions only to dash any hopes for progress when the second session convened in a hotel in the same city the following day. Jong, however, made a request for Japan,s assistance in the DPRK's quest for membership in the Asia Development Bank (ADB), for a resumption of export/import insurance coverage for Japanese firms trading with the North, and for economic assistance prior to normalization. Regarding the insurance issue, Takano reportedly told Jong that prerequisite to the resumption of trade insurance coverage is the payment by the North of its trade debts to Japan, on which Pyongyang had defaulted in the mid-1970s.[124]

The second and final session of the tenth round convened shortly after 10 a.m. on August 24, lasting seven and a half hours, including lunch. Its length exceeded the original schedule by four hours. While the two sides' basic positions remained unchanged, there were nonetheless a few notable developments. First, Japan indicated for the first time a willingness to use the same approach it had used vis-a-vis the ROK in 1965 toward the DPRK—namely, substituting "economic cooperation" for "property claims." Second, while rejecting the "ROK formula," the North intimated that it might cease to insist on "reparations" but settle for "compensation." Third, both sides agreed to implement exchanges between their diplomatic authorities and concurred in the desirability of interchanges between non-governmental economic personnel.[125]

---

124 "Kita Chosen, Nihon ni kokko seijoka mae no keizai shien o yosei" [North Korea Requests Japan's Economic Assistance Prior to Normalization of Relations], ibid., August 25, 2000; "Chongch'i kyoldan namun puk-il sugyo" [Political Decision Remains for North-Japan Normalization], *Joongang ilbo*, August 27, 2000.

125 "Nihon, keizai kyoryoku hoshiki o teian hosho setten kento de itchi" [Japan Proposes Economic Cooperation Formula, Agreement on Exploring Compensation Contact Point], *Yomiuri shinbun*, August 25, 2000; "Cho-il chongbugan che 10-ch'a pon hoedam urich'uk taep'yodan tanjang i kijadul kwa hoegyon" [Head of Our Side's Delegation to the 10th Regualr Meeting between the Governments of the DPRK and Japan Meets Reporters], *Nodong sinmun*, August 25, 2000, 5; "Cho-il chongbugan che 10-ch'a pon hoedam:

The joint press announcement issued at the end of the tenth round on August 24 showed that the North once again had its way in describing the issues discussed during the talks; the only issue that was specifically mentioned was the "settlement of the past." It said that both sides had confirmed their desire to "make progress" in normalization talks in the future, agreeing to hold the 11th round in October in a "third country" to be determined later.[126]

Both sides tried to put a positive spin on the results of the tenth round. North Korea characterized it as a "forward-looking, realistically-oriented" meeting that would help pave the way for the resolution of bilateral issues in the future.[127] Japan was encouraged by the North Koreans' eagerness to press for an early normalization. As Foreign Minister Kono put it, the "positions of both sides have become clear, thus providing a foundation for substantive discussions."[128]

On September 3 the Japanese government was reported to have decided to provide 400,000 tons of rice to the North through the World Food Program.[129] A response to Jong's request to Takano during their

> kwangye kaeson e nasonun hyonsiljok munje p'urogal kich'o rul maryon" [The Tenth Regular Meeting between the Governments of the DPRK and Japan Prepares Foundation for Solving Practical Problems Pertaining to Improving Improved Relations], *Choson sinbo*, August 30, 2000.
> 126 "Cho-il chongbugan che 10-ch'a pon hoedam kwa kwallyon han kongdong podomun" [Joint Press Announcement on the Tenth Main Meeting between the Governments of the DPRK and Japan], *Nodong sinmun*, August 25, 2000, 5.
> 127 "Cho-il chongbugan che 10-ch'a pon hoedam kwangye kaeson e nasonun hyonsiljok munje p'urogal kich'o rul maryon" [The Tenth Regular Meeting between the Governments of the DPRK and Japan Prepares Foundation for Solving Practical Problems Related to Improving Relations], *Choson sinbo* (Tokyo), August 30, 2000; "Nitcho kosho o 'senshinteki to hyoka, Kita Chosen medeia" [North Korean Media Assess Japan-DPRK Talks as Forward-looking], *Asahi shinbun* (Tokyo), August 27, 2000.
> 128 "Hanashiai no koso dekita Kono gaisho Nitcho kosho hyoka" [Foundation for Negotiation Forged, Foreign Minister Kono Assesses Japan-DPRK Talks], *Yomiuri shinbun*, August 28, 2000. Kono made the assessment in an NHK program on August 27.

informal get-together noted above, the Japanese decision, which, as we shall see, was later modified, was designed to ensure that the talks would continue in the months ahead. Whether any real headway could be made in the talks anytime soon, however, hinged on whether both sides would be willing to show more flexibility in their respective positions than had been the case thus far. That, in turn, was a function of internal political dynamics, which defined the scope and limits of their respective "win sets."

Prelude to the Eleventh Round

Determined to make the next round of the talks more productive than its predecessors, Japan took an extraordinary measure. In early October the Japanese government announced a decision to donate 500,000 tons of rice to the North through the World Food Program (WFP). What was extraordinary about this decision was that the quantity of the proposed rice aid would surpass the WFP's target from doners around the globe by the ratio of 2.6 to 1. For the WFP had appealed for a total donation of 195,000 tons. Moreover, Japan decided to donate Japanese rice, which is 12 times more expensive than Thai or Chinese rice. The total cost would be 120 billion yen (about $1 billion).[130]

There were a few other notable developments that preceded the eleventh round of the Japan-DPRK normalization talks, which were held

---

129 N. Korea to Get Japan Rice Aid, Asahi Evening News, September 3, 2000.
130 "Nitcho kankei: Jimin bukai '50-man ton no kome shien o ryosho seishiki happyo e" [Japan-DPRK Relations: LDP Officially Announces Approval of 500,000 tons of Rice Aid], *Mainichi shinbun* (Tokyo), October 4, 2000; "Rice Aid to North Appears to be the Result of a Secret Promise," *Asahi Evening News*, October 7, 2000, an editorial. The Japanese press reported that the LDP "zoku-giin (ministry protectors and beneficiary) of the Ministry of Agriculture, Forestry, and Fisheries" played a key role in the aid decision. With the prospect of the largest rice harvest in three years, the Japanese government would be "hard-pressed to dispose of the glut in rice."

in Beijing from October 30 to 31. One was the revelation that Prime Minister Mori had sent a personal letter to Kim Jong Il "via contact who had close ties to a top member of the North Korean Workers' Party" expressing his desire to hold a summit meeting. Mori apparently acted without consulting anyone in his government or ruling coalition; Foreign Minister Kono said in a news conference that the "prime minister acted according to his own judgment." The advice offered by ROK President Kim Dae Jung may have influenced Mori's decision.[131] Another revelation, made by Mori himself while attending an Asia-Europe Meeting (ASEM) in Seoul on October 20 was that he had previously offered to the North Koreans an option on how to resolve the abduction issue: Pyongyang could release the Japanese kidnap victims in a third country so that they might be "found" as missing persons. The offer, Mori said, was made during his visit to Pyongyang in 1997 as a member of a Japanese Diet delegation.[132]

Also noteworthy was the visit by Vice Marshall Jo Myong Rok, the first deputy chairman of the DPRK National Defense Commission, to the US, from October 9 to 12. The highest-level North Korean official ever to visit the US, Jo held talks with Secretary of State Madeleine Albright, Secretary of Defense William Cohen, and President Clinton. A joint communiqué issued on October 12 signaled that the US-DPRK relations had entered a new stage, in which both sides would "work to remove mistrust, build mutual confidence, and maintain an atmosphere in which they can deal with issues of central concern." They would "make every effort in the future to build a new relationship free from past enmity." The communique also said that Secretary Albright would visit the DPRK with the aim of conveying Clinton's views directly to Kim Jong Il and preparing for a possible Clinton visit to the North."[133] Albright visited

---

131 "Mori Letter to Kim Bothers Officials," *Asahi Evening News*, October 4, 2000.
132 "Mori shusho gaiko 'bikkuri hatsugen' tsugi tsugi tabitabi mizukara kyuchi ni" [Prime Minister Mori: A Succession of "Startling Statements" Often Paints Himself into Corner], *Asahi shinbun*, October 21, 2000.
133 U.S. Department of State, Office of the Spokesman, *U.S.-D.P.R.K. Joint*

North Korea from October 23 to 25, spending more than 12 hours with Kim Jong Il. She reported that she and Kim "had serious, constructive, and in-depth discussions of proposals on diplomatic relations, missile restraint, and security issue." On her way back to Washington, Albright stopped over in Seoul to attend a trilateral foreign ministers' meeting with her counterparts from the ROK and Japan.[134]

All this could only have bolstered Japan's resolve to redouble its efforts to make headway in its diplomatic negotiations with the North. The acceleration of diplomacy involving the other states, on the other hand, may have made the North less accommodating toward Japan in the normalization talks than would have been the case otherwise. It was against this backdrop that eleventh round of the talks convened in Beijing on October 30.

The Eleventh Round of Normalization Talks

Although the cast of the players remained the same—with Takano Kojiro and Jong Thae Hwa heading their respective negotiating teams—, there was nonetheless a striking difference between the eleventh and the preceding two rounds: a virtual news blackout. The Japanese side let it be known that it was the North Korean side that had requested that no details be released about the two-day negotiations. Neither joint press statement nor press conference was forthcoming at the end of the eleventh round. What could not be hidden from public view, nonetheless, was that no substantive breakthrough had occurred. Accounts in the Japanese press suggest that very little progress had been

---

Communique (Washington, DC: October 12, 2000), http://www.state.gov/www/regions/eap/001012.usdprk.jointcom.html.
134 Idem, *Secretary of State Madelein K. Albright: Press Availability with Korean Foreign Minister Lee, Japanese Foreign Minister Kono at Shilla Hotel after the Trailateral Meeting* (Seoul: October 25, 2000), http:// secretary.state.gove/www/statements/2000/001025.html.

made.

The North Koreans were reported to have adhered to their previous position on apology and compensation for Japanese colonial rule. They insisted that an apology addressed explicitly to the Korean people must be accompanied by compensation, for, in their view, an apology without payment of compensation would be hollow. The North Koreans, moreover, were said to have flatly rejected the so-called Japan-ROK formula under which Japan would provide "economic cooperation" consisting of a grant and a loan; nothing less than "compensation" would suffice. Pressed by the Japanese side to make good faith effort to resolve the abduction issue, the North Koreans reportedly adhered to their previous position that no such issue existed. When the Japanese reformulated it as one of "missing persons," the North Koreans asserted that it should be discussed in Red Cross talks.[135]

In sum, neither Japan's goodwill gesture of offering 500,000 tons of rice to the North nor Japan's eagerness for measurable progress in negotiations appeared to have made any difference in the outcome of the eleventh round. The bottom line was that neither side displayed any willingness to make concessions on the key issues, which in turn reflected political constraints both faced at home. None of the developments that had preceded the eleventh round, including Japan's generous side payments, had changed the structure of the two-level games; neither side had experienced an expansion of their "win-sets."

---

135 "Nitcho kosho Kita Chosen ga 'Nikkan hoshiki' o kyohi" [Japan-DPRK Talks: North Korea Rejects "Japan-ROK Formula"], *Yomiuri shinbun*, November 1, 2000; "'Koko no seisan' heikosen no mama Nitcho kosho shuryo, jikai wa rainen ka" [Japan-DPRK Talks End With Parallel Lines on "Settling the Past," Next Round Next Year?], *Asahi shinbun*, November 1, 2000; "North Korea Talks Restart in Beijing," *Japan Times*, October 31, 2000; "Japan-North Korea Talks," *Mainichi Daily News*, November 4, 2000, an editorial.

Conclusion

From the preceding survey of the key events and episodes in the evolution of Japan-DPRK relations from 1993 to 2000, can one find impressionistic confirmations of some of the ideas and insights proposed by the contending schools of thought? The rationality assumption shared by neorealism and neoliberalism, it may be argued, does seem to receive support in a number of instances. A case in point is the success with which North Korea fortified its capacity to act in the international arena by availing itself of opportunities spawned by the nuclear issue. For, both in the short and long term, the North gained much more than it lost. The gains were both material and ideational, ranging from the commitment to supply 500,000 metric tons of HFO a year to measures aimed, from Pyongyang's perspective, at bolstering the latter's state identity. Although Japan was only an indirect participant in the negotiations involving the nuclear issue, it had high stakes and ended up shouldering a major share of the financial burden for the LWR project. Most important, none of the North's gains would have materialized had it not been for Pyongyang's "nuclear card." North Korea's decision to fire a rocket over Japan in August 1998 is more difficult to assess than its handling of the nuclear issue. Even though it suffered short-term losses, it probably came out ahead in the long term. All of the sanctions Japan had imposed on the North in the wake of the rocket launch have been lifted, and Pyongyang's bargaining leverage vis-à-vis Washington and Tokyo alike has increased. The 1998 missile/satellite incident, too, then may be adjudged to have reflected "rational" calculations on Pyongyang's part. This assessment is bolstered when ideational factors are taken into account.

Another example of North Korea's "rationality" may be found in its success in extracting humanitarian food assistance from Japan in exchange for resuming inter-governmental dialogue. The cost for the North in such cases was minimal, for agreeing to resume negotiations entailed no commitment to produce any substantive agreement. The North, of course, paid a high price in an ideational sense when it first requested food aid from Japan, South Korea, and the international community in 1995. It had to set aside its vaunted *chuch'e* ideology, the centerpiece of its state identity. Having paid the price, however, Pyongyang may have become immune to further embarrassment. Vis-a-vis Japan, however, the logic of victim versus wrongdoer the North has enunciated repeatedly, may well give Pyongyang a sense of entitlement. If that is the case, its repeated requests for aid from Japan may not adversely affect its self-identity.

Can Japan's behavior also be appraised as rational? Did its policy of unstinting cooperation with the US and South Korea with respect to the nuclear issue bespeak rationality? What of its response to the North's rocket launch? Finally, did Japan gain more than it lost in raising the abduction issue with the North, in lifting all the sanctions on the North, and in resuming food aid to the North? Given its stakes in terms of national security and postwar state identity, all of Japan's actions could be construed to have been well calculated to produce patent gains.

As we have seen previously, however, it was absolute gains, not relative gains, that seem to have dictated Japan's policy in most of the preceding examples. For it can be argued that the North gained more than Japan did in most cases. Even in the rocket launch Pyongyang may have scored more gains than Japan. Although it is true that Japan was jolted to appreciate the magnitude of North Korea's security threat and to take countermeasures accordingly, whether such "gains" eclipsed what the North gained both materially and ideationally is open to question.

On another issue in the neorealist-neoliberal debate, namely capabilities versus intentions, the record of Japan-North Korea interactions is inconclusive. Is Japan's concern over North Korea's missile development program symptomatic of the greater weight of capabilities than intentions or vice versa? What the North has actually demonstrated is its capability, not intentions. Given the North's track record in the use of violence in the international arena, however, Japan's policy planners may be amply justified in attributing sinister intentions to the North and in positing worst-case scenarios. What does all this prove about the relative weight of capabilities and intentions? Since capabilities are markedly more transparent than intentions, it may be the former, not the latter, that may help shape policy. This may be particularly true when the potential adversary is as opaque as North Korea.

The neoliberal insight that power resources are non-fungible, that the value of power depends on goals sought, is abundantly supported by the evidence presented in the preceding pages. It was not the overwhelming superiority of the aggregate power of the US, the sole superpower in the post-Cold War world, nor of Japan, the second largest economy in the world, that helped to mold the outcome in the nuclear standoff or in other disputes and negotiations involving the tiny and feeble North Korea. What mattered most was the latter's issue-specific power, its ability to leverage opaque nuclear and missile programs or the humanitarian concerns of Japan regarding Japanese women married to North Korean nationals.

Another core idea in liberal institutionalism, namely the role of regimes and institutions in promoting international cooperation, may arguably receive some support from the preceding narrative. A major factor in the evolution of the standoff on the nuclear issue was the high priority the US government had placed on extending the NPT regime. The NPT was up for renewal in 1995, and the US was concerned that allowing North Korea to openly flout it might adversely affect the chances of its renewal for an indefinite period. The role of the IAEA in the unfolding of the events should also be noted, even though it is unclear whether the IAEA really facilitated cooperation, rather than exacerbating discord. What did facilitate cooperation, however, was a newly-created international organization, the KEDO. It was an ingenious device that helped to allay Pyongyang's identity-related concerns about the proposed role of its arch-rival Seoul in the LWR project. The KEDO also proved to be an indispensable instrument of cooperation among the US, the ROK, and Japan. With the participation of the European Union as a core member—that is, a member of the executive board along with the three founding members—, the KEDO's international complexion, not to mention its financial base, has been strengthened.

As adumbrated above, state identity, a core concept in constructivism, figures prominently as an important explanatory variable in the foregoing narrative. Significantly, the chief North Korean representative in the ninth round of the Japan-DPRK normalization talks explicitly referred to his country's identity in explaining why the issue of cultural treasures constituted part of what Pyongyang saw as the process of settling Japan's past. State identity also played a role in the various stages of the evolution of the nuclear issue—from Pyongyang's March 1993 announcement of intention to withdraw from the NPT to its acceptance of the Geneva Agreed Framework in October 1994 and beyond. The increasingly intrusive actions of the IAEA and the apparent collusion between it and the US posed a serious challenge to the DPRK's systemic integrity, i.e., its identity as a sovereign state that values independence, national pride and dignity.

Both identity and domestic structure affected developments in some cases. Japan's identity as a peace-loving state dependent on an alliance with the US may have influenced the timing and contents of the four-party agreement of March 1995. The October 1994 Geneva accords on nuclear issues heralded a measurable improvement in US-DPRK relations, which in turn provided a strong incentive for Japan to seek ways of resuscitating the stalled normalization talks. The emergence of a coalition government headed by a Socialist prime minister in Japan appeared to enhance the chances of a breakthrough. At a minimum, it may have encouraged the North to believe that it would fare better in negotiations than before.

The contents of the four-party agreement, however, were ambiguous enough to allow both sides to feel that they had extracted concessions from the other side. The agreement by both sides not to attach any precondition to normalization talks and to act independently during such talks ratified the North's preferences. The de facto downgrading of the September 1990 three-party declaration from a binding agreement to a mere historical event that opened the way for normalization talks bespoke the North's grudging acceptance of Japan's view. In a word, the four-party agreement was a classic compromise in which both sides gave some and gained some.

The crucial part the operational environment plays in shaping foreign policy decisions is highlighted by Japan's rice aid to the North. Pyongyang's decision to ask Tokyo for rice aid in May 1995 was triggered by the severity of food shortages stemming from policy failures and structural weaknesses of the North Korean economy. As already noted, It was most probably the North's sense of entitlement vis-à-vis Japan—the belief that as a victim of ruthless Japanese exploitation during the colonial period and of hostile policy during the postwar period, North Korea has a right to demand and receive both an apology and compensation from Japan—that prompted Pyongyang to turn to Tokyo for help. An admission of food shortages and a request for aid were so contrary to the reigning ideology of North Korea, *chuch'e sasang*, that they caught not only Japan but most observers around the world by surprise. What was even more surprising was the North's ready acceptance of Japan's preconditions for aid—that the North seek and receive aid from the South first. All this clearly signaled the triumph of pragmatism over ideology in the North.

Pragmatic considerations affected Japan's decisions on the issue as well. Saddled with a huge surplus of imported rice that necessitated substantial storage costs on a continuing basis, the Murayama government could not pass up an opportunity to kill two birds with a single stone. First, providing rice aid to the North would reduce storage costs for Japan. Second, it might bolster the chances of resuming normalization talks. No less important, Japan could ill afford to antagonize North Korea or to create an impression of insensitivity in the world arena, especially after the two arch-enemies on the Korean peninsula had reached an agreement on rice aid.

North Korea's differing reaction to Japan and South Korea for their rice aid can be explained in terms of identity-related internal political dynamics in the North. Ever since ROK President Kim Young Sam cracked down on South Korean citizens who attempted to show their respects to the late Kim Il Sung following his death in July 1994, the DPRK stepped up *ad hominem* attacks against Kim Young Sam. Although dire necessity dictated temporary tactical retreat and compelled the North to engage in negotiations with the South for rice aid, it apparently failed to diminish the North's animosity toward Kim Young Sam and his government. No one who insulted its "Great Leader" could be forgiven, no matter how generous his gift might be. The North, as previously noted, not only failed to thank the South for 150,000 metric tons of rice but actually harassed South Korean ships bringing free rice to its ports. Japan, by contrast, received an expression of appreciation from the North for rice aid.

Internal politics affected Japan's North Korea policy as well. The notoriety given to alleged abductions of Japanese nationals by North Korean agents and the fresh attention given to the plight of Japanese women married to North Koreans in Japanese media in 1997 led the Hashimoto government to withhold any humanitarian food aid to the North. The ability of North Korea to turn an initially unfavorable event into an opportunity to be exploited, however, was on display once again. The North grabbed the Japanese wives issue, turning it into a bargaining chip. By signaling to Japan that it would be willing to allow home visits by selected Japanese wives of North Koreans, the North induced change in Japanese policy. Resumption of Japan's humanitarian aid to the North became politically feasible, and more important, the way was finally opened for the resumption of the long-stalled normalization talks. The sharp deterioration of the North's food crisis occasioned by a severe drought contributed to Pyongyang's tactical accommodation.

Internal political dynamics of Japan and North Korea interacted to produce an impasse over the issue of alleged abductions. Mounting pressure for the rescue of alleged kidnap victims or at least a credible accounting of their fate sharply delimited the win-set for the Japanese government, which in its Level I game was compelled to pursue the matter with North Korea. North Korea, for its part, had domestic constraints of its own—namely, its need to safeguard its perceived dignity. At a bare minimum, that dictated a refusal to admit any wrongdoing, of which sending agents to a foreign country to kidnap foreign citizens would be the most serious kind. All this was functionally equivalent to a Level II game delineating the boundaries of Pyongyang's win-set.

Although the compromise formula under which the North agreed to look into the matter under the innocuous rubric of missing persons was one of the few options that fell in the intersection of the two sides' win-sets, it was nonetheless foredoomed to failure; for it did not really address North Korea's political need. North Korea's delayed response that its investigation had failed to shed any light on the "missing persons" was as predictable as it was necessary for the Pyongyang regime whose identity had to be safeguarded.

All in all, the ideas and insights of the contending paradigms, when selectively deployed, can help elucidate events and episodes that may elude plausible explanation at first glance. The reality nonetheless is so complex and, in many cases, so opaque that one must always keep an open mind. We need, therefore, to examine whether the developments in the subsequent years bolster the impressionistic assessment essayed above.

CHAPTER 4

The Persistence of Discord and the Limits of Cooperation

As we saw in the preceding chapter, the long-stalled normalization talks resumed in 2000, thus signaling a mutual policy adjustment in the direction of tactical cooperation. Three rounds of the talks, however, failed to produce any tangible results. The positions of the two sides remained as far apart as they were when the tenth round started.

In 2001 both external and internal factors helped to plunge Japan-North Korea relations to a new low. Externally, the emergence of the George W. Bush administration in the US appeared to nudge Pyongyang toward a waiting game vis-à-vis all of its adversaries, including Japan. Internally, the salience of the abduction issue in the media and public opinion alike compelled Tokyo to place a high priority on the issue, which effectively ruled out any concessions to the North.

In September 2002, however, an unprecedented summit meeting between Prime Minister Koizumi and North Korea's supreme leader Kim Jong Il materialized in Pyongyang. This development, nonetheless, proved to be a double-edged sword, for it both raised, albeit temporarily, the level of cooperation between the two countries and escalated conflict.

Symptomatic of the former was the resumption of normalization talks after a two-year hiatus. Although the return of five Japanese kidnap victims to Japan shortly after the summit could also be cited as an example of cooperation, the Japanese government's decision to allow them to stay in Japan for good gave rise to controversy anew. It was primarily to realize the reunion of the returned kidnap victims and their family members who had remained in the North that Koziumi went to Pyongyang again in May 2004.

Meanwhile, the initiation in August 2003 of six-party talks, in which the two Koreas, the US, China, Russia and Japan participated, provided Tokyo with a potentially useful dialogue channel with Pyongyang. For, although the multilateral process focused on the resolution of the crisis sparked by North Korea's nuclear weapons development program—specifically, the revelation in October 2002 that the North had not really frozen its program as stipulated by the 1994 Geneva accords but was engaged in a covert program utilizing highly-enriched uranium (HEU)—, it nonetheless spawned bilateral contacts on the sidelines. In terms of both frequency and importance, the latter sometimes eclipsed formal sessions of the talks.

Japan's hopes to take advantage of the opportunities for bilateral talks with the North in order to make some headway on the abduction issue, however, were dashed for over two years. It was not until the fifth round of the talks held its first session in November 2005 that the two sides managed to agree to hold "comprehensive and parallel" inter-governmental talks. This led to the first-ever three-track talks in Beijing in February 2006.

2001: Stalemate and Skirmishes

One thing Japan and North Korea have in common is that both regard the year 2001, rather than 2000, as the dawn of a new millennium, a practice that differs from what is prevalent in the West. For the two countries, then, the new millennium began not in an upbeat mood but with a resurrection of the familiar impasse in bilateral relations. There was neither forward movement nor major setbacks—unless one equates the suspension of normalization talks with the latter.

A few things that made waves, in a literal sense in one case, did happen. One was the rash of bankruptcies on the part of credit unions owned and operated by *Chosoren*, the North Korea-oriented association of Korean residents in Japan, which led to an unprecedented raid of *Chosoren* offices by Japanese law enforcement officials. Another was the successful test firing of a rocket by Japan designed to launch a surveillance satellite, which immediately triggered a protest by Pyongyang. Finally, there was the case of a suspicious ship discovered in waters near Kyushu. Suspecting it to be a North Korean spy ship, Japan's coast guard staged a hot pursuit, which led to an explosion and sinking of the ship in the East China Sea.

Incidents of cooperation were not totally absent during the year. Two Japanese delegations visited North Korea on separate occasions—one to ascertain the status of victims of the atomic bombs dropped in Japan in August 1945 who might be living in the North and the other to verify the distribution of Japan's rice aid to the North. Finally, working-level contacts were reported to have occurred in Beijing between foreign ministry officials of the two countries.

To examine these and related events chronologically, let us begin with a February visit to North Korea by a Japanese government delegation to collect information on atomic bomb victims in the North. The delegation, led by Sato Shigekazu, deputy director-general of the Japanese Foreign Ministry's Asian and Oceanian Affairs Bureau, interviewed a dozen surviving victims as well as North Korean health officials and medical workers. They found that a total of 1,353 victims had returned to the North at the end of World War II, of whom 926 were still alive. The average age of surviving victims was 69.[1]

---

1 "Atomic Bomb Victims in DPRK Demand Japan's Aid," *The People's Korea* (Tokyo), March 28, 2001, http://www1.korea-np.co.jp/pk/158th_issue/

To the extent that the Japanese visit reflected a desire to provide compensation to the surviving victims, it exemplified cooperation. In March, however, the North found a cause to launch verbal attack against Tokyo. On March 12 the DPRK Mission to the UN issued a communique expressing strong objections to Japan's permanent membership in the Council. The communique called on the international community to "take issue with Japan's past crimes against humanity," rather than "discussing the country's [candidacy] for permanent membership" in the Council and to "pay due attention to the danger of Japan's moves to revive militarism." "Before seeking a permanent seat in the Security Council," the North asserted, "Japan should gain the trust of the international community by, among other things, recognizing, apologizing and compensating for its invasion of Korea and [other] Asian countries and [for] the crimes committed in the past." [2]

In July, during his visit to Russia, Kim Jong Il was quoted by the Russian news agency, *ITAR-TASS*, as accusing Japan of trying to "justify its past crimes." "As long as Japan persists in glossing over its past," Kim told the news agency, "normal bilateral relations [between the DPRK and Japan] cannot be forged." [3]

On August 28 Japan's National Space Development Agency "successfully sent a rocket into space in 21 months following two failed attempts." The H-2A rocket was designed to "launch a 2-ton rocket at a cost of 8.5 billion yen sometime in the future." This program, it should be noted, got under way on the heels of the August 1998 launch of a North Korean rocket discussed in the preceding chapter. Japan's goal is to build an independent capability to collect intelligence on such launches. Prime Minister Koizumi reportedly "hailed the long-awaited success,

---

2001032802.htm. This paper is published by *Chosoren*, the pro-DPRK federation of Korean residents in Japan.

2 "Pyongyang Rejects Tokyo's Bid for UNSC Permanent Seat: Permanent Mission to UN Issues Communique," ibid.

3 "Kim soshoki ga Nihon seifu o hihan 'kako no hanzai o seitoka" [General Secretary Kim Criticizes the Japanese Government, "It Justifies Past Crimes"], *Asahi shinbun*, July 27, 2001.

saying that it lifts Japan into the ranks of the world's top space-vehicle developers."[4]

To no one's surprise, North Korea lashed out against the Japanese rocket launch. In a statement issued on September 10, a spokesman for the DPRK Foreign Ministry noted that the "Japanese authorities······are not hiding the fact that the rocket can be used exclusively for military purposes" and that its aim "is to cope with North Korea's missiles." "It is," according to the spokesman, "a well-known fact" that Japan considers the DPRK as its "No. 1 target." "Japan's moves to develop missiles······ targeted against the DPRK have reached a dangerous stage," "This serious development compels the DPRK to reconsider its moratorium on satellite launch," the North proclaimed.[5]

Meanwhile, from September 18 to 22, a Japanese delegation visited North Korea for the second time in 2001. Although it was led by the same Foreign Ministry official who had headed the earlier mission in February, the delegation included, in addition to other officials, members of the Japanese Diet as well. Its goal was to monitor the distribution of Japan's rice aid to the North. Of the 500,000 metric tons of rice Japan had pledged in October 2000, over 400,000 metric tons had already arrived in North Korean ports. The delegation "confirmed that Japan's rice aid was being distributed as intended at the various places observed." It reported that the "North Korean institutions accepting the aid and those places the mission observed expressed gratitude for Japan's assistance."[6]

In November it was reported that working-level contacts between Japan and North Korea took place in Beijing. Hiramatsu Kenji, the

---

[4] "Mission Success—H-2A Rocket Soars into Orbit," *Mainichi Daily News*, August 29, 2001.

[5] "DPRK Hits Japan's H-2A Rocket Test Firing," *The People's Korea*, September 15, 2001, http://www1.korea-np.co.jp/pk/168th_issue/2001091503.htm.

[6] "Kita Chosen: Nihon seifu no shien kome shisatsudan 18 nichi kara 22 nichi made hoCho" [North Korea: The Japanese Government's Rice Aid Monitoring Mission Visits North Korea From 18th to 22nd], *Mainichi shinbun*, September 18, 2001; see also Ministry of Foreign Affairs of Japan, *Diplomatic Bluebook* 2002 (Tokyo, 2002), 35.

director of the Northeast Asia Division of the Japanese Foreign Ministry, held unannounced talks with his North Korea counterpart with the apparent aim of resuscitating the stalled normalization talks.[7]

In the same month, however, the first-ever search of the headquarters of *Chosoren*, the General Association of Korean Residents in Japan, which acts as a de facto embassy of the DPRK, occurred. The search was in response to a series of collapses of *Chosoren*-affiliated financial institutions—namely, *Chogin* (Korea Bank) and credit unions under its umbrella—and the "problems of illicit financing" by them.[8]

According to a statement issued by the Central Standing Committee of *Chosoren* (*Ch'ongnyon* in Korean) a day after the search, "over 300 prosecution and police agents" had "ransacked" the Tokyo headquarters of the federation. The "Japanese investigation authorities' repressive campaign," the statement asserted, "involved searching 47 places on 56 occasions, arresting 15 persons and 'questioning' more than one hundred people for no reason." "This," it added, "was nothing but political suppression of Koreans in Japan and national financial institutions of [*Ch'ongnyon*], a crackdown prompted by national discrimination."[9]

---

7 "Nitcho kachokyuga Peking de setshoku" [Japan and North Korea Have Contacts in Beijing at the Division Director Level], *Yomiuri shinbun*, November 24, 2001; "Puk-il sugyo silmu hyopsang idalch'o Beijing so" [Working-Level Negotiation between North Korea and Japan Held in Beijing Early This Month], *Dong-A ilbo*, November 26, 2001.

8 Ministry of Foreign Affairs of Japan, *Diplomatic Bluebook 2002*, 35; James Simms, "North Korean Ties Complicate Japan's Efforts to Clean Up Banks," *Wall Street Journal*, April 4, 2002. According to this article, "Tokyo has spent more than 500 billion yen ($3.8 billion) guaranteeing *chogin* deposits……" Among those arrested in late 2001 were "scores of former *chogin* executives and a former finance official at *Chosoren* [or *Ch'ongnyon* in Korean]." Allegations against them included "embezzlement and covering up bad loans."

9 "Anti-Chongryon Campaign in Japan Under Fire," *Korean News Service* (KNS)-*Korean Central News Agency* (KCNA), November 29, 2001, Tokyo, http://www.kcna.co.jp/contents/30.htm While KNS is operated by *Ch'ongnyon*, KCNA is North Korea's official—and only—news agency. Please note that North Korea uses its own system of Romanizing Korean words, which differs

On the following day, a spokesman for the DPRK Foreign Ministry issued a statement condemning the Japanese action. It claimed that the problems faced by Chogin and credit unions under its control had been "caused by the overall Japanese economy in depression, not by any illegal transactions or 'evasion of inspection.'" "We cannot but follow this incident with particular vigilance," the statement said, "as this was the first undisguised political suppression of [Ch'ongnyon] since its formation." Equating the suppression of Ch'ongnyon with "an infringement upon the dignity and sovereignty of the DPRK," the statement warned that Pyongyang would not "remain a passive onlooker to the escalating anti-DPRK moves."[10]

North Korea's decision in December to suspend the project to investigate the situation pertaining to "missing persons,"—a project ostensibly initiated by its Red Cross Society at the request of Japan—[11] is not unrelated to the preceding warning. It exemplified Pyongyang's familiar tactic of *tit for tat*.

On December 22 Japan Coast Guard patrol boats spotted a suspicious ship in the East China Sea near Kyushu. When the ship ignored orders to stop and sped away, Japanese patrol boats began a hot pursuit, and an exchange of fire occurred. Finally, the suspicious ship caught fire and sank outside Japan's territorial waters.[12]

---

from the McCune-Reischauer system I am using here.

10 "DPRK FM Spokesman on Japan's Unprecedented Suppression of Chongryon," *Korean Central News Agency* (Pyongyang), November 30, 2001, http://www.kcna.co.jp/contents/30.htm.

11 Ministry of Foreign Affairs of Japan, *Diplomatic Bluebook 2002*, 35; "Report of DPRK Red Cross Society," *Korean Central News Agency* (Pyongyang), December 17, 2001. http://www.kcna.co.jp/ item/2001/200112/news12/17.htm. The announcement by the DPRK Red Cross Society, however, did not mention Tokyo's actions against the pro-North Korean organizations in Japan. Instead, it cited the enactment by the Japanese Diet of anti-terrorism law, which allows the dispatch of Japan's Self-Defense Forces overseas in connection with the US-led war on terrorism.

12 "27 'Spy' Ships Operating in Waters Around Japan," *Daily Yomiuri*, December 31, 2001; Kaijo Hoancho, *Kyushu nansei kaiiki fushinsen ni kakaru chosa jokyo ni*

Denying that it had anything to do with the incident, North Korea denounced Japan in harsh terms. In its words, "this was an incident unprecedented in history. This……is nothing but brutal piracy and unpardonable terrorism……that could be committed only by Samurais of Japan in defiance of international law." Asserting that "the Japanese reactionaries are spreading a sheer rumor that the unidentified ship might be a 'spy ship from North Korea,'" the North characterized Japanese behavior as a "trite charade," "a grave provocation," and a product of Japan's "hostile policy" toward the DPRK. Recalling the Japanese government's actions against *Ch'ongnyon* noted earlier, North Korea repeated the warning: "we will never remain a passive onlooker to such moves of the Japanese authorities."[13]

It should be noted that this was not the first time that unidentified ships suspected of being North Korean spy ships were spotted in waters surrounding Japan, nor would it be the last.[14]

The Resumption of Official Dialogue

The suspension of inter-governmental dialogue between Japan and North Korea should not be equated with the absence of any dialogue whatsoever. If dialogue is defined loosely, then one can say that the two Japanese delegations that visited the North in 2001 conducted dialogue of sorts with their North Korean hosts. What is more, at least one case of covert contacts between working-level officials of both sides did make news in the same year. More noteworthy was the revelation in 2002 that

---

tsuite [On the Investigation Relating to Suspicious Ships In the Sea Area Southwest of Kyushu] (Tokyo, October 4, 2002), 1, http://www.kaiho.mlit.go jp/info/news/h14/fushinsen/joukyou.html.

13 "Japan's Fuss About 'Unidentified Ship' Refuted," *Korean Central News Agency*, December 26, 2001, http:// www.kcna.co.jp/item/2001/200112/news12/26.htm.

14 For more information, please consult the Web site of the Japan Coast Guard (*kaijo hoancho*), http://www.kaiho.mlit.go.jp.

sub rosa contacts at a higher level occurred at frequent intervals, regardless of the state of official relations.¹⁵

North Korea's decision to break the impasse in its relations with Japan in early 2002 needs to be viewed against the backdrop of what Pyongyang must have seen as deterioration in its strategic environment. Most important was US policy. The George W. Bush administration completed a three-month review of its policy toward the North in June 2001 but failed to allay the North's apprehensions. Although on June 6 the Bush administration offered to resume negotiations with North Korea "without any preconditions," Washington made it clear that it would pursue three goals: "improved implementation of the Agreed Framework relating to North Korea's nuclear activities; verifiable restraints on North Korea's missile programs and a ban on its missile exports; and a less threatening conventional military posture."¹⁶ To Pyongyang, however, Washington's motives were suspect; the reference to conventional military posture was something new, for only missiles and nuclear weapons had

---

15 Interestingly, it was not simply the Japanese media that reported on the covert, high-level negotiations that had paved the way for the historic Koizumi-Kim Jong Il summit in September 2002 but North Korea's official news agency that made a reference to "on-going unofficial contacts" between the two governments nearly two months before the summit. See "Asean chiyok yondan sanggup hoeui kigan e Cho-Il oemusang hoedam chinhaeng/ Choson Oemusong taebyonin Cho-Il kwangye munje e ongup" [The Foreign Ministers of the DPRK and Japan To Hold Talks During the ASEAN High-level Meeting/The DPRK Foreign Ministry Spokesman Comments on Issues in Korea-Japan Relations], *KCNA* (Pyongyang), July 25, 2002, http://www.kcna.co.jp/contents2/25.htm; "'Rachi' kado de kane hiki dasu hoshin 2-nen chikaku maeni katamaru?" [The Plan to Use the "Abduction" Card to Draw Out Money May Have Been Firmed Up Nearly Two Years Ago?], *Asahi shinbun*(Tokyo), October 14, 2002; "Nitcho kosho aratana 'madoguchi' o mosaku 'Tanaka ruto tsukaezu'" [Searching for New "Window" for Japan-North Korea Negotiations, "The Tanaka Channel Will Not Be Used"], *Yomiuri shinbun*, November 7, 2002.
16 Steven Mufson, "U.S.Will Resume Talks with N. Korea," *Washington Post*, June 7, 2001, A01.

been the subject of discussion up to that point.

While working-level contacts between US officials and North Korean diplomats at the United Nations occurred in the ensuing weeks, no progress was made toward the resumption of bilateral talks.[17] Immediately after the September 11 terrorist attacks on New York and Washington, DC, however, North Korea took the unusual step of sending a "private communication" to the US State Department via the Swedish Embassy in Pyongyang, informing Washington that "it regretted the attacks and didn't have anything to do with them."[18] A day after the attack, the DPRK Foreign Ministry spokesman called the attack "very regretful and tragic," stressing that "as a UN member the DPRK is opposed to all forms of terrorism."[19]

What seems to have jolted and angered the North was President Bush's inclusion of North Korea in an "axis of evil," along with Iran and Iraq, in his State of the Union address in January 2002.[20] With chances of

---

17 "U.S., North Koreans Talk in New York," ibid, July 13, 2001.
18 Oh Young-jin and Son Key-young, "N.K. Sent US Private Cable on Anti-Terrorism," *Korea Times*, September 23, 2001.
19 "DPRK Stance Towards Terrorist Attacks on U.S.," *Korean Central News Agency*, September 12, 2001, Pyongyang, http://www.kcna.co.jp/item/2001/200109/news09/12.htm. On the same day, however, *Nodong sinmun* [Labor News], the daily organ of North Korea's ruling Workers' Party of Korea (WPK), published a commentary denouncing the alleged scheme of the US to "stifle" North Korea to death and warning that "the people's army and people of Korea [will mercilessly wipe out the aggressors' war provocateurs." "U.S. Invariable Design to Stifle DPRK Slammed," ibid.
20 The North Korean leadership may have been doubly alarmed that Bush mentioned their country ahead of the other two. In his words, "Our second goal is to prevent regimes that sponsor terror from threatening America or our friends and allies with weapons of mass destruction. Some of these regimes have been pretty quiet since September the 11th. But we know their true nature. North Korea is a regime arming with missiles and weapons of mass destruction, while starving its citizens." After mentioning Iran and Iraq, Bush continued: "States like these, and their terrorist allies, constitute *an axis of evil*, arming to threaten the peace of the world. By seeking weapons of mass destruction, these regimes pose a grave and growing danger. They could

The Persistence of Discord and the Limits of Cooperation 201

reconciliation with the US diminishing—and with the latter's perceived threat to Pyongyang increasing—the North must have realized the importance of ending its "cold war" with Japan as soon as possible.

The first sign that change was in the offing came on February 12, when Pyongyang suddenly released a Japanese journalist it had been holding for more than two years on espionage charges. Since it happened without any apparent quid pro quo, the gesture could be seen as an olive branch of sorts. It was, however, later revealed that the North Korean move was related to secret negotiations then under way.[21]

When the abduction issue leaped to the top of both media and public attention in Japan in March, however, breaking the stalemate in its relations with Tokyo became a pressing necessity, not a mere option for Pyongyang. The catalyst for the escalation of Japan's attention to the abduction issue was a stunning testimony by a former wife of one of the nine Japanese Red Army members who hijacked a Japan Airlines plane (*Yodo*) to Pyongyang in 1970 that she had participated in the abduction of a 23-year-old Japanese student, named Aritomo Keiko, from Europe in 1983.[22]

---

provide these arms to terrorists, giving them the means to match their hatred. They could attack our allies or attempt to blalckmail the United States. In any of these cases, the price of indifference would be catastrophic." *New York Times*, January 30, 2002 (Italics are not in the original text).

21 "Analysis: N. Korea Offers an Olive Branch," *Asahi.com*, February 14, http://www.asahi.com/ english/internatinal/K2002021400546.html. Tanaka Hitoshi, director general of the Japanese Foreign Ministry's Asian and Oceanian Bureau, needed to find out how much power the North Korean official with whom he began secretly negotiating actually had in his country. "So Tanaka asked him to arrange the unconditional release of a Japanese reporter who was detained there in 1999 for allegedly spying on the communist nation." "The Nihon Keizai Shimbun reporter was released in February 2002." Kanako Takahara, "New Pyongyang Approach Needed: Summit Architect," *Japan Times*, December 30, 2005.

22 "Arimoto-san rachi: Tamiya moto kanbuno shijide, Tokyo chisaide rachi o shogen" [Arimoto Kidnaping: Under the Instruction of Former Leader Taimya, Testimony on Kidnaping at the Tokyo District Court], *Mainichi shinbun*, March

This was the first time that an insider's account of how the abduction of a Japanese national was carried out became available. The witness, Yao Megumi, said that "North Korea and the [Japanese] hijackers orchestrated Aritomo's abduction." Yao told the Tokyo District Court that she was instructed by Tamiya Takamaro, the leader of the *Yodo* hijacking, to "trick Japanese in Europe and lure them to Pyongyang." Yao was sent to London, where in May 1983 she met Aritomo, a language student. "Yao told the student about a job opening at a trading company, and the two traveled to Copenhagen in July that year to meet Yao's contact." The latter, a *Yodo* group member, introduced Aritomo to a North Korean agent, who provided her with a North Korean passport and accompanied her to Pyongyang.[23]

A few days after the Aritomo story made headlines in the Japanese press, secret working-level contacts materialized in Beijing. Hiramatsu Kenji, director of the Japanese Foreign Ministry's Northeast Asia Division, was believed to have asked his North Korean counterpart, a division director-level official in charge of Japan affairs, to "reveal the whereabouts" of Arimoto.[24] Shortly thereafter Prime Minister Koizumi told Aritomo's mother, at a meeting with 14 relatives of kidnap victims, that while the government "will make every effort" to obtain the release of their loved ones, it "will not make any compromises with North Korea." Koizumi later told reporters that the "issue is not only related to the families of the missing people but also to 'Japan as a country.'"[25]

On March 22, the DPRK Red Cross Society issued a statement categorically denying that North Korea had anything to do with the alleged kidnapping of Aritomo. Nonetheless, the statement added, the

---

13, 2002; "Arimoto Traveled out of Denmark Using a Passport from North Korea," *Japan Times*, March 14, 2001.
23 "Yodo Ex-wife Duped Aritomo," *Asahi.com*, March 13, 2002, http://www.asahi.com/english/national/K2002031300587.html.
24 "Japan Asks North for Aritomo's Location," *Japan Times*, March 18, 2002.
25 "No Compromises with N. Korea Over Abductions: Koizumi," *Mainichi Daily News*, March 19, 2002.

North Korean Red Cross had decided to resume the work of investigating "missing persons" and was willing to hold talks with its Japanese counterpart on "issues of mutual concern at a convenient time."[26]

This paved the way for the resumption of Red Cross talks in Beijing on April 29. The two-day meeting, however, failed to produce any tangible results on the abduction issue. The Japanese delegates "urged their North Korean counterparts to confirm the safety of the 11 Japanese [who the Japanese government believes were abducted by North Korean agents between 1977 and 1983] and handed them details of [Aritomo's] court testimony." All the North Korean delegates did, however, was to pledge to "carry out a thorough search" of all the missing persons. One hopeful outcome was the agreement on the visits to Japan of Japanese wives of North Koreans sometime in the summer.[27]

On July 31 the foreign ministers of Japan and the DPRK met in Brunei on the sidelines of the Association of Southeast Asian Nations Regional Forum (ARF). The meeting between Kawaguchi Yoriko and Paek Nam Sun marked the second time that such high-level meeting had taken place. According to a joint statement issued at the end of the talks, the two sides agreed to "make serious efforts" to resolve the various bilateral issues, including the "settlement of the past" and "humanitarian issues." Most important, the two sides agreed to resume their stalled normalization talks in principle and to hold both inter-governmental talks at the director-general level and another round of Red Cross talks in August.[28]

---

26 "Choson Choksipjahoe Ilbon Choksipja wa hoedam hal yongui p'yomyong/ Aritomo Keiko 'rapch'i' pujong" [The Korean Red Cross Society Expresses a Willingness to Hold Talks with the Japanese Red Cross/ Denies Aritomo Keiko "Abduction"], *Choson chungang t'ongsin* (KCNA), March 22, 2002, Pyongyang, http://www.kcna.co.jp/contents2/22.htm.
27 "Japanese Wives of North Koreans Granted Home Visits," *Mainichi Daily News*, April 30, 2002.
28 "Nitcho gaisho kaidan: jindojo ken'an no soki kaiketsu ni kyodo shomei" [Japan-DPRK Foreign Ministers' Meeting: Joint Signature on the Early Resolution of Pending Humanitarian Issues], *Mainichi shinbun*, July 31, 2002.

The Red Cross talks that were held in Pyongyang from August 18 to 19, however, failed to make any headway on the abduction issue. The North's confirmation of the identities of six "missing" Japanese nationals was not related to the issue, for none of them was on Japan's official list of the 11 suspected abduction victims. Members of the Japanese delegation, who included a senior Foreign Ministry official, were briefed by North Korean officials responsible for investigations into "missing Japanese nationals." Both sides agreed to realize the home visit of Japanese wives of North Korean men in late October.[29]

The director general-level talks took place in Pyongyang from August 25 to 26. The head of the Japanese delegation, Tanaka Hitoshi, who was the director-general of the Foreign Ministry's Asian and Oceanian Bureau, had been conducting secret negotiations with an unnamed senior North Korean official since October 2001. His counterpart at the senior-level talks in Pyongyang was Ma Chol Su, director-general of the DPRK Foreign Ministry's Asian Affairs Bureau. Although he was carrying a verbal message from Prime Minister Koizumi to Chairman Kim Jong Il, Tanaka's rank was not high enough for a face-to-face meeting with Kim. The message, therefore, was conveyed to Premier Hong Song Nam, ranked fourth in North Korea's power hierarchy.[30]

Although published reports of the first senior-level talks between the two countries in almost two years indicated that the whole range of issues—from the alleged abductions of Japanese nationals to the "settlement of the past," with the North demanding an apology and compensation from Japan—were discussed, the most important item that was concealed from public view pertained to the summit meeting that would occur in three weeks.

---

29 "Nitcho kaidan 'rachi' shinten nashi" [Japan-DPRK Talks: No Progress on "Abduction"], *Yomiuri shinbun*, August 20, 2002; "Pyongyang Finds 6 'Missing' Japanese, None on Abduction List," *Mainichi Daily News*, August 19, 2002.

30 "Kita Chosen: rachi mondai no Koizumi messeji 'soshoki ni tsutaeru'" [North Korea: Koizumi's Message on the Abduction Issue Conveyed to the General Secretary], *Mainichi shinbun*, August 25, 2002.

The First Koizumi-Kim Jong Il Summit

On September 17 Koizumi Junichiro became the first Japanese prime minister to set foot in North Korea. By mutual agreement, the one-day summit was a no-frills affair, consisting of morning and afternoon sessions lasting two and a half hours. There was neither ceremony of any kind nor luncheon or banquet. Although a joint declaration was adopted, only Koizumi held a press conference.

Substantively, however, the summit produced stunning results. Most notable was Kim Jong Il's admission of and apology for the abduction of 13 Japanese nationals by North Korean agents. One way of analyzing the outcome of what turned out to be the first of two Koizumi-Kim Jong Il summits is to assess (1) the gains and losses on the part of the two sides, (2) the motives or aims of each side, and (3) the extent to which they achieved their goals.[31]

---

31 Principal sources for the first Koizumi-Kim Jong Il summit include: Gaimusho, *Koizumi Sori Daijin kaiken yoshi, Heisei 14-nen 9-gatsu 17-nitchi (o: Pyongyang)* [Summary of Prime Minister Koizumi's Press Conference, September 17, 2002 (Pyongyang)], http://www.mofa.go.jp/mofaj/kaidan/ s_koi/ n_korea_02/summary.html; idem, *Nitcho Pyongyang sengen, Heisei 14-nen 9-gatsu 17-nitchi* [Japan-DPRK Pyongyang Declaration, September 17, 2002], http://www.mofa.go.jp/mofaj/kaidan/s_koi/ n_korea_02/ sengen.html; Ministry of Foreign Affairs of Japan, Opening Statement by Prime Minister Junichiro Koizumi at the Press Conference on the Outcome of his Visit to North Korea, Pyongyang, North Korea, September 17, 2002 (Provisional Translation), http://www.mofa.go.jp/region/asia-paci/ n_korea/pmv0209/press.html; idem, *Japan-DPRK Pyongyang Declaration* (Provisional Translation), http://www.mofa.go.jp/region/asia-paci/n_korea/pmv0209/pyongyang.pdf ; "Kim Jong Il tongjiwa Koizumi Junichiro ch'ongni sai ui hoedami issotda" [Conference Held Between Comrade Kim Jong Il and Prime Minister Koizumi Junichiro], *Choson chungang t'ongsin* (KCNA), September 17, 2002; "Ilbonin haengbang pulja turui sosigi hwagin toeottanungosul Ilbon ch'uge t'ongji/Choson Oemusong taebyonin" [Japanese Side Notified of the Confirmation of the Status of Japanese Missing Persons/ DPRK Foreign Ministry Spokesman], ibid; "Choil Pyongyang sonon" [DPRK-Japan Pyongyang Declaration], ibid.,

To consider Japan's gains first, the summit marked an important milestone in the resolution of the abduction issue. Kim Jong Il's admission that North Korean agents had indeed kidnapped a dozen Japanese nationals and, more important, his unprecedented apology, as subsequent developments showed, signaled not the end of the long-running dispute between Japan and the DPRK over the abduction issue but only the beginning of the process by which it can be resolved once and for all.

A closely related gain for Japan was the first-ever apology by the North Korean leader. Never before had Pyongyang's supreme leader admitted a wrong-doing or made an explicit apology to anybody, let alone a foreign leader. The closest the DPRK, albeit not its paramount leader, had come to apologizing was to express regret, as happened in July 2002 in the wake of a naval clash in the West Sea between the two Koreas. In this connection, Kim Jong Il acknowledged to Koizumi that the "unidentified" ship that had entered waters near Japan in 2001 was a North Korean ship as Tokyo had suspected, promising that it would not happen again.

A third gain for Tokyo, which could be counted as a gain for Seoul and Washington as well, was Pyongyang's commitment to extend its moratorium on missile testing beyond 2003. Finally, the North's pledge to abide by all international agreements pertaining to the Korean Peninsula, which inferentially included the 1994 Agreed Framework between the DPRK and the US as well as other agreements relating to nuclear weapons, appeared at the time to be a big plus for Japan, the ROK, and the US.

Turning to Japan's losses, one may note the conspicuous omission of any direct reference to the abduction issue in the joint declaration signed by the two leaders in Pyongyang. The declaration instead referred to the "issues of concern related to the lives and security of Japanese nationals"

---

http://www.kcna.co.jp/ contents2/17.htm . See also the articles in *Asahi shinbun, Yomiuri shinbun, Mainichi shinbun, Japan Times, Asahi Evening News, Daily Yomiuri, Mainichi Daily News,* August 30 through September 18, 2002.

noting that the North would take "appropriate measures" to prevent such "regrettable incidents" from recurring in the future. This contrasted with the inclusion of a reference to Koizumi's "deep remorse and heartfelt apology" to the Korean people for the injury and suffering Japan inflicted on them during its colonial rule.

Japan's commitment to provide "economic cooperation" to the North—in the form of grants-in-aid and long-term, low-interest loans—and humanitarian assistance through international organizations may also be counted as a cost of the bargain struck in Pyongyang.

Finally, Koizumi's failure to obtain more information on the circumstances under which the eight Japanese kidnap victims allegedly died in the North could only belong to the debit column in the balance sheet of his summit diplomacy in Pyongyang.

Let us turn to North Korea's gains and losses. A patent gain for Pyongyang was the inclusion in the joint declaration of Koizumi's apology for colonial rule. Next, Japan's commitment to provide economic cooperation and humanitarian assistance, while lacking in specificity, was nonetheless a gain for the North. Last but not least, the agreement to resume normalization talks was a mutual gain, for both sides could potentially benefit from such talks and, especially, from their successful conclusion.

What, then, were the costs or losses for North Korea? As noted, until September 17, 2002, the DPRK had never admitted a wrongdoing in the international arena. What the North admitted to Japan and, inferentially, to the whole world on that day, moreover, was not a mere "wrongdoing" but state-sponsored terrorism. Over a dozen Japanese nationals, Kim Jong Il admitted to Koizumi, had been kidnapped by North Korean agents, eight of whom had lost their lives under circumstances that have yet to be clarified and verified. For a country that extols *chuch'e*, whose hallmarks are national pride, dignity, sovereignty, and independence, such an admission must surely have been a bitter medicine to swallow.

The unusually hostile reaction by the Japanese public and, especially, by the families of the kidnap victims, was bound to affect the Japanese government's ability or willingness to make concessions to the North and, particularly, to provide sizable economic and humanitarian assistance in the future.

As subsequent events have demonstrated, however, North Korea continued to possess bargaining leverage with Japan in negotiations. The DPRK's commitment to abide by international agreements relating to the Korean Peninsula, moreover, not only lacked specificity but also proved to be insincere. Nor was its pledge to extend the moratorium on missile testing iron-clad or precise. What did Pyongyang mean, for instance, by the phrase, "beyond 2003"? It could mean anywhere from a year to several years. There was, furthermore, no mention of the North's export of missiles, missile parts, and technology.

Koizumi's motives or aims in making the bold decision to visit Pyongyang and hold a summit meeting with Kim Jong Il may have included not only breaking the impasse on the abduction issue and paving the way for the resumption of normalization talks but, as Young C. Kim suggests, meeting his political needs at home. In Kim's words, "he sought to divert public opinion from his inability to move ahead with key domestic agenda and to consolidate his political position by a spectacular foreign policy accomplishment." Additionally or alternatively, Koizumi's "desire for a major political legacy" may have played a part. Finally, Kim notes that Kozumi's "virtual ignorance about the complexities of international security issues and limited foreign policy experience may help explain the ease with which he was prevailed upon by Tanaka [who had conducted secret negotiations with the North] and the 'boldness' with which he moved."[32]

What Kim Jong Il hoped to accomplish in the summit may have included the following: (1) jump-start the stalled normalization talks, with the prospects of obtaining substantial economic assistance, (2) send a message to the Bush administration that high-level dialogue needs to occur without too much delay, and (3) demonstrate to the North Korean

---

32 Young C. Kim, "North Korea Confronts Japan: Politics of Normalization and Rice," in *North Korea and the World: Explaining Pyongyang's Foreign Policy*, ed. B. C. Koh (Seoul: Kyungnam University Press, 2004), 178-79.

people that the visit by the leader of such an economic giant as Japan implies a recognition of his stature in the world arena.

Both leaders may have partially attained their objectives. For Koizumi, although the goal of breaking the impasse was attained, it came with a stiff price—the revelation that eight Japanese nationals had perished in North Korean captivity. The task of ascertaining the circumstances under which that happened has proved to be singularly elusive. The resumption of normalization talks, moreover, did not really herald improved bilateral relations. Finally, Koizumi's domestic political standing did receive a boost. Polls taken immediately after the summit showed that over 80 percent had a positive assessment of his summit diplomacy, and approval rates for his cabinet increased dramatically as well.[33]

Kim Jong Il did succeed in jump-starting normalization talks but if he had hoped for a relatively smooth sailing, he did not get it. His calculation that his admission of and apology for the abduction of Japanese nationals would help resolve the abduction issue proved to be hopelessly off the mark. The goal of sending a message to the Bush administration, on the other hand, was accomplished, for it announced on September 25 that it would send an envoy to Pyongyang "at an early date." As will be shown below, however, that entailed unanticipated—and, from Pyongyang's perspective, unwelcome consequences. Finally, whether the summit produced any political dividends at home for Kim Jong Il is debatable. The persistence of food shortages and other economic woes may well have offset whatever boost Kim may have received in the propaganda arena.

---

33 "Nitcho kaidan 'hyoka' 81%, rachi 'nattoku dekinu' 76%" [Japan-DPRK Talks "Positively Appraised" 81%, Abduction "Not Convincing" 76%], *Asahi shinbun*, September 19, 2002; "*Mainichi shinbun* seron chosa: Nitcho kosho saikai 'datona handan' 54%" [*Mainichi shinbun* Poll: Resumption of Japan-DPRK Negotiations, "Appropriate Decision" 54%], *Mainichi shinbun*, September 23, 2002.

Prelude to the Resumption of Normalization Talks

On the heels of the summit, Japan dispatched a fact-finding mission to the North to collect information on the kidnap victims, both surviving and dead. During a four-day visit (September 28-October 1), members of the mission interviewed five survivors and collected DNA samples of a 15-year-old girl identified by North Koreans as the daughter of a kidnap victim named Yokota Megumi who had allegedly committed suicide. After reviewing the taped interviews, the Japanese government confirmed the identities of the five surviving Japanese. The fact-finding mission, however, was "unable to gather remains of most of the deceased for DNA testing to support Pyongyang's statement that eight are really dead." [34]

The information the DPRK Foreign Ministry provided the Japanese mission concerning how the eight had died and why their remains could not be located—all of their graves were allegedly washed away during floods—failed to convince Tokyo. The North Koreans also told the Japanese mission that "those responsible for the abductions" had been punished, pledging to "fully cooperate in efforts to completely resolve the abduction cases."[35]

Shortly thereafter, North Korea agreed to allow the five surviving Japanese kidnap victims to return to Japan for two weeks.[36] Before the visit materialized, however, an important development unfolded in Pyongyang-Washington relations, which would affect Pyongyang-Tokyo relations as well.

From October 3 to 5, US Assistant Secretary of State James Kelly visited Pyongyang as President Bush's special envoy. On October 4, North Korea's First Deputy Foreign Minister Kang Sok Ju allegedly admitted the existence of a nuclear weapons development program utilizing highly-

---

34 Taro Karasaki, "Team Returns With Remains, Photos from North Korea," *Asahi Evening News*, October 4, 2002.
35 "Details about Deaths of Abductees Dubious," *Japan Times*, October 3, 2002.
36 "Extension of Abduction Visit: Concessions Tied to U.S.-North Korea Stalemate," ibid., October 11, 2002.

enriched uranium (HEU). According to a US State Department press statement, when "Kelly and his delegation advised the North Koreans that [the United States] had recently acquired information that indicates that North Korea has a program to enrich uranium for nuclear weapons in violation of the Agreed Framework and other agreements, North Korean officials acknowledged that they have such a program. The North Koreans attempted to blame the United States and said that they considered the Agreed Framework nullified."[37]

North Korea, however, disputes the preceding claim, arguing that Kelly either misunderstood or even "fabricated" what he heard in Pyongyang. The North Korean version of what actually transpired in the Kang-Kelly meeting is as follows: After explaining why the North believes that the US had failed to implement the key provisions of the Agreed Framework, Kang allegedly asserted that the DPRK "has a right to possess not only nuclear weapons but even more powerful things" [*haengmugi nun mullon kuboda tohan gotto kajige toeyo itta*] in order to protect its sovereignty and right of survival. The North underscored in particular the adoption of a "hostile policy" by the George W. Bush administration toward the DPRK, notably its designation of the North as part of an "axis of evil" and as a potential target of "pre-emptive nuclear attack."[38]

Although the North proposed dialogue on the issue—setting forth three conditions: (1) recognize its sovereignty, (2) conclude a non-aggression treaty, and (3) do not impede its economic development—the Bush administration insisted that the North must dismantle its nuclear weapons program before any dialogue can occur. Since neither side

---

37 U.S. Department of State, *North Korean Nuclear Program, Press Statement by Richard Boucher, spokesman* (Washington, DC: October 16, 2002). Available from the Web site of the US State Department, http://www.state.gov.

38 "Chomi saiui pulgach'im choyak ch'egyori haengmunje haegyol ui hamnijogigo hyonsiljogin pangdo/Choson Oemuson taebyonin" [Conclusion of a Non-aggression Treaty Between the DPRK and the United States Is the Reasonable and Realistic Approach], *Choson chungang t'ongsin* (KCNA), October 25, 2002, http://www.kcna.co.jp/item2/2002/200210/news10/25.htm .

showed any inclination to compromise, the dispute escalated. Thus was born the second standoff between North Korea on the one hand and the US and its allies on the other over the nuclear issue.

To return to Japan-North Korea relations, on October 15, five Japanese nationals abducted by North Korea in 1978 arrived in Japan for what were initially billed as temporary reunions with their families. There were two couples in the group. All five were in their 40s but four of them had been in their early 20s and one 19 when they were abducted to the North 24 years ago. The two couples were married in the North, and the fifth who came alone had married an American deserter there. All five had children who were born in the North.[39]

On October 24, the Japanese government announced that the five abductees would not return to the North, vowing that it would ask Pyongyang to allow the children of the five who remained in the North to join their parents as soon as possible. The Japanese government made the decision on its own—that is, without ascertaining the wishes of the abductees—, primarily because of deep distrust of North Korea. Although North Korea had taken the position that whether the abductees would return to Japan for good would depend on their own wishes, the Koizumi government concluded that the abductees were not free to make up their own mind. Their behavior since arriving in their homeland—their refusal to divulge any information about their abductions or about other abductees who the North claims were no longer alive—raised the suspicion that North Korea controlled their words and deeds. Allowing them to return to the North, therefore, might end up giving the regime negotiating leverage in normalization talks.[40]

---

39 "Rachino 5-nin kikoku, 24-nen buri kazoku saikai" [Five Abductees Return Home, Reunite with Families for the First Time in 24 Years], *Asahi shinbun*, October 16, 2002; "Abductees Come Home," *Japan Times*, October 16, 2002.

40 "Government to Keep Abductees, Call For North Korean-born Kids to Visit," ibid, October 25, 2002;"'Eiju' kettan no urani Kita Chosen eno nukigatai fushinkan, shusho" [Behind the "Permanent Residence" Decision Is Deep-seated Mistrust of North Korea, Prime Minister], *Asahi shinbun*, October 26, 2002.

Finally, on October 27, the leaders of the US, the ROK and Japan—President George W. Bush, President Kim Dae Jung, and Prime Minister Koizumi Junichiro—issued a joint statement in Los Cabos, Mexico, where they were attending a meeting of the Asia-Pacific Economic Cooperaton (APEC) forum, agreeing that "North Korea's program to enrich uranium for nuclear weapons is a violation of the Agreed Framework and the South-North Joint Declaration on Denuclearization of the Korean peninsula." They "called upon North Korea to dismantle this program in a prompt and verifiable manner and to come into full compliance with all its international obligations in conformity with North Korea's recent commitment in the Japan-North Korea Pyongyang Declaration."[41]

It was against this backdrop—the emergence of the nuclear issue and a new turn in the abduction issue—that normalization talks resumed in Kuala Lumpur, Malaysia on October 29.

The Twelfth Round of Normalization Talks

Two years had elapsed since the last round of Japan-DPRK normalization talks ended inconclusively in Beijing. Although the chief North Korean delegate was Jong Thae Hwa, who represented the North in the last three rounds, the Japanese delegation had a new head: Suzuki Katsunari.[42] Each side had different priorities and goals, and, as a result, two days of talks failed to produce any agreement on substantive matters.

Japan placed the highest priority on the abduction issue, strenuously

---

41 Ministry of Foreign Affairs of Japan, *Joint US-Japan-ROK Trilateral Statement*, http://www.mofa. go.jp/region/asia-paci/n_korea/nt/joint0210.html.
42 Suzuki was a veteran diplomat with 40 years of service in the Japanese Foreign Ministry. Although an experienced and "tough" negotiator, he compared the difficulty of his new task to "trying to pass an elephant through the eye of a needle." Jong was a veteran of the Korean War, having served with the "Chinese People's Volunteers." A 32-year veteran of the DPRK Foreign Ministry, he was fluent in Chinese—he was born in China—, French, and Japanese. *Mainichi shinbun*, October 30, 2002.

demanding that the North allow the reunion of the five abductees in Japan and their family members in the North. It also gave the North a list of questions regarding the eight "dead" abductees based on the explanations the North had given to the Japanese fact-finding team. Next, Japan pressed the North to stop the HEU-based nuclear weapons program, reiterating the gist of the Bush-Kim-Koizumi joint statement issued at the APEC meeting in Mexico.[43]

North Korea, on the other hand, was primarily interested in the issue of "settling the past" and compensation from Japan for colonial-era misdeeds. For Pyongyang, in other words, normalization of relations was the top priority. To the Japanese demand for an early reunion of the five abductees and their family members, the North reacted by accusing Tokyo of having broken the commitment to return the abductees to the North after two weeks. This, the North asserted, led to Pyongyang's loss of trust in Japan. The North called on Tokyo to send the five abductees back to Pyongyang so that they may decide on their own whether to return to Japan with their family members. As far as the nuclear issue was concerned, the North insisted that it was strictly a bilateral issue between Pyongyang and Washington. Because it was rooted in the US's "hostile policy" toward the DPRK, the North argued, the issue can only be resolved through dialogue between the two countries.[44]

---

43 Gaimusho, *Nitcho kokko seijoka kosho dai 12-kai hon kaidan (hyoka to gaiyo)* [The 12th Round of Japan-North Korea Normalization Talks: An Evaluation and a Summary] (Tokyo: October 31, 2002), http://www.mofa.go.jp/mofaj/area/n_korea/abd/nego12_html.
"Nit-Cho kosho: 29-nichino naiyo yoshi" [Japan-North Korea Talks: Gist of Developments on 29th,], *Mainichi shinbun*, October 30, 2002.

44 Ibid.; "Nitcho kosho: Kita Chosen kawa, kazoku kikoku kaito sakeru, kaku mondai wa Bei to kyogi" [Japan-North Korea Talks: North Korean Side: No Reply on Family's Return to Japan, Will Discuss Nuclear Issue with America], *ibid*, October 30, 2002; "Urinun Cho-Il kukkyo chongsanghwa hoedam kwa kwallyon hayo chosongdoen sat'aerul ommiri komt'o hago itta/ Choson Oemusong taebyonin" [We Are Carefully Examining the Situation Created by the DPRK-Japan Normalization Talks/ DPRK Foreign Ministry Spokesman].

Concerning the North's argument regarding Japan's breach of an agreement on the five abductees, Japan's chief delegate Suzuki reminded his counterpart, Jong, that the problem had originated in the "criminal act of kidnapping" by North Korea, implying that that indisputable fact had freed Japan of any obligation to the North on the matter. Initially, Jong tried to brush aside the abduction issue, asserting that Kim Jong Il's apology to Koizumi during the Pyongyang summit had "resolved it in its broad context." Suzuki was quick to reject Jong's interpretation.[45]

The only thing the two sides could agree on was procedural. They agreed to conduct "security consultations" in November in order to discuss all the security-related issues—nuclear weapons, missiles, and others—in accordance with the Japan-DPRK Pyongyang Declaration. When the North proposed to hold the next round of normalization talks in late November, however, the Japanese reportedly asked for more time "before setting a specific date for more talks."[46]

After the talks ended, Koizumi tried to give a positive spin to what had or had not happened. In his words, "it's just beginning, and it takes efforts by both sides. Both of us at least are eager to continue talks, and we just have to be patient."[47] While North Korea, too, welcomed the "reaffirmation by both sides of the will to implement" the Pyongyang declaration, it also criticized Japan for placing the abduction and nuclear issues ahead of the "settlement of the past," which Pyongyang equates with the "fundamental issue in diplomatic normalization." In North

---

Choson chungang t'ongsin (KCNA), November 5, 2002, http://www.kcna.co.jp/item2/2002/200211/news11/05.htm.

45 "Rachi, kaku kaihatsu wa heikosen, Nitcho kokko seijoka kosho hajimaru" [Parallel Lines on Abduction and Nuclear Development, Japan-North Korea Normalization Talks Begin], *Asahi shinbun*, October 30, 2002; "Tokyo, Pyongyang Trade Accusations as Talks Commence," *Japan Times*, October 30, 2002.

46 "Japan, North Korea End Talks Without Making Any Progress," ibid., October 31, 2002.

47 Eric Talmadge, "Japan Seeks Return Date for Families," *Washington Post*, October 31, 2002.

Korean view, "it is because Japan has thus far failed to account for the grave crimes it committed against our people in the past that unsavory things continue to happen in our bilateral relations." The North issued a veiled threat that should its normalization talks with Japan continue to be unproductive and drag on indefinitely, it might reconsider its moratorium on test-firing missiles.[48]

Back to Stalemate

As things turned out, normalization talks would not drag on indefinitely but enter another prolonged hiatus. One day after the twelfth round ended, Japan announced that it would not set a date for the next round until North Korea indicates when the family members of the five abductees can come to Japan to join their parents and spouse.[49] Two weeks later the North warned that the security consultations that had been agreed on at the twelfth round would be postponed indefinitely and that there would be other serious consequences unless Japan returned the five abductees to the North.[50] The North subsequently carried out its threat, thus ensuring that no official dialogue would occur.

Unofficial contacts, nonetheless, continued. From November 23 to 24, two senior members of the Japanese Foreign Ministry—Tanaka Hitoshi and Hiramatsu Kenji—, both of whom had played a pivotal role in arranging the first Koizumi-Kim Jong Il summit, held talks with North

---

48 "Urinun Cho-Il kukkyo chongsanghwa hoedam kwa kwallyon hayo chosongdoen sat'aerul ommiri komt'o hago itta/ Choson oemusong taebyonin." See note 44 above for full citation.
49 "Talks on Hold Until Pyongyang Affirms Family Reunions," *Japan Times*, November 1, 2002.
50 "Ilbon ch'ugun anbo kwallyon hoedami mugihan yongi toendanun kosul araya handa/ Chson oemubu taebyonin" [Japan Needs to Know That Talks on Security and Related Issues Will be Postponed Indefinitely/ DPRK Foreign Ministry Spokesman], *Choson chungang t'ongsin* (KCNA), November 14, 2002, http://www.kcna.co.jp/item2/2002/200211/news11/14.htm.

Korean officials in China but failed to make any progress. Tanaka told Japanese reporters that negotiating with North Koreans was difficult, adding: "The Japanese side cannot change its principles. We have to continue the talks tenaciously."[51]

Meanwhile, the standoff between North Korea on the one hand and the US, South Korea, and Japan on the other over the nuclear issue escalated, when the Executive Board of the Korean Peninsula Energy Development Organization (KEDO) decided on November 14 to suspend delivery of heavy fuel oil (HFO) to the North in December. Whether deliveries would resume in the ensuing months would hinge on whether the North dismantles its HEU-based nuclear weapons development program.[52] Pyongyang responded by announcing that it would no longer abide by the freeze of its nuclear facilities in Yongbyon, proceeding to remove seals and disable monitoring devices from nuclear facilities, expelling International Atomic Energy Agency (IAEA) inspectors, and, finally, withdrawing from the Nuclear Non-proliferation Treaty (NPT).[53]

North Korea's "nuclear brinkmanship" had the effect of strengthening cooperation among the US, Japan, and South Korea. Their cooperation was institutionalized in the Trilateral Coordination and Oversight Group (TCOG), which held frequent meetings at the director-general (assistant secretary in the US government)-level.[54]

---

51 "Nitcho tokyoku, Chugoku de seijoka kosho no hikoshiki kyogi" [North Korean and Japanese Authorities Hold Unofficial Talks on Normalization Talks in China], *Asahi shinbun,* November 25, 2002; "Unofficial Japan, N. Korea Talks 'Difficult'," *Washington Post,* November 24, 2002.
52 Ministry of Foreign Affairs of Japan, *Diplomatic Bluebook* 2004 (Tokyo, 2004), 26.
53 *Nodong sinmun,* December 12, 21, 27, 2002; January 10, 2003; see also *Korean Central News Agency* (KCNA) dispatches for the same dates at http://www.kcna.co.jp.
54 Ministry of Foreign Affairs of Japan, *TCOG Joint Press Statement,* January 7, 2003, http://www.mofa.go. jp/region/asia-paci/n_korea/nt/joint0301.html; ibid., June 13, 2003, http://www.mofa.go.jp/region/asiapaci/

Japan's overall strategy toward the North, however, was summed up in two words: dialogue and pressure. While assiduously seeking dialogue with the North with the aim of making progress on the abduction issue, Japan also stepped up pressure on the North in numerous ways.

Japan's Pressure Tactics

The pressure tactics Japan employed vis-à-vis North Korea included (1) re-interpreting laws to facilitate the imposition of sanctions on the North, (2) tightening inspections on North Korean ships that dock in Japanese ports, (3) cracking down on firms tied to the North, (4) levying taxes on property owned by *Ch'ongnyon* (or *Chosoren*), (5) strengthening aerial surveillance capabilities, and (6) refusing to provide humanitarian aid to the North.

To elaborate on these measures, in May 2003 the Japanese government decided that, should the need to impose financial sanctions on the North arise, it would rely on the Foreign Exchange and Foreign Trade Law. Article 16 of the law allows the government to suspend remittances to foreign countries if the government "deems it necessary to back international efforts toward global peace." In the past, this provision had been construed to require either a UN resolution or efforts by a large number of countries. By interpreting "international efforts" as cooperation between two or more countries, however, Japan would be able to suspend remittances to North Korea. The statement released in December 2002 by the Japan-US Security Consultative Committee, for example, would meet such requirement, for it called on North Korea to "abandon its nuclear program and suspend its ballistic missile development and related activities." In order for the Japanese government to invoke this clause, however, the North must first cross a red line—by either launching a missile or reprocessing spent fuel rods in order to extract weapons-grade plutonium. Remittances by Korean residents in

---

n_korea/nt/joint0306.html.

Japan to their relatives in the North are estimated to total 200 million to 600 million dollars annually.[55]

Another area in which Japan chose to exert "pressure" on North Korea pertained to the monitoring of North Korean ships, of which about 150 make over 1,300 port calls in Japan each year. In the first four months of 2003, Japan's Land, Infrastructure and Transport Ministry conducted port state control (PSC) inspections, which check whether a ship meets international safety standards, on 50 North Korean ships and "ordered the captains of 40 of them to rectify" various problems relating to structure and safety.[56]

One North Korean ship in particular, the 9,672-ton Mangyongbong-92, was subjected to a rigorous scrutiny in August 2003. Upon its arrival at Niigata on Japan's west coast, more than 100 officials from the Land, Infrastructure and Transport Ministry, the Japan Coast Guard, and Tokyo customs boarded the ship to conduct inspections. While the coast guard and customs did not find any problems, a PSC inspection conducted separately by the land ministry turned up a few, and the ship was allowed to leave for the North only after all the improvements ordered by the ministry had been carried out.[57]

Japan also began cracking down on companies "suspected of providing North Korea with equipment that can be used to develop weapons of mass destruction." In May, Japanese authorities "raided a

---

55 "Seifu, Kita Chosen eno sokin teishi······misairu hassha, kaku saichorishi" [Government: Will Suspend Remittances to North Korea When Missile is Fired or Nuclear Reprocessing Occurs], *Yomiuri shinbun*, May 19, 2003; Kanako Takahara, "Japan Lowers Hurdle for North Korea Sanctions," *Japan Times*, May 20, 2003.

56 "Japan Steps Up N. Korea Crackdown," *Mainichi Daily News*, June 10, 2003; "Seifu, Kita Chosen funeno kanshi kyoka—sujunin kibode zeikan nado zoin" [Government Strengthens Monitoring of North Korean Ships······Vastly Increases Custom Personnel], *Yomiuri shinbun*, June 11, 2003.

57 "Show of Force Greets North Korean Ferry," *Japan Times*, August 26, 2003; "Japan Allows N. Korean Ship to Sail Home," *Mainichi Daily News*, August 26, 2003.

Tokyo trading company and worked with Hong Kong officials to seize electronic equipment bound for North Korea." The equipment in question—specialized power-supply devices—"could have aided North Korea's uranium enrichment program or been used in missile-launch devices." In the same month, a "North Korean who claimed to have worked at a munitions plant in North Korea" testified in a Congressional hearing in Washington that "90 percent of the North's nuclear program is based on Japanese parts."[58] The Japanese government is reported to have received a list of Japanese companies "suspected of exporting chemicals, electronic parts and machinery that can be used in missile production and nuclear development programs to North Korea, which led to a "stepped up monitoring of politically sensitive exports to Pyongyang."[59]

Additionally, facilities belonging to the pro-Pyongyang General Association of Korean Residents in Japan (*Ch'ongnyon*), which had long been tax-exempt, began receiving tax bills from local governments. *Ch'ongnyon's* headquarters in Tokyo, for example, received an exemption from real estate tax in 1972, when the then Governor Minobe Ryokichi decided that it was a de facto embassy of the DPRK. Governor Ishihara Shintaro, however, refused to accord *Ch'ongnyon* diplomatic status, imposing "fixed-asset and urban-planning taxes of about 60 million yen [about 500,000 dollars] on the group's properties in July [2003]." When it failed to pay the taxes, the Tokyo Metropolitan Government seized the properties. In September *Ch'ongnyon* paid "22 million yen of the taxes in two installments." In June a municipal government in Ibaraki prefecture became the first local government to impose a real estate tax on a *Ch'ongnyon* facility, which had been tax-exempt since 1989. The revocation of the exemption stemmed from the city's discovery that the facility, a hall, was not open to the public.[60]

---

58 Sachiko Sakamaki and Doug Struck, "Japan Cracks Down on Firms Tied to N. Korea," *Washington Post*, May 22, 2003.
59 "CIA Tracks Japanese 'Military' Exports to N. Korea," *Mainichi Daily News*, March 7, 2003.
60 "City Imposes Real Estate Tax on Chongryun," *Japan Times*, June 15, 2003;

Whether Japan's launch of an H-IIA rocket carrying two spy satellites into space on March 28, 2003 can be viewed as part of Tokyo's concerted campaign of exerting pressure on Pyongyang is debatable. It may have been more of a defensive measure. One of the satellites is "equipped with an optical sensor and the other with a synthetic-aperture radar [capable of distinguishing] objects on Earth 1 to 3 meters in size." Their primary objective is "to keep an eye on North Korea," and the latter lost no time in denouncing the rocket launch. The DPRK Foreign Ministry spokesman accused Japan of "sparking a new arms race in Northeast Asia," adding that the launch "deprived Japan of any justification and qualification to talk about the DPRK's satellite launch."[61]

Finally, Japan continued to withhold any humanitarian aid to the North. When Maurice Strong visited Japan in February 2003 as a special envoy of UN Secretary General Kofi Annan, he inquired whether Japan would be willing to provide rice aid to the North. Strong was told that as long as the abduction issue remained unresolved, Japan was in no position to consider such aid. In the following month Annan himself "urged Japan to consider providing food aid to North Korea," but Japan did not budge.[62]

In the short term, none of these tactics appeared to be effective in persuading Pyongyang to accommodate Tokyo's wishes regarding the abduction issue and, to a lesser extent, the nuclear issue. On the contrary, Pyongyang was as defiant as ever. To cite but two examples, during three-

---

"Tokyo Deaf to Chongryun Tax Gripes," ibid, November 14, 2003.

61 "H-IIA Deploys Japan's First Spy Satellites," ibid, March 29, 2003; "Choson Oemusong taebyonin, Ilbon ui chongt'am wisong palsanun Cho-Il Pyongyang son'on ui chongsin wiban" [DPRK Foreign Ministry Spokesman: Japan's Launch of Spy Satellites Violates the Spirit of the DPRK-Japan Pyongyang Declaration," *Choson chungang t'ongsin* (KCNA), March 28, http://www.kcna.co.jp/calendar/2003/03/03-29/2003-03-29 -02.html.

62 "Kokuren tokushi, Kita Chosen kome shien dajin, Abe fuku chokan kyohi" [UN Special Envoy Inquires about Rice Aid to North Korea, Vice Minister Abe Refuses], *Asahi shinbun*, February 22, 2003; "Annan Asks Japan to Aid Pyongyang," *Japan Times*, March 9, 2003.

party talks involving North Korea, the US, and China that were held in Beijing in April 2003, North Korea's chief delegate, Li Gun, reportedly told his US counterpart, James Kelly, that Pyongyang already had nuclear weapons and would be prepared to conduct a demonstration or even to transfer them to a third country.[63]

On four separate occasions in 2002, North Korea fired short-range missiles toward the East Sea (or the Sea of Japan). Believed to be anti-ship "Silkworm" missiles with a range of up to 100 kilometers, they did not pose any threat to Japan's security, Tokyo concluded. Similar test-firings occurred three times in 2000 and once in 2001, and they could be part of Pyongyang's annual military exercises.[64]

Japan's Quest of Dialogue

As for dialogue, the second component of Japan's North Korea policy, a window of opportunity opened in August 2003, when Japan began participating in six-party talks in Beijing. As already noted, these talks featured bilateral talks on the sidelines of main sessions, and Japan managed to hold such talks with North Korea on a number of occasions. At the first round of the talks, Japan's chief delegate, Director-General of the Foreign Ministry's Asian and Oceanian Bureau Yabunaka Mitoji, mentioned the abduction issue in his opening statement to the plenary session on August 27. Stressing the importance of solving the "nuclear problem, missile development and the abduction issue" in a comprehensive manner, Yabunaka pointed out that the resolution of these issues must precede normalization of diplomatic relations between Japan and the DPRK and Tokyo's economic assistance to Pyongyang.

---

63 Kanako Takahara, "Japan Divided Over How to Respond," *Japan Times*, April 26, 2003.
64 "Kita Chosen ga taikan misairu hassha, Nihonkai ni muke kotoshi 4-dome" [North Korea Launches Anti-ship Missile, Toward the Sea of Japan, for the 4th Time This Year], *Yomiuri shinbun*, October 21, 2003.

Although Yabunaka held bilateral talks with his North Korean counterpart, Vice Foreign Minister Kim Yong Il, on the sidelines on the following day, they turned out to be too brief—lasting mere 20 minutes each on two occasions—to be useful. The talks proceeded on parallel lines: Yabunaka demanded an early "return" of the former abductees' family members to Japan as well as an investigation into ten Japanese who Tokyo believes were abducted by the North—they include the eight who, the North says, died there—, while Kim insisted that Japan had broken its promise to return the five abductees to Pyongyang and that all the issues, including the abduction issue, should be resolved one by one in accordance with the DPRK-Japan Pyongyang Declaration. The contacts nonetheless marked the first time that dialogue had occurred at the official level since the 12th round of normalization talks in Kuala Lumpur in October 2002, which in itself was symbolically significant.[65]

As the year 2004 dawned, the pace of official contacts quickened. In mid-January four Japanese Foreign Ministry officials visited Pyongyang in order to interview two Japanese nationals there—a man in North Korean custody charged with drug smuggling and a woman who was allegedly seeking asylum in the North. Around the same time another Japanese official—from the Cabinet Secretariat—visited the North with the aim of "pressing [Pyongyang] to agree to government-to-government negotiations." Since all this was occurring in the midst of moves by the Japanese Diet to enact "legislation to empower the government to restrict trade and financial remittances to North Korea," it could be construed as a sign that Japan's dual strategy of "pressure and dialogue" may finally have begun to show some results.[66]

---

65 "Rachi kaiketsu mondai de Nitcho monowakare, Kita Chosen wa jurai shucho kaezu" [Japan and North Korea Fail to Agree on the Abduction Issue, North Korea Does Not Alter Previous Claims], ibid, August 29, 2003; "North Korea Says Japan Broke Promise," *Japan Times*, August 29, 2003.

66 James Brooke, "North Korea Reaches Out to Japan in a Series of Quiet Signals," *New York Times*, January 18, 2004; "Abduction Aide Made Secret Trip to North," *Asahi.com*, February 5, 2004, http:// www.asahi.com/english/politics/TKY200402050157.html.

In mid-February, what the Japanese Foreign Ministry called "high-level Japan-DPRK talks" materialized in Pyongyang. Japan was represented by Tanaka Hitoshi, who now held the position of Deputy Foreign Minister, and Yabunaka Mitoji, while North Korea was represented by First Vice Foreign Minister Kang Sok Ju and Vice Foreign Minister Kim Yong Il.[67]

Both sides discussed the abduction and nuclear issues during these talks. Japan stressed the importance of resolving the abduction issue, reiterating its demand for an unconditional "return" of all the family members of the five kidnap victims now in Japan and for disclosure of information about the "missing" victims. The North Korean side reacted strongly to the Japanese Diet's revision of foreign exchange law on the eve

---

[67] It is noteworthy that while the Japanese Foreign Ministry listed Kang Sok Ju and Kim Yong Il as the "principal dialogue partners" in the high-level talks, the DPRK Foreign Ministry spokesman stated that the Japanese delegation "paid a courtesy call" on Kang and "held talks with our delegation headed by Vice Minister Kim Yong Il." The North is undoubtedly sensitive to the fact that Kang, who is number two in its foreign ministry, outranks Tanaka, who is below the administrative vice-minister in the Japanese Foreign Ministry. The Japanese press reported that although Kim Yong Il spent the largest amount of time with the Japanese delegation, Kang Sok Ju had two and a half hour-long talks with Tanaka and Yabunaka. Gaimusho, *Nitcho haireberu kyogi no gaiyo* [Summary of Japan-North Korea High-level Talks], (Tokyo: February 14, 2004), http://www.mofa.go.jp/mofaj/area/n_korea/abd/ jn_kaigi_g.html ; "Choson Oemusong taebyonin: Ilbon oemusong taep'yodan ui Choson pangmun e ongup" [DPRK Foreign Ministry Spokesman Comments on the Visit of the Japanese Foreign Ministry Delegation], *Choson chungang t'ongsin* (KCNA), February 14, 2004, http://www.kcna.co.jp/calendar/2004/02/02-17/2004-02-17-001.html ; "Nitcho kosho: seifugan kyogi no keizokude goi" [Japan-North Korea Talks: Agree to Continue Inter-governmental Negotiations], *Mainichi shinbun*, February 14, 2004; "Rachi kyogi, keizokude goi" [Agree to Continue Negotiations on Abductions], *Yomiuri shinbun*, February 14, 2004; "Kim soshoki sokkin, kazoku demukae an genkyu Nitcho, kosho keizokude itchi" [General Secretary Kim's Close Aide Mentions the Idea of Fetching Family Members, Japan and North Korea Agree to Continue Negotiations], *Asahi shinbun*, February 14, 2004.

of the high-level talks, calling it an attempt to stifle the North. As for the family members of the five abductees, the North Korean side repeated its past stance that the abductees must return to the North first and then confirm the wishes of their family members. The North also contended that the issue of the "missing" Japanese has already been settled. The Japanese side's emphatic assertion that normalization of diplomatic relations would be impossible without the resolution of the abduction issue fell on deaf years.[68]

When the Japanese side raised the nuclear issue, the North Korean side stated that since the DPRK was already committed to the denuclearization of the Korean Peninsula, the most important thing was how the US and other participants in six party talks would react to Pyongyang's proposal on freezing nuclear activities. Unveiled on December 9, 2003, the proposal enumerated three conditions for a freeze of the North's nuclear activities and facilities: (1) its removal from Washington's list of states sponsoring terrorism, (2) a termination of political, economic, and military sanctions and "blockade" against the North, and (3) provision of energy assistance to the North, such as heavy fuel oil and electricity.[69]

In short, these talks gave both sides a chance to explain their positions in detail. Although nothing tangible was accomplished, both sides nonetheless reaffirmed the need to seek a resolution of the various pending issues on the basis of the Pyongyang Declaration and to continue inter-governmental negotiations.

At the second round of six-party talks that opened in Beijing on February 25, Japan had another chance to hold bilateral talks with the

---

68 Gaimusho, *Nitcho haireberu kyogi no gaiyo*.
69 Ibid. For North Korea's proposal, see "Choson Oemusong taebyonin 6-ja hoedam chaegae munje e ongup, ch'oesohan 'mal tae mal' kongyak, ch'otdangye choch'I ui habui che'an" [DPRK Foreign Ministry Spokesman Comments on the Issue of Resuming Six-Party Talks: Proposes an Agreement on "Word for Word" Commitment and First-stage Actions As a Minimum], *Choson chungang t'ongsin* (KCNA), December 10, 2003, http://www.kcna.co.jp/calendar/2003/12/12-10/2003-12-10-002.html.

North. Yabunaka and his North Korean counterpart, Vice Foreign Minister Kim Kye Gwan, held an 80-minute meeting on the sidelines of the talks. Although this was twice as long as the two contacts the two sides had at the first round of the talks in August 2002, it was equally unproductive. Apart from the recitation of familiar demands and replies, there was a Japanese proposal to set up a joint committee to investigate the ten abductees who were either declared dead or unaccounted for. Kim promised to "convey Japan's views to Pyongyang." The only agreement reached was to hold further dialogue.[70]

The seeming sterility of dialogue fueled moves to step up pressure. On February 26, Japan's revised Foreign Exchange and Foreign Trade Law went into force. The requirement for "international efforts" was deleted, and the government was given the green light to "halt trade and money remittances to a particular country," if, in its own judgment, such measures are "necessary for the maintenance of the peace and safety of our country."[71] On April 5, the Liberal Democratic Party (LDP) and its coalition partner Komeito submitted a bill aimed at banning North Korean ships from Japanese ports. The bill would empower the government to prohibit ships from specific countries designated at a Cabinet meeting from calling on Japanese ports; such decision can be made when it is "necessary to maintain our country's peace and safety."[72] Finally, on April 14, the Diet enacted a "law requiring shipowners to have insurance for oil-spill damage, a measure that may effectively bar access to Japanese ports by North Korean ships." A revised version of an existing law, the law "expands coverage obligation to include ships of 100 tons or

---

70 "Rachi mondaide Nitcho kyogi, kazoku no kikoku wa heikosen" [Japan and North Korea Hold Talks on the Abduction Issue, Parallel Lines on the Return of Family Members], *Yomiuri shinbun*, February 26, 2004; "Tokyo, Pyongyang Discuss New Bilateral Talks in March," *Japan Times*, February 27, 2004.

71 Reiji Yoshida, "Japan Set to Play Sanction Card," *Japan Times*, February 27, 2004.

72 "Coalition Partners Move to Block Visits by N. Korean Ships," *Mainichi Daily News*, April 6, 2004; Joseph Coleman, "Japan to Toughen Stance on North Korea," *Washington Post*, April 6, 2004.

more that want to enter Japanese waters. Previously, the obligation was limited to tankers." Whereas "73 percent of all the ships that entered Japanese ports" in 2002 had such insurance, "only 2.8 percent of visiting North Korean ships" did so.[73]

Against this backdrop Japan and North Korea held another round of inter-governmental talks in Beijing on May 4-5. Even though they were not called "high-level talks," the same two senior Foreign Ministry officials who had gone to Pyongyang for such talks two and a half months ago showed up in Beijing. Tanaka Hitoshi and Yabunaka Mitoji, however, had different North Korean officials as dialogue partners this time—Jong Thae Hwa, the veteran diplomat who had represented the DPRK in the last four rounds of normalization talks, and Song Il Ho, a vice bureau director in Pyongyang's foreign ministry.[74]

After holding talks for nearly ten hours on two consecutive days, both sides were reported to be in an upbeat mood. Yabunaka told reporters: "Last time······we just repeated our respective principles. But this time, we discussed in considerable depth how to resolve the issue." A "senior" Japanese Foreign Ministry official was quoted as saying: "We were able to discuss issues that will lead to a new round of talks," adding that "North Korea made it clear that it 'intends to let the families go to Japan." After receiving reports from Tanaka and Yabunaka, Prime Minister Koizumi confirmed that the two sides had "talked in detail, including the issue of allowing the family members of the five to come to Japan." Asked whether he "planned to visit Pyongyang to collect the kin of the five repatriated abductees," Koizumi did not rule out the possibility.[75]

---

73 "Diet Targets North Korean Ships via Oil-spill Insurance Law," *Japan Times*, April 15, 2004.
74 "Nitcho seifukan kosho hajimaru, rachi higaisha kazoku no kikoku jitsugen o yosei" [Inter-governmental Talks Between Japan and North Korea Begin, Requests Return of Kidnap Victims' Family Members], *Asahi shinbun*, May 5, 2004.
75 "Pyongyang Drops Hint It Will Let Kin of Abductees Come to Japan to Settle," *Asahi.com*, May 7, 2004, http://www.asahi.com/english/nation/TKY200405070176.html; Kanako Takahara, "Koizumi Lauds Abductions

The Second Koizumi-Kim Jong Il Summit

On May 14, Koizumi announced that he would indeed make a second visit to Pyongyang on May 22. He revealed that he had been preparing for the trip for a month. In April, Yamasaki Taku, a former LDP vice president and "political ally" of Koizumi had an informal meeting with North Korean officials—Jong Thae Hwa and Song Il Ho—in Dalian, China. Yamasaki reportedly broached the idea that "a senior Japanese government official could go to Pyongyang to accompany the family members [of the abductees] to Japan." Although Yamasaki had someone other than Koizumi in mind, Jong and Song "inquired about the possibility of Koizumi making a second visit to Pyongyang." After receiving Yamaski's report, Koizumi reportedly instructed Tanaka Hitoshi to inform the North of his wish to go to Pyongyang again, and that was done during Tanaka and Yabunaka's meeting wih Jong and Song in Beijing in early May.[76]

The second Koizumi-Kim Jong Il summit that materialized in Pyongyang on May 22 set a new record in a dual sense: no leader of a Group of Seven (G-7) nation had ever visited North Korea twice, and two consecutive summits between leaders of countries that do not recognize each other are without precedent in diplomatic history. What were the main differences between the two summits? How shall we assess gains and losses (or costs) for both sides?[77]

Progress; Second Pyongyang Visit Not Ruled Out," *Japan Times*, May 7, 2004.

76 "'Watashi ga iku' shusho saihocho ni kake" ["I Will Go" Prime Minister Gambles on a Second Visit to North Korea], *Yomiuri shinbun*, May 15, 2004; "North Korea Visit Slated for May 22," *Asahi.com*, May 15, 2004, http://www.asahi.com/english/politics/TKY200405150158.html.

77 Principal sources for the second Koizumi-Kim Jong Il summit include: Shusho Kantei, *Nitcho shuno kaidangono kisha kaiken, Heisei 16-nen 5-gatsu 22-nichi* [Press Conference Following Japan-North Korea Summit Meeting, May 22, 2004], http://www.kantei.go.jp/jp/koizumispeech/2004/05/ 22press.html; "Nitcho shuno kaidan (yoshi)" [Japan-North Korea Summit Meeting (Summary)], *Yomiuri shinbun*, May 23, 2004; "Kim soshoki, kaku mondai

The two Koizumi-Kim Jong Il summits had several common features. First, both were one-day affairs. Second, they were "no-frills, strictly business-oriented" events. There were not even working lunches. Third, both took place in Pyongyang, not in Tokyo or even a third country. Finally, both produced results that entailed costs and benefits for each side.

On balance, however, differences eclipsed similarities. If the first summit produced unanticipated consequences—notably, Kim Jong Il's stunning admission that North Korean agents had abducted 13 Japanese nationals in the 1970s and 1980s and his apology to Koizumi—the second summit lacked any real surprises. For both the Japanese government and public expected the main result of Koizumi's second North Korea visit to be the reunion of the kidnap victims' families—that is, Koizumi would bring to Japan the children and spouse of the five abductees who had returned to Japan in the wake of the first summit. Such expectation, to be sure, was only partially fulfilled, for three of the eight family members chose not to join the others in accompanying Koizumi to Japan. Bringing the five children of four kidnap victims to Japan, nonetheless, was a tangible outcome of the second summit, which could not be minimized.

Coupled with the absence of any surprises, the second summit was also notable for the absence of any joint statement. The two sides merely

---

'heiwateki kaiketsu ni doryoku' to hyomei" [General Secretary Kim Will Endeavor to Resolve the Nuclear Problem Peacefully], *Asahi shinbun*, May 23, 2004; Kanako Takahara, "Koizumi Gets Four Abductees' Kids," *Japan Times*, May 23, 2004; idem, "Jury Not In Yet on Who Came Out Ahead at Summit," ibid., May 23, 2004; "Kim Jong Il ch'ongbiso wa Koizumi Junichiro ch'ongni sangbong kwa hoedam" [General Secretary Kim Jong Il and Prime Minister Koizumi Junichiro Hold Talks], *Choson chungang t'ongsin* (KCNA), May 22, 2004, Pyongyang; "Cho-Il sunoe hoedam, 'Pyongyang son'on' chae hwaginui uimiwa p'yongka" [DPRK-Japan Summit Meeting: The Significance and Assessment of the Reaffirmation of the "Pyongyang Declaration"], *Choson sinbo* [Korea News] (Tokyo), May 24, 2004, http://www.korea-np.co.jp/news/ArticlePrint.aspx?ArticleID=10716.

reaffirmed their commitments to the 2002 Pyongyang Declaration. Another difference pertains to the specificity with which Japan pledged humanitarian aid to the North. Although, at the first summit, Japan did enumerate the categories of "economic cooperation" it would provide the North after the normalization of diplomatic relations—notably, "grant aids, long-term loans with low interest rates" and "humanitarian assistance through international organizations"—, there was no mention of the type or quantity of aid. At the second summit, however, Japan specifically promised to provide the North with 250,000 tons of food aid and medical equipment valued at $10 million through international organizations.

The subtle snub Koizumi received during his second visit to Pyongyang is also noteworthy. During his first visit, Koizumi was greeted by a high-powered North Korean welcoming party headed by Kim Yong Nam, the president of the presidium of the Supreme People's Assembly, who is ranked number two in Pyongyang's power hierarchy and performs the functions of the DPRK's head of state. In stark contrast, the highest-ranking official who greeted Koizumi at Pyongyang's Sunan Airport on May 22 was Kim Yong Il, a vice foreign minister (who is outranked by such other vice foreign ministers as Kang Sok Ju and Kim Kye Gwan). The second summit was also shorter than the first, lasting only 90 minutes. If the translation time is factored in, this means that the two leaders had only 45 minutes in which to exchange their views and find some common ground.

What did Koizumi gain from his second encounter and talks with Kim Jong Il? Did his gains outweigh the costs he had to incur? As already noted, the most important gain for Koizumi and his country alike was the "return" of five North Korea-born children of four Japanese kidnap victims to their parents' country, putting an end to the humanitarian tragedy of 18 months of separation among members of the two families. Koizumi later revealed that Pyongyang had made it clear that only his visit would bring about that result.

Although Koizumi failed to help reunite the family of the fifth kidnap victim, he obtained a commitment from Kim Jong Il that they would have a chance to have a temporary reunion in a third country. Since he spent an hour trying in vain to persuade Charles Robert Jenkins, the husband of Soga Hitomi, to come to Japan with their two daughters, however, Koizumi cannot be faulted for Jenkins' decision to stay in the North. Nor can one fault Jenkins for fearing that he might be extradited to the US to face a court martial for desertion once he stepped foot in Japan. Washington had refused to assure Tokyo that Jenkins would not be subject to prosecution.

Whether Koizumi's extraction of a commitment from Kim Jong Il to conduct a "full-scale reinvestigation with the participation of Japan" into the ten "missing Japanese nationals" can be rated as a gain is problematical. As we shall note below, this would prove to be totally unsatisfactory from Japan's perspective.

On the North Korean nuclear issue, Koizumi had a chance to convey to Kim Jong Il the consensus of Japan, South Korea, and the US on the necessity of the North's complete, verifiable, and irreversible dismantlement (CVID) of its nuclear program. Although Kim is undoubtedly familiar with the three countries' unified position, it was nonetheless useful to explain the importance and ramifications of the nuclear issue face to face with the North's supreme leader, the only person who can change the DPRK's policy in a fundamental way. One patent gain was Kim's explicit commitment to maintain a moratorium on missile tests.

On a personal level, the second summit may have served Koizumi's political needs at home. For one thing, it may have helped to "deflect public criticism over [the] revelation that he had not signed up for the national pension program for close to seven years."[78] Another by-product of the summit, which may not have entered into Koizumi's calculus when he was planning for it but which nonetheless materialized, had to do with its effects on the House of Counselor election, which coincided with the dramatic reunion of Soga Hitomi and her husband and two

---

78 "Return to North A Big Gamble," *Asahi.com*, May 17, 2004, http://www.asahi.com/english/politics/ TKY200405170122.html.

daughters. Also helpful to Koizumi was the boost he received in opinion polls. Nearly 70 percent of respondents in a Kyodo news agency poll gave a positive assessment of his second North Korea visit, even though a higher percentage of them indicated that the abduction issue remained unresolved.[79] Koizumi, it must be stressed, also encountered harsh criticisms from the families of the "missing" abductees and politicians, including a few in his own political party.[80]

Losses or costs Koizumi incurred included Japan's multiple commitments: (1) to provide 250,000 metric tons of food aid and medical equipment worth $10 million, (2) resume the stalled normalization talks and (3) refrain from imposing sanctions on the North as long as the provisions in the Pyongyang declaration are upheld. Since these translate into Kim Jong Il's gains, let us examine them under that rubric.

The single most important gain for Kim and his country was the promise of economic or humanitarian aid. Should the food aid promised by Koizumi materialize, it would mark the first time in four years that Japan provided such aid to the North. As we saw in the preceding chapter, in 2000 Japan supplied the North a total of 600,000 tons of rice on two separate occasions. The worsening of the abduction issue in the subsequent years, however, led to a complete suspension of Japan's humanitarian aid to Pyongyang. For a country suffering from a severe shortage of food and foreign exchange alike such as North Korea, the aid promised by Koizumi would go a long way toward meeting its dire need. Medical equipment valued at $10 million, too, would be most useful to the North, whose medical facilities and supplies are woefully deficient.

The agreement to resume normalization talks was good news for the North as well. Should they ever bear fruit, the North is certain to receive a big payoff—in the form of "economic cooperation" that may well total $10 billion. Although it will most likely be stretched over a decade or so,

---

79 "70% Positive on Koizumi Trip: Poll," *Japan Times*, May 25, 2004.
80 "Families of Missing Persons Call Koizumi's N. Korea Visit 'Worst Case Scenario'," *Mainichi Daily News*, May 23, 2004.

the Japanese assistance, or "compensation" as the North is certain to view it, will nonetheless become the largest infusion of foreign capital into the North in recent decades.

Kim Jong Il also took advantage of his second summit with Koizumi to underscore that the US remains a major factor in the equation. He did so directly, or perhaps inferentially, by stressing that whether Pyongyang-Tokyo relations would make headway would hinge largely on the attitudes and positions of Japan's ally, meaning the US. Indirectly, Kim drove home to Koizumi the role of the US in preventing Jenkins and his two daughters from going to Japan to join his wife and their mother. Kim Jong Il may have hoped either to drive a wedge between Tokyo and Washington or to induce Tokyo to help moderate the Bush administration's unbending hard line toward the North.

Symbolically, Kim Jong Il got another chance to demonstrate to the North Korean people that the leader of the world's second largest economy took the trouble to come to Pyongyang. Koizumi was portrayed in the North Korean media as visiting the North primarily to reaffirm commitments to implementing the Pyongyang declaration, which includes his apology to the Korean people, and to transform hostile relations into friendly ones.[81]

The price Kim Jong Il paid for all this was minimal. The agreement to allow the five children of the four Japanese kidnap victims to join their parents in Japan didn't really cost the North much. Keeping them in the North, actually, would have been more costly. One possible adverse consequence would be the revelation of the mistreatment the kidnap victims had received during their long involuntary stay in the North. The four former abductees who were fortunate enough to be reunited with their children might, as they eventually did, feel free to speak about

---

81 "Cho-Il sunoe hoedam, 'Pyongyang son'on' chaehwaginui uimi wa p'yongka," *Choson sinbo*, May 24, 2004. This paper is published by the pro-North Korea Ch'ongnyon in Tokyo and can be regarded as a mouthpiece of the DPRK. Additionally, the article cited here draws heavily on coverage in the North Korean press.

conditions in the North as they saw and experienced them.

Kim's promise to reopen an investigation into the ten Japanese abductees cannot be regarded as a major cost, either. On the other hand, the issue remains as a symbol of the persistence of the abduction issue and continues to serve as a stumbling block on the path toward an improvement in Japan-DPRK relations.

In sum, the second Koizumi-Kim Jong Il summit was a noteworthy event, which entailed gains and losses for both sides. Implementing all the agreements, however, proved to be singularly elusive. A dispute over the authenticity of what the North claimed were the remains of one of the abductees would become acrimonious, plunging the bilateral relationship into an impasse once more.

Post-Summit Developments

The most positive development in the immediate aftermath of the second Koizumi-Kim Joing Il summit was the reunion of the family members of Soga Hitomi. As noted, Koizumi had failed to bring her husband and two daughters to Japan with him but had secured a commitment from Kim Jong Il to arrange a reunion in a third country. The reunion finally materialized in Jakarta, Indonesia on July 8. A plane chartered by the Japanese government had gone to Pyongyang to pick up Soga's husband, Charles Jenkins, and their two daughters, Mika, 21, and Belinda, 18. Accompanied by both Japanese and North Korean diplomats, they then flew to Jakarta, where Soga had arrived a day earlier. Thanks to North Korea's cooperation, Japanese TV networks were able to broadcast both the family members' departure from Pyongyang and their emotional reunion with Soga in Jakarta. Since this happened two days before an upper house (House of Councilors) election in Japan, it gave the strong impression that its timing had been calculated to generate support for Koizumi's ruling coalition.[82]

---

82 "Sogasan ikka saikai: 'gomen' kurikaeshi namida to atsui hoyo" [The Soga

The Soga family flew to Japan nine days later. Jenkins, a former US Army sergeant who deserted to the North while serving in South Korea in 1965, was court-martialed in Japan but released from a military jail on November 27 after serving only 25 days of a 30-day sentence.[83]

Meanwhile, Japan implemented a part of its commitment to provide food and medical assistance to the North. In August it provided 125,000 tons of food aid to the North through the World Food Program (WFP).

Family Reunion: Repeatedly Saying "I'm Sorry," Tearful and Warm Embrace], *Mainichi shinbun*, July 10, 2004; Kanako Takahara, "Is Pyongyang Trying to Win the Election for the Coalition?" *Japan Times*, July 10, 2004; Jane Perlez, "Diplomacy Reunited Ex-G.I. and His Japanese Wife," *New York Times*, July 10, 2004; Young C. Kim, "North Korea Confronts Japan: Politics of Normalization and Rice," 194. Kim writes that North Korean Foreign Minister Paek Nam Sun reportedly told his Indonesian counterpart that "the Japanese government wanted to ensure that the reunion take place before July 11." He adds: "As expected by the Koizumi camp, the Japanese media gave frenzied extensive, continuous live coverage of the developments leading up to that emotive scene of the reunion at the airport. Several television stations in Japan kept broadcasting the fascinating story with dramatic images of the tearful reunion right through the day the ballots were being cast." In the July 11, 2004 election, the ruling coalition of the Liberal Democratic Party and the New Komeito retained a majority in the upper house (139 seats in the 242-member chamber). "Upper House Election Results," *Nikkei.net.interactive* (Tokyo), July 12, 2004, http://www.nni.nikkei.co.jp/FR/FEAT/upper_elec04/results.html

83 James Brooke, "Wanted G.I. Surrenders To U.S. Army in Japan," *New York Times*, September 12, 2004; idem, "G.I. Deserter Tells of Cold, Hungry Times in North Korea," ibid., November 4, 2004; Eric Talmadge, "U.S. Deserter Weeps Upon Release in Japan," *Washington Post*, November 27, 2004. "After hearing bleak testimony about his harsh life in North Korea, an Army judge seemed to accept a defense lawyer's argument that Sergeant Jenkins, 64, had 'already suffered 40 years of confinement.' The judge, Col. Denise Vowell, then demoted him to private, stripped him of four decades of back pay and benefits, and gave him a dishonorable discharge and a 30-day jail sentence." "But the trial and sentencing seemed to reflect American political needs to mollify Japan public opinion, which has been moved by the drama" of Jenkins and his Japanese wife, the kidnap victim. Brooke, "G.I. Deserter……"

Although the North wanted rice, Tokyo decided to provide a mixture of wheat, rice, corn, soybeans, sugar and cooking oil, valued at $40 million. Additionally, Tokyo gave Pyongyang $7 million in medical supplies through the United Nations Children's Fund (UNICEF) and the World Health Organization.[84] Later in the year, Japanese government officials accompanied the monitoring missions of the WFP and other international organizations in the North on two separate occasions and reported that Japan's food aid "has been distributed properly and reached ordinary people in the country."[85]

If the Japanese government had high hopes that positive results might be reaped from the reinvestigation into the ten "missing" Japanese abductees promised by Kim Jong at the second summit, it was bitterly disappointed. After two rounds of working-level talks held in Beijing in August and September failed to yield any new information, the two sides agreed to hold the third round in Pyongyang where Japan hoped to meet with North Korea's security officials who presumably may be able to throw more light on the situation as well as any other relevant individuals.[86]

The third round of the talks held in Pyongyang in November was not only longer—seven days (initially planned for four days) instead of two days in the preceding two rounds—but also upgraded to the director general-level. Headed by Yabunaka Mitoji, director-general of the Foreign Ministry's Asian and Oceanian Bureau, the Japanese delegation was the biggest ever. It consisted of 19 officials from three government agencies, including forensic experts from the National Policy Agency. North Korea was represented by Ma Chol Su, director of its foreign ministry's Asian

---

84 "Tokyo Readies First Aid Bound for North," *Japan Times*, August 6, 2004.
85 Gaimusho, *Gaiko seisho, Heisei 17-nenban*, [*Diplomatic Bluebook*, 2004] (Tokyo: K.K. Taiyo Bijutsu, 2005), 30
86 Ibid., 24-25; "Nitcho jitsumu kyogi 'fumeisha ni shin joho nashi, jikai wa raigetsu de yosei" [Japan-North Korea Working-Level Talks: No New Information on the Missing Persons, Requests to Hold the Next Round Next Month], *Yomiuri shinbun*, August 13, 2004; "Rachi mondai shinten sezu, Nitcho jitsumusha kyogi ga shuryo" [No Progress on the Abduction Issue, Japan-North Korea Working-level Talks End], *Asahi shinbun*, September 27, 2004.

affairs bureau, and included a high-ranking official from Pyongyang's security agency who was said to be in charge of the reinvestigation into the missing persons.[87]

The duration of the talks was extended from four to seven days in order to allow members of the Japanese team to visit various sites, including a hospital where the North alleged one of the abductees, Yokota Megumi, committed suicide in March 1993; they also conducted interviews with 16 individuals who had contacts with the "missing" abductees. One of those who met with the Japanese visitors was Kim Chol Jun, who claimed to be the husband of Yokota. The Japanese team was given what were alleged to be the remains (bone fragments) of his late wife, who was said to have been cremated. The Japanese team also received some documents and other items that Pyongyang claimed were related to the missing abductees.[88]

After a careful analysis of all the material the Japanese delegation brought from North Korea, the Japanese government concluded that none of them supported Pyongyang's claims that eight of the ten "missing" Japanese were dead and that two had never entered the North. Most stunning was the government's finding on the bone fragments allegedly extracted from the remains of Yokota. DNA analysis, it announced, revealed that the fragments were not hers but belonged to two unidentified men. The Japanese government lodged a strong protest

---

[87] "Nitcho kyogi, rachi saichosa no sekininsha ga kekka hokoku" [Japan-North Korea Talks, Official in Charge of Abduction Re-investigation Reports on Results], *Yomiuri shinbun*, November 11, 2004.

[88] "Delegates Visit Sites Linked to Abductees," *Japan Times*, November 14, 2004; "Sanctions Against North Korea Under Study, Machimura Says," ibid, November 15, 2004; "N. Korea's Explanations Said to be Questionable," *Daily Yomiuri*, November 17, 2004; Gaimusho, *Anpi fumeino rachi higaisha ni kansuru saichosa (Kita Chosen kara teishi sareta joho, bussho no seisa kekka* [Re-investigation Into Kidnap Victims Whose Whereabouts Are Unknown (Results of An In-depth Analysis of Information and Itemls Provided by North Korea)] (Tokyo: December 24, 2004), http://www.mofa.go.jp/mofaj/area/n_korea/abd/sai_chosa.html.

to the North on December 8 via diplomatic channels in Beijing.[89]

Predictably, Pyongyang rejected Tokyo's claims about Yokota's alleged remains. After stating its objections through a statement by its foreign ministry spokesman, the North issued a lengthy memorandum by its official news agency, KCNA, on January 25, 2005. The KCNA memorandum argued, among other things, that cremation at an extremely high temperature (around 1,200 degree Celsius) makes it next to impossible to extract DNA from bone fragments. The Japanese government published a lengthy rebuttal on February 10, purporting to show that extracting DNA is still possible from certain fragments that are not sufficiently burned and that one of the two laboratories to which it had given different sets of fragments for analysis had succeeded in doing so. A non-technical argument in the KCNA memorandum shifted the responsibility for the abduction issue to Japan, on the ground that the latter's consistently hostile policy toward the North had engendered a surge of anti-Japanese sentiment among the North Korean people.[90]

The revelation of the Yokota case inflamed anger and animosity among the Japanese people and politicians alike toward the North,

---

89 Ibid.; "8-nin shibo urazuke kaimu, rachi higaisha shiryo no bunseki kekka happyo" [No Evidence That Eight Died, the Results of Analysis of Materials on Kidnap Victims Announced], *Yomiuri shinbun*, December 25, 2004; Reiji Yoshida, "Japan Doesn't Buy North's 'Evidence'," *Japan Times*, December 25, 2004.

90 "Choson Oemusong taebyonin tamhwa, Ilboni palp'yohan yugol 'kamjong kyolgwa' e uihok" [Statement by DPRK Foreign Ministry Spokesman: Doubts on the "Results of Analysis" of the Remains Announced by Japan], *Choson chungang t'ongsin* (KCNA), December 14, 2004, http://www.kcna.co.jp/calendar/2004/12/12-15/2004-12-15-002.html; "Choson Chungang T'ongsin pimangnok 'Ilbonun pan konghwaguk moryakguk ul chojakhan chaegim eso choltaero posonalsu opta" [KCNA Memorandum: "Japan Can Never Escape Responsibility for Fabricating Plot to Defame our Republic], idem, January 24, 2005, http://www.kcna.co.jp/calendar/2005/01/01-25/2005-01-25-001.html; Gaimusho, *Kita Chosen gawa "hiboroku" ni tsuite* [On the "Memorandum" by the North Korean Side] (Tokyo: February 10, 2005), http://www.mofa.go.jp/mofaj/area/n_korea/abd/notgebook.html.

stepping up pressure on the government to impose sanctions on Pyongyang. A non-binding resolution passed by a Diet panel "called on the government to strongly consider sanctions" and to "suspend all food and humanitarian aid" until the North provides the truth about the missing Japanese nationals. Foreign Minister Machimura Nobutaka agreed with the panel on the aid issue. In his words, "even if we are asked by the World Food Program [to provide food aid], it is difficult to respond." Prime Minister Koizumi called Pyongyang's apparent deception "extremely regrettable" but was ambiguous about sanctions, merely saying that "We'll use both pressure and dialogue." As for the sentiment of the Japanese people, a Kyodo news agency poll released on December 10 showed that "three in four Japanese voters" supported imposing economic sanctions on the North.[91]

Even before the Yokota case erupted, the Japanese Diet had enacted a law that would allow the government to ban port calls by North Korean ships.[92] Following the first two rounds of working-level talks that produced no new information on the missing Japanese, a Liberal Democratic Party panel approved an interim report that envisages a five-stage sanction process vis-à-vis Pyongyang. In the first stage, Japan would "freeze or suspend humanitarian aid to North Korea." In the second stage, "it would beef up current measures to ensure that those who remit cash to or do business with North Korea would be reported to the government." In the third stage, "the government would conditionally prohibit cash remittances and trade, while the fourth would involve an all-out ban." In the fifth and final stage, the government would "ban North Korean ships from sailing to Japan."[93]

---

91 Elaine Lies, "Japan Lawmakers Urge North Korea Sanctions," *Washington Post*, December 10, 2004; Joseph Coleman, "N. Korea Remains Are Not of Japan Citizen," ibid, December 8, 2004. Koizumi's reaction is from the latter article.
92 "Tokutei senpaku nyuko kinshi ho'an, Shu'in honkaigi de kaketsu" [The Lower House Passes the Law That Would Ban Specific Ships from Entering Ports], *Yomiuri shinbun*, June 3, 2004, evening edition.
93 Kanako Takahara, "Panel OKs Sanctions on North," *Japan Times*, November 6, 2004; "Tai Kita Chosen Jimin ga dankaiteki keizai seisai o sakusei e" [LDP

When a law passed in 2004 entered into force in March 2005, what the Japanese press called "stealth sanction—a de facto sanction without formal declaration"—became a reality. The law "bans vessels of 100 gross register tons or larger unless they carry sufficient insurance to cover all damage caused by an oil spill." Since North Korea could ill afford to purchase such insurance for its ships, its trade with Japan might suffer[94] On the other hand, Japan-North Korea trade, as Table 2 shows, had been declining steadily in the past few years, which may well turn the "stealth sanction" into a mirage, an illusory one having minimal impact on the North. One area in which de facto trade sanction can have some effect is fisheries trade. In 2003 Japan imported 4.48 billion yen (about $38 million) worth of "asari" (littleneck) clams from the North, which "accounted for 22.2 percent of the country's exports [to Japan], behind queen crabs, at 8.4 percent, and men's suits, at 7.7 percent." The Association of the Families of Victims Kidnapped by North Korea urged Japanese consumers to boycott North Korean clams.[95]

In April 2005 a resolution on the human rights situation in the DPRK drafted by Japan and co-sponsored with the European Union was adopted by the UN Commission on Human Rights. This was the third year in a row that the commission had adopted such resolution. What was new in the 2005 resolution, however, was that it contained specific language on Japanese abductees, notably "requesting the immediate return of the abductees [to Japan] and urging other UN bodies, in

---

Drafts a Phased Sanctions Plan Vis-à-vis North Korea], *Yomiuri shinbun*, October 20, 2004.
94 "'Stealth Sanction' Starts in March," *Daily Yomiuri*, February 9, 2005. A 100-ton ship must be insured for at least 106,700,000 yen (about $900,000), which would require up to 10 million yen (about $85,000) a year in premiums. What is more, most insurance companies are known to show little or no interest in insuring North Korean ships. "Ilbon, taebuk kyongje chejae sasilsang sijak" [Japan Begins De Facto Economic Sanctions vis-à-vis the North], *Joongang ilbo*, February 1, 2005.
95 Reiji Yoshida, "Japan Could 'Clamp Down' on N. Korea," *Japan Times, January* 20, 2004.

particular the General Assembly, to take up the question······if improvement of the situation is not observed." In November 2005, the Third Committee of the UN General Assembly approved a similar resolution, expressing "serious concern" over "the situation of human rights in the DPRK, including the abduction issue."[96]

Meanwhile, the Japanese government added another name to its list of Japanese abductees to the North. On April 27, Tanaka Minoru, from Kobe, Hyogo prefecture, was officially recognized as the 16th kidnap victim. He disappeared in 1978 at the age of 28 but the Japanese government found evidence that Tanaka's boss at a noodle shop, who was a North Korean agent, "deceived him into being taken to the communist country." This meant that Japan would now seek information on 11 missing Japanese, instead of ten.[97]

Not all was bleak in Tokyo-Pyongyang relations, however. On May 18 the North Korean ferry Mangyongbong-92 arrived in Niigata "for the first visit to a Japanese port in five months, after meeting insurance requirements" under the new Japanese law noted above. When the 9,672-ton ship applied for entry permit on April 12, the Land, Infrastructure and Transport Ministry took the precaution of confirming the "solvency

---

96 Ministry of Foreign Affairs of Japan, *Statement by the Press Secretary/Director-General for Press and Public Relations, Ministry of Foreign Affairs, on the Adoption of the Resolution on the Situation of Human Rights in the Democratic People's Republic of Korea at the U.N. Commission on Human Rights* (Tokyo: April 15, 2005), http://www.mofa.go.jp/announce/announce/2005/4/0415-2.html; idem, *Statement by the Press Secretary/Director-General for Press and Public Relations, Ministry of Foreign Affairs, on the Adoption of the Resolution on the Situation of Human Rights in the Democratic People's Republic of Korea at the Third Committee, United Nations General Assembly* (Tokyo: November 18, 2005), http://www.mofa.go.jp/announce/announce/2005/11/1118.html.

97 Gaimusho, *Kita Chosen ni yoru Nihonjin rachi mondai* [The Issue of Japanese Kidnapped by North Korea] (Tokyo: January 2006), http://www.mofa.go.jp/mofaj/area/n_korea/abd/rachi_mondai. html; "Japanese Noodle Shop Employee Was Kidnapped by North Korea 28 Years Ago, Tokyo Says," *Yahoo! News Asia*, April 27, 2005, http://asia.news.yahoo. com/050427/ap/d89nnrvg0.html

of a Burmuda-based insurance company that has a contract with the ship's owners" through the British government. All told, 20 North Korean cargo ships were approved by the ministry following verification of their insurance status.[98]

On May 24 Prime Minister Koizumi sent a congratulatory message to a reception commemorating the 50th anniversary of the founding of *Ch'ongnyon*, the pro-DPRK Korean residents association in Japan. Koizumi had sent a message to the same organization in the preceding year, too, after returning from his summit meeting with Kim Jong Il in Pyongyang. On both occasions, Koizumi took pains to sign his name as the president of the LDP, not prime minister of Japan. The 2005 message conspicuously omitted any reference to "making maximum efforts" to realize diplomatic normalization, which was in the previous year's message, but instead underscored the need for the North to take steps to resolve the impasse over the abduction issue. He also requested *Ch'ongnyon*'s cooperation in "helping Japan to resume dialogue with North Korea."[99]

In July, Koizumi reportedly indicated to former LDP Vice President Yamasaki Taku his desire to normalize diplomatic relations with the DPRK before his term as LDP President expires in September 2006. According to Yamasaki, Koizumi told him that "I want to solve the nuclear and abduction issues······during my term and normalize relations with North Korea." Koizumi "apparently is intent on breaking the impasse in Japan-North Korea relations after six-party talks resume on July 26."[100]

---

98 "North Korean Ferry Clears Hurdle to Get Entry Permit," *Japan Times*, May12, 2005; "North Korea Ferry Calls, Insurance in Hand," ibid, May 19, 2005.

99 "Chosen Soren 50-nen kinen pati, kyori oku kaku seito" [The General Association of Korean Residents' 50-Year Anniversary Party, Parties Distance Themselves], *Asahi shinbun*, May 25, 2005; "Chongryun Marks 50 Years of Promoting North Korea," *Japan Times*, May 25, 2005.

100 "Koizumi Seeks Normalized Ties with DPRK by End of His Terms," *Daily Yomiuri*, July 20, 2005.

The Resumption of Dialogue

Koizumi's hope that the fourth round of Six-Party Talks would pave the way for the resumption of dialogue between his country and the North would be attained but the road proved to be bumpy. The fourth round turned out to be the longest round ever. Whereas the first three rounds lasted three days on average, the fourth consisted of an astounding 20 days of negotiations. What is more, it occurred in two phases, separated by a 37-day recess. On the eve of its opening on July 26, however, Pyongyang issued an ominous warning to Tokyo. Referring to remarks by senior officials of the Japanese government, notably Chief Cabinet Secretary Hosoda Hiroyuki, Foreign Minister Machimura Nobutaka, and Acting LDP Secretary-General Abe Shinzo, that expressed Japan's intention to raise the abduction issue at the six-party talks, North Korea accused Japan of attempting to turn the talks from a forum for seeking the denuclearization of the Korean Peninsula into an arena in which to pursue its self-interests. The North, therefore, saw no need to sit face-to-face with Japan at the forthcoming talks, even going so far as to label Japan a "political pigmy that cannot escape ridicule and condemnation by others for being narrow-minded."[101]

In his opening statement at the talks on July 26, Sasae Kenichiro, Japan's chief delegate and director-general of the Foreign Ministry's Asian and Oceanian Bureau, mentioned the abduction issue "despite earlier criticism from other participants to stay focused on the nuclear issue." His repeated attempts during brief encounters with North Korea's chief delegate, Vice Foreign Minister Kim Kye Gwan, to set up a bilateral meeting, however, failed.[102]

---

101 "Minju Choson: 'Kut'aeyo Ilbon kwa majusol p'iryoga ikkenunga'" [*Minju Choson* (Democratic Korea): "Is It Really Necessary to Sit Face-to-Face with Japan?"], *Choson chungang t'ongsin* (KCNA), July 23, 2005, Pyongyang. *Minju Choson* is the daily organ of the DPRK government.

102 "Rachi mondaide Nihon ni koritsukan 6-sha kyogi, Chu Kan Ro mo gidai hantai" [Six-Party Talks: Japan Feels Isolated Due to the Abduction Issue,

It was only after the first phase adjourned on August 7 that Sasae held a 20-minute meeting with Kim Kye Gwan. This marked the first time since November 2004 that official bilateral talks materialized. Substantively, however, very little was accomplished. Kim merely promised that he would report to his country what Sasae had requested: (1) the return of all surviving Japanese kidnap victims in the North to Japan as soon as possible, (2) an ascertainment of the truth about the abductions, and (3) the handover of those who carried out the abductions to Japanese authorities.[103]

Two days before the second phase of the fourth round convened, Koizumi won a landslide victory in Japan's general election. The LDP won 296 seats in the 480-seat House of Representatives, a gain of 86 seats. Although the LDP's coalition partner, the New Komeito, saw a net loss of three seats, its 34 seats were nonetheless sufficient to give the ruling coalition a two-thirds majority in the lower house of the Diet, the more powerful of its two chambers.[104]

This must have influenced Pyongyang's calculus in its policy toward the Koizumi government, for there was a marked change in North Korean behavior when the second phase opened on September 13. For a bilateral meeting materialized on the second day of the resumed six-party talks on the sidelines. Moreover, the meeting lasted 80 minutes, which was four times longer that the previous one, and Kim Kye Gwan appeared to be more attentive when Sasae underscored Japan's commitment to a comprehensive resolution of the nuclear, missile, and abduction issues as

---

China, South Korea, Russia Oppose Agenda], *Asahi shinbun*, July 27, 2005; Yu Yoshitake, "Japan Focuses More on Nukes," *Asahi.com*, July 27, 2005, http://www.asahi.com/english/Herald-asahi/TKY200507270373.html.

103 "Yaku 9-kagetsu buri Nitcho kyogi, rachi higaisha no kikoku nado yosei" [Japan-North Korea Talks After a 9-month Hiatus, Requests the Repatriation of Kidnap Victims], *Yomiuri shinbun*, August 8, 2005.

104 Norimitsu Onishi, "Koizumi's Party, Backing Reforms, Wins by Landslide," *New York Times*, September 12, 2005; "Koizumi's LDP Wins Big," *Japan Times*, September 12, 2005; "2005 sosenkyo: kaihyo kekka" [2005 General Election: Results of Vote Tally], *Asahi shinbun*, September 12, 2005.

a precondition for normalization of diplomatic relations with North Korea. Sasae also called for a resumption of full-fledged inter-governmental negotiations. While repeating the North's previous line, Kim assured Sasae that he would communicate Japan's concerns to Pyongyang.[105]

At North Korea's request, bilateral meetings on the sidelines of the six-party talks were held for five days in a row. Following the adoption on September 19 of a joint statement by the six-party talks, in which the agreement of the DPRK and Japan "to take steps to normalize their relations" is mentioned, Japan's Foreign Minister Machimura confirmed in Tokyo that Japan and North Korea had agreed to resume inter-governmental talks.[106]

The inter-governmental talks that were held in Beijing on November 4-5, however, failed to make any progress. Conducted at the deputy director general-level, Japan was represented by Saiki Akitaka of the Foreign Ministry's Asian and Oceanian Bureau, while the North Korean team was headed by Song Il Ho, vice director of the DPRK Foreign Ministry's Asian Affairs Bureau. To the dismay of the Japanese delegation, Song reiterated the North's previous stance that the abduction issue "has been settled" and questioned the reliability of the DNA test conducted in Japan on what the North claimed were the bone fragments of Yokota. Song made it clear that North Korea was interested primarily in the question of "settling the past," which would accompany diplomatic normalization. Saiki's proposal to conduct negotiations on three topics—

---

[105] "Nitcho ga kobetsu kyogi, rachi mo kyogika, 6-sha kyogi 2-nichime de jitsugen" [Japan and North Korea Hold Separate Talks on the Second Day of Six-Party Talks, Abductions Discussed], ibid., Setember 14, 2005, evening edition; "Tokyo, Pyongyang Hold Meeting," *Japan Times*, September 15, 2005.

[106] "Nitcho, seifukan taiwa o saikai e, sakunen matsu irai" [Japan and North Korea To Resume Inter-Governmental Dialogue, For the First Time Since the End of Last Year]. *Asahi shinbun*, September 20, 2005; "Japan, North Korea Agree to Continue 2002 Talks," *Japan Times*, September 20, 2005; "Editorial: Patience Has Paid Off So Far," ibid., September 21, 2005.

namely, (1) the abduction issue, (2) nuclear and missiles issues, and (3) the settlement of the past—, however, failed to elicit a favorable response. The two sides agreed to continue the talks.[107]

Saiki and Song returned to Beijing in the following month to continue the inter-governmental talks. Although the focus of the two-day meeting (December 24-25) was on the format of future negotiations, Saiki also reiterated Japan's past demands for a full accounting of the missing persons, a "convincing" explanation of the Megumi case, and the handover of North Koreans suspected of involvement in the abductions. Song, for his part, reiterated the North's position that the abduction issue had been resolved and refused to provide any new information. In the end, however, Song stated that Pyongyang would make "sincere efforts and take concrete measures" to settle "issues of concern" to Japan. Most important, the North accepted Japan's proposal for holding "three separate consultations concurrently and promptly upon the establishment of a comprehensive framework for the consultations."[108]

---

107 "Nitcho, 1-nen buri kyogi" [Japan and North Korea Hold Talks After 1-Year Hiatus], *Asahi shinbun*, November 4, 2005; "Nitcho kosho keizoku de koi" [Japan and North Korea Agree to Continue Negotiations], ibid, November 5, 2005; "Shasetsu: 'Kita' e kokusaitekina atsuryoku o tsuyomeyo" [Editorial: Intensify International Pressure on the North], *Yomiuri shinbun*, November 6, 2005.

108 "Kita Chosen, heiko kyogi ukeire e, rachi wa 'kaiketsu sumi' to shucho" [North Korea Accepts Parallel Talks, Asserts "Abductions Have Already Been Solved"], *Asahi shinbun*, December 25, 2005; "Nitcho kokkyo seijoka kosho saikai de koi, rachi, kaku to heiko kyogi" [Japan and North Korea Agree to Resume Negotiations on Diplomatic Normalization, Abductions and the Nuclear Issue To Be Discussed in Parallel], ibid., December 26, 2005; "Japan, N. Korea Agree on Talks' Format," *Japan Times*, December 26, 2005; "Cho-Il chongbugan chopch'ok chinhaeng, 3 punkwabyol hoedam 1-wol chung kaech'oe habui" [Inter-governmental Talks Between the DPRK and Japan Held, Agreement on Convening Three Parallel Talks in January], *Choson chungang t'ongsin* (KCNA), December 26, 2005, Pyongyang; Gaimusho, *Nitcho seifukan kyogi (12-gatsu 24-25-nichi, o: Peking) (Gaiyio)* [Inter-governmental Talks between Japan and North Korea (December 24-25, Bei-

Three-track Talks

In accordance with the preceding agreement, Japan and North Korea held inter-governmental talks in Beijing from February 4 to 8, 2006. The two sides used different names for the three-track talks. Whereas Japan labeled them "the first round of Japan-North Korea Comprehensive and Parallel Talks" (*Dai 1-kai Nitcho hokatsu heiko kyogi*), North Korea referred to them as the "DPRK-Japan Inter-governmental Talks for Diplomatic Normalization" (*Kukkyo chongsanghwa rul wihan Cho-Il chongbugan hoedam*).[109]

On the first day of the talks, the two sides held the opening session in the afternoon. Lasting only 75 minutes, the session featured statements by the heads of the two delegations, Haraguchi Koichi, Japan's ambassador in charge of normalization talks with the North, and Song Il Ho, who had represented the DPRK in the inter-governmental negotiations leading up to the three-track talks. Haraguchi stressed that Japan placed the highest priority on the abduction issue and that without its resolution, coupled with the resolution of the nuclear and missile issues, Japan would not agree to diplomatic normalization with the North. Song, for his part, left little doubt that Pyongyang was interested first and foremost in the issue of settling or liquidating the past, which would entail diplomatic normalization with and compensation from Tokyo.[110]

---

jing) (Summary)] (Tokyo: December 27, 2005), http://www.mofa.go.jp/mofaj/area/n_korea/abd/seifkan_0512.html.

109 Gaimusho, *Dai 1-kai Nitcho hokatsu heiko kyogi (gaiyo)* [The First Round of Japan-North Korea Comprehensive and Parallel Talks] (Tokyo: February 2006), http://www.mofa.go.jp/mofaj/ area/n_korea/abd/hokatsu.html ; "'Cho-Il chongbugan hoedam chinhaeng 4~8 il" ["DPRK-Japan Inter-governmental Talks Held, 4th~ 8th], *Choson chungang t'ongsin* (KCNA), February 9 2006, Pyongyang, http://www.kcna.co.jp/calendar/2006/02/02-10/2006-0208-012.html; "DPRK-Japan Inter-governmental Talks Held," *KCNA*, February 9, 2006, http://www.kcna.co.jp/item/2005/200602/news02/10.htm.

The most important outcome of the first session, however, was an agreement on how to conduct the talks. The North proposed, and Japan accepted, a "one theme a day" format in lieu of strictly parallel negotiations in which three panels would have held talks simultaneously. Under this format, the second day of the talks would take up the abduction issue, the third day diplomatic normalization, and the fourth day the nuclear issues, missiles, and other security-related issues. A plenary session would wrap up the talks on the fifth and final day.

The first substantive session thus occurred on the following day, February 5, Even though it was Sunday, the session lasted nine hours, including a lunch break. The Japanese team was led by Umeda Kunio, deputy director of the Foreign Ministry's Asian and Oceanian Bureau, while the North Korean team was headed by Kim Chol Ho, vice director of the Asian Affairs Bureau in the DPRK Foreign Ministry. Umeda reiterated Japan's demands for (1) the return of all surviving abductees, (2) a full disclosure of information on all the abductees, and (3) the handover of those suspected of involvement in the abductions. Regarding the last item, Umeda named specific individuals—Sin Gwang Su, Kim Se Ho, and one of the Japanese hijackers of the Japanese airliner, Yodo-go. Umeda also named three other Japanese hijackers as well as the widow of

---

110 "Nihonkawa 'rachi o saiyusen' Kita Chosen wa seijoka chushi, Nitcho kyogi" [Japan-North Korea Talks: Japan Places "Highest Priority on Abductions," North Korea Stresses Normalization], *Asahi shinbun*, February 5, 2006; "Nitcho kyogi: Pyongyang sengen o rikode kyogi o kakunin, Peking shinai" [Japan-North Korea Talks in Beijing: Confirms Negotiations Will Uphold the Implementation of the Pyongyang Declaration], *Mainichi shinbun*, February 5, 2006; "Nitcho kyogi, saiyusen no rachi mondaiga saishono gitai ni" [Japan-North Korea Talks: The Highest Priority Abduction Issue To Be the First Agenda Item], *Yomiuri shinbun*, February 5, 2006; "Japan, N. Korea Open Three-track Talks," *Japan Times*, February 5, 2006; "'Cho-Il kukkyo chongsanghwa hoedam' ch'onnaljae chonch'e hoeui, Pyongyang son'on rihaeng ui chase hwagin" ["DPRK-Japan Normalization Talks: Plenary Session on the First Day Confirms the Will to Implement the Pyongyang Declaration], *Choson sinbo*, February 5, 2006, http://www.korea.np.co.jp/news/Article:Print.aspx?ArticleID=20535.

a former hijacker who died in the North.[111]

Kim Chol Ho refused to budge from Pyongyang's stance that the abduction issue had already been settled, insisting that the North had made "sincere efforts" on it. He also reiterated Pyongyang's doubts about the reliability of the DNA tests on Yokota's remains (ashes), demanding that the latter be returned to the North and that the Japanese scientist who conducted the test and North Korean scientists should get together to re-examine the test results. In the end, both sides agreed to take up the abduction issue again during the fourth session on February 7.

When the third session convened on February 6, it marked the first time since October 2002 that negotiations on diplomatic normalization had resumed. The five and a half hours of talks between the two sides—led, respectively, by Haraguchi and Song Il Ho—could be labeled the 13th round of Japan-DPRK normalization talks. While agreeing that the principles enunciated in the Pyongyang declaration should guide normalization, the two sides nonetheless disagreed on what should accompany it. Haraguchi underlined that the declaration referred to "economic cooperation" Japan would provide "after the normalization," enumerating "grant aids, long-term loans with low interest rates," and "other loans and credits by such financial institutions as the Japan Bank for International Cooperation." He told Song that such "economic

---

111 Sources for the second day of the talks include:"Rachi mondai wa heikosen, saikyogi e mukae chotei, Nitcho kyogi 2-nichime" [The Second Day of Japan-North Korea Talks: Parallel Lines on the Abduction Issue, Schedule Adjusted for Re-negotiation], *Asahi shinbun*, February 6, 2006; "Rachihan no migara hiki watashi o yokyu, Kita wa kyohi······Nitcho kyogi" [Japan-North Korea Talks: Demands Handover of Kidnappers, North Refuses], *Yomiuri shinbun*, February 6, 2006; "Nitcho kyogi: rachi mondai meguri heikosen, 6-nich ikomo keizokude itchi" [Japan-North Korea Talks: Parallel Lines Concerning the Abduction Issue, Agree to Continue Discussions Even After the 6th], *Mainichi shinbun*, February 6, 2006; "Japan, North Korea Discuss Abductions for Nine Hours," *Japan Times*, February 6, 2006; "'Cho-Il kukkyo chongsanghwa hoedam' it'uljae, 'rapch'i' tullossakgo 9-sigan hyopsang" [The Second Day of DPRK-Japan Normalization Talks: Nine Hours of Negotiation on "Abductions"], *Choson sinbo*, February 6, 2006,

cooperation" will be the only way to "settle the past."[112]

Citing "crimes against humanity" committed by the Japanese against the Koreans during the colonial period—notably "conscripting 8.4 million people" for hazardous work, "massacring a million people," and forcing "200,000 women" into sexual slavery as "comfort women for Japanese soldiers"—Song stated that Japan needed to provide "compensation," in addition to "economic cooperation." He also called for an improvement of the status of Korean residents in Japan who profess loyalty to the North and a return of all "cultural relics" Japan plundered during the occupation period. If they have been damaged, he stressed, the relics must restored to their original condition. Should that prove to be impossible, Japan must pay compensation, he added.[113]

On February 7, the fourth day of the talks, the two sides held two sessions. During the morning session devoted to security issues, the Japanese team was headed by Yamamoto Tadamichi, the Foreign Ministry's ambassador in charge of the North Korean nuclear issue, while the North Korean team was led by Jong Tae Yang, vice director of the DPRK Foreign Ministry's American affairs bureau. This marked the first time that Japan and North Korea conducted bilateral talks dealing

---

http://www.korea-np.co.jp/news/ArticlePrint.aspx?ArticleID=20538.

112 Sources for the third session on normalization include: "Nitcho kokkyo seijoka kosho, keizai kyoryoku, koi sezu" [Japan-North Korea Talks on Diplomatic Normalization, Disagree on Economic Cooperation], *Asahi shinbun*, February 7, 2006; "Nitcho seijoka kosho, 3-nen 3-kagetsu buri saikai" [Japan-North Korea Normalization Talks Resume After a Hiatus of 3 Years and 3 Months], *Yomiuri shinbun*, February 7, 2006; "Pyongyang Normalization Talks Deadlock," *Japan Times*, February 7, 2006; "'Cho-Il kukkyo chongsanghwa hoedam' 3-iljae, kwago ch'ongsane kwanhan t'oui sijak" [The Third Day of DPRK-Japan Normalization Talks: Discussion on the Settlement of the Past Begins], *Choson sinbo*, February 6, 2006, online at http://www.korea-np.co.jp/news/ArticlePrint.aspx?ArticleID=20545.

113 These details are found in the North Korean account of what its delegation said during the talks. In addition to the articles in *Choson sinbo*, "Cho-Il chongbugan hoedam chinhaeng 4-8 il," *Korean Central News Agency* (KCNA), February 9, 2004 (cited in note 109) is useful for this purpose.

exclusively with security issues, for an agreement reached at the 12th normalization talks in Kuala Lumpur in October 2002 for such talks was never implemented. Yamamoto strongly urged the North to return to the six-party talks and stop the development and deployment of ballistic missiles that threaten Japan's security.[114]

The fifth round of the six-party talks, which held the first session in Beijing in November 2005 for three days, had entered into an impasse due to Pyongyang's anger over Washington's imposition of de facto sanctions on a Macao bank with which the North had close ties. The US Treasury Department charged that Banco Delta Asia in the former Portuguese colony of Macao had "worked surreptitiously with North Korea for 20 years and helped it traffic in drugs."[115] There was also a suspicion that the bank had helped the North launder counterfeit US hundred-dollar bills by allowing North Korean officials to "make surreptitious deposits and withdrawals." A ban on US financial institutions doing business with the bank led it to freeze all accounts linked to North Korea and eventually to sever its relationship with Pyongyang altogether. Japan's largest bank "voluntarily ceased all transactions with Banco Delta Asia."[116] Banks in Germany and Singapore, discontinued doing business with the "only foreign-run bank in North Korea," creating enormous problems for Pyongyang.[117]

---

114 "6-sha kyogi e mujoken fukki yobikake, Nitcho, anzen hosho meguri kyogi" [Call for An Unconditional Return to Six-Party Talks, Japan and North Korea Hold Talks on Security], *Asahi shinbun*, February 7, 2006; "'Cho-Il kukkyo chongsanghwa hoedam' 4-iljae, 'anbo' rul tandok uijero sangjong" [The Fourth Day of DPRK-Japan Normalization Talks, "Security" Is the Only Agenda Item], *Choson sinbo*, February 7, 2006, http://www.korea-np.co.jp/news/ArticlePrint.aspx?ArticleID=20574.
115 Joseph Kahn, "North Korea and U.S. Spar, Causing Talks to Stall," *New York Times*, November 12, 2005.
116 "Makao Banko Deruta Ajia: ote hoginga torihiki teishi—Kita Chosen kanren giwakude" [Macao Banco Delta Asia: Major Japanese Banks Stop Transactions—Because of Suspected Links With North Korea], *Mainichi shinbun*, February 2, 2006.

Against this backdrop, Song reminded Yamamoto that it was the US, not the North, that had erected a stumbling block to Six-Party Talks; hence Japan should ask its US ally to remove it. What Pyongyang wanted, in other words, was for the US to lift de facto sanctions impeding its financial transactions abroad.

The afternoon session took up the abduction issue, which nine hours of discussions on February 5 had left in limbo. Umeda Kunio and Kim Chol Ho thus returned to the conference table for additional negotiations, which lasted only 90 minutes. Whereas Umeda repeated Japan's triple demands pertaining to missing Japanese nationals, Kim not only reiterated Pyongyang's demands relating to the disputed DNA test of Yokota's remains but also introduced a new one. Kim claimed that there were Japanese nationals who were responsible for kidnapping North Koreans, demanding the handover of seven members of Non-governmental Organizations (NGOs) who were helping North Korean refugees in China.[118]

Five days of the talks came to an end on February 8, when all the delegates attended a 40-minute plenary session. The heads of the two delegations, Haraguchi and Song Il Ho, concurred in the view that although the talks exposed a wide chasm between Japan and North Korea, they nonetheless provided a useful forum in which to deepen mutual understanding. As Song Il Ho put it, "this type of negotiations is necessary in order to narrow the differences between the two sides and

---

117 "North Korea's Nuclear Push May Be Stymied by U.S. Banking Rules," *Bloomberg.com*, March 6, 2006, http://www.bloomberg.com/apps/news?pid=10000080&sid=akMjhbFt2TAI.

118 "Nitcho kyogi: rachi, matamo shinten sezu, 6-kakoku kyogi fukki ojizu" [Japan-North Korea Talks: Still No Progress on Abductions, Also Refuses to Return to Six-Party Talks], *Mainichi shinbun*, February 8, 2006; "Nitcho kyogi: rachi mondai, kochaku taiwa rosen hihan ya keizai seizai ron mo" [Japan-North Korea Talks: The Abduction Issue Deadlocked, Dialogue Policy Criticized, Even Economic Sanctions Considered], ibid., February 8, 2006; Kanako Takahara, "North's Abduction Charge Irks NGOs," *Japan Times*, February 10, 2006.

make progress in [North] Korea-Japan relations." The only agreement to come out of the talks turned out to be an agreement to continue the three-track talks, with the date of the next round to be set through diplomatic channels.[119]

Pressure Eclipses Dialogue

In the aftermath of the failure of another attempt at inter-governmental dialogue, Japan-North Korea relations entered into stalemate again. With rising calls for sanctions from the public and politicians alike, Tokyo began to exert pressure on Pyongyang in various ways. Realistically, full-fledged sanctions were not an available option, as long as the six-party process was under way. Washington's de facto sanctions on the North noted above can best be described as pressure of the kind Tokyo has been trying to exert on Pyongyang. The main difference is that the former appears to hurt Pyongyang much more than the latter.

Nearly all of the various pressure tactics Japan deployed vis-à-vis the North that were discussed earlier were still available. Thus North Korean ships arriving in Japan continued to receive stringent inspections.[120] A

---

119 "Nitcho kyogi, zentai kaiko hiraki shuryo, kyogi keizokude itchi" [Japan-North Korea Talks End With a Plenary Session, Agree to Continue Talks], *Asahi shinbun*, February 8, 2006; Nitcho hokatsu heiko kyogi: 8-nichi heimaku Nihon, senryaku yari naoshi semarare" [Japan-North Korea Comprehensive Parallel Talks: Closes on 8th, Japan Pressed to Overhaul Strategy], *Mainichi shinbun*, February 9, 2006; Takaharu Yoshiyama and Kyoji Fukushima, "Japan-N. Korea Talks End in Stalemate," *Daily Yomiuri*. February 9, 2006; Takaharu Yoshiyama, "Japan Walks Away Empty-handed as Talks Close," ibid., February 10, 2006; "Abduction Impasse Keeps Pyongyang Talks Fruitless," *Japan Times*, February 9, 2006; "Cho-Il kukkyo chongsanghwa hoedam kyolsok, 'kyesokjogin hyopsang' p'iryosong injong" [DPRK-Japan Normalization Talks Wrap Up: The Need for "Continuous Negotiations" Recognized], *Choson sinbo*, February 8, 2006, http://www.korea-np.co.jp/news/Articl ePrint.aspx?ArticleID=20583.

scrutiny of facilities owned by *Ch'ongnyon* was stepped up with the aim of levying property taxes on them, a move that received a boost by a Fukuoka High Court decision that nullified the Kumamoto city government's exemption of taxes on a *Ch'ongnyon* facility.[121]

Alarmed by a "sharp increase in the number of postal remittances to North Korea in recent years," Japan Post, a public corporation under the jurisdiction of the Ministry of Internal Affairs and Communications, decided to investigate details of the remittances. The number of postal remittances to the North increased from 306 in fiscal 2002 (April 2002-March 2003) to 1,560 in fiscal 2004 (April 2004-March 2005). Although the maximum amount allowed per remittance to the North is about 480,000 yen (about $4,000), whether that limit is always observed or enforced was not known.[122]

Since cash can also be sent to the North in registered mail, the government decided to monitor registered mail bound for the North. In addition, the government would conduct random inspections of 100 or so export firms with a view toward preventing illegal exports of dual use—both civilian and military use—machinery to North Korea.[123]

---

120 "Kita Chosen kamotsusen: fusei yushutsu kan'yode kankei kikanga tachi iri kensa" [North Korean Freighter: Entrance Inspection by Related Agencies for Ties to Illegal Exports], *Mainichi shinbun*, March 7, 2206.

121 "Japanese High Court's Ruling Against Chongryon Assailed," *KCNA*, March 1, 2006, http://www.kcna.co.jp/item/2006/200603/02.htm. This article presents excerpts from a commentary that appeared in *Minju Choson*, the daily organ of the DPRK government, which assails the Japanese court decision as "totally unfair." It warned that the "DPRK will never look with folded arms on Japan's unjustifiable suppression of *Chongryon*," adding that "if Japan persists in these actions against *Chongryon*, it will be entirely accountable for the ensuing grave consequences."

122 "Spike in Postal Remittances to North Korea Scrutinized," *Japan Times*, February 17, 2006.

123 "Kita Chosen mondai: yubinbutsu no kensa kyoka fusei sokin boshi e—seifu hoshin" [North Korea Problem: Government Intends to Strengthen Inspection of Mail to Prevent Illegal Transfer of Cash], *Mainichi shinbun*, March 13, 2006.

The Persistence of Discord and the Limits of Cooperation 255

In early March, a task force on the abduction issue under the rubric of the Prime Minister's Office decided to create two new groups with a view toward increasing pressure on the North. One group will explore "stricter enforcement of existing laws" on "immigration control, foreign exchange and customs services, partly to clamp down on illegal exports to North Korea." This group will also examine ways of dealing with Pyongyang's "alleged money laundering, drug trafficking and counterfeiting." The other group will be in charge of facilitating exchanges of information among the various government agencies regarding the various aspects of the abduction issue, including information on North Korean agents, both past and present, who are believed to have been involved in abductions[124]

Japan also flexed its muscle when it and its ally the US "successfully conducted the first test of a jointly developed ballistic missile defense system off Hawaii" on March 8. The SM-3 missile vehicle "incorporates a new nose cone developed by Japan," which "is expected to boost [its] accuracy rate." The joint test's success was hailed by the director of the US Missile Defense Agency as an "'important milestone' in the development of a missile defense system to down incoming enemy missiles."[125]

This development coincided with North Korea's test-firing of two short-range missiles, something the North has done often in the past. What must have alarmed the North's potential adversaries, however, was the assessment by the commander of the US Forces Korea, General B. B. Bell, that the latest North Koren missiles were a "qauantum leap forward from the kind of missiles that they have produced in the past." In a testimony before the US House Armed Services Committee on March 9,

---

124 "Kita Chosen rachi mondai: rachi kanjikai, 2-bunkakai o setchi" [North Korea Abduction Issue: Abduction Task Force Establishes Two Groups], *Mainichi shinbun*, March 14, 2006; "Gov't Abduction Team to Set Up 2 Groups to Add Pressure on N. Korea," *Yahoo! Asia News*, March 6, 2006, http:// asia.news.yahoo.com/060306/kyodo/d8g621s80.html.
125 Aya Igarashi, "Japan-U.S. Missile Test Successful," *Daily Yomiuri*, March 10, 2006.

Bell revealed that the "missiles were boosted by solid fuel, rather than liquid fuel, providing greater reliability, mobility and precision." Noting that the North "was also moving ahead with the development of longer-range ballistic missiles that could hit Alaska and targets in the continental United States," Bell asserted that "North Korea is a significant threat that still must be deterred."[126]

On March 23 the Japanese police raided six *Ch'ongnyon*-affiliated sites in Osaka in connection with an investigation into the case of Hara Tadaaki, one of the abductees Pyongyang claimed to have died in the North. The raids were aimed at unveiling a "network of collaborators" who took orders from Sin Gwang Su, a former North Korean agent who was arrested in South Korea in 1985 for impersonating Hara. Sin confessed that he had abducted Hara to the North and was imprisoned in the South but was later repatriated to the North. Sin and another North Korean agent suspected by Japan of involvement in the abductions of Japanese nationals were placed on the Interpol's international wanted list.[127]

Finally, given all this, there was little or no chance that the North would receive the remainder of the food aid Koizumi pledged to Kim Jong Il during their second summit anytime soon. As noted, Japan provided 125,000 tons of assorted food aid through the WFP in August 2004 but suspended delivery of the remaining 125,000 tons four months later over a dispute regarding the alleged remains of Yokota.

---

126 "North Korea Launches Land-to-Air Missiles," *Mainichi Daily News*, March 8, 2006; Jack Kim, "N. Korea Missiles Tested Are Quantum Leap: US General," *Yahoo! News*, March 10, 2006, http://news.yahoo.com/s/nm/20060310/ts_nm/korea_north_missiles_dc_4.

127 "Police Search Chongryun Affiliate Over '80 Abduction," *Japan Times*, March 24, 2006; "Sin Guang Su's North Korean Spy Ring Under Investigation," *Asahi.com*, March 24, 2006, http://www.asahi.com/ english/Herald-asahi/TKY200603240377.html; "Kita Chosen rachi mondai: Harasan jiken sosaku, borayku koi to hinan?Kiita Chosen" [North Korean Abduction Issue: Search in Mr. Hara's Incident, North Korea Denounces It as a Plot], *Mainichi shinbun*, March 24, 2006, evening edition.

North Korea reacted to these pressure tactics with the familiar tactic of *tit for tat*. Harsh denunciation of Japanese actions was coupled with the issuance of arrest warrants for four members of Japanese NGO's for their alleged involvement in abducting North Korean citizens. The four were among the seven persons the North had called on Japan to hand over to Pyongyang during the three track talks in Beijing.[128]

The North asserted that Japan's "moves to hush up the settlement of the past with the 'abduction issue' are a shameful plot to evade the responsibility for [its] past crimes." Arguing that Tokyo was intentionally "driving the DPRK-Japan relations to confrontation and conflict," Pyongyang labeled the "frantic campaign conducted by the Japanese reactionaries against the DPRK under an unreasonable pretext" a "foolish" move that will "make a mess of the future of Japan."[129]

Conclusion

What do these developments suggest regarding the sources and patterns of North Korea's policy toward Japan and vice versa? Do the concepts and insights deployed in the preceding chapter still help illuminate Japan-DPRK relations in the 21st century?[130]

Let us begin with the rationality postulate advanced by both

---

128 "Rodong sinmun 'pan konghwaguk, pan *ch'ongnyon* passho moryak ch'aekdong'" [Nodong sinmun: "Anti-DPRK, anti-Ch'ongnyon fascist maneuvers"], *Chson chungang t'ongsin* (KCNA), March 26, 2006, Pyongyang, http://www.kcna.co.jp/calendar/2006/03/03-27/2006-0326-005.html ; "Kita Chosen: Nihon no NGO 4-nin ni taihosho, seifuni hiwatashi yokyu" [North Korea: Arrest Warrants for Four Japanese NGO Members, Demands the Government to Hand Them Over], *Mainichi shinbun*, March 28, 2006.
129 "Moves of Japanese Reactionaries to Evade Liquidation of Past Flailed," *Korean Central News Agency* (KCNA), March 26, 2006, http://www.kcna.co.jp/item/2006/200603/news03/27.htm.
130 As noted at the outset of this chapter, both Japan and North Korea count 2001 as the first year of the new millennium.

neorealism and neoliberalism. Since neither Japan nor North Korea appears to care too much about relative gains, we may consider whether each side scored absolute gains in some of the more noteworthy transactions. To the extent that they did, one can argue that their behavior fulfilled the criteria of rationality.

We have already seen that the first Koizumi-Kim summit of September 2002 offered both sides an opportunity to score gains while incurring costs. While none of the bargains struck during that summit were embedded in zero-sum games in a strict sense, their unanticipated consequences may nonetheless have produced effects approximating zero-sum. Take, for example, Koizumi's most prized gain—bringing home the five abductees. Kim Jong Il clearly did not anticipate the manner in which their home-coming would be achieved. Japan's decision to renege on its commitment to return them to the North after two weeks deprived Kim of potent bargaining leverage. In the short term, therefore, Koizumi's gain on that score spelled Kim's loss.

What, then, were the most important gains Kim scored in his first tete-a-tete with Koizumi? With the benefit of hindsight, one can see that most of his gains were ideational rather than material. Koizumi's apology for the "tremendous damage and suffering" Japan caused to the Korean people "through its colonial rule," his pledge to provide "economic cooperation" to the North after diplomatic normalization, and his commitment to "make every possible effort for an early normalization" of relations with the DPRK—all of these were soothing words that proved to be hollow in light of subsequent events.

Did Kim's own apology to Koizumi for the abductions of 13 Japanese nationals by North Korean agents in the 1970s and 1980s amount to an ideational loss, given the apotheosis of national pride in the DPRK's reigning ideology of *chuch'e*? If it was such a loss in an absolute sense, however, Kim did manage to control damage to a large degree. For one thing, his apology was conspicuously absent in the Pyongyang Declaration; nor did his admission that the abductions were the "work of persons affiliated with North Korea in the past" find its way into the joint declaration. Second, this meant that the North Korean people were left in the dark, at least in the short run.

One of the goals Kim may have pursued, as we hypothesized earlier, may have been to send a message to the Bush administration that it should hasten to open dialogue with the North. That goal was attained within a little over two weeks following the summit, when Bush's special envoy, James Kelly, visited Pyongyang to hold high-level talks. This, too, turned out to be a short-lived gain, for the Kelly visit spawned unforeseen consequences, leading to the second standoff over the nuclear issue between Pyongyang and Washington.

None of this implies that either Japan or North Korea did not behave rationally as far as the first Koizumi-Kim Jong Il summit was concerned. From a medium to long-term perspective, it provided a turning point in their bilateral relations—a turning point that was as necessary as it was painful. Progress toward an eventual normalization of diplomatic relations, albeit excruciatingly slow, would be inconceivable had it not been for the beginning of the catharsis Kim Jong Il's "confession" to Koizumi signaled.

The second Koizumi-Kim summit, too, produced gains for both sides, while entailing costs as well. Koizumi's most ostentatious gain was bringing home five children of the four kidnap victims, closely followed by the reunion of the fifth kidnap victim and her spouse and children. To the extent that the latter event, occurring as it did practically on the eve of general elections, played a role in helping Koizumi's ruling coalition retain its control in the upper house, it spelled a domestic political payoff as well.

What Kim Jong Il gained from the second summit was more material than ideational. For he extracted specific commitments from Koizumi regarding the type and amount of humanitarian assistance Japan would provide to the North. Even though the controversy over the alleged remains of a kidnap victim led Tokyo to suspend delivery of the aid, the North had nonetheless received a half of what had been promised—a material gain of sizable magnitude for the impoverished country.

For both sides, the gains may well have eclipsed the costs; hence the rationality assumption can be sustained in this instance as well. What of the three-track talks? What did each side gain from that novel experiment? What Japan officially dubbed "comprehensive and parallel talks" proved to be comprehensive talks that ran along parallel lines. For both side adhered to the positions they had previously articulated and refused to make any concessions whatsoever. If anything, positions appeared to harden in some cases, notably, the North's demand for the handover of Japanese NGO workers for allegedly kidnapping North Korean citizens, who are in fact refuges who fled the North to escape hunger and oppression.

As both sides grudgingly admitted, the talks did give them an opportunity to understand each other better and to appreciate how far apart they really are on the key issues. Their mutual commitments to continue the talks using the same format may be viewed as a gain loosely defined. Since neither side foresaw how the talks would actually proceed and, especially, their abject failure, however, their decision to hold the inter-governmental talks should not be faulted as proof of irrationality.

The impact of external events on the behavior of both sides was also on display during the period under review here. External events, however, usually interacted with internal circumstances. The timing of the first Koizumi-Kim summit may have been dictated by the convergence of external pressure on the North and internal pressure on Japan. For Pyongyang, the need to break the impasse in its relations with Washington must have been pressing, and the symbolic value of the leader of the world's second largest economy paying a visit for a meeting with the supreme leader must have been too tempting to bypass. For Tokyo, the growing agitation in the domestic political arena for resolving the abduction issue may have been the single most important variable in the equation.

The hardening of Japan's position in the immediate aftermath of the summit stemmed not merely from the deterioration of the abduction issue following the revelation of the alleged deaths of eight kidnap victims and the furor it sparked among the Japanese public but also from the eruption of the second standoff over the nuclear issue. The need to maintain a united front with its US ally and quasi-ally, South Korea, coupled with its own "nuclear allergy" and threat perception, figured prominently in Japan's policy calculus.

The concept of two-level game is useful in deciphering the international behavior of Japan and North Korea alike. A key difference may lie in the relative malleability of the "win-set" in the totalitarian North as compared to the democratic Japan. This may help explain Kim Jong Il's bold decision to "come clean" on the abduction issue to some extent but not all the way. To reveal the whole truth on the abduction issue, however, would require going beyond the win-set for the North, for it would be tantamount to compromising its state and regime identity. Evidence South Korea's intelligence agency—now called the National Intelligence Service—has collected shows that contrary to what he told Koizumi in September 2002, Kim Jong Il personally ordered abductions. Sin Gwang Su, the North Korean agent Japan put on the international wanted list for the abduction of Japanese national Hara Tadaaki, reportedly told South Korean intelligence in 1985 that "in 1980 he [was] instructed by Kim to kidnap a Japanese national and steal his identity."[131]

It is conceivable that the eleven "missing" kidnap victims about whom Japan assiduously seeks the "truth" from the North may not have died by illness or accident as Pyongyang claims but may actually have been killed by North Korean security personnel. It is also possible that the North may have destroyed evidence relating to their deaths. The North's irreducible need to safeguard its state identity, which includes not only the dignity and pride of the state but also a personality cult centered on Kim Jong Il, his late father (the constitutionally anointed "eternal president" of the DPRK), and their entire clan, precludes the option of disclosing the unvarnished truth about the abductions. To a regime that flaunts "military first" policy, of which a major pillar is the exhortation to defend the supreme leader with one's life, disclosing any information that will tarnish his image and reputation is not an option at all. No less

---

131 Yuichiro Nakamura, "Kim Jong Il Directly Tied to Abductions / ROK Documents Say He Instructed Spy to Kidnap Japanese Man, Steal His Identity," *Daily Yomiuri*, February 5, 2006.

important, in the leader-centered (*suryong-je*) political system that is North Korea today, the only person who can make key decisions is Kim Jong Il himself.

As long as Japan, driven by its own domestic political dynamics, persists in seeking a full disclosure of information from the North, then, the stalemate is exceedingly unlikely to be broken. No less important is the nuclear issue, the resolution of which is a prerequisite to the normalization of diplomatic relations between Japan and the DPRK, as Tokyo has repeatedly emphasized. The chances of a compromise being reached on that issue may be somewhat greater than is the case with the abduction issue.

PART II

Japan and South Korea

CHAPTER 5

Between Discord and Cooperation: Japan-ROK Normalization and Its Aftermath

Inter-governmental negotiations, as we saw in the preceding chapters, often turn out to Janus-faced. While they are not only aimed at increasing cooperation but also evidence of cooperation in their own right, the process of negotiation is frequently marred by discord. This leads to a prolongation of negotiations and, should the parties fail to find common ground, to an exacerbation of discord.

Unlike the on-again and off-again normalization talks between Japan and the DPRK, however, the negotiations between Japan and the ROK did bear fruit. Hence their conclusion of the normalization and related treaties in 1965 marked the most important watershed in the annals of Japan-ROK relations. Although the normalization paved the way for a marked increase in bilateral cooperation, it did not put an end to discord, which continued to erupt intermittently on issues large and small.

Even a cursory overview must therefore differentiate between the pre-normalization period (1948-1965) and the post-normalization period

(1965-present). Since the focus of this study is on the developments since 1985, however, a review of the early years will necessarily be brief.

The Pre-normalization Period, 1948-1965

Japan's relations with the ROK began shortly after the latter came into being, even though Japan was still under the Allied occupation. An ROK mission was set up in Tokyo in January 1949, which was headed by an ambassador from January 1949 to May 1950 and from December 1961 to December 1965. In the intervening years it was headed by a minister.[1] Since there was no Japan mission in Seoul, however, this was an anomalous arrangement. Initially, the ROK mission was accredited to the Supreme Commander for the Allied Powers (SCAP), as was the case with the missions from other countries. Inasmuch as the foremost function of the mission was the protection of Korean residents in Japan, it promptly established a branch office in Osaka where a large number of Koreans lived.[2]

Even though preliminary negotiations for diplomatic normalization began in October 1951, six months before Japan regained its sovereignty, the ensuing 14 years were marked more by discord—strains and hostility—than by harmony or cooperation between Tokyo and Seoul.[3] There were

---

1 Oemubu, *Han'guk oegyo samsimnyon, 1948-1978* [30 Years of Republic of Korea Diplomacy 1948-1978] (Seoul: Oemubu, 1979), 439-40.
2 Kim Tong-jo, *Hoesang 30-nyon Han'il hoedam* [30-Year Reminiscences: Republic of Korea-Japan Negotiations] (Seoul: Joongang ilbosa, 1986), 19. Kim was a participant in ROK-Japan negotiations and served as ambassador in both the ROK mission and embassy in Japan. He also served as the ROK ambassador to the United States, the ROK foreign minister, and the special assistant to the ROK president on foreign policy.
3 At the request of the ROK government, SCAP instructed the Japanese government to hold talks to discuss all pending issues between the two sides, and the preliminary meeting convened in the conference room of the SCAP headquarters on October 20, 1951. The San Francisco Peace Treaty had been signed in the preceding month and was scheduled to enter into force on April 28, 1952. Ibid., 21.

nonetheless intermittent negotiations, of which seven rounds were held between 1952 and 1965, ultimately producing a settlement of nearly all outstanding issues, which in turn paved the way to normalization.

The level of discord or animosity in Tokyo-Seoul relations remained consistently high during the tenure of President Syngman Rhee (1948-1960) due to a number of factors. The single most important factor was Rhee's intense distrust of Japan, which was rooted in his long experience as a leader of anti-Japanese activities aimed at regaining Korea's independence. As Chong-Sik Lee points out, however, the refusal or inability of influential Japanese politicians to heed the South Korean people's demand for expressions of remorse for the wrongs inflicted on the latter during the colonial period served to aggravate the situation.[4]

Emblematic of the Japanese attitude were the remarks made by Kubota Kanichiro, the chief Japanese delegate, during the third round of the Japan-ROK talks on diplomatic normalization in October 1953. During an acrimonious exchange with a South Korean delegate on the issue of property claims, Kubota stated that Japan had actually contributed to the Korean economy by carrying out such projects as reforestation, irrigation, port and railway construction, and others. He also stated that had Japan not taken control of Korea, either China or Russia would have done so, adding that the Koreans would have suffered far more under Chinese or Russian occupation than they did under Japanese. His remarks so enraged the South Koreans that the talks were suspended for four and a half years.[5]

---

4 Chong-Sik Lee, *Japan and Korea: The Political Dimension* (Stanford, CA: Hoover Institution Press, Stanford University, 1985), 23-42. In Lee's words, "Korea's approach to Japan was spiritual, moral, holistic, and Oriental, whereas the Japanese approach was legalistic, pragmatic, piecemeal, and Western. The Koreans talked of human sufferings and indignities, and the Japanese talked of material benefits they had brought to the Koreans." See ibid., 24-25.
5 Ibid., 39; Nagano Nobutoshi, ed., *Nihon gaiko handobukku: juyo shiryo, kaisetsu, nenpyo* (A Handbook of Japanese Diplomacy: Selected Documents with Comments and Chronology of Events) (Tokyo: Saimaru Shuppankai, 1981), 190. For a detailed summary of the heated exchange between Hong Chin-gi, a

A key move by the Rhee government also fueled Japanese animosity toward South Korea: Rhee's proclamation of the "Peace Line" in January 1952 extending the ROK's sovereignty to 50-60 nautical miles from its coastline infuriated Tokyo. According to Kim Tong-jo, a key player in Seoul-Tokyo negotiations, however, the "Peace Line," which the Japanese called the "Rhee line," actually raised the stakes for Japan, thus increasing the latter's need to reach a comprehensive settlement with South Korea.[6]

Of the actions taken by the Japanese government, the most damaging to Seoul was the repatriation of Korean residents to North Korea, which we discussed in Chapter II. Carried out under an agreement between the Red Cross organizations of Japan and the DPRK, which remained in effect from August 1959 to November 1967, the repatriation program allowed 88,611 Korean residents in Japan to resettle in North Korea.[7] While the Japanese government justified its decision to permit the repatriation on humanitarian grounds—i.e., respect for the Korean residents' right to choose their own place of residence—,[8] it actually helped to alleviate the problems caused by the Korean residents in Japan.

Quoting government and Red Cross statistics, the *Asahi shinbun* noted on February 5, 1959 that one out of every four Korean residents was a recipient of "livelihood protection" subsidies, costing the Japanese

---

South Korean delegate, and Kubota at the second session of the subcommittee on property claims on October 15, 1953, see Kim Tong-jo, *Hoesang* 30-nyon, 53-59.

6 Ibid., 35-39. During the 13 years when the "Peace Line" was in effect, it exacted the following tolls from Japan: 233 fishing vessels seized by the ROK, of which 173 were not returned; three ships sank by the ROK; 2,791 crew members of Japanese fishing vessels detained by the ROK; and five killed. Nagano, ed., *Nihon gaiko handobukku*, 189.

7 Gaimusho, ed., *Waga gaiko no kinkyo, 1968* [The Recent Condition of Our Diplomacy, 1968], (Tokyo: Okurasho Insatsu-kyoku, 1968), 166. The number refers only to those who were repatriated under the agreement. Since repatriation continued after the agreement expired, however, the actual number of all repatriates may surpass 90,000.

8 Gaimusho. ed., *Waga gaiko no kinkyo, 1960* (Tokyo: Okurasho Insatsu-kyoku, 1960), 29-31 and *1961* (Tokyo, 1961), 67-71.

government 2.6 billion yen. Proportionately, according to the Japanese daily, ten times as many Koreans as Japanese were on "livelihood protection" (or welfare). The paper added that about 80 percent of Koreans were unemployed and that in 1957 about 22,000 Koreans had committed larceny, battery, and other felonies; in proportional terms the Korean residents' crime rate was five times that of the Japanese.[9]

What annoyed the ROK most, however, was that the repatriation program enabled the DPRK, its arch-rival, not only to score a major propaganda victory in the contest for legitimacy but also to strengthen its foothold in Japan immeasurably. The relatives of the repatriates have proved to be the principal source of continuing support, both ideological and financial, for the DPRK in the subsequent years.

The end of the Rhee era, which came abruptly in the wake of student-led demonstrations in April 1960, helped to improve the prospects for Japan-ROK normalization. Even though Huh Chung, who headed the caretaker government for four months and who had previously served as the chief delegate in Japan-ROK talks, was well aware that the hard-line policy of the Rhee government had not been effective, he nonetheless refrained from taking any policy initiative during his brief tenure other than to underscore his wish to see normalization at the earliest possible date.[10] It therefore remained for the Chang Myon government, which emerged in August 1960, to signal a new direction in Seoul's Japan policy.

On September 6, 1960 a new leaf was turned in Japan-ROK relations when a special Japan Air Lines plane carrying Foreign Minister Kosaka Zentaro touched down at Kimpo International Airport. He was the first Japanese government official to set foot on Korean soil since the ROK came into being, and his arrival marked the first time since Korea's liberation that the Japanese national flag, the rising sun, appeared in

---

9 Kim Tong-jo, *Hoesang 30-nyon*, 141-42; Tessa Morris-Suzuki, "Exposing Japan's Dark Role in Koreans' Return," *Asahi com*, November 26, 2004, http://www.asahi.com/english/opinion/TKY200411260122.html.
10 Gaimusho. ed., *Waga gaiko no kinkyo, 1961*, 63.

Korea, first as an emblem on his airplane and then on his limousine. He was not, however, the first Japanese citizen to be admitted to the ROK. He had been preceded by Yatsugi Kazuo, who visited Seoul as a special emissary of Prime Minister Kishi Nobusuke in May 1958, meeting with President Syngman Rhee.[11]

Kosaka, however, scrupulously avoided using any words that might suggest remorse or apology for Japanese colonial rule, saying that "Japan fully respects the feelings of the Korean people toward Japan and wishes to move in the direction of co-prosperity." He also disappointed Seoul by insisting that since the repatriation of Korean residents to North Korea was being handled by Red Cross organizations, the Japanese government could not intervene in the matter. Given all this, the Chang government was hardly in a position to approve his request for the establishment of a Japan mission in Seoul.[12] It is worth noting that the absence of reciprocity from the ROK gave Japan the right to demand the closing of the ROK mission in Japan; pending normalization, however, the mission served a useful function not only for Seoul but for Tokyo as well, which is why the Japanese government chose not to exercise its right.

Although the fifth round of the Japan-ROK talks, which convened in Tokyo in the following month, failed to make any notable headway, it was nonetheless plain that the general atmosphere had become distinctly cordial and even optimistic. In May 1961 another symbolically important event occurred when the first ever delegation of Japanese Diet members made a week-long visit to Seoul. Led by Noda Uichi, the three-man delegation consisted of veteran members of the House of Representatives who had served as cabinet members; Tanaka Kakuei, who would become prime minister in 1972, was one of them. The Chang government's decision to invite such heavy-weight politicians reflected its desire to make a breakthrough in the Japan-ROK talks.[13]

---

11 Ibid., 63-64; Kim Tong-jo, *Hoesang 30-nyon*, 203. For Yatsugi's visit, see ibid., 117-20.
12 Ibid., 202-5.
13 Ibid., 210.

Three days after the Japanese politicians left Seoul, the Chang government was overthrown in a coup d'etat led by Major General Park Chung Hee. That turn of events, however, did not impede but actually facilitated Japan-ROK talks. For Park, a graduate of the Japanese Military Academy and a Japanophile, was no less eager than Chang Myon to normalize relations with Japan. If anything, Park had more compelling reasons for wanting a speedy normalization of Seoul-Tokyo relations. The need to establish legitimacy in the eyes of his compatriots as well as his deep personal convictions made economic modernization the highest priority on his political agenda; pursuit of that goal in turn would necessitate a massive infusion of capital and technology, of which Japan appeared to be the ideal source.[14]

Unlike his predecessor, however, Park could match his determination with power; he was a strong leader who could overcome widespread, vociferous opposition and strike a deal with Japan. As Chong-Sik Lee shows, this was precisely why ardent supporters of normalization in Japan, notably former Prime Minister Kishi and his colleagues, welcomed Park's seizure of power.[15] In contrast to the reaction of the Kishi group, however, the Japanese government initially took a wait-and-see attitude toward the military junta in Seoul. Yi Tong-hwan, whom the junta appointed to head the ROK mission in Japan as minister in July 1961, thus found it necessary to expend a considerable amount of time and energy on trying to convince Tokyo that the coup was something that needed to happen and that the coup leaders had absolutely no sympathy for socialism but were totally dedicated to economic modernization.[16]

---

14 For the elaboration of a hypothesis linking his early background to his quest for modernization, see Byung Chul Koh, *The Foreign Policy Systems of North and South Korea* (Berkeley: University of California Press, 1984), 82-85.
15 Lee, *Japan and Korea*, 47-49.
16 Kim Tong-jo, *Hoesang 30-nyon*, 212-13. Yi Tong-hwan and Kim Tong-jo were classmates at Kyongsong Commercial Higher School, the precursor of the College of Commerce (later renamed the College of Business Administration) of Seoul National University. In naming Yi, who was neither a career diplomat nor a heavyweight politician, to the Tokyo post, the junta appeared to have

The zeal with which the Park regime sought normalization, then, was but one factor, albeit an important one, in the equation.[17] The United States, by all accounts, played a key role in the process. As Chong-Sik Lee points out, the Vietnam War gave the US "reason to prod both the Japanese and the Koreans to normalize their relationship."[18] In Bruce Cumings's view, Washington's push for Japan-ROK normalization was linked to "Acheson's strategy of pushing Japan toward a regional economic effort in Northeast Asia."[19]

---

taken into account Yi's extensive network of friends and acquaintances in Japan; Yi, for example, was a graduate of Tokyo College of Commerce (later renamed Hitotsubashi University) and could count on the cooperation of two fellow alumni in the Ikeda cabinet—namely, Chief Cabinet Secretary Ohira Masayoshi and Foreign Minister Kosaka Zentaro.

17 In November 1961 Park made a 30-hour visit to Japan on his way to the United States for a meeting with President John F. Kennedy. Park was royally treated by the Japanese government and had a two-hour meeting with Prime Minister Ikeda Hayato. At a press conference immediately following the meeting, Park indicated that he was extremely pleased with the meeting, saying that should the Japanese government show sincerity on the issue of property claims, the Korean government would be prepared to resolve the issue of the Peace Line in a flexible manner. The Japanese Foreign Ministry noted that the Ikeda-Park meeting marked the first time since the Japan-ROK talks began ten years ago that the top leaders of both countries had a friendly and candid discussion, thereby bolstering mutual trust. See Gaimusho. ed., *Waga gaiko no kinkyo, 1962* (Tokyo: Okurasho Insatsu-kyoku, 1962), 77-78. Documents declassified by the ROK government in August 2005 reveal that it was Prime Minister Ikeda who had taken the initiative to arrange the unprecedented meeting. The two leaders reached a broad agreement in principle on the key issues with the aim of expediting negotiations at the "working-level." "Han'il hoedam munso palch'ue, VIP sangbong" [Excerpts from Documents on ROK-Japan Normalization Talks: VIP Encounter], *Chosun ilbo*, August 27, 2005.
18 Lee, *Japan and Korea*, 53.
19 Cumings, *Korea's Place in the Sun*, 319. For new information based on declassified US government documents on US role in the normalization, see "Nikkan joyaku teiketsu zen'ya Beigoku ga soki teiketsu motome Nikkan soho e kainyu" [U.S. Intevens On Eve of Japan-ROK Treaty Conclusion Asking Both

Visits to Tokyo and Seoul by such high-ranking US officials as Secretary of State Dean Rusk (January 1964) and Assistant Secretary of State William Bundy (September-October 1964) for the express purpose of "encouraging Japanese-South Korean normalization" as well as the active involvement of American ambassadors in Tokyo and Seoul bespoke American commitment.[20] In addition to prodding the two parties to expedite their negotiations, the US also tried to help neutralize strong domestic opposition to normalization in South Korea. Another index of US role was the Park government's decision to jettison its plan to go for "normalization first, the resolution of pending issues later" when the US expressed reservations about its feasibility.[21]

Domestic opposition in South Korea, which forced the resignation of Park Chung Hee's cabinet in May 1964 and led to Park's declaration of martial law on June 3, 1964, affected both the timing and contents of the eventual settlement. The need to counter, if not forestall, the charge of a sellout by opponents of normalization was always uppermost in the minds of South Korean negotiators.

The signing of the Treaty on Basic Relations Between Japan and the Republic of Korea and five other agreements dealing, respectively, with (1) fishery, (2) property claims and economic cooperation, (3) the legal

---

Sides to Conclude Treaty Early], *Asahi shinbun*, August 21, 2000.
20 Lee, *Japan and Korea*, 53.
21 Kim Tong-jo, *Hoesang 30-nyon*, 248-54; 266-68. Documents declassified by the ROK government in August 2005 confirm that Washington played a major role. Former Vice Foreign Minister Chong In-yong, who was a member of South Korea's negotiating team from 1960 to 1964 goes so far as to suggest that the "US choreographed the negotiations." "Han'il Hoedam munso palch'ue, Miguk ui ipjang" [Excerpts from Documents on Japan-ROK Normalization Talks: The United States' Position], *Chosun ilbo*, August 27, 2005; "Han'il Hyopjong tangsi oemubu ch'agwan Chong Il-yong-si 'sasilsang Miga chudo······musang 3-ok, Yusang 2-ok an Miso naondut'"[Mr. Chong Il-yong, Vice Foreign Minister at the Time of Negotiations: "The US Actually Led······The Idea for 300 Million Dollars in Grants-in-Aid and 200 Million Dollars in Loans Probably Emanated from the US], ibid., January 22, 2005.

status of Korean residents in Japan, (4) cultural property and cultural exchanges and (5) peaceful settlement of disputes; and various related documents at the Prime Minister's Residence on June 22, 1965 formally signaled the end of the long, arduous, and cantankerous negotiations and the beginning of a new era between Japan and the ROK.[22]

The basic treaty, in addition to providing for the establishment of ambassadorial-level diplomatic relations and consular relations between the two countries, contains two key provisions regarding the status of pre-1910 treaties and of the Republic of Korea. Article II reads: "It is confirmed that all treaties or agreements between the Empire of Japan and the Empire of Korea on or before August 22, 1910 are already null and void." Article III confirms that "the Government of the Republic of Korea is the only lawful Government in Korea as specified in Resolution 195 (III) of the United Nations General Assembly."[23]

Article II is the result of a compromise between Seoul's insistence that the treaties in question were null and void *ab initio* and Tokyo's claim that they were nullified by Japan's defeat in World War II and the conclusion of the San Francisco peace treaty. The ambiguous phraseology of the article leaves the dispute unresolved. No less ambiguous is the precise meaning of Article III. As noted in Chapter II, it lends itself to varying interpretations; it can support either Seoul's claim that it is the only lawful government on the entire Korean peninsula or Tokyo's

---

22 Gaimusho. ed., *Waga gaiko no kinkyo, 1966* (Tokyo: Okurasho Insatsu-kyoku, 1966), 107; Gaimusho Sengo Gaikoshi Kenkyukai. ed., *Nihon gaiko 30-nen: sengono kiseki to tenbo, 1952-1982* [Thirty Years of Japanese Diplomacy: The Postwar Record and Prospects, 1952-1982] (Tokyo: Sekaino Ugoki-sha, 1982), 90. The basic treaty and other agreements entered into force on December 18, 1965 upon an exchange of the instruments of ratification, which took place in a formal ceremony at the Central Government Building in Seoul attended by the foreign ministers and chief delegates of both sides.

23 For the English-language text of the basic treaty, see Kagoshima Heiwa Kenkyujo. ed., *Nihon gaiko shuyo bunsho, nenpyo, dai-2-ken* [Basic Documents of Japanese Foreign Relations, vol. 2], *1961-1970* (Tokyo: Hara Shobo, 1984), 570-572.

interpretation that UN General Assembly Resolution 195 (III) limits the jurisdiction of the ROK to the southern half of the peninsula.

The fishery agreement recognizes both countries' right to establish 12-miles exclusive fishery zones; it also provides for an additional zone that will be subject to joint regulations. The controversial "Peace Line" thus evaporated. The centerpiece of the agreement on property claims and economic cooperation was Japan's commitment to provide the ROK with (1) a grant of $300 million, (2) an Official Development Assistance (ODA) loan of $200 million at the interest rate of 3.5 percent per annum repayable in 20 years, and (3) private commercial credits of $300 million or more. All of these would be spread over ten years.[24]

The agreement on the legal status of ROK nationals in Japan confers the right of permanent residence on all ROK nationals who have lived in Japan since before the end of World War II—August 15, 1945—and their children who were born in Japan between August 16, 1945 and January 16, 1971 and lived continuously in Japan. The agreement calls for renegotiation of the status of all others—i.e., those born after January 17, 1971—between Japan and the ROK after 25 years have elapsed since its entry into force.[25]

It should be noted that economic relations between Japan and South Korea did not follow but preceded the establishment of diplomatic relations. What diplomatic normalization did was to pave the way for a dramatic increase in economic and other interactions. Even during the Rhee era there was bilateral trade on a very modest scale, ranging from $49 million in 1955 to $116 million in 1953, averaging about $75 million a year.[26] The pace of economic intercourse increased appreciably in the post-Rhee era. Barely four months after Rhee's ouster, the Chang Myon government issued visas to representatives of the Mitsubishi Trading Company, opening the door to visits by employees of other

---

24 Gaimusho. ed., *Waga gaiko no kinkyo, 1966*, pp.108-10.
25 Ibid., 110-11; *Zainichi Kankokujin no kyojuken* [The Residency Right of Republic of Korea Nationals in Japan] (Tokyo: Zainichi Taikanminkoku Seinenkai, 1989), 9.
26 See Table 4 in Lee, *Japan and Korea*, 57.

<Table 5> Japan-South Korea Trade

(in millions of dollars; custom clearance basis)

Year	Exports	Imports	Total	Balance
1961	126	22	148	104
1962	138	28	166	110
1963	160	27	187	133
1964	109	42	151	67
1965	180	41	221	139
1966	335	72	407	263
1967	407	92	499	315
1968	603	102	704	501
1969	767	134	901	633
1970	818	229	1,047	589
1971	858	274	1,130	581
1972	980	426	1,406	554
1973	1,789	1,207	2,996	582
1974	2,656	1,568	4,224	1,088
1975	2,248	1,308	3,556	940
1976	2,824	1,917	4,741	908
1977	4,080	2,114	6,193	1,966
1978	6,003	2,591	8,594	3,412
1979	6,247	3,359	9,606	2,887
1980	5,368	2,996	8,365	2,372
1981	5,658	3,389	9,047	2,269
1982	4,881	3,254	8,135	1,627
1983	6,004	3,365	9,369	2,639
1984	7,227	4,213	11,440	3,014
1985	7,097	4,092	11,189	3,005
1986	10,475	5,292	15,766	5,183
1987	13,229	8,075	21,305	5,154
1988	15,441	11,811	27,252	3,631
1989	15,920	12,994	28,914	2,926
1990	17,457	11,707	29,164	5,750
1991	20,605	12,339	32,944	8,266
1992	17,770	11,577	29,347	6,193
1993	19,124	11,681	30,805	7,443
1994	24,339	13,490	37,829	10,849
1995	32,622	17,049	49,671	15,573

1996	29,339	15,948	45,287	13,390
1997	26,086	14,590	40,676	11,496
1998	15,401	12,117	27,518	3,284
1999	23,072	16,166	39,238	6,906
2000	30,699	20,452	51,451	10,247
2001	25,405	17,307	42,712	8,098
2002	28,547	15,454	44,001	13,093
2003	34,675	17,841	52,516	16,834
2004	44,200	22,027	66,227	22,173
2005	46,880	24,536	71,416	22,344

SOURCES: Gaimusho, Hokuto Ajia-ka, *Kankoku keizai kankei deta-shu*, July 1990; Gaimusho, *Gaiko seisho*, 1990 through 1993 (Tokyo: Okurasho Insatsu-kyoku, 1990-1994);Tsusho Sangyosho (ed.), *Tsusho hakusho*, 1998,1999, 2000, 2001(Tokyo: Okrasho Insatsu-kyoku, 1998,1999, 2000, 2001); Nihon Boeki Shinko Kiko, *Boeki, toshi, kokusaishushi tokei*, on line at http://www.jetro.go.jp ; Hanguk Unhaeng, *Kyongje t'onggye yonbo 2005* (Seoul, 2005). The 1996 figures were converted from yen at the rate of108.81 yen to $1.00.

trading companies and businessmen of all stripes.[27] In 1964 the value of bilateral trade totaled $151 million; in 1965 the amount had reached $221 million.

The Post-normalization Period

The most tangible effect of normalization occurred in the economic realm. The pace of growth in bilateral trade accelerated, with Japanese exports to South Korea growing at a phenomenal rate. Within three years of normalization, South Korea became Japan's second largest export market next to the United States, retaining that status for the next ten years. Since South Korean exports to Japan lagged behind its imports by considerable margins, the growing trade imbalance became a chronic issue in bilateral relations.

Bilateral consultations increased sharply. In the first two and a half years since normalization, government-level meetings related to trade and

---

27 Ibid., 46.

economic issues were held 16 times, which, according to the Japanese Foreign Ministry, bespoke not only the rapid expansion and deepening of Tokyo-Seoul economic ties but also their complexity.[28] Structures of bilateral consultations sprang up, of which the most important is the annual conference of cabinet ministers, which began to be held in Tokyo and Seoul on an alternating basis every year since 1967. As will be noted shortly, however, the cabinet conference was either postponed or canceled altogether when political relations were strained or some unforeseen events occurred.

Japan became one of the two most important sources of both public and private loans for South Korea, along with the United States.[29] In 1973 Japan surpassed the United States as source of direct investment, accounting for 60 percent of all foreign direct investment in South Korea on a cumulative basis.[30]

Of the numerous projects for which South Korea sought and received Japanese assistance in capital and technology, one of the most important was the construction of an integrated iron and steel complex in Pohang. South Korea requested Japanese assistance for the project at the third cabinet conference in August 1969. After conducting an on-site study, Japan agreed to provide financial aid in the form of grants and loans totaling $124 million.[31] In 1972 South Korea requested an additional $130 million for the same project, which Japan agreed to provide in principle.[32] In 1993 the Pohang Iron and Steel Company

---

28 Gaimusho, ed., *Waga gaiko no kinkyo, 1968* (Tokyo: Okurasho Insatsu-kyoku, 1968), 225.
29 Oemubu, *Han'guk oegyo 30-nyon*, 158-60. If international organizations are taken into account, then Japan's rank as a source of loans for South Korea slips to a third place.
30 Gaimusho, ed., *Wagan gaiko no kinkyo, 1974* (Tokyo: Okurasho Insatsu-kyoku, 1974), 244.
31 Gaimusho, ed., *Waga gaiko no kinkyo, 1970* (Tokyo: Okurasho, Insatsu-kyoku, 1970), 85-86.
32 Yamamoto Tsuyoshi, "Nihon to Kankoku" [Japan and the Republic of Korea] in Yamamoto Susumu et al, *Sengo Nihon gaikoshi, VI: Namboku mondai to*

(POSCO), with a steel-making capacity of 30 million tons, became the second largest steel company in the world, next to Nippon Steel Corporation (NSC) of Japan.[33] In 1997 POSCO's actual steel output of 26.43 million tons was only 520,000 tons less than that of NSC. In 1998 POSCO surpassed NSC in steel outputs for the first time, and by 1999 POSCO's annual output reached 28 million tons. In August 2000 POSCO and NSC announced the formation of a strategic alliance under which they would jointly develop technology and cooperate in other ways.[34]

One noteworthy aspect of Japan-ROK economic relations in the years immediately following normalization pertains to Seoul's request for rice from Tokyo. Both in 1969 and in 1970 Seoul asked Tokyo to lend rice to deal with serious shortages; Tokyo complied by providing 333,000 tons in 1969 and 300,000 tons in 1970.[35] This episode is worth noting because, as we saw in Chapter 4, in 1995 North Korea took the unusual step of making a similar request to Japan, a country with which the DPRK has yet to establish diplomatic relations. Upon Seoul's insistence that Tokyo should not oblige unless and until Pyongyang receives rice from Seoul first, the two Korean states engaged in negotiations in Beijing in June 1995 for the first time in a year, producing an agreement under which Seoul would provide, free of charge, 150,000 tons of rice to Pyongyang.[36] Tokyo promptly indicated a willingness to follow suit, reaching an agreement with Pyongyang to supply 300,000 tons of rice, of which 150,000 would be free and the remainder would be provided on a

---

Nihon [History of Japan's Postwar Diplomacy, vol. 6: The South-North Problem and Japan] (Tokyo: Sanseito, 1984), 158.

33 *Korean Industry in the World 1994* (Seoul: Korea Development Bank, 1994), 40.

34 P'ohang Chech'ol, *Hoesa hyonhwang* [The Company's Current Situation], August 2000, Http://www.posco.co.kr/ kr/pr/sum/sum.html; "Shin Nittetsu to Kankoku Pohang Sogo Seitetsu ga bubun teikei o seishiki happyo" [Nippon Steel and Korea's POSCO Officially Announce Partial Cooperaion], *Asahi shinbun*, August 3, 2000.

35 Gaimusho, ed., *Waga gaiko no kinkyo, 1970*, 84.

36 *Hankook ilbo*, June 22, 1995, 1.

deferred payment basis.[37]

Until 1973 Japan-ROK relations were developing relatively smoothly. That is not to say that they were trouble-free. One issue that was left unresolved in 1965, namely, the territorial dispute centered on a small island off the eastern coast of South Korea which is called Takeshima by the Japanese and Tokdo by the Koreans, remained a source of continuing friction. Beginning in 1970, when Japan discovered that the island was occupied by South Koreans, the Japanese government began to protest to Seoul regularly, and the latter clung to the position that it had sovereignty over the island.

As noted, the chronic trade imbalance in Tokyo's favor prompted Seoul to seek remedies. Seoul sought a liberalization of imports of primary industrial goods, a lowering of tariffs and other measures. The main source of the imbalance, however, was structural: because South Korean industries relied heavily on Japanese machinery and parts, which were more expensive than the primary goods and light-industrial products Seoul exported to Japan, the imbalance was hard to rectify. What is more, the more South Korea exported to the rest of the world, the more it needed to import Japanese goods. Given all this, it was almost a small miracle that South Korean exports to Japan continued to grow. In 1974 South Korea even accomplished the feat of making Japan its number one export market, surpassing the United States.[38]

Strains soon developed, however, in political relations, which

---

37 *Japan Times Weekly International Edition*, July 3-9, 1995, 3. The Japan-North Korea agreement was reached in Tokyo on June 27, six days after the signing of the inter-Korean agreement in Beijing.

38 This was duly noted in the Japanese Foreign Ministry's annual publication. See Gaimusho, ed., *Waga gaiko no kinkyo, 1974* (Tokyo: Okurasho, Insatsu-kyoku, 1974), 243. The Foreign Ministry prefers to use ratios between Japanese exports and imports to measure progress in rectifying the trade imbalance. Thus even though Japan's trade surplus vis-a-vis South Korea increased from $554 million in 1972 to $582 million in 1973, Gaimusho saw an improvement in the picture: the export-import ratio decreased from 2.3:1 to 1.5:1. Ibid.

temporarily put a damper on economic relations as well. The main source of the problems that erupted in 1973-1975 could be traced to internal politics in South Korea, specifically, to the growing authoritarianism of President Park Chung Hee. The extra-constitutional measures he adopted in 1972 in the name of "revitalizing reforms" (*yusin*) led to a sharp increase in his own powers and coercive controls over the citizenry.[39]

In August 1973 agents of the Korean Central Intelligence Agency (KCIA) kidnapped Kim Dae Jung from a Tokyo hotel. Kim had come very close to defeating Park in the presidential election of 1971 and had been in self-imposed exile abroad since the proclamation of *yusin* in 1972. He was forcibly taken by a high-speed patrol boat to South Korea and set free near his house in Seoul. His life had apparently been saved thanks to U.S. intervention. The Japanese authorities collected fingerprints of Kim Tong-un, a first secretary in the ROK Embassy in Tokyo, and ascertained that the automobile used in the kidnapping belonged to a vice-consul in the ROK consulate in Yokohama; they also knew that both of these men were actually KCIA agents operating under diplomatic or consular cover.[40]

---

39 For an analysis of the October 1972 "revitalizing reforms" in South Korea and their implications, see B. C. Koh, "*Chuch'esong* in Korean Politics," *Studies in Comparative Communism*, 7, no. 1 and 2 (Spring/Summer 1974), 83-97.

40 Yamamoto, "Nihon to Kankoku," 182. On May 11, 1979 the Japanese news agency, *Kyodo Tsushin*, published documents it obtained from the US State Department proving that the US was aware of KCIA involvement in the kidnapping. The documents, some of which were classified but mistakenly released by the State Department, included a cable from US Ambassador Philip Habib, dated August 21, 1973, confirming the accuracy of press reports that KCIA was behind the Kim Dae Jung incident and another cable from U.S. Ambassador Snyder, dated January 10, 1975, reporting that ROK Foreign Minister Kim Tong-jo had confidentially told him that "Kim Tong-un, the KCIA agent responsible for the Kim Dae Jung kidnapping, was quietly dismissed from KCIA." Nagano, ed., *Nihon gaiko handobukku*, 193-194. A week before Kim Dae Jung's inauguration as ROK president in February 1998, a major South Korean daily, *Dong-A ilbo*, obtained secret KCIA documents that proved conclusively that the agency had planned and carried out his

Notwithstanding all this, the Japanese government opted for a course of action aimed at minimizing damage to Tokyo-Seoul relations. Refraining from raising the issue of the violation of Japan's sovereignty by agents of the ROK government, Tokyo relied on emissaries to reach a political settlement with Seoul. The so-called "first political settlement" that materialized during ROK prime minister Kim Jong Pil's visit to Japan in November 1973 consisted of Seoul's expression of regret to the Japanese government and people, Seoul's pledge to investigate Kim Tong-un with a view toward punishing him in accordance with law should his role in the kidnapping be proven, and Seoul's commitment not to hold Kim Dae Jung liable for his words and deeds during his ill-fated visit to Japan and to allow him to exercise his freedom, including the freedom to leave the country.[41]

The Kim Dae Jung incident nonetheless had adverse effects on Tokyo-Seoul relations. The Japanese government postponed the 7th Japan-ROK cabinet conference, which had been scheduled for September, and suspended economic assistance to Seoul. Not only did Seoul fail to receive the 150 million-dollar loan that had been approved in the 1972 cabinet conference but Seoul also missed the opportunity to engage in negotiations with Tokyo on a new loan request for $270-280 million.[42] Following the political settlement, however, the 7th Japan-ROK cabinet conference was held in December.[43]

---

kidnapping. "Kim Dae Jung napch'i, chungjong chojikjok pomhaeng······ponbo tandok ipsu" [Kim Dae Jung Kidnapping Was KCIA's Well-planned Crim······ This Paper Has Exclusive Information], *Dong-A ilbo*, February 19, 1998.

41 Yamamoto, "Nihon to Kankoku," 184-187. Diplomatic documents declassified by the ROK government in February 2006 show that Japanese Prime Minister Tanaka Kakuei told South Korean Prime Minister Kim Jong Pil that Japan's demand for a continued investigation of the incident embodied in the political settlement was simply "*tatemae*" [for appearance only], not "*honne*" [real intention]. "Kim Dae Jung jiken, motto shinzo ga shiritai" [The Kim Dae Jung Incident: We Want to Know the Truth], *Asahi shinbun*, February 7, 2006, editorial.

42 Yamamoto, "Nihon to Kankoku," 189.

The deterioration of the political situation in South Korea spawned more problems in Tokyo-Seoul relations. In January 1974 President Park Chung Hee proclaimed a series of emergency decrees aimed at stifling all manner of political dissent. Under the decrees anyone who criticized the *yusin* constitution that had been adopted following the declaration of martial law in October 1972 would be subject to arrest without warrant for trial in an emergency court martial. The maximum penalty would be 15 years of imprisonment. In April the maximum penalty was increased to death.[44]

The South Korean authorities arrested scores of students, implicating them in an alleged plot to overthrow the ROK government. Among those arrested were two Japanese citizens—Hayakawa Yoshiharu, a graduate student at Seoul National University, and Tachikawa Masaki, a freelance writer. They were later sentenced to 20 years of imprisonment by a special military court for participating in an alleged plot spearheaded by an underground student organization called the National Democratic Youth Student League (*Minch'ong Hangnyon*). The uncooperative and evasive behavior of the South Korean authorities in dealing with the Japanese diplomats in Seoul, who attempted in vain to protect the rights of their compatriots, elevated the arrest to a diplomatic issue.[45]

Then, on August 15, the anniversary of Korea's liberation from Japanese colonial rule, a serious incident erupted. A 22-year-old Korean resident in Japan named Mun Se-gwang tried to assassinate President Park, killing his wife in the process. Mun had entered South Korea with an illegally-obtained Japanese passport. He had stolen the handgun that he used to fire the fatal shot from a police box in Osaka, Japan. A Japanese national, Mrs. Yoshii Mikiko, had helped Mun to obtain the passport. What is more, according to the South Korean authorities, the preparations for the terroristic act had taken place in Japan under the

---

43 Gaimusho, ed., *Waga gaiko no kinkyo, 1974*, 243.
44 B. C. Koh, "South Korea, North Korea, and Japan," *Pacific Community* (Tokyo) 6, no. 2 (Jan. 1975), 209.
45 Ibid., 209-210; Gaimusho, ed., *Waga gaiko no kinkyo, 1975* (Tokyo: Okurasho,

guidance of North Korea-oriented Korean residents' organization, *Ch'ongnyon* (or *Chosoren* in Japanese).[46]

All this suggested to South Korea that while North Korea was the ultimate culprit, Japan also bore a measure of responsibility. Tokyo's perspective, however, was entirely different. On the day the incident occurred, the director of the Northeast Asia Division of the Japanese Foreign Ministry stated in a press briefing that the Japanese government bore no responsibility for crimes committed by individual Japanese citizens abroad, let alone for the acts of a Korean resident in Japan, a foreigner. He added that obtaining a passport illegally means that an individual, not the government, has done something bad. Two days later, the Japanese Foreign Ministry reiterated its view that the Japanese government was not directly liable, either legally or morally, for the Mun Se-gwang incident; it nonetheless expressed regret that Mun was a Korean resident in Japan, pledging that the Japanese police would thoroughly investigate all matters relating to the incident.[47]

In order to defuse the crisis, Japan took the extraordinarily conciliatory step of sending its prime minister to the funeral of Mrs. Park on August 19. Tanaka Kakuei was the only prime minister and the highest-ranking foreign dignitary at the funeral. He personally conveyed condolences to President Park and had a 30-minute talk with the South Korean leader.[48]

The Tanaka visit, however, failed to produce the desired effect for Japan. Underscoring the Japanese government's responsibility, South Korea demanded not only an official apology but also the extradition of Mun's alleged collaborators in Japan to South Korea and, failing that, their prompt prosecution and the suppression of the activities of *Ch'ongnyon*. Tokyo's failure to comply with these demands led to widespread demonstrations in South Korea. Given the stringent controls

---

Insatsu-kyoku, 1975), 68-69.
46 Koh, "South Korea, North Korea, and Japan," 210.
47 Yamamoto, "Nihon to Kankoku," 192-93.
48 Koh, "South Korea, North Korea, and Japan," 213-14.

over public assembly in South Korea, foreign observers, including Japanese newsmen, were quick to surmise that the outbursts of mass anger over Japan were either staged or inspired by the Park government. The most serious demonstration occurred on September 6, when a group of 200 South Korean youths invaded the Japanese embassy in Seoul, tore down a Japanese flag, ransacked a number of offices, and set fire to an embassy car.[49] The ransacking of the Japanese embassy had been fueled by remarks made by Japanese Foreign Minister Kimura Toshio on the previous day suggesting that the ROK was not the only legitimate government on the entire Korean peninsula and that he saw no military threat to the South emanating from the North.[50]

After intense negotiations, during which Seoul reportedly bypassed the Japanese Foreign Ministry and appealed directly to former Prime Minister Sato Eisaku and Shiina Etsusaburo, the vice-president of the LDP and a former foreign minister, the two sides reached a compromise on defusing the crisis. Prime Minister Tanaka dispatched Shiina as his special envoy carrying his personal letter to President Park. The letter, which Shiina delivered to Park on September 19, reiterated Japan's official position on the Mun Se-gwang incident. It expressed regret that the preparations for Mun's acts in Seoul had occurred in Japan, pledged appropriate measures to prevent similar occurrences in the future, promised full cooperation with Seoul's investigation of the incident, and assured Seoul that Japan would do its best to punish illegal acts aimed at overthrowing the ROK government.[51]

At Seoul's insistence and pursuant to a previous agreement, Shiina made a supplemental verbal explanation, specifically mentioning *Chosoren* as a possible object of governmental regulation. He told President Park that Japan "understands" the hostile nature of *Chosoren* toward Seoul, frowns upon its utilization by North Korean agents for

---

49 Ibid., 215.
50 Gaimusho, ed., *Waga gaiko no kinkyo, 1975*, 67.
51 Yamamoto, "Nihon to Kankoku," 193-95; Gaimusho, ed., *Waga gaiko no kinkyo, 1975*, 68.

subversive activities directed against Seoul, and will take stern measures if its members violate Japan's domestic laws.[52] These remarks were recorded by the Seoul side and initialed by Ushiroku Torao, the Japanese ambassador to Seoul who had accompanied Shiina to the Blue House. While the two sides disagreed sharply on the nature of the minutes of the Park-Shiina meeting—with Seoul asserting that it was a legally binding diplomatic document, and Tokyo insisting that it was not—,[53] the result nonetheless represented a classic diplomatic compromise. Seoul scored a symbolic victory for which Tokyo paid a relatively low price; by promising to take stern measures against *Chosoren* if and only if its members violate Japan's domestic laws, Tokyo did not really assume a new obligation vis-a-vis Seoul.

In February 1975, citing the importance of South Korea's "friendly relations with Japan," the Park government released the two Japanese citizens who had been waiting for a review of their verdict by the ROK supreme court.[54] In July of the same year the so-called "second political settlement" of the Kim Dae Jung incident occurred when Foreign Minister Kim Tong-jo handed Ambassador Nishiyama a note verbale, which stated that although the ROK government had failed to find sufficient evidence to indict Kim Tong-un, the diplomat implicated in the Kim Dae Jung kidnapping, it had stripped him of his position as a government employee. With Tokyo's acceptance of Seoul's explanation as evidence that the latter had done its best, the incident was officially closed.[55] As will

---

52 Koh, "South Korea, North Korea, and Japan," 216.
53 Yamamoto, "Nihon to Kankoku," 195-96. South Korean diplomatic documents declassified in January 2005 reveal that the Park Chung Hee government even considered breaking off diplomatic relations with Japan over the issue but the US intervened to forestall such a turn of events. Sang-Hun Choe, "Attempts to Kill Park in '74 Strained Ties with Seoul, Papers Show," *Japan Times*, January 21, 2005; "Chongbu, Mun se-gwang sakon tung oegyo munso konggae" [Government Makes Public Diplomatic Documents Relating to Mun Se-gwang and Other Incidents], *Chosun ilbo*, January 20, 2005.
54 Gaimusho, ed., *Waga gaiko no kinkyo, 1975*, 69.

be noted below, however, Kim Dae Jung would become a factor in Japan's Korea policy in 1980.

The last few years of the Park Chung Hee era saw a marked improvement in Tokyo-Seoul relations. One of the more notable developments was the entry into force of two Japan-ROK agreements on continental shelf in June 1978, four and a half years after they were signed. One delineated the boundaries of the continental shelf and the other provided for its joint exploration for oil and natural gas. Over China's protest, Japan-ROK joint exploration of the continental shelf in the South China Sea began in October 1979. This not only marked the beginning of a long-term cooperation between the two countries but also signaled the dawning of a "new era of cooperative relations."[56]

The assassination of Park Chung Hee in October 1979 did not disrupt Tokyo-Seoul relations. Prime Minister Ohira Masayoshi, in expressing his government's condolences, stressed that Japan would continue to pursue the policy of "maintaining and strengthening a friendly cooperative relationship" with the ROK.[57] The unexpected event did, however, force the postponement of the 11th Japan-ROK cabinet conference.

When the Seoul government, which was under the control of Chun Doo Hwan since his seizure of power in December 1979, arrested, tried, and sentenced Kim Dae Jung to death in September 1980 on charges of having violated national security and anti-communist laws, it created a new problem for Tokyo. If, as had been reported in the Japanese press, one of the charges against Kim pertained to his alleged role in the establishment of what Seoul views as an anti-state organization in Japan in 1973, that would constitute a violation of the terms of the political settlement of his kidnapping case between Tokyo and Seoul. For Seoul

---

55 Yamamoto, "Nihon to Kankoku," 196-97; Nagano, ed., *Nihon gaiko handobukku*, p. 193.
56 Ibid., 182, 184 and 196; Gaimusho, ed., *Wagan gaiko no kinkyo, 1979* (Tokyo: Okurasho Insatsu-kyoku, 1979), 50-51; ibid., *1980* (Tokyo, 1980), 52.
57 Ibid., 18 and 52.

had pledged not to make an issue of what Kim had said or done during his stay in Japan prior to the kidnapping.[58]

Under domestic political pressure, the Japanese government therefore asked the Seoul government to provide the full text of the trial military court's verdict. After initially pledging cooperation, Seoul later changed its mind, informing Tokyo on October 7, 1980 that "because the general practice in [South] Korean trials is to limit access to the text of judgments to prosecutors, the accused, defense attorneys, and others concerned with the trial, it will be difficult to comply with the Japanese government's request."[59]

It was only after Chun Doo Hwan commuted Kim Dae Jung's sentence to life imprisonment in January 1981 after the ROK Supreme Court had confirmed the original verdict that Tokyo-Seoul relations returned to a normal state.[60] This was signaled by Japanese foreign

---

[58] *Yomiuri shinbun* reported on August 15, 1980 that the indictment read by the prosecutor in the courtroom listed Kim's 1973 activity in Japan, even though a summary of the indictment published by the Seoul government omitted it. See Aochi Shin, "Kim Dae Jung gunji saiban to Nihon seifu no shisei" [Kim Dae Jung's Court Martial and the Posture of the Japanese Government], I, *Gekkan Shakaito* [The Socialist Party Monthly], no. 291 (November 1980), 14.

[59] Aochi Shin, "Kim Dae Jung gunji saiban to Nihon seifu no shisei," II, *Gekkan Shakaito*, no. 292 (December 1980), 118.

[60] Chun Doo Hwan's commutation of Kim Dae Jung's death sentence was part of a deal with the US under which President Reagan would receive Chun as one of the first foreign heads of state since his inauguration. Chun saw that as an opportunity to bolster his shaky legitimacy. Kim Dae Jung himself, however, felt that his commutation owed to the efforts of those in Japan who supported his cause and exerted pressure on the Japanese government to save his life. See Kim Dae Jung and Yamahana Sadao, "Sokoku minshuka no tameni tatakau" [Struggling for the Democratization of the Fatherland], *Gekkan Shakaito*, No. 328 (September 1983), 125-31. This is a transcript of an interview Yamahana conducted in the US where Kim was spending what amounted to his second exile since December 1982, when the Chun regime released him and allowed him to go the US for medical treatment. Yamahana, a Japan Socialist Party (JSP) member of the House of Representatives, served as the chairman of the JSP in 1993-94.

minister Ito's attendance of Chun Doo Hwan's inauguration as the ROK president in March 1981.[61] In September of the same year the bilateral cabinet conference was held in Seoul for the first time in three years. The main agenda of this conference was the Chun government's request for $6 billion loan from Japan to finance the fifth five-year plan that was scheduled to begin in 1982; the request had been unveiled during the foreign ministers' meeting in Tokyo in the preceding month.[62]

Seoul's loan request had at least two novel features. First, its size was bigger than anything Japan had previously encountered. It was, in fact, many times—7.5 times, to be exact—the total "economic cooperation" package accompanying the Japan-ROK normalization in 1965. Second, Seoul explicitly linked its request to Tokyo's security interests. Seoul argued that since Seoul was spending an inordinate amount of money to protect the security not only of itself but also of Japan, Tokyo had an obligation to provide economic assistance to Seoul, which would be tantamount to burden-sharing.[63]

Seoul's linking of its loan request with Tokyo's security interests was based in no small measure on their shared perception that the security of the ROK is a pivotal factor in Japan's security equation. This notion had been repeatedly reaffirmed in Japan-U.S. joint communiques as well as in the joint communiques of Japan-ROK cabinet conferences. Even though the words used in these communiques had changed over the years, the underlying concept had remained more or less intact.[64]

---

61 Gaimusho, ed., *Waga gaiko no kinkyo, 1981* (Tokyo: Okurasho Insatsu-kyoku, 1981), 57. Chun, who had been the ROK president since September 1980, was inaugurated anew in March 1981 after being elected under a new constitution.
62 Gaimuho, ed., *Waga gaiko no kinkyo, 1982* (Tokyo: Okurasho Insatsu-kyoku, 1982), 24 and 64.
63 For an in-depth analysis of the negotiations between Seoul and Tokyo on the former's loan request, see Chong-Sik Lee, *Japan and Korea*, 103-39.
64 For an insightful analysis of subtle change in the phraseology of communiques as well as of statements in the annual publications of the Japanese Foreign Ministry, see Gong Yooshik, "Hanbando t'ong'il kwa Ilbon

Nonetheless, Tokyo resisted Seoul's attempt to make the linkage between loan and security; nor would it agree to the amount and terms of the loan Seoul had initially put forth. After protracted negotiations, the two sides finally reached an agreement, which was announced during Prime Minister Nakasone Yasuhiro's historic visit to South Korea in January 1983. Tokyo agreed to provide Seoul with a $4 billion loan over seven years beginning retroactively in 1982. Of the total, $1.85 billion would be an Official Development Assistance (ODA) loan in yen, $1.8 billion would come from the Export-Import Bank, and $350 million would be commercial bank loans.[65]

Nakasone's visit to Seoul marked a historic milestone in Japan-ROK relations, because it was the first time that a Japanese prime minister had made a state visit. None of the three previous visits by Japanese prime ministers to South Korea had been on that august level. Prime Minister Sato Eiskaku attended President Park Chung Hee's inaugurations in 1967 and 1971, and Prime Minister Tanaka Kakuei attended Mrs. Park's funeral in 1974. Nakasone was given an exceptionally warm welcome by Chun Doo Hwan, and the two hit it off. The apparent ease with which the two leaders developed rapport owed in part to Nakasone's meticulous preparations, which included learning some Korean phrases and songs.[66]

Nakasone also created much goodwill in Seoul by mentioning the "need for a penitent attitude toward the unfortunate past" and underscoring Korea's contributions to the early development of Japanese culture and society.[67] Even though, in the view of many South Koreans, he

---

ui yokhal: Ilbon ui tae Hanbando chongch'aek ui pyonhwa wa ap'uro ui chonmang" [The Reunification of the Korean Peninsula and the Role of Japan: Change in Japan's Policy toward the Korean Peninsula and Future Prospects], a paper presented to the Fall Conference of the Korean Sociological Association, December 13-14, 1990, Seoul.

65 Lee, *Japan and Korea*, 132; for a summary of the loan negotiations, see Table 12 on p. 133. See also Nabatame Tadao et al, "Gaiko rongi no shoten" [Focal Points in Discussion on Diplomacy], *Rippo to chosa* [Legislation and Investigation] (Tokyo), no. 117 (August 1983), 9-10.

66 Lee, *Japan and Korea*, 131-32.

did not go far enough, it was clear that his visit had elevated Japan-ROK relations to a "new plane"—*shinjigen* in Japanese and *sinch'awon* in Korean—as the Nakasone-Chun joint statement stressed.[68]

Nakasone's decision to place a top priority on Tokyo-Seoul ties was most probably related to his political needs. With a relatively fragile power base in the LDP, he turned to diplomacy to fortify his leadership credentials. Japan's $4 billion loan to South Korea, to which Nakasone's political will made a decisive contribution, was linked to the Tokyo-Washington alliance. The *Mainichi shinbun* went so far as to characterize the Nakasone visit to Seoul as part of his strategy toward the US, noting that Japan's $4 billion economic cooperation with South Korea would indirectly lighten both Seoul's military expenditures and Washington's security burden.[69]

When Chun Doo Hwan returned the Nakasone visit by making a three-day state visit to Japan in September 1984, it marked another milestone in the annals of Japan-ROK relations. Chun became the first head of state of the ROK to make a state visit. One of the symbolically important highlights of the Chun visit was the Japanese emperor's expression of regret. At a banquet in honor of Chun and his entourage on September 6, the Emperor said: "It is truly regretful (*makotoni ikan de ari*) that during this century there was a time when an unfortunate past between our two countries existed; I think that it must never be repeated." A product of negotiation among the Prime Minister's Office, the Foreign Ministry and the Imperial Household Agency, this statement fell

---

67 Ibid., 132.
68 Asked to explain the meaning of the phrase in the joint statement, "Japan-ROK relations will develop to a new plane," Nakasone said in the House of Representatives on January 28, 1983 that since his visit marked the first time that a Japanese prime minister made an official visit (*koshiki homon*) to the ROK, it helped to "elevate Japan-ROK relations to friendly relations that have not existed until now." Nabatame et al, "Gaiko rongi no shoten," 10.
69 Ishikawa Sho, "'Nikkan shinjidai' to shinbun hodo" ["New Era in Japan-ROK Relations" and the Newspaper Coverage], *Sekai* [The World] (Tokyo), no. 468 (November 1984), 114-15.

considerably short of being an apology.⁷⁰

Nonetheless, it was the first time that the emperor had expressed regret over the "unfortunate past" between the two countries. Chun Doo Hwan's positive response needs to be understood in that context. In his words, "there is a common proverb in both of our countries that says 'the ground hardens after the rain.' I understand it to mean that although friends may fight sometimes, they open their hearts to each other after the moment passes, becoming closer friends than before. I believe that the unfortunate past between our two countries must become a valuable foundation on which to seek a future ROK-Japan relationship that is brighter and friendlier than now."⁷¹

The joint communique issued by Nakasone and Chun on September 8 used such phrases as "a new chapter in the history of Japan-ROK relations," "building an ever-lasting relationship of neighborly friendship and cooperation······from a global perspective," and "the maintenance and development of a cooperative relationship by Japan and the ROK, [both of which] pursue the common ideologies of freedom, peace and democracy, will not only be in the interest of both peoples but also contribute to the peace and stability of East Asia and to the world peace."⁷²

The communique noted that the two leaders had agreed on the importance of expanding people-to-people exchanges, particularly those involving the youths of both countries, economic cooperation and cooperation in industrial technology. Under the latter rubric the two leaders applauded the program under which South Korean technicians

---

70 Ibid., 116-118. According to Yamamoto Tsuyoshi, the Prime Minister's Office ended up imposing its will on the other two agencies in drafting the Emperor's remarks known in Japanese as *okotoba*. The Emperor first noted Japan's indebtedness to Korea in scholarship, culture, and technology during the early period, especially the sixth and seventh centuries before expressing his regret over the "unfortunate past." Yamamoto, "Nihon to Kankoku," 224-25.

71 Ibid., 325-26.

72 For the Japanese-language text of the joint communique, see Gaimusho, ed., *Waga gaiko no kinkyo, 1985* (Tokyo: Okurasho Insatsu-kyoku, 1985), 477-80.

receive training in Japan. The two leaders also discussed the issue of improving the legal status and treatment of Korean residents in Japan, taking into account their special historical background. No specifics were disclosed, however, suggesting that much remained to be ironed out in that arena.

In short, the beginning of mutual visits by the top leaders of Japan and the ROK did herald the dawn of a new era (*shinjidai*) in their bilateral relations. There were, however, skeptics and critics on both side of the Sea of Japan (or the East Sea [*Tonghae*] as the Koreans call it). In Japan people in progressive circles were displeased with the accentuation of Japan's one-sided policy—that is, the policy favoring the ROK at the expense of the DPRK—and with the hollowness of the Emperor's *okotoba*. In the words of the distinguished historian of Korea, Hatada Takashi, "words alone are not enough; there remain many, many things which call for reflection in daily behavior [of the Japanese people] such as textbook description [of history] and the employment of Korean residents in Japan." In South Korea Kim Young Sam, then leader of the opposition camp, asserted that "the aim of President Chun's visit to Japan is to build a political and material base for maintaining and strengthening his repressive system." Kim Dae Jung, who was in the US at the time, told the *Asahi shinbun* that "while the Emperor's apology [sic] is a great present, Chun Doo Hwan should apologize, too. That would make his visit to Japan a success."[73]

As the two countries marked the 20th anniversary of their diplomatic normalization in 1985, they shared the assessment that their bilateral relations had grown markedly during the preceding two decades. Not only had the two countries become each other's major trading partners, but governmental consultations and exchanges had multiplied at a steady rate. Notwithstanding periodic disputes over a variety of issues, the

---

73 Ishikawa, "'Nikkan shinjidai' to shinbun hodo," 112-13; 116-18. Kim Dae Jung apparently meant to say that Chun Doo Hwan should apologize for his bloody suppression of the Kwangju uprising in May 1980 and for his repression of dissidents such as Kim Dae Jung.

bilateral relationship on the whole had been mutually beneficial.

Most notable among the sources of continuing discord, however, were the perennial imbalance in trade and related issues and the failure to "settle the unfortunate past" once and for all. During the 1965-1985 period, the bilateral trade grew an astounding 50.6 times—from $221 million to $11,189 million. (See Table 3) In none of the 20 years, however, did South Korea enjoy a surplus in its balance of trade with Japan. The cumulative deficit for the period stood at $30.3 billion.

As noted previously, a major source of the trade imbalance was South Korea's heavy reliance on Japanese capital and intermediate goods in manufacturing goods for export. In Seoul's view, nonetheless, visible and invisible trade barriers as well as the reluctance of Japanese companies to transfer technology to South Korean firms were key variables in the equation. Even though the Japanese government adopted an "action program" in July 1985 with a view toward facilitating foreign exports to Japan, Seoul found the program more cosmetic than substantive.[74]

The issue of "settling the past" proved to be singularly resilient. Periodic pronouncements by high-ranking Japanese politicians and officials justifying Japan's colonial rule over Korea or extolling its alleged benefits grated on the sensibilities of the Koreans. The textbook controversy, which erupted in the summer of 1982, served to aggravate the situation.[75] Public expressions of regret by the emperor and prime ministers at periodic intervals, while helping to alleviate the South Koreans' outrage, had nonetheless fallen short of mollifying them. These issues would continue to haunt Tokyo-Seoul relations during the third decade of normalization and beyond.

---

74 Gaimusho, *Waga gaiko no kinkyo, 1985*, 82; for Seoul's reaction, see "Ilbon-sik olbomurigi: sijang kaebang haendong kyehoek silsok opta" [Japanese-style equivocation: the action program for market opening lacks substance], editorial, *Hankook ilbo*, August 1, 1985.
75 For an illuminating account of the textbook controversy, see Lee, *Japan and Korea*, 141-64.

Conclusion

Of the various concepts and ideas proposed by the contending schools of thought, none appears as potent as identity, a core concept in constructivism, in generating plausible explanations of many of the developments examined in this chapter. One must, however, differentiate between state identity and regime identity. Unlike the former, which, once constructed, is relatively durable, the latter is constructed anew each time a new leader takes the reins of power. Regime identity is less important to states marked by relative political stability than it is to states where regime changes occur in the aftermath of a revolution or a coup d'etat or where even transitions based on elections usher in regimes that differ markedly from their predecessors. Japan exemplifies the former, while South Korea illustrates the latter.

South Korea's regime identities during the decades reviewed in this chapter were molded by the background, personal proclivities, and political needs of its leaders, and they profoundly affected Seoul's policy toward Japan, either directly or indirectly. The most salient aspects of regime identity during the First Republic (1948-1960) of Syngman Rhee were his anti-communism and anti-Japanism. The former was a function of his strong desire to reunify the peninsula by prevailing over the Communists in the North, the bitter experiences of the Korean War, the tenacity of Communist resistance in the South, and the internal political uses to which he put anti-communism. Rhee's anti-Japanism, another hallmark of his regime identity, was traceable to his long experience as an independence movement leader during the Japanese colonial period. His unflinching hard-line vis-a-vis Japan both reflected and reinforced such identity.[76]

---

76 On Syngman Rhee's background and political career, see Richard C. Allen, *Korea's Syngman Rhee: An Unauthorized Portrait* (Richmond, VT & Tokyo: Charles E. Tuttle Co., 1960); Robert T. Oliver, *Syngman Rhee: The Man Behind the Myth* (New York: Dodd Mead & Co., 1960); Chong-Sik Lee, *The Politics of Korean Nationalism* (Berkeley: University of California Press, 1965); Lew

Of the probable sources of the identity of the Park Chung Hee regime, two stand out: his Japanese background and his need to legitimize his coup d'etat. Noteworthy aspects of Park's Japanese background are his early education in a Japanese controlled normal school, subsequent training in the Japanese Military Academy, and service as an officer in the Japanese Imperial Army, all of which helped him to appreciate Japan's potential value in his quest for modernization. Park's May 1960 coup, the first forcible seizure of power in South Korea's political history, had not only trampled upon South Korea's constitutional order but violated his own *mobomsaeng* [model student] norms, which valued discipline, obedience to superiors, duty, and self-sacrifice. Justifying his coup as a "radical but unavoidable surgery to save the life" of Korea, Park had pledged to dedicate his life to fulfill the goals of his "revolution"—to construct a fatherland that is both prosperous and free from humiliation and poverty.[77]

Launching South Korea on the path to economic growth, then, was Park's chosen means of vindicating his coup d'etat, bolstering his shaky legitimacy, and constructing his regime identity. Such political needs, when coupled with his Japanese background, may help us understand Park's all-out push for Japan-ROK diplomatic normalization. A related dimension of his regime identity was authoritarianism, to which his *mobomsaeng* norms and military background contributed and which was deemed necessary to carry out his state-led modernization scheme. His increasingly authoritarian rule, culminating in the sweeping change of the rules of the political game in October 1972, known as the October Revitalizing Reforms (*Siwol yusin*), spawned the Kim Dae Jung kidnapping incident. Although it created the first serious crisis in Japan-ROK relations since normalization, the crisis was eventually defused by a "political settlement," a product of the shared perception by the two sides

---

Young Ick, *Yi Sung-man ui salm kwa kkum: taet'ongnyong'i toegi kkaji* [The Life and Dreams of Syngman Rhee: Pre-Presidential Years] (Seoul: Joongang Ilbosa, 1996).

77 Koh, *The Foreign Policy Systems of North and South Korea*, 82-85.

that the stakes were too high to permit any disruption in their bilateral, especially economic, ties.

Another incident, also traceable to Park's authoritarian rule, temporarily strained Tokyo-Seoul relations—namely, the Mun Se-gwang incident in which a Korean resident of Japan killed Park's wife in an abortive assassination attempt on Park. Mun's numerous links with Japan gave the Park government an excuse to demand Japan's crackdown on *Ch'ongnyon*, the pro-North Korean residents' federation in Japan. In the end, this, too, produced a political settlement in which Tokyo provided symbolic relief to Seoul without really yielding anything substantive.

The problem Park's successor, Chun Doo Hwan, faced in constructing his regime identity was not fundamentally different from what Park had to cope with—namely, establishing legitimacy. For Chun, too, had seized power in a coup. In one significant respect, however, Chun's problem was more serious than Park's. Whereas Park's coup had been relatively bloodless, Chun's path to power had been strewn with hundreds of dead bodies both from the December 12, 1979 coup and, more important, from the suppression of the May 1980 uprising in Kwangju. Nothing therefore was more important for Chun than to gloss over the image of a murderer and a usurper and to construct a regime identity that bore the stamp of approval from Seoul's principal ally, Washington, and quasi-ally and major trading partner, Tokyo.

All this helps to explain Chun's decision to spare the life of Kim Dae Jung, whom his regime had sentenced to death. Japan's firm stand on the issue was an important, albeit not a decisive, factor in the decision. Chun's need to seek the help of the United States in shoring up his legitimacy also played a major role in his decision. Having consolidated his power beyond challenge, Chun attempted to put pressure on Japan to provide a massive loan, making an explicit linkage between the loan request and Japan's security. In the end, it was the political will of Japanese Prime Minister Nakasone that was instrumental in resolving the new dispute.

Japan's dual identity as a trading state and a peace-loving state dependent on an alliance with the US is also noteworthy in understanding its policy toward Seoul. The resolution of the disputes revolving around Kim Dae Jung during both the Park Chung Hee and Chun Doo Hwan eras, the Mun Se-gwang incident during the Park era, and, finally, the loan dispute during the Chun era owed primarily to political decisions by the top leaders in Seoul and Tokyo, who were driven by identity needs of varying intensity.

The concept of two-level games is also relevant to an elucidation of some of the events delineated above. The constraints of Level II game clearly delimited the scope of "win-sets" for Japan and the ROK alike during their protracted normalization talks. Despite or because of its authoritarian nature, the Park regime encountered virulent popular opposition to normalization on what the public perceived as humiliating terms. That compelled the regime to draw a line beyond which it would not retreat. As a democracy, Japan was more constrained by public opinion than South Korea was. The need to appease public opinion and secure support for Diet ratification, therefore, defined the boundaries of Japan's win-set. The compromise reached in the end plainly fell in the intersection of the two sides' win-sets.

Japan's response to the incidents involving Kim Dae Jung—first, his kidnapping by KCIA agents during the Park era and next, his near execution on grounds of treason during the early months of Chun Doo Hwan's rule—was also shaped to a considerable extent by the dynamics of its Level II game. Pressure exerted by a coalition of groups, including opposition politicians, prominent intellectuals, and religious leaders, helped to define the Japanese government's win-set, from which the final outcome could not digress. In both cases, however, one may argue that Level II game was either nonexistent or negligible in South Korea. External pressure emanating from Tokyo and, especially, Washington played a pivotal role in shaping Seoul's behavior. Pressure alone, however, would not have sufficed. It was the convergence of external pressure and identity-related internal interests that helped to mold the outcome, which proved to be beneficial to all concerned—the regime in Seoul, Japan, the US, and, most important, Kim Dae Jung himself.

The role of historical legacy or historical memory was forcefully displayed during the long, intermittent negotiations on diplomatic normalization. Its continuing salience is shown by the frequency with which emotions are aroused in South Korea by Japanese political leaders' statements that are perceived in that country as glossing over Japan's past misdeeds and by the attention paid in both countries to the Japanese emperor's *okotoba* on the "unfortunate past" between them.[78]

Finally, none of this should obscure the effects of economic factors on Japan-ROK relations, which are closely linked to identity—Japan's trading state identity and regime identity constructed by successive South Korean leaders.[79] The single most important explanatory variable for their diplomatic normalization was the convergence of perceived economic interests, and two decades of interactions proved that the mutual perceptions had been right on the mark. The political settlement of the crises spawned by Kim Dae Jung, Mun Se-gwang, and the loan request, too, was intertwined with economic considerations. None of these factors, however, was potent enough in isolation. It was the conjunction of two or more factors, such as political dynamics underpinning regime identity and related economic needs, that helped to ameliorate conflict and generate cooperation.

---

78 For an informative discussion of the role of historical legacies in Japan-Korean relations, see Bridges, *Japan and Korea* in the 1990s, 6-19.
79 An in-depth discussion of the economic dimension of Tokyo—Seoul relations may be found in ibid., 87-117.

CHAPTER 6

Japan-ROK Summit Diplomacy, 1990-1995

Japan-ROK relations continued to expand during the third decade of normalization. In the political arena inter-governmental exchanges and consultations multiplied, of which the most notable emblem was summit diplomacy. In the 1990s North Korea's nuclear weapons program, whether imaginary or real, helped to bring Tokyo and Seoul closer, spawning new mechanisms for consultations and cooperation. Notwithstanding such wide-ranging cooperation, discord erupted at periodic intervals. Statements by heavyweight Japanese politicians concerning Japan's past relations with Korea helped to fuel friction.

In the economic realm perpetual trade imbalance in Tokyo's favor strained the bilateral relations. Nonetheless, that did not prevent the volume of trade from increasing at a steady rate. Technology transfer and fisheries also provided grist for friction. On the whole, however, the third decade was notable for the prevalence of cooperation.

Summit Diplomacy

If, by "summit diplomacy," we mean the mechanism by which top leaders of nations get together with the aim of exchanging views and finding solutions to pending issues, then it can take a variety of forms. In the context of Japan-ROK relations, two principal ways in which summit meetings can occur are visits by top leaders to each other's country and their get-togethers in a third country on the sidelines of multilateral international conferences.

The former in turn can be divided into (1) state or official visits, (2) working visits, (3) unofficial visits occasioned by special circumstances. As Table 6 shows, if one were to count all three types, then one would get a total of 34 during the 57-year period, 1948-2005.

Two of the three unofficial visits by President Syngman Rhee, however, occurred during the period when Japan was under US military occupation; the sovereign power in Japan in those years, therefore, was the US, specifically the Supreme Commander for Allied Powers (SCAP). Rhee was therefore a guest of SCAP, not the Japanese government. It was

<Table 6> Visits by Top Leaders between Japan and South Korea

Date	Nature of Visit
1948.10.10	ROK President Syngman Rhee makes an unofficial visit to Japan
1950. 2.16	" "
1953. 1. 6	" "
	Rhee meets Prime Minister Yoshida Shigeru
1961.11.11	Park Chung Hee, chairman of the Supreme Council for National Reconstruction, stops over in Tokyo en route to Washington; Park meets Prime Minister Ikeda Hayato
1967. 6.30	PM Sato Eisaku attends Park's inauguration as ROK president in Seoul
1971. 7. 1	Sato attends Park's inauguration again
1974. 8.19	PM Tanaka Kakuei attends the funeral of Mrs. Park Chung Hee in Seoul
1983. 1.11-12	PM Nakasone Yasuhiro makes a state visit to South Korea

1984. 9. 6- 8	Pres. Chun Doo Hwan makes a state visit to Japan
1986. 9.20-21	PM Nakasone attends the opening ceremony of the Asian Games in Seoul
1988. 2.24-25	PM Takeshita Noboru attends the inauguration of Pres. Roh Tae Woo in Seoul
1988. 9.16-17	Takeshita attends the opening ceremony of the Seoul Olympic Games
1990. 5.24-26	Pres. Roh Tae Woo makes a state visit to Japan
1991. 1. 9-10	PM Kaifu Toshiki makes a state visit to S.Korea
1992. 1.16-18	PM Miyazawa Kiichi makes a state visit to S. Korea
1992.11. 8	Pres. Roh Tae Woo makes a working visit to Kyoto, Japan
1993.11. 6- 7	PM Hosokawa Morihiro makes a working visit to Kyongju, S. Korea
1994. 3.24-26	Pres. Kim Young Sam makes a state visit to Japan
1994. 7.23-24	PM Murayama Tomiichi makes a state visit to S. Korea
1995.11.17-20	Pres. Kim Young Sam attends an Asia Pacific Economic Cooperation (APEC) meeting in Osaka, Japan; Kim holds a 45-minute meeting with Murayama on November 18
1996. 6.22-23	PM Hashimoto Ryutaro makes a working visit to Cheju, S. Korea
1997. 1.25-26	Pres. Kim Young Sam makes a working visit to Beppu, Japan
1998.10.7 -10	Pres. Kim Dae Jung makes a state visit to Japan
1999. 3.19-21	PM Obuchi Keizo makes a state visit to S.Korea
2000. 5.29	PM Mori Yoshiro makes a working visit to South Korea
2000. 9.22-24	Pres. Kim Dae Jung makes a working visit to Atami, Japan
2001. 10.15	PM Koizumi Junichiro makes a working visit to South Korea
2002. 3.12-13	PM Koizumi makes an official visit to S. Korea
2002. 6.30-7.2	Pres. Kim Dae Jung visits Japan to attend the closing ceremony of the 2002 FIFA World Cup Korea/Japan and holds a summit meeting with PM Koizumi
2003. 2.24-25	PM Koizumi attends the inauguration of Pres. Roh Moo Hyun and holds a summit meeting.
2003. 5.6-9	Pres. Roh Moo Hyun makes a state visit to Japan
2004. 7.21-22	PM Koizumi makes a working visit to Cheju, S. Korea
2004. 12.17	Pres. Roh Moo Hyun makes a working visit to Ibusuki city, Kanagawa prefecture, Japan.
2005. 6.20-21	PM Koizumi makes a working visit to S. Korea

only after Japan regained sovereignty that Rhee held a brief meeting with a Japanese Prime Minister—Yoshida Shigeru—during a visit with General Mark W. Clark, commander-in-chief, United Nations Command. No meaningful exchange of views, let alone negotiation, took place.[1]

Of the four meetings between the top leaders of Japan and South Korea during the ensuing two decades were, all but one were, strictly speaking, not so much meetings as encounters. Park's brief stopover in Tokyo was the lone exception, for he and Japanese Prime Minister Ikeda Hayato held two hours of talks that proved to be a milestone in the conduct of normalization talks.[2] It is worth noting that in November 1972, seven years after normalization, Park had agreed to make a state visit to Japan but abruptly canceled it, citing domestic circumstances. The cancellation was announced just three days after Park had declared martial law that set in motion a chain of events leading to sweeping political change in South Korea euphimistically labeled the "October [1972] revitalizing reforms."[3]

---

1 Oemubu, *Ilbon kaehwang*, 1990. 5 [The General Condition of Japan, 1990. 5] (Seoul: Oemubu, 1990), 159.
2 The significance of the Park-Ikeda meeting was revealed for the first time in January 2005, when the South Korean government declassified diplomatic documents related to the ROK-Japan normalization talks. A careful preparation preceded the meeting, including an exchange of letters by the two leaders, which were hand-carried by a Japanese emissary, the head of the Japanese delegation to the normalization talks. Park was greeted at Haneda International Airport by Ikeda. The two leaders held talks for two hours at the Prime Minister's Residence (*kantei*), covering the whole gamut of issues affecting diplomatic normalization. At the end of the talks, Ikeda proposed announcing that the two sides had reached a "99.9-percent agreement" but Park toned it down to a "broad agreement." "Park Chung Hee, Ilbon chagum yu'ip t'onghan 'kyongje ch'imnyak' uryo" [Park Chung Hee Expressed Concern About "Economic Aggression" through Influx of Japanese Capital], *Chosun ilbo*, January 21, 2005; "Han'il hoedam munso palch'ue, VIP pangmun" [Excerpts from Documents on the ROK-Japan Normalization Talks: VIP Visits], ibid, August 26, 2005.
3 Ibid., 160.

None of the three visits to Seoul by Japanese prime ministers between 1967 and 1983 were designed to deal with pending issues. All three were ceremonial visits, two of them congratulatory and the third an expression of condolences. Prime Minister Tanaka's extraordinary gesture of going to Seoul to attend the funeral of the late Mrs. Park Chung Hee was aimed at ameliorating the poisoned atmosphere between the two countries on the heels of her assassination by a Korean resident in Japan who had used both a forged Japanese passport and a pistol stolen from a Japanese police box.[4]

Since we have already examined the historic state visit by Prime Minister Nakasone to South Korea in January 1983 and President Chun Doo Hwan's state visit to Japan in September 1984 and since our focus in this chapter is on the 1986-1995 period, we shall begin with President Roh Tae Woo's state visit to Japan in May 1990.

Roh Tae Woo's Visit to Japan, May 1990

The Roh visit, the second state visit to Japan by a ROK president, materialized at Seoul's initiative. Shortly after taking office, Roh conveyed to Tokyo his wish to visit Japan, and Tokyo extended an invitation.[5] Originally

---

4 Yamamoto Tsuyoshi, "Nihon to Kankoku" [Japan and the Republic of Korea] in Yamamoto Susumu et al, *Sengo Nihon gaikoshi, VI: Namboku mondai to Nihon* [History of Japan's Postwar Diplomacy, vol. 4: The South-North Problem and Japan] (Tokyo: Sanseito, 1984), 192-93. For a summary of declassified South Korean documents on the incident, see "Chongbu, Mun Se-gwang sakon tung oegyo munso konggae" [Government Discloses Diplomatic Documents on Mun Se-gwang and Other Incidents], *Chosun ilbo*, January 21, 2005; "'Mun Se-gwang sakon' Han'il susa kyolgwa tallatta" ["Mun Se-gwang Incident" Results of Investigations Differ Between the ROK and Japan], ibid.; Choi Soung-ah, "Attempts on Park's Life in 1974 Caused Near-break in Japan Ties," *Korea Herald*, January 21, 2005.
5 Kamiya Fuji and Tanino Sakutaro, "Taidan: mada futomeina Chosen hanto no seiji josei" [Conversation: The Still Opaque Political Situation on the Korean Peninsula], *Gaiko foramu* [Diplomatic Forum] (Tokyo), No. 21 (June 1990), 37.

scheduled for the Fall of 1988, the visit, however, had to be postponed twice due to circumstances in Japan, including the emperor's illness.[6]

In many cases a state visit can serve as a catalyst for resolving pending bilateral issues. Rarely, however, is this done through direct negotiations between heads of state or government. Substantive negotiations typically occur at the "working level" prior to a state visit. Summit meetings, then, frequently serve to ratify and confirm agreements and compromises that have already been hammered out. If length of summit meetings is an indicator of how much serious negotiation has transpired, then the lengths of the two summit meetings between Roh and Prime Minister Kaifu Toshiki are suggestive: the first, held on May 24, the first day of Roh's visit, lasted an hour, while the second, held on the morning of Roh's departure two days later, lasted 90 minutes.[7]

The single most important substantive issue, the legal status of the "third generation" Korean residents, had in fact been under discussion between the two countries since December 1988 and resolved three weeks before Roh's visit at the 5th regular consultative meeting of their foreign ministers.[8]

This issue had the following background. When Japan and South Korea normalized their relations in 1965, they agreed that Japan would confer permanent residency rights on the "first generation" Korean residents, defined as (1) those who had resided in Japan continuously from before August 15, 1945 until the time of application for residency

---

Tanino, who revealed that Roh had taken the initiative for his Japan visit, was the director-general of the Asian Affairs Bureau of the Japanese Foreign Ministry at the time.

6 Gaimusho, ed., *Gaiko seisho: waga gaiko no kinkyo, 1989* [Diplomatic Blue Book: The Recent Condition of Our Diplomacy, 1989] (Tokyo: Okurasho Insatsukyoku, 1989), 163.

7 Ch'ongwadae, *Che 1-ch'a Han'il chongsang hoedam kyolgwa podo charyo* [Press Release on the Results of the First ROK-Japan Summit Meeting], May 24, 1990; idem, *Che 2-ch'a Han'il chongsang hoedam kyolgwa podo charyo* [Press Release on the Results of the Second ROK-Japan Summit Meeting], May 26, 1990.

8 Gaimusho, ed., *Gaiko seisho, 1990*, 148.

and (2) their children and grandchildren who were born in Japan between August 16, 1945 and January 16, 1971 and who had continuously resided in Japan until the time of application for residency. The children of the preceding two categories of people born in Japan after January 17, 1971 were defined as the "second generation" and would be entitled to permanent residency. Known as *kyotei eiju* [permanent residency based on an agreement], theirs would be a special type of residency entailing more favorable conditions than *ippan eiju* [general permanent residency].[9]

The 1965 agreement between Japan and South Korea on the legal status of Koreans in Japan, however, deferred action on the status of the "third generation,"—defined as the children of the "second generation" born in Japan—until 25 years after its entry into force; the agreement stipulates that the two sides shall settle the issue through negotiation by its 25th anniversary, which would fall on January 16, 1991. When negotiations commenced between delegations headed by the directors-general of the Asian bureaus of the two countries' foreign ministries in December 1988, South Korea put forth a set of ten specific demands, including (1) the granting of permanent residency to all descendants of ROK nationals in Japan who have acquired permanent residency; (2) the exemption of all ROK permanent residents in Japan from forcible expulsion and from the requirement for re-entry permits; (3) the abolition of the finger-printing requirement in alien registration; (4) an expansion of job opportunities for ROK permanent residents in teaching, local government, and other fields; and (5) the granting of the right to vote and run for office in local elections to ROK permanent residents.[10]

---

9 Ito Naoki, "Zainichi Kankokujin 'sansei' mondai" [The Problem of "Third Generation" Republic of Korea Residents in Japan], *Gaiko foramu*, April 1990, 74-75. To cite one difference between *kyotei eiju* and *ippan eiju*, whereas those granted the latter will be expelled from Japan after receiving and serving sentences of one year imprisonment or more, those enjoying the former will be expelled only after seven years or more of imprisonment.

10 Ibid. For a justification of these demands, see *Zainichi Kankokujin no kyojuken* [The Residency Right of Republic of Korea Citizens in Japan] (Tokyo: Zainichi

At the foreign ministers' meeting held in Seoul in April 1990, the two sides reached a compromise in which Japan accepted some of the preceding demands, agreed to go a half way on others, and promised to engage in further negotiations on the remainder. Most important, Japan agreed to allow permanent residency to "third generation" ROK citizens in Japan on condition that they undergo "simplified procedures." On the question of expulsion, only "grave crimes," such as rebellion and crimes that impinge on state and diplomatic interests, would trigger it. Japan also committed itself to the abolition of the fingerprinting requirement as well as the requirement for the carrying of alien registration certificates for "third generation" Koreans in Japan as soon as suitable alternatives are found. As for the requirement for reentry permits, while it will remain in effect, the maximum length of stays outside Japan would be increased to five years.[11]

Another issue that had to be tackled prior to Roh's visit pertained to what the new emperor would say about Japan's past aggression against and harsh colonial rule over the Korean people. The Japanese government had not given any serious thought to the issue until it became a focal point of speculation in the media in Tokyo and Seoul alike. In early May, in response to a question by a Japanese journalist, a South Korean

---

Taikan Minkoku Seinenkai Chuo Honbu, 1989). See also the special issue on the legal status of both ROK and DPRK (Democratic People's Republic of Korea) citizens in Japan, *Horitsu jiho* [Law Review] 62, no. 7 (June 1990) (Tokyo), 6-43. For a summary of how the issue of the legal status of Korean residents in Japan was handled during the ROK-Japan normalization talks, see "Han'il hoedam munso palch'ue, chae'il Hangugin popjok chiwi" [Excerpts from Documents on the ROK-Japan Normalization Talks: Legal Status of ROK Citizens], *Chosun ilbo*, August 27, 2005.

11 Tanaka Hiroshi, "Nikkan sansei kyogi no sengo sayu" [The Front, Rear, Left, and Right of the Japan-Republic of Korea Negotiations on the Third Generation], *Horitsu jiho* 62, no. 7 (June 1990), 31; Gaimusho, Ajia-kyoku, Hokuto Ajia-ka, *"Sansei mondai" taisho hoshin (gaisho teiki kyogide matomatta mono* [Plan for Dealing With the "Third Generation" Problem (Principles Agreed at the Regular Consultative Meeting of Foreign Ministers)], an unpublished document. No date given.

Foreign Ministry official said that there was strong public opinion in his country demanding a more specific statement from the new emperor than the one made by the late emperor in September 1984. The official pointed out that the latter had two problems from Seoul's perspective: (1) by saying that "[i]t is truly regrettable……," the emperor had failed to indicate whether he himself regretted what Japan had done in Korea; (2) the word "regrettable" was not sufficient; what South Korean public opinion demanded was an apology.[12]

Even though the South Korean official was careful to stress that it was public opinion, not his government, that was clamoring for a specific statement from the new emperor, press reports failed to note the distinction. The ruling Liberal-Democratic party (LDP) in Japan reacted strongly to what appeared to be Seoul's new demand. A consensus of opinion, shared by even Socialist members of the Diet, was that the emperor's ability to make statements was limited, for he was merely a symbol of the Japanese state under the constitution. The Japanese government, it was argued, should not and could not use the emperor as a tool of diplomacy.

When Roh Tae Woo told Japanese journalists that the emperor's statement should be clear and contain an apology, he irritated both Japanese politicians and officials. It was only after the Japanese government had made it crystal clear that the emperor could not make the kind of statement Seoul wanted but that the prime minister would make a strong statement that the ROK government tacitly accepted Tokyo's position on the issue. A statement was then drafted by the Japanese Foreign Ministry, reviewed by the Imperial Household Agency, and discussed and approved at the prime ministerial level—with the

---

12 This account, which will be continued in the following paragraphs, is based on my interview with Mr. Yamamura Eiji, Deputy Director of the Northeast Asia Division of the Japanese Foreign Ministry in Tokyo on August 8, 1990. The South Korean Foreign Ministry official was identified by Mr. Yamamura as Moon Bong Ju, the director of the First Northeast Asia Division, which deals with Japan.

Prime Minister, the Chief Cabinet Secretary, and top LDP leaders participating in discussion.

The statement, known as *okotoba*, was delivered by Emperor Akihito at a banquet in honor of Roh and his wife on the evening of May 24. After recalling and quoting verbatim the 1984 statement by his late father, Emperor Showa, the new emperor said:

> I think of the sufferings your people underwent during this unfortunate period, which was brought about by my country, and cannot but feel the deepest regret (*tsuseki no nen*).[13]

The preceding differs from the 1984 statement in two respects: First, unlike the latter, it leaves no doubt as to who is expressing regret. Second, the Japanese words used for regret are different: *tsuseki no nen* as opposed to *ikan*. While the Chinese characters for *tsuseki* imply pain, that in no way connotes an apology. Had the statement not been followed a day later by a clear-cut statement by Prime Minister Kaifu, therefore, Roh Tae Woo and, especially, South Korean public opinion, would not have been mollified. In a speech at a banquet in Roh's honor at the prime minister's official residence, Kaifu said:

> I would like to take the opportunity of Your Excellency's visit to express my sincre remorse and honest apologies [*kenkyoni hanseishi, sotchokuni owabino kimochi o moshi nobetaito zonjimasu*] for the fact that there was a period in our history in which Japanese actions inflicted unbearable suffering and sorrow on the people of the Korean peninsula.[14]

---

13 For the Japanese text of the emperor's statement and an English translation thereof by the Japanese government, see Oemubu, *No T'ae-u taet'ongnyong Ilbon-guk kongsik pangmun yonsolmun-jip, 1990. 6* [Collection of Speeches by President Roh Tae Woo During His State Visit to Japan, 1990. 6] (Seoul: Oemubu, 1990), 19-25.

14 Ibid., 158 and 166.

Notwithstanding the positive spin the Roh Tae Woo government put to the above, however, the South Korean press remained critical. Focusing on the emperor's *okotoba*, major South Korean newspapers ran editorials expressing displeasure over the "use of ambiguous phrase" by the emperor, the "limits of Japanese response, and its failure to measure up to our people's expectations."[15]

Another noteworthy event during the Roh visit was his speech to the joint session of the Japanese Diet. He became the first ROK president to be given that privilege. Saying that Japan and South Korea will form the core of the emerging Asia-Pacific era, Roh argued that the two countries must go beyond bilateral relations and cooperate actively in regional affairs. He called for a genuine partnership between the two countries based on true understanding of the past and mutual respect, using the expression "*kakkapgodo kakkaun tongbanja.*"[16] The phrase, which can be translated as "truly close partners," is meant to put an end to the notion

---

15 In his statement at Kimpo International Airport upon returning from Japan on May 26, Roh took the liberty of translating *tsuseki no nen* as "the feeling of pain in [the emperor's] heart," which is considerably different from the official Japanese translation, "the deepest regret." In Roh's words, "through······ statements by Emperor Akihito who is the symbol of the Japanese state and Prime Minister Kaifu who represents the Japanese government, Japan has candidly acknowledged that it had given us such an unfortunate past and clearly apologized and repented for the pain and sorrow our people have experienced due to Japanese actions. Oemubu, *No T'ae-u taetongnyong Ilbon-guk kongsik pangmun yonsolmun-jip*, 11. Emphasis added. For a summary of and excerpts from South Korean newspaper editorials, see Nagamori Yoshitaka, "Okotoba de fukamatta Nikkan gyappu" [The Gap Between Japan and South Korea That Has Deepened Due to the Emperor's Statement], *Gendai Koria* [Modern Korea] (Tokyo), no. 303 (July 1990), 50-55; "Roh daitoryo honichiwa do uketomeraretaka: Kankokuji futatsuno shasetsu kara" [How Was President Roh's Japan Visit Received? From the Editorials of Two South Korean Newspapers], *Sekai* [The World] (Tokyo), July 1990, 118-21.

16 For the text of Roh's speech in Korean and its official Japanese and English translations, see Oemubu, *No T'ae-u taetongnyong Ilbon-guk kongsik pangmun yonsolmun-jip*, 44-98.

that Japan and Korea are "so near and yet so far" (*kakkapgodo mon nara* in Korean; *chikakute toi kuni* in Japanese). The latter phrase implies that while the two are close geographically, they are far apart in terms of feelings and attitudes toward each other.

There were other tangible outcomes of the Roh visit as well. The Japanese government announced that it would allocate four billion yen (about $28 million in 1990) for assistance to Korean victims of the atomic bombs dropped in Hiroshima and Nagasaki.[17] An estimated 23,000 Korean victims returned to South Korea after the war, of whom about 1,600 were registered with an organization of atomic bomb victims in South Korea as of June 1989.[18]

Japan and South Korea signed a "letter" pertaining to visas: in addition to exempting visa fees to each other's citizens, the two sides agreed to issue one-year multiple-entry visas to qualified applicants. With the lifting of restrictions on foreign travel in South Korea, the number of visitors between the two countries was increasing rapidly, reaching 2 million in 1989.[19] The new agreement was expected to increase the two-way traffic further in the years ahead.

Roh and Kaifu agreed on some specific measures to promote cooperation in science and technology, including cooperation in automation technology among small and medium-sized business firms; technical cooperation in the prevention of occupational disease among industrial workers; the conclusion of an agreement on atomic energy, and

---

17 Gaimusho (ed.), *Gaiko seisho, 1990*, 148.

18 Oemubu, *Ilbon kaehwang, 1990.5*, 174-75. An estimated 40,000 Koreans were killed in Hiroshima and Nagasaki. The issue of assistance to atomic bomb victims has a long history dating back to 1967. On December 1, 1981 Japan and South Korea reached an agreement under which Japan would allow South Korean victims to receive medical care in Japan during a five-year period effective immediately. A total of 345 Koreans went to Japan to take advantage of that agreement during the period. In October 1988, Japan offered to provide 42 million yen annually, with the money being donated to the ROK Red Cross. Ibid., 175-76.

19 Ibid.

the establishment of Japan-ROK joint committee on the basic sciences.[20]

Not to be minimized is another goodwill gesture on the part of Japan. The Japanese government decided to return some Choson dynasty relics—those that belonged to the last king and queen—that had been kept at the Tokyo National Museum. Thanking his host for this decision, Roh expressed the hope that the Japanese government would take positive steps in the future to facilitate the return of Korean cultural property shipped to Japan during the colonial period.[21]

All in all, the Roh visit proved to be quite productive for South Korea and mutually beneficial for both countries. Notwithstanding the controversy surrounding the *okotoba*, the visit was instrumental in resolving or laying the groundwork for the resolution of pending issues and in creating goodwill. An assessment by the Japanese Foreign Ministry concluded that the visit produced a "huge result" (*okina seika*) for the construction of a "new Japan-ROK era" (*Nikkan shinjidai*). It noted that the two top leaders had shared the perception that the two countries had put the past behind them, adding that the two countries would strive to build a new era as true partners in the days ahead.[22]

Kaifu's Visit to South Korea, January 1991

In January 1991 it was Japan's turn to send its top leader to South Korea. When Prime Minister Kaifu arrived in Seoul on January 9 for a two-day visit, he became the second Japanese prime minister to make a state visit to South Korea. The visit signaled that the pace of summit diplomacy between Tokyo and Seoul had picked up. Whereas nearly six years had elapsed between the Chun and Roh visits to Japan, the Kaifu

---

20 Ch'ongwadae, *Che 2-ch'a Han'il chongsang hoedam kyolgwa podo charyo*, 5.
21 Ibid.
22 Gaimusho, Ajia-kyoku, Hokuto Ajia-ka, Roh Tae Woo daitoryo honichino hyoka to seika [Appraisal and Results of President Roh Tae Woo's Visit to Japan], May 26, 1990, an unpublished document.

visit to South Korea occurred within eight months of the Roh visit. The timing of the Kaifu visit was related to a new development: the first round of the Japan-DPRK normalization talks was about to begin in Pyongyang in two weeks.

Although the Kaifu visit was one day shorter than the Roh visit, the length of "summit meetings" was identical in both: one 60-minute session followed by another 90-minute session. During the first session the two leaders exchanged views on the rapidly changing international environment, most notably, the end of the Cold War and the emergence of a new world order; they agreed that both countries should work together to ensure that in the 1990s the tide of peace, reconciliation, and cooperation would reach the shores of the Asia-Pacific region as well.[23]

On the sensitive and potentially momentous issue of Japan-DPRK diplomatic negotiations, Kaifu assured Roh that Japan would continue to keep in mind the five principles Roh had previously articulated, conducting the forthcoming talks in close consultation with Seoul and with the aim of making a contribution to the peace and stability of the Korean peninsula. As noted in Chapter II, the five principles, which were conveyed to Japan through Kanemaru Shin in October 1990, called for (1) consultation in advance, (2) linking progress in Japan-DPRK talks to progress in inter-Korean dialogue, (3) urging Pyongyang to conclude a safeguard agreement with the IAEA, (4) refraining from either paying compensation or giving economic aid to the North prior to normalization, and (5) encouraging the North to embrace a policy of openness and cooperation with the international community.[24]

During the second session the two leaders adopted "three principles of Japan-ROK friendship and cooperation" or, as the Japanese Foreign Ministry put it, "three principles of the new Japan-ROK era."

First, the two countries will strengthen exchanges, cooperation, and mutual understanding in order to build a true partnership.

---

23 Ch'ongwadae, *Che 1-ch'a chongsang hoedam kyolgwa podo charyo* [Press Release on the Results of the First Summit Meeting], January 9, 1991.
24 Ibid.

Second, they will redouble their contributions to peace and reconciliation as well as prosperity and openness in the Asia-Pacific region.

Third, they will increase cooperation in the quest for the solution of global problems.[25]

Additionally, the two leaders reviewed progress in the implementation of agreements and understandings reached during Roh's visit to Japan in May 1990. They noted with satisfaction that much had been accomplished during the preceding seven months. The resumption of regular cabinet-level meeting in November 1990 following a four-year hiatus, they agreed, had been very helpful. With regard to the "third-generation" problem, Kaifu informed Roh that the Japanese government planned to substitute a family registration system for fingerprinting; the latter would be abolished for ROK residents in Japan within two years. The Japanese government, Kaifu added, would gradually reduce the nationality requirement in the hiring of local government employees and teachers in national and public schools.[26] A memorandum of understanding incorporating these points as well as others that had previously been articulated was signed by the foreign ministers of the two countries on the second and final day of the Kaifu visit.[27]

The two leaders reaffirmed their conviction that the promotion of mutual understanding between the peoples of their countries was a sine qua non for the building of a "future-oriented" partnership. With that in mind, they agreed to implement a Japan-ROK 21st century exchange project (*Nikkan 21 seiki seishin koryu jigyo*). In addition to expanding the youth exchange program already under way, the project would initiate an exchange program between local governments of the two countries and

---

25 Ch'ongwadae, *Che 2-ch'a chongsang hoedam podo charyo* [Press Release on the Results of the Second Summit Meeting], January 10, 1991; Gaimusho, *Gaiko seisho, 1991*, 212.
26 Ibid.; Ch'ongwadae, *Che 2-ch'a chongsang hoedam kyolgwa podo charyo*, 2.
27 For the text of the memorandum in Korean, see Oemubu, *Ilbon kaehwang*, 1994. 3, 350-53.

sponsor various cultural events aimed at introducing each other's cultures to their general publics.[28]

Miyazawa's Visit to South Korea, January 1992

With Prime Minister Miyazawa Kiichi's state visit to South Korea in January 1992, Japan-ROK summits were well on their way to becoming annual affairs. As things turned out, in fact, there would be another summit before the year was out. To discuss the Miyazawa visit first, it had both symbolic and substantive aspects. Symbolically, by choosing South Korea as his first foreign destination since taking office, Miyazawa signaled to Seoul that he attached a high priority to Tokyo-Seoul ties. Miyazawa also became the first Japanese prime minister to address the ROK National Assembly. His speech, entitled "Japan-ROK Relations in the Asian and Global Context," will be examined shortly. Miyazawa's apology to the Korean people for the pain and sufferings Japan had inflicted on them during the colonial period was also symbolically noteworthy in view of the salience of the "comfort women" issue. Substantively, the twin issues of trade imbalance and technology transfer had gained new urgency and needed to be tackled anew.[29]

In his historic speech to the ROK National Assembly on January 17, the second day of his three-day visit, Miyazawa first congratulated the Republic of Korea on two recent developments: its entry, together with the DPRK, into the United Nations and the signing of two potentially epochal agreements between the two Korean states following protracted

---

28 Gaimusho, *Gaiko seisho, 1991*, 212. A literal translation of the project's name, given in Japanese in the parentheses, would be "Japan-ROK 21st Century Whole-hearted Exchange Project."

29 See the text of an opening statement by Roh Tae Woo (in Korean) at the news conference held in the Blue House on January 18, 1992 (distributed by the Blue House). See also Gaimusho, ed., *Gaiko seisho: tenkanki no sekai to Nihon, 1992* [Diplomatic Blue Book: The World in Transition and Japan, 1992] (Tokyo: Okurasho Insatsu-kyoku, 1992), 178-80.

negotiations at the prime ministerial level. Noting that the UN would and should play an increasingly important role in the post-Cold War world, Miyazawa expressed hope that Japan and the ROK would cooperate closely in that world organization.[30]

Miyazawa saw enormous potential for the growth of Northeast Asia in a world where Cold War rivalry no longer hampers cooperation among its members and argued that Japan and South Korea should play a central role in the region's transformation into one marked by cooperation, prosperity, and openness. He went so far as to assert that whether a new Northeast Asia can be created would hinge on cooperation between Japan and South Korea.

The need for the two neighbors to work together to promote peace and well-being not only in the Asia-Pacific region but also in the world was the main theme of Miyazawa's speech. A sine qua non for close collaboration between them, Miyazawa underscored, was a deepening of mutual trust, which in turn requires a correct understanding of the past. In his words:

> Never should we allow ourselves to forget the fact that, at certain moments in the history of our relations with your country for the past couple of millennia, our country was the assailant [*kagaisha*] and your country was the victim [*higaisha*]. Allow me to take this opportunity to express anew my sincere remorse and apology [*kokoro karano hanseino i to owabino kimochi o hyomei itashimasu*] for past Japanese actions that inflicted unbearable suffering and sorrow

---

30 "Miyazawa Naikaku Daijin no Taikanmingoku homon ni okeru seisaku enzetsu (o souru) (Ajia no naka, sekai no nakano Nikkan kankei)" [Prime Minister Miyazawa's Policy Speech During His Visit to the Republic of Korea (in Seoul) (Japan—ROK Relations in the Asian and Global Context) in Gaimusho, ed., *Gaiko seisho, 1992*, 383-88. The translation of the title of the speech is from a "provisional and unofficial translation" of the entire text of the speech by the Japanese Foreign Ministry, which I have obtained from its Northeast Asia Division in the summer of 1992.

on the people of the Korean peninsula. Recently, the issue of the so-called comfort women in the service of the [Japanese Imperial] Army [*jugun ianfu*] has come into light. I cannot help feeling acutely distressed over this, and I express my sincere apology.[31]

Not only did Miyazawa make an unequivocal apology but he also made it plain that he was extending his apology to "the people of the Korean peninsula," which, of course, included those who live in the North. The "comfort women" issue gained notoriety in December 1991, when several Korean women who claimed to have been forced to work as sex slaves for Japanese soldiers during World War II sued the Japanese government for compensation. Shortly before Miyazawa went to Seoul, Chief Cabinet Secretary Kato Koichi acknowledged that the Japanese government could not deny that the Japanese Imperial Army was involved in the matter. In July 1992, Kato announced the results of an investigation conducted by government ministries and agencies concerned, which concluded that the government had participated in the comfort women program during the war; he stated that the government would "examine with sincerity how to express our feelings" toward the victims.[32]

Returning to Miyazawa's speech, he enumerated measures for promoting mutual understanding: (1) promoting research in Japanese universities on the culture and language of the Korean peninsula and related topics as well as joint research by Japanese and Korean universities; (2) translating into Japanese books dealing with Korean history, culture and thought as well as biographies; (3) expanding youth exchange—500 South Korean youths would be invited to Japan over a five-year period beginning in the next fiscal year.

---

31 "Miyazawa naikaku sori daijin……," 386-387. I have drawn on the "provisional and unofficial translation" of the speech by the Japanese Foreign Ministry noted earlier, making several revisions based on the original Japanese text.
32 Gaimusho, ed., *Gaiko seisho, 1992*, 179-80.

Noting that South Korea had become a doner of economic aid to developing countries, Miyazawa called for cooperation between Tokyo and Seoul in helping "the developing world by taking advantage of the rich experiences both of us have." Other areas of bilateral cooperation he mentioned included environment and the Uruguay Round negotiations on trade liberalization.

In their tete-a-tetes, Miyazawa and Roh reconfirmed that their two countries would continue to consult on the ongoing Japan-DPRK normalization talks. The two leaders agreed that trade imbalance and cooperation in industrial technology and science merited the highest priority. They decided that the Japan-ROK committee on cooperation in trade and industrial technology should make a concerted effort to formulate and submit concrete proposals to them by the end of July.[33] In accordance with this decision, an action plan was formulated and adopted in July, of which the key components were the establishment of a foundation for the promotion of cooperation in industrial technology, the inauguration of a Japan-ROK businessmen's forum, the improvement of the climate for investment and technology transfer by South Korea, and the improved treatment of Japanese trading companies operating in South Korea.[34]

Roh Tae Woo's Working Visit to Kyoto, November 1992

As already noted, 1992 saw not one but two visits by the top leaders of Japan and South Korea to each other's country. For within ten months of the Miyazawa visit, Roh Tae Woo made a one-day "working visit" to Kyoto, Japan. As the first of its kind, the visit symbolized the maturity of Japan-ROK relations. Occurring as it did five days after the Presidential election in the U.S., the first-ever summit unencumbered by formality was

---

33 Roh Tae Woo's opening remarks at a news conference, January 18, 1992, Seoul in a transcript distributed by the Blue House.
34 Gaimusho (ed.) *Gaiko seisho*, 1992, 180.

meant to reaffirm the common interests, perceptions, and approaches of the two neighboring countries toward international affairs. The historic normalization of relations between Seoul and Beijing in August was also part of the backdrop against which the Kyoto summit took place.[35]

Miyazawa and Roh agreed that Japan, South Korea, and the US, which shared democracy and the market economy, should keep intact their security relationships and that the continued role of the US in Northeast Asia was essential to the stability of the region. They also agreed that the continuing pursuit by China of the policies of reform and openness was desirable from the standpoint of regional stability; hence stepped-up dialogues and interchanges between Japan and South Korea on the one hand and China on the other would be in the best interests not only of the three countries but also of the region as a whole. They further shared the view that Russia's reform process merited support.

Regarding bilateral issues, the two leaders took note of the action plan for the amelioration of trade imbalance, agreeing to make continuing efforts to correct the imbalance and expand bilateral trade. Although the issue of "comfort women" did not loom large in the working summit, the two leaders nonetheless pledged to continue to work hard to resolve it. Finally, Miyazawa and Roh agreed that the new type of meeting they experimented with in Kyoto was most beneficial, desirable, and worthy of routinization. They felt that it was peculiarly suited to the tasks of developing a future-oriented Japan-ROK relationship and responding efficaciously to the rapidly changing international environment.

---

35 *Han'il chongsang hoedam kyolgwa tae'oe palp'yomun* [Press Release on the Results of the ROK-Japan Summit Meeting], released in Kyoto on November 8, 1992 by Kim Hak-joon, the chief Presidential press secretary.

Hosokawa's Working Visit to Kyongju, November 1993

The working-visit model would be used again exactly a year later when Prime Minister Hosokawa Morihiro made a two-day visit to Kyongju, Korea. It was Hosokawa who had suggested a working visit and a site other than Seoul. That both Hosokawa and Kim Young Sam were not only newly elected leaders of their respective countries but also harbingers of significant change in their respective political systems helped to enhance the value of their encounters and tete-a-tetes. What is more, Hosokawa provided a breath of fresh air to the South Korean people. Not only did he go further than any of his predecessors in expressing his desire to rectify the past but he did not shrink from acknowledging the existence of trade barriers in Japan and bureaucratic resistance to their removal.[36]

Hosokawa's statement on Japan's past actions in Korea was as follows:

> Regarding the myriad ways in which our country, through colonial rule, has inflicted unbearable sorrow and sufferings on the people of the Korean peninsula—such as depriving them of the opportunity to receive education in their mother tongue and forcing them to change their names from Korean to Japanese—I am deeply remorseful and express my heartfelt apology *[fukaku hanseishi kokorokara chinsha moshi ageru]*.[37]

Two things differentiated Hosokawa's statement above from those of

---

36 Ch'ongwadae, *Han'il chongsang hoedam kyolgwa podo charyo* [Press Release on the Results of the ROK-Japan Summit Meeting], November 7, 1993; Gaimusho, Ajia Kyoku, Hokuto Ajia-ka, *Nikkan shuno kaidan (gaiyo oyobi hyoka)* [The Japan—ROK Summit Meeting (Summary and Appraisal)], November 8, 1993, an unpublished document; idem, *Hosokawa sori boto hatsugen (kyodo kisha kaiken)* [Prime Minister Hosokawa's Opening Statement (Joint Press Conference), November 7, 1993.
37 Gaimusho, Ajia Kyoku, Hokuto Ajia-ka, *Hosokawa sori boto hatsugen.*

his predecessors: first, he was more specific about what Japan had actually done during the colonial period than any of his predecessors, citing things that touched the very identity of the Korean people and thus had become the source of acute pain and resentment;[38] second, the word he used for apology, *chinsha*, conveyed to the Koreans more sincerity than those used by his predecessors. This was due to the fact the Chinese characters for *chinsha* were also used in Korean for apology (pronounced as *chinsa*) and signified the highest form of apology.

Kim and Hosokawa exchanged views on both international and bilateral issues, ranging from North Korea's nuclear and missile programs to economic cooperation and cultural exchange. They affirmed the importance of the upcoming unofficial APEC (Asia Pacific Economic Cooperation) summit in Seattle, pledging to work together to promote the common interests and welfare of the Asia-Pacific region. They noted with approval a report submitted by the Japan-ROK businessmen's forum, promising to cooperate in implementing its recommendations. They agreed in principle to set up a new high-level structure for bilateral economic cooperation, to be known as the New Initiative for Economic Partnership (NIEP), leaving the details to be hammered out at the working level. Hosokawa proposed the installation of a hot line between the Blue House and the Japanese Prime Minister's Residence to supplement the one that already existed between the foreign ministries of the two countries, and Kim Young Sam accepted the proposal.

In sum, while nothing really new came out of the Kyongju summit in material or substantive terms, its ideational or symbolic value was nonetheless considerable. Both sides viewed it as an unqualified success. In the words of the Japanese Foreign Ministry, it was "the first step toward making fresh progress in Japan-ROK relations" (*Nikkan kankeino aratana*

---

38 In his talks with Kim Young Sam, Hosokawa mentioned not only those two things cited in the preceding quotation but also forcing Korean women into sex slavery for Japanese soldiers and forcible conscription of Korean men to work in mines and other hazardous places. Ch'ongwadae, *Han'il chongsang hoedam kyokgwa podo charyo*, November 7, 1993, 3.

shinten eno dai ippo).³⁹

Kim Young Sam's Visit to Japan, March 1994

Four and a half months later President Kim Young Sam made a state visit to Japan. The three-day visit (March 24-26, 1994) was the first state visit by a ROK president in nearly four years. What set the Kim visit apart from his predecessors' was that what the Japanese emperor would say about the past Japanese actions toward the Korean people did not become an issue. It was, in fact, the first time that Seoul had not made any request on the matter, leaving it entirely to Tokyo's discretion. Despite or perhaps because of such an unusual circumstance, the emperor did make a statement on the past that was well received in South Korea. At a banquet he hosted on March 24, 1994 Emperor Akihito said:

> There was a period during the long and close intercourse between our two countries when our country brought great sufferings to the people of the Korean peninsula. A few years ago I expressed my profound feelings of sorrow on this matter, and I have the same feelings now. In the postwar period our citizens have endeavored to create trust and friendship with your citizens based on a deep remorse [*fukui hansei*] about the past history.⁴⁰

The South Korean press noted that this marked the first time that a Japanese emperor had ever used the word *hansei* (*pansong* in Korean) in reference to Japan's past behavior; the latest statement, therefore, was an improvement over the emperor's 1990 statement. One newspaper,

---

39 Gaimusho, Ajia Kyoku, Hokuto Ajia-ka, *Nikkan shuno kaidan (gaiyo oyobi hyoka)*, November 8, 1993, 1.
40 "Kuchu bansankai okotoba" [The Emperor's Statement at a Banquet in the Imperial Palace] in *Taet'ongnyong pang'il charyo* [Materials on the President's Visit to Japan], Oemubu, undated and unpaged.

Hangyorye sinmun, perhaps the most progressive daily in South Korea, however, pointed out that the emperor had not really expressed his own remorse but merely referred to the remorse on the part of the Japanese people.[41]

Speaking at the banquet following the emperor's statement, Kim Young Sam described the latter as "remarks overflowing with friendship toward our country and people." But Kim's repeated reference to "your imperial majesty" (*tenno heika*) did not sit well with his own people. *Hangyorye sinmun* reported that it had been deluged with calls from its readers protesting Kim's "excessive deference" to the emperor.[42]

The general atmosphere surrounding the Kim visit, particularly the two sessions he had with his host, Prime Minister Hosokawa, could not have been more amicable. The number one topic of their discussion was not any bilateral issue but North Korea's nuclear program. For Pyongyang had precipitated a new crisis by restricting an IAEA inspection team's access to one of its seven nuclear facilities in Yongbyon, and the U.S. had begun a diplomatic campaign to have the UN Security Council adopt a resolution imposing sanctions on North Korea. Against this background, Kim wanted to consult with Hosokawa on how to deal with the North Korean challenge. That the two had common interests and perceptions helped them to shape a common strategy, which was to present a united front on the part of Seoul, Tokyo, and Washington and to exert pressure on Pyongyang to change its policy on inspections, while leaving the door open for negotiations. The friendly tone of the Kim-Hosokawa talks on the North Korean problem, during which no disagreement whatsoever surfaced, reportedly surprised even the diplomats involved.[43]

---

41 "Han'il chongsang hoedam ul ponun kungmin ui sigak" [How the People See the ROK-Japan Summit Meeting], an editorial, *Hankyoreh sinmun* (Seoul), March 26, 1994.

42 Ibid., March 26, 1994. The paper reported that the protest calls came in on the evening of March 24 following the broadcast of Kim Young Sam's banquet speech in South Korea.

43 "Kotkotso silgam nanun 'mirae chihyang' Kim taet'ongnyong pang'il songkwa-Ilbon ui sigak" [The "Future-Orientation" That Is Palpable Everywhere; the

Regarding bilateral relations, the two leaders agreed that both countries should accelerate exchanges, diversify relations, and cooperate in the international arena more closely than ever before. Apart from coordinating strategy toward North Korea, South Korea wanted to secure stronger and, if possible, specific commitments from Japan on economic cooperation. Seoul's pressing need for Japanese cooperation, in fact, was cited by the Japanese Foreign Ministry as one of the major factors underlying Seoul's laissez-faire attitude toward the issue of an imperial statement on the past; another factor, in the Foreign Ministry's view, was the Kim Young Sam government's self-confidence stemming from its legitimacy and popular support.[44]

Kim secured from Hosokawa commitments to step up efforts to reduce trade imbalance, to provide assistance to small and medium companies manufacturing industrial parts, to study the option of dispatching to South Korea a delegation to explore investment opportunities, to foster cooperation in the fields of automobile, airplane, and high-speed electronic communication networks, and to conclude an agreement on the prevention of double taxation. Although the ROK Foreign Ministry described the above as "specific commitments to cooperate," none of them actually entailed any binding commitments.[45] What is more, Hosokawa was to step down as prime minister a month later, even though neither he nor Kim Young Sam could have anticipated that development at the time of their Tokyo summit.

Following in the footsteps of his predecessor, Roh Tae Woo, Kim Young Sam addressed the Japanese Diet. In a speech entitled "Toward a

---

Results of President Kim's Japan Visit: the View from Japan], *Joongang ilbo*, March 26, 1994.

44 Gaimusho, Ajia Kyoku, Hokuto Ajia-ka, *Kim Young Sam daitoryo honichi no hyoka, 3-gatsu 24-nichi—26-nichi, o: Tokyo* [An Assessment of President Kim Young Sam's Visit to Japan, March 24-26 in Tokyo], March 28, 1994, an unpublished document.

45 Oemubu, Aju-guk, "Taet'ongnyong pang'il, pangjung kyolgwa, '94.4.4" [The Results of the President's Visits to Japan and China, April 4, 1994], *oegyodan purip'ing charyo* [Briefing Material for the Diplomatic Corps] (Seoul), 3.

New History of Friendship and Cooperation" delivered on the second day of his visit, Kim underlined the need for a shared dream between the Korean and Japanese peoples, "a dream [to build] a new ROK-Japan relationship, a new Asia-Pacific region, and a new world." He added that "to make such a dream come true would require a new posture and new cooperation."[46]

Saying that both his compatriots and the Japanese people must open their minds completely and "wipe away the remnants of the past," Kim nonetheless called for the courage to come to grips with historical truths and learn from the lessons of history. His main message, however, was the importance of a "mature partnership" between the two countries and of not allowing the past or national prejudice to block its realization. What impressed one seasoned observer of the Korean scene, Okonogi Masao of Keio University, was Kim's insistence that Korean unification would be consistent with Japan's national interest; in Kim's words, "I firmly believe that a unified Korea will become a reliable partner of Japan."[47]

As noted previously, however, perhaps the single most important aspect of the Kim visit was that for the first time Japan was not under any pressure to agonize over how to formulate an imperial statement on past Japanese actions toward the Korean people. As one Japanese editorial put it, the visit marked the "first step toward maturity in Japan-ROK relations [and showed that] they are now on the future-oriented track. They must not be allowed to leave the track."[48]

---

46 "Ilbon kukhoe eso han Kim Young Sam taet'ongnyong yonsolmun, 1994 nyon 3 wol 25 il Tonggyong" [The Text of President Kim Young Sam's Speech Before the Japanese Diet, March 25, 1994, Tokyo] in *Taehan min'guk oegyo yonp'yo, 1994* [Chronology of Diplomacy by the Republic of Korea, 1994], Oemubu (Seoul: Oemubu, 1995), 487-492; for a Japanese-language version, see ibid., 493-501.

47 For Okonogi's assessment of the Kim visit, see "Nikkan 100-nen no yuko kizuku toki" [Time to Build Friendship For 100 Years of Japan and Korea], *Yomiuri shinbun* (Tokyo), March 27, 1994. Okonogi said that Kim had brought "three messages" to Japan: (1) "future-orientation," (2) "internationalization" and (3) the North Korean nuclear problem.

Murayama's Visit to South Korea, July 1994

In late April Hata Tsutomu succeeded Hosokawa as prime minister but the brevity of his tenure in office—two months—prevented Hata from visiting Seoul, although it was Japan's turn to send its top leader to its neighboring country.[49] It befell on Murayama Tomiichi, Hata's successor and the first Socialist prime minister in 27 years, to return Kim Young Sam's March 1994 visit to Japan. An unexpected development helped to determine the timing of Murayama's visit. The death of DPRK President Kim Il Sung on July 8 made it imperative that Murayama and Kim Young Sam get together to formulate or confirm a common strategy toward North Korea. The resumption of the third round of the US-DPRK high-level talks in Geneva added a sense of urgency. No less pressing was Japan's need to reassure South Korea that the inauguration of a Socialist-led coalition government would not signal change in Japan's policy toward the Korean peninsula.

Against this backdrop Murayama made a state visit to South Korea from July 23 to 24, 1994. Seoul's uneasiness was fueled by the record of the Social Democratic Party of Japan (SDPJ), which, until recently, had been implacably hostile toward the ROK, echoing the DPRK's views on all key issues. The SDPJ had refused to recognize the validity of the Japan-ROK normalization treaty (basic treaty), rejected the claim of the ROK to be the sole legitimate government on the peninsula, and supported DPRK positions on unification and related issues. The SDPJ, however, began to soften its hard-line posture toward the ROK, and in September 1993, shortly after it had joined a coalition government, the then chairman of the party, Yamahana Sadao, visited Seoul.[50]

---

48 "Seijuku eno kidoni noru Nikkan kankei" [Japan—ROK Relations That Have Entered the Track Toward Maturity], an editorial, *Yomiuri shinbun*, March 27, 1994.
49 See Hata's letter to Kim Young Sam dated July 1, 1994, in which he expresses his regret for not being able to visit South Korea due to his resignation as prime minister, in *Taehanmin'guk oegyo yonp'yo, 1994*, Oemubu, 662-63.

When Prime Minister Murayama assured President Kim Young Sam that there would be no change in Japanese policy toward the Korean peninsula, South Korea breathed a collective sigh of relief. Not only did Murayama confirm the key elements of Japan's Korea policy that were already in place, but he also echoed Kim Young Sam's hard line regarding North Korea's suspected nuclear program. The two agreed that the provision of light-water reactors (LWRs) to the North must be contingent upon Pyongyang's cooperation not only in removing the present and future threats of nuclear proliferation but also in ascertaining its past nuclear activity.[51]

Even though Seoul did not ask for a statement on Japanese colonial rule, Murayama followed the precedent set by his predecessors in making one just the same. He said that he wanted to express a "heartfelt apology and severe remorse" (*kokoro karano owabi to kibishii hansei no kimochi*) for the "unbearable sufferings and grief our country's colonial rule inflicted on many people on the Korean peninsula."[52]

On the issue of "comfort women," however, Murayama said that the Japanese government was examining the various ways of expressing "apology and remorse" to the surviving victims. On the issue of the Koreans in Sakhalin—those who had been forcibly taken there by the Japanese government during World War II and abandoned at the end of the war—, the two leaders agreed that the time was running out on those in their 70s and older and that therefore those people merited priority assistance. They acknowledged the need to seek the cooperation of the Russian government in the matter as well.[53]

All in all, the Murayama visit proved to be a success, for it

---

50 For a brief chronological summary of the evolution of the Socialists' policy toward the ROK, see *Yomiuri shinbun*, July 24, 1994, 2.
51 *Asahi shinbun* (Tokyo), July 24, 1994, 1.
52 "Nikkan shuno kaidan omona yaritori" [Main Items in the Give and Take in the Japan-ROK Summit Meeting," *Yomiuri shinbun*, July 24, 1994, 3.
53 "Nikkan shuno kaidan no omona yaritori," *Mainichi shinbun* (Tokyo), July 24, 1994, 2.

accomplished its main goals: reassuring the Kim Young Sam government of the continuity of Japan's Korea policy and confirming a common approach to North Korea. Additionally, the visit reportedly helped to bolster Murayama's self-confidence, a sense that he could be an effective leader in diplomacy.[54] Most important, it demonstrated that Tokyo-Seoul relations were on track, making steady progress toward the lofty goal of a "truly future-oriented relationship."[55]

Statements and Strains

As Kim Young Sam and his predecessors took pains to point out, however, from Seoul's perspective, a "future-oriented" relationship could only be built on the foundation of coming to grips with the past misdeeds and trying to learn the lessons of history. The occasional appearance of signs that such a foundation was shaky, therefore, was bound to cause strains in Tokyo-Seoul relations. That is precisely what happened in 1995, the 50th anniversary of Korea's liberation from Japanese colonial rule.

Actually, ominous signs began to surface in 1994 but the quickened pace of summit diplomacy helped to eclipse them. In May of that year, Justice Minister Nagano Shigeru told *Mainichi shinbun* that it was wrong to label the Pacific war an aggressive war, that what Japan did had been both permissible and justifiable, that Japan did sincerely try to liberate colonies and establish a Greater East Asia Co-prosperity Sphere, and that the Nanjing massacre had not really happened (because, he claimed, he

---

54 "Shusho kikoku: gaiko 'michisu'kara jishin e, naisei niwa nanmon sanseki [The Prime Minister Returns Home: From an "Unknown Quantity" to Self-Confidence in Diplomacy, Difficult Problems Abound in Domestic Policy," *Sankei shinbun* (Tokyo), July 25, 1994, 3.
55 "Makoto ni mirai shiko no Nikkan kankei o" [Wanted: A Truly Future-Oriented Japan-ROK Relationship], an editorial, ibid., July 23, 1994, 2. This editorial appeared on the day of Murayama's departure for Seoul.

went there immediately after the "alleged incident" and did not see any evidence of a massacre.) In an interview with *Kyodo* news agency on the same day (May 3, 1994), Nagano said that since the "comfort women" were public prostitutes at the time, they should not be viewed as the product of discrimination against Koreans or women, adding that the US and British armed forces had also provided prostitutes for their soldiers. Faced with a storm of protests from Japan's former victims, including South Korea, Nagano retracted his remarks and then resigned from his cabinet post.[56]

In August 1994 Sakurai Shin, Director-General of the Environment Agency, told the journalists assigned to his agency that from Japanese standpoint, the Pacific war had not been an aggressive war and that while Japan did inconvenience the countries of Asia, it also helped them win independence and reap benefits in education, resulting in higher rates of literacy in those countries than in Africa which was under European domination. Seoul immediately lodged a strong protest with Tokyo, and Sakurai resigned from his cabinet post within two days of the publication of his remarks.[57]

In October 1994 Hashimoto Ryutaro, who was the Minister of International Trade and Industry at the time but who would succeed Murayama as prime minister in January 1996, made a statement in the House of Representatives that stirred controversy. While acknowledging on the one hand that Japan did commit an act of aggression against China and imposed colonial rule in Korea, doing things in Korea that by today's standards could only be described as aggressive, Hashimoto argued on the other hand that whether an aggressive war occurred in a particular region was a matter of definition; in his view, Japan had not

---

56 "Ilbon chongbu insa mit chongch'iga tung'ui kwago yoksa kwallyon pujongjok paron kirok" [The Record of Negative Statements by Japanese Government Personnel, Politicians and Others Regarding the Past History] in *Ilbon kaehwang, 1996. 2* [The General Condition of Japan, 1996. 2], (Seoul: Oemubu, 1996), 375-76.
57 Ibid., 376.

waged an aggressive war during World War II. Since these comments were not as provocative as those of Nagano and Sakurai, the ROK Foreign Ministry merely expressed its regret and requested a clarification from the Japanese government.[58]

No matter how much goodwill had been generated by summit diplomacy and how much actual progress had been made in bilateral relations, the recurrence of statements by Japanese politicians aimed at glossing over Japan's past misdeeds in the year in which South Korea was marking a double anniversary—the 50th anniversary of liberation and the 30th anniversary of ROK-Japan normalization—was certain to grate on the sensibilities of the South Korean people. That the remarks did not always emanate from incumbent cabinet members offered but meager consolation to the Koreans. What mattered most was that they came from heavy-weight politicians, people who had once been cabinet ministers.

The opening salvo in the anniversary year came from Okuno Seisuke, a former Justice Minister. In an interview with *Asahi shinbun* on March 16, Okuno asserted that Japan had fought a "self-defensive war" during World War II, that Japanese occupation of Asian countries was linked to its war against the US and Britain whose colonies these countries were, and that even though Japan did cause sufferings in these countries, it also liberated them from white people's colonial rule. In a rally held on the same day in opposition to a "no war" resolution encompassing Japanese apology for its actions in the Pacific war, Okuno pointed out that although An Chung-gun, who assassinated Ito Hirobumi in 1909, was revered in Korea as an independence fighter, from a Japanese standpoint, he was no better than a "murderer."[59]

On June 3, Watanabe Michio, a former Deputy Prime Minister and Foreign Minister, told a gathering in Utsunomiya that while it is indisputable that Japan ruled Korea once, the phrase "colonial rule" is a misnomer, for one cannot find a single reference to it in the San Francisco Peace Treaty or in any official document. He went on to say that proper

---

58 Ibid., 377.
59 Ibid.

procedures, not force, had been used in concluding the annexation treaty between Japan and Korea in 1910. Since Watanabe was not officially affiliated with the Japanese government, all the ROK Foreign Ministry could do was to express "strong regret" over his remarks.[60]

The "no war" resolution the House of Representatives of the Japanese Diet passed on July 9 failed to satisfy South Korea. A product of compromise among the three coalition partners—the LDP, the SDPJ, and the New Party Sakigake—, the resolution had encountered stiff opposition in the Japanese Diet itself. Not only did all 171 members of the opposition New Frontiers party (*Shinshinto*) boycott the session that approved it but about 70 members of the governing coalition did not attend the session either. In the resolution the House of Representatives "offer[ed] its sincere condolences to those who fell in action [in World War II] and victims of wars and similar actions all over the world" and "express[ed] a sense of deep remorse." It also stated: "We must transcend the differences over historical views of the past war and learn humbly the lessons of history so as to build a peaceful international society."[61]

ROK Ambassador to Japan Kim Tae Zhee called the Diet resolution a "retreat" from what former prime ministers had acknowledged. The reaction of the South Korean media was more direct. The Korean Broadcasting System (KBS) commented that "the resolution contains only ambiguous phrasing without using the word 'apology' for Japan's past wrongdoings and fails to say [Japan] will never again engage in armed conflict." This assessment was echoed in major newspapers such as *Chosun ilbo* and *Hankook ilbo*.[62]

The statement issued by Prime Minister Murayama on August 15, the 50th anniversary of the end of World War II, was aimed at mollifying adverse reaction to the Diet resolution noted above. In his statement Murayama described Japan's "colonial rule and aggression" and the "tremendous damage and suffering" (*tadaino songai to kutsu*) they had

---

60 Ibid., 378.
61 *Japan Times*, weekly international edition, June 19-25, 1995, 1 and 6.
62 Ibid., 3.

caused to the "people of many countries, particularly those of Asian nations" as "irrefutable facts of history." He then expressed "once again my feelings of deep remorse and state[d] my heartfelt apology," adding that he also wished to "express my feelings of profound mourning for all victims, both at home and abroad, of that history." Finally, Murayama stated that "building from our deep remorse······Japan must eliminate self-righteous nationalism, promote international cooperation as a responsible member of the international community and, thereby, advance the principles of peace and democracy."[63]

In the second half of the year, however, a succession of cabinet ministers, including the prime minister himself, made remarks that irked the Korean people. On August 8, two weeks before Murayama issued his statement of remorse, the newly appointed Education Minister, Shimamura Yoshino, told reporters that whether an act of aggression has occurred is subject to debate inasumuch as a war always entails one side attacking another and one of them emerging victorious. Although couched in general terms, these comments nonetheless triggered an expression of "deep regret" from the ROK Foreign Ministry.[64]

Then, on October 5, Prime Minister Murayama made a comment in the House of Councillors Budget Committee that touched off a frenzied reaction in South Korea. Responding to a question concerning the Japan-Korea annexation treaty, Murayama said that his understanding was that "in the context of······international relations at the time the treaty was concluded and implemented in a legally effective manner." Not only did the South Korean government lodge a formal protest but the ROK National Assembly adopted a resolution demanding a "correct historical understanding" from Japan, and 106 members, over a third of the entire

---

[63] Gaimusho, *Murayama sori daizin danwa: sengo 50-shunen no shusen kinenbi ni atatte* [Statement by Prime Minister Murayama: On the Occasion of the 50th Anniversary of the End of the War], August 15, 1995 (Tokyo); Ministry of Foreign Affairs of Japan, *Statement by Prime Minister Tomiichi Murayama* (15 August 1995) (Tokyo).

[64] Oemubu, *Ilbon kaehwang,* 1996. 2, 378.

membership, submitted a proposal to seek the repeal and renegotiation of agreements between the ROK and Japan pertaining to normalization and related issues.[65]

In an unusual move, even President Kim Young Sam joined the chorus of criticism. He told the *New York Times* on October 14 that Murayama had disappointed the Korean people with his comments, adding that it would be impossible to build a future-oriented ROK-Japan relationship without a correct understanding of history. According to a highly-placed South Korean source, Kim went so far as to call Japanese politicians "liars." Kim was also reported to have accused Japan of impeding Korean unification.[66]

On October 17, Foreign Minister Kono Yohei stated in a news conference that Japan bore no responsibility for the division of the Korean peninsula. He was referring to the argument by many Koreans that by starting the Pacific war and by not surrendering sooner, Japan had induced the Soviet Union's entry into the war during its final days, which in turn had led to the peninsula's partition after Japanese surrender. The ROK Foreign Ministry's spokesman issued a statement on the same day expressing profound regret at what it called Kono's "distortion of history" and "glossing over" Japanese actions.[67]

Against this backdrop, South Korea canceled a "summit" meeting between Kim Young Sam and Murayama that had been scheduled to take place in New York on October 22 while both were attending the UN's celebration of its 50th anniversary. Also canceled was a plenary meeting of the Japan-ROK Parliamentary Union, which had been scheduled for the same month in Seoul.[68]

---

65 Gaimusho, Ajia Kyoku, Hokuto Ajia-ka, *Chosen hanto josei to Nikkan kankei* [The Situation on the Korean Peninsula and Japan-ROK Relations], May 22, 1996, an unpublished document, 8.

66 "T'ong'il chongch'aek panghae tung kanghan pulk'oegam: Kim taet'ongnyong taeil kangkyong paron paegyong" [Strong Displeasure Over Impeding Unification Policy, etc: Background of President Kim's Hardline Statement Toward Japan], *Hankook ilbo*, October 16, 1995, 4.

67 Oemubu, *Ilbon kaewhang*, 1996. 2, 379.

Finally, on November 8, the South Korean press reported that Eto Takami, the director-general of the Management and Coordination Agency, had told Japanese reporters that Japan had done "good things for Korea during the colonial period" and that the Japan-Korea treaty of annexation had been valid. To call it invalid, he said, would mean that no international agreements are possible. The ROK Foreign Ministry reacted strongly to the report, saying that if Eto had indeed made these remarks, then it could "not suppress [a sense of] shock and indignation." It added that it "expect[ed] the Japanese government to take an appropriate action." On November 13, Eto resigned from his cabinet post.[69]

On the following day, Japan took the initiative to halt a further deterioration of the climate in Tokyo-Seoul relations. Since the APEC ministerial and summit meetings were about to get under way in Osaka, sending a conciliatory signal to South Korea might help ensure that a meeting between Prime Minister Murayama and President Kim Young Sam would not fail to materialize for the second time in as many months. A copy of a letter from Murayama addressed to Kim Young Sam was transmitted by Japan's ambassador to the ROK Yamashita Shintaro to Foreign Minister Gong Ro-myung in Seoul on November 14, with the original being hand-delivered by Foreign Minister Kono Yohei to Gong the next day in Osaka.[70]

---

68 *Hankook ilbo*, October 19, 1995, 1.
69 Oemubu, *Ilbon kaehwang, 1996. 2*, 379; Gaimusho, Ajia Kyoku, Hokuto Ajia-ka, *Chosen hanto josei to Nikkan kankei*, 8. In January 1995 Eto made remarks that "outraged" ROK President Kim Young Sam. In a speech at Kita Kyushu University, Fukuoka prefecture on January 13, Eto asked rhetorically: "Why is a treaty between countries [signed] in 1910 called an invasion now? What is the difference between that and the merger of a town and a village?" Kim told Japanese Foreign Minister Ikeda Yukihio at the Blue House on January 15 that "the remarks are regretable," urging the Japanese government to "take steps to prevent any recurrence of such remarks." *Japan Times*, weekly international edition, January 27-February 2, 1997, 3.
70 Gaimusho, Ajia Kyoku, *Hokuto Ajia-ka, Murayama sori hatsu Kim Young Sam Kankoku daitoryo ate shokan* [Prime Minister Murayama's Letter to ROK

In his letter, Murayama implied that the Japan-Korea annexation treaty was an unequal treaty. In his words, "the treaty annexing Korea and other treaties preceding it were concluded at a time when the relations between the two sides had become unequal against the background of a widening gap in power in the latter half of the 19th century. It is beyond doubt that these treaties were those of the imperialistic era that did not recognize [the right to] national self-determination or national dignity."[71]

Recalling that on August 15 he had humbly acknowledged as a historical fact Japan's misdeeds in the not too distant past that had inflicted great losses and sufferings on other nations and peoples, Murayama expressed anew his "deep remorse and heartfelt apology" to "the people of the Korean peninsula" for the "unbearable hardship and grief" they suffered under colonial rule brought about by the annexation treaty." "I have engraved anew in my heart the depth of the injury that treaty has left in the minds of the ROK citizens, an injury that cannot really be healed," he wrote.[72]

Murayama went on to express his "unshakable conviction" that a future-oriented Japan-ROK relationship can only be built on a foundation of an "acute remorse toward the past" [*kakoni taisuru tsusekina hansei*]. Finally, Murayama reassured Kim Young Sam that the keystone of Japan's Korea policy was the strengthening of friendly relations with the ROK. Tokyo's policy toward Pyongyang—that is, any movement in Japan-DPRK relations—, he wrote, would continue to be guided by the "principle of harmonizing with progress in North-South [Korea] relations."[73]

President Kim Young Sam], November 17, 1995, an unpublished document.
71 Ibid., 1.
72 Ibid.
73 Ibid., 2.

The Murayama-Kim Meeting in Osaka, November 1995

Thanks in large part to the preceding letter, Murayama and Kim Young Sam did hold a 45-minute meeting in Osaka on November 18. On its agenda were four issues: (1) historical legacy, (2) North Korea, (3) APEC and (4) bilateral trade, with emphasis on the first two. Regarding history, the two leaders reaffirmed the importance of correctly understanding the past but being future-oriented (*kako o chokushi shi, mirai o shiko suru koto*), agreeing to provide government assistance to collaborative historical research between Japanese and Korean scholars.[74]

As for North Korea, the two leaders discussed the problem of supplying rice to the North, which both countries had done earlier in the year and which the North were asking them to continue. Kim stressed the need to be on guard against Pyongyang's tactic of trying to foment division between Seoul and Tokyo. Murayama explained that Japan's policy toward North Korea was guided by two principles: (1) rectifying the abnormal relations between Japan and the DPRK that have existed in the post-World War II period and (2) making a contribution to the peace and stability of the Korean peninsula. He assured Kim that Japan would maintain close consultation with South Korea in pursuing its policy toward the North.[75]

The two leaders concurred on the importance of trilateral consultations among the ROK, Japan, and the U.S and reaffirmed the shared view of the two sides that how Japan-ROK relations evolve would affect not merely the Korean peninsula but the entire Asia-Pacific region as well. Since the whole world was watching the bilateral relationship, they agreed, the two countries had an obligation to pursue a forward-looking cooperative relationship. In this connection, Kim Young Sam expressed both agreement with and appreciation for the ideas embodied

---

74 Gaimusho, Ajia Kyoku, *Hokuto Ajia-ka, Nikkan shuno kaidan no gaiyo (11-gatsu 18-nichi 11:15-12:00)* [A Summary of the Japan-ROK Summit Meeting, 11:15-12:00, November 18], November 18, 1995, an unpublished document.
75 Ibid.

in Murayama's letter noted above.[76]

Its brevity notwithstanding, the Osaka summit signaled the thawing of the frosty climate that had threatened to impede cooperation between Tokyo and Seoul. The stakes were high for both sides, and in the end reason appeared to prevail over emotions. Nonetheless, the deterioration of Japan-ROK relations in 1995, the 30th year of their normalization, served as a reminder that three decades of economic interactions, cultural exchanges, and cooperation in political and security affairs had failed to exorcise the ghost of Japanese colonial rule in Korea. No amount of rhetoric could conceal the reality that historical legacy has an amazing staying power, that nationalistic emotions can be aroused by seemingly trivial incidents, and that the edifice of Japan-ROK relations remained precariously fragile.

Conclusion

Regime identity, a modified constructivist variable, can help explain many aspects of summit diplomacy during the third decade of normalization. The defining characteristic of the Roh Tae Woo regime was democratic transition. Not only did his election signify the first direct presidential election in South Korea in 16 years but his inauguration heralded the first peaceful transfer of power in the turbulent history of the ROK. Roh, moreover, could claim a large measure of credit for the outcome, since it was his dramatic declaration on June 29, 1987 that paved the way for reasonably free and fair electoral competition, in which the opposition camp had a good chance of winning but missed it due to its failure to unite behind a single candidate.[77]

The bottom line, nonetheless, was that South Korea had finally crossed the threshold of democratic transition.[78] A concomitant of

---

76 Ibid.
77 Im Yong-t'ae, *Taehan Minguk 50-nyonsa*, 2 [The 50 Year History of the Republic of Korea, vol. 2] (Seoul: Tullyok, 1998), 246-53.

democratic transition was an expansion of the freedom of the press and the role of public opinion in policymaking, both domestic and foreign. This was the backdrop against which the Roh government was constrained to raise the issue of the Japanese emperor's *okotoba* in conjunction with Roh's May 1989 state visit.

Another aspect of Roh's regime identity was his aspiration to project an image of *pot'ong saram* (ordinary man), which entailed measures, most of them more cosmetic than substantive, aimed at toning down the trappings of authoritarianism and the "imperial" presidency. It was therefore not coincidental that the first-ever "working visit" in Tokyo-Seoul summit diplomacy occurred when Roh made a one-day visit to Kyoto in November 1992.

The identity of the Kim Young Sam government was officially proclaimed as *munmin chongbu* (civilian government), signaling that he was the fist civilian to be elected president in 30 years. With his election, South Korea was well on its way toward democratic consolidation. Unlike his predecessors, moreover, Kim's legitimacy was beyond question. During the first year of his tenure in office, he enjoyed an unprecedented popularity rating of over 90 percent in public opinion polls. The confidence all this gave him may help explain his government's decision not to request an *okotoba* from the emperor in connection with his state visit to Japan in March 1994.

As noted in the preceding chapter, the concept of regime identity is less germane to Japan than it is to South Korea. Nonetheless, to the extent that a prime minister can influence the tone or even contents of his rhetoric in summit meetings, regime identity can be assumed to play a role. A case in point is Prime Minister Hosokawa Morihiro, who was refreshingly direct in expressing his remorse and apology for Japan's past behavior toward the Korean people. By specifically mentioning and atoning for Japan's colonial policy that sought to destroy the identity of

---

78 For an excellent overview of the theoretical and empirical literature on democratization, see Larry Diamond, *Developing Democracy:Toward Consolidation* (Baltimore: Johns Hopkins University Press, 1999).

the Korean people, Hosokawa struck a responsive chord among his Korean audience.

In the case of Prime Minister Murayama Tomiichi, however, regime identity had mixed results. The coalition government he headed was the outcome of a marriage of convenience, and he needed to perform a delicate balancing act so as not to alienate diverse constituencies, including the numerically superior coalition partner, the LDP. This may help account for the apparent inconsistency in his statements pertaining to Japanese colonial rule over Korea, which led to unprecedented diplomatic snubs by the Kim Young Sam government.

Closely related to the above is the concept of two-level game. The dynamics of domestic politics, especially the configuration and relative influence of interest groups broadly defined, helped to mold the win-sets of the regimes in Tokyo and Seoul alike. The discrepancy between promise and performance often reflected what Putnam calls "involuntary defection"—the Level I player's inability to "deliver on a promise because of failed ratification" at Level II.[79] The bureaucracy, by dragging its feet in implementing an international agreement, had the de facto power to veto ratification. Uncertainty about ratification often led to ambiguity in commitments made, which typically lacked specific targets. The brevity of the prime minister's tenure in office, another aspect of internal politics, contributed to the misfit between outcomes and effects as well.

The timing of summit diplomacy was sometimes dictated by developments in external setting—such as the initiation of Japan-DPRK negotiations on diplomatic normalization and the death of Kim Il Sung. External events, notably those related to North Korea's suspected nuclear program, provided a major topic for discussion, invariably producing a consensus on counter-measures. This was true even when a socialist prime minister headed the ruling coalition in Japan, which may have reflected, inter alia, the power of Japan's foreign policy bureaucracy and Prime Minister Murayama's pragmatism. The adage that "where one

---

79 Putnam, "Diplomacy and Domestic Politics," 440.

stands depends on where one sits" appeared to be apropos here.

How may one account for the frequency with which Japanese politicians utter what Koreans call *mang'on* (reckless remarks) concerning history? Are they slips of tongue or do they bespeak the speakers' true convictions *(honne* in Japanese)? While the answer may vary from speaker to speaker, the possibility cannot be ruled out that they not only betray the speakers' *honne* but also are shared by the latter's age cohorts. If that is the case, a true reconciliation between the Japanese and Korean people may have to await a thoroughgoing generational change in Japanese politics, a total eclipse of the "colonial" or World War II generation by the postwar generation in the political arena.

CHAPTER 7

The Resilience of Conflict in Japan-ROK Relations

As Japan and South Korea entered the fourth decade of normal inter-state relations,[1] the two countries had become closer to each other than ever before. Economically, South Korea was Japan's third largest export market in the world, next to the U.S. and Hong Kong, and fourth largest source of imported goods. Japan retained its position as the number one source of South Korean imports for the 12th consecutive year, eclipsing the U.S.

In the realm of security the perception of a common threat emanating from North Korea had brought the two neighbors together, institutionalizing trilateral consultations among the two and their

---

1 In a strict sense, the fourth decade began on December 18, 1995, because the Japan-ROK normalization treaty (the basic treaty) entered into force on December 18, 1965 upon an exchange of the instruments of ratification. Oemubu, *Han'guk oegyo samsimnyon, 1948-1978* [30 Years of Republic of Korea Diplomacy, 1948-1978] (Seoul: Oemubu, 1979), 28-29.

common ally, the US. Linked by two alliance treaties—the US-Japan security treaty and the US-ROK mutual defense treaty—, the three were partners in a de facto tripartite strategic alliance.

Close interactions in the economic and security arenas, however, had failed to dissipate the lingering feelings of distrust rooted in the bitter experience of colonial rule. Repeated verbal pledges at the highest level had not really helped to settle the past once and for all.

Nationalistic emotions, exacerbated by historical memory, also fueled a territorial dispute. A long-simmering dispute over a group of islets in the Sea of Japan (or the East Sea) known as Takeshima in Japan and Tokdo in South Korea flared up in February 1996, plunging Tokyo-Seoul relations to a new low.

From early 1996 to early 1998, then, discord overshadowed cooperation in Japan-ROK relations. The situation began to change, however, with the inauguration of the Kim Dae Jung government in Seoul in February 1998, which marked the first peaceful transfer of power between the ruling and the opposition camps in South Korean political history. Kim's visit to Japan in October 1998 appeared to herald a turning point in Seoul-Tokyo relations, ushering in an era of a genuine partnership.

The ensuing two and a half years witnessed a blossoming of cooperation between the two countries. Mutual visits and consultations among officials accelerated. Security cooperation, both bilateral and trilateral (including their common ally, the US), increased measurably. Economic ties were strengthened. South Korea began to lift a long-standing ban on the import of Japanese popular culture in stages. The two countries became the top destinations of each other's tourists going abroad.

The hope that Japan-ROK relations really had turned a corner—that cooperation would eclipse discord on an enduring basis—, however, was rudely dashed in early 2001, when disputes erupted anew on old issues—history textbooks and fishing. Dramatic development in the global environment—the terrorist attacks on the United States in September 2001—, however, helped to set in motion a process of a rapprochment in

October after six months of strained relations.

In sum, the period 1986-2001 saw an amazing resiliency of conflict in Japan-ROK relations. Conflict was their salient, albeit not dominant, feature over 80 percent of the time, reappearing on the scene after a brief interlude of cooperation. The return of cooperation after six months suggests, however, that the overall relationship between Tokyo and Seoul should not be characterized as conflictual, even when conflict seemed to be more pervasive than cooperation. Cooperation in economic and security relations has remained largely intact, and summit meetings and other high-level inter-governmental contacts have continued.

The Territorial Dispute

The conflicting claims by Tokyo and Seoul over the Takeshima/Tokdo island were so irreconcilable that they remained unresolved at the time of normalization in 1965,[2] and both sideshad steadfastly maintained their claims during the ensuing four decades. Tokyo's claim is based in part on old Japanese documents and maps showing that "Matsushima," which, according to the Japanese, was the ancient name for Takeshima, had been controlled by the Tokugawa bakufu (military government) and in part on the formal incorporation of

---

2 Gaimusho Sengo Gaikoshi Kenkyukai, ed., *Nihon gaiko 30-nen: sengono kiseki to tenbo, 1952-1982* [Thirty Years of Japanese Diplomacy: The Postwar Record and Prospects, 1952-1982] (Tokyo: Sekaino Ugoki-sha, 1982), 89-90. South Korean diplomatic documents declassified in August 2005 reveal that in September 1962 Iseki Yujiro, director-general of the Japanese Foreign Ministry's Asian Bureau, even suggested blowing up the island as an extreme solution to the dispute over its ownership, noting that it was "about the size of Hibiya Park" in Tokyo and "practically worthless." See "Han'il hoedam munso palch'ue, Tokdo munje" [Excerpts from Documents on ROK-Japan Normalization Talks: Tokdo Issue], *Chosun ilbo*, August 27, 2005; Yuichiro Nakamura, "ROK Releases Secret Papers/ Documents Detail Talks over Takeshima," *Daily Yomiuri*, August 27, 2005.

the island into Shimane prefecture in February 1905 pursuant to a decision of the cabinet. Tokyo's assertions that the cabinet decision had "reconfirmed the Japanese government's intention as a modern state to possess Takeshima" and that the failure of the Korean government to protest the Japanese action was tantamount to acquiescence, however, are challenged by Seoul.[3]

Seoul, citing historical documents, argues that Korea had exercised jurisdiction over the island from as early as the sixth century and that in 1905 Korea was in no position to lodge protest to Japan. Seoul also cites Directive No. 677 of the Supreme Commander for Allied Powers issued to the Japanese government in 1946, which explicitly excluded "Liancourt Rocks (Take Island)" from Japanese jurisdiction. The disputed island was then called Liancourt Rocks, named after a French ship which reported discovering it in 1849.[4]

After the Syngman Rhee government included the island inside the boundary of the Peace Line in January 1952,[5] the Japanese government delivered its first diplomatic note of protest to Seoul asserting Japanese sovereignty over Takeshima. South Korea, however, dispatched "volunteer guards" (*uiyong subidae*) to the island in April 1953, replacing them with police guards (*Tokdo kyongbidae*) in February 1956. In August 1954 South Korea installed a lighthouse on the island, fortifying it in August 1955. South Korea also built a helicopter landing facility on it in December

---

3 Gaimusho, Ajia-kyoku, Hokuto Ajia-ka, *Takeshima mondai* [Takeshima Issue] (Tokyo: undated); Ministry of Foreign Affairs of Japan, *The Issue of Takeshima* (Tokyo: March 2004), http://www.mofa.go.jp/region/ asia-paci/takeshima/position.html.

4 Oemubu, *Tokdo kwallyon ch'amgo charyo* [Reference Material Relating to Tokdo], April 1996 (Seoul); Ministry of Foreign Affairs and Trade, *Dokdo: Korean Territory Since the Sixth Century* (Seoul: July 2005), http://www.mofat.go.kr/mofat/ICSFiles/afieldfile/2005/07/18/Dokdo.pdf For a list of both Korean and Japanese documents that Koreans claim "prove" Tokdo's status as Korean territory, see Kukbangbu, *Kukbang paekso, 1998* [Defense White Paper, 1998] (Seoul, 1998), appendix 8.

5 For the background of Rhee's "Peace Line," see Lee, *Japan and Korea*, 37-38.

1981 and a radar station in December 1993.[6]

Tokyo has sent Seoul a memorandum of protest every year, to which Seoul has always responded with a memorandum refuting the Japanese claim. Until 1993 the *Diplomatic Bluebook* published annually by the Japanese Foreign Ministry included the following statement: "It is clear that Takeshima, over which we have a jurisdictional dispute with the Republic of Korea, is a Japanese territory both legally and historically; we therefore regularly protest to the Republic of Korea, conveying [our] position."[7]

Under international law, consolidation of title to territory requires a continuous and peaceful display of authority. Notwithstanding South Korea's occupation of Tokdo/Takeshima continuously since 1953, Japan's lodging of protests to South Korea at periodic intervals would therefore leave the issue of who has sovereignty over the disputed island unsettled. Protest has the legal effect of making South Korea's display of authority less than peaceful.[8]

When South Korea began to take steps to build a wharf on one of the islets comprising the island in February, 1996, Japanese Foreign Minister Ikeda Yukihiko expressed Japan's objections, reiterating Japan's claim to sovereignty over the island and asking South Korea to stop the project. This move occurred as part of Japan's preparation to declare a 200-mile exclusive economic zone (EEZ) in conjunction with its ratification of the United Nations Convention on the Law of the Sea.[9]

---

6 Oemubu, *Tokdo kwallyon ch'amgo charyo*, 9-10.
7 Gaimusho, ed., *Gaiko seisho: tenkanki no sekai to Nihon, 1992* [Diplomatic Bluebook: The World in Transition and Japan, 1992] (Tokyo: Okurasho, Insatsu-kyoku, 1993), 180-81. Nearly identical statements are found in the earlier editions as well.
8 Two most frequently cited cases pertaining to this issue are "Island of Palmas case" (United States v. the Netherlands), Permanent Court of Arbitration, 1928 and "Legal Status of Eastern Greenland case" (Denmark v. Norway), Permanent Court of International Justice, 1933. For excerpts from the courts' decisions, see Louis Henkin et al, *International Law: Cases and Materials*, 3rd ed. (St.Paul, MN: West Publishing Co., 1993), 309-20.
9 *Japan Times*, weekly international edition, February 19-25, 1996, 3.

South Korea's response to Ikeda's statement was both swift and stern. The ROK Foreign Ministry's spokesman said on February 9: "We have repeatedly reaffirmed that Tokdo is our territory from the standpoint of both history and international law and that we have effective control over it." Labeling the Japanese protest an "infringement of our sovereignty," Seoul indicated that it would proceed with the project for building a wharf. Seoul also canceled a meeting between President Kim Young Sam and a delegation of Japan's ruling coalition headed by Yamasaki Taku, chairman of the Liberal Democratic party's Policy Affairs Research Council, which had been scheduled for February 12. The Japanese delegation, which had been planning to raise the island issue with Kim Young Sam, canceled its plan to visit Seoul altogether.[10]

The South Korean press quoted a government source as saying that the ROK government might be compelled to seek a revision of the 1965 normalization treaty as well as a review and adjustment of the whole gamut of bilateral issues, including the "comfort women" issue, fisheries, the return of cultural properties, and the status of ROK residents in Japan. All South Korean political parties were united in their denunciation of Japan, and many organizations, including radical student organizations, not only issued statements critical of Japan but also staged rallies and demonstrations, some of which featured the burning of Ikeda's effigies.[11]

The ROK government unveiled a plan to conduct a military exercise in the vicinity of the disputed island and to increase the number of police guards stationed on it from 26 to 34. The exercise had actually been planned before the dispute erupted and was a regular occurrence. It took place on February 15, with three naval vessels, one high-speed patrol boat, and four combat aircraft taking part.[12] The Japanese government appeared to take all this in strides. Prime Minister Hashimoto reportedly stressed in an informal meeting of cabinet members the importance of "continu[ing] talks calmly to prevent each country's different position

---

10 *Hankook ilbo* (Seoul), February 10 and 11, 1996.
11 *Ibid.*, February 12 and 13, 1996.
12 *Ibid.*, February 16, 1996.

from undermining friendly relations."[13]

South Korea, however, refused to engage in any negotiations with Japan over the island dispute, insisting that it was not a negotiable issue. When the Japanese cabinet on February 20 approved a plan to proclaim an EEZ, the ROK government responded by officially proclaiming an EEZ of its own on the same day.[14] Since there would be considerable overlap between the two EEZs, however, neither side was in a position to delineate its EEZ boundaries unilaterally; negotiation would become unavoidable.

The opportunity to find a modus vivendi arrived in early March. With both sides concluding that they had more to lose than gain by continuing the island dispute, they conducted behind-the-scenes negotiations to prepare for a summit meeting between Prime Minister Hashimoto and President Kim Young Sam in Bangkok, Thailand, where both were scheduled to attend the Asia-Europe Meeting (ASEM), the inaugural summit of Asian and European leaders, from March 1 to 2. Although a Hashimoto-Kim meeting had been agreed to prior to the outbreak of the island dispute, the latter had placed its occurrence in jeopardy.

When the two leaders finally did meet in Bangkok on March 1, they reiterated their respective governments' claims to the island but agreed to separate the issue from other pending bilateral issues. Hashimoto stressed that the two countries "share such fundamental values as freedom, democracy and a market-economy," voicing "the hope that Tokyo can forge a 'future-oriented' relationship with Seoul based on repentance for

---

13 *Japan Times*, weekly international edition, February 19-25, 1996, 3. and February 26-March 3, 1996, 7.
14 *Hankook ilbo*, February 21, 1996; *Japan Times*, weekly international edition, February 26-March 3, 1996, 1. Both countries had already enacted laws on EEZ following their ratification of the UN Convention on the Law of the Seas. A South Korean law on EEZ entered into force in September 1996, and a Japanese law on EEZ took effect in July 1996. Oemubu, *Han'il kwan'gye hyon'an mit Ilbon chongse, 1997. 8* [Issues in ROK-Japan Relations and the Situation in Japan, Augast 1997], (Seoul, 1997), 4.

its wrongs up to and including World War II." Kim replied that Seoul, too, "attaches importance to its relations with Tokyo and mentioned the need to cement ties further." The two leaders "reaffirmed that Tokyo and Seoul would continue to explore specific ways to help promote private-sector studies on the history of relations between Japan and Korea." They also exchanged their views on their handling of North Korea. Hashimoto informed Kim of his government's decision to contribute $19 million to the Korean Peninsula Energy Development Organization (KEDO) to help pay for the heavy fuel oil that will be supplied to the North in accordance with the 1994 Geneva accords.[15]

The Bangkok summit signaled that the island dispute, although far from being resolved, would remain dormant for the time being. A crisis of major proportions was thus averted in Tokyo-Seoul relations. Only by bypassing the island issue would the two sides manage to hammer out a new fisheries agreement two and a half years later.

World Cup 2002 and the Cheju Summit

On May 31, 1996 the Federation of International Football Associations (FIFA) announced a decision on the co-hosting of the 2002 World Cup by Japan and South Korea. One of the two most popular athletic events in the world, along with the Olympic games, the quadrennial soccer tournament in the year 2002, the first such event in the 21st century, had been the focus of intense diplomatic competition between the two countries. Not only was FIFA's surprising decision unprecedented but it would have significant implications for Tokyo-Seoul relations as well.[16]

---

15 *Japan Times*, weekly international edition, March 11-17, 1996, 1 and 6; *Hankook ilbo*, March 4, 1996; Gaimusho, Ajia Kyoku, Hokuto Ajia-ka, *Chosen hanto josei to Nikkan kankei* [The Situation on the Korean Peninsula and Japan-ROK Relations], May 22, 1996, an unpublished document, 9. The quotations are from *Japan Times*.

Co-hosting would necessitate close cooperation between the two countries. In order to make it an unqualified success, which both countries undoubtedly want, they would need to leave no stone unturned. Meticulous preparations would necessarily entail frequent and extensive consultations. In a word, the two countries would need to work together for a common goal until the year 2002.

Although the reaction in the two countries was mixed, editorial commentaries were generally positive. Japan, which had the backing of FIFA President Joao Havelange, had resisted the idea of co-hosting until the last minute but, according to Naganuma Ken, president of the Football Association of Japan, forcing "a straight two-way vote" in the 21-member FIFA executive committee carried the risk of "losing everything;" hence Japan accepted "half a world cup."[17] *Asahi shinbun* editorially welcomed FIFA's decision, saying that it "offers an opportunity to build a new Japan-South Korea relationship······Mutual understanding and cooperation between our two countries will go a long way toward peace and stability in Asia." *Yomiuri shinbun* called the decision "a realistic compromise," calling on the two countries to "work together in a spirit of fair play" to make the co-hosting a success.[18]

In South Korea *Hankook ilbo* summed up the prevailing mood when it labeled the co-hosting decision a "test of ROK-Japan reconciliation" . Noting that many difficulties lie ahead—such as choosing the sites for the matches, dividing the revenues, deciding on sponsorships and television rights, and the composition of organizing committees—, the South Korean daily cautioned that co-hosting the tournament might aggravate rather than ameliorate Seoul-Tokyo relations. Should the two countries approach their tasks with empathy and in a spirit of reciprocity, the paper

---

16 *Japan Times*, weekly international edition, June 10-16, 1996, 1 and 5; *Hankook ilbo*, June 1 and 3, 1996.
17 Kumi Kinohara, "Half a World Cup Better Than None," *Japan Times*, weekly international edition, June 24-30, 1996, 18.
18 "Editorial Sampler: FIFA Decision Brings Rare Opportunity," ibid., July 1-7, 1996, 20.

wrote, they would not only succeed in their common goal of successfully co-hosting the tournament but also find solutions to other pending bilateral issues.[19]

Against this backdrop the top leaders of the two countries held another summit meeting, their second in the year, in Cheju island from June 22 to 23. According to the ROK Foreign Ministry, Kim Young Sam, desirous of utilizing the FIFA decision to work toward elevating the ROK-Japan relationship to a higher level in the 21st century, proposed a summit to Hashimoto. The first visit by a Japanese prime minister to South Korea in nearly two years, the Hashimoto visit symbolized the determination of both countries to set aside differences and accentuate shared interests.[20]

Welcoming the co-hosting decision as desirable for the development of Japan-ROK relations, the two leaders agreed to set up a structure for facilitating consultations and cooperation so as to make the 2002 World Cup, the first such event to be held in Asia, the "most successful in history." They also reaffirmed their agreement at the Bangkok summit on the need to separate the territorial issue from other bilateral issues, noting the urgency of stepping up negotiations on the delineation of the boundaries of the two countries' EEZs as well as on fisheries. Hashimoto underscored the need to create an atmosphere conducive to "friendly and dispassionate dialogue."[21]

A key item on the agenda of the Cheju summit was North Korea. The two leaders affirmed the importance of maintaining close consultations and a united front among Seoul, Tokyo, and Washington. Hashimoto

---

19 "Han'il hwahap ui sihomdae" [Test of ROK-Japan Reconciliation," an editorial, *Hankook ilbo*, June 3, 1996.
20 Oemubu, *Han'il kwan'gye hyonhwang* [The Present Condition of ROK-Japan Relations], June 1996 (Seoul), 2.
21 Gaimusho, Ajia Kyoku, Hokuto Ajia-ka, *Hashimoto sori no hokan* (shuno kaidan) [Prime Minister Hashimoto's Visit to the Republic of Korea (Summit Meeting)], June 24, 1996; idem, *Kyodo kisha kaiken: Kankoku gawa boto hatsugen* [Joint Press Conference: the ROK Side's Opening Statement], June 23, 1996; idem, *Hashimoto sori kyodo kisha kaiken boto hatsugen* [Prime Minister Hashimoto's Opening Statement at the Joint Press conference], June 23, 1996.

reiterated his government's support of the Kim-Clinton proposal for four party peace talks involving the two Koreas, the US and China; Hashimoto had endorsed the proposal on April 16 immediately after it was unveiled in Cheju by the two presidents.[22] Kim and Hashimoto also exchanged views on cooperation in the economic and cultural spheres as well as in international organizations. They concurred on the need to strengthen cooperation in industrial technology and to increase investment. They agreed on the desirability of organizing a structure for joint historical research by scholars from both countries and reaffirmed the value of exchange among the youth. They discussed the possibility of increasing the number of youths that are exchanged from 5,000 to 10,000 a year. In this connection, Hashimoto noted that 37,000 Japanese students make field trips to South Korea each year, which is separate from the youth exchange project.[23]

Regarding cooperation in international organizations, the two leaders agreed to work closely in the UN, the Asia-Pacific Economic Cooperation (APEC), ASEM, the World Trade Organization (WTO), and other forums. Hashimoto asked Kim to support Japan's bid to become a nonpermanent member of the UN Security Council for the 1997-98 term, and Kim pledged his support. Hashimoto promised to make an effort to convey the two countries' common position on North Korea to the G-7 summit in Lyon, France as well as to seek support for KEDO. Hashimoto's effort was reflected in the statement by the chairman of the Lyon summit issued on June 29, which included two paragraphs on the Korean peninsula endorsing the position of the US, Japan, and the ROK.[24]

---

22 For the text of Hashimoto's endorsement of the four party talks proposal, see Gaimusho, Ajia Kyoku, Hokuto Ajia-ka, *Chosen hanto no eizokuteki heiwani kansuru shisha kaigo ni tsuiteno Hashimoto soridaizin no komento* [Prime Minister Hashimoto's Comments on the Proposal for a Four Party Meeting Concerning Permanent Peace on the Korean Peninsula], April 16, 1996 (Tokyo).
23 Gaimusho, Ajia Kyoku, Hokuto Ajia-ka, *Hashimoto sori no hokan*, 2.
24 Gaimusho, Ajia Kyoku, Hokuto Ajia-ka, *Riyon samitto gicho seimei Chosen hanto kanren bumon* [Lyon Summit Chairman's Statement: the Part Relating to the Korean Peninsula], June 29, 1996 (Tokyo).

During a joint press conference, Hashimoto revealed that he had made his first visit to South Korea in 1965 shortly after the Japan-ROK normalization treaty was signed. He was leading a group of Japanese students at the request of the then President of the Liberal Democratic party Sato Eisaku and had a chance to meet Kim Young Sam, who was an opposition member of the ROK National Assembly at the time. But what touched him most, Hashimoto said, was his discovery during talks with South Korean students that there were many aspects of the Korean people's experience under Japanese colonial rule that he had not learned in school. During his first two years of primary school before Japanese surrender, Hashimoto had not learned that the Korean people had been forced to adopt Japanese names; the sufferings inflicted by the Japanese on the Korean people, he said, were beyond imagination. He expressed his heartfelt apology and remorse for the "comfort women" issue, saying that "nothing injured the honor and dignity of women more than [being forced into sex slavery]." He reminded his audience that since becoming prime minister he had repeatedly said that "we must not evade the weight of the past or our responsibilities for the future."[25]

Hashimoto's remarks at the joint press conference were well received in South Korea. Yoo Chong Ha, the chief presidential secretary for foreign affairs and national security who would become the foreign minister later in the year, said that they "may be seen as progress from the previous Japanese stance." Yoo characterized the Cheju summit as "historic," adding: "The two leaders got together with a certain sense of purpose to forge personal rapport and seek ways to elevate bilateral relations to a new level, especially in co-hosting the 2002 World Cup soccer finals."[26]

---

25 Gaimusho, Ajia Kyoku, Hokuto Ajia-ka, *Nikkan shuno kyodo kisha kaiken* (shitsugi oto) [Joint Press Conference by the Top Leaders of Japan and the Republic of Korea (Qustions and Answers)], June 23, 1996, 1-2; *Japan Times*, weekly international edition, July 1-7, 1996, 1 and 5.
26 *Japan Times*, weekly international edition, July 1-7, 1996, 5.

The Hashimoto-Kim Meeting in Manila

Pursuant to an understanding reached at the Cheju summit that the two leaders should try to have frequent face-to-face meetings, they got together for the third time in 1996 on November 24 in Manila where they were attending the annual APEC summit. A key topic of their discussion was North Korea, for the North's dispatch of a submarine to the South in September had precipitated a crisis in inter-Korean relations. When the two leaders met, all but two of the 26 North Korean infiltrators who had sneaked into the South aboard the disabled submarine had been killed, eleven of them apparently at the hands of their comrades. One commando had been captured and another was still at large. The infiltrators, however, had not only tied up 60,000 South Korean soldiers for seven weeks but also caused the death of 17 South Korean soldiers, policemen, and civilians and the injury of over a dozen soldiers.[27]

The Kim Young Sam government took a hard-line stance toward the incident, calling on the North to apologize for the intrusion. Seoul also announced that it would suspend all economic cooperation with Pyongyang, including participation in KEDO's light-water reactor (LWR) project. Since Seoul was the principal financier of and the pivotal player in that project, its decision meant that the project would be on hold. During his talks with Kim Young Sam in Manila, Hashimoto said that he understood Seoul's position and expected the North to take measures that would satisfy the South. The two leaders reaffirmed the importance of preserving a united front among Seoul, Tokyo, and Washington vis-a-vis Pyongyang.[28]

---

27 For the submarine incident, see B. C. Koh, "South Korea in 1996: Internal Strains and External Challenges," *Asian Survey* 37, no. 1 (Jan. 1997), 1-9; for the Hashimoto-Kim meeting in Manila, see *Japan Times*, weekly international edition, December 2-8, 1996, 1 and 5 and *Hankook ilbo*, November 25, 1996.

28 Gaimusho, Ajia Kyoku, Hokuto Ajia-ka, *Nikkan shuno kaidan no gaiyo (11-gatsu 24-nichi, Manira)* [A Summary of the Japan-Republic of Korea Summit Meeting (November 24, Manila)], November 24, 1996, 1.

Earlier in the day, Bill Clinton and Kim Young Sam had agreed that the North would need to take "acceptable measures" before the implementation of the LWR project could go forward. The phrase "acceptable measures" was more flexible than the word "apology," thus giving the North more leeway. Clinton and Kim had also explicitly stated that their joint proposal for four-party peace talks was unconditional, meaning that it was not linked to any North Korean action regarding the submarine incident.[29]

Hashimoto and Kim reaffirmed their previous commitment to the building of a "future-oriented" bilateral relationship, discussing the means of expanding cooperation in various fields. They reiterated their common determination to cooperate fully to make the 2002 World Cup a success. Not wishing to inject any negative note into their meeting, the two leaders refrained from bringing up the island dispute in their talks.[30] Hashimoto renewed an invitation he had extended to Kim during the June Cheju summit to visit Japan, and Kim confirmed his acceptance of the invitation; the two leaders agreed that Kim would visit Japan in the early part of 1997. In deference to Hashimoto's wish to meet with Kim "in a casual setting, [the meeting] will probably be held outside of Tokyo," a senior Japanese official revealed.[31]

The "Comfort Women" Issue

In early January 1997, before another Hashimoto-Kim summit could take place, however, the "comfort women" issue emerged as a source of strain between Tokyo and Seoul. To note its background first, when the issue surfaced in the Japanese Diet for the first time in June 1990, the Japanese government took the position that since "comfort women" had

---

29 Ibid.; *The Korea Herald*, November 25, 1996.
30 Gaimusho, Ajia Kyoku, Hokuto Ajia-ka, *Nikkan shuno kaidan no gaiyo* (November 24, 1996), 2.
31 Ibid.; *Japan Times*, weekly international edition, December 2-8, 1996, 5.

nothing to do with the government but had been under the control of civilian entrepreneurs, there was no need for either government apology or compensation. The discovery of former Japanese Imperial Army documents implicating it in the Defense Agency Library in January 1992, however, compelled the government to initiate an inquiry.[32]

In July 1992 the Japanese government issued its first report on "comfort women" in which it admitted that there had been government involvement in the running of "comfort stations" during World War II. The report said, however, that the government had failed to find any evidence to prove that comfort women were forced to provide sex to Japanese soldiers. Faced with criticisms from Asian countries, especially South Korea, the Japanese government decided to continue its investigation, releasing its second report on the issue in August 1993.[33]

In its second report, which was unveiled on the day before the Miyazawa administration ended, the Japanese government reversed its earlier position and admitted for the first time that force had been used in recruiting "comfort women." Basing its conclusions in part on interviews with 16 former "comfort women" from South Korea, the report carefully avoided using the word *subete* (in every respect) regarding the use of coercion (*kyosei*), choosing instead the more restricted expression, *sojite* (on the whole or generally). The report did say, however, that the Japanese military authorities were in constant control of "comfort women," adding that "it is apparent that comfort women under military control must have been forced to live in miserable conditions without freedom."[34]

In a statement accompanying the release of the report, Chief Cabinet

---

32 Ajia Josei Shiryo Senta, ed., *"Ianfu" mondai* Q & A: *"Jiyushugishikan" e onnatachino hanron* [Questions and Answers on the "Comfort Women" Issue: Women's Refutation of "Liberal View of History"] (Tokyo: Meiseki Shoten, 1997), 26.
33 *Asahi shinbun*, August 5, 1993; *Japan Times*, August 5, 1993.
34 Ibid. On the background on the choice of the word *sojite* over *subete*, see "'Kyosei' hyogen saigo mate fushin" [Agonizing Until the Last Moment Over the Expression "Coercion"], *Asahi shinbun*, August 5, 1993, 27.

Secretary Kono Yohei offered his "heartfelt apology and remorse" to "all who have received humiliating injuries on their body and soul," saying that "we must not turn away from this type of historical truth but come to grips with it as a lesson of history." South Korea reacted favorably to the second report. ROK Foreign Minister Han Sungjoo, while giving a generally positive assessment, pointed out that the report lacked any information on the total number of "comfort women." Han expressed the hope that the Japanese government would continue to pay attention to the issue and throw light on those aspects that remain unexplained.[35]

In July 1995 the Japanese government established a private fund called the Asian Women's Fund (AWF)—*Josei no tameno Ajia Heiwa Kokumin Kikin (Ajia Josei Kikin)* in Japanese—with the aim of providing compensation to the 300 or so surviving former "comfort women" out of an estimated 200,000. After a special investigator for the UN Commission on Human Rights, Radhika Coomaraswamy of Sri Lanka, released a report in February 1996 calling for a Japanese *government* apology and compensation, a group of former "comfort women" urged Tokyo to halt the AWF's activities. They said that anything short of a formal government apology and compensation would "disgrace their honor and dignity."[36]

When the UN Commission on Human Rights met in Geneva in April 1996 to discuss the Coomaraswamy report, delegates from both North and South Korea hailed it, urging Japan to accept its recommendations. This represented a change in South Korea's position, which had been to decline government compensation; since July 1993 the ROK government had a program of its own for subsidizing the livelihood of the surviving victims.[37] Seoul's unqualified endorsement of

---

35 "Kankoku seifu wa ichio hyoka" [The ROK Government Gives a Generally Positive Assessment], *Asahi shinbun*, August 5, 1993, 1.
36 *Japan Times*, weekly international edition, February 12-18, 1996, 3 and May 27-June 2, 1996, 3.
37 The ROK National Assembly enacted a law on providing livelihood support to the "comfort women for the Japanese army during the Japanese imperialist period" in May 1993, and a government decree implementing the law was

the UN special investigator's report, therefore, was a significant reversal of its previous policy. Approval of government compensation meant, however, rejection of the "consolation money" from the AWF, a non-governmental organization, albeit under government auspices.

Prime Minister Hashimoto's decision to send a letter of apology to each surviving victim failed to mollify either the victims or their governments. In a letter drafted in August 1996 Hashimoto wrote:

> The issue of comfort women, with an involvement of the Japanese military authorities at the time, was a grave affront to the honor and dignity of large numbers of women. As Prime Minister of Japan, I thus extend anew my most sincere apologies and remorse to all the women who underwent immeasurable and painful experiences and suffered incurable physical and psychological wounds as comfort women.
>
> ......I pray from the bottom of my heart that each of you will find peace for the rest of your lives.[38]

Against this background the South Korean government was stunned to learn that on January 11, 1997 representatives of the AWF had distributed certificates guaranteeing payment of two million yen ($17,000) each to seven former "comfort women" in Seoul. All of the women also received letters of apology from Hashimoto. One of the AWF representatives who went to Seoul said that the seven Korean women had written to the Fund in December expressing their desire to receive the money. Indicating that there were more Korean women who wanted to receive compensation from the Fund, the representative hinted that the Fund would not cease its activities vis-a-vis Korean women.[39]

---

promulgated two months later. Under the decree, each surviving victim was given a lumpsum payment of five million won (about $6,250) and a monthly stipend of 150,000 won ($188). Oemubu, *Ilbon kaehwang*, 1994. 3 [The General Condition of Japan, March 1994] (Seoul: Oemubu, 1994), 239.

38 *Japan Times*, August 14, 1996, an "unofficial government translation."

ROK Vice Foreign Minister Lee Ki-Joo summoned Japanese ambassador Yamashita Shintaro to lodge a formal protest against the Japanese action. "Lee conveyed the South Korean government's opposition to the Fund's action of doling out compensation to the victims through a private channel." Yamashita reportedly told Lee that "the Japanese government had tried to stop the action but could not [do so] since the action was made by a private group." The ROK Foreign Ministry spokesman also issued a statement on the incident: "We regard the Fund's actions as a stop-gap payment, turning a blind eye to the demands of our government and the victims." The spokesman reiterated Seoul's request that "Japan voluntarily carry out" the recommendations of the 1995 UN special investigator's report. "A government official who requested anonymity" was more blunt: "Tempting some of the victims who are suffering from financial difficulties to accept the compensation was a provocative act which ignored the pride of the Korean people." He added: "We will use all means available from international law to counter the act."[40]

In a meeting with his Japanese counterpart, Ikeda Yukihiko, in Seoul on January 15, ROK Foreign Minister Yoo Chong Ha reiterated his government's position on the incident. Yoo expressed "extreme regret" at

---

39 *Dong-A ilbo* (Seoul), January 12, 1997. On January 20 the AWF deposited 5 million yen in the bank account of each of the seven women. The additional 3 million yen was intended for "medical and welfare expenses." Oegyo T'ongsangbu, *Ilbon kaehwang* [The General Condition of Japan] (Seoul: March 1998), 235.

40 *Korea Herald*, Jaunary 13, 1997; *Joongang ilbo* (Seoul), January 13, 1997. In July two AWF officials entered South Korea on tourist visas, met with seven former "comfort women," and obtained the latter's written consent to accept compensation from the Fund. This prompted an organization in the South called *Chongdaehyop* (Korean Council for Comfort Women) to denounce the Japanese government for its "fraudulent ploy······to shirk its responsibility for the war crimes." Ibid., July 30, 1997. A fund-raising drive to help the surviving Korean comfort women was subsequently launched by *Chondaehyop* in cooperation with South Korean news media.

the AWF's action, urging Japan to have the Fund revoke its action and stop payment of compensation to former sex slaves. Ikeda stressed that since the AWF's decision had been based on the wishes of the individuals concerned and on humanitarian considerations, it could not be revoked. He said, however, that in the future, there would be consultations between the foreign ministries of the two countries.[41]

The Beppu Simmit

On the eve of the Kim-Hashimoto summit in Beppu, Oita prefecture, Chief Cabinet Secretary Kajiyama Seiroku made comments on the "comfort women" issue that implied that "it would be wrong for people to only stress the cruel nature of the issue without taking the social background at that time into consideration," adding that "the younger generation [in Japan] is not taught about the 'once-authorized system' of licensed prostitution."[42] Since Kajiyama was the principal spokesman for the Hashimoto government, his comments could not but cast a dark shadow over the summit.[43]

---

41 Gaimusho, Ajia Kyoku, Hokuto Ajia-ka, *Nikkan gaisho kaidan no gaiyo (1-gatsu 15-nichi, Souru)* [Summary of the Japan-Republic of Korea Foreign Ministers' Meeting, January 15, Seoul], January 15,1997, 2.
42 "Kajiyama Elabortes on Sex-slave Comments," *Japan Times*, January 27, 1997. Kajiyma's original comments were made on January 24 but on January 27 he offered an apology to the South Korean people. "But," according to the *Japan Times*, "he then repeated his earlier comment that prostitution was legal in Japan before and during World War II, when the Imperial Japanese Army apparently operated brothels for its soldiers. Many of these women came from the Korean Peninsula and worked against their will in the military brothels."
43 A *Japan Times* editorial described Kajiyama's comments as "catastrophically ill-timed," "insensitive and irrelevant." In its words, "the social mores of the time have nothing to do with the abduction and forced sexual servitude of many women, most of them Korean." Asking "what would end South Korean protests over the past," the *Japan Times* said that "an honest and frank assessment of Japanese behavior in the past is part of the answer." See "Taking

362   *Between Discord and Cooperation*

One of the very first things Hashimoto did in Beppu was to reiterate his heartfelt apology to the Korean people. Hashimoto's action came on the heels of Kim Young Sam's reference to the Kajiyama comment, which Kim characterized as "something that is terribly wrong and requires an acceptable explanation." The South Korean press noted that Hashimoto made an apology not once but three times. The two leaders held two sessions—one at a lunch and another in the form of an "expanded meeting"—followed by a joint press conference on January 25. They held their final meeting during a breakfast the following day.[44]

A close reading of what Hashimoto said in reference to the Kajiyama comment reveals, however, that he actually tried to clarify it. During the joint press conference with Kim Young Sam on January 25, Hashimoto said the following:

> At the outset of today's summit meeting, I stated that if the press reports on Chief Cabinet Secretary Kajiyma's comments had created displeasure [*fukaini omowaretato sureba*], I was very sorry. I then explained what had actually happened. That is to say, [the comments in question] were made not during a press conference but in response to reporters' questions while [Kajiyma was] walking. He merely recounted what some Japanese Diet member had said during a visit to China, namely,······the existence of public brothels in our country in those days should be kept in mind as the backdrop for the period when there was the comfort women problem. [Kajiyama] explained [all this] to young reporters who had not even been born at the time. That is what happened.

Hashimoto added that he had reiterated to Kim Young Sam his

Things for Granted," ibid., January 29, 1997, an editorial.
44 *Dong-A ilbo*, January 25, 1997; *Chosun ilbo*, January 25, 1997; "Shushoga daitoryoni chinsha, kanbo chokan jugun ianfu hatsugen" [Prime Minister Apologizes to President on Chief Cabinet Secretary's Comment on Comfort Women], *Asahi shinbun*, January 25, 1997.

heartfelt apology and remorse for the injury done to the honor and dignity of women due to the comfort women problem, which he had expressed during the Cheju summit in June 1996, assuring Kim that there was no change either in his own thinking or in that of the Japanese government on the issue.[45]

Since both sides were eager to produce positive results, the two leaders did not pursue either the Kajiyama comment or the comfort women issue any further. During working-level negotiations in preparation for the summit, the two sides had actually agreed to avoid such sensitive issues as comfort women and the territorial dispute over Takeshima/Tokdo in the summit per se. They would, however, be discussed during foreign ministers' talks that would be held in conjunction with the summit. Hashimoto raised the territorial issue by saying that "I will not repeat the Japanese government's position on the Takeshima issue since you know it well," adding that "this issue should not be allowed to damage the friendly relationship between our two countries." He then requested that the bilateral fisheries agreement be renewed by the end of the year. Kim Young Sam responded by reiterating the consistent ROK position that "Tokdo is a Korean territory both historically and under international law, over which the Republic of Korea currently exercises effective control."[46]

North Korea received priority attention during the summit, with both leaders reconfirming their previous agreement to present a united front vis-a-vis Pyongyang. They would work together to induce North Korea to accept the proposal for a four-party peace talks. Hashimoto assured Kim that Japan would consult closely with South Korea on improving relations with North Korea, basing its policy on an assessment of the overall situation on the Korean Peninsula. Hashimoto also

---

45 Gaimusho, Ajia Kyoku, Hokuto Ajia-ka, *Nikkan shuno kyodo kisha kaiken (shitsugi oto)* [Joint Press Conference by the Top Leaders of Japan and the Republic of Korea (Questions and Answers)], January 25, 1997, 2.
46 "'Han'il chongsang hoedam' musun yaegi nawanna······" [The ROK-Japan Summit: What Was Discussed······], *Chosun ilbo*, January 25, 1997.

supported South Korea's opposition to the plan by Taiwan to ship low-grade nuclear waste to the North.[47] The Taiwan Power Company and North Korea signed a contract on January 11, under which the North would receive 60,000 barrels of radioactive waste from Taiwan over the next two years. The volume could reach 200,000 barrels. The North "will be paid US $1,150 per barrel in addition to an undisclosed lump sum for site preparation and shipping (assuming North Korean freighters are used)."[48]

The two leaders agreed to hold a "Japan-ROK Youth Exchange Network Forum" in Osaka in March and to revive annual soccer games between the two countries that had been suspended in order to promote closer cooperation for World Cup 2002. The first game would be held in Seoul in May, and the second in Tokyo in September. While the foreign ministers held separate talks on a wide range of issues including the renewal of the fisheries agreement and the delineation of boundaries in the EEZs proclaimed by both countries, no tangible progress was reported.[49]

All in all, the Beppu summit, which was designed to minimize formalities and maximize results, appeared to have been a largely symbolic affair. Neither side changed its previously held positions but reiterated them. Hashimoto's statement on what Koreans perceived as highly insensitive remarks by a key member of his cabinet on the eve of the summit did not seem to mollify South Korean public opinion. The

---

47 Gaimusho, Ajia Kyoku, Hokuto Ajia-ka, *Kim Young Sam daitoryo no honichi (shuno kaidan no gaiyo)* [President Kim Young Sam's Visit to Japan (A Summary of Summit Meeting)], January 25, 1997, 3; "Tai kita Chosen de renkei o kakunin ······Nikkan shuno kaidan" [Cooperation Toward North Korea Confirmed······Japan-ROK Summit], *Yomiuri shinbun*, January 25, 1997; "Nikkan shuno, tai kita Chosen kinmitsuni renkeide itchi" [Top Leaders of Japan and the ROK Agree on Close Cooperation Toward North Korea], *Asahi shinbun*, January 26, 1997.

48 Lee Wha Rang, "In Defense of N. Korea's Waste Dump Deal with Taiwan," February 9, 1997, http://kimsoft.com/korea/nk-waste.htm, February 12, 1997.

49 *Joongang ilbo*, January 26, 1997.

editorial reaction in the South Korean press tended to be critical. Editorials in the Japanese press, too, underlined the need to translate words into action. As a *Yomiuri* editorial put it: "The most difficult task ahead will be to turn the talk of improved bilateral ties into reality. The expression "future-oriented relationship" is a political catchphrase that has been used repeatedly during Japan-South Korea summits in the past. Such a relationship between the two nations, however, continues to be elusive."[50]

Friction Over Fishing

Just how difficult it is to "turn the talk of improved bilateral ties into reality" was demonstrated in the months following the Beppu Summit by a growing dispute over fishing. Negotiations by working-level officials from both countries on a new fisheries agreement to replace the 1965 pact and on drawing up boundaries of their respective exclusive economic zones (EEZs) entered into an impasse as neither side showed any flexibility.

The conflicting territorial claims on the Takeshima/Tokdo Island continued to impede negotiations on EEZs. Faced with mounting pressure from its fishing industry and politicians allied with it, Japan sought to expedite the conclusion of a new fisheries agreement by delinking it from the EEZ issue. South Korea, however, stuck to the position that the two should not be separated but be pursued in tandem.

Japan proposed establishment of "joint management fishing waters" around the disputed island under a new fisheries agreement but South Korea initially rejected it. During separate negotiations on EEZs, South Korea proposed a delineation of a "provisional EEZ border line, putting

---

50 "Make 'Future-oriented' Ties Reality," an editorial, *The Daily Yomiuri*, January 27, 1997; this is a translation of "Mirai shikoteki Nikkan kankei" [Future-oriented Japan-ROK Relations], *Yomiuri shinbun*, January 27, 1997, an editorial.

the issue of sovereignty over [Tokdo/Takeshima] on the shelf." Japan rejected the proposal, for it would simply prolong the status quo, namely South Korean control over the island.[51]

To increase pressure on South Korea, Japan adopted two tactics. First, it told South Korea that due to domestic pressure, failure to reach an agreement on a new fisheries pact by July 20, the first anniversary of Japan's declaration of its EEZ, would result in Japan's unilateral renunciation of the old fisheries treaty. Second, in the second half of June and early July, Japanese patrol boats seized five South Korean fishing boats for allegedly violating Japanese territorial waters. Japan had expanded its territorial waters by adopting a straight baseline method of delineating territorial waters effective January 1, 1997. Arguing that the use of straight baseline method without an agreement with adjacent states was inconsistent with international law, however, South Korea refused to recognize the Japanese action. South Korea insisted that it would continue to recognize Japan's old territorial waters drawn in accordance with the "normal method"—that is, encompassing 12 nautical miles from the coastline at low tide. The South Korean fishing vessels seized by Japan, South Korea claimed, were outside Japan's territorial waters as recognized by Seoul.[52]

After subjecting the captains of the seized vessels to summary trials and imposing a fine of 500,000 yen (about $4,500) on each of them, Japan freed the vessels and their crew except for two captains, who faced further judicial proceedings.[53] Significantly, the seizure of the fifth vessel

---

51 Kim Kyung-ho, "Korea, Japan Split on Fishing Pact; Tokyo Threatens to Abandon Treaty," *Korea Herald*, June 14, 1997.
52 "Ilbon ilbangjok yonghae hwakdae - Han'guk oson ittan nap'o" [Japan Unilaterally Expands Territorial Sea - Keeps Seizing Korean Fishing Vessels], *Chosun ilbo*, June 30, 1997; Kim Kyung-ho, "Japan Seizes Korean Boat for Fifth Time in a Month; Tension Expected Over Fisheries Accord," *Korea Herald*, July 9, 1997.
53 Ibid.; "Oop hyopjong: Han'guk omin pyollon chaeil tongp'o Pae Hun pyonhosa intobyu" [Fisheris Negotiations: An Interview With Korean Resident in Japan, Attorney Pae Hun, Who Is Defending Korean Fishermen], *Hankyoreh*

occurred only a week after South Korean Foreign Minister Yoo Chong Ha asked his Japanese counterpart, Ikeda Yukihiko, to delay enforcement of Japan's new territorial sea regulations until a new fisheries agreement is adopted. Ikeda rejected Yoo's request. At the foreign ministers' meeting, which occurred in Hong Kong on July 1, Yoo noted that during the six meetings the two had thus far, no topic had received more attention than fisheries. Both underscored the entanglement of domestic politics with the issue in their respective countries.[54] The Japanese action precipitated a strong reaction in South Korea. All political parties were united in their denunciation of it: the ruling New Korea Party called it a "worrisome and serious matter that threatens the existing Republic of Korea-Japan relations as well as a violation of international law;" the largest opposition party, the National Council for New Politics, labeled "the Japanese government's unilateral delineation of territorial waters" not only a "clear violation of international law" but also a manifestation of "diplomacy of expansionism and force that disregards neighboring countries;" the United Liberal Democrats, the number two opposition party, was even more blunt, describing the Japanese action as an "act of militaristic tyranny" and a "challenge to all peace-loving humanity."[55]

Prime Minister Hashimoto's reported defense of the seizure further inflamed South Korean public opinion. Hashimoto was quoted by Japan's Jiji Press (*Jiji tsushin*) as having told Japanese reporters on July 10 that it was "natural [*tozen*] to seize foreign ships that are engaged in fishing in Japan's territorial waters" and that the straight baseline method was a rule of international law. A "high ranking" official of the ROK

---

sinmun, July 20, 1997.

54 Gaimusho, Ajia Kyoku, Hokuto Ajia-ka, *Nikkan gaisho kaidan no gaiyo (7-gatsu 1-nichi, Hong Kong)* [A Summary of the Meeting Between the Foreign Ministers of Japan and the Republic of Korea, July 1, Hong Kong], July 1, 1997, 2. See also *Korea Herald*, July 9, 1997. The Hong Kong meeting was actually the seventh between Yoo and Ikeda.

55 "Yoya Ilbon ui Han'guk oson nap'o kangnyok pinan" [Government and Opposition Parties Strongly Denounce Japan's Seizure of Korean Fishing Vessels], *Chosun ilbo*, July 1, 1997.

Foreign Ministry on July 11 refuted Hashimoto's claim by pointing out: "Article 1 of the [Japan-ROK] fisheries agreement stipulates that one contracting party must consult with the other before adopting a straight baseline method." He added that South Korea had explicitly objected to Japan's use of the method several times. Reiterating his government's stance that it would not recognize Japan's unilateral delineation of its territorial waters based on the straight baseline method, he demanded not only an immediate release of two South Korean captains still being held in Japan but also an apology for the alleged beating of South Korean crew members by Japanese officials while their ships were being seized as well as the punishment of those who participated in the beating.[56]

Emblematic of the priority the Kim Young Sam government placed on the matter was the unusual decision of the Council for the Coordination of Unification and Security Policies (*T'ongil Anbo Chongch'aek Hoeui*), chaired by the prime minister and consisting of the deputy prime minister for unification, the defense and foreign ministers, and the director of the Agency for National Security Planning, to take it up. The maritime-fishery minister was invited to the meeting, which usually discusses issues relating to North Korea. President Kim Young Sam was reported to have "ordered the relevant authorities to 'actively deal with' the Japanese action in consideration of 'the usual Korean public feelings against Japan.'"[57] Nationalistic feelings in both countries clearly helped to raise the stakes in the negotiations. Fueling and sustaining them were the demands of fishing industries in both, which were intent on protecting their vested interests with the help of their respective governments.[58]

---

56 "Oemubu: Han'il oop hyopjong kwallyon Hashimoto paron pip'an" [Foreign Ministry Criticizes Hashimoto's Statement Regarding ROK-Japan Fisheries Agreement], *Hankyoreh sinmun*, July 11, 1997. I was in Tokyo at the time this controversy arose but neither Hashimoto's statement nor South Korean reaction thereto were reported in Japanese mass media, print or other. *Jiji tsushin's* dispatch was carried in the South Korean press only.

57 "Korea-Japan Fishery Talks Suspended; Seoul Angry with Continued Seizure of Trawlers," *Korea Herald*, July 14, 1997.

On July 28 ROK Foreign Minister Yoo Chong Ha and his Japanese counterpart, Ikeda Yukihiko, held talks in Kuala Lumpur where both were attending an expanded foreign ministers' meeting of the Association for Southeast Asian Nations (ASEAN). Yoo requested both an immediate release of the two South Korean captains in Japanese custody and a clarification of allegations that South Korean crew members had been beaten by Japanese authorities. Ikeda stated that the seizure of South Korean fishing boats had occurred in accordance with Japanese law. The two sides agreed to hold both a working-level meeting to ascertain the facts concerning the incidents and a meeting of specialists to deal with the straight baseline issue. Most important, both foreign ministers expressed regret that the incidents had undesirable effects on their two countries' "friendly, cooperative relations" and agreed to "make an effort to prevent the recurrence of such incidents in the future."[59]

Then, on August 15, a Japanese court—the Hamada branch of the Matsue District Court in Shimane prefecture—handed down an unexpected ruling. It dismissed an indictment against one of the two South Korean captains in Japanese custody on the ground that his seizure had been illegal. Noting that the Japan-ROK fisheries agreement "guarantees exclusive fishing rights in waters 12 nautical miles from either coast," presiding judge Hasegawa Yasuhiro held that the South Korean captain's trawler was "not in Japanese waters at the time of its seizure because it was fishing more than 12 nautical miles from the actual coast."

---

58 For an articulation of the stakes and stance of the Japanese fishing industry, see Hidaka Kanji, "Kanchu ryogoku to shin gyogyo kyotei o isoge" [Expedite New Fishery Agreements With Both the Republic of Korea and China], *Asahi shinbun*, July 8, 1997, 14, a commentary (*rondan*). The writer is the President of the National Federation of Fishing Cooperatives (*Zenkoku Gyogyo Kyodo Kumiai Rengokai*).

59 Oemubu, "Han'il oemu changgwan hoedam kyolgwa" [The Results of A Meeting Between the Foreign Ministers of the Republic of Korea and Japan], *Oegyo charyosil* [Diplomatic Archives], August 1997 (Seoul). The meeting the two foreign ministers were attending was officially called the Post-Ministerial Meeting (PMC) of the ASEAN.

"In principle," the judge added, "treaties and established international laws always have priority regardless of when they were established."[60]

The Matsue District Public Prosecutor's Office immediately filed an appeal to a higher court, asserting that the district court had "erred" in its interpretation of the Japan-ROK fisheries treaty and the relevant Japanese laws. An official of Japan's Maritime Safety Agency said: "we will not change our policy (of patrolling waters around Japan) because it was decided upon after consultations with the Foreign Ministry and others." The South Korean captain, however, was released and allowed to return to Seoul on August 16. Meanwhile, the case of the other South Korean captain remained to be adjudicated at the Hagi Summary Court in Yamaguchi prefecture.[61] In subsequent negotiations South Korea indicated a willingness to consider Japan's demand for a provisional fisheries agreement provided two conditions were met: (1) South Korea's claim to Tokdo must not be affected and (2) the existing rights of South Korean fishermen must be guaranteed. Japan did not accept these conditions, and the impasse persisted. Japan also rejected South Korea's demand for an investigation of the alleged beating of South Korean crew members by Japanese officials, asserting that violent behavior by the Koreans had necessitated some restraining measures while they were being taken into custody.[62]

On October 29 a South Korean fishing boat was seized by a Japanese patrol boat off Tsushima. The South Korean trawler with four crew members had been fishing in Japan's newly-drawn territorial waters that Seoul refuses to recognize. The incident sparked an angry response from South Korea, which construed it as a violation of an understanding reached between Foreign Ministers Yoo and Ikeda in Kuala Lumpur in

---

60 "District Court Dismisses Indictment against South Korean Ship Captain," *Daily Yomiuri*, August 16, 1997.
61 Ibid.; "Court Drops Territorial Waters Case," *Japan Times*, August 16, 1997; "Kim Sun-gi Taedong-ho sonjang kwiguk" [Captain Kim Sun-gi of Taedong-ho Returns Home], *Chosun ilbo*, August 17, 1997.
62 "Korea, Japan to Reopen Fishery Talks," *Korea Herald*, September 6, 1997.

July. The two, after expressing regret over the adverse consequences of Japan's seizure of five South Korean trawlers, had agreed to "make an effort to prevent the recurrence of such incidents in the future."[63]

The vague wording of the Kuala Lumpur "agreement," however, left room for disagreement in interpretation. The Japanese side could plausibly have construed it as implying a commitment by South Korea to prevent its fishing boats from entering disputed waters. It is also possible that the seizure of the ship by a Japanese Maritime Safety Agency patrol boat may have reflected either inter-agency rivalry or the lack of coordination between government agencies in Japan. The release of the captain after a two-week detention, however, served to defuse the crisis. The other crew members and the ship had been released earlier.

As the year drew to a close, the pace of negotiations visibly accelerated. With differences between the sides having been narrowed substantially, Japan made a special effort to wrap up a new fisheries agreement before a new government is inaugurated in Seoul in February 1998. Some South Korean observers speculated that Japan's eagerness to wrap up an agreement might be related to its perception of increased leverage stemming from its major role in the IMF-organized bailout of South Korea after a currency crisis erupted in November. Tokyo's dispatch of its parliamentary vice foreign minister, Komura Masahiro, to Seoul twice in a week—on November 30 and December 4—and Foreign Minister Obuchi Keizo's two-day visit to Seoul on December 30 and 31, however, failed to produce an agreement. The most contentious issue remained the demarcation of a joint fishing zone where fishing ships from both countries would be allowed to fish under certain restrictions. To ensure its fishermen's continued access to the "golden fishing ground" called *Taehwat'oe* in South Korea and *Yamatotai* in Japan, South Korea insisted on drawing the eastern boundary of the zone at 136 degrees east

---

63 "Sin'ui choborin Ilbon ui oson nap'o" [Japan's Seizure of Fishing Boats That Betrays Trust], *Dong-A ilbo*, November 1, 1997, an editorial; Kim Kyung-ho, "Seoul May Delay Fisheries Talks; If Tokyo Refuses to Release Seized Boat, Crew," *Korean Herald*, November 1, 1997.

longitude but Japan adhered to 135 degrees east longitude.[64]

An unusual aspect of Obuchi's visit to Seoul was his meeting with President-elect Kim Dae Jung, an unprecedented event. The revelation that the Japanese Foreign Ministry had conducted negotiations with the Kim Dae Jung camp without informing the ROK Foreign Ministry annoyed the latter. Neither Obuchi nor Kim Dae Jung could have known at the time that nine months later they would be holding a summit meeting.

On January 23, 1998 Japan officially notified Seoul of Tokyo's decision to unilaterally terminate the 1965 fisheries agreement, which stipulates that such a notice shall take effect one year later. Three days earlier, Japan had seized another South Korean fishing boat for violating its expanded territorial waters that the ROK continues to regard as international waters. The 139-ton trawler with 15 crew members aboard was the seventh and largest South Korean fishing boat seized by Japan since June 1997.[65]

South Korea demanded an immediate release of the fishing boat and its crew members and on January 23 Foreign Minister Yoo Chong Ha summoned Japanese Ambassador to the ROK Ogura Kazuo to his office to protest the Japanese decision to scrap the fisheries agreement and to give notice of Seoul's retaliatory measure. Seoul would immediately suspend self-imposed regulations governing South Korean fishing boats

---

64 "Nikkan gyogyo kyogi, Komura seimujikan ga Kankoku gaimujikan to sessho" [Japan-ROK Fisheries Talks, Paliamentary Vice-Minister Komura Negotiates With ROK Foreign Vice-Minister], *Asahi shinbun*, December 1, 1997; "Ooup hyopjong: Komura Ilbon ch'agwan oop hyopsang wihae chae panghan" [Fisheries Agreement: Japan's Vice Minister Komura Revisits ROK for Fisheries Negotiation], *Hankyoreh sinmun*, December 5, 1997; "Korea-Japan Fishery Talks End in Failure," *Korea Herald*, December 6, 1997; "Kim Dae Jung OKs Japan-N. Korean Talks," *Daily Yomiuri*, January 1, 1998.

65 Kim Kyung-ho, "Japan Seizes Korean Fishing Boat Again," *Korea Herald*, January 2, 1998; "Government Decides to Scrap Fisheries Accord with ROK," *Daily Yomiuri*, January 23, 1998; "Seoul Told Pact Is Being Scrapped," ibid., January 24, 1998.

operating in the vicinity of Japanese waters. The "autonomous regulations," adopted in 1980 following a Seoul-Tokyo agreement, prohibited South Korean fishing boats from operating in *international* waters adjacent to Japan's territorial waters during specified periods. Japan adopted reciprocal regulations concerning Japanese fishing boats operating near South Korean waters. Although the suspension of the 1980 agreement would give both South Korean and Japanese fishing boats access to wider fishing zones, it was expected to benefit South Korean fishermen more than it would Japanese fishermen.[66]

Yoo called Japan's unilateral action a "very unfriendly act," adding that Japan should assume full responsibility for any negative effects it might produce on ROK-Japan relations. Two committees of the ROK National Assembly—one on unification and foreign affairs and another on agriculture, forestry, maritime and fisheries—adopted resolutions condemning the Japanese move and calling for strong counter-measures. The National Assembly also summoned ROK Ambassador to Japan Kim Tae Zhee to give testimony on the matter. At a hearing of its unification and foreign affairs committee on January 26, both Ambassador Kim and Foreign Minister Yoo testified. Yoo, while reconfirming the Kim Young Sam government's position that the Japanese *government*, not a private fund, should pay compensation to surviving "comfort women," stressed the need to confine counter-measures to fisheries.[67]

A perception gap between Seoul and Tokyo also surfaced regarding

---

[66] "Ohyop p''agi: Han,Il kinjang kungmyon······'modun ch'aegim Ilboni choya'" [Termination of Fisheries Agreement: Tension Between ROK and Japan······"Japan Must Bear All Responsibility"], *Chosun ilbo*, January 24, 1998; "Kankoku no jishu kisei chudan ga akueikyo no kenen" [Worry Over Adverse Effects of the ROK's Suspension of Autonomous Regulations], *Yomiuri shinbun*, January 24, 1998.

[67] "Kukhoe, Han'il hyopjong chaekomt'o ch'okku" [National Assembly Demands Reconsideration of ROK-Japan Treaty], *Hankyoreh sinmun*, January 27, 1998; "Haesol/oop hyopjong: Kukhoe, Il ui oophyopjong p'agi maeng pinan" [Analysis/Fisheries Agreement: National Assembly Strongly Criticizes Japan's Scrapping of Fisheries Agreement], ibid.

what had or had not transpired during the weeks preceding the Japanese action. In a statement issued on January 23, the spokesman for the ROK Foreign Ministry stated that "it is difficult to understand why Japan's political circles (*chongch'i-kwon*) refused to accept a compromise agreed upon by high-level representatives of both countries who had full powers to negotiate."[68] Foreign Minister Yoo also referred to this in a press conference, implying that a compromise had been reached during Vice Foreign Minister Komura's second visit to Seoul but that it had later been rejected by the Japanese government.[69]

The Japanese Foreign Ministry, however, contradicted the preceding interpretation, asserting that Komura had never agreed to anything and that he was in no position to do so. What had really happened, it said, was that Komura had simply brought Seoul's final offer and reported it to his superiors, who, upon examining it, found it unacceptable.[70]

President-elect Kim Dae Jung told *Asahi shinbun* that he found the Japanese action "insulting." He questioned its timing, noting that his country was not only in the midst of an economic crisis but also on the eve of inaugurating the first truly democratic government in 50 years. Kim said that "Japan's greatest problem is that it is not trusted by its neighbors," implying that the Japanese action on fisheries would exacerbate the problem."[71]

---

68 Oemubu, Tongbuga 1-kwa, *Oemubu taebyonin songmyong (Ilbon ui Han'il oop hyopjong chongnyo t'ongbo kwallyon)* [Statement by the Spokesman for the Ministry of Foreign Affairs (Concerning Japan's Notification on the Termination of the ROK-Japan Fisheries Agreement)], January 23, 1998 (Seoul).
69 *Chosun ilbo*, January 24, 1998.
70 "'Komura seimujikan wa Kankoku-an ni goi sezu'—gyogyo kyotei de Gaimusho" ["Parliamentary Vice Minister Komori Did Not Agree to ROK Proposal"—Foreign Ministry on Fisheries Agreement], *Asahi shinbun*, January 27, 1998.
71 Both President Matsushita Muneyuki and Managing Editor Oguri Keita of *Asahi shinbun* took part in its interview with Kim Dae Jung in Seoul on January 22, 1998. See *Asahi shinbun*, January 23, 1998, for a front-page article, excerpts

Given the importance of its relations with Japan, painfully underscored by Tokyo's participation in the IMF-organized bailout of South Korea, however, the ROK government made plain its desire to contain the adverse effects of the fisheries dispute. For its part, Japan publicly expressed the hope that negotiations would resume in the near future. At a press conference, Chief Cabinet Secretary Muraoka Kanezo said that the decision to scrap the treaty was made "in response to a request from the ruling bloc" in order to protect the interests of Japanese fisheries workers. He cautioned that the "emotional reaction of some Koreans to Japan's decision would benefit neither country."[72]

In a statement issued on January 23, Foreign Minister Obuchi stressed that Japan's decision "to notify the ROK Government of Japan's intention to terminate" the 1965 fisheries treaty was in accordance with Article 10, paragraph 2 of that agreement. Noting that ten rounds of working-level consultations as well as negotiations at "a number of summit and foreign ministers' talks" during the past two years had failed to produce an agreement, Obuchi stated that Japan's decision reflected its determination to put an end to the "old fishery order," which was established more than 30 years ago, and to "promptly establish a new fishery order based on the purport of the United Nations Convention on the Law of the Sea." Obuchi made clear his government's intention to cooperate with the incoming ROK government under Kim Dae Jung, to "further develop the friendly and cooperative bilateral relationship into the 21st century, as well as to promote the cooperation of the two countries in the international community."[73]

---

from the interview, and related articles. In an editorial that appeared on the following day, the paper concurred in Kim's view on the questionable timing of the Japanese move. See "Daido o miushinauna" [Don't Lose Sight of the Main Road], ibid., January 24, 1998, editorial.

72 "Seoul Retaliates As Tokyo Scraps 1965 Fishery Pact," *Japan Times*, January 23, 1998.

73 Ministry of Foreign Affairs of Japan, *Statement by Foreign Minister Keizo Obuchi on the Termination of the Japan-R.O.K. Fishery Agreement*, January 23, 1998 (Tokyo).

Conclusion of a New Fisheries Agreement

Despite his criticism of the Japanese action on the fisheries treaty, Kim Dae Jung turned out to be a catalyst for significant progress in ROK-Japan relations. Convinced that a genuine partnership between Seoul and Tokyo would be a sine qua non for a new international order in Northeast Asia in the 21st century, Kim placed a top priority on improving ties with Japan after his government was formally launched on February 25, 1998. Pursuant to his wishes, Seoul and Tokyo agreed that President Kim would make a state visit to Japan from October 7 to 10.

This made it imperative that the two countries work together diligently to clear all or most of the hurdles on the path to a fully cooperative relationship, of which the impasse on a new fisheries agreement was one. In other words, potent political will by top leadership emerged as a new variable in the equation.

Also noteworthy was the election of Obuchi as prime minister on July 30, after Hashimoto Ryutaro resigned to take responsibility for the LDP's failure to win a majority in the House of Councillors election.[74] As Foreign Minister, Obuchi had been personally involved in negotiations with Seoul on a new fisheries agreement and thus was committed to resolving the dispute. As will be noted below, he would play a key role in breaking the impasse on September 24.

The Kim Dae Jung government actually reached an agreement to resume negotiations on a fisheries pact with the Japanese government on March 21, less than a month after its inauguration. Negotiations resumed on April 29 and, a day before the second round of working-level talks began on July 2, the Kim Dae Jung government restored the "autonomous regulations" imposing restrictions on South Korean fishing boats operating in international waters adjacent to Japan's territorial waters.[75]

---

74 Hisane Masaki, "Hashimoto Steps Down," *Japan Times*, Weekly International Edition, July 20-26, 1998, 1 and 5; "Obuchi Names First Cabinet," ibid., August 10-16, 1998, 1 and 6.

By the time the fourth round of the working-level talks convened on August 14, Obuchi had replaced Hashimoto as Japan's prime minister. As the prospective host of Kim Dae Jung, Obuchi had a strong incentive to settle the fisheries dispute before the Kim visit materialized. It would, however, take three more rounds of working-level talks and negotiations at higher levels involving politicians and cabinet ministers to produce an agreement.

To mention the role of politicians first, Sato Koko, chairman of an LDP committee on international fisheries issues, visited South Korea from September 15 to 17, meeting with President Kim Dae Jung, Foreign Minister Hong Soon Young, and Minister of Maritime Affairs and Fisheries Kim Sun Kil. A 12-term member of the House of Representatives, Sato is one of the most influential politicians shaping Japan's policy toward fisheries. As for South Korea, Deputy Speaker of the National Assembly Kim Bong Ho, a member of Kim Dae Jung's National Congress for New Politics, visited Japan in July and September on a mission to seek a mutually acceptable compromise.[76]

In the final high-level negotiations that took place in Tokyo on September 24, both Sato and Kim Bong Ho joined their respective fisheries ministers, Nakagawa Shoichi and Kim Sun Kil. It was, however, not until after Prime Minister Obuchi invited all four to his official residence that a breakthrough materialized. Obuchi then virtually presided over final negotiations lasting over two hours, in which Chief Cabinet Secretary Nonaka Hiromu also participated. The meeting ended at 40 minutes past midnight—on September 25—with "basic agreement" on the contours of a new fisheries pact. ROK Maritime Affairs and Fisheries Minister Kim Sun Kil characterized Obuchi's active role in the negotiations as "unimaginable," saying that it bespoke the commitment

---

75 "Han'il oop hyopjong kaejong kwallyon kyosop ilji" [Chronology of Negotiations on the Revision of ROK-Japan Fisheries Agreement], *Joongang ilbo*, September 25, 1998.

76 Jun Kwan-woo, "Lawmakers Work on Sidelines to Conclude Fisheries Accord," *Korea Herald*, September 17, 1998.

and "sincerity" of the Japanese side.[77]

In what ways did the stakes and interests of the two sides diverge? And how did they resolve their differences? Simply put, South Korea sought to maximize the area in which its fishermen could fish and to preserve their right to catch various species of fish as long as possible. Japan, on the other hand, wanted to reduce the area in which South Korean fishing boats could operate and shorten the period during which they would be allowed to catch fish in waters adjacent to Japan. Both sides, moreover, had to find ways of ironing out their differences without aggravating their territorial dispute over Takeshima/Tokdo and without agreeing on the boundaries of their respective EEZs.

A practical way out of such predicament was to set up a joint fishing zone in the middle of the sea dividing the two countries, which the Japanese call *Nihonkai* (the Sea of Japan) and the Koreans *Tonghae* (the East Sea). That in turn raised two issues. First, what would be the status of Tokdo/Takeshima in relation to such zone? Second, where would they draw the zone's outer boundaries? Regarding the first, South Korea accepted Japan's proposal to include the disputed island in the zone on condition that its 12-nautical-mile "territorial waters" would remain off limits to Japanese fishing boats, a price Japan considered worth paying. Although Japan wanted the zone to be "jointly managed," South Korea insisted on treating it as if it were international waters, meaning only the "flag state" would exercise jurisdiction over its vessels. In the end, Japan agreed to the principle of flag-state jurisdiction on condition that a joint committee (*Nikkan gyogyo kyodo iinkai*) be created to deal with the conservation of marine resources and other issues that might arise between the two countries.[78]

---

77 "Han'il oop hyopsang imojomo" [Aspects of ROK-Japan Fisheries Negotiations], *Joongang ilbo*, September 25, 1998.
78 "Nikkan shin gyogyo kyotei de kihon goi - kyodode shigen kanri, Takeshima niwa zantei suiiki" [Japan and ROK Basically Agree on New Fisheries Pact - Resources Will Be Managed Jointly, Provisional Water Zone Surrounding Takeshima], *Asahi shinbun*, September 25, 1998; Oegyo T'ongsangbu, Kukje

South Korea, however, succeeded in diluting the authority of the committee in such a way that as far as the joint fishing zone in the East Sea (the Sea of Japan) was concerned, the committee would be empowered merely to make recommendations. Only in the second joint fishing zone that would be established near Cheju island in the southern tip of the Korean peninsula would the committee have the authority to make binding decisions.[79]

The second issue relating to the joint fishing zone in the Sea of Japan (or the East Sea) proved to be the most contentious of all. Whereas South Korea insisted that the zone's eastern boundary should be 135 degrees east longitude, Japan indicated that it would only accept 136 degrees east longitude. In the end, the two sides split the difference, settling on 135 degrees 30 minutes east longitude. Actually, this compromise had been worked out between Sato and Kim Bong Ho on Cheju island a week earlier during Sato's visit to South Korea but the reluctance of the Japanese side to endorse the idea had created a snag during the final high-level negotiations in Tokyo.[80]

This issue was entangled with the disposition of a "golden fishing ground" known as *Yamatotai* in Japan and *Taehwat'oe* in Korea, which is located between 134 degrees east longitude and 136 degrees east longitude and between 39 degrees north latitude and 40 degrees north latitude. Had Japan had its way, *Yamatotai* would have been excluded *in toto* from the joint fishing zone. By contrast, South Korea, whose fishermen caught 20,000-25,000 tons of squid in *Taehwat'oe* a year, wanted to include all of it in the zone. Japan's final acceptance of 135 degrees 30 minutes east longitude was contingent upon South Korea's

---

Popkyukwa, *Han'il o'op hyopjong charyo surok* [Collection of Materials on ROK-Japan Fisheries Agreement] (Seoul: October 1998).

79 Ibid.

80 "Han'il o'op hyopjong t'agyol anp'ak, Kim Bong Ho pu-uijang, Obuchi chikjop tamp'an" [Inside Story of Successful Conclusion of ROK-Japan Fisheries Negotiations, Deputy Speaker Kim Bong Ho and Obuchi Face Off Directly], *Dong-A ilbo*, September 26, 1998.

concession, which permitted the eastern boundary line to be "bent" so that less than a half of *Yamatotai* would be encompassed by the joint fishing zone.[81]

Next in importance was the issue of exclusive fishing zones (EFZs). Whereas South Korea proposed 35 nautical miles from coastline, Japan insisted on 36 nautical miles. Japan prevailed not only on this issue but on the issue of grace periods as well. That is, South Korea had to settle for three years, instead of five, during which its fishermen would be able to continue fishing in Japanese waters beyond 135 degrees 30 minutes east longitude and off Japan's EEZ. To be able to operate in these waters, which would be part of Japan's EEZ, South Korean fishing boats must obtain licenses from Japan, pay fees, observe Japanese laws and regulations, and not exceed assigned fishing quotas. Overall, South Korean fishermen will be permitted to catch 15,000 tons of pollack for one year, king crabs for two years, and other fish for three years.[82]

It is noteworthy that the new fisheries agreement refers to the disputed island of Takeshima/Tokdo by coordinates only—at 131.52-53 degrees east longitude and 37.14.00-37.14.45 degrees north latitude. Nor does it name the joint fishing zone, which, too, is described by coordinates only. Japan nonetheless began calling it zantei suiiki

---

[81] "Han'il o'op hyopjong t'agyol uimi, Han'il kwangye chongsang-hwa kyegi maryon" [Significance of Conclusion of ROK-Japan Fisheries Agreement, Catalyst for Normalizing ROK-Japan Relations], ibid., September 26, 1998; "Sae Han'il o'op hyopjong, Taehwat'oe nun otton kot" [New ROK-Japan Fisheries Agreement, What Kind of Place is Taehwat'oe], *Joongang ilbo*, September 26, 1998; "Fisheries Accord," *Korea Herald*, September 28, 1998, an editorial. A straight boundary line would have encompassed 70 percent of the fertile fishing ground.

[82] "Han'il sae o'op hyopjong t'agyol, ch'oejongan habui" [Conclusion of New ROK-Japan Fisheries Agreement, Final Version Adopted], *Chosun ilbo*, September 25, 1998. For details regarding what is permitted in each other's EFZs, see Norin Suisansho, Suisancho, Kokusaika, *Nikkan gyogyo kosho ni tsuite* [On Japan-ROK Fisheries Negotiations] (Tokyo: February 10, 1999), http://www.maff.go.jp/work/990215-02.htm.

(provisional water zone), while South Korea coined the term, *chunggan suyok* (intermediate water zone).[83]

The agreement encountered vocal opposition in both countries, where fishermen, their spokesmen and allies expressed displeasure, accusing their respective governments of having short-changed their interests. The Obuchi government nonetheless succeeded in obtaining Diet approval on December 11. The Kim Dae Jung government had a more difficult time but finally rammed through a bill authorizing ratification in the National Assembly on January 6, 1999 with only members of the ruling coalition parties present and voting.[84]

Following an exchange of ratification instruments by ROK Foreign Minister Hong Soon Young and Japan's ambassador to the ROK Ogura Kazuo on January 22, 1999, the agreement entered into force on the same day. If, after three years, either side notifies the other of its intention to terminate the agreement, then it will expire six months after such notice.[85] In other words, it will remain in effect for at least three and a half years.

Due to a failure of working-level negotiations on details pertaining to implementation, however, the agreement did not take effect for several months. Only the provisions on the joint fishing zones became

---

83 "Nikkan shin gyogyo kyotei······," *Asahi shinbun*, September 25, 1998; Gaimusho, *Komura gaimu daijin danwa: Aratana Nikkan gyogyo kyotei ni tsuite* [Foreign Minister Komura's Statement: On the New Japan-ROK Fisheries Agreement], September 25, 1998 (Tokyo); Oegyo T'ongsangbu, Kukje Popkyukwa, *Han'il o'op hyopjong charyo surok*.

84 "Nikkan shin gyogyo kyotei, Jimin naino ryosho ga nanko, Nihonkai gawa senshutsu giin ga hampatsu" [New Japan-ROK Fisheries Agreement Face Rough Sailing Within LDP, Diet Members From Sea of Japan Area Rebel], *Yomiuri shinbun*, November 16, 1998; "Nikkan shin gyogyo kyotei o shonin - Shuin" [House of Representatives Approves New Japan-ROK Fisheries Agreement], *Nihon keizai shinbun*, December 12, 1998; "Sae Han'il o'op hyopjong 22-il kke parhyo toelttut" [New ROK-Japan Fisheries Agreement May Take Effect on January 22], *Joongang ilbo*, January 7, 1999.

85 Oegyo T'ongsangbu, Kukje Popkyukwa, *Sin Han'il o'op hyopjong pijunso kyohwan mit parhyo, 1.22* [Exchange of Ratification Instruments and Entry into Force of the New ROK-Japan Fisheries Agreement, January 22] (Seoul).

immediately enforceable. What is more, the seizure of a number of South Korean fishing boats by Japan's Maritime Safety Agency patrol boats marred what would otherwise have been a momentous occasion.

What is the balance of issue-specific power in the negotiations between the Obuchi and Kim Dae Jung governments? To begin with alternatives, Japan appeared to be in a stronger position than South Korea was. For Japan had already given one-year notice on the 1965 agreement, which would therefore cease to be effective on January 22, 1999. In the absence of a new bilateral pact, the UN Convention on the Law of the Sea would become the sole legal basis for a fisheries order between the two countries. That multilateral treaty, to which both Japan and the ROK are parties, gives coastal states far-reaching rights in their EEZs, rights that border on sovereignty. Although the absence of mutually recognized EEZ boundaries between the two neighboring states would complicate matters, one thing was certain—that the area in which South Korean fishing boats would be allowed to operate would shrink to an almost vanishing point in waters controlled by Japan.

That meant that South Korea would incur greater losses than would Japan in the alternative scenario. Since, under the 1965 pact, South Korean fishermen caught twice as much fish in Japan's EEZs than their Japanese counterparts—220,000 tons vs. 110,000 tons—, the former had much to lose. South Korea, in short, had no realistic alternative to a new fisheries agreement with Japan.[86]

As for commitments to negotiation, South Korea's appeared to be somewhat stronger than Japan's. Kim Dae Jung placed high priority on improving relations with Japan, and his vision of a ROK-Japan

---

86 "Han'il sae o'op hyopjong t'agyol, ch'oejong-an habui," *Chosun ilbo*, September 25, 1998; Sohn Tae-soo, "Fisheries Accord Deal Blow to Fishermen; Fishing Industry Reeling from Narrower Zone, Tougher Restrictions," *Korea Times*, September 26, 1998; Haeyang Susanbu, *Hanil oop hyopjong* [ROK-Japan Fisheries Agreement] (Seoul, 1998), http://www.momaf.go.kr/doc/news/fishery3/FISHERY1.htm. South Korean fishing boats operating in Japan's EEZ in 1998 totaled 1,600, including large vessels and trawl boats.

"partnership" was in danger of dying a premature death should the fisheries dispute linger on. Shaken by North Korea's stunning display of missile power, Japan had acquired a new appreciation of the value of cooperation with South Korea. Additionally, Obuchi not only understood the importance of resolving the fisheries dispute with Seoul better than most of his colleagues in the LDP leadership but was eager to have a successful summit with Kim Dae Jung. Nonetheless, its high stakes probably made the Kim government's commitments outweigh the Obuchi government's.

Finally, Japan had control over its alternative. The clock was ticking, and all Japan needed to do was wait. It, of course, had the option of rescinding its January 1998 decision and stopping the clock. That, however, bespoke its control over the alternative, not the opposite. By contrast, South Korea lacked any control. The only realistic option it had was to strike a deal with Japan on a compromise that would help protect the rights of its fishermen to the maximum feasible degree.

In short, the balance of issue-specific power may have marginally favored Japan. The final compromise the two sides hammered out reflected such reality. Although the eastern boundary of the joint fishing zone in the Sea of Japan (or the East Sea) appeared to be a textbook example of diplomatic compromise, its actual shape favored Japan more. The inclusion of Takeshima/Tokdo in the zone spelled a clear gain for Japan. Additionally, Japan prevailed over South Korea on the length of EFZs and the grace periods. Finally, South Korea allowed Japan to have its way regarding the establishment of a joint fishing zone south of Cheju island.[87]

Before we examine the results of Kim Dae Jung's October 1998 state visit to Japan, for which the conclusion of a new fisheries agreement

---

87 Yi Sang-myon, "Han'il o'op hyopjong nomu manhi irotta" [Too Much Was Lost in the ROK-Japan Fisheries Agreement], *Hankook ilbo*, September 29, 1998. The author, a professor of international law at Seoul National University, contends that South Korea inexplicably gave up most of the waters in the ROK-Japan joint continental shelf development zone in the south to Japan.

prepared the way, we need to examine two other dimensions of Japan-ROK interactions—security cooperation and economic relations.

Security Cooperation

Although Japan and South Korea have been strategically linked to each other through their respective military alliances with the US for several decades, bilateral security cooperation remained rather limited until the 1990s. During the Cold War era, the two countries maintained but a modest exchange program between their defense establishments.

Diplomatic normalization in 1965 opened the way for the stationing of military attaches in each other's embassies, which South Korea began to do in 1966, with Japan following suit in 1967. It was not until 1979, however, that Japan's defense chief (*boei chokan* or the director-general of the Defense Agency) visited South Korea for the first time. Eleven years were to elapse before another Defense Agency director-general would visit South Korea.[88]

In April 1994 Lee Byung Tai became the first ROK defense minister to visit Japan. His meeting with Tamazawa Tokuichiro, the director-general of Japan's Defense Agency, occurred against the backdrop of escalating tensions on the Korean peninsula fueled by North Korea's suspected nuclear weapons development program. The two defense ministers agreed to expand exchanges of students, realize mutual port calls by training naval vessels, and hold dialogues between working-level defense officials.[89]

---

88 The first Japanese defense chief to visit South Korea was Yamashita Ganri, who made a two-day visit from July 25 to 26, 1979. From December 7 to 9, 1990, Ishikawa Yozo visited South Korea, becoming the second Defense Agency head to do so. Boeicho, ed., *Boei hakusho, Heisei 3-nenban* [Defense of Japan, 1991] (Tokyo: Okurasho Insatsu-kyoku, 1991), 320 and 332. The English title is Boeicho's.
89 Idem, *Boei hakusho, Heisei 6-nenban* [Defense of Japan, 1994] (Tokyo: Okurasho, Insatsu-kyoku, 1994), 178-79.

Ministerial meetings have since become annual affairs. Port calls by naval cadets during their cruise training exercises occur periodically. Working-level conferences on defense policy began to be held annually. In July 1995 the two sides exchanged an official letter of agreement to help prevent military aircraft accidents and in September 1996 their air forces established a special communication channel (hot line).[90]

When Japan and the US were conducting a review of the "guidelines for US-Japan defense cooperation" in 1997, Tokyo took pains to keep Seoul informed of progress. Appreciative of Tokyo's gesture and finding the general direction and contents of the proposed revision of the guidelines compatible with its own interests, Seoul merely requested Japan to consult with the ROK on all matters affecting the Korean peninsula. That part of the guidelines pertaining to US-Japan "cooperation in situations in areas surrounding Japan" was of particular interest to South Korea. Seoul also requested maximum transparency during the stage of formulating concrete plans by Japan and the US to facilitate the implementation of the guidelines, and both sides agreed that they would step up consultations between their foreign and defense ministries with respect to issues impinging on South Korea's sovereignty.[91]

The two countries subsequently began holding annual consultative meetings on security policy attended by the directors-general of their respective foreign ministries' Asian affairs bureaus and defense officials at the deputy director-general level. The inaugural meeting was held in Seoul in June 1998, followed by the second meeting in Tokyo in July 1999.[92]

---

90 Idem, *Boei hakusho, Heisei 10-nenban* [Defense of Japan, 1998] (Tokyo: Okurasho, Insatsu-kyoku, 1998), 202-203; Kukbangbu, *Kukbang paekso*, 1998 [Defense White Paper, 1998], part 2, chap. 4.

91 "Mi Il pangwi hyomnyok chich'im: Il Hanguk e pangwi chich'im solmyonghoe" [US-Japan Defense Cooperation Guidelines: Japan and ROK Hold an Explanatory Meeting on Guidelines], *Hankyoreh sinmun*, September 16, 1997.

92 Oemubu, Asia Taepyongyang-guk, Tongbuga 1-kwa, *Che 2-hoe Hanil anbo chongch'aek hybuihoe kaech'oe*, 7. 8 [The 2nd ROK-Japan Consultative Meeting on Security Policy Convenes, July 8)] (Seoul: July 8, 1999), http://www.mofat. go.kr/korean/data/press/press9907/012.htm.

North Korea's missile/satellite launch over Japan on August 31 had the effect of underscoring the importance of security cooperation between Japan and South Korea. ROK Defense Minister Chun Yong Taek was in Tokyo a few days after the incident, as was ROK Foreign Minister Hong Soon Young. Although their visits had been scheduled prior to the incident, they nonetheless discussed its implications and appropriate counter-measures with their Japanese counterparts.

The director-general of Japan's Defense Agency, Norota Hosei visited South Korea from January 6 to 8, 1999. Noteworthy aspects of the visit included the following. First, Japan took the initiative of asking South Korea to hold the annual defense ministerial talks in advance of US Defense Secretary William Cohen's visits to Tokyo and Seoul. Second, Norota was accompanied by an unusually large number of top defense officials—15. This contrasted with the entourage of four aides that accompanied Chun to Tokyo in September 1998. Third, Norota became the first Japanese defense minister to pay a courtesy call on a ROK president. He also met with Prime Minister Kim Jong Pil, Foreign Minister Hong Soon Young, and Unification Minister Kang In Duk. An unnamed ROK defense ministry official was quoted in the South Korean press as saying that since the missile/satellite incident Japan began to view South Korea as a "new military partner."[93]

Although the ministerial meeting reaffirmed the two countries' joint policy of maintaining close trilateral consultations involving the US and both on North Korea while cooperating bilaterally, it also revealed that Japan adhered to a somewhat harder line toward Pyongyang than South Korea did. After Norota warned that Japan would be compelled to withdraw from the LWR project in the event of another missile launch by North Korea, President Kim Dae Jung reportedly asked him to take into

---

93 "Ol ch'ot kukbang changgwan hoedam, Han'il kunsa kyoryu kasok yego" [First Meeting of Defense Ministers This Year - Heralds Acceleration of ROK-Japan Military Exchanges], *Joongang ilbo*, January 6, 1999; Boeicho Jieitai, *Oshirase: Norota boei chokan no Kankoku homon ni tsuite* [Notice: On Defense Agency Director-General Norota's Visit to the ROK], January 5, 1999 (Tokyo).

account both "negative and positive aspects of situations surrounding North Korea" and not to make any hasty decisions. Norota was said to have told Kim that North Korea lacked credibility among the Japanese people due to the suspicions about abductions of Japanese nationals and the missile incident.[94]

Among tangible results of the Norota-Chun talks were the decision to establish an emergency communication network to deal with emergencies triggered by incursions of North Korean submarines into the waters between South Korea and Japan and other provocative incidents and the decision to expedite the preparation for a joint naval exercise solely for the peaceful purpose of conducting search and rescue operations in accordance with the agreement reached between Chun and Nukawa Fukushiro, Norota's predecessor, during Chun's September 1998 visit to Tokyo.[95]

Actually, since 1994 the navies of the two countries have periodically conducted what they call "goodwill exercises"(*shinzen kunren*). The fifth such exercise occurred in the vicinity of Tokyo Bay in December 1998 with an escort vessel from Japan's Maritime Self-Defense Forces and a supply ship from the ROK navy participating. They conducted training in communications, tactical maneuvers, and approaches.[96]

---

[94] "Kim taet'ongnyong Ilbon e KEDO chagum chiwon tonggyol-ron chaego yoch'ong" [President Kim Requests Japan to Reconsider Option of Freezing Financial Support for KEDO], *Joongang ilbo*, January 9, 1999. During his visit to Japan in October 1998, Kim Dae Jung consistently referred to the North's August 31 rocket launch over Japan as the "launch of an artificial satellite," thus displaying a subtle difference in interpretation of the incident between Seoul and Tokyo.

[95] "Han'il kukbang changgwan, puk misail tobal tung kongdong taech'o habui" [ROK, Japan Defense Ministers Reach Agreement on Joint Measures Against the North's Missile and Other Provocations], *Dong-A ilbo*, January 8, 1999; "Han'il kongdong ch'ot haesang hullyon—naenyon konghaeso kunan hwaltong silsi" [First ROK-Japan Joint Naval Exercise—Rescue Operation To Be Conducted in International Waters Next Year], ibid., September 3, 1998.

[96] Boeicho, Jieitai, *Oshirase: Kankoku kaigun tono shinzen kunren ni tsuite* [Notice: On Goodwill Exercise with the ROK Navy] (Tokyo: Kaibaku Kohoshitsu,

In terms of scale and duration, however, the joint naval exercise conducted by the two navies in August 1999 was unprecedented. For a total of five ships, five aircraft, and 1,200 sailors participated in the exercise that lasted five days. Held in the East China Sea between Kyushu and Cheju Island, the exercise was a "mock search and rescue of a wrecked civilian vessel in international waters." [97]

The joint naval exercise was followed two months later by another joint exercise simulating a rescue operation in international waters near Pusan. This time, however, the participants were non-military personnel: about 500 persons from Japan's Maritime Safety Agency and South Korea's Maritime Police Agency, 15 ships, and five helicopters. [98]

In addition to all this, the ROK Joint Chiefs of Staff and Japan's Staff Council held talks in 1999, as did the ROK Navy and Japan's Maritime Self Defense Forces. There is also a military "hot line" between Seoul and Tokyo. In sum, security cooperation between the two "quasi-allies" has markedly increased, and trilateral consultations among the two and their common alliance partner, the US, have been institutionalized by the formation of the Trilateral Coordination and Oversight Group (TCOG).

December 1998).

[97] "Japan, S.Korea Hold Naval Exercise," *Associated Press*, Seoul, August 4, 1999; "Nikkan ga hatsuno kyodo kunren, Kaiji wa shorai no kunji kyoryoku mo shiyani" [First Joint Exercise by Japan and ROK: Maritiame SDF Eyes Future Military Cooperation], *Asahi shinbun*, August 4, 1999. The ships consisted of a destroyer and an escort vessel from South Korea and three destroyers from Japan, while the aircaft consisted of a helicopter from South Korea and one patrol plane and three helicopters from Japan. Although no breakdown of sailors is available, one may surmise that Japanese sailors outnumbered their South Korean counterparts.

[98] "Kankoku no Pusan okide hatsuno Nikkan kyodo kyunan bojo kunren" [First Japan-ROK Joint Rescue and Extermination Exercise Off Pusan, Korea], ibid, October 7, 1999.

Economic Issues

Trade is a key dimension of the bilateral relations between Japan and South Korea, serving simultaneously as a symbol of cooperation and a source of discord. In 2000 Japan remained South Korea's number two trading partner, accounting for 15.7 percent of Seoul's global trade. In the same year South Korea was Japan's fourth largest trading partner, accounting for seven percent of Tokyo's global trade. The precipitous decline in Tokyo-Seoul trade in 1998 was attributable to a combination of the currency crisis in South Korea and the continuing recession in Japan. In 1999, however, improved economic conditions in both countries helped to restore their bilateral trade to the 1997 level. In 2000 the value of Japan-ROK trade set a new record, surpassing that of 1995 (See Table 5).

South Korea's trade deficit vis-a-vis Japan, however, continued to be an issue. In 1996 the cumulative deficit since normalization surpassed the $130 billion mark, which exceeded South Korea's total exports in that year—$129.7 billion. That prompted Seoul to ask Tokyo to lower import duties on South Korean footwear, textile and agricultural products, to increase the quota on South Korean fisheries products, and to lower other non-tariff barriers. South Korea also requested Japan to "extend its general system of preferences (GSP) tariff favors to [South] Korean exporters through the next year."[99] In 1997 the value of total trade between South Korea and Japan declined by over 10 percent but South Korea incurred a deficit of $11.5 billion, which was 3.6 times South Korea's total deficit in its global trade.[100]

---

99 '"Total Shortfall against Japan Surpasses Annual Export Figure," *Korea Herald*, August 15, 1997; "Yoo Chong-ha oemu: Ilbon T'onsangsang myondam taeil muyok chokja haeso yogu" [Foreign Minister Yoo Chong-ha Asks for Reduction of Trade Deficit With Japan in Talks with Japan's Trade Minister], *Hankyoreh sinmun*, July 30, 1997.

100 T'onggyech'ong, *Hanguk chuyo kyongje chip'yo*, 1998. 9 [Major Statistics of the Korean Economy, 1998. 9], (Seoul, 1998), 234, 244, and 256.

<Table 7>Japanese & U.S. Investment in South Korea

(in thousands of dollars)

Year	(A) Japan	(B) U.S.	(C) Total FDI[a]	(D) A as % of C	(E) B as % of C
1990	235,895	317,465	802,635	29,4	39.6
1991	226,239	296,229	1,395,959	16.2	21.2
1992	155,161	379,182	894,476	17.3	42.4
1993	285,943	340,669	1,044,274	27.4	32.6
1994	428,438	310,909	1,316,505	32.5	23.6
1995	418,288	644,934	1,941,423	21.5	33.2
1996	254,676	676,026	3,202,646	8.0	21.1
1997	265,753	3,189,523	6,970,908	3.8	45.8
1998	504,171	2,972,930	8,852,356	5.7	33.6
1999	1,749,691	3,738,338	15,541,269	11.3	24.1
2000	2,448,222	2,915,494	15,689,857	15.6	18.6
2001	772,184	3,889,094	11,291,994	6.8	34.4
2002	1,403,542	4,999,522	9,101,324	15.4	49.4
2003	540,661	1,239,925	6,467,861	8.4	19.2

SOURCE: T'onggyech'ong, *Hanguk t'onggye yongam*, 2004 (Seoul, 2005), p. 525.
a Foreign Direct Investment

As noted already, the single most important source of the trade imbalance between Japan and South Korea is their industrial structure—specifically, South Korea's heavy dependence on Japanese intermediate and capital goods and technology. In 1996, for example, while Japan's overall share of South Korean imports valued at $150.3 billion was 21 percent, its share of intermediate goods and finished products was between 45 and 55 percent.[101] In 1997 over 60 percent of South Korean imports from Japan consisted of machinery.[102] This pattern did not change much in subsequent years: machinery accounted for 56, 58 and 61

---

101 "Kwangbok 52 tol: k'ojinun tae-Il chokja, kyongje yesok t'alp'i ajik yowon" [52nd Anniversary of Liberation: Growing Deficit with Japan, Prospect of Freedom from Economic Subjugation Still Remote], *Dong-A ilbo*, August 14, 1997.
102 Tsusan Sangyosho, ed., *Tsusho hakusho, Heisei 10-nenban* [White Paper on

percent of South Korean imports from Japan in 1998, 1999, and 2000, respectively.[103] In 1998, however, South Korea recorded not only a suplus in its global trade for the first time since 1993 but the amount of surplus, $39 billion, was the largest ever. The deficit of $3.3 billion in its trade with Japan, therefore, did not really hurt Seoul. Although the deficit in Seoul's trade with Tokyo more than doubled in absolute terms in 1999, it was once again dwarfed by a sizable surplus in Seoul's global trade—$24 billion. In 2000, however, Seoul's surplus in global trade declined to $11.8 billion, barely eclipsing its deficit with Tokyo.[104]

Another contributing factor to the trade imbalance is a decline in South Korea's competitiveness due to its high labor costs relative to productivity. A precipitous decline in Japan's direct investment in South Korea in 1996 was symptomatic of the problem. As Table 7 shows, Japan's direct investment in South Korea, which surpassed that of the US in 1994, began to decline in 1995, plummeting to a single digit in 1996 in terms of share of total foreign direct investment (FDI) in South Korea. In 1997 Japan lost its position as the number two source of FDI in South Korea to the Netherlands, slipping to a fourth position after France and Germany. Beginning in 1998, Japan rose to the third position, nearly doubling its share of FDI in South Korea in 1998 and more than tripling it in 1999. In 2000 Japan recovered its traditional number two position.[105]

Trade and Commerce, 1998], (Tokyo: Okurasho, Insatsu-kyu, 1998), 253-54.
103 Tsusan Sangyosho, ed., *Heisei 11-nenben Tsusho hakusho* [White Paper on International Trade, 1999], (Tokyo: Okurasho Insatsu-kyoku, 1999), 214; idem., *Tsusho hakusho, 2000* [White Paper on International Trade, 2000], (Tokyo: Okurasho Insatsu-kyoku, 2000), 171; Keizai Sangyosho, *Tsusho hakusho, 2001 (kakuron)* [White Paper on International Trade, 2001 (Details)] (Tokyo: K.K. Gyosei, 2001), 147-48. The translation of the titles, as indicated by parentheses instead of brackets, is MITI's. In 2001 MITI was replaced by the Ministry of Economics and Industry.
104 For South Korea's global trade balance, see T'onggye-ch'ong, *Hanguk chuyo kyongje chip'yo, 2001. 3,* [Major Statistics of Korean Economy, March 2001] (Seoul: T'onggye-ch'ong, 2001), 261.
105 Ibid., 298-99.

The turnaround in Japan's direct investment in South Korea in 1998 and its dramatic increase in 1999 owe to a major effort by the Kim Dae Jung government to improve South Korea's investment climate. Some of the impediments to FDI in South Korea that came to its attention are revealing. At the 30th annual meeting of Japan-ROK economic personnel (*Han'il kyongje-in hoeui*) held in Seoul in April 1998, many of the 120 Japanese participants complained about barriers to FDI in South Korea. Among other things, they cited (1) the difficulty of setting up factories in South Korea, including exorbitant rents for land, (2) the tendency of South Korean conglomerates to invest in the same areas where Japanese companies have invested and the resultant erosion of profitability, (3) the general difficulty of doing business in South Korea—a Mitsui representative pointed out that none of the eleven companies in which Mitsui has invested has succeeded—and (4) the limited utility of "one stop" service for FDI Seoul operates. A Sumitomo representative pointed out that "one stop" service counters usually lack Japanese-speaking staff and merely direct their foreign clients to relevant government agencies.[106]

During his visit to Japan in October 1998, President Kim Dae Jung told Japanese business leaders: "as a result of recent drastic changes in related laws, almost all Korean industries are open to foreign investors. International investors can now buy Korean real estate and financial products without limit and buy businesses through mergers and acquisitions." He also pointed to changes in labor-management relations, notably continuing tripartite dialogue among labor, management, and government, and the legalization of layoffs.[107] The three-and-a-half-fold increase in Japanese investment in 1999 over the previous year is a

---

106 Oegyo T'ongsangbu, Aju T'ongsang-tim, "*Han'il kyongje-in hoeui*" *kija purip'ing charyo* [Press Briefing Material on "ROK-Japan Economic Personnel Meeting], April 20, 1998 (Seoul), 2-3.

107 "Ilbon kyongje tanch'e kongdong chuch'oe och'an yonsol" [Speech at a Luncheon Co-hosted by Japanese Economic Organizations], October 8, 1998, New Otani Hotel, Tokyo, in *Kim Dae Jung taet'ongnyong Ilbon kongsik pangmun kyolgwa*, Oegyo T'ongsangbu, 155-56.

graphic demonstration of the effects of changed investment climate in South Korea.[108]

The issue of perennial trade imbalance, however, was eclipsed by the currency and financial crisis that engulfed South Korea in late 1997. Compelled to seek a bailout from the IMF, South Korea swallowed the IMF's stringent conditions mandating austerity and a wide-ranging restructuring of financial system and corporate management. The IMF-organized rescue plan consisted of loans from multiple sources—the IMF itself ($21 billion), the World Bank ($10 billion), the Asian Development Bank ($4 billion), and all of the G-7 countries plus a number of other Western countries ($20 billion). What was striking was that Japan accounted for a half of the loan commitment from individual countries; its 10-billion-dollar commitment was not only the largest but twice that of the US.[109]

The size of Japan's commitment reflected its relative stake in South Korea. It was estimated that "Japanese lenders hold about 40 percent of South Korea's total external debt," which the South Korean government estimated at the end of 1997 at $156.9 billion, using a method of calculation approved by the IMF. This would make Japan the largest single source of loans to South Korea; Western European lenders collectively hold about 45 percent and US lenders hold about 15 percent of Seoul's external debt.[110] A default by South Korea or the collapse of its

---

108 Tsusho Sangyosho, ed., *Tsusho hakusho 2000*, 170.
109 International Monetary Fund, *IMF Approves SDR 15.5 Billion Stand-by Credit for Korea*, Press Release No. 97/55, December 4, 1997 (Washington, DC); Andrew Pollack, "Package of Loans Worth $55 Billion Is Set for Korea," *New York Times*, December 4, 1997, A1 and C6; Michael Schuman and Bob Davis, "South Korea Agrees to IMF's Bailout Terms," *Wall Street Journal*, December 4, 1997. The size of the bailout package was subsequently increased to $57 billion.
110 Timonthy L. O'Brien, "Lenders to Allow Koreans to Delay Debt Repayments," *New York Times*, December 30, 1997, A1 and C3; Yoo Cheong-mo, "Korea's Foreign Debts Total $156.9 Billion by IMF Standards," *Korea Herald*, December 31, 1997.

financial system, in other words, would deal a crushing blow to Japan.

It is noteworthy that Japan had actually contributed to South Korea's currency crisis. Apparently anticipating a serious shortage of foreign exchange in Seoul, Japanese banks began recalling short-term loans from South Korean financial institutions in October 1997 and collected $8 billion before the IMF bailout was announced. Japanese action, in other words, became a self-fulfilling prophecy. When Prime Minister Hashimoto held a meeting with President Kim Young Sam at the APEC summit in Vancouver on November 24, Hashimoto reportedly conveyed to Kim his regret over the Japanese action.[111]

In January 1999 the finance ministers of both countries signed an agreement on a short-term financing facility, under which Japan would provide up to $5 billion liquidity to the Bank of Korea through "swap transaction" between US dollar and South Korean won in the event of another currency crisis. This arrangement would have the effect of increasing South Korea's foreign currency reserve by $5 billion. South Korea thus became the first beneficiary of the Miyazawa Initiative, under which Japan pledged to make $30 billion available to Asian countries experiencing currency crises.[112] In sum, although it is patently asymmetric, the Japan-ROK economic relationship is nonetheless marked by mutual dependence.

Kim Dae Jung's Visit to Japan, October 1998

Kim Dae Jung's state visit to Japan from October 7 to 10, 1998 may well prove to be the most productive of the five state visits to that country

---

111 "Il 80-ok talo changnyon kingup hoesu, Hanguk hwallan puch'aejil" [Japan Suddenly Recalled $8 Billion Last Year, Fanning ROK Currency Crisis], *Dong-A ilbo*, May 20, 1998.

112 Okurasho, *Kyodo puresu sutetomento: Lee Kankoku zaikeibu chokan to Miyazawa okura daijin tono kaidan (1999-nen 1-gatsu 15-nichi o Frankufuruto)* [Joint Press Statement: Meeting Between ROK Finance-Economy Minister Lee and Finance Minister Miyazawa (January 15, 1999, Frankfurt)] (Tokyo).

by an ROK head of state that have occurred to date.(See Table 6) As already noted, the settlement of the fisheries dispute, that is, the conclusion of a new fisheries agreement, materialized as a prelude to, perhaps as a precondition for, the visit. Thanks to painstaking preparatory work by the diplomats of both countries, moreover, the visit produced a joint declaration and an action plan designed to pave the way for a genuine reconciliation between Japan and South Korea and for the forging of a truly cooperative relationship, a partnership not merely in name but in substance as well.

Japan extended to Kim Dae Jung one of the warmest welcomes ever accorded a visiting foreign dignitary. His speech to the joint session of the two houses of the Diet was attended by 527 Diet members out of a total of 751, a record surpassed only once before when US President Ronald Reagan was the speaker in the 1980s. Most unusual was the presence of a large number of Diet members' wives, including those of five former prime ministers, among the general audience in the gallery.[113] Kim's speech, which was interrupted 12 times by applause, was broadcast live by NHK (*Nihon Hoso Kyokai* or Japan Broadcast Corporation), Japan's state-owned broadcast network.

Kim's expression of both personal thanks to the Japanese government and people for their role in saving his life and official thanks for helping his country tide over the currency crisis, coupled with his praise of Japan's accomplishments and contributions to the global community, were well received by his audience. Recalling his experience of having been kidnaped from Tokyo in 1973 and receiving a death sentence in 1980, Kim said:

---

113 "Kim taet'ongnyong pang-Il twit yaegi" [Behind the Scenes Stories of President Kim's Visit to Japan], *Joongang ilbo*, October 11, 1998. It should be noted that poor attendance is the norm for speeches given to parliaments by visiting heads of state or government in Japan and the US. In the US Congress, staff members are frequently asked to fill the empty seats left by members of Congress so as not to embarrass foreign speakers.

> I have never forgotten the debt of gratitude I owe the Japanese people and press, as well as the Government, for the efforts you all made to protect my life and safety over long years. I am extremely happy for this opportunity today to fulfill my long-held dream of expressing my gratitude to you, the representatives of the Japanese people. To the Japanese people, I say, thank you very much.[114]

In another memorable part of the speech, Kim noted that Korea and Japan had interacted with each other for over 1,500 years, sharing religion and many aspects of culture. Even their languages, he pointed out, belong to the same Ural-Altaic language group. During the Tokugawa era, when Japan pursued a closed-door policy, he said, Japan and Korea continued mutual exchanges. Kim stressed that there were only two periods during which Japan-Korea relations were "unfortunate"—a seven-year period in the 16th century when Japan invaded and occupied Korea and 35 years of colonial rule in the first half of the 20th century. He then stated:

> It is truly infantile to regard 1,500 years of exchanges and cooperation as insignificant because of unfortunate periods that totaled fewer than 50 years. Isn't it something we should be ashamed of and something we should be reproached for by our ancestors, who forged such a history, and by our descendants?[115]

Referring to Japan's assistance to South Korea, Kim had this to say:

> In the process of overcoming [our] foreign currency crisis, Japan's assistance was great indeed. Japan rolled over loans of US $7.9 billion, or over one third of total short-term loans of US $21.7 billion that were to mature early this year. You have given us more

---

114 "Ilbon kukhoe yonsol" [Speech to the Japanese Diet], October 8, 1998 in Oegyo T'ongsangbu, *Kim Dae Jung taet'ongnyong Ilbon kongsik pangmun kyolgwa*, 65. I have used the ROK Foreign Ministry's translation in ibid., 88-99.
115 Ibid., 67 and 91.

support than any other country. A friend in need is a friend indeed, they say. I take this opportunity to express my heartfelt thanks to Japan, once again, for its active and genuine assistance.[116]

The summit meeting between Kim and Obuchi that had preceded Kim's Diet speech turned out to be a mere formality where the agreements that had already been reached were confirmed. It consisted of two back-to-back sessions—a "one-on-one summit" and an "expanded summit." The former, in which both leaders were accompanied by two top aides each and interpreters, lasted an hour, while the latter, in which other people joined, making the total participants about two dozen, lasted 45 minutes.[117]

The centerpiece of the visit was the publication of a joint statement and an action plan immediately following the summit. The "Japan-Republic of Korea Joint Declaration: A New Japan-Republic of Korea Partnership towards the 21st Century" proclaimed the "common determination" of Obuchi and Kim to raise to a "higher plane" (*shin jigen* in Japanese *and sin ch'awon* in Korean) the "close, friendly and cooperative relations between Japan and the Republic of Korea" with a view towards building a new Japan-ROK "partnership." To do so, according to the declaration, both countries must "squarely face the past and develop relations based on mutual understanding and trust."[118]

Then came Obuchi's apology:

---

116 Ibid., 72-73 and 97.
117 "Kim taet'ongnyon pang-Il twit yaegi," *Joongang ilbo*, October 11, 1998.
118 For the Japanese text of the declaration, see Gaimusho, *Nikkan kyodo sengen - 21 seiki ni muketa aratana Nikkan patonashippu*, October 8, 1998 (Tokyo); for the Korean text, see "21 segi ui saeroun Han'il patunosuip ul wihan kongdong sonon" in Oegyo T'ongsangbu, *Kim Dae Jung taet'ongnyong Ilbon kongsik pangmun kyolgwa*, 11-16; for an English translation, see Ministry of Foreign Affairs of Japan, *Japan-Republic of Korea Joint Declaration: A New Japan-Republic of Korea Partnership towards the Twenty-first Century*, October 8, 1998 (Tokyo). The Japanese Foreign Ministry has translated *shin jigen* as "higher dimension."

Looking back on the relations between Japan and the Republic of Korea during this century, Prime Minister Obuchi regarded in a spirit of humility [kenkyoni uketome] the historical fact that Japan caused during a certain period in the past tremendous damage and suffering [tadaino songai to kutsu o ataeta] to the people of the Republic of Korea through its colonial rule, and expressed his deep remorse and heartfelt apology for that fact [koreni taishi tsusetsuna hansei to owabi o nobeta].[119]

Obuchi's words were virtually identical to those contained in Prime Minister Murayama's August 15, 1995 statement. The main difference was Obuchi's explicit reference to the people of the Republic of Korea. His apology, which Kim Dae Jung "accepted with sincerity," was actually the only statement of its kind generated during the Kim visit. For, in his speech at a banquet welcoming Kim and his wife on October 7, Emperor Akihito did not offer any apology, saying only that "in contrast to a history of intimate exchanges, there was a period when our country imposed immense sufferings on the people of the Korean peninsula. Deep sorrow concerning it [sono koto ni taisuru fukai kanashimi] always remains in my memory."[120]

The joint declaration went on to list various measures aimed at translating the two leaders' shared commitment to usher in a new era of genuine partnership. As elaborated in the supplementary "action plan," the measures were broken down into five broad categories: (1) expansion of channels of bilateral dialogue, (2) cooperation to promote world peace and security, (3) strengthening cooperation in the economic field, (4) increasing cooperation on global issues, and (5) promotion of people's exchanges and cultural exchange.

---

119 Gaimusho, *Nikkan kyodo sengen*, 1; Ministry of Foreign Affairs of Japan, *Japan-Republic of Korea Joint Declaration*, 1. I have edited the Japanese Foreign Ministry's translation.
120 "Kuchu bansan deno tenno heika no okotoba" [His Majesty Emperor's Remarks at an Imperial Palace Banquet], *Asahi shinbun*, October 8, 1998.

To give a few examples, the two sides agreed to hold a summit meeting at least once a year. Japan pledged to provide an Export-Import Bank (EXIM Bank) loan of $3 billion to South Korea to help the latter overcome its current economic difficulties. This would be in addition to the $1 billion EXIM Bank loan Japan had already provided earlier in the year. The two sides signed an agreement on a "working holiday program," under which youths of both countries would be allowed to visit the other country to learn its culture and life style while working for up to a year. The two sides also set a target of 10,000 primary and middle school students visiting each other's country in the next ten years. Finally, Japan agreed to increase the number of South Korean engineering students in Japanese universities to 1,000 in ten years.

In a joint press conference following their summit meeting and the release of the joint declaration and action plan, both Obuchi and Kim Dae Jung sounded an upbeat note. Expressing his "great pleasure" (*okina yorokobi*) at having had a heart-to-heart talk with the president "who understands the importance and possibilities of Japan-ROK relations," Obuchi said that the summit meeting would "adorn a page of history" and that the two countries had taken a "first step toward developing friendly and cooperative relations that are on a higher plane" than before. Kim Dae Jung said that he had found the summit meeting "most useful" and was satisfied with its results, adding that it had confirmed that a "solid foundation was being laid for future-oriented, friendly, neighborly relations between the Republic of Korea and Japan." He was, Kim said, "deeply moved by the Prime Minister's enthusiasm for and knowledge concerning the further development of ROK-Japan relations."[121]

Asked by a reporter whether, given the past track record of summit meetings, the two leaders' commitment to put the issue of history to rest and begin a new relationship towards the 21st century would produce tangible results, both Obuchi and Kim stressed that unlike in the past,

---

121 *Gaimusho, Obuchi naikaku daijin, Kim Dae Jung Kankoku daitoryo kyodo kisha kaiken-roku* [Record of Joint Press Conference by Prime Minister Obuchi and ROK President Kim Dae Jung], October 8, 1998 (Tokyo).

Japan's apology had become part of a formal diplomatic document and that the Republic of Korea had been explicitly mentioned as the intended recipient of that apology. They were therefore confident that the ghost of history would cease to haunt Tokyo-Seoul relations in the years to come.[122] Their optimism, however, proved to be premature, for the issue of Japanese history textbooks would strain the bilateral relations in early 2001.

To return to the joint news conference, Kim Dae Jung stressed that the necessity for ROK-Japan cooperation in security and economic fields was greater now than at any time in the past. He also noted a "fundamental difference" between the 20th and 21st centuries. Whereas the former could be considered an era of nation-states, he said, the latter is certain to become an era of globalization in which the world will become one. "The legacy of the 20th century," in his words, "must be liquidated here and now, and closest neighbors must joint hands and cooperate and sometimes compete with all the nations of the world in the era of globalization."[123]

The press reaction to the Kim visit was generally favorable in both countries. The South Korean press, however, pointed to the lack of specificity in Obuchi's apology. As an editorial in *The Korea Herald*, put it, "the 'comfort women' issue will likely serve as a major yardstick in gauging whether Japan is truly repentant of its past crimes. Japan has never accepted the crime and never offered a formal apology. It has also refused to make official compensation for the victims, arguing that all Korean claims were settled under the 1965 normalization treaty. If Japan

---

122 Ibid. Former prime minister Murayama, whose August 15, 1995 statement was virtually reproduced in Obuchi's apology, concurred in the view that Obuchi's apology would carry greater weight than his because the former had become part of a diplomatic document. "Han'il kongdong sonon kakkuk panung" [Reaction from Various Countries to the Joint ROK-Japan Declaration], *Joongang ilbo*, October 11, 1998.

123 "Kongdong kija hoegyon kirok" [Record of Joint Press Conference], October 8, 1998 in Oegyo T'ongsangbu, *Kim Dae Jung taet'ongnyong Ilbon kongsik pangmun kyolgwa*, 55.

continues to refuse to faithfully confess, it will certainly be objurgated and accused of playing with words in its 'apologies' to Korea and other Asian countries."[124]

The Japan Times was unmistakably upbeat in its assessment. Calling Kim Dae Jung a "visionary" and a man who understands the Japanese better than any other Korean leader, the Japanese daily declared that Kim "has already inaugurated a new era in relations with Japan." The paper continued:

> His forward-looking attitude was evident in the speeches he made during the summit. He focused on challenges that lay ahead rather than the stains of the past. His decision to have the Seoul government assume the financial responsibility for the "comfort women"—and the subsequent request that Japan assume the moral burden of that tragedy—has shifted the political and ethical terrain.[125]

The Kim Dae Jung government's "forward-looking" posture toward Japan was also reflected in its decision to refer to the Japanese emperor by his official title and to gradually remove restrictions on the import of Japanese films, popular music, comic books, and other items subsumed

---

124 "Japan's Apology," *Korea Herald*, October 9, 1998, an editorial.
125 "Building a Future with South Korea," *Japan Times*, October 10, 1998, an editorial. Reversing its predecessor's policy, the Kim Dae Jung government decided in April 1998 not to seek compensation directly from the Japanese government for "comfort women" but to make payments of 31.5 million won (about $23,000) to each of the women. On May 7, all but 32 of the 152 surviving "comfort women" were paid both the government subsidy and an additional 34.5 million won each from funds raised by *chongdaehyop* (Korean Council for Women Drafted for Military Sexual Slavery by Japan), a non-governmental organization in South Korea. The 32 women who didn't receive any payment had either turned down the offer or could not be located. "Pokjibu wianbu 120 myong chiwongum 3,450-man won ssik chigup" [Welfare Ministry Pays 34.5 Million Won of Support Money to Each of 120 Comfort Women], *Joongang ilbo*, May 9, 1998.

under "popular culture."[126] Another sign of change appeared when Fuwa Tetsuro, chairman of the Japan Communist Party (JCP) attended the banquet in honor of Kim Dae Jung hosted by Prime Minister Obuchi. Three JCP Diet members also attended a reception following Kim's speech to the Diet. Finally, the Kim Dae Jung government granted *Akahata*, the JCP newspaper, permission to establish a bureau in Seoul.[127]

Obuchi's Visit to South Korea, March 1999

Within five months of the Kim Dae Jung visit, Prime Minister Obuchi made a three-day *state* visit to South Korea. It was the first *state* visit by a Japanese prime minister to the ROK in five years, for Prime Minister Hashimoto's visit to Cheju in June 1996 had been a "working visit." The main purpose of the Obuchi visit was to hold a summit meeting with Kim Dae Jung, of which two sessions were held on March 20, 1999. On their agenda were (1) bilateral issues and (2) policy toward North Korea.[128]

On bilateral issues, the two leaders noted with satisfaction that the

---

126 Angered by Japan's imposition of fingerprinting on Korean residents in 1989, the South Korean government stopped using the phrase "Ilbon ch'onhwang" (Japanese emperor), replacing it with "Ilhwang," an abbreviation of the phrase that has a less exalted connotation than emperor, in its internal documents. The Korean press, meanwhile, began using the word "Ilwang" (King of Japan), a deliberate downgrading of emperor. "Chongbu 'ch'onhwang' hoch'ing chonhwan paegyong" [Background on Government's Policy Change in Referring to "Emperor"], *Hankyoreh sinmun*, September 12, 1998.
127 *Daily Yomiuri*, October 9, 1998.
128 Ministry of Foreign Affairs of Japan, Press Conference by the Press Secretary, 23 March 1999, *Archives on Press Conferences* (Tokyo), http://www.mofa.go.jp./announce/press/1999/3/323.html; "Han'il munhwa kyoryu sinsol: chongsang hoedam kongdong palp'yomun yoji" [ROK-Japan Forum on Cultural Exchange To Be Established: Gist of Joint Announcement on Summit Meeting], *Chosun ilbo*, March 22, 1999, 4.

joint declaration and action plan adopted in Tokyo in October 1998 were being implemented smoothly. Of many examples of expanding channels of dialogue, they cited the first "gathering of Japan-ROK cabinet ministers" (*Nikkan kakuryo kondankai*) held in Kagoshima in November 1998, confirming that another would be held in South Korea in the fall of 1999.[129]

The two leaders also took note of measures aimed at economic cooperation, including the initiation of inter-governmental negotiations on a bilateral investment agreement, agreeing to step up efforts to remove barriers and increase cooperation under a new umbrella, "Agenda 21 for Japan-ROK Economic Cooperation." They reviewed progress in expanding youth exchange, noting that all the projects were on track, including that on "working holidays" scheduled to begin in April 1999. Obuchi and Kim decided to set up a forum on cultural exchange and to support exchange projects connected with the joint sponsorship of World Cup 2002. Obuchi welcomed Seoul's moves to open its markets to Japanese popular culture, and Kim promised further measures in the coming months.[130]

In sum, as far as bilateral issues were concerned, Obuchi and Kim found virtually no area of disagreement. Obuchi was reported to have told Kim that there was widely shared belief among the Japanese people that a new era in Japan-ROK relations could really begin, adding his own assessment that the bilateral relationship had never been better.[131]

---

129 Oegyo T'ongsangbu, *Han'il kongdong son'on mit haengdong kyehoek ui ch'ujin hyonhwang e kwanhan kongdong ollon palp'yomun* [Joint Press Communique on the Implementation of the ROK-Japan Joint Declaration and Action Plan] (Seoul: March 20, 1999). *Kondankai (kandamhoe in Korean)* implies less formality than does *kaidan* (or *hoedam*) [meeting]. Prime Minister Obuchi attended both the Kagoshima gathering and its sequel held in Cheju in October 1999. Oegyo T'ongsangbu, Asia T'aep'yongyang-guk, Tongbuga 1-kwa, *Ilbon yaksik kaehwang* [Brief Overview of Japan] (Seoul: June 21, 2000), 3.
130 Oegyo T'ongsangbu, *Han'il kongdong son'on* ......
131 The source of this information was Lim Dong Won, the chief presidential secretary for foreign affairs and national security, who participated in Kim-

The second item on the agenda of the summit was North Korea. In the words of the press secretary of the Japanese foreign ministry, Obuchi and Kim "discussed issues related to North Korea in considerable depth and they saw eye to eye on a number of points." Obuchi, he added, expressed support for Kim's engagement (or "sunshine") policy toward the North, and the "two leaders agreed on the importance of Japan, the [ROK], and the [US] working in close coordination and cooperation." Obuchi "expressed his view that this policy of engagement or a comprehensive approach should include elements of dialogue as well as elements of deterrence."[132]

It was no secret, nonetheless, that the two leaders diverged somewhat in their respective views of Pyongyang's threat and, more important, of how to counter it. Kim Dae Jung was known to favor a more conciliatory approach than Obuchi, who underscored the need to combine diplomacy with deterrence. When he was asked about this at a post-summit news conference in Tokyo, the foreign ministry press secretary pointed out that the "agreements and convergence of views far outweigh the perceived areas of difference." He hastened to add that it was important for Seoul, Tokyo, and Washington "to work hand in hand towards the same objectives," underscoring that they did indeed "share the same objectives" vis-a-vis Pyongyang. He nonetheless conceded that these three countries that were linked by two military alliances might not "necessarily adopt identical policies at all times" but stressed that their differences existed mainly in the realm of relative "emphasis."[133]

At Korea University where he gave the only substantive public speech of his visit, Obuchi said that "it is difficult to build amicable relations with North Korea if it does not clear suspicions over nuclear weapons development [or] halt the development, test-firing, deployment and, export of ballistic missiles." Kim Dae Jung, however, "publicly urged

---

Obuchi talks. *Chosun ilbo*, March 22, 1999, 3.
132 Ministry of Foreign Affairs of Japan, *Press Conference by the Press Secretary*, 23 March 1999, 1-2.
133 Ibid., 3-4.

Obuchi and the Japanese public not to harden their position only because of the missile problem, which he said poses a bigger threat to South Korea than to Japan."[134]

Prime Minister Mori Yoshiro's Visit to Seoul, May 2000

Prime Minister Mori Yoshiro's one-day working visit to Seoul on May 29, 2000 was linked to the historic inter-Korean summit. For it occurred two weeks before President Kim Dae Jung was scheduled to go to Pyongyang. While officially welcoming the impending inter-Korean summit, Japan appeared nonetheless to be apprehensive about its possible adverse effects on issues of concern to Tokyo. In a more positive vein, the Mori government could use Kim Dae Jung's help in letting the DPRK's supreme leader, Kim Jong IL, know of its desire for the continuation of normalization talks as well as its need for an early resolution of the missile and abduction issues.[135]

As was the case with the Obuchi-Kim summit in March 1999, however, the two leaders discussed both bilateral relations and issues related to North Korea. On the former, both affirmed that the state of the Japan-ROK relations was excellent, that the agreements signed in October

---

134 Chon Shi-yong, "Kim, Obuchi Reaffirm N.K. Engagement Stance," *Korea Herald*, March 22, 1999, 1. For the text of Obuchi's speech, see Gaimusho, *Koryo Daigaku ni okeru Obuchi sori dajin enzetsu - Shin seiki no Nikkan kankei - aratana rekishi no sozo* [Prime Minister Obuchi's Speech at Korea University: Japan-ROK Relations in the New Century:Creating a New History] (Tokyo: March 20, 1999), http://www.mofa.go.jp/mofaj/gaiko/happyo/enzetsu/enze_0320.html. The statement quoted here is not in the text of Obuchi's speech but from his response to a question after the speech.

135 Gaimusho, "Mori sori daijin no Kankoku homon ni tsuite" [On Prime Minister Mori's Visit to the ROK], *Shuno, gaisho kaidan (Mori sori daijin)* [Summit and Foreign Ministers' Meetings (Prime Minister Mori)] (Tokyo: May 9, 2000), http://www.mofa.go.jp/mofaj/gaiko/kaidan/s_mori/korea_00/homon.html.

1998 were being faithfully implemented, and that a "new era in Japan-ROK relations" had indeed opened, simultaneously increasing and deepening mutual exchanges at the governmental and people's levels. They noted with satisfaction progress in negotiations on an investment agreement; Seoul's phased lifting of restrictions on the import of Japanese popular culture, including music and movies; and cooperation in connection with the hosting of World Cup 2002. Citing the warm personal relationship his predecessor had forged with Kim Dae Jung, Mori vowed to honor Obuchi's legacy by working with Kim to keep up the momentum of progress in Japan-ROK relations.[136]

With respect to North Korea, Mori and Kim concurred on the importance of close bilateral cooperation between the two countries as well as of trilateral consultations among the two and the US. Mori expressed full support for the impending inter-Korean summit, describing it as the fruit of the engagement policy Kim Dae Jung had pursued with a great deal of perseverance. Asked by a Japanese reporter whether he intended to raise the missile and abduction issues with the North Korean leader Kim Jong Il, Kim Dae Jung avoided a direct answer but stated that since the agenda of the summit had not been fixed, he expected that it would cover any and all issues, both bilateral and international, including those in which the US and Japan have special interests.[137]

Mori was well prepared for a question asked by a South Korean reporter about the controversial statement on "divine nation (*kami no kuni*) with the emperor at the center" Mori had made in Japan. Reading from a prepared text, Mori expressed his "deep remorse" for the misunderstanding his remark had caused. He said that the expression "divine nation" had been designed to refer to Japan's tradition dating from ancient times of believing in the existence of forces that transcend human beings in such natural objects as land, mountains, rivers, and sea.

---

136 Idem, "Nikkan shuno kaidan (kyodo kisha kaiken)" [Japan-ROK Summit Meeting (Joint Press Conference), ibid (Tokyo: May 29, 2000), http://www.mofa.go.jp/mofaj/gaiko/kaidan/s_mori/korea_00/kaiken.html.
137 Ibid.

His reference to the emperor, Mori added, was meant to point out the changing position of the emperor who, under the postwar constitution, is the symbol of Japan and of the unity of the Japanese people.[138]

Kim Dae Jung conveyed to Mori his hope that the Group of Eight (G-8) summit that was scheduled to be held in Okinawa in July "would jointly voice support for increased dialogue between North and South Korea."[139] Mori was instrumental in having the G-8 summit adopt a statement on the Korean peninsula on July 21, 2000, which expressed "strong support" for "all efforts by the ROK and the DPRK to reduce tensions and establish lasting peace that contribute to stability in Northeast Asia" and for "the ROK's engagement policy, which is contributing to positive developments." The G-8 statement also described the DPRK's "reconfirmation of its moratorium on missile-launch as a positive step," calling on the DPRK "to continue such efforts." "We look forward," it said, "to a constructive response to international concerns over security, non-proliferation, humanitarian and human rights issues".[140]

What is striking about the G-8 statement is that it is substantially more than an expression of support for the dramatic improvement of inter-Korean relations following the Pyongyang summit. It is also an endorsement of Japan's concerns over the missile and abduction issues, with the latter being euphemistically referred to as "humanitarian and human rights issues." Mori, it must be stressed, did not obtain such an explicit endorsement from Kim Dae Jung notwithstanding their commitment to bilateral and trilateral consultations and coordination.

If, as the Japanese foreign ministry concluded, the Mori-Kim summit

---

138 Ibid; *Korea Herald*, May 30, 2000.
139 Richard Maeki, "Japan, ROK Agree to Approach N. Korea Ties in Coordination," *Daily Yomiuri*, May 30, 2000.
140 Ministry of Foreign Affairs of Japan, "G8 Statement on Korean Peninsula (Okinawa, 21 July 2000)," *Kyushu-Okinawa Summit Meeting 2000: Official Documents* (Tokyo), http://www.g8kyushu-okinawa.go.jp/e/documents/korea.html.

helped to build a personal relationship based on trust, then, its value in developing bilateral relations could not be minimized. Since, despite its setback in the June 25 parliamentary election, the LDP retained its reigns of power and Mori was re-elected as prime minister, such a relationship would be beneficial to the process of strengthening Japan-ROK relations. This was shown during the summit held in Atami from September 22 to 24.[141]

Kim Dae Jung's Visit to Japan, September 2000

From September 22 to 24 Kim Dae Jung made his second visit to Japan since becoming the ROK president. Unlike his first visit in October 1998, however, this was an "official working visit," and the summit meeting between Kim and Obuchi took place not in Tokyo but in the hot springs resort city of Atami in Shizuoka prefecture. During two sessions— an "expanded" session on September 23 and a one-on-one session on the following day—the two leaders reviewed the progress their two countries had made toward the implementation of the commitments contained in the October 1998 joint declaration and action program, noting both accomplishments and areas in which more work remained to be done. Kim welcomed a marked increase in Japanese investment in South Korea and pledged to continue efforts to improve his country's investment climate with a view toward encouraging more investment. Both sides agreed to accelerate efforts to conclude a bilateral investment protection agreement.[142]

The two leaders also discussed the idea of a Free Trade Agreement

---

141 "Kim Dae Jung daitoryo raigetsu 22-nichi rainichi" [President Kim Dae Jung to Visit Japan on the 22nd of Next Month], *Yomiuri shinbun*, August 16, 2000.
142 Gaimusho, *Kim Dae Jung taitoryo no honichi* (hyoka to gaiyo) [President Kim Dae Jung's Visit to Japan (Appraisal and Summary)] (Tokyo: September 24, 2000); Ch'ongwadae, *Ilbon kongsik silmu pangmun, 2000 9. 22-24* [Official Working Visit to Japan, 2000. 9. 22-24] (Seoul: October 6, 2000).

(FTA), in which Japan showed more interest than South Korea. Seoul feared that an FTA might have the effect of widening the gap in its trade balance with Tokyo—that is, Seoul's perennial deficits. In a characteristic diplomatic fashion, the two sides agreed to set up a bilateral forum to study the matter further. One area in which there was a meeting of minds was cooperation in information technology (IT). This was an area in which both countries had made substantial advances and could engage in mutually beneficial collaborative projects; some cooperation had already taken place. An agreement to promote more cooperation in E-commerce, research and development, IT human resource interaction, and related fields was unveiled.[143]

Other issues discussed during the summit meeting included the problem of the availability of seats in the civil aviation route between the two countries, which would become acute with the co-hosting of the World Cup soccer tournament in 2002, and the issue of participation in local elections by Korean residents in Japan. Regarding the latter, Mori told Kim that since it concerned a basic structure of Japanese politics, the issue would require careful deliberation in the Diet; the best he could do was to make an effort to encourage the Diet to pay attention to the issue. Mori informed Kim that Korean would become one of the foreign languages students could choose for the examination required of all applicants to national and public universities by 2003 at the latest.[144]

---

143 Ibid.; Ministry of Foreign Affairs of Japan, *Japan-R.O.K/R.O.K/Japan Information Technology (IT) Cooperation Initiative* (Unofficial Translation) (Tokyo: September 23, 2000); "Han'il chongsang hoedam: IT hyomnyok shipke habui, tongp'o ch'amjong-kwon igyon" [ROK-Japan Summit: Easy Agreement on IT Cooperation, Disagreement on Korean Residents' Right to Vote], *Chosun ilbo*, September 24, 2000; "Han'il IT hyomnyok, kiop chehyu botmul yego" [ROK-Japan IT Cooperation: Collaboration Expected to Yield Huge Benefits for Business], *Joongang ilbo*, September 23, 2000.

144 "Kankokugo senta shiken ni, shuno kaidan de shusho hyomei e" [Korean To Be Included in "Center" Exam, Prime Minister Reveals in Summit Meeting], *Asahi shinbun*, September 22, 2000; "Kim taitoryo chiho senkyo hoan no nennai seiritsu yobo, Nikkan shuno kaidan" [President Kim Wants

A major topic of discussion between Mori and Kim was North Korea. Kim advised Mori to seek a summit meeting with Kim Jong Il, pointing out that as the supreme leader with absolute power, Kim Jong Il alone would be in a position to make a decisive move. Kim Dae Jung underscored that breakthroughs in negotiations with the DPRK had usually occurred when its supreme leader was directly involved, citing as examples the Kim Il Sung-Carter meeting in June 1994 and his own meeting with Kim Jong Il in June 2000.¹⁴⁵

Kim Dae Jung urged Japan to provide food aid to the North, saying that "North Korea would probably appreciate it very much." The issue, actually, was already under review in Tokyo and, as we saw in Chapter 4, the Mori government decided in October to provide Pyongyang with 500,000 tons of rice. During the summit, nevertheless, Mori told Kim Dae Jung that it was "difficult to gain public support for such an idea in Japan as there are concerns that economic assistance might end up strengthening North Korean military power." Regarding Kim Dae Jung's proposal for joint assistance by Seoul and Tokyo to the North's infrastructure modernization, Mori reportedly stressed that a normalization of Japan-DPRK relations must precede such assistance.¹⁴⁶

All in all, the most notable aspect of the Atami summit was the warm affection shown by the two leaders toward each other. They were eager to please and support each other and to accentuate the positive, even when they did not agree with each other. The value of such a warm personal relationship, however, turned out to be limited. With weak political base and, more important, prone to committing gaffes, Mori was continually

---

Enactment of Law on Local Elections, Japan-ROK Summit Meeting], ibid., September 24, 2000.

145 "Nikkan shuno kaidan: Nitcho kokkyo seijoka itsuyoi kitai, Kankoku taitoryo" [Japan-ROK Summit Meeting: ROK President Has High Expectations for Japan-DPRK Normalization], *Mainichi shinbun*, September 23, 2000.

146 Junko Takahashi, "Japan-South Korea Summit: Kim Urges Mori to Help Feed North Korea," *Japan Times*, September 25, 2000.

embroiled in controversy and by April 2001, was replaced by Koizumi Junichiro.

The Escalation of Conflict in Tokyo-Seoul Relations

In a strict sense, the seeds of conflict were planted during the last months of the Mori administration. The most serious of the three issues that would plunge Japan-ROK relations to a new low for six months in 2001 was the history textbook controversy, and the critical phase in its evolution occurred in April 2001 when Mori, though a lame duck, was still officially the head of the Japanese government.

On April 3, 2001 the Ministry of Education, Culture, Sports, Science and Technology (MEXT) approved a controversial history textbook for middle (or junior high) schools prepared by the Japanese Society for History Textbook Reform (*Atarashii Rekishi Kyokasho o Tsukurukai* [*Tsukurukai*]). The MEXT, acting through its Textbook Authorization Research Council, also approved seven other history textbooks for use by middle schools in 2002.[147]

The MEXT justified its decision on grounds that Tsukurukai had fully complied with its request for revision of 137 entries in the first draft. A civics (*komin*) textbook prepared by Tsukurukai was also approved. The ROK government, which had repeatedly urged the Japanese government not to approve *Tsukurukai's* "New History Textbook" (*Atarashii Rekishi Kyokasho*), immediately protested Tokyo's action. In Seoul's view

---

147 Monbu Kagakusho, *Heisei 12-nendo kyokayo tosho kentei kekka ni kansuru taijin danwa* [Minister's Statement on the Results of the 2000 Screening of Books for Use in Teaching] (Tokyo: April 3, 2001), http://www.mext.go.jp/ b-menu/houdou/13/04/010402.htm; "'Tsukurukai' kyokasho Monbu-kagakusho no kentei ni gokaku" [*Tsukurukai's* Textbook Passes Education-Science Ministry's Screening], *Asahi shinbun*, April 4, 2001. The English translation of *tsukurukai* is its own; a literal translation would read "Society for Making a New History Textbook."

Tsukurukai's textbook distorts history, glossing over the aggression and atrocities committed by the Japanese Imperial Army. Reflecting one of the key aims of its authors, the textbook conspicuously omits any reference to the "comfort women," those who had been forced to serve as sex slaves for Japanese soldiers during World War II, of whom more than a hundred thousand had come from Korea.[148]

Tsukurukai was formed in January 1997 by those who rebelled against descriptions of "comfort women" contained in social studies and history textbooks that had been approved by the Education Ministry for selection by middle schools. They advocated deletion of all references to "comfort women" from middle school textbooks. Decrying what they called the "masochistic tendency" (*jigyaku-teki keiko*) in history education in postwar Japan, they committed themselves to the goal of writing a textbook that contains a "self-portrait of the Japanese state and people from the perspective of world history," presenting a "story of the Japanese people" whose ancestors experienced successes and failures, achievements and sufferings. Theirs, they vowed, would be a textbook marked by "dignity" (*hinkaku*) and balance, which would not only be used in classrooms but also be read and discussed by parents and children.[149]

In the "New History Textbook" Japan's annexation of Korea in 1910 is portrayed as something the Japanese government found it necessary to accomplish "in order to safeguard Japan's security and interests in Manchuria." What is more, "since England, America, and Russia were wary of each other's attempt to expand influence on the Korean

---

148 Nishio Kanji et al, *Atarashii rekishi kyokasho* (Shihanbon) [New History Textbook (General Sales Edition)] (Tokyo: Fusosha, 2001). Fourteen persons are listed as co-authors, of whom nine are writers (*shippitsu-sha*) and five are editorial supervisors (*kanshu-sha*).

149 "'Tsukurukai no shucho" [*Tsukurukai's* Arguments] in *Tsukurukai Q & A* [Questions and Answers About *tsukurukai*] (Tokyo: January 30, 1997), http://www.tsukurukai.com/argument.htm; Fujioka Nobukatsu, "Why Middle School Student Should Not Be Taught About 'Military Comfort Women'," (Tokyo, December 1996), http://www.tsukurukai.com/english2.html.

Peninsula, none of them objected" to the Japanese action. "Suppressing opposition in Korea with military force," the textbook adds, "Japan carried out the annexation."[150]

Regarding the origins of the Pacific war, the new history textbook underscores the "encirclement by ABCD"—America, Britain, China, and Dutch—aimed at the economic strangulation of Japan. It mentions the "Hull note" of November 1941, in which U.S. Secretary of State Cordell Hull is said to have demanded Japan's immediate, unconditional withdrawal from China. Since "complying with the demand would mean capitulation to the US," the "Japanese government ultimately decided to go to war against the US." Japan's sneak attack against the US ships and airplanes at Pearl Harbor is depicted as "air raid" by Japan's "mobile naval unit against the US Pacific Fleet." In explaining Japan's early successes in Southeast Asia, which it calls a "great victory," the book asserts that it was made possible by the cooperation of the local people who resented several hundred years' colonial rule by white people. "Japan's victory in these battles nurtured both a dream of independence and courage for many people in Southeast Asia and India." "Japan's war aims," the book states, "consisted of self-reliance and self-defense, liberating Asia from domination by Europe and America," and building a "Great East Asia Co-prosperity Sphere."[151]

The word "aggression" (*shinryaku*) never appears in the textbook; instead the word "military occupation" (*kunji senryo*) is used.[152] The Nanjing massacre is called the "Nanjing incident," in which the Japanese troops occupying Nanjing in 1937 "killed a large number of Chinese civilians." The book hastens to add, however, that there are doubts about evidence concerning the incident, that there are many different points of view, and that debate on the incident continues to this day.[153]

By the time the ROK government prepared a detailed analysis of all

---

150 Nishio et al, *Atarashii rekishi kyokasho*, 240.
151 Ibid., 274-77.
152 Ibid., 266.
153 Ibid., 295.

eight history textbooks and formally requested Japan to make changes in 35 entries, of which 25 were from Tsukurukai's textbook, Koizumi Junichiro had succeeded Mori as prime minister. Given Koizumi's reputation as a hard-line nationalist, however, Seoul confronted a more daunting challenge than before. To complicate the matter, Koizumi had made a commitment to visit Yasukuni Shrine, where 14 Class A war criminals are enshrined, on the anniversary of Japanese defeat on August 15. As we shall see shortly, a dispute over fishing would soon be added to the sources of Japan-ROK discord.

On July 9 the MEXT announced that it had found only two of Seoul's 35 requests for revision meritorious. Both of them were minor factual errors: only one of them was from the Fusosha textbook by *Tsukurukai*, and the other was from a section on ancient Korean history in a different textbook. The error in the Fusosha textbook, moreover, was one of nine passages the publisher had already decided to rewrite.[154] To no one's surprise, the Kim Dae Jung government rejected "Tokyo's attempt to close the chapter on the controversial textbook issue," insisting that Tokyo should "go back to the drawing board." A delegation consisting of secretaries-general of the three ruling coalition parties that had been scheduled to meet President Kim was told that the meeting had been cancelled. The delegation had hoped to discuss the textbook issue with Kim.[155]

Kim Dae Jung was reported to have told a Cabinet meeting on July 10 that he had found Japan's stance "totally unacceptable." "I'm shocked. That Japan distorts historical facts and teaches them to people will have no positive effects on bilateral relations at all," a Blue House spokesman

---

154 Monbu Kagakusho, *Chugaku rekishi kyokasho shusei yokyu ni kakaru kento kekka ni kansuru Monbu Kagaku daijin komento* [Education and Science Minister's Comments on the Results of the Review of the Request for Revision of Middle School History Textbooks] (Tokyo: July 9, 2001), http://www.mext.go.jp/b-menu/houdou/13/07/ 010799.htm.

155 "Seoul Insists Japan Rewrite History Textbooks," *Mainichi Daily News,* July 9, 2001.

quoted Kim as saying.[156] The Kim government announced a suspension of any further opening of the South Korean market to Japanese popular culture. Since October 1998 it had been lifting restrictions on the import of Japanese popular culture in stages; after three waves of liberalization, only a few items remained on the list of banned items, such as compact disks for Japanese songs, video tapes of movies and television dramas, adult movies, and animated movies that have not won awards at international film festivals. All of these items were scheduled to be removed from the banned list in 2001.[157] Additionally, over 125 projects involving bilateral people's exchange were scrapped, many of them at Seoul's request. The number of Japanese tourists visiting South Korea also began to decline, with a growing number of groups canceling their reservations.[158] In absolute terms, however, the number of Japanese visitors to South Korea was still larger than in the preceding year. What was decreasing was the rate of growth, which was 32 percent between 1998 and 1999 and 13.2 percent between 1999 and 2000. During the first seven months of 2001 the rate remained 5.2 percent. The strain in Tokyo-Seoul relations adversely affected their economic intercourse as well: Japan's direct investment in South Korea during the first five months of 2001 totaled $307 million, which was only 45.8 percent of the record during the comparable period in 2000. During the same period South Korean exports to Japan declined 6.8 percent compared to the previous year.[159] By the end of July Japan's position as Seoul's second largest

---

156 "Kim Dae-jung Outraged at Textbook Snub," *Mainichi Daily News*, July 10, 2001.
157 "Mado wa hiraita bakari nanoni······Kankoku no Nihon bunka kaiho chudan de hamon" [Window Had Just Opened······ROK's Interruption of Opening to Japanese Culture Creates Ripple], *Ashahi shinbun*, July 15, 2001, 9.
158 "Kyokwaso munjero Han'il kyoryu saop 125-kon chungji" [125 ROK-Japan Exchange Projects Stopped Due to Textbook Problem], *Chosun ilbo*, July 21, 2001; "Ilbon kwangwanggaekdul 'Kyokwaso kyut'an e Hanguk kagi komna'" [Japanese Tourists: "Afraid to Go To Korea Due to Textbook Protests], *Joongang ilbo*, July 23, 2001.
159 "Han'il kyoryu−kyonghyop pinghagi ······tae-Han t'uja-aek changnyon ui

destination of export goods after the US was in jeopardy, for Seoul's exports to China ($10.69 billion) had surpassed its exports to Japan ($10.37 billion) for the first time.[160]

In mid-August the textbook issue receded into the background as it became clear that the controversial Fusosha textbook had failed to meet its professed goal of being selected for use by ten percent of middle school students. Only a handful of national or public middle schools had selected the New History Textbook, and most of them were schools for students with disabilities. Only seven private middle schools had selected the book but they had also chosen Fusosha's civic textbook. Two other private schools had chosen the latter only. All told, the proportion of all middle school students who will be using the Fusosha textbook in 2002 will be less than 1 percent of their population; some estimates were as low as 0.1 percent.[161]

This development, which was welcomed by South Korea, however, was overshadowed by Prime Minister Koizumi's decision to visit Yasukuni Shrine on August 13. That the visit occurred not on August 15, the anniversary of Japan's surrender in World War II, as he had originally planned, but two days earlier did not really mitigate its adverse repercussions in South Korea. Koizumi, who since April had repeatedly stated his determination to visit the shrine on August 15, had been under pressure not only from Seoul and Beijing but also from domestic critics and coalition partners. Secretaries-general of the three parties participating in the ruling coalition—the LDP, the New Komeito, and the

---

cholban" [ROK-Japan Intercourse - Glacial Period for Economic Cooperation……Investment in Korea Is Half of Last Year's], *Dong-A ilbo*, August 27, 2001.
160 Kim Mi-hui, "China Rises as 2nd Biggest Export Mart," *Korea Herald*, August 31, 2001.
161 "Rekishi kyokasho: 'Tsukurukai' saitaku-ritsu wa 0.1% miman ni" [History Textbook: Tsukurukai's Selection Rate Is Less Than 0.1%], *Mainichi shinbun*, August 16, 2001; "Tsukurukai hen 1% miman, chugaku kyokasho no saitaku shuryo" [*Tsukurukai's* Book Falls Below 1%, Selection of Middle School Textbook Ends], *Asahi shinbun*, August 16, 2001.

Conservative party—had urged him not to make the visit.[162]

In addition to choosing what he hoped would be a less sensitive date, Koizumi issued a statement in which he acknowledged Japan's responsibility for causing "incalculable pain and suffering to the neighboring Asian countries through colonial rule and aggression," which essentially reiterated Murayama's 1995 statement. Koizumi also said that Japan "should never repeat the mistake of going to war" and expressed "hopes to meet with leaders of China and the Republic of Korea in the near future to explain the intentions behind his visit." To conform to the principle of separation of religion and state embodied in the Japanese constitution, moreover, Koizumi did not follow the Shinto ritual of bowing twice, clapping hands twice, and then bowing again but bowed only once. He nonetheless signed his name as Prime Minister Koizumi Junichiro. Faced with mounting criticisms both at home and abroad, however, his government on August 16 indirectly characterized his visit as "private."[163]

In South Korea, all newspapers ran editorials denouncing the visit, politicians in both ruling and opposition camps were united in their condemnation, and anti-Japanese demonstrations erupted throughout

---

162 "Koizumi Drops Wartime Anniversay Visit to Yasukuni," *Mainichi Daily News*, August 14, 2001; "Koizumi Visits Yasukuni Shrine," *Japan Times*, August 14, 2001; "Koizumi shusho Yasukini jinja o sanpai" [Prime Minister Koizumi Visits Yasukuni Shrine], *Yomiuri shinbun*, August 14, 2001.

163 Ibid.; "Koizumi shusho Yasukuni jinja o maetaoshi sanpai" [Prime Minister Koizumi Visits Yasukuni Shrine Ahead of Schedule], *Asahi shinbun*, August 14, 2001; "Koizumi shusho wa 'shiteki sanpai' no ninshiki, seifu ga tobensho" [Prime Minister's Understanding Is "Private Visit," Government Replies], ibid., August 17, 2001. In a written reply, approved by the cabinet on August 16, to a question posed by a Social Democratic member of the House of Councillors, the Koizumi government referred to the "government's unified view issued on October 17, 1985," according to which two criteria must be met for an official visit: (1) decision by the government that it is an official function and (2) an expenditure of public money. Since neither of these criteria was met, the Koizumi visit by implication was private.

the country. The most restrained but nonetheless poignant criticism came from President Kim Dae Jung. In an address commemorating the 56th anniversary of Korea's liberation from Japan on August 15, Kim noted that ROK-Japan relations were in trouble. In his words:

> To our surprise, some people in Japan are attempting to distort history, thereby casting dark clouds over ROK-Japan relations again. History does not concern the past alone but it impinges on the present and the future as well. How can we become good friends with people who would forget or ignore the countless pains that they have inflicted on us, and how can we live with them in the future with any degree of trust? These are the questions our people are asking.[164]

Kim hastened to add that there were "many conscientious Japanese people who are concerned about the distortion of history and the prime minister's visit to [Yasukuni] shrine." The Korean people, he stressed, "fervently hope that our bilateral relations will develop in the right direction on a foundation of correct historical understanding."[165]

When Koizumi subsequently tried to arrange a meeting with Kim in New York where both were planning to attend the special session of the UN General Assembly on children in mid-September, however, he was rebuffed by Seoul. Koizumi dropped his plan to attend the UN meeting, opting instead to make a tour of four member states of ASEAN—Thailand, Malaysia, Singapore, and Indonesia. Seoul also turned down Tokyo's request for a meeting between Kim and Foreign Minister Tanaka Makiko at the UN meeting. Due to the terrorist attacks on the World Trade Center and the Pentagon on September 11, however, the UN General Assembly indefinitely postponed its special session on children.

---

164 Ch'ongwadae, "Che 56 chunyon kwangbok-jol taet'ongnyong kyongch'uk-sa" [President's Address Commemorating the 56th Anniversary of Liberation], *Poto charyo* [Press Release], August 15, 2001 (Seoul), 2.
165 Ibid.

Finally, Tokyo's proposal for Koizumi's visit to Seoul was countered by Seoul's insistence on preconditions—that Koizumi must demonstrate his sincerity by deeds, based on the Japanese people's virtual rejection of the Fusosha history textbook, Murayama's 1995 statement, and the October 1998 ROK-Japan joint declaration. Although what specific deeds would meet Seoul's conditions remained unclear, it was reported that a reiteration of Japan's "1998 apology for wartime atrocities" and an acknowledgment of "the correctness of the decision by almost all local school boards in Japan to reject the use of the controversial textbook approved by the national government" might suffice. A Japanese Foreign Ministry source, however, was quoted as saying that "those conditions were pretty tough to meet."[166]

The third source of discord in Tokyo-Seoul relations was fishing. In June Japan tried to prevent the implementation of an agreement between South Korea and Russia allowing South Korean trawlers to catch 15,000 tons of saury for a fee of $55 per ton in waters around southern Kuril Islands. Japan claimed that since it had sovereignty over the islands and waters surrounding them belonged to its exclusive economic zone (EEZ), South Korean action was tantamount to a violation of its territorial sovereignty. South Korea countered that since Russia exercised actual control over the disputed islands, it was simply following international practice by concluding an agreement with Russia and that such action in no way signified recognition of Russian sovereignty. As the fishing was scheduled to commence in July, Japan took a counter-measure: it rescinded the permission it had previously granted South Korean fishermen to catch 9,000 tons of saury in the Sanriku region in northeastern Japan beginning on August 20.[167]

---

166 Douglas Struck, "Japan's Neighbors Cool to Koizumi," *Washington Post*, August 25, 2001, A13; "Kankoku seifu Tanaka gaisho to Kim Dae Jung taitoryo no kaidan kyohi" [ROK Government Refuses Meeting between Foreign Minister Tanaka and President Kim Dae Jung], *Yomiuri shinbun*, September 8, 2001.
167 Oegyo T'ongsangbu Taebyonin, *Ilbon chongbu ui uri kkongch'i cho'op hoga yubo*

From a strictly economic standpoint, Japan's stakes were rather low. Japanese fishermen caught 135,000 tons of saury in 2000, which was more than 16 times what South Korean fishermen caught in the same year in the same disputed area. In the Sanriku region South Korean fishermen caught only 92 tons of saury in 1999 and 240 tons of saury in 2000. This meant that the impact of Japan's countermeasures would be minimal as well. What is more, Japan, too, paid Russia a fee for fishing saury around southern Kurile islands, although Japan officially characterized its payment as money intended to foster cooperation in fishing and conservation of marine life.[168]

In 1999 and 2000, however, South Korean fishing in the Russian-controlled waters was based on an ostensibly non-governmental agreement, in which private parties from both sides took part. It was the emergence of the Russian government as a party to an agreement that had raised the stake for Japan from a symbolic or, perhaps, legal standpoint. Anything that bordered on a tacit acceptance of Russian sovereignty over the disputed islands triggered alarm in Tokyo. Domestic politics may also have played a role. The House of Councillors' election, which took place on July 29, may have contributed to the hard-line stance of the Koizumi government, for public opinion had become distinctly conservative and nationalistic.[169]

---

e kwanhan oegyobu tanggukja nonp'yong [Foreign Ministry Official's Remarks on the Japanese Government's Suspension of Permission to Fish Given to Our Saury Tawlers] (Seoul: Ministry of Foreign Affairs and Trade: June 19, 2001); "Ryoto kosho ni aratana nandai: sanma gyo mondai de nosuisho ga Kan, Ro hihan" [New Obstacle in Territorial Negotiations: Agriculture-Fisheries Minister Criticizes ROK and Russia Regarding Saury Fishing Problem], *Asahi shinbun*, June 20, 2001.

168 "Hoppo shito oki sanmagyo Nikkan tomo 'jitsugai' nashi" [Saury Fishing Off Northern Four Islands: No Real Loss to Either Japan Or ROK], *Asahi shinbun*, August 2, 2001.

169 "Nam K'uril yolto choop nangiryu······Ilbon kanggyong chasero sonhoe" [Turbulence for South Kuril Islands Fishing······Japan Adopts Hard Line], *Joongang ilbo*, June 20, 2001; Oegyo T'ongsangbu Taebyonin, *Ilbon chongbu······*, 1.

South Korea rejected Japan's offer to permit fishing around the disputed Kuril islands on condition that South Korea recognize Japan's sovereignty over them and seek a fishing permit. Twenty-six South Korean vessels started fishing for saury in the disputed waters on August 1. South Korea did not "retaliate" against Japan's ban on South Korean fishing in the Sanriku region by banning Japanese fishing in its EEZ. Apart from Seoul's desire not to escalate the fishing dispute with Tokyo, the prospect that such a retaliatory measure would have very little impact on Japan must have influenced Seoul's decision. In 2000, the quantity of fish Japanese vessels caught in South Korean EEZ totaled only 1,000 tons. The two sides agreed to "continue consultations on the fishing issue······in a sincere manner."[170]

In early October, however, the fishery dispute took a new twist. Faced with Seoul's refusal to back down on the Kurile islands issue, Tokyo had turned to Moscow for relief, reaching an agreement in principle under which Moscow would bar all "third" countries from fishing in the disputed area in 2002. In 2001, in addition to South Korea, North Korea, Taiwan, and Ukraine had obtained Russia's permission to catch fixed quantities of saury in waters surrounding southern Kurile islands for fee. The Japanese press reported that only the amount of compensation Japan would pay Russia remained to be negotiated and that a formal agreement would be signed by Prime Minister Koizumi and President Putin in the latter part of October when they were scheduled to hold talks in Shanghai on the sidelines of an Asia-Pacific Economic Cooperation (APEC) summit.[171]

---

170 Haeyang Susanbu, *Che 225-hoe Kukhoe (chonggihoe) Haeyang Susanbu kukjong kamsa chirui tapbyon charyo, 2001. 09. 14* [Material for Questions and Answers During the 225th National Assembly (Regular Session) Audit of the Ministry of Maritime Affairs and Fishery, September 14, 2001] (Seoul, 2001); Ministry of Foreign Affairs of Japan, *Statement by Ms. Makiko Tanaka,* Minister for Foreign Affairs, on Fishing Operations by Fishing Boats of the Republic of Korea in Waters Around the Four Northern Islands (Tokyo: August 3, 2001).

171 "Japan, Russia New Accord on Saury Fishing Dispute," *Daily Yomiuri,* October 10, 2001.

Shortly before the stunning news hit Seoul, South Korea and Japan had agreed on a visit by Koizumi to Seoul on October 15. The terrorist attacks on the US on September 11 had altered the calculus of diplomacy in Japan and South Korea alike. With the scheduled co-hosting of World Cup soccer championship games in 2002, the two countries faced a pressing need to cooperate on measures to combat terrorism. Both, moreover, felt obligated to provide assistance to their common alliance partner, the US, in the latter's anti-terrorist campaign. Japan's repeated requests—Koizumi had written letters to Kim Dae Jung on two occasions—and China's decision to welcome Koizumi's visit led Seoul to set aside its preconditions and consent to a one-day visit by the Japanese prime minister.[172]

The revelation of the impending agreement by Russia and Japan on saury fishing, however, precipitated an uproar in South Korea, casting a dark cloud over Koizumi's visit, which was scheduled to take place on October 15. South Korea's stakes were high, for it relied on the disputed area for a third of its annual supply of saury. Given Japan's hard line on South Korean fishing in the Sanriku region, South Korea would be hard put to find alternate fishing ground to make up for the loss of Kurile island fishing rights.[173]

The Beginning of a Rapprochement

When the Koizumi visit did materialize, however, it marked a significant first step toward a rapprochement between Japan and South Korea, heralding an end to six months of strained relations. In a symbolic gesture reminiscent of his visit to the Marco Polo bridge in Beijing a week

---

172 "Koizumi pang Han songsa kkaji" [Background on Koizumi's Visit to ROK], *Joongang ilbo*, October 15, 2001.
173 "Tonggangnan kkongch'I oegyo, yon 350-ok hwanggum ojang nunddugo nallilp'an" [Failed Diplomacy on Saury, Golden Fishing Ground Worth 35 Billion Annually About to Slip Away], *Dong-A ilbo*, October 12, 2001.

earlier, Koizumi visited a former Japanese prison, in which exhibits documenting Japan's brutality against Koreans during the colonial period are displayed, prior to his summit meeting with Kim Dae Jung. Koizumi told the press that he had observed the exhibits "with a heartfelt remorse and apology"(*kokorokara hansei to owabino kimochi o motte*) for the pain and suffering Japanese colonial rule had inflicted on the Korean people. He added that "the pain the Korean people must have felt amid unbearable difficulties such as foreign invasion and the division of their country" defied his imagination. "We must mutually reflect [*otagai hanseishi tsutsu*] and cooperate so as not to repeat the painful history twice."[174]

By mentioning the need for "mutual reflection," however, Koizumi stirred a controversy in the South Korean press and among opposition politicians. From a Korean point of view, there was no need for the victim of aggression to engage in any reflection; it was only the aggressor or the perpetrator of misdeeds that needed to do so. Koizumi's aides explained that the adjective "*otagai*" (mutually) had inadvertently been misplaced. The translation provided by the ROK Foreign Ministry omitted the word "reflect" altogether, and among Japanese newspapers, *Asahi shinbun* was the only paper to report the controversial statement intact. The transcript issued by the Japanese Foreign Ministry also contained the words in question.[175]

---

[174] "Koizumi shusho to Kankoku Kim taitoryo ga kaidan, 'owabi' takaku hyoka" [Prime Minister Koizumi and ROK President Kim Hold Talks, "Apology" Highly Appraised], *Asahi shinbun*; October 15, 2001; Gaimusho, "Koizumi Sori no Kankoku homon (Heisei 13-nen 10-gatsu 15-nichi): Sodemun Tokuritsu Koen ni okeru hatsugen" [Prime Minister Koizumi's Visit to the ROK (October 15, 2001): Remarks at Sodaemun Independence Park], *Shusho, gaisho kaidan* [Summit and Foreign Ministers' Meetings] (Tokyo: October 2001); "Koizumi pang-Han, 'kwago pulmi suroun yoksa' aemaehan sagwa" [Koizumi's Visit to ROK, Vague Apology for "Unfortunate Past"], *Chosun ilbo*, October 15, 2001; Shin Yong-bae, "Kim, Koizumi Fail to Resolve Issues Straining Korea-Japan Ties," *Korea Herald*, October 16, 2001.

[175] Gaimusho, "Koizumi Sori no Kankoku homon……"

During two hours of talks, which consisted of an 85-minute one-on-one meeting and a 30-minute "expanded summit meeting," Koizumi and Kim discussed such contentious bilateral issues as history textbooks, Yasukuni Shrine visits, and saury fishing as well as issues related to the co-hosting of World Cup 2002, economic cooperation, and the need to cooperate with the US in the latter's war on terrorism. On the textbook issue the two leaders agreed to set up a joint research organization consisting of historians and other experts from both countries with the aim of forging a consensus on the interpretation of Japan-Korea interactions in the past. As for the Yasukuni Shrine issue, Koizumi explained that he had visited the shrine on August 13 with a strong feeling that war should not occur again and with the aim of paying respects to those who had lost their lives in past wars. When Kim Dae Jung pointed out that the shrine also honored Class A war criminals, Koizumi pledged to find an alternative that would allow anyone from any place to pay respects to those who perished in wars. Finally, the two leaders agreed to conduct high-level talks to resolve the saury fishing dispute as soon as possible.[176]

As for the other issues, the two leaders agreed to "make efforts" to solve them. They agreed, for example, to do their best to conclude a bilateral investment agreement by the end of the year; to work toward enabling South Korean nationals to visit Japan without visa for a limited period—as Seoul already permits Japanese tourists to visit South Korea without visa up to 30 days, Seoul was seeking reciprocity from Tokyo in connection with the co-hosting of World Cup 2002—; to cooperate in easing the problem of insufficient air links between the two countries; and to initiate close bilateral consultations on combating terrorism

---

176 Gaimusho, "Nikkan shuno kaidan (gaiyo)" [Japan-ROK Summit Meeting (Summary)], *Shuno, gaisho kaidan* [Summit and Foreign Ministers' Meetings] (Tokyo: October 16, 2001); Ch'ongwadae, "Il ch'ongni wa tandok mit hwakdae chongsang hoedam" [One-on-One and Expanded Summit Meeting with Japanese Prime Minister], *Ch'ongwadae kaelindo* [Blue House Calendar] (Seoul: October 15, 2001).

during the World Cup games.

On the issue of cooperating with the US war against terrorism, Koizumi sought to reassure Kim that Japan's Self-Defense Forces (SDF), when deployed overseas under the new SDF law expected to be enacted soon, would not be involved in any combat-related operations but confine their activities to humanitarian assistance and logistical support. Saying that he understood Japan's intentions, Kim nonetheless stressed that Japan should do everything within the framework of its peace constitution.[177]

All this meant that no concrete agreements had come out of the first summit between Koizumi and Kim Dae Jung. What is more, Koizumi's statements and pledges regarding the textbook and Yasukuni Shrine issues had failed to measure up to the expectations of South Korean public opinion. Both the South Korean press and opposition parties expressed their disappointment. The threat by the main opposition party, Grand National Party, to disrupt his visit led Koizumi to cancel his plan to visit the National Assembly.

The governments in Tokyo and Seoul, however, lost no time in taking follow-up measures. Vice-ministers and directors-general of their respective foreign ministries held talks in Tokyo within two days of the Koizumi visit. In addition to discussing the implementation of the agreements reached in principle on various issues during the Seoul summit, they also worked on the agenda and other details of another Koizumi-Kim summit that would occur on the sidelines of the Asia-Pacific Economic Cooperation (APEC) forum in Shanghai on October 20.

During the Shanghai summit Koizumi made a firm commitment to establish an expert panel to study the feasibility of an alternative to Yasukuni Shrine within this year. Koizumi also reiterated his commitment to "easing visa regulations for South Koreans who visit Japan and even make their trips visa free in the future." [178] Although high-level talks to

---

177 Gaimusho, "Nikkan shuno kaidan (gaiyo)"; Ch'ongwadae, "Il ch'ongni wa tandok mit hwakdae chongsang hoedam."

resolve the saury fishing dispute failed to make any headway, Tokyo and Moscow decided to postpone the signing of an agreement banning third parties from catching saury in Russia-controlled waters around the southern Kurile islands. The Kim Dae Jung government was reported to be seriously considering lifting all the sanctions it had imposed on Japan in July, gradually resuming exchanges between military and other personnel and re-examining a further liberalization of imports of Japanese popular culture. In a word, ROK-Japan relations were clearly on their way toward "normalization."[179]

Conclusion

The coexistence of discord and cooperation that marked the first half of the fourth decade of the Japan-ROK normalization may actually signify that the bilateral relations have indeed been "normalized" in the sense that the two neighboring countries experience progress as well as setbacks in their dealings with each other as is the norm in inter-state relations. Emblematic of progress were the frequency of summit and ministerial meetings and the continuing security cooperation among Tokyo, Seoul, and Washington, including their close collaboration in KEDO. The manifest success of the summit meeting between Kim Dae Jung and Obuchi in October 1998 is particularly noteworthy.

While economic ties remained strong, the persistence of trade imbalance made them a source of friction. When the currency crisis drove

---

178 "Kim Pushes Koizumi To Create Yasukuni Alternative," *Mainichi Daily News*, October 20, 2001.

179 Hwang Jang-jin, "Seoul Moving to Normalize Ties With Tokyo Following Summit," *Korea Herald*, October 17, 2001; "Ro-Il chongsang, kkongch'i hyopsang ch'oejong yongi······Hanguk panbal koryo" [Top Leaders of Russia and Japan Postpone Final Agreement on Saury Negotiations······Response to ROK Backlash], *Dong-A ilbo*, October 22, 2001; "Han'il kkongch'i hyopsang songkwa opsi kkunna" [ROK-Japan Talks on Suary End Inconclusively], ibid., October 28, 2001.

Seoul to the brink of bankruptcy in late 1997, however, Tokyo joined other developed countries and international financial institutions in crafting a rescue plan. What is more, Tokyo's commitment of $10 billion in standby loans was the largest of its kind among individual countries.

In other areas, however, distrust and disagreement not only lingered on but appeared to deepen at times. The intensification of the territorial dispute over Takeshima/Tokdo, the eruption of friction over fishing, and the controversy over the comfort women issue came dangerously close to setting back the two countries' mutually shared goal of forging a new relationship.

The intensity of discord that accompanied these disputes calls for an explanation, as does the ascendancy of cooperation since 1998. All three principal schools of thought—neorealism, neoliberalism, and constructivism—contribute ideas that may be useful in generating a plausible explanation. As was true in the previous chapters, however, neorealism is the least useful of the three approaches. The main insight it provides is actually shared with neoliberalism—that states are rational actors in the sense of seeking optimal outcomes within the constraints of limited information and resources. The manner in which the sticky territorial dispute was handled and the fisheries dispute was resolved lends support to the preceding proposition.

Elite images, nationalism, and internal political dynamics, all of which can be subsumed under constructivism, also played their part in the unfolding of the events. Bureaucratic politics and the press in South Korea were important factors in the equation. South Korea's decision to build a wharf on the disputed island of Tokdo/Takeshima in February 1996 stemmed less from a real need than from the desire of the Ministry of Maritime Affairs and Fisheries to raise its visibility and assert its jurisdictional prerogative.[180] The Japanese government was understandably provoked by the South Korean decision and felt compelled to issue a statement reiterating its claim to the island.

---

180 This interpretation was offered to me by a high-ranking official of the ROK government who must remain anonymous.

Democratization has served to enhance not only the freedom of the press but also the role of public opinion in Seoul's policymaking. Once Ikeda's statement on the disputed island made banner headlines in the South Korean press, it aroused nationalistic emotions among the South Korean people, leaving the Kim Young Sam government no choice but to take a hard line. Since Ikeda had merely reiterated Japan's long-standing position, his statement need not have stirred up so much controversy had it not been so prominently reported.

Having long maintained physical control over the island, South Korea had an upper hand in the dispute. Its show of force illustrated both Seoul's capacity and willingness to act with the aim of not only reaffirming its claim to sovereignty but of placating South Korean public opinion as well. Japan's restraint reflected the ascendancy of pragmatism over emotions.

When Japan had a capacity to act, on the other hand, it did not hesitate to use it. That is what happened in the fisheries dispute in which the capture of South Korean trawlers and fishermen in waters newly claimed by Japan as its own demonstrated that Japan could play a hardball, too. Whether such Japanese behavior was tactically efficacious, however, is open to question. If it showed South Korea Japan's determination and capability to protect its perceived national interests, it also inflamed South Korean public opinion, drastically reducing options for the Kim Young Sam government in its negotiations with Japan.

What is more, South Korea scored an unexpected "victory" of sorts in its battles with Japan when a Japanese court handed down a decision that in effect vindicated Seoul's position in the fisheries dispute. What happened in that case demonstrated how internal political dynamics can produce outcomes that benefit the adversary in international relations. Although it was an isolated, lower court decision that was later overturned,[181] the verdict nonetheless had the effect of freeing the South

---

181 On September 12, 1998 the Hiroshima Higher Court held that the lower court had erred in interpreting the relevant laws and remanded the case to the Hamada branch of the Matsue Discount Court. *Joongang ilbo*, September

Korean captain from detention and providing symbolic relief to Seoul. That it happened at all was a testimony to the maturity of Japanese democracy. Such an assertion of judicial independence in a case fraught with nationalistic emotions is unthinkable in South Korea where democratic consolidation is still under way.

Japan's decision in January 1998 to notify South Korea of its decision to terminate the 1965 fisheries agreement reflected the potency of internal political dynamics. Under intense pressure from the fishing industry and politicians allied with it, the Japanese government had stepped up both the pace and level of negotiations with the ROK government in the closing weeks of 1997.

Frustrated by the lack of results, Tokyo decided to take the unilateral action, which was authorized by the 1965 agreement and hence fully consistent with international law, hoping that the one-year deadline would provide Seoul with an added incentive to resume negotiations for a new treaty. If Japan's notice were to take effect in January 1999, the UN Convention on the Law of the Sea, to which both Japan and the ROK are parties, would provide the only source of law governing fisheries between the two countries. While clashes and incidents would undoubtedly multiply, the UN Convention would also benefit Japan. For, unlike the 1965 Japan-ROK fisheries agreement, which enshrines the principle of the flag state's jurisdiction over ships, the UN Convention gives the coastal states jurisdiction over ships involved in disputes.

South Korea's emotional reaction to Japan's notice showed both the strength of nationalism and the limits of economic leverage in international relations. Contrary to what neorealism would predict, Japan's overwhelming advantage in economic power over South Korea, which was graphically demonstrated in the former's stellar role in bailing out the latter in the 1997 currency crisis, failed to be translated into an asset in the unfolding of the territorial and fisheries disputes. It could be argued, nonetheless, that Japan's participation in the IMF-led bailout of

12, 1998.

South Korea was dictated by pragmatic considerations, namely, the need to protect its economic interests vis-a-vis Seoul where Japanese banks had the largest exposure of all international lending institutions. It was Seoul's awareness of that fact which undercut Tokyo's leverage. What happened, in other words, was further proof of the neoliberal proposition on the nonfungibility of power—that aggregate power needs to be distinguished from issue-specific power.

Regime identity, the modified constructivist concept that was introduced in the preceding chapters, may provide an important clue to understanding the manner in which the fisheries dispute was resolved in September 1998. The identity of the Kim Dae Jung government was defined by his unique background. The best-known dissident during South Korea's authoritarian era, whom both Park Chung Hee and Chun Doo Hwan tried unsuccessfully to liquidate and whose last-minute reprieve owed to the intervention of the US and Japan, Kim was elected President in his fourth attempt. As noted, his election signaled the first inter-party transfer of power in the annals of South Korean politics and, as such, it marked a giant stride in the consolidation of the hard-won democracy in that country.

With the official label of *kungmin ui chongbu* (the people's government), the Kim Dae Jung government's most salient hallmark was his fervant ambition to make the most of what he, a devout Catholic, viewed as a God-given opportunity to leave a mark in history by discharging his duties to the best of his ability. The most pressing task he faced was overcoming the economic crisis in which South Korea was mired since November 1997. No less important was completing the task of democratic consolidation. Finally, Kim wanted to make a signal breakthrough in inter-Korean relations, ushering in a new era of reconciliation and cooperation, which would lead eventually to unification.

All this required the invigoration of diplomacy, a redoubled effort to solidify Seoul's relations with the major powers surrounding the Korean peninsula as well as the European Union. Kim placed particular emphasis on improving relations with Japan, a country from which he had been kidnapped by KCIA agents in 1973 and which, together with the US, helped to save his life in 1980. Widely read and possessed with a keen sense of history, moreover, Kim believed that his country and Japan should enter the new century with a clean slate, which called for resolving all the issues and disputes that originated in the 20th century before it ended.

These considerations, which one may encapsulate in Kim Dae Jung's regime identity, underlay his determination to resolve the fisheries dispute with Japan and to neutralize that perennial source of discord, Japan's colonial rule in Korea, once and for all. Kim's regime identity alone, however, would not have sufficed. A convergence of interests between Seoul and Tokyo was a sine qua non. If the Obuchi government had a regime identity, it was no doubt influenced by his political experience and interests.

Notable among his political experience was his long association with Korean affairs, including his involvement as foreign minister in Japan's attempts to settle the fisheries dispute with South Korea. Obuchi was a key member of the Japan-ROK Parliamentary League, of which he was vice chairman on the Japanese side in 1998.[182] Like any politician, moreover, Obuchi had a strong interest in building a record of accomplishment as prime minister. He therefore had a high stake in removing any obstacle that might lie on the path to the success of the summit meeting with Kim Dae Jung. One should, of course, keep in mind the constraints on prime minister in parliamentary systems of government in general and in Japanese polity in particular. Nonetheless,

---

182 Obuchi told *Joongang ilbo* in March 1998, when he was still foreign minister, that he had visited South Korea so many times that he had lost count. "Ilbon, taebuk oegyo chokkuk nasol kot, Obuchi oesang ponji hoegyon" [Japan Will Actively Pusue Diplomacy vis-a-vis North - This Paper Interviews Foreign Minister Obuchi], ibid., March 20, 1998. In his speech at the banquet he hosted for Kim Dae Jung on October 8, 1998, Obuchi described himself as "shinkan-ha no ushi" (a cow that belongs to the pro-ROK faction). The Japanese press, he reminded his audience, referred to him as *ushi* (cow). Oegyo T'ongsangbu, *Kim Dae Jung taet'ongnyong Ilbon pangmun kyolgwa*, 123.

the available evidence suggests that Obuchi's commitment may have been a factor in shaping the manner and timing of the fisheries compromise.

Nor should one overlook the role of politicians in the negotiations. Seoul's invitation and red-carpet treatment of Sato Koko, the veteran LDP lawmaker and leader of the LDP politicians tied to fishing industry, proved to be an astute tactical move. For he had played a key role in preventing a settlement in December 1997.

In addition to regime identity in Seoul and Tokyo alike, external environment played a role as well. By launching a rocket that flew over Japan on August 31, the DPRK may inadvertently have helped to cement Japan-ROK ties. North Korea gave both Tokyo and Seoul strong incentives to strengthen their security cooperation, which was intertwined with economic cooperation and political linkages.

The tenacity with which the comfort women issue continues to bedevil Japan-ROK relations, as it did in 1997, underscores the strength of historical legacy. The manner in which the controversy triggered by Chief Cabinet Secretary Kajiyama's remarks was contained showed the effect of internal politics as well. Prime Minister Hashimoto's apology was carefully crafted to satisfy two sets of audiences with incompatible demands—those in South Korea and Japan. By recalling an apology he had previously made multiple times, Hashimoto succeeded in placating his South Korean audience without expending any new political capital. By clarifying what he said were the actual circumstances surrounding the controversy, Hashimoto may also have managed to placate his Japanese audience.

What Hashimoto did in this case exemplifies a "two-level game," which posits that "statesmen are typically trying to do two things at once; that is, they seek to manipulate domestic and international politics simultaneously." In this view, "diplomatic strategies and tactics are constrained both by what other states will accept and by what domestic constituencies will ratify."[183]

---

183 Andrew Moravcsik, "Introduction: Integrating International and Domestic

How may one explain the surge of discord in 2001, which plunged Japan-ROK relations to a new low, resulting in a six-month stalemate? How is one to understand the impetus for the rapprochement that began to unfold in October 2001? A notable aspect of what happened in 2001 is that the sources of discord were all old issues—history textbooks, Yasukuni Shrine visits, and fishing.

Equally noteworthy is that these issues were largely ideational. Even in the fishery dispute, the only one that was not wholly ideational, however, material ramifications were not primary but secondary. From the Japanese standpoint, economic considerations were so marginal as to be all but irrelevant. At stake was territorial sovereignty, a patently ideational factor but one that eclipses material considerations.

Last but not least, domestic politics played a large part in the escalation of discord. In Japan's case, regime identity may help account for its behavior to a large degree, for it was the advent of a new regime, the Koizumi government, which accelerated the process by which conflict eclipsed cooperation between Tokyo and Seoul. A maverick politician, Koizumi is strongly nationalistic. He had no previous exposure to Korea: not only had he never visited either Seoul or Pyongyang but he had not shown any interest in any issues related to Korea. Although billed as a reformer, his track record lags behind his rhetoric.[184] More than any of his predecessors, however, he is media-savvy. Appearing "before the TV cameras on a daily basis," Koizumi "comes up with short, snappy phrases and recites them like mantras until they become embedded in the public consciousness." The success with which he projects a fresh image and his

---

Theories of International Bargaining" in *Double-Edged Diplomacy: International Bargaining and Domestic Politics,* eds. Peter B. Evans, Harold K. Jacobson, and Robert D. Putnam (Berkeley: University of California Press, 1993), 15. For an elaboration of the two-level games approach, see Robert D. Putnam, "Diplomacy and Domestic Politics: The Logic of Two-Level Games" in ibid., appendix, 431-68.

184 Ken Belson, "Setback for Overhaul Campaign in Japan," *New York Times,* December 18, 2001; idem, "For Japan's Would-Be Reformer, Little Traction," ibid., December 26, 2001.

ability to "play the public relations game like a pro" may help explain his extraordinary popularity; eight months into his job, he maintained in December 2001 "an extraordinarily high 80 percent public approval rating."[185]

The confidence generated by his phenomenal popularity, coupled with his desire not to tarnish his reputation for keeping promises, may go a long way toward explaining Koizumi's decision not to cancel but make only a marginal adjustment to his plan to visit Yasukuni Shrine. Polls conducted both before and after his Yasukuni visit showed that over 60 percent of those surveyed supported the visit—69 percent in June and 65 percent on August 18, five days after the visit took place. Koizumi himself cited the post-visit poll in a news conference on August 23, expressing the hope that "people in foreign countries would understand" what he had done in light of Japanese public opinion.[186]

As for South Korea, the Kim Dae Jung government's strong desire to maintain good relations with Japan clashed with the emotional, nationalistic backlash of politicians, the general public, and the media, with the latter fueling the first two. Democratization had substantially narrowed the government's "win-set." In the fishery dispute South Korea's stakes were economic, and Seoul appeared to have failed to anticipate Tokyo's strong reaction. The latter's failure to protest similar agreements in the preceding years and the knowledge that Tokyo, too, paid fees to Moscow for fishing in the disputed waters may have contributed to Seoul's miscalculation. Once the dispute erupted, however, Seoul was in no position to yield to Tokyo's demands. Domestic political constraints

---

185 Toshi Maeda, "Koizumi Play Public Relations Game Like a Pro," *Japan Times*, December 29, 2001.
186 "Seiron chosa: Yasukuni sanpai maetaoshi 'yokatta' 65%, 15-nichi kaihi hyoka" [Opinion Poll: 65% Approves Yasukini Visit Ahead of Schedule, Avoiding the 15th Appreicated], *Mainichi shinbun*, August 19, 2001; "Koizumi shusho: seiron chosa kekkani jishin, Yasukuni sanpai maetaoshi" [Prime Minister Koizumi: Confidence Boosted By Opinion Poll Results, Visiting Yasukuni Ahead of Schedule], ibid., August 23, 2001.

all but precluded that option.

While both internal and external factors helped to lay the groundwork for the rapprochement in October, it may be argued that external factors outweighed internal ones. The latter were the September 11, 2001 terrorist attacks on the US and the scheduled co-hosting of World Cup soccer tournament in the summer of 2002. Both underscored the need for bilateral and multilateral cooperation to counter terrorism, tasks that could not be performed without breaking the stalemate in bilateral relations. Internally, both the Koizumi and Kim Dae Jung governments were acutely aware of the economic and political costs of the strained relations. Neither had anything to gain from the continuing impasse.

What stands out in all of these developments is not the intensity or intractability of disputes between Japan and South Korea but their manifest determination, fueled by their respective regime identities, to contain the adverse fallouts from intermittent friction and to get on with the job of managing their multifaceted relationship. The shared perception that both have more to gain than lose by maintaining cooperative ties and working together to forge a truly new relationship underpinned the policies of Japan and South Korea toward each other during the fourth decade of their normalization.

CHAPTER 8

Forging a Future-oriented Japan-ROK Relationship: A Long Road Ahead

The pattern of cooperation interspersed with discord continued unabated in the second half of the fourth decade of the Japan-ROK normalization. Whereas the first three years—2002 through 2004— witnessed the prevalence of cooperation, with only faint echoes of discord, however, the year 2005, officially designated as the Japan-Korea Friendship Year, saw a surge of discord that reverberated throughout the year and beyond. Nonetheless, that did not seriously hamper people-to-people exchanges. Nor did it disrupt cooperation at the working-level. Sub-cabinet and cabinet-level meetings continued to be held.

The Year of Japan-ROK National Exchange

To commemorate the co-hosting of the 2002 FIFA World Cup soccer games, to "give a strong boost to the atmosphere of friendship between the two countries in the new century and to further cement the firm partnership between them by means of richly varied events," Japan and South Korea designated the year 2002 as the "Year of Japan-ROK National Exchange" (*Nikkan Kokumin Koryunen* in Japanese; *Han'il Kungmin Kyoryunyon* in Korean). On January 1, Prime Minister Koizumi and President Kim Dae Jung took the unprecedented step of sending New Year's greetings to the people of both countries.[1]

Noting that the number of people who travel between the two countries had grown from about 10,000 per year before 1965 to 10,000 *per day* 37 years later, Koizumi pledged to do his best to further strengthen the bilateral relations. He also expressed the hope that the people of the two countries would have a chance to show the world the "firm bonds of friendship and trust between them." Kim Dae Jung underlined the importance of the two neighboring peoples' meeting and exchanging views, saying that dialogue begets understanding, which in turn promotes cooperation. He expressed the confidence that vigorous human and cultural exchanges would contribute immensely to the "future-oriented partnership" between the two countries and their common prosperity.

Nearly 100 events were held in both countries, marking the first time since normalization that so many cultural exchange events occurred. Inter-governmental contacts also increased in frequency, including three meetings between Koizumi and Kim Dae Jung, of which two were connected with the co-hosting of the 2002 FIFA World Cup soccer finals.

Before turning to the third and fourth summit meetings between the two leaders, however, we need to note a seemingly minor but nonetheless interesting episode. On December 23, 2001 Emperor Akihito made a

---

1 Ministry of Foreign Affairs of Japan, *The Year of ROK-Japan Exchange in 2002* (Tokyo: October 2001), http://www.mofa.go.jp/region/asia-paci/korea/culture.html; Shusho Kentei, *Koizumi sori daijin no Nikkan ryokokumin eno messeji* [Prime Minister Koizumi's Message to the Peoples of Japan and the Republic of Korea] (Tokyo: January 1, 2002), http://www.kantei.go.jp/ koizumispeech/2002/01/01/message.html; Kim Dae Jung Taikan Minkoku taitoryo no 'Kan'nichi kokumin koryunen' messeji [ROK President Kim Dae Jung's "ROK-Japan National Exchange Year" Message] (Seoul: January 1, 2002), http://www.kantei.go.jp/ jp/koizumispeech/2002/01/01message_ k.html.

surprising statement about "historical and ethnic ties that bind Japan and the Korean Peninsula," which was largely ignored by the Japanese press. Nine days before Koizumi's trip to Seoul, however, the *Japan Times* published a lengthy article on the incident. The Japanese emperor revealed that according to a historical document, "one of his eighth-century ancestors was born to a descendant of immigrants from the Korean Peninsula. In doing so, he said he felt a close 'kinship' with Korea." According to the paper, the "Emperor, quoting from the 'Shoku Nihongi' ('Chronicles of Japan'), compiled in 797, said the mother of Emperor Kinamu (737-806) had come from the royal family of Paekche, an ancient kingdom of Korea."[2]

Koizumi Visits South Korea, March 21-23, 2002

During his three-day official visit to South Korea in late March, Koizumi not only had a summit meeting with Kim Dae Jung but also engaged in what he described as "some Japan-ROK exchange," visiting a traditional performing arts center in Seoul and going to Pusan and Kyongju to "personally experience some of the history and culture of the Republic of Korea."[3] The short (85-minutes) summit meeting, coupled

---

2 Hiroshi Matsubara, "Emperor's Remark Pours Fuel on Ethnic Hot Potato," *Japan Times*, March 12, 2002. To quote further from this article, "Voicing his desire to see the two countries deepen their cooperation before co-hosting the 2002 World Cup soccer finals, the Emperor also noted that those who emigrated or were invited to come to Japan from Korea in ancient times brought their culture and technology with them. 'I believe it was truly fortunate that such culture and technology was brought to Japan through the friendly attitudes of the Korean people,' he was quoted as saying on the agency's transcript."
3 "Koizumi's Schedule Full, Rich before Parley with Kim," *Korea Herald*, March 21, 2002; "Koizumi shusho Kankoku no koto Kyongju o mankitsu" [Prime Minister Koizumi Enjoys Korea's Ancient Capital Kyongju Fully], *Asahi shinbun*, March 24, 2002; "Koizumi Tests New International Telephone Link," *Japan Times*, March 24, 2002.

with a signing ceremony for the Japan-ROK Investment Agreement and a joint press conference, was notable for the extraordinary cordiality displayed by the two leaders toward each other.[4]

While both expressed respect for each other, Koizumi went much further than Kim Dae Jung.[5] In his opening statement at the joint press conference, Koizumi said that he had read Kim's memoirs and learned that "President Kim's life has truly been an extraordinary one." He added: "I believe President Kim is a man who will be remembered in history and in talks with him today, I could keenly feel his passion······for the importance of peace, nation-building efforts of the Republic of Korea, democratic systems, a market economy······and reunification of the Korean Peninsula." Through his multiple meetings with Kim—the October 2001 summit in Seoul, the APEC leaders' meeting in Shanghai in the same month, the Association of Southeast Asian Nations (ASEAN) plus 3 (Japan, China, and the ROK) meeting in Brunei Darussalam in November 2001, and finally, the March 2002 summit—Koizumi "was overwhelmingly impressed by the deep insight and acumen of President Kim, who has experienced so many difficult and challenging episodes in

---

4 Ministry of Foreign Affairs of Japan, *Prime Minister Junichiro Koizumi's Visit to the Republic of Korea* (Tokyo: March 2002), http://www.mofa.go.jp/region/asia-paci/korea/pmv0203/index.html; idem, *Overview of the Japan-Republic of Korea Summit Meeting* (Tokyo: March 2002), http://www.mofa.go.jp/region/asia-paci/korea/pmv0203/summit.html; idem, *Opening Statements by Prime Minister Junichiro Koizumi and President Kim Dae Jung of the Republic of Korea at the Joint Press Conference* (Tokyo: March 22, 2002), http://www. mofa.go.jp/region/asia-paci/korea/pmv0203/state.html; "Kita kaze shimiru mirai shiko, Nikkan shuno kaidan" [Future Orientation Pierced by the North Wind, ROK-Japan Summit Meeting], *Asahi shinbun*, March 23, 2002; "Nikkan shuno kaidan, rachi mondai de kyoryoku yosei" [ROK-Japan Summit Meeting: Requests Cooperation on the Abduction Issue], *Yomiuri shinbun*, March 23, 2002; "Stronger Ties with Seoul Bears Fruit," *Mainichi Daily News*, March 24, 2002.

5 Kim Dae Jung referred to Koizumi as "friend" several times during his joint press conference with the prime minister. "Chongsang hoedam hoegyon, DJ, Koizumi e such'a 'ch'ingu' ra pullo" [Summit Meeting Press Conference: Kim Dae Jung Calls Koizumi "Friend" Several Times], *Chosun ilbo*, March 23, 2002.

his life and this has left a strong impression on me."⁶

Substantively, the two leaders agreed to cooperate on a wide range of issues. Most important, they agreed to leave no stone unturned in order to make the 2002 FIFA World Cup Korea/Japan an "unprecedented success." As Kim Dae Jung put it, "in doing this, we must demonstrate to history and the world the new relations of friendship between Japan and the Republic of Korea." Koizumi indicated "his intention to attend the opening ceremony of the World Cup, to be held on May 31 in Seoul," and Kim expressed his hope to "attend the final match and closing ceremony of the tournament, to be held on June 30 in Yokohama."⁷

Additionally, Japan will waive visa requirements for ROK citizens for a fixed period, including the time of the World Cup. South Korea already waives visa requirements for Japanese tourists and travelers in transit without insisting upon reciprocity.

Exchange programs that are already in place—such as the working holiday program for youths, the project to exchange elementary and junior high school teachers, sports exchange, and the support for mutual language learning—will be expanded. For example, the number of working holiday visas issued will increase from 1,000 to 1,800 per year.

The two leaders also agreed to strengthen cooperation in the international arena, notably, the fight against terrorism, East Timor, the World Trade Organization (WTO), and environmental protection.

They concurred in the assessment that agreements made in their "summit talks in Shanghai last year are being smoothly implemented," including the "textbook issue, the visit to Yasukuni Shrine, the conclusion of the investment agreement, visa waiver and the issue of saury fishing."⁸

With the aim of strengthening the "future-oriented economic relations" between Japan and South Korea, the two leaders pledged to

---

6 Ministry of Foreign Affairs of Japan, *Opening Statement by Prime Minister Junichiro Koizumi*.
7 Ibid.
8 Ministry of Foreign Affairs of Japan, *Overview of the Japan-the Republic of Korea Summit Meeting*.

expedite the implementation of the investment agreement they signed in conjunction with the summit. They also agreed to "establish a study group composed of representatives from industry, government and academia in order to consider a Japan-Republic of Korea free trade agreement (FTA)."[9]

With respect to North Korea, the two leaders agreed that both bilateral cooperation and "trilateral cooperation among the United States, the Republic of Korea and Japan [are] vital." Koizumi expressed support for Seoul's engagement policy with the North, and both leaders "agreed on the need to seek a resolution of the situation on the Korean Peninsula through dialogue." In short, this was a most amicable summit meeting in which the spirit of friendship and cooperation was highlighted."[10]

Bones of Contention

The display of mutual respect and amity by Koizumi and Kim Dae Jung, however, did not mean that old bones of contention had vanished. Such issues as the name of the sea separating the two countries—the Sea of Japan or the East Sea—, history textbooks that Seoul believes whitewash Japan's record of aggression and atrocities committed against its neighboring countries and peoples, visits to Yasukuni Shrine by leading Japanese politicians, fishing, and North Korean refugees in China continued to trigger discord.

Within a month of his trip to South Korea, for example, Koizumi stirred up controversy again by visiting Yasukuni Shrine. The timing of the visit—five weeks before the opening of the World Cup—appears to have reflected Koizumi's careful calculation, for the need for Japan and the ROK to cooperate in the joint hosting of the tournament was so pressing as to preclude the visit from sparking a diplomatic feud between the two

---

9 "Koizumi, Kim Look into FTA," *Japan Times*, March 23, 2002.
10 Ministry of Foreign Affairs of Japan, *Overview of the Japan-the Republic of Korea Summit Meeting*.

countries. South Korean Foreign Minister Choi Sung-hong was thus constrained to tell Terada Terusuke, Japan's ambassador to Seoul whom he had summoned to lodge an official protest, that the South Korean government "is determined to separate the Yasukuni issue from World Cup preparations."[11]

2002 FIFA World Cup Korea/Japan

Koizumi kept his promise to attend the opening ceremony of the World Cup on May 31. Also attending the ceremony as Seoul's guests of honor were Prince and Princess Takamado, who became the first members of Japan's Imperial family to visit South Korea since the end of World War II. Although Seoul's first preference had been Crown Prince Naruhito, it was nonetheless satisfied with the visits of both Koizumi and the Takamodo couple.[12]

Had it not been for his Yasukuni visit in April, Koizumi most probably would have held another meeting with Kim Dae Jung but none materialized. They only exchanged greetings at the opening ceremony. That they would meet again at the final match and closing ceremony a month later was given as an unofficial excuse by both sides.[13]

---

11 Kim Ji-ho, "Seoul Protests Koizumi Shrine Visit," *Korea Herald*, April 23, 2002.
12 "Prince, Princess Arrive in Seoul for Cup Opening," *Daily Yomiuri*, May 30, 2002; "World Cup Opens in Spectacular Seoul Style," *Mainichi Daily News*, May 31, 2002.
13 "Sakka W-hai: egao no Koizumi shusho Nikkan no mirai shiko e no kiwado" [Soccer World Cup: Smiling Prime Minister Koizumi, Future-Oriented ROK-Japan as Keyword], *Mainichi shinbun*, June 1, 2002. There was another incident that had strained Tokyo-Seoul relations in the weeks before the World Cup opening. On May 10, five North Korean asylum seekers entered the Japanese Consulate General in Shenyang but were seized by Chinese police officers with the apparent approval of the Japanese consular officials. An internal investigation by the Japanese Foreign Ministry revealed that "communication problems and an inadequate command system (at the Consulate) may have

The World Cup itself proved to be an unqualified success for both of the host countries. Both the Japanese and South Korean teams did well, too. Japan qualified for the round of 16 of the 32-team tournament, while South Korea joined the final four, an amazing feat for a country that had not won a single game in the five previous trips to World Cup soccer finals. In doing so, South Korea became the first Asian team to reach the semifinals.

Tangible byproducts of the tournament included the conclusion of an extradition treaty between Japan and South Korea, Japan's waiver of visa requirements for Korean tourists—which would later be extended—and another summit meeting between Koizumi and Kim Dae Jung.[14]

Kim Dae Jung and his wife, Lee Hee Ho, visited Japan from June 30 to July 2. On the first day they watched the final match between Brazil and Germany in the royal box at the International Stadium in Yokohama with Emperor Akihito and Empress Michiko as well as Koizumi. The summit meeting took place on July 1, followed by a dinner hosted by Prime Minister Koizumi. Kim and his wife also had a luncheon with the royal couple on the following day.[15]

At the summit meeting, the two leaders adopted a "joint message toward the future," entitled "Beyond the Successful Co-hosting of the 2002 FIFA World Cup Korea/Japan." In it, they declared that "Japan and

---

resulted in the consulate general appearing to have given tacit approval to Chinese police officers to enter and take away" the North Korean asylum seekers. Since the episode had a happy ending—the asylum seekers were allowed to go to a "third country."—, however, it did not escalate to a diplomatic feud between Seoul and Tokyo. See "China Police Entered Consul 'With Consent'," *Japan Times*, May 12, 2002; "Report Hints Staff Confused," *Daily Yomiuri*, May 15, 2002.

14 "Japan, South Korea Sign Extradition Pact Ahead of World Cup," *Japan Times*, April 9, 2002; "Han'il naedal 12-il put'o biza myonje" [ROK-Japan to Exempt Visas from May 12th], *Dong-A ilbo*, April 9, 2002.

15 "Kim Invites Emperor to South Korea," *Japan Times*, July 3, 2002; Ministry of Foreign Affairs of Japan, *Visit to Japan of His Excellency President Kim Dae-jung of the Republic of Korea and Mrs. Kim Dae-jung* (Tokyo: July 2002), http://www.mofa.go.jp/region/asia-paci/korea/pv0206/index.html.

the Republic of Korea have displayed solid ties of friendship to the world." The "successful" and "safe" co-hosting of the 2002 FIFA World Cup, they stated, "will undoubtedly be a valuable asset of the two countries in enhancing Japan-ROK relations to a higher level." "Based on friendship and trust," they continued, "our two countries will continue to deepen cooperation and expand the exchange between the two peoples in the political, economic, social and cultural fields. To this end, we will promote various ways including joint projects for the enhancement of sports and youth exchanges" Additionally, the two countries "will study in depth the idea of a Japan-ROK free trade agreement" and "enhance our cooperation in the international arena."[16]

One of the topics the two leaders discussed at their summit was North Korea. They reaffirmed the importance of trilateral coordination (the US, Japan, and the ROK). Koizumi stated that he would step up efforts to revive normalization talks and to resolve security and humanitarian issues, including the abduction issue, through dialogue with the North. With respect to the promotion of the post-World Cup bilateral cooperation, Kim Dae Jung stated that he would consider taking further steps toward the liberalization of Japanese popular culture—that is, an additional lifting of Seoul's restrictions on its import—taking into account progress in the implementation of the commitments Koizumi had previously made regarding the various bilateral issues.

The two leaders agreed to give full support to the joint history study project, which had already been launched in accordance with their

---

16 Idem, *Joint Message Toward the Future by Prime Minister Koizumi and President Kim Dae-jung "Beyond the Successful Co-hosting of the 2002 FIFA World Cup Korea/Japan"* (Tokyo: July 1, 2002), http://www.mofa.go.jp/region/asia-paci/korea/pv0206/joint.html; Gaimusho, *Nikkan shuno no mirai ni muketa kyodo messeji: 2002-nen sakka warudo kappu kyodo kaisai seiko o koete* [Joint Message Toward the Future by the Leaders of Japan and the ROK, "Beyond the Successful Co-hosting of the 2002 FIFA World Cup Korea/Japan"] (Tokyo: July 1, 2002), http://www.mofa.go.jp/mofaj/area/korea/world_cup.html. I have made slight changes in the unofficial translation of the message based on the Japanese text.

previous agreement. Kim Dae Jung requested Japan (1) to grant suffrage to Korean residents in Japan in local elections and (2) to make visa exemptions for Korean visitors to Japan permanent. Koizumi responded that the suffrage issue was being considered in the Diet. On the visa issue, "he expressed his delight over the smooth implementation of visa exemptions during the World Cup," while indicating his intention to "make a full assessment" of Kim's request. He stated that the two countries "should conduct further consultations" on the issue.[17]

Koizumi and Kim also agreed to accelerate inter-governmental exchanges, including mutual visits of foreign ministers, the holding of a gathering of the two countries' cabinet ministers that had been suspended due to a dispute over history textbooks, and high-level economic consultation. In the international arena, the two leaders agreed that they should strengthen cooperation in international organizations on such issues as peacekeeping operations in East Timor and counter-terrorism. All in all, this final summit between Koizumi and Kim Dae Jung was a great success.

Post-World Cup Developments

Cooperation between Japan and South Korea continued in the subsequent months. Most of the things the two leaders agreed on in their July 2002 summit were implemented. Koizumi's surprise visit to Pyongyang in September, discussed in some detail in Chapter 5, could be seen as an implementation of his pledge to step up his efforts to resolve the various issues between Japan and North Korea and to jump-start the stalled normalization talks. Kim Dae Jung, an ardent believer in the wisdom of dialogue with the North, welcomed Koizumi's bold initiative. As we have already noted, however, the abduction issue sparked a storm of controversy and anger in Japan, thereby aggravating, rather than

---

17 Ministry of Foreign Affairs of Japan, *Visit to Japan of His Excellency Kim Dae-jung*.

ameliorating, Tokyo-Pyongyang relations.

The revelation in October that the North had tacitly acknowledged the existence of a nuclear weapons program utilizing highly-enriched uranium (HEU), while adding another contentious issue to the agenda of Japan-DPRK normalization talks, had the effect of increasing the frequency and intensity of both bilateral coordination between Japan and the ROK and trilateral coordination involving the latter two and the US. The meeting of the leaders of the three countries—Bush, Kim Dae Jung, and Koizumi—on the sidelines of the Asia-Pacific Economic Cooperation (APEC) summit meeting in Los Cabos, Mexico, in October 2002 exemplified trilateral coordination at the highest level. That meeting, as we saw in Chapter 5, produced a joint trilateral statement calling upon the North to dismantle the HEU-based nuclear weapons program "in a prompt and verifiable manner and to come into full compliance with all its international obligations in conformity with North Korea's recent commitment in the Japan-North Korea Pyongyang Declaration."[18]

Trilateral coordination was in full swing in November to hammer out a compromise at the KEDO Executive Board meeting on the issue of suspending delivery of heavy fuel oil to the North in response to the latter's violation of the 1994 Geneva accords (the US-DPRK Agreed Framework). It also proved to be indispensable in dealing with the escalation of the standoff between the North on the one hand and the US, South Korea, and Japan on the other, as Pyongyang expelled IAEA inspectors, dismantled or disabled monitoring devices and seals from its nuclear facilities in Yongbyon, and, finally, withdrew from the NPT.

The Koizumi-Roh Moo Hyun Summit, February 2003

The inauguration of a new government in Seoul in February 2003

---

18 Ministry of Foreign Affairs of Japan, *Joint US-ROK-Japan Trilateral Statement* (Tokyo: October 2002), http://www.mofa.go.jp/region/asia-paci/n_korea/nt/joint0210.html.

gave Koizumi an opportunity to visit South Korea again and hold a summit meeting with the new president, Roh Moo Hyun. Before embarking on his second trip to South Korea, however, Koizumi made a carefully calculated move. On January 14, he made a surprise visit to Yasukuni Shrine, which honors 2.5 million Japanese who died in wars, including 14 executed Class A war criminals.[19] The timing of the visit was related to a confluence of external and internal events. Externally, new administrations were being launched in Seoul in late February and in Beijing in March. Internally, unified local elections were scheduled to be held in April. Making the controversial move before the inauguration of new presidents in South Korea and China, in Koizumi's calculus, might help minimize adverse effects on Japan's relations with the two countries. Having a "buffer" of three months might also help reduce repercussions in elections and allay the misgivings of the LDP's coalition partner, the New Komeito.[20]

Protests and expressions of anger nonetheless emanated from Seoul, Beijing, and the New Komeito. In Seoul, the foreign ministry issued a statement expressing "anger and disappointment" and Vice Foreign Minister Kim Hang Kyung summoned Urabe Toshinao, deputy chief of mission at the Japanese embassy, to lodge a protest.[21] More serious was the abrupt cancellation of a meeting between President Kim Dae Jung and Japanese Foreign Minister Kawaguchi Yoriko, who was visiting Seoul "to cement bilateral cooperation over North Korea's nuclear development program. Kawaguchi, however, was able to meet with her South Korean counterpart, Choi Sung Hong, and "pay a courtesy call······ on President-

---

19 For the history of the shrine (called *Yasukuni Jinja* in Japanese) and the controversy surrounding it, see "Yasukuni Shrine," *Wikipedia, the free encyclopedia,* http://en.wikipedia.org/wiki/Yasukuni_Shrine. In addition to the 14 Class A war criminals who were responsible for waging the Pacific phase of World War II, the shrine also honors over a thousand convicted Japanese war criminals.

20 "Yasukuni Visit Was Carefully Orchestrated," *Daily Yomiuri,* March 16, 2003.

21 "Koizumi Stirs Diplomatic Row With Surprise Yasukuni Visit," *Japan Times,* January 15, 2003.

elect Roh Moo Hyun."²²

It was during her meeting with Roh that Kawaguchi "proposed that Koizumi and Roh meet as soon as possible and invited Roh to visit Japan." Roh accepted the proposal but "described Koizumi's Yasukuni Shrine visit as 'regrettable.'" He hastened to add: "It's one thing to respond emotionally to a problem, but when the problem is complicated, it's important to hold talks between both parties to solve the issue."²³

Against this backdrop, Koizumi arrived in Seoul on the eve of Roh Moo Hyun's inauguration, attended the inauguration ceremony and held his first summit meeting with Roh on February 25. It is noteworthy that among the dozens of foreign dignitaries attending the inauguration ceremony, Koizumi was the only incumbent head of government. There were two former Japanese prime ministers—Nakasone Yasuhiro and Mori Yoshiro—and a former president of Germany, Richard von Weizsacker, but the US was represented by Secretary of State Colin Powell, China by Vice Premier Qian Qichen and Russia by Federation Council Speaker Sergei Mironov and Deputy Foreign Minister Alexander Locyukov.²⁴

Roh held meetings with the representatives of all four major powers with special ties to the Korean Peninsula but Koizumi, who outranked the representatives of the other three powers, was given precedence. The 50-minute-long Roh-Koisumi meeting reportedly proceeded in a most amicable atmosphere. When Koizumi told Roh that he had been concerned about the weather and was relieved that it didn't rain and praised Roh's inaugural address as "ambitious and full of vigor," Roh replied that "the Heaven has given us good weather as a special present to

---

22 "South Korea's Kim Snubs Kawaguchi Over Yasukuni Shrine Controversy," ibid., January 16, 2003.
23 "Roh Wants to Meet Koizumi," *Daily Yomiuri*, January 17, 2003.
24 "'Roh Moo Hyun chongbu ch'ulbom' Han'il chongsang hoedam" ["The Launching of the Roh Moo Hyun government" ROK-Japan Summit Meeting], *Joongang ilbo*, February 26, 2003. The inauguration ceremony and related events were scaled down as South Korea remained in mourning for the death of hundreds of commuters in an arson attack in the Taegu subway during the preceding week.

mark the visit of the most honored guest from Japan."[25]

Since Roh understandably was eager to make his first summit meeting an unqualified success, he did not raise any sensitive issues, notably, Koizumi's January visit to Yasukuni Shrine. Roh simply said that "even though there were unfortunate events in ROK-Japan relations in the past," he wished to "build a future-oriented cooperative relationship based on a correct understanding of history." Neither side, moreover, mentioned the North's firing of a short-range ground-to-ship missile several hours before Roh was sworn in.[26] Defense analysts viewed it as a failed test, for the "missile apparently exploded in midair before reaching its dummy target in the Sea of Japan [the East Sea]."[27]

In order to build a "future-oriented" relationship, the two leaders agreed that fostering friendship and trust between the two peoples would be pivotal and that the youths should be the centerpiece of such endeavor. Hence sports and other exchanges between the youths of both sides would be expanded. Noting that the number of people traveling between the two countries totaled 3.6 million annually, Koizumi called the situation "one of the closest [human] exchanges in the world." He nonetheless stressed the importance of promoting tourism. Koizumi expressed the hope for Roh's visit to Japan at an early date, and Roh

---

25 Ibid.; "Nichi-Bei-Kan kobetsu kaidan: omowaku no sa fuji kessoku" [Bilateral Talks Among Japan, US and ROK: Solidarity After Sealing Differences of Opinion], *Mainichi shinbun*, February 26, 2003. I have translated "*hwagi ae'aehan punwigi*" (Korean) and "*nagoyakana fun'iki*" (Japanese) as "most amicable atmosphere." Other adjectives that may be used are "peaceful," "harmonious," and "congenial."

26 Gaimusho, *Nikkan shuno kaidan (gaiyo)* [ROK-Japan Summit Meeting (Summary)] (Tokyo: February 25, 2003), http://www.mofa.go.jp/mofaj/kaidan/yojin/arc_03/korea_kaidan.html; "Nichi-Bei-Kan no renkei o kakunin, Nikkan shuno kaidan" [Cooperation Among Japan, the US, and the ROK Confirmed, ROK-Japan Summit Meeting], *Asahi shinbun*, February 26, 2003.

27 Don Kirk, "North Korea Fires Antiship Missile in Test Launch," *New York Times*, March 10, 2003.

replied that he would be delighted to do so.[28]

Regarding North Korea, the two leaders shared the view that its nuclear weapons development program posed a serious threat and reconfirmed the importance of trilateral coordination among the US, Japan, and the ROK in their quest for a peaceful, diplomatic solution. They agreed to maintain close bilateral coordination as well and to continue efforts to persuade North Korea to dismantle its nuclear program with the cooperation of the international community, including China, Russia, and the European Union.[29]

The appearance of unity, however, was deceptive, for Roh and Koizumi actually had somewhat different priorities. Whereas Roh's foremost priority was inter-Korean exchanges and cooperation, as his decision to continue his predecessor's engagement or Sunshine policy suggested, Koizumi's was the Japan-US alliance. Koizumi's emphasis on trilateral coordination reflected, in part, his desire to "act as go-between" (hashiwatashi) in US-ROK relations, which appeared to be a little strained as the Roh government was being launched. The Koizumi-Roh summit, in a sense, was a carefully choreographed affair aimed at accentuating areas of agreement while glossing over differences.[30]

Roh Moo Hyun's Visit to Japan, June 2003

In early June, Roh Moo Hyun, accompanied by his wife, made a state visit to Japan. The four-day visit, however, generated a controversy and criticisms at home on a number of grounds. One was the timing of the visit, for Roh's departure for Japan on June 6 coincided with Memorial

---

28 "'Roh Moo Hyun chongbu ch'ulbom' Han'il chongsang hoedam," *Joongang ilbo*, February 26, 2003; Gaimusho, *Nikkan shuno kaidan (gaiyo)* (Tokyo: February 25, 2003).
29 Ibid.
30 "Nichi-Bei-Kan no renkei o kakunin, Nikkan shuno kaidan," *Asahi shinbun*, February 26, 2003.

Day in South Korea, a day on which the nation remembers and pays tribute to all those who gave their lives for the country in wars. The Roh government's obsession with securing a "state visit," a notch higher than "official visit," had left it virtually no other choice.[31]

Another thing that fueled anger and criticism in South Korea was that "Roh's visit also coincided with the enactment of war contingency bills [on June 6] that define the rules under which Japan can respond to attacks by a foreign country." Roh was constrained to point out that

---

31 Because a "state visit" entails a meeting with the Emperor and a state dinner hosted by him and because the Emperor's schedule is usually set a year in advance, the Japanese government told Seoul that Roh had to come on June 8 or settle for an official visit. See Shin Ji-ho, "Siron: 'Il kyollye' chach'ohan Hanguk oegyo" [Commentary: "Japan's Lack of Courtesy" Was Brought About by Korean Diplomacy], *Dong-A ilbo*, June 9, 2003. Roh was not alone in wanting a "state visit" even at a high cost. For Chinese President Hu Jintao's pursuit of the same diplomatic "prize" in connection with his visit to the US in the latter part of April 2006, see Jim Yardley, "Set Out the Good China, the President's Coming," *New York Times*, April 9, 2006. In Hu's case, the US and China "agreed to disagree," meaning China will call the visit a "state visit," while the US will treat it as an "official visit." In Roh's case, too, there was a subtle difference in how both sides characterized his visit. The joint statement issued after the summit meeting on June 7, 2003, said that "President Roh Moo Hyun of the Republic of Korea and Mrs. Roh paid an official visit (*koshiki homon*) to Japan as "Japan's state guests" (*Nihonkoku kokuhinto shite*) from 6 to 9 June 2003." Gaimusho, "Nikkan shuno kyodo seimei: Heiwa to han'ei no Hokuto Ajia jidai ni muketa Nikkan kyoryoku kiban no kochiku" [ROK-Japan Summit Joint Statement: Building the Foundation of ROK-Japan Cooperation Toward an Era of Peace and Prosperity in Northeast Asia] (Tokyo: June 2003), http://www.mofa.go.jp/mofaj/kaidan/yojin/ arc_03/j_k_seimei.html. By contrast, Seoul's version of the joint statement read: "As state guests of Japan, President Roh Moo Hyun and the First Lady of the Republic of Korea paid a *state visit* to Japan from June 6 to 9, 2003." Office of the President, Republic of Korea, *Joint Statement by President Roh Moo Hyun of the Republic of Korea and Prime Minister Junichiro Koizumi of Japan Following a Summit Meeting* (Seoul: June 7, 2003), http://www.president. go.kr/warp/app/ en_speeches/view?group _id=en_archive&meta _ide=en_speeches&id=3156d7 (Italics are the author's).

"people in neighboring nations are alarmed by the change in Japan's defense policy."[32]

Roh was the first South Korean leader who belonged to the post-World War II generation, who had no first-hand memory of Japan's colonial rule. Not only did he choose not to raise the issue of Japan's misdeeds during the colonial period but he had not sought any expressions of regret from the Emperor. Even though this did not attract much criticism, Roh's "failure" to obtain specific commitments from Koizumi regarding such issues as shuttle flights between Haneda and Kimpo Airports and visa exemptions for South Korean tourists to Japan was duly noted in the South Korean press.[33]

Both during the two-hour-long summit meeting and the joint press conference that followed it, the two leaders betrayed a difference of emphasis on how to deal with the North Korean nuclear issue. Whereas Koizumi took a distinctly hard-line approach, Roh displayed a more conciliatory stance. At the joint press conference, Koizumi spoke of the need for close trilateral coordination among Tokyo, Seoul, and Washington and for dealing with the North in a "strict manner," should it escalate the crisis. While recognizing the need to combine dialogue and pressure vis-à-vis the North, however, Roh said that his government "puts greater weight on dialogue."[34]

Such difference, actually, could be detected in the joint statements emanating from the summit meeting the two leaders had separately with US President Bush in the weeks preceding their own summit. In the US-ROK joint statement, Roh agreed with Bush that "increased threats to peace and stability on the [Korean] peninsula would require consideration of *further steps*."[35] In the US-Japan joint statement, however,

---

32 Kanako Takahara, "Koizumi, Roh Set Pyongyang Policy," *Japan Times*, June 8, 2003.
33 "News Analysis: N.K., History Still Fault Line," *Korea Herald*, June 9, 2003; "Hannara, 'kuch'ejok songkwa opta" [Grand National Party: No Concrete Results], *Dong-A ilbo*, June 9, 2003.
34 Takahara, "Koizumi, Roh Set Pyongyang Policy," *Japan Times*, June 8, 2003.

"Koizumi and Bush said North Korea will face 'tougher measures' if the [nuclear] problem escalates."[36]

Other issues on the agenda of the summit meeting pertained to economic and cultural relations. One was a bilateral free trade agreement, for which the two countries had already established a joint study group. The two leaders, however, merely agreed to begin government-level talks "at an early date," without setting a specific timetable. At a breakfast meeting with Korean journalists covering the summit meeting on the final day of his Japan visit, Roh conceded that Seoul was dragging its feet on the issue. In the short run, an FTA would increase South Korea's trade deficit with Japan but there would be long-term benefits, he said. Japan, he added, needed to take certain steps, such as a waiver of visa requirements, technology transfer, and more investment in South Korea, before the process of concluding an FTA could be accelerated.[37]

Regarding the visa exemption issue, however, the two sides were no more specific than they were on the FTA issue. They agreed to "make further efforts to realize visa exemptions at an early date for ROK nationals traveling to Japan." As a new step toward that goal, Japan would "consider" waiving visa requirements for South Korean students visiting Japan on school trips. The issue of establishing shuttle flights between Kimpo and Haneda airports, too, received the same treatment, with both sides agreeing to work toward its "early realization."[38]

---

35 White House, Office of the Press Secretary, *Joint Statement Between the United States of America and the Republic of Korea* (Washington: May 14, 2003), http://www.whitehouse.gov/news/releases/2003/05/ print/20030514-17.html (Italics are supplied by the author).
36 Takahara, "Koizumi, Roh Set Pyongyang Policy," *Japan Times*, June 8, 2003.
37 "Roh pang'il kyolsan kija kandamhoe mundap" [Q & A at Roh's Informal Meeting with Reporters on the Results of his Japan Visit], *Joongang ilbo*, June 10, 2003.
38 Ministry of Foreign Affairs of Japan, *Japan-Republic of Korea Summit Joint Statement—Building the Foundations of ROK-Japan Cooperation toward an Age of Peace and Prosperity in Northeast Asia* (Tokyo: June 7, 2003; provisional translation by the Government of Japan), http://www.mofa.go.jp/region/ asia-paci/korea/pv0306/pdfs/joint.html.

In sum, the second Koizumi-Roh Moo Hyun summit accentuated the lofty, if vague, goal of forging a "future-oriented" bilateral relationship. The rhetoric of harmony and cooperation emanating from it, however, could not mask the reality that a gap existed between the perceptions and interests of not only the two leaders but of the countries they respectively led as well.

During the ensuing months, the pace of cultural exchange and cooperation in other areas quickened. Many of the agreements, no matter how vaguely worded, began to be implemented as well. In mid-September the Seoul government announced that it would "further relax its ban on imports of Japanese cultural products" in January 2004, which would allow the entry of Japanese compact disks (CDs), game software, and movies in the South Korean market.[39] In late October Koizumi and Roh met again on the sidelines of an APEC summit in Bangkok, Thailand, and agreed to launch full negotiations on an FTA before the year was out; that agreement was carried out in December, when the first round of such negotiations occurred in Seoul.[40]

2004: Cooperation Eclipses Discord

As the New Year dawned, old contentious issues re-emerged but were kept under control. Cooperation continued in the cultural and economic realms. The holding of summit meetings in July and again in December showed that cooperation at the highest level was on track as well. The continuing need to deal with the North Korean nuclear issue, primarily within the framework of Six-Party Talks, was instrumental in sustaining trilateral cooperation involving the US, Japan, and South Korea.

The old issue that sparked controversy on the New Year's Day was

---

39 "South Korea to Ease Ban on Japan Cultural Goods," *Japan Times*, September 17, 2003.
40 "Onun 22-il Han'il FTA ch'ot hyopsang kaesi" [ROK-Japan Negotiations on FTA to Begin on the 22nd], *Chosun ilbo*, December 15, 2003.

Koizumi's visit to Yasukuni Shrine on that day. Not only was it the first time that he had visited the shrine on the New Year's Day but he was wearing ceremoniall Japanese kimono and conspicuously affixed his official title when he signed the shrine's guest book. Once again, Koizumi's timing seemed to have been well calculated. Making the move so early would serve to minimize its adverse effects on Japan's relations with its neighbors, especially South Korea and China. The latter two would, and did, lodge strong protests but their anger would wear off as time progressed. Another factor was the scheduled dispatch of Japan's Self-Defense Forces contingent to Iraq. If Koizumi were to visit the controversial shrine, widely viewed as a symbol of Japanese militarism, after the dispatch had occurred, that would conceivably send a wrong signal. Domestically, his act might help win the favor and support of conservative voters in the upper house election scheduled for July.[41]

The shrine visit, the fourth since Koizumi became prime minister in 2001, however, triggered opposition within the ruling coalition as well. Kanzaki Takenori, leader of the coalition partner New Komeito, criticized the visit as a violation of the Constitutional principle of the separation of state and religion and on the ground that it would have "serious diplomatic implications."[42] *Asahi shinbun*, an influential daily, labeled the visit a manifestation of "self-conceit" that did not serve Japan's national interest.[43]

Another old issue that reared its head in the first month of the New Year pertained to Tokdo, which the Japanese call Takeshima. On January 8, Korea Post, which operates South Korea's postal service, announced

---

41 "Koizumi, Yasukuni sinsa ch'ambae: saehae ch'onnal kisup……kyesandoen 'ugyonghwa'" [Koizumi Visits Yasukuni Shrine: Sneak Attack on the New Year's Day……Calculated "Tilt toward the Right"], *Dong-A ilbo*, January 3, 2003; "Shrine Visit Strains Relations," *Asahi com*, January 3, 2004, http://www.asahi.com/ english/politics/TKY200401030070.html.
42 Ibid.
43 "Yasukuni sanpai—hitoriyogari ni kokueki nashi" [Yasukuni Visit: Self-Conceit, No National Interest Served], *Asahi shinbun*, January 4, 2004, an editorial.

that it would issue "four types of stamps depicting Tokdo's birds and plants on January 16." Japan immediately protested, calling on Seoul not to proceed with its plan. Japan cited Article 6 of the Universal Postal Union (UPU) Convention, which stipulates that "the subjects and designs of postage stamps shall be in keeping with the spirit of the preamble to the······Convention and in compliance with the consensus of UPU members." This, actually, was not the first time that Seoul had issued Tokdo stamps; it did so in 1954 and 2002. Japan, however, protested only in 1954 but not in 2002.[44]

When the stamps went on sale in South Korea's post offices on January 16, they sold out in three hours. With a supply of 2.2 million sheets, each consisting of 16 stamps, the post offices had rationed them to one sheet per customer. "Within days, sheets of the stamps, with a total face value of $2.45, were selling on Yahoo Korea's auction site for $39."[45] Regrets were voiced by Foreign Minister Kawaguchi Yoriko—who summoned ROK Ambassador to Japan Cho Se-Hyung to express regret—, Chief Cabinet Secretary Fukuda Yasuo, and Posts Minister Aso Taro.[46] The dispute, however, did not "create major diplomatic friction," which observers in Seoul attributed to the possibility that rhetoric and behavior surrounding the affair were linked primarily to internal politics in both countries—namely, South Korea's general elections in April and Japan's upper house elections in July.[47]

On April 7 a district court in Japan handed down a decision that, while encouraging to Seoul, Beijing, and other Asian victims of past Japanese aggression, had little effect on Koizumi. The Fukuoka District

---

44 Kim Tae-gyu, "Seoul Rebuffs Tokyo's Criticism on Tokto Stamps," *Korea Times*, January 9, 2004: "Seoul Snubs Tokyo over Stamps," *Japan Times*, January 9, 2004.
45 James Brooke, "A Postage Stamp Island Sets Off a Continental Debate," *New York Times*, January 27, 2004.
46 Kanako Takahara, "Seoul Issues Controversial Stamp, Draws Flak from Irate Kawaguchi," *Japan Times*, January 17, 2004.
47 "[News Analysis] Experts See No Change in Tokyo Ties," *Korea Herald*, March 3, 2004.

Court ruled that Koizumi's visit to Yasukuni Shrine in August 2001 was "unconstitutional because it violated the separation of state and religion." Actually, this was not the first time that a Japanese court had held a prime minister's visit to Yasukuni Shrine unconstitutional. In January 1991 the Sendai High Court made the same ruling, which was upheld by Japan's Supreme Court when it "dismissed an appeal by the state." Koizumi reacted to the Fukuoka District Court's ruling by vowing to keep visiting the shrine.[48]

The Koizumi-Roh Moo Hyun Summit, July 2004

Neither Koizumi's controversial Yasukuni visit nor the dispute over Tokdo (or Takeshima) proved to be serious enough to disrupt summit diplomacy. Koizumi thus made his first working visit to South Korea in July to hold a summit meeting with Roh Moo Hyun again. This was Koizumi's second visit to the Korean Peninsula in 2004, for he had visited North Korea in May for his second summit meeting with Kim Jong Il.

The two-day summit (July 21-22), held on the resort island of Cheju, was touted by Roh's aides as the beginning of "shuttle diplomacy" among the leaders of Northeast Asia. Its "working meeting" format—in which leaders wore casual clothes even during official banquets, their entourages were scaled down to a bare minimum, and "expanded meetings" that typically follow "summit meetings" were dispensed with—was aimed at increasing the frequency and efficiency of summits.[49]

A key item on its agenda was North Korea. The third round of Six-Party Talks, held in Beijing a month earlier, was viewed by its participants, which included Japan and South Korea, as encouraging. For the first time

---

48 "Koizumi Shrine Visit Ruled Unconstitutional," *Japan Times*, April 8, 2004; Reiji Yoshida, "Prime Minister Pledges Yasukuni Return," ibid.
49 "[Han'il chongsang hoedam] 'uijon p'agoe' not'ai ch'arim kyogomnun taehwa" [ROK-Japan Summit Meeting, "Protocols Set Aside," No-tie Attire, Free-flowing Dialogue], *Chosun ilbo*, July 22, 2004.

since the multilateral process began in August 2003, the US put forth a proposal spelling out what North Korea needed to do in the short run and what it would get in return. The North, too, was a little more specific than in the past in delineating what it called a "reward for freeze" formula. Given this, there was a good chance that real progress, if not a breakthrough, would materialize in the fourth round of the talks, which was expected to be held in September.

Koizumi and Roh Moo Hyun agreed to redouble cooperation, both bilateral and trilateral, in finding a peaceful solution to the North Korean nuclear issue. They confirmed their common goal, shared with the US, China, and Russia, of inducing the North to dismantle its nuclear weapons program "completely, verifiably, and irreversibly." In return for this, they would join the other participants in providing large-scale economic assistance, including energy aid, to the North. Koizumi also indicated his wish to realize normalization of relations with the North at an early date, before his term as LDP president expires in September 2006. "If North Korea implements the Pyongyang declaration [which Kim Jong Il and Koizumi signed after their first summit in September 2002] in a sincere manner, relations could be normalized within two years, or even as quickly as one year," Koizumi said during a joint press conference in Cheju. The declaration covers the abduction issue as well as Pyongyang's nuclear program and missiles."[50]

On bilateral issues, the two leaders, noting that the year 2005 marks the 40th anniversary of the normalization of Japan-ROK relations, agreed to designate that year as the Year of Japan-ROK Friendship and to step up exchange programs that are already under way and initiate new programs. Cultural exchanges involving TV dramas and movies between the two countries were already increasing at an impressive rate. The popularity of Korean popular culture in Japan had even been christened as the "Korean Wave (*Kanryu*)", and even Koizumi mentioned a popular South Korean

---

50 Tatsuya Fukumoto, "Koizumi, Roh, Discuss Trade, N. Korea Nukes," *Daily Yomiuri*, July 22, 2004; Seo Hyun-jin, "Roh, Koizumi to Cooperate on N.K.," *Korea Herald*, July 22, 2004.

TV drama shown in Japan under the title, "Winter Sonata" (*Fuyu no sonata*).[51]

Regarding visa exemptions, Koizumi announced that Japan would waive visas for ROK nationals visiting Japan during a world exposition to be held in Aichi prefecture from March to September 2005. He promised that permanent visa exemptions for Korean visitors to Japan would be considered afterward.[52]

The two leaders renewed their commitment to continue efforts toward an early conclusion of a bilateral free trade agreement. Koizumi invited Roh to visit Japan later in the year for another round of "working summit," and Roh accepted the invitation. Regarding the issue of history, which is a perennial stumbling block in forging a "future-oriented" bilateral relationship, Koizumi stated that it was the responsibility of "us, who are living in the present to come to grips with the past history [*kako no rekishi o chokushishi*]; reflect on it when necessary; and develop future-oriented relations with neighboring countries."[53]

At the post-summit joint press conference, Roh Moo Hyun stated that during the remainder of his term of office, the "ROK government would not raise the issue of past history as either an official agenda item or a contentious issue." This pledge, which he would break in 2005, was widely criticized in South Korea, especially among opposition politicians, who labeled Roh's conduct during the Cheju summit "diplomacy of humiliation." [54]

---

51 Gaimusho, *Nikkan shuno kaidan (gaiyo)* (Tokyo: July 22, 2004), http://www.mofa.go.jp/mofaj/area/ korea/kaidan0407_gai.html. On the popularity of Korean "pop culture" as well as "all things Korean" in Japan, see Andrew Ward, "Pop Songs to Heal a Historical Rift," *Financial Times*, August 7/August 8, 2004; Mari Yamaguchi, "All Things Korean Now Popular in Japan," *Washington Post*, November 22, 2004.
52 "Shusho, Nikkanbei no domei kankei no chuyosei kyocho, Nikkan shuno kaidan" [Prime Minister Stresses the Importance of the Alliance Relationship among Japan, the ROK, and the US: *ROK-Japan* Summit Meeting], *Asahi shinbun*, July 22, 2004.
53 Gaimusho, *Nikkan shuno kaidan (gaiyo)* (Tokyo: July 22, 2004).

Roh's pledge to Koizumi did not cover contemporary issues, and the name of the sea lying between their two countries is one of them. In September it was reported that Japan planned to "send experts to the U.S. Library of Congress to examine 19th century maps in a bid to strengthen its position in the dispute with south Korea over the name of the Sea of Japan." South Korea, after examining old maps in the same library in 2002, asserted that "more than 60 percent show 'East Sea' or 'Sea of Korea.'" The Japanese Foreign Ministry "claims to have proved the inaccuracy of similar South Korean assertions based on Seoul's examinations of old maps at the British Library, the Cambridge University Library and the Bibliotheque Nationale de France."[55]

Nothing that was said and done during the Cheju summit suggested that Japan and South Korea had become true friends who really trust each other and lend full support to each other's endeavors in the international arena. This became evident at the first Asia-Europe Meeting (ASEM), held in Hanoi in October. Leaders from 38 participating nations and the European Union, including Roh Moo Hyun and Koizumi, approved a chairman's statement issued on October 8 expressing their support for the reform of the United Nations and its principal organs. The statement endorsed the goal of "strengthening and enhancing the representativeness, transparency and effectiveness of the U.N. system." This, Seoul said, "echoed Roh's statement during the meeting," which stressed that "any nation wishing to acquire permanent membership of the Security Council should first obtain trust from the relevant regional nations."

---

54 "Imgijung sinsa ch'ambae munje chegi anhalkot" [I Won't Take Issue With Shrine Visit During The Remainder of My Term], *Joongang ilbo*, July 22, 2004; "[Han'il chongsang hoedam] Koizumi 'Shwiri yonghwa pomyo Nambuk kinjanggam nukkyo" [ROK-Japan Summit Meeting, Koizumi Felt Tension Between North and South While Watching the Movie "Shwiri"], *Dong-A ilbo*, July 23, 2004. Roh also irked many of his countrymen by referring to Dokto as Takeshima at the joint news conference. He was repeating the word a Japanese journalist had used in a question.

55 "Experts to Seek Evidence over Sea of Japan Name," *Japan Times*, September 6, 2004.

Roh's secretary on foreign policy, Chung Woo-sung, who had accompanied Roh to the ASEM meeting, was more blunt: "Japan has to obtain trust from nations first," before it can generate support in its bid for permanent Security Council membership.[56]

Cooperation nonetheless occurred in the arena of denuclearization. When the six-party talks entered into an impasse due to North Korea's refusal to allow a fourth round to be held on schedule, the foreign ministers of Japan and South Korea met in Seoul in November to discuss ways of breaking the impasse. Japanese Foreign Minister Machimura Nobutaka held talks with both Roh Moo Hyun and Foreign Minister Ban Ki Moon, and they agreed to keep the freeze on the project to build two light-water reactors (LWRs) in the North, a multibillion-dollar project financed mainly by Seoul and Tokyo. Machimura "also warned of economic sanctions against North Korea," an option on which the Roh government has some reservations.[57]

Koizumi and Roh Hold Another "Working Summit," December 2004

When it was announced that Koizumi and Roh Moo Hyun would hold another "working summit" in Kagoshima in December, a controversy arose in Seoul over the choice of the site. Although Kagoshima had already hosted an informal meeting of cabinet members of both countries in November 1998, questions surfaced this time regarding its suitability for a summit meeting. Two things appeared to bother Seoul. First, during World War II, Kagoshima had served as Kamikaze pilots' base. Second, Saigo Takamori, proponent of Japanese conquest of Korea, was born there. While ROK Foreign Minister Ban Ki

---

56 Shim Jae-yun, "Seoul Puts Brake on Tokyo's UN Bid," *Korea Times*, October 11, 2004.
57 "Tokyo, Seoul Want Six-Way Talks Resumed," *Japan Times*, November 7, 2004.

Moon openly suggested the possibility of "changing the venue," his Japanese counterpart, Machimura Nobutaka said that "it was beyond common sense to change something that had been diplomatically decided." [58]

Roh disclosed later that Koizumi had actually offered to change the venue but he decided to go ahead with the summit in Kagoshima, because he believed that by making a small concession, he would eventually gain more. "What counts in diplomacy," Roh was quoted as saying, "is substance, not making big noise; they say that diplomacy should be conducted without paying excessive attention to what the people are saying behind your back." [59]

In terms of format and dress code, the two-day summit that opened in the hot spring resort of Ibusuki, Kagoshima prefecture on December 17 was identical to the summit held in Cheju five months earlier. While Koizumi and Roh agreed on many things, they also displayed differences in their approaches toward the North. Both the nuclear and abduction issues had reached a difficult stage. North Korea's refusal to return to Six-party Talks had created an impasse, which the other participants in the talks were trying hard to break. From Japan's vantage point, however, the abduction issue was more pressing. The finding that the alleged remains of one of the kidnap victims provided by the North belonged to other people, had shocked and angered the Japanese people. When Koizumi sought Roh's support in dealing with this problem, Roh expressed an understanding of Japan's frustration but counseled caution. Roh even raised the possibility that the North might have made an honest mistake and applauded "Koizumi's pledge to consider the imposition of sanctions carefully." [60]

---

58 "Han 'pakkuja' Il 'motbakkwo'" [ROK: "Let's Change," Japan: "Cannot be Changed], *Chosun ilbo*, November 6, 2004.
59 "Roh taet'ongnyong palk'in Han'il chongsang hoedam twit yaegi" [Behind-the-Scene Story about ROK-Japan Summit Disclosed by President Roh], *Joongang ilbo*, December 30, 2004.
60 "Koizumi, Roh Back Six-way Talks, In No Hurry for Sanctions," *Japan Times*,

The two leaders concurred on the need to exert efforts to make the "Year of Japan-ROK Friendship" in 2005 truly memorable. Both pledged to attend its "grand opening"—scheduled for January 25 in Tokyo and January 27 in Seoul—in their respective countries. Koizumi set the goal of increasing the human traffic between Japan and South Korea from an estimated four million in 2004 to five million in 2005. To facilitate the attainment of this goal, the two leaders agreed to consider doubling the number of shuttle flights between Haneda and Kimpo Airports.[61]

Koizumi also confirmed Japan's plan to consider (1) waiving visa requirements for ROK nationals visiting the 2005 World Exposition in Aichi from March to September and (2) giving permanent exemption to South Korean visitors based on the results of the Aichi experiment. On the FTA issue, both leaders reiterated their previous commitments to strive for its early conclusion. In the arena of "working-level cooperation," the two leaders welcomed the signing on December 13 of a bilateral agreement on mutual assistance in customs matter. They confirmed that efforts would be made to wrap up negotiations on a treaty on mutual legal assistance in criminal matters as soon as possible. Finally, they agreed to begin negotiations for an agreement for the protection of migratory birds.[62]

The two leaders also discussed issues beyond bilateral relations, notably the formation of an East Asian Community (EAC), cooperation for reconstruction assistance to Iraq, and United Nations reform. The last issue was related to Japan's wish to become a permanent member of an expanded UN Security Council. If Koizumi had hoped to get Roh's support, however he must have been disappointed. For Roh told Koizumi that since the two countries did not really share the same interests, Seoul needed to study the matter further.[63]

December 18, 2004.
61 Gaimusho, *Gaiko seisho, Heisei 17-nenban* [Diplomatic Bluebook 2005] (Tokyo: K.K. Taiyo Bijutsu, 2005), 34-35.
62 Idem, *Nikkan shuno kaidan (gaiyo)* (Tokyo: December 17, 2004).
63 Ibid.

The joint press conference following the two-hour-long summit meeting provided glimpses of differences between the two leaders. When a Japanese reporter posed a question about the issue of past history, Roh said that he "came here thinking that I would not want to pose issues such as those relating to history that could prompt Japanese citizens to react emotionally and negatively." He went on to state that he did not think that asking Japan to apologize again would be conducive to friendly bilateral relations. In his view, the time had come for the Japanese people to make their own decisions regarding Japan's past behavior. He struck a positive note as well, noting that the current bilateral atmosphere was "healthy," adding "we constantly look back on history and discuss historical issues in order to contribute positively to a correct future." He had no doubt that the "future for the two countries [spells] peace and coexistence."[64]

To a Korean reporter's question about ways of preventing what the Korean press calls "reckless remarks" (*mang'on*) by Japanese politicians—that is, remarks that gloss over Japan's misdeeds during colonial rule—, Koizumi acknowledged that "there have been remarks offensive to the Korean people" but underlined the need to maintain "friendly, cooperative relations." He echoed Roh's reference to the on-going joint historical study, implying that it might help alleviate the problem. Koizumi was less equivocal about the Yasukuni Shrine issue. He made clear his intention to continue visiting the shrine and asked for an understanding. He stated that many Japanese citizens had gone to battlefields involuntarily and lost their lives. "The peace and prosperity Japan enjoys today," he said, "owe not merely to the efforts of the people today but also to the efforts and sacrifices of the earlier generation." His visits to the shrine, Koizumi insisted, were an expression of his "respect

---

64 "Koizumi, Roh Back Six-Way Talks, In No Hurry for Sanctions," *Japan Times*, December 18, 2004; "Roh taet'ongnyong, 'Il kungmin'i kyoltan'ul' Koizumi, 'Han kungmin's ihaerul'" [President Roh: "The Japanese People Should Decide" Koizumi: "The Korean People Should Understand"], *Chosun ilbo*, December 18, 2004.

and appreciation to those predecessors who traveled on the path of hardship." The visits should never be equated with an implicit support for war or militarism, he said.[65]

All in all, although the Kagoshima summit could not be rated as a rousing success, it nonetheless proved the vitality of Japan-ROK relations. The two leaders jointly coined a new term, "shuttle summit meeting," agreeing to continue it in the future. Koizumi proposed two such meetings a year.[66]

2005: The Year of "Friendship" Marred by Friction

The year 2005, as already noted, was designated as the "Year of Japan-ROK Friendship" to mark the 40th anniversary of the normalization of their bilateral relations. Although over 250 cultural events were held without a hitch, however, inter-governmental relations were strained by old issues related to history—the dispute over Tokdo/Takeshima, history textbooks and Prime Minister Koizumi's pointed refusal to stop visiting Yasukuni Shrine. Notwithstanding this, two summit meetings—a "shuttle summit meeting" in Seoul and a short meeting on the sidelines of an international conference in Pusan—were held, and cooperation continued in other areas as well.

What triggered a surge of anti-Japanese rhetoric and activities in South Korea was the decision by the Shimane prefectural assembly to designate February 22 as "Takeshima Day" with the aim of asserting Japan's sovereignty over the South Korea-controlled group of islets. As soon as it became known that a draft ordinance for this purpose had been submitted to the assembly, South Korea reacted with an outburst of anger and protests. Comments by Japanese ambassador to Seoul, Takano Toshiyoki, reaffirming Japan's official position on the disputed island— that it belongs to Japan on both historical and legal grounds—added fuel

---

65 Ibid.
66 Gaimusho, *Gaiko seisho* (2005), 38, including note 18.

to the controversy.[67]

On February 24, the second anniversary of his inauguration, Roh Moo Hyun reneged on his July 2004 pledge not to raise historical issues vis-à-vis Japan. In a speech at the National Assembly, he said: "The different attitude in Japan and Germany in handling their past history is giving us a lot of lessons to learn. [Japan] should be candid about the past and, only by doing so would Japan move toward the future without being tied to the past."[68]

Meanwhile, the "disclosure of distortions in a new Japanese history textbook for use in secondary schools" in 2007 sparked nationwide protests in South Korea. The textbook, "compiled by right-wing nationalist scholars, describes Japan as having helped the modernization of Korea with its 1910-45 colonization and explains it was the Korean people who wished to change their surnames to Japanese during colonial rule."[69]

On March 17, a day after the Shimane prefectural assembly adopted the "Takeshima Day" ordinance, the standing committee of the ROK National Security Council (NSC) adopted a "new doctrine" on Seoul's Japan policy. In announcing the doctrine, Unification Minister Chung Dong Young, who concurrently serves as the chairman of the NSC standing committee, stated that the Roh government "has decided to take stern counter-measures" against the developments relating to Tokdo and historical issues, because it "views them as equivalent to past colonial aggression." Japan's assertion of sovereignty over "our territory," which Japan had forcibly taken over in the process of seizing Korea but which South Korea had "recovered following Liberation," Chung said, "is not

---

67 "'Takeshima no hi' mondai de Kankoku kokan, '40 shunen gyojini shishomo" [ROK High Official: "Takeshima Day" May "Hinder 40th Anniversary Events"], *Asahi shinbun*, February 26, 2005; Anthony Failola, "Islands Come Between South Korea and Japan," *Washington Post*, March 17, 2005.

68 "Roh Tells Japan to Make Clean Breast of Past Misdeeds," *Japan Times*, February 26, 2005.

69 Lee Joo-hee, "Korea-Japan Row Widens over Textbook," *Korea Herald*, March 11, 2005.

merely a territorial issue but tantamount to the negation of the history of our liberation."[70]

Key points in the newly-enunciated doctrine included the following:
- The ROK government will forge its relations with Japan based on humanity's universal values and common sense. It will resolve issues relating to past history in accordance with the universal historical formula of seeking truth, genuine apology, and forgiveness and reconciliation
- Recognizing that Japan is and will remain our fate-decreed partner in the quest for peace and prosperity in Northeast Asia, the ROK government will maintain political and diplomatic exchanges that have already been agreed on and will continue to promote economic, social, cultural, and human exchanges.
- The ROK government will call on the Japanese government to pay compensation to individuals who have suffered damages during colonial rule based on respect for human rights and humanity's universal norms.
- Japan must recognize that winning the trust of its neighbors is the first step toward earning respect as a leading country in the United ations and in the world community.[71]

Japan lost no time in responding to Seoul's "new doctrine" on its Japan policy. On the same day it was unveiled, Foreign Minister Machimura Nobutaka issued a statement. He underlined Japan's "strong determination to develop a future-oriented Japan-ROK relationship" based on the principles enunciated in previous unilateral and joint statements, "facing the past squarely and reflecting where reflection is needed." Machimura reiterated Japan's previous pledge "to humbly

---

70 "Chongbu 'Il Tokdo chorye, che-2 ui Hanbando ch'imt'al'" [Government: "Japan's Ordinance on Tokdo Is Equivalent to a Second Seizure of the Korean Peninsula], *Chosun ilbo*, March 18, 2005.
71 "NSC sangim wiwonhoe Han'il kwangye songmyong chonmun" [Full Text of NSC Standing Committee's Declaration on ROK-Japan Relations], *Chosun ilbo*, March 18, 2005.

recognize the historical fact that Japan caused enormous damage and suffering to the peoples of the various Asian countries, to show deep understanding and sympathy toward the [South] Korean people, and to help each other as neighbors with patience and generosity."[72]

Regarding Seoul's demand for compensation to victims of Japan's colonial rule, Machimura stated that the "issue of property claims" was settled at the time of Japan-ROK normalization in 1965. Japan, however, was prepared to cooperate with Seoul concerning the "investigation into and return of the remains of the people born on the Korean Peninsula." As for the "Takeshima" issue, Machimura stated that having an "emotional confrontation" was beneficial to neither side, underscoring the need to approach the issue from a broader perspective, taking into account Japan-ROK relations as a whole, including the fishery issue." He also assured Seoul that the "authorization of school textbooks will be carried out in a fair and appropriate manner."[73]

Machimura's reference to the fishing issue is noteworthy, for the latter is a key factor in the Dokto/Takeshima dispute. As we saw in Chapter 8, Japan and South Korea set up a joint fishing zone in waters adjoining the disputed island in 1999. However, "Japanese fishermen have been overwhelmed by South Korean fishing boats and unable to operate freely." This was an important part of the backdrop against which Shimane prefecture decided to enact the ordinance that ignited the latest round of controversy.[74]

A week later Chief Cabinet Secretary Hosoda Hiroyuki renewed Japan's long-standing proposal for adjudication of the dispute by the International Court of Justice, an option Seoul has consistently rejected.[75]

---

72 Gaimusho, *Machimura gaimu daijin danwa: Kankoku kokka anzen hosho kaigi jonin iinkai seimeimun ni tsuite* [Statement by Foreign Minister Machimura: On the Declaration by the Standing Committee of the ROK National Security Council] (Tokyo: March 17, 2005), http://www.mofa.go.jp/mofaj/press/danwa/17/dmc_0317.html.

73 Ibid.

74 "Takeshima—Kankoku no minasan e"[Takeshima: To the People of the Republic of Korea], *Asahi shinbun*, March 17, 2005, an editorial.

Apart from rhetoric, South Korea took a series of "counter-measures" aimed at Japan. Foreign Minister Ban Ki Moon canceled a visit to Tokyo. The government announced that it would reverse its previous policy and allow visits by ordinary citizens to Tokdo. ROK Air Force fighter jets began flying daily patrols of the island, and on March 17, "two Japanese Air Self-Defense Force reconnaissance jets" that "strayed too close to the volcanic outcroppings" were warned to leave the airspace.[76]

As for the battle of words, both sides attributed domestic political needs to the other side for escalating it. A "senior" Japanese Foreign Ministry official was reported to have asserted that "Roh Moo Hyun's weak political footing prompted him to play up historical issues to gain support from right-wingers."[77] Another unnamed Japanese government official was quoted as saying that Roh's conduct "has exposed the weakness of the President who is prone to be swayed by public opinion." He showed his displeasure by comparing Roh's rhetoric to that of North Korea, saying that they were both replete with "emotional expressions."[78] In Seoul, Machimura's statement was described as designed for "domestic consumption," reiterating Japan's familiar positions and offering nothing new to South Korea.[79]

In April the textbook issue became the focus of attention after the Japanese government approved a new series of textbooks. A spokesman

---

75 "'Tokdo, kukje sabop chaep'anso kaja'" ["Tokdo: Let Us Go to the International Court of Justice"], *Chosun ilbo*, March 25, 2005.
76 Reiji Yoshida, "Government Downplays Jets Warned Off by Seoul," *Japan Times*, March 18, 2005; Faiola, "Japanese Claim Touches Nerve in South Korea," *Washington Post*, March 20, 2005.
77 Kanako Takahara, "New Strain, Historical Baggage Cloud What Was To Be a Celebratory Year," *Japan Times*, March 17, 2005. "'Roh taet'ongnyong tamhwa' Ilbon chongbu, ollon panung" [Statement by President Roh: Reaction by the Japanese Government and Press], *Joongang ilbo*, March 25, 2005.
78 "'Tokdo, kukje sabop chaep'anso kaja'," *Chosun ilbo*, March 25, 2005.
79 "Kiro e son Han'il kwangye······yangguk oegyo songmyong-jon" [ROK-Japan Relations at a Crossroads······War of Diplomatic Statements], *Dong-A ilbo*, March 19, 2005.

for the ROK Foreign Ministry issued a statement on April 5 calling on Japan to make an effort to revise those textbooks that "both justify and glorify Japan's past misdeeds." The statement noted that while some textbooks seriously distort historical facts concerning contentious issues, others attempt to provide relatively objective descriptions, including the forcible nature of the Japanese annexation of Korea and the resistance of the Korean people against their colonial occupiers. This, the statement continued, is congruent with the historical knowledge of conscientious Japanese intellectuals and citizens. It gives hope that the "Japanese people's conscience will be confirmed in the textbook adoption stage in the months ahead." Finally, the statement expressed "serious concerns" about the assertion of Japanese sovereignty over Tokdo in some of the civics textbooks that were approved.[80]

Meanwhile, the Roh government's hard line toward Japan began to draw criticisms at home from former government officials and scholars. Gong Ro Myong, former Foreign Minister and ambassador to Japan, for example, questioned the wisdom of undermining a "de facto alliance" forged between the "only liberal democracies in Northeast Asia." He pointed out that Tokyo's claim of sovereignty over Tokdo will have no effect on Seoul's de facto control over it and that the controversial textbooks have a very low rate of adoption by schools. He then questioned whether a policy that "in effect conveys to the people fantasized, hence unattainable, outcomes" could be regarded as responsible.[81]

As if he was heeding the counsel for moderation, Roh Moo Hyun on April 27 offered Japan what the *Japan Times* called an "olive branch to the

---

80 "[Il kyogwaso p'amun] Oegyo T'ongsangbu taebyonin songmyong chonmun" [Japanese Textbook Controversy: the Full Text of the Statement by the Spokesman for the Ministry of Foreign Affairs and Trade], *Chosun ilbo*, April 6, 2005.

81 "Gong Ro Myong chon oemu, tae'il kangyong hurume ilch'im" [Former Foreign Minster Gong Ro Myong Criticizes Hard Line toward Japan], *Dong-A ilbo*, April 16, 2005.

future." In a congratulatory message to the 2,500th edition of *Mindan*, the organ of the pro-Seoul Korean Residents Union in Japan, Roh said that the ROK and Japan "are a community with common destiny [*kongdong unmyongch'e*] bound to open up together the future of Northeast Asia." While he saw the future of ROK-Japan relations as marked by "peace" and "coexistence," however, he took pains to stress the importance of resolving historical and other issues in such a way as to facilitate the building of a new future between the two neighbors.[82]

Before another round of "shuttle summit meeting" between Roh and Koizumi materialized in Seoul in the latter part of June, two incidents symbolizing the strained bilateral relations occurred. On May 11 Vice Foreign Minister Yachi Shotaro reportedly told members of the ROK National Assembly in an informal breakfast meeting that "Japan was reluctant to share intelligence with their nation because the U.S. does not trust the South on Pyongyang's nuclear ambitions." Seoul reacted with anger, with its foreign ministry summoning Japanese ambassador to lodge a protest and the Blue House issuing a statement calling on the Japanese government to take a disciplinary action against Yachi. His superior, Foreign Minister Machimura, told him to be "careful," and Yachi himself said "it was 'regrettable' if his remarks 'caused misunderstanding.'" "The true intention of my remarks," he said, "was to stress the importance of reinforcing cooperation between Japan and South Korea as well as among Japan, South Korea and the U.S."[83]

A second incident involved a 36-hour standoff between patrol ships from Japan and South Korea in the East Sea (or the Sea of Japan) in early

---

82 "Roh Offers Japan an Olive Branch to the Future," *Japan Times*, April 28, 2005; "Roh taet'ongnyong Han'il kwangye paron 'sinjung'" [President Roh's Remarks on ROK-Japan Relations: "Cautious"], *Dong-A ilbo*, April 28, 2005.

83 "Seoul Calls Envoy Over Yachi's Alleged Slur," *Japan Times*, May 27, 2005; Kanako Takahara, "Yachi 'Perplexed' Remarks Got Play, Is Issued Warning," ibid., May 28, 2005; "'Gokai o maneki ikan' tai-Kankoku hatsugen de Yachi gaimujikan" ["Regret Inviting Misunderstanding" Vice Minister Yachi's Comments on South Korea], *Asahi shinbun*, May 28, 2005.

June. In the early hours of June 2, a 77-ton South Korean fishing boat with eight crew members aboard was trying to flee three Japanese patrol boats after being accused of fishing illegally in Japan's Exclusive Economic Zone (EEZ). The boat was spotted by South Korean patrol boats, and a standoff between them and the Japanese patrol boats ensued. They "docked against opposite sides of the fishing vessel about 16 miles off the coast of South Korea's southern port city of Ulsan for most of the 34-hour confrontation" in the sea. The standoff ended peacefully after diplomats from both sides reached an agreement, under which the South Korean maritime authorities would conduct an investigation. Should it reveal a violation of Japan's EEZ by the South Korean vessel, its owner would pay a fine of 500,000 yen to the Japanese authorities. Roh reportedly had "urged an early end to the standoff, saying it should be resolved rationally with sovereignty of both countries respected."[84]

The Third "Shuttle Summit Meeting," June 2005

The summit meeting between Roh Moo Hyun and Koizumi that was held in Seoul on June 20 was one of the least productive meetings of its kind. Although preparations had been under way at the working-level for several weeks, the Roh government could not make up its mind about the wisdom of holding the summit until six days before its scheduled date. Roh took the precaution of consulting leaders of political parties, who counseled him to go ahead. Anticipating that the summit would fail to produce substantive results, Roh wanted to share the burden of failure with other politicians. Although billed as the third "shuttle summit," it was held in the Blue House, rather than at a resort. The two leaders wore not informal attire but business suits and neckties. Nor was there a

---

84 "Korea, Japan Strike Deal After 34-hour Standoff at Sea," *Korea Herald*, June 3, 2005; "Han'il haesang taech'i hyopsang t'agyol······Il ch'olsu hagiro" [Compromise Reached in ROK-Japan Standoff at Sea······Japan to Withdraw], *Chosun ilbo*, June 3, 2005.

friendly stroll in the morning after the summit meeting.

The joint press conference following the summit meeting did not feature a carefully choreographed display of harmony but revealed a gaping chasm between the two leaders. Roh Moo Hyun revealed that all but ten minutes of the two-hour meeting had been spent on history-related issues. He said that he and Kozumi had reached two "minuscule-level agreements" (*aju chom najun sujunui habui*). One was to set up a joint historical study panel, which will have under its umbrella a sub-committee on textbooks. The other was that Koizumi would "consider" building another memorial to honor the Japanese citizens who died in wars after considering Japanese public opinion. Roh had initially used the word "agreed" but hastened to retract it.[85]

Roh said that all the issues that had been raised between Seoul and Tokyo—Yasukuni Shrine visits, textbooks, and the differing perspectives on key aspects of colonial rule—had been covered during the meeting. Although both sides made an effort to understand each other through a "candid and sincere exchange of views," Roh said, "nothing has been agreed on" with regard to the issues discussed. There was nonetheless a "definite consensus between Prime Minister Koizumi and me" about the importance of "respecting peace and ceaselessly developing exchanges and cooperative relations."[86]

Roh, then, went on to disclose that he had told Koizumi that "emphasizing peace, expanding exchanges and enhancing cooperation" would not be sufficient to ensure "peace in the future." They need to be accompanied or supplemented by measures to achieve genuine reconciliation based on the shared understanding of the past history and the forging of a consensus regarding the future, Roh said. Finally, turning to Koisumi, Roh said that "unless we resolve the fundamental issues relating to history, small incidents can ignite conflict and [deepen] mutual distrust," expressing his hope that such goal can be attained

---

85 "Han'il chongsang kongdong kija hoegyon palp'yo naeyong" [ROK-Japan Summit, Contents of Joint Press Conference], *Dong-A ilbo*, June 21, 2005.
86 Ibid.

during the tenure of "such a decisive leader as the prime minister."[87]

Koizumi stated at the joint news conference, which, for the first time, did not allow reporters to ask any questions, that "I take very seriously the sentiments held by the South Korean public on issues related to the past, based on a reflection of the course of bilateral relations over the past few months."[88] In contrast to Roh, however, Koizumi highlighted positive aspects of the summit meeting, noting Japan's plan to take certain steps from a humanitarian perspective—notably, (1) the investigation into and return of the remains of people from the Korean Peninsula who were conscripted during World War II, (2) assistance to Koreans in Sakhalin, and (3) assistance to atomic bomb victims living in South Korea. Koizumi also mentioned the agreement to increase the number of daily flights between Haneda and Kimpo airports, which began in November 2003, from four to eight effective August 1. Finally, noting that the next summit meeting would be held in Japan within the year, Koizumi concluded that "it was a fruitful meeting, because we had a frank exchange of opinions."[89]

The press reaction both in Seoul and Tokyo, however, was harsh. It was variously described as the "worst dialogue concerning history,"[90] a "meeting in which not a single forward step was taken,"[91] a "meeting that

---

87 Ibid.; "Han'il chongsang hoedam imochomo—2" [Sketches from the ROK-Japan Summit Meeting—Part 2], ibid., June 21, 2005.

88 "Koizumi, Roh Fail to Agree on History Issues," *Asahi.com*, June 20, 2005, http:// www .asahi.com/english/Herald-asahi/TKY200506200272.html.

89 "Han'il 'yoksa kongdongwi sanha kyokwaso wiwonhoe sinsol'" [Korea and Japan: To Establish Textbook Committee Under the Umbrella of Joint History Research Committee], *Dong-A ilbo*, June 21, 2005; "Han'il chongsang kongdon kija hoegyon palp'yo naeyong," ibid.; Gaimusho, *Koizumi Sori Hokan no Gaiyo, 6-gatsu 20-nichi - 21-nichi, o: Seoul* [A Summary of Prime Minister Koizumi's Visit to the Republic of Korea, June 20-21, Seoul] (Tokyo: June 20, 2005), http://www.mofa.go.jp/mofaj/kaidan/s_koi/ korea_05/ gaiyo.html.

90 "Roh Moo Hyun-Koizumi habui monnirum 'ch'oe'agui yoksa taehwa'" ["The Worst Dialogue Concerning History" In Which Roh Moo Hyun and Koizumi Failed to Reach an Agreement], *Chosun ilbo*, June 21, 2005.

apparently did not produce any substantive agreement,"[92] and a summit "characterized by a heavy atmosphere unfit for two nations marking the 40th anniversary of normalizing diplomatic ties."[93] While *Asahi shinbun* faulted both sides—saying "We are vexed at the way both leaders are obsessed with their ideas and lack flexibility" and "Koizumi needs to show a sincere attitude to lead public opinion"—the *Japan Times* agreed with Roh's statement that "although a willingness for peace, enhanced exchanges and strengthened cooperation are helpful, they will not guarantee peace. Concrete action is necessary. On this account, the heavier responsibility is Mr. Koizumi's."

Post-summit Developments

The persistence of discord did not hamper exchanges and cooperation in bilateral relations. One positive development was Emperor Akihito's surprise visit to a monument honoring Koreans killed on the tiny Pacific island of Saipan during his visit there on June 28. Even though the visit appeared to have been arranged "after Koreans living on Saipan threatened to stage protests over" the Emperor's trip, it nonetheless marked the first time that a Japanese emperor had "paid tribute at a monument dedicated soley to Koreans killed in the war."[94]

On the 60th anniversary of Japan's defeat in World War II on August

---

91 "Chotgarak tulgido 'mugowotdon' manch'an" [Banquet at Which Even Chopsticks Appeared to be "Heavy"], ibid, June 22, 2005.
92 "Agreement At a 'Minuscule Level,'" *Japan Times*, June 22, 2005, an editorial.
93 "Editorial: Japan-S. Korea Summit," *Asahi.com*, June 22, 2005, http://www.asahi.com/english/Herald-asahi/TKY200506220143.html.
94 "Emperor Honors Saipan War Dead," *Japan Times*, June 29, 2005; "Saip'an e kan Akihito Il-wang 'Hanguk wiryongt'ap' chon'gyok pangmun" [Emperor Akihito Visiting Saipan Pays Surprise Visit to "Korean Memorial"], *Joongang ilbo*, June 29, 2005. It should be noted that as this article follows the South Korean press's practice of referring to the Japanese emperor as "Japanese king," I have taken the liberty of replacing it with "emperor."

15, Koizumi apologized for Japan's "past militarism in Asia" and pledged to "uphold its postwar pacifism." Borrowing from the apology Prime Minister Murayama Tomiichi delivered on the 50th anniversary of the war's end in August 1995, Koizumi said: "Our country has caused tremendous damage and pain to the peoples of many countries, especially Asian countries, through colonial rule and invasion. Humbly acknowledging such facts of history, I once again reflect most deeply and offer apologies from my heart." He also reiterated his often-expressed wish to "forge a future-oriented relationship of cooperation based on mutual understanding and confidence with Asian countries by squarely facing up to the past and correctly understanding history."[95]

Koizumi's explicit apology contrasted with a resolution adopted by Japan's House of Representatives on August 2, which merely expressed "regret" (or "reflection"—*hansei* in Japanese) and conspicuously omitted any reference to "colonial rule" and "invasion."[96]

Another noteworthy development pertains to the textbook controversy. When the "selection period for textbooks to be used for four years starting [in] April in public junior high schools ended [on] August 31," opponents of a contentious revisionist history textbook—compiled by the Japanese Society for History Textbook Reform (*Tsukurukai*) and published by Fusosha—learned that it had been adopted by less than 1 percent of junior high schools. A leader of a Japanese civic group that participated in a campaign against the textbook declared a victory for "our grassroots campaign," saying that "the result also showed other

---

95 Norimitsu Onishi, "Koizumi Apologizes for War; Embraces China and South Korea," *New York Times*, August 16, 2005; Shusho Kantei, "Zenkoku Senbotsusha Tsuitoshiki: Naikaku Soridaijin Shikiji"[Prime Minister's Address at the Memorial Service for the Nation's War Dead] (Tokyo: August 18, 2005), http:// www.kantei.go.jp/jp/koizumispeech/2005/08/15sikiji.html.

96 Norimitsu Onishi and Howard W. French, "Ill Will Rising Between China and Japanese," *New York Times*, August 3, 2005; "Sengo 60-nen ketsugi, shu'inde saitaku 'shokuminchi shihai'mararezu" [Resolution on the 60th Year After the War Adopted by the House of Representatives, "Colonial Rule" Omitted], *Asahi shinbun*, August 3, 2005.

Asian people that many Japanese do not support 'the distorted version of historical facts' in the textbook and seek friendship with Japan's neighbors." He also "credited civic groups from South Korea for contributing to the victory by requesting local boards of education not to adopt the textbook and putting ads against the text[book]" in Japan's national and local newspapers.[97]

On September 11, Koizumi won a landslide victory in a general election; his party, the LDP, won 296 seats in the 480-seat House of Representatives. With the addition of 31 seats won by his coalition partner, New Komeito, Koizumi now controlled a two-thirds majority in the lower house of the Japanese Diet.[98] Although the election was largely a referendum on Koizumi's postal reform (privatization) plan, it undoubtedly helped to boost his self-confidence and ability to conduct foreign policy as well.

On September 22, Koizumi and Roh Moo Hyun talked over the telephone for about ten minutes, which were labeled "Japan-ROK summit talks on the telephone" (*Nikkan shuno denwa kaidan*). It was Roh who had called Koizumi to congratulate Koizumi on his landslide victory in the general election. Roh also expressed his appreciation for Japan's contribution to the adoption of a joint statement at the six-party talks. The fourth round of the talks—held in Beijing from July 26 to August 7 and from September 13 to 19—had adopted the first-ever joint statement enumerating broad principles designed to guide the resolution of the North Korean nuclear issue. Koizumi thanked Roh and confirmed that both governments would continue to cooperate closely in the talks. The two leaders also talked about Japan-North Korea relations, with Roh

---

97 Akemi Nakamura, "Groups Against Revisionist History Text Call Campaign a Success," *Japan Times*, September 2, 2005; "Fusosha kyogwaso sasilsang p'aebae" [Fusosha Textbook Practically Defeated], *Hankook ilbo*, August 31, 2005.

98 Kanako Takahara, "Reform Mandate May Help Boost Diplomacy, Experts Say," *Japan Times*, September 13, 2005; "Sosenkyo 2005: tobetsu tosenshasu" [2005 General Election: Number of Elected Candidates by Party], *Yomiuri shinbun*, September 13, 2005.

expressing support for Japan's policy and Koizumi reaffirming his commitment to maintain collaboration with both Seoul and Washington in conducting dialogue with Pyongyang. Finally, Koizumi told Roh that he was looking forward to welcoming Roh to Japan within the year.[99]

As things turned out, however, Koizumi would be denied the pleasure of welcoming Roh to Japan again. For, within a month of the telephone summit, Koizumi caused consternation and anger in Seoul, Beijing and other parts of Asia by visiting Yasukuni Shrine for the fifth time since becoming prime minister in 2001. Mindful of a ruling on September 30 by the Osaka High Court that "his visits to the shrine's main hall of worship had strong religious connotations" and therefore violated the "constitutional provision that stipulates the separation of state and religion," Koizumi did not enter the main hall. He "eliminated much of the pomp of his prior appearances there, wearing a dark suit and blue tie rather than the ceremonial kimono he donned" in 2004. Departing from his previous practice, he did not add his title, prime minister, to his signature in a shrine register.[100]

Predictably, South Korea lodged a strong protest, canceled its foreign minister's scheduled visit to Tokyo for a meeting with his Japanese counterpart, and indicated that Roh might not go to Japan for a summit

---

99 "Kankoku taitoryo, nenmatsu ni honichino mitoshi, Nikkan shunoga denwa kaidan" [ROK President Is Likely to Visit Japan at Year's End, The Leaders of Japan and the ROK Hold Talks on the Telephone], *Asahi shinbun*, September 23, 2005; Gaimusho, *Puresu ririsu: Nikkan shuno denwa kaidan* [Press Release: ROK-Japan Summit Talks on the Telephone] (Tokyo: September 22, 2005), http://www.mofa.go.jp/mofaj/ press/release/17/ris_0922d.html.

100 Martin Fackler, "Japanese Court Rules Premier's Visits to War Shrine Illegal," *New York Times*, October 1, 2005; Norimitsu Onishi, "Asians Angered, Again, by Visit to War Shrine by Japan Leader," ibid., Anthony Faiola, "Koizumi's Shrine Visit Angers Asians, Again," *Washington Post*, October 18, 2005; Nahohito Maeda, "Koizumi's Latest Shrine Visit Has Everyone Looking to His Successor," *Asahi.com*, October 17, 2005, http://www.asahi.com/english/Herald-asahi/TKY200510170373.html; "Shusho no Yasukuni sanpai, Chugoku, Kankoku ga hanpatsu tsuyomeru" [Prime Minister's Yasukuni Visit: Protests in China and South Korea Intensify], *Asahi shinbun*, October 18, 2005.

meeting anytime soon.[101]

The *Japan Times* published an editorial critical of the visit, entitled "What Is Mr. Koizumi Thinking?,"[102] and even the *New York Times* editorially labeled the visit "pointless provocation." To quote a few passages from the latter, "Fresh from an election that showcased him as a modernizing reformer, Prime Minister Junichiro Koizumi of Japan has now made a point of publicly embracing the worst traditions of Japanese militarism······The shrine visit is a calculated affront to the descendants of those victimized by Japanese war crimes, as the leaders of China, Taiwan, South Korea and Singapore quickly made clear······This is exactly the wrong time to be stirring up nightmare memories among the neighbors······It is time for Japan to face up to its history in the 20th century so that it can move honorably into the 21st."[103]

On October 21, South Korea decided at a high-level strategic meeting presided over by Roh to follow a two-track policy toward Japan—that is, Seoul would draw a distinction between areas in which cooperation with Tokyo is indispensable and those in which choice is available. Under this policy, Foreign Minister Ban's visit to Japan was deemed as "indispensable," because it would deal with the issue of bilateral coordination in the six-party talks. Summit meetings, on the other hand, might fall in the discretionary category in the absence of unanticipated developments. This opened the way for Ban's visit to Japan from October 27 to 29.[104]

---

101 "Ban oegyo 'uri chongbu, chwajolgam majo nukkyo'" [Foreign Minister Ban: "Our Government Feels Frustrated"], *Chosun ilbo*, October 18, 2005; "Koizumi sinsa ch'ambae······Han'il kwangye kupsok naenggak" [Koizumi's Shrine Visit······ROK-Japan Relations Cool Rapidly], *Dong-A ilbo*, October 18, 2005.
102 "What Is Mr. Koizumi Thinking?" *Japan Times*, October 19, 2005.
103 "Pointless Provocation in Tokyo," *New York Times*, October 18, 2005, an editorial.
104 "'Orak karak' Ban changgwan kyolguk Ilbon kanda" [Minister Ban "Who Cannot Make Up His Mind" Will Go To Japan After All], *Chosun ilbo*, October 25, 2005; "Kankoku gaisho 'Hisshu fukaketsuna koshowa keizoku'" [ROK Foreign Minister: "Will Continue Indispensable Negotiations"], *Asahi shinbun*, October 27, 2005.

During his visit, Ban conferred with both Foreign Minister Machimura and Prime Minister Koizumi. Ban told Koizumi about the strong opposition by both his government and compatriots to Koizumi's Yasukuni visits but Koizumi repeated his familiar defense of his controversial action. In his talks with Machimura, Ban implied that Roh might not visit Japan for another summit by the year's end.[105]

Instead of going to Tokyo, Roh met Koizumi again in Pusan on the sidelines of an APEC summit on November 19. The meeting, which lasted only 30 minutes, gave Roh another opportunity to criticize Koizumi face-to-face for his visits to Yasukuni Shrine. Roh told Koizumi that the South Korean people deem the visits "totally unacceptable." Koizumi reiterated his well-known justification of his shrine visits. Roh stated that although his government had no intention of asking Japan to apologize again or pay further compensation for damages and sufferings inflicted on the Korean people during colonial rule, it was necessary to resolve the three issues straining bilateral relations—namely, Yasukuni Shrine visits, history textbooks, and Tokdo (Takeshima). On North Korea, Koizumi reiterated Japan's position on the abduction issue, and Roh expressed hope for a peaceful resolution of the issue through working-level negotiations.[106]

The brevity of the Roh-Koizumi meeting contrasted sharply with the Roh-Hu Jintao meeting, which lasted an incredible eight hours. Hu had

---

105 "Kankoku gaisho, Koizumi shusho no Yasukuni sanpai o hinan giron wa heikosen" [ROK Foreign Minister Denounces Prime Minister Koizumi's Yasukuni Visit, Debate Proceeds Along Parallel Lines], *Yomiuri shinbun*, October 29, 2005; "Kankoku gaisho, shin tsuito shisetsu o yokyu, Nikkan gaisho kaidan" [ROK Foreign Minister Demands New Memorial Facility, ROK-Japan Foreign Ministers' Talks], *Asahi shinbun*, October 28, 2005.

106 Norimitsu Onishi, "South Korean Tells Japan's Leader to Stop Visiting Shrine," *New York Times*, November 19, 2005; "Roh Raps Koizumi Anew on Yasukuni," *Japan Times*, November 19, 2005; Gaimusho, *Koizumi Sori Daijin: Pusan APEC shuno kaidan no sai no Nikkan shuno kaidan (gaiyo)* [Prime Minister Koizumi: ROK-Japan Summit Meeting In Conjunction With Pusan APEC Summit (Summary)] (Tokyo: November 18, 2005), http://www.mofa.go.jp/mofaj/kaidan/s_koi/apec_05/s_jk_gai.html.

pointedly refused to hold a one-on-one meeting with Koizumi.[107]

In the ensuing weeks, more things happened that showed the depth to which Japan-ROK relations had plummeted. On November 30, Koizumi said in a speech commemorating the 50th anniversary of the founding of the LDP that visits to Yasukuni Shrine are not subject to diplomatic negotiation. He also stated that the only country in the world that equates an attack against Japan with an attack against itself is the United States; "if we review the past 60 years and think about who can be trusted and with which country we should form an alliance," he continued, "there is no other other country but the United States." Referring to constitutional revision, Koizumi underscored his belief in the indispensability of military capability, arguing that a country that lacks it would be looked down upon by others and anything could happen to such a country.[108]

On December 14 Roh Moo Hyun leveled a thinly-veiled criticism at Koizumi at an international conference. Speaking at the first East Asia Summit (EAS), Roh predicted that East Asian states will follow in the footsteps of the European Union but that a core requirement of such process is a thorough-going reflection (or contrition) on the past order. In his words, "Germany so completely liquidated its past as to give up a part of its territory; nor did it build any memorial facility to honor those who went to war in the name of state and inflicted suffering on their neighbors." [109]

On December 23 Chief Cabinet Secretary Abe Shinzo disclosed that

---

107 "Chongsang hoedam, Hanjung 8-sigan—Han'il un ttag 30-bun" [Summit Meetings: 8 Hours between ROK and China, Mere 30 Minutes between ROK and Japan], *Chosun ilbo*, November 22, 2005.
108 "Han, chung sinsa ch'ambae bip'an ihae mothae, silloe hago tongmaeng maejul nara Migukbbun" ["Cannot Understand Criticism of Shrine Visit by South Korea and China, The US is the Only Country That Is Worthy of Trust and an Alliance Relationship], *Joongang ilbo*, December 2, 2005.
109 "Roh taet'ongnyong, kukje hoe'ui soksangso Il ch'ongni 'myonbak'" [President Roh Reproaches Japanese Prime Minister at an International Conference], *Chosun ilbo*, December 15, 2005.

there would be no budget allocation for a feasibility study concerning a new war memorial during Koizumi's term in office. Abe did not cite public opinion—which Koizumi had promised would be the basis of decision on the memorial—but "the view that it should be a facility where anyone can pay respects without reservations—and not something to be built at the request of other countries." Citing "government sources," *Asahi shinbun* reported that "Koizumi decided on Dec. 8 in consultations with Abe not to include funds for the feasibility study in the budget."[110]

As already noted, cooperation continued unabated at the working-level and in areas that did not stir nationalistic emotions. Japan complied with South Korea's request for a return of a monument honoring Korean volunteers who fought against Japanese invaders led by Toyotomi Hideyoshi in the late16th century. The monument, called the Pukkwan Grand Battle Monument, was presumed to "have been brought to Japan by an Imperial Army officer during the Russo-Japanese War (1904-05)" and stood "on the grounds of Yasukuni Shrine." South Korea planned to return it to North Korea, for it was originally erected in what is now North Hamgyong province. On October 20, the 187 centimeter-high stone monument was flown from Narita to Inchon international airport.[111]

On December 17, Kitagawa Kazuo, Minister of Land, Infrastructure and Transport, revealed that the Japanese government had decided to make the visa waiver for Korean tourists permanent effective February 2006, when the temporary exemption is scheduled to expire.[112] Another

---

110 "Analysis- Koizumi's Scorn Further Delays Study of New War Memorial," *Asahi.com*, December 24, 2005, http://www.asahi.com/english/Herald-asahi/TKY200512240142.html.

111 "South Korea Asks Japan to Return Monument Taken As War Spoils," *Daily Yomiuri*, July 1, 2005; "Pukkwan taech'opbi 100-nyon mane koguk p'umuro" [Pukkwan Grand Battle Monument Returns Home After 100 Years], *Dong-A ilbo*, October 21, 2005.

112 "Kankokujin kankokyaku, biza menjo kokyuka e, Kitagawa kokkyosho ga hyomei" [Visa Exemptions for ROK Tourists to Become Permanent, Tansport Minister Kitagawa Reveals], *Asahi shinbun*, December 18, 2005, evening

example of cooperation is an agreement reached on December 22 at the eighth fisheries talks in Seoul to cut the annual fishing quotas in the exclusive economic zones (EEZs) of Japan and South Korea. The maritime officials of both countries agreed to reduce the quotas from 67,000 tons in 2005 to 63,500 in 2006. The two sides also agreed to trim the number of vessels allowed to operate in their respective EEZs by 36, to 1,050 in 2006.[113] Additionally, on December 24 Japan and South Korea agreed to "allow their airlines to open four new routes between the two countries, including a service linking Hakodate in northern Japan and Seoul." The other new routes will link Asahikawa and Seoul, Sapporo and Pusan, and Hiroshima and Pusan. The two sides also agreed to "increase the number of flights on existing routes between the two countries, including the Akita-Seoul route."[114]

2006: No Sign of a Thaw

As the New Year dawned, the frosty relations between Japan and South Korea continued. The three "old" issues bedeviling the bilateral relationship—Yasukuni Shrine, Takeshima/Tokdo, and textbooks—remained as intractable as ever. Nor did the coexistence of discord and cooperation abate, let alone vanish altogether.

The opening shot in the battle—or, given its intensity and duration, the "war"—of words was fired by Koizumi on January 4 during his New Year's news conference. Defending his visits to Yasukuni Shrine, he said: "I can't understand why foreign governments would intervene in a spiritual

---

edition.
113 "S. Korea, Japan Agree to Cut EEZ Fishing Quotas for 2006," *Yahoo! Australia & NZ Finance*, December 23, 2005, http://au.biz.yahoo.com/051223/17/p/fv4m.html.
114 "Japan, S. Korea Agree to Open 4 New Flight Routes," *Yahoo! News Asia*, December 24, 2005, http:// asia.news.yahoo.com/051224/kyodo/d8emc940c.html.

matter and try to turn it into a diplomatic problem." ROK Foreign Minister Ban Ki Moon responded to Koizumi by saying that the leaders of the Japanese government should listen to their neighbors more carefully to gain a correct understanding of history. "Our government," he added, "believe that it is important for the Japanese government to make an effort to gain trust and respect of other governments."[115]

On January 16, Ban told Japanese reporters in Seoul that unless Koizumi or his successor "makes clear that they will not visit Yasukuni Shrine," Roh would most likely not go to Japan for a summit meeting.[116] Two days later, ROK ambassador to Japan, Ra Jong Yil, called Koizumi's Yasukuni visits a "nightmare" and the "sole issue damaging what could have been more amicable ties between the two neighbors." Ra also expressed his disappointment over "Japan's reluctance to build a secular war memorial," which could help solve the problem.[117]

On January 23, Koizumi again criticized China and South Korea for impeding summit diplomacy using his Yasukuni visits as an excuse. In response to a question in the upper house of the Japanese Diet, he noted that these two Asian countries were the only countries that had problems with his visits. "No [other] national leaders have criticized my visiting Yasukuni Shrine," he said. He suggested he was exercising the Constitutionally guaranteed "freedom of thought."[118] On February 7, it was the lower house's turn to hear Koizumi's criticism of China and

---

115 "Yasukuni mondai 'gaikoku seifu kainyu, rikai dekinai' shusho nento kaiken" [Yasukuni Issue: "Cannot Understand Foreign Government's Interference" Prime Minister's New Year's News Conference], *Asahi shinbun*, January 4, 2005; "Ban oegyo 'Il, chubyonguge kwi kiuryoya'" [Foreign Minister Ban: "Japan Should Listen to Neighboring Countries"], *Dong-A ilbo*, January 5, 2006.
116 "Ban: Roh Visit Won't Happen As Long As PMs Visit Yasukuni," *Daily Yomiuri*, January 17, 2006.
117 Kanako Takahara, "Yasukuni 'Nightmare' for Ties: Seoul Ambassador," *Japan Times*, January 20, 2006.
118 Tetsushi Kajimoto, "Koizumi Not Backing Down on Yasukuni," ibid., January 26, 2006.

South Korea. He called their refusal to hold summit meetings with him "rather abnormal." If he were to heed their call and stop visiting the shrine, then summit talks would materialize, he said. But, he asked rhetorically, would it be good for Japanese diplomacy?[119]

As noted, Koizumi's visits to Yasukuni Shrine has not only irked Japan's neighbors but also drawn criticisms from the Japanese press. In his New Year's news conference, in fact, Koizumi said he didn't understand "why opinion leaders and intellectuals who don't want politics to meddle with freedom of spirit and thought criticize [my action]." This prompted *Asahi shinbun* to publish an editorial entitled, "It Is We Who Cannot Understand."[120]

On February 11, the *New York Times* published an article based on a two-hour interview with what it called a "shadow shogun"—Watanabe Tsuneo, who was the editor-in-chief of Japan's largest newspaper, the *Yomiuri shinbun*. Widely regarded as "Japan's most powerful media baron," Watanabe knew Koizumi well. But he "has railed against [the prime minister], who he says just doesn't listen to him anymore." In his words, "this person Koizumi doesn't know history or philosophy, doesn't study, doesn't have any culture. That's why he says stupid things, like 'What's wrong about worshiping at Yasukuni?' Or, 'China and Korea are the only countries that criticize Yasukuni.' This stems from his ignorance."[121]

On March 1, Roh Moo Hyun devoted more than a half of his speech commemorating the 87th anniversary of the March 1 independence

---

119 "'Yasukuni sanpai shinakereba kaidan—ijoda' Shusho, hihanni mohanron" ["If No Visits to Yasukuni, then Talks—This Is Abnormal" Prime Minister Strongly Refutes Criticism], *Asahi shinbun*, February 8, 2006; "Koizumi Calls Refusal of Summits by China, S. Korea 'Abnormal'," *Kyodo News*, February 8, 2006. http://www.home.kyodo.co.jp/modules/fstStory/index.php.
120 "Shusho nento kaidan, watashi koso rikai dekinu" [Prime Minister's New Year's News Conference: It Is We Who Cannot Understand], *Asahi shinbun*, January 5, 2006, an editorial.
121 Norimitsu Onishi, "Shadow Shogun Steps into Light, to Change Japan," *New York Times*, February 11, 2006.

movement to Seoul-Tokyo relations. He noted that during the preceding year, nothing had changed in Japan's conduct vis-à-vis South Korea, citing "visits to [Yasukuni] Shrine by leaders, distortions in history textbooks, and the Tokdo issue." Japan "is now going so far as to commemorate the day on which it forcibly occupied Tokdo through an aggressive war," he added. "Under these circumstances, one cannot but wonder whether Japan is not moving in the direction of asserting hegemony by justifying its history of aggression and domination."[122]

Without mentioning Koizumi's name, Roh dismissed the Japanese leader's mantra that visits to Yasukuni Shrine were meant to express opposition to wars and personal matters in which other countries should not interfere. The words and deeds of a state's leader, Roh argued, are not something to which he can assign meaning himself but subject to evaluation against objective yardsticks. The latter include "universal human conscience" and "historical experience," he said. Since "Japan has already apologized" for its misdeeds during colonial rule, Roh was asking Japan to "translate apology into practice." "What we oppose is conduct that nullifies apology," he said, citing Germany as an example of a state that has set a "precedent and a standard" for conforming action to apology. "If Japan wishes to become a 'normal state' or a 'leading state in the world,' then it should win the trust of the international community by behaving in accordance with humanity's conscience, instead of changing law and fortifying military capabilities," Roh said.[123]

Koizumi expressed his annoyance to members of the press corps attached to the Prime Minister's Residence by saying that "it is our country's Constitution, which we Japanese shape with our own hands."

---

122 Ch'ongwadae, *Che 87-junyon kinyomsa* [Speech Commemorating the 87th Anniversary] (Seoul: Office of the President, the Republic of Korea, March 1, 2006), http://cwd.go.kr/cwd/kr/archive/popup_archive_print.php?meta_id=sp.

123 Ibid., By the expression "changing laws," Roh was referring to moves in Japan to revise its US-drafted "no war" constitution (Art. 9). The translation I have provided here is not literal but meant to convey Roh's intended meaning.

Roh's comments, he said, amounted to an "interference in [Japan's] internal political affairs." Koizumi also pointed out that the consideration of constitutional amendment by the various political parties has nothing to do with the "fundamental ideology of pacifism," which enjoys wide support from the people." He implied that Roh's remarks reflected a lack of understanding of Japan.[124] Chief Cabinet Secretary Abe Shinzo urged Roh to "take a close look at Japan's path to protect freedom, democracy and human rights and its efforts to establish peace in the world."[125]

On March 30 the textbook issue emerged as a bone of contention again. The revelation that Japan's education ministry—officially called the Ministry of Education, Culture, Sports, Science and Technology—"ordered revisions to most references made to two groups of islets at the center of territorial disputes"—the Senkaku Islands and the Takeshima (Tokdo) islets—so that they would be called Japanese territory infuriated Seoul. Although there were other revisions repugnant to Japan's Asian neighbors, South Korea focused its attention on Tokdo. Foreign Minister summoned Japan's ambassador to Seoul, Oshima Shotaro, to lodge a strong protest, describing as "unacceptable" Japan's "infringement upon our sovereignty." There was a chorus of condemnation from politicians, the public, and the media as well.[126]

---

124 "Kankoku taitoryo no Nihon no kenpo kaisei hihan, Koizumi shushoga fukaikan" [ROK President's Criticism of the Revision of Japan's Constitution, Prime Minister Koizumi Feels Displeasure], *Asahi shinbun*, March 2, 2006.
125 "Roh Raps Constitutional Change," *Japan Times*, March 2, 2006.
126 "Textbooks Given State Makeover," ibid., March 30, 2006; "Kyokasho kentei, Mombusho ga nanshoku, Yasukuni sosho no kijutsu meguri" [Textbook Screening, Education Ministry Disapprove, A Tour of Description of Yasukuni Lawsuits], *Asahi shinbun*, March 30, 2006, evening edition; "Ban Ki Moon Oegyo 'Tokdo chukwon hueson padadurilsu opsso'" [Foreign Minister: "Infringement of Tokdo Sovereignty Unacceptable], *Chosun ilbo*, April 1, 2006; "Yoya 'Il kyogwaso Tokdo p'amun' kangnyok pip'an" [Government and Opposition Parties Strongly Criticize Japanese Textbook Tokdo Controversy], ibid; "Sasol; Ilbon ui anha mu'in ape Taehan minguk chongbu nun odi innunga"[Editorial: Where is the ROK Government in the Face of Audacious Japan], ibid; "Japan's New Provocation Over Dokdo,"

On April 6 the South Korean press reported than an internal report prepared by Japan's foreign ministry concluded that Roh Moo Hyun's hard line toward Japan was related to South Korea's domestic politics. Roh's principal motive in pursuing a hard-line Japan policy, the report allegedly asserted, was to "avoid being labeled a lame duck president." Given this, Roh was most likely to adhere to such policy for a long time, perhaps until his term ends. With regard to Tokdo, the report saw a series of actions by the Roh government—such as making the islets a tourist destination, the flight of a squadron of fighter jet led by the air force chief of staff over them, and visits by members of the Cabinet and the National Assembly—as being aimed at stirring up domestic public opinion and fanning nationalistic sentiments.[127]

South Korea requested Japan to confirm the veracity of the press report but Tokyo declined to do so. Chief Cabinet Secretary Abe Shinzo said at a press conference in Tokyo that it was "international common sense" not to clarify either the existence or the contents of such reports. All this made Seoul suspicious. Foreign Minister Ban said in a press briefing that if the alleged report is authentic and its contents jibe with what has been reported, then it was a grave matter; he could not contain his anger.[128] On April 13, Ambassador Oshima said in Seoul that the Japanese government's thinking differed from what the South Korean press had reported as the contents of an internal report. He did not, however, confirm whether such report really exists, invoking the policy of the Japanese Foreign Ministry that prohibits either confirmation or

---

Korea Herald, April 1, 2006.

127 Although the report on the alleged internal report first appeared in *Joongang ilbo*, it quickly made headlines in all newspapers and news broadcasts. "Seoul Protests Japanese Report on Roh as Lame Duck," *Korea Herald*, April 6, 2006; "Il oemusong naebu pogoso 'p'amun'······Han'il kwangye 'asul asul'" [Commotion Over the Japanese Foreign Ministry's Internal Report······ Perilous Moment for ROK-Japan Relations], *Chosun ilbo*, April 6, 2006.

128 "Ban oegyo: 'Il oemusong pogoso punno kumhalsu opta'" [Foreign Minister Ban: "I Cannot Contain Anger Over the "Japanese Foreign Ministry Report"], *Chosun ilbo*, April 6, 2006.

denial.[129]

Hardly had the "internal report" controversy subsided when another dispute loomed on the horizon. On April 14 the Japanese government announced a plan to "send a Japan Coast Guard vessel to conduct maritime surveys in the Sea of Japan near" Takeshima (or Tokdo). In Seoul Vice Foreign Minister Yu Myung Hwan summoned Ambassador Oshima to the Foreign Ministry and "demanded an immediate halt to the survey, saying it would intrude upon South Korea's Exclusive Economic Zone." Oshima rejected the demand on the ground that "the survey will be conducted within Japan's EEZ and in accordance with international maritime law."[130]

Actually, the "EEZs claimed by the two countries overlap near the island." Four rounds of talks, held from 1996 to 2000, broke down, leaving the overlapping claims unresolved. Seoul saw the Japanese plan as "the latest in its efforts to draw international attention to the territorial dispute over the islands located in a rich fishing area and near natural gas deposits."[131] While Japan urged Seoul to take a "cool-headed" approach, respect each other's rights, and conform to international law, South Korea threatened to use force to block Japan from conducting the survey. Roh Moo Hyun accused Japan of scheming to "justify its history of aggression," seeing the planned survey in the context of a surge of chauvinistic nationalism in Japan.[132] The stakes were high, and tensions were rising. As Japan's *Jiji* Press speculated, "if Tokyo decides to go for the

---

129 "Oemusong pogoso podo naeyong Il chongbu saenggak kwa talla" [Reported Contents of Foreign Ministry Report Differ From What the Japanese Government Thinks], *Joongang ilbo*, April 14, 2006.
130 "Oshima Rejects South Korean Request to Cancel Survey Near Disputed Islets," *Japan Times*, April 15, 2006; Ryu Jin, "S. Korea Urges Japan to Scrap Survey Plan Near Dokdo," *Korea Times*, April 14, 2006.
131 "Seoul Protests Japanese Survey near Dokdo Islets," *Korea Herald*, April 15, 2006.
132 "Roh taitoryo: Takeshima mondai de hihan 'shinryaku no rekishi o seitoka suru koi'" [President Roh: Criticizes Takeshima Issue "Behavior Aimed At Justifying History of Aggression"], *Mainichi shinbun*, April 19, 2006.

plan despite South Korea's warnings……, it could lead to seizures of vessels and end up with a helpless situation for the two neighboring countries."[133]

Two days of intense negotiations in Seoul between the vice foreign ministers of the two countries, however, produced a compromise settlement, in which both sides made concessions. In exchange for South Korea's commitment to postpone its plan to "push for the registration of Korean names for seabed topography near the Dokdo islets……at an international ocean-mapping conference to be held in June in Germany," Japan agreed to suspend its plan to conduct the survey Seoul had objected so vehemently. Neither side, however, abandoned their respective plans. Hence their agreement was tantamount to a stop-gap measure. The seeds of conflict remained intact. Their agreement to resume negotiations on drawing up EEZ boundaries did not appear too promising, given the irreconcilable differences between them.[134]

Cooperation Continues Despite Friction

Notwithstanding the unending series of unpleasant incidents and the seeming intractability of the key disputes, bilateral relations between Japan and South Korea plodded along. Trade and other economic interactions remained robust, and cultural and human exchanges continued to expand. In 2005, for example, the value of merchandise trade between Tokyo and Seoul increased 11.4 percent, although the persistence of imbalance in favor of Japan continued to pose a problem for South Korea. (See Table 5). As for human exchange, the number of visitors traveling between the two countries increased 5 percent over the

---

133 "S. Korea Ready to Use Force to Block Japan's Survey Near Disputed Isles," *Mainichi Daily News*, April 17, 2006.
134 Jung Sung-ki, "Japan Withdraws Maritime Survey Plan," *Korea Times*, April 24, 2006; "Sighs of Relief over Takeshima Deal," *Daily Yomiuri*, April 24, 2006.

preceding year—to 4.2 million.¹³⁵

To note some of the positive developments in the early months of 2006, we may begin with the agreement signed on January 20 to gradually increase Japan's import quota on South Korean *nori* (laver). Under the agreement, the quota in 2015 will be five times the 2004 quota. This agreement prompted Seoul to drop its complaint against Japan filed with the World Trade Organization.¹³⁶ On January 20, the two countries signed a treaty on mutual legal assistance in criminal matters. The treaty obligates Japan and South Korea to "provide mutual legal assistance in connection with investigations, prosecutions and other proceedings in criminal matters."¹³⁷

On February 4, the finance ministers of Japan and South Korea agreed in Tokyo to more than double the "amount of funds they can swap in emergency situations." Their "emergency currency swap" ceilings will increase from $7 billion to $15 billion. Under the new bilateral swap agreement, the two countries will be able to "swap their local currencies against the U.S. dollar in times of emergency, with Japan committing $10 billion and Korea $5 billion."¹³⁸

On February 6, the Japanese government decided to "exempt visas of ROK nationals, who wish to enter Japan as temporary visitors for a period of 90 days or less, from March 1, on the premise that the ROK government will take the same measure for Japanese nationals."¹³⁹

---

135 "Han'il 'chollyak taehwa': uimi wa chonmang" [ROK-Japan "Strategic Dialogue": Significance and Prospects], *Joongang ilbo*, February 25, 2006.
136 "Nikkan nori funso kaiketsu taketsu, yunyu waku no dankaiteki kakudai de koi" [ROK-Japan Dispute on Laver Resolved, Agreed on Phased Expansion of Import Quotas], *Asahi shinbun*, January 21, 2006.
137 Ministry of Foreign Affairs of Japan, *Signing of a Mutual Legal Assistance Treaty between Japan and the Republic of Korea* (Tokyo: January 20, 2006), http://www.mofa.go.jp/announce/announce/2006/1/ 0120.html.
138 "Korea, Japan to Double Currency Swaps," *Korea Herald*, February 6, 2006.
139 Ministry of Foreign Affairs of Japan, *Exemption of Temporary Visitors' Visa for Nationals of the Republic of Korea* (Tokyo: February 6, 2006), http://www.mofa.go.jp/announce/announce/2006/2/ 0206.html.

On March 6, the second round of "strategic dialogue" between the two countries occurred in Tokyo. The first round was held in Seoul in October 2005. Representing both countries were Yu Myung Hwan, Seoul's First Vice Minister for Foreign Affairs and Trade and Yachi Shotaro, Tokyo's Vice Foreign Minister. The two sides exchanged views on "how the two countries can cooperate in building peace and stability in Northeast Asia, in achieving early resumption of the Six Party Talks" as well as their respective bilateral relations with the US. They also discussed their own bilateral relations with emphasis on how to improve them, noting that they "share the fundamental value of liberal democracy and market economy and are also allies of the United States."[140]

On March 29, Japan and South Korea exchanged *Notes Verbale* concerning working holiday visas, which "will increase the number of annual issuance of working holiday visas by both governments under the Japan-ROK Working Holiday Program from the current 1,800 to 3,600 in 2006." This increase 'will be implemented as part of the Japan-ROK Joint Project for the Future that supports youth, sport and grass-root exchanges."[141]

In sum, in the first four months of 2006, the bilateral relations between Japan and South Korea remained close and in some ways were becoming closer. As long as the history-related sources of strain persist, however, the two neighboring countries' laudable goal, repeatedly reaffirmed in summit meetings, of forging a future-oriented bilateral relationship will remain elusive.

---

140 Idem, *Visit to Japan of Mr. Yu Myung-Hwan, First Vice Minister for Foreign Affairs and Trade of the Republic of Korea* (Tokyo: March 6, 2006), http://www.mofa.go.jp/announce/announce/2006/3/0306-2.html.
141 Idem, *Expanded Issuance of Visas under ROK-Japan Working Holiday Program* (Tokyo: March 30, 2006), http://www.mofa.go.jp/announce/announce/2006/3/0330-3.html.

Conclusion

How may one account for the resilience of discord in Japan-ROK relations? Why do the old issues—Yasukuni Shrine visits, history textbooks, and the dispute over Tokdo/Takeshima—continue to haunt the two states that are de facto allies so tenaciously? To what extent do the insights of the contending schools of thought in the International Relations literature help illuminate the patterns of behavior displayed by Japan and South Korea toward each other?

Does the postulate of rationality, for example, find support, however feeble, in the behavior of either Japan or South Korea or both? What is the relative weight of ideational versus material factors in deciphering each state's conduct? What of the relative influence of external setting as opposed internal political dynamics? Does the concept of two-level game help explain the behavior of Koizumi and Roh Moo Hyun?

To begin with the Yasukuni Shrine issue, it is not an exaggeration to say that during the period covered in this chapter, the issue has been synonymous with Koizumi. To be sure, other politicians in Japan, including lawmakers and Cabinet members, have visited the shrine but it is Koizumi's visit that Seoul, Beijing, and other victims of Japanese militarism find most infuriating. For, in their eyes, he personifies the Japanese nation, and his plea that he is not acting as prime minister when he "prays for peace" at the shrine is not convincing even to his own compatriots, let alone to those who live in lands colonized or occupied by Japan in the past..

Koizumi's perception of his own identity as a man who keeps his campaign pledge, who is not swayed by foreign reaction, and who is intensely nationalistic at heart may go a long way toward explaining the obstinacy with which he has made his annual visits to the shrine. Domestic politics also appear to have played a role. His need to appease or appeal to the conservative constituency and confidence gained by a landslide victory in a general election may have influenced the timing of his visits.

The singular durability of the textbook issue—which has bedeviled

Japan's relations with the former victims of its colonial rule and aggressions since the 1970s—owes in part to the conservative proclivity of the education ministry and in part to the growing strength of nationalism in Japan. The low adoption rate of the most controversial history textbook published by Fusosha shows, however, the kind of chauvinistic nationalism espoused by Japan's right-wing revisionist historians does not appeal to the mainstream of Japanese society. The development in early 2006, in which Japan's education ministry emerged as the principal proponent or guardian of nationalistic historiography, is mystifying. Did it signal the ascendancy of ultra-conservatism in the traditionally nationalistic ministry?

The territorial dispute surrounding Takeshima/Tokdo is fueled by a complex array of factors, both ideational and material. Ideationally, nationalism is a potent driving force for both Japan and South Korea. The timing of Japan's formal incorporation of the disputed group of islets leads Koreans to equate it with Japanese colonialism. Had this not been the case, the dispute would have become purely territorial. Material considerations also enter into the equation. The waters near the islets are rich fishing grounds. The possibility also exists that the adjoining subsoil may contain valuable mineral deposits, including crude oil.

Can the behavior of the two states be adjudged rational? Japan's periodic assertion of sovereignty over Takeshima meets the criteria of rationality, for it is the only way to prevent South Korea that controls the islets *de facto* from becoming their *de jure* owner as well. Under international law, title to *terra nullius* can be consolidated only through "continuous and peaceful" display of authority over a long period of time. Protests by other states have the effect of making display of authority less than peaceful. Failure to protest, on the other hand, will over time be construed as acquiescence—that is, an implicit acceptance of another state's claim of ownership.[142]

---

142 For an exposition of the relevant legal principles and case-law, see Lori Fisler Damrosch et al., *International Law: Cases and Materials*. 4th ed. (St. Paul: MN, 2001), 315-46.

From this perspective, then, South Korea's response to Japan's periodic assertion of sovereignty over Tokdo may not necessarily be rational. Not only do protests and condemnation have no effect on Japan's policy on the issue but they can be counter-productive as well. For South Korea may end up accentuating the non-peaceful nature of its *de facto* control of the islets.

Just as Koizumi's stubborn refusal to heed the pleas or advice regarding visits to Yasukuni Shrine can be construed as being driven in part by his identity and in part by political needs, so Roh Moo Hyun's transformation from a pragmatist into a hard-liner in his Japan policy lends itself to an interpretation highlighting his identity and political needs.

As the first member of the post-World War II generation to be elected South Korea's president, Roh Moo Hyun did not have a visceral distrust of Japan. He was the first ROK president not to seek an apology or an expression of regret from the emperor during a state visit. His promise not to raise any history-related issue vis-à-vis Japan during his term of office was as unprecedented as it was imprudent. As things turned out, he broke the promise after seven months in a way that jolted Koizumi. For in his speech to the nation on March 1, 2006, Roh did not simply raise historical issues but harshly criticized Koizumi as well. Roh's relations with Koizumi deteriorated rapidly. Koizumi, of course, provided ammunition to Roh by making his annual pilgrimage to Yasukuni Shrine.

Roh's political problems at home were much worse than what Koizumi faced in Japan. One needs only to recall that he was the only president ever impeached in South Korean political history. Koizumi's provocative behavior and, in Seoul's eyes, self-serving rhetoric justifying his Yasukuni visits, then, gave Roh an opportunity to rally his compatriots to the flag. Except for a lonely voice or two in the wilderness, few criticisms were hurled at Roh's hard-line policy toward Japan. The furor over the Japanese Foreign Ministry's alleged internal report in April 2006 takes on a new meaning in this context. What the report is alleged to have contained—e.g., Roh's hard line toward Japan was related to his weak political base and lame-duck status—was not off the mark by any means.

The report, if it really existed as seems to have been the case, was, in effect, expounding the theory (or, more accurately, hypothesis) of "two-level game" a la Robert Putnam.

Finally, the ascendancy of cooperation in 2002 owed, to a striking extent, to an external factor—the co-hosting of FIFA World Cup Korea/Japan. It was a classic win-win situation, in which both of the co-hosts basked in the limelight of global publicity and enjoyed the thrills of victory in the playing fields. In the process, the two countries and peoples became a little closer, too.

In sum, not only do the patterns of interaction between Japan and South Korea in the second half of the fourth decade of their diplomatic normalization remain strikingly consistent but they lend themselves to a theoretically-oriented or conceptually-informed interpretation as well.

CHAPTER 9

Conclusion

What does the preceding record of interactions between Japan and the two Korean states reveal about the sources, patterns, and consequences of cooperation and conflict? What are the most notable differences between the two dyads, Japan-ROK and Japan-DPRK? What effect, if any, did political succession or change in each of the three countries have on their respective policies? Did North Korean policy toward Japan change to any measurable degree in the post-Kim Il Sung era? What difference did South Korea's transition to democracy make in its relationship with Japan? Did Japan's policy toward the two Korean states manifest any notable change after the four decades of LDP hegemony ended and the era of coalition politics began in 1993?

Japan-DPRK vs. Japan-ROK

Notwithstanding fundamental differences, the Japan-DPRK and the

Japan-ROK relationships share the principal source of discord that has proved to be singularly durable: the historical legacy of colonial rule. The specific issues that legacy has spawned, such as "comfort women" and history textbooks, continue to provide grist for controversy and acrimony, causing disruptions of inter-state and even non-governmental intercourse.

Differences between the two sets of relationships, however, are far-reaching. First and foremost, the presence or absence of diplomatic relations sets them apart. Whereas Japan and the ROK established full diplomatic relations in 1965, Japan and the DPRK have yet to make any notable headway in their intermittent negotiations for diplomatic normalization, which began in the early 1990s, were suspended for seven and a half years, resumed in early 2000 but suspended again by the fall of the same year. This pattern continued in the subsequent years, with normalization talks resuming in the fall of 2002 in the aftermath of a historic summit meeting between Kim Jong Il and Koizumi Junichiro but entering an impasse anew. One more round, the 13th, was held in February 2006, leaving open the possibility that more will follow.

Second, the two dyads differ sharply in security relations. Whereas Japan and the ROK are quasi-allies sharing a common alliance partner, the United States, Japan and the DPRK count each other as potential adversary, a source of perceived threat to their respective national security.

Finally, the magnitude of economic relations defies comparison. In 2005 the value of trade between Tokyo and Seoul was 365 times that of Tokyo-Pyongyang trade. Japan and South Korea count each other among their most important trading partners. The perennial imbalance in trade in Tokyo's favor means, however, that the Japan-ROK economic relationship can best be described as one of asymmetric interdependence.

What all this suggests, then, is that Japan's relations with the ROK is marked more by cooperation than by conflict, while the reverse is true of Japan's relations with the DPRK. The sources of conflict differ, too. Even though, as noted, historical legacy is shared by the two dyads, other issues are specific to each. Between Japan and North Korea, abductions of Japanese nationals by North Korean agents and North Korea's firing of a missile over Japan in 1998 have caused a great deal of discord, with the former remaining as the single most important hurdle to be overcome.

Between Japan and South Korea, on the other hand, in addition to historical legacy, the territorial dispute over Takeshima/Tokdo and fishing in waters claimed but not controlled by Japan have strained bilateral relations. Nor were the manner in which historical legacy manifested itself as a source of discord in Tokyo-Seoul relations and the intensity with which the dispute was waged duplicated in Tokyo-Pyongyang relations. The controversy over Japanese history textbooks that, in Seoul's eye, whitewash Japanese aggression and colonial-era misdeeds and Prime Minister Koizumi's visits to Yasukuni Shrine that have bedeviled Japan-DPRK relations since 2001 have no parallel in Japan-DPRK relations, in which the abduction issue has eclipsed all others. The North's demand for a liquidation of the legacy of Japanese colonial rule, to be sure, is a bone of contention in Pyongyang-Tokyo relations but the degree to which it directly affects their bilateral relations does not even begin to compare with the situation in Seoul-Tokyo relations. This difference may be attributable to the absence of diplomatic relations between the two countries.

North Korea's Japan Policy

Did political succession in North Korea following the death of Kim Il Sung in July 1994 produce any change in its policy toward Japan? At the most basic level, that is to say, in terms of strategic goals, one sees continuity, not change. The single most important change, it must be stressed, occurred during the final years of Kim's 36-year rule: North Korea's decision to seek diplomatic normalization with Japan. Eight rounds of inter-governmental talks on normalization spanning two years occurred under Kim's watch. The goal the DPRK pursued tirelessly, albeit unsuccessfully, was to extract maximum compensation from Japan coupled with an explicit official apology for Japan's misdeeds during its colonial rule in Korea. In other words, the North sought both material and ideational gains in its diplomatic negotiations with Japan.

Tactically, however, change has occurred in the post-Kim Il Sung era. Kim Jong Il's decision to seek food assistance from Japan in 1995 marked a departure from his late father's policy. More dramatic was his bold decision, perhaps a gamble, to host a summit meeting with Japanese Prime Minister Koizumi in September 2002. His stunning admission that North Korean agents had kidnapped 13 Japanese nationals in the 1970s and 1980s and apology to Koizumi, have helped to transform Pyongyang-Tokyo relations in a major way. The revelation that eight of the 13 abductees had died in the North and Pyongyang's failure to provide a convincing explanation of the circumstances of their deaths have strained the bilateral relations ever since.

In North Korean foreign policy, ideational considerations play a pivotal role, frequently outweighing material ones. Concern for national pride and dignity and the need to preserve the integrity of its unique political system—in short, the DPRK's state identity—have helped to shape its tactical behavior. Had it not been for the priority given to ideational concerns, the North could have made more headway in its normalization talks with Japan and reaped sizable economic benefits in the short and medium term. Pyongyang's reluctance, perhaps inability, to divulge the full truth about the deaths of the Japanese abductees is most probably related to its state identity.

The North's tactical repertoire has also included its deft utilization of unanticipated developments, turning them into opportunities to bolster its bargaining position but this exemplifies continuity rather change.

To the extent that continuity has eclipsed change between the Kim Il Sung and post-Kim Il Sung eras, one can see the effects of the manner in which political succession was implemented in the North. The first-ever hereditary succession in a Communist country, the transfer of power from Kim Il Sung to his elder son, Jong Il, occurred incrementally in accordance with a carefully-crafted plan over two decades. In a substantive sense, political succession appeared to have been completed before Kim Il Sung's death. For, due to his failing eyesight, he was unable to read any reports or documents but depended on oral reports and tape-recorded material prepared by Jong Il. This, coupled with Kim Jong Il's control over the military, meant that Kim Jong Il actually *ruled* the DPRK, with Kim Il Sung's role being elevated to that of *reigning*.[1]

Add to the above Kim Jong Il's pressing need not only to keep intact but to constantly draw on the legacy of his father, the principal source of his own legitimacy. Against this backdrop, continuity in the fundamental complexion of the North Korean state, its reigning ideology, and strategic objectives is as natural as it is imperative.

As already noted, however, the Kim Jong Il regime has displayed a somewhat higher degree of flexibility and pragmatism in its tactical behavior than its predecessor did. In 1995 North Korea requested and received rice aid from both Japan and South Korea. Although the magnitude of food shortage may have been the key factor in the equation, the North Korean action nonetheless showed that, while continuing to pay lip service to *chuch'e sasang*, the post-Kim Il Sung regime was prepared to set aside national pride, a core concept of *chuch'e*, in quest of pragmatic solutions to a national crisis.

On the other hand, inasmuch as the basic nature of the political system has remained unchanged, the Kim Jong Il regime has continued to manifest a hard line as well. The rocket launch over Japan in August 1998 and the tactical behavior displayed in the second stage of normalization talks with Japan in 2000 and beyond exemplify this reality. All in all, while political succession in North Korea appears to have produced only marginal changes in the idiosyncrasies of its political system, its policy toward Japan has entered a new stage of intermittent but contentious inter-governmental negotiations at levels, high and low. The two summit meetings between Kim Jong Il and Koizumi may well mark a watershed in Pyongyang-Tokyo relations, should they eventually lead to diplomatic normalization.

---

1 B. C. Koh, "The North Korean Political System Under Kim Jong Il: A Comparative Perspective" in *North Korea in Transition and Policy Changes: Domestic Structure and External Relations*, ed. Jae Kyu Park (Seoul: Kyungnam University Press, 1999), 28-57.

South Korea's Policy toward Japan

If one were to use South Korea's transition to democracy as a benchmark, can one find any notable differences in its policy toward Japan between the pre-transition and the post-transition periods? Democratic transition began in the waning months of Chun Doo Hwan's Fifth Republic, with Roh Tae Woo's June 29, 1987 declaration laying the groundwork and becoming a reality when he was elected as president in December of the same year and inaugurated in February of the following year. Although South Korea has been making steady progress toward consolidating its hard-won democracy ever since, it still has some distance to travel before the goal is fully attained. South Korea, in other words, can best be described as a democratizing state, rather than a full-fledged democracy.

To note continuity first, one is struck by the resiliency of old issues—historical legacy and territorial dispute. One also finds the potency of ideational factors, which on many occasions appear to have outweighed material considerations. The role of regime identity in shaping Seoul's policy toward Tokyo has remained undiminished, even though its relative strength and, in particular, thrust have varied.

In the realm of change one can discern the growing potency of public opinion and bureaucratic politics in post-transition South Korea. The decision to build a wharf on the disputed island of Tokdo/Takeshima in February 1996 appears to have been shaped less by a real need than by the desire of a new government agency, the Ministry of Maritime Affairs and Fisheries, to raise its visibility and assert its jurisdictional prerogative. When Japanese Foreign Minister Ikeda criticized Seoul's move, reiterating Tokyo's long-standing claim of sovereignty over the island, it made banner headlines in the South Korean press. This in turn provoked a nationalistic reaction from the public, leaving the Kim Young Sam government little choice but to take a hard line.

Can the Kim Dae Jung government's quest for a new "partnership" with Japan be construed as a fruit of democratization as well? While his election as president owed in no small measure to the fragmentation of the vote among multiple candidates, it also signaled the triumph of democracy. South Korea's most prominent dissident who had narrowly escaped death at the hands of authoritarian regimes twice, Kim Dae Jung enjoyed a visibility and respect abroad, especially in Japan, which proved to be a great asset in his conduct of summit diplomacy.

Roh Moo Hyun, Kim's successor, began his presidency with a relatively open mind. As the first ROK president who had no personal memory of Japanese colonial rule, Roh must have been a breath of fresh air from Japan's perspective. His decision not to seek an expression of regret from the Emperor during his state visit to Japan and promise not to raise history-related issues vis-à-vis Japan in his term of office bespoke a regime identity that was tailor-made to strengthen Seoul-Tokyo relations. Both external and internal factors helped to change all this. Externally, the frequency with which disputes erupted in the bilateral relations—centering on the old issues of Tokdo/Takeshima, history textbooks, and Yasukuni Shrine—has generated a need for a firm response. Internally, both public opinion and his weak political base drove him to embrace a hard line toward Japan.

Japan's Policy toward the Korean Peninsula

Although the Liberal Democratic party's loss of power in 1993 proved to be short-lived, for it managed to return to power within a year in coalition with the Socialists and Sakigake, the end of the LDP's monopoly of power that year marked a watershed in Japanese politics. One may therefore be justified in labeling the period since 1993 as the post-hegemonic era. Has Japan's policy toward the two Koreas, then, been affected by the end of LDP hegemony in any way?

If anything changed in Japan's Korea policy in the post-hegemonic era, it was confined largely to the realm of rhetoric and style. Substantively, very little appears to have changed. A number of factors help account for this. First, the non-LDP government, one in which the erstwhile ruling party was relegated to the sidelines, lasted less than a year, which is far too brief for any new policy to crystallize. Second, the difficulty of forging a consensus on key policy issues among the seven coalition parties allowed the bureaucracy to exercise more influence than ever before, thus sharply limiting the probability of any new initiative being launched.

Third, although the LDP returned to power in June 1994 as a member of a three-party coalition government, it was nonetheless the dominant coalition partner. The appearance of a Socialist prime minister, therefore, seemed to make little difference in Japan's Korea policy. If anything, it was during Murayama Tomi'ichi's 18-month tenure as prime minister that Tokyo-Seoul relations witnessed a serious diplomatic setback: Seoul's unprecedented canceling of a summit meeting between Murayama and Kim Young Sam.

One must hasten to add that the dichotomy between rhetoric and substance can sometimes be misleading in analyzing foreign policy. In Japan's relations with the two Koreas, in particular, rhetoric can serve as either a source of discord or a catalyst of cooperation. The diplomatic setback noted above, in fact, stemmed not from any substantive actions but from rhetoric emanating from Tokyo that Seoul found offensive. It would, therefore, be a mistake to minimize the significance of Prime Minister Hosokawa Morihiro's rhetoric when he visited South Korea in November 1993 as the head of the first non-LDP coalition government. For Hosokawa went further than any of his predecessors in expressing his desire to liquidate Japan's negative historical legacy in Korea. Not only was he more specific about what Japan had actually done during the colonial period than any of his predecessors, citing things that touched the very identity of the Korean people such as forbidding the use of Korean and forcing the Korean people to adopt Japanese names, but he was also unstinting in his apology for Japan's misdeeds.

On balance, however, there were more occasions when rhetoric served to generate ill feelings and strain bilateral relations than those when the opposite happened. As noted, Murayama's 18-month tenure as prime minister witnessed a rash of statements by heavy-weight politicians, including the prime minister himself, that Koreans perceived as glossing over Japan's past aggression and misdeeds.

The strains in Tokyo-Seoul relations during Koizumi's long tenure as prime minister, on the other hand, owed not to rhetoric alone but to a combination of events that had both material and ideational ramifications. The dispute over Takeshima/Tokdo, for example, was fueled not only by nationalistic emotions but also by fishing interests and access to mineral resources, either imagined or real. The controversy generated by history textbooks and Koizumi's annual visits to Yasukuni Shrine, however, had very little to do with material interests. It was predominantly, even exclusively, ideational factors that were at stake.

The Relative Importance of "Explanatory" Variables

Although it is unwise, if not reckless, to generalize about the relative weights of different variables, can we nonetheless hazard a brief impressionistic assessment based on our survey in the preceding chapters? National interests plainly affect the behavior of all three states. National interests, however, can be objectively defined only at a very high level of abstraction—such as security, development, and legitimacy. The actual linkage between each of these components on the one hand and policy outputs on the other is contingent upon each state's perceptions— that is, how the components are defined and perceived. Security, for example, has a strong subjective dimension. How a state sees its own security is the ultimate determinant of its behavior. This, as is well known, gives rise to the vicious circle of an arms race and a security dilemma. In the Japan-ROK dyad, security in terms of mutual threat perception plays a negligible role. It is mainly because they have a common ally that security becomes an issue or a context in which bilateral relations are conducted. Sharing a common threat, i.e., North Korea, can also be important but the surge of inter-Korean cooperation since 2000 has spawned a perception gap between Seoul and Tokyo vis-à-vis Pyongyang.

What of power? One thing that is beyond question is that diffuse power is less important than issue-specific power. The overwhelming superiority of Japan's economic power, for example, has not always given Tokyo an edge in its relations with either Seoul or Pyongyang. Issue-specific power, however, is another matter. The abduction issue has given the North bargaining leverage, although Japan's economic power looms large in Pyongyang's calculus as well—that is, the latter's hope for a huge economic payoff has helped to keep normalization talks alive.

Ideational factors help shape the behavior of all three states but they are more salient in North Korea than in the other two. Pyongyang's state identity, as already noted, plays a pivotal role, eclipsing material interests. Domestic politics can be a potent variable in international relations, as one can see in the linkage between Koizumi's visits to Yasukuni Shrine and South Korea's policy toward Japan, especially the latter's refusal to hold a summit meeting in Japan.

External setting obviously conditions the policies of all three states to varying degrees. The salutary effects of co-hosting FIFA World Cup Korea/Japan 2002 on the two countries' relations in the political and cultural realms have already been noted. A change in North Korea's posture toward Japan during Six-party Talks—a reversal of the policy of refusing to hold bilateral talks on the sidelines of the multilateral conference—also signaled the impact of external setting, for the reversal occurred on the heels of Koizumi's landslide victory in a general election.

If one were to assign relative weights to the preceding variables, one might be excused for placing ideational variables at the top. The role played by history-related issues in Japan-ROK relations, with both sides being driven primarily by ideational considerations, lends support to such choice. North Korean behavior in its dispute with Japan clearly points to a similar conclusion.

Domestic politics, encapsulated in the vocabulary of "two-level game," may merit a distant second place. In the case of North Korea, however, domestic politics take on a different meaning—the idiosyncrasies of its leader-dominated system that extols the national ideology of *chuch'e* (autonomy, self-reliance) and related values of national pride and dignity. Although, as noted, pragmatism overrides ideology from time to time, the need to safeguard state identity has proved to be the dominant factor in molding Pyongyang's international conduct.

On a less exalted plane, the distinction between relative and absolute gains does seem to matter, albeit to a lesser degree than neorealism would have us believe. All three states have demonstrated a willingness to adjust policy in quest of absolute gains. Relative gains, however, do seem to enter the equation once in a while. Roh Moo Hyun's explanation of why he was ambivalent about a bilateral free trade agreement with Japan—that Japan would gain more than South Korea in the short-run because the trade imbalance would widen in Tokyo's favor—provided a textbook example of the primacy of relative over absolute gains in foreign policymaking.

On balance, the potency of ideational variables suggests that insofar as Japan and the two Korean states are concerned, cooperation on large issues—notably, the resolution of the abduction issue between Tokyo and Pyongyang and the fundamental resolution of history-related issues between Tokyo and Seoul—remains tantalizingly elusive. This is not to suggest that such cooperation is unattainable, for nothing is impossible in a changing and increasingly interdependent world.

Nonetheless, change of seismic proportions may be necessary before cooperation blossoms in the two sets of bilateral relations. A steady expansion of human and cultural exchanges between Japan and South Korea may conceivably, or even ineluctably, lead to attitudinal change. Coupled with generational change in political leadership, that may well pave the way for a genuine reconciliation between the two countries during the fifth decade of their diplomatic normalization. The prognosis for Japan-DPRK relations, on the other hand, cannot be as optimistic as above. Since a breakthrough is still possible, however, we may be excused for ending this study on a cautiously optimistic note.

Appendix 1

Treaty of Basic Relations between Japan and The Republic of Korea

Japan and the Republic of Korea,

Considering the historical background of relationship between their peoples and their mutual desire for good neighborliness and for the normalization of their relations on the basis of the principle of mutual respect for sovereignty;

Recognizing the importance of their close cooperation in conformity with the principles of the Charter of the United Nations to the promotion of their mutual welfare and common interests and to the maintenance of international peace and security; and

Recalling the relevant provisions of the Treaty of Peace with Japan signed at the city of San Francisco on September 8, 1951 and the Resolution 195 (III) adopted by the United Nations General Assembly on December 12, 1948;

Have resolved to conclude the present Treaty on Basic Relations and have accordingly appointed as their Plenipotentiaries,

- Japan:
  Etsusaburo Shiina,
  Minister for Foreign Affairs of Japan
  Shinichi Takasugi

• The Republic of Korea:
Tong Won Lee,
Minister for Foreign Affairs of the Republic of Korea
Dong Jo Kim,

Ambassador Extraordinary and Plenipotentiary of the Republic of Korea

Who, having communicated to each other their full powers found to be in good and due form, have agreed upon the following articles:

Article I

Diplomatic and consular relations shall be established between the High Contracting Parties. The High Contracting Parties shall exchange diplomatic envoys with the Ambassadorial rank without delay. The High contracting Parties will also establish consulates at locations to be agreed upon by the two Governments.

Article II

It is confirmed that all treaties or agreements concluded between the Empire of Japan and the Empire of Korea on or before August 22, 1910 are already null and void.

Article III

It is confirmed that the Government of the Republic of Korea is the only lawful Government of Korea as specified in the Resolution 195 (III) of the United Nations General Assembly.

Article IV

(a) The High Contracting Parties will be guided by the principles of the Charter of the United Nations in their mutual relations.

(b) The High Contracting Parties will cooperate in conformity with the principles of the Charter of the United Nations in promoting their mutual welfare and common interests.

Article V

The High Contracting Parties will enter into negotiations at the earliest practicable date for the conclusion of treaties or agreements to place their trading, maritime and other commercial relations on a stable and friendly basis.

Article VI

The High Contracting Parties will enter into negotiations at the earliest practicable date for the conclusion of an agreement relating to civil air transport.

Article VII

The present Treaty shall be ratified. The instruments of ratification shall be exchanged at Seoul as soon as possible. The present Treaty shall enter into force as from the date on which the instruments of ratification are exchanged.

IN WITNESS WHEREOF, the respective Plenipotentiaries have signed the present Treaty and have affixed thereto their seals.

DONE in duplicate at Tokyo, this twenty-second day of June of the year one thousand nine hundred and sixty-five in the Japanese, Korean, and English languages, each text being equally authentic. In case of any divergence of interpretation, the English text shall prevail.

• FOR JAPAN:
Etsusaburo Shiina
Shinichi Takasugi

• FOR THE REPUBLIC OF KOREA:
Tong Won Lee
Dong Jo Kim

SOURCE: Kagoshima Heiwa Kenkyujo (ed.), *Nihon gaiko shuyo bunsho, nenpyo, dai 2-ken* (Basic Documents on Japanese Foreign Relations, Vol. 2), 1961-1970 (Tokyo: Hara Shobo, 1984), pp. 569-572. The English translation of the title is the editor's.

Appendix 2

Japan-DPRK Pyongyang Declaration

Japanese Prime Minister Junichiro Koizumi and Chairman Kim Jong Il of the DPRK National Defense Commision met and had talks in Pyongyang on September 17, 2002.

Both leaders confirmed the shared recognition that establishing a fruitful political, economic and cultural relationship between Japan and the DPRK through the settlement of both the unfortunate past between them and the outstanding issues of concern would be consistent with the fundamental interests of both sides, and would greatly contribute to the peace and stability of the region.

1. Both sides determined that, pursuant to the spirit and basic principles laid out in this Declaration, they would make every possible effort for an early normalization of their relations, and decided that they would resume the Japan-DPRK normalization talks in October 2002.

Both sides expressed their strong determination that in the course of achieving normalization, they would sincerely tackle outstanding problems between Japan and the DPRK based upon their mutual trust.

2. The Japanese side regards, in a spirit of humility, the facts of history that Japan caused tremendous damage and suffering to the people

of Korea through colonial rule in the past, and expressed deep remorse and heartfelt apology.

Both sides shared the recognition that providing economic cooperation after the normalization by the Japanese side to the DPRK side, including grant aids, long-term loans with low interest rates and such assistance as humanitarian assistance through international organizations, over a period of time deemed appropriate by both sides, and providing other loans and credits by such financial institutions as the Japan Bank for International Cooperation with a view toward supporting private economic activities, would be consistent with the spirit of this Declaration, and decided that they would sincerely discuss the specific scales and contents of the economic cooperation in the normalization talks.

Both sides, pursuant to the basic principle that when the bilateral relationship is normalized, both Japan and the DPRK would mutually waive all their property claims and those of their nationals that had arisen from causes which occurred before August 15, 1945, decided that they would sincerely discuss the specific scales and contents of the economic cooperation in the normalization talks.

Both sides decided that they would sincerely discuss the issue of the status of Korean residents in Japan and the issue of cultural property.

2. Both sides confirmed that they would comply with international law and would not commit acts threatening the security of the other side. With respect to the outstanding issues of concern related to the lives and security of Japanese nationals, the DPRK side confirmed that it would take appropriate measures so that these regrettable incidents, which took place under the abnormal bilateral relationship, would never happen in the future.

3. Both sides confirmed that they would cooperate with each other in order to maintain and strengthen the peace and stability of Northeast Asia.

Both sides confirmed the importance of establishing cooperative relationships based upon mutual trust among countries concerned in this region, and shared the recognition that it is important to have a framework in place in order for these regional countries to promote confidence-building, as the relationships among these countries are normalized.

Both sides confirmed that, for an overall resolution of the nuclear issue on the Korean Peninsula, they would comply with all related international agreements. Both sides also cofirmed the necessity of resolving security problems, including nuclear and missile issues, by promoting dialogues among countries concerned.

The DPRK side expressed its intention that pursuant to the spirit of this Declaration, it would further maintain the moratorium on missile launching in and after 2003.

Both sides decided that they would discuss issues relating to security.

Prime Minister of Japan
Junichiro Koizumi

Chairman of the DPRK National Defense Commission
Kim Jong Il

September 17, 2002
Pyongyang

SOURCE: Ministry of Foreign Affairs of Japan (Provisional Translation), online at http://www.mofa.go.jp/region/asia-pac/n_korea/pmv0209/pyongan...

Bibliography

Ahn, Byung-joon. "Japanese Policy toward Korea." In *Japan's Foreign Policy after the Cold War: Coping with Change*, edited by Gerald L. Curtis, 263-273. Armonk, NY: M.E. Sharp, Inc., 1993.

Ajia Josei Shiryo Senta, ed. *"Ianfu"* mondai Q & A: *"Jiyushugishikan" e onnatachino hanron* [Questions and Answers on the "Comfort Women" Issue: Women's Refutation of "Liberal View of History"]. Tokyo: Meiseki Shoten, 1997.

Aochi, Shin. "Kim Dae Jung gunji saiban to Nihon seifu no shisei." [Kim Dae Jung's Court Martial and the Posture of the Japanese Government], I and II. *Gekkan Shakaito* [The Socialist Party Monthly] (Tokyo), no. 391 (November 1980), and no. 292 (December 1880).

Arai, Toshiaki. *Nikkan, Nitcho kankei no kadai* [Tasks of Japan-ROK and Japan-DPRK Relations]. Tokyo: Nitchu Shuppan, 2005.

Asahi, Motofumi. "Chosen mondai to Nihon gaiko" [The Korea Question and Japanese Diplomacy]. *Gekkan Shakaito*, no. 396 (December 1988): 150-64.

Bae, Chong-ho. *Ilbon ui kukka chollyak kwa Hanbando* [Japan's National Strategy and the Korean Peninsula]. Seoul: T'ongil Yonguwon, 2001.

Banno, Masataka. *Gendai gaiko no bunseki- joho, seisaku kettei, gaiko kosho* [Analysis of Modern Diplomacy: Intelligence, Policymaking, and

Diplomatic Negotiation]. Tokyo: Tokyo Daigaku Shuppankai, 1991.
Boeicho, ed. *Boei hakusho* [Defense White Paper]. Tokyo: Okurasho Insatsu-kyoku, annual.
Boeicho, Jieitai. *Oshirase: Kita Chosen no misairu hassha no bunseki kekka ni tsuite* [Report: On the Results of Analysis of North Korea's Missile Launch]. Tokyo: October 30, 1998.
Brecher, Michael. *The Foreign Policy Systems of Israel: Setting, Images, Process.* New Haven: Yale University Press, 1972.
Bridges, Brian. *Japan and Korea in the 1990s: From Antagonism to Adjustment.* Aldershot, England: Edward Elgar Publishing, Ltd., 1993.
Ch'oe, Kyong-nak and Hi-wan Cho. *Han'il kwangye-ron* [On Republic of Korea-Japan Relations]. Seoul: T'aebaeksa, 1985.
Choi, Chungmoo, ed. "Comfort Women." Special issue, *Positions* (Durham, NC) 5, no. 1 (1997).
Chon, Yo-ok. *Ilbon un opta*, 1 [There Is No Japan. vol. 1]. Seoul: P'urun Sup, 1997.
Ch'ongwadae. *Che 1-ch'a Han'il chongsang hoedam kyolgwa podo charyo* [Press Release on the Results of the First ROK-Japan Summit Meeting]. Seoul: May 24, 1990.
―――. *Che 2-ch'a Han'il chongsang hoedam kyolgwa podo charyo* [Press Release on the Results of the Second ROK-Japan Summit Meeting]. Seoul: May 26, 1990.
―――. *Che 1-ch'a chongsang hoedam kyolgwa podo charyo* [Press Release on the Results of the First Summit Meeting]. Seoul: January 9, 1991.
―――. *Che 2-ch'a chongsang hoedam kyolgwa podo charyo* [Press Release on the Reults of the Second Summit Meeting]. Seoul: January 10, 1991.
―――. *Han'il chongsang hoedam kyolgwa podo charyo* [Press Release on the Results of the ROK-Japan Summit Meeting]. Seoul: November 7, 1993.
―――. *Taet'ongnyong yonsolmun* [Text of the President's Speech]. Seoul: June 9, 2003. http://www.president.go. kr.
―――. *Joint Statement by President Roh Moo-hyun of the Republic of Korea and Prime Minister Junichiro Koizumi of Japan Following a Summit Meeting.* Seoul: June 7, 2003.

Chosen Jiho Tokubetsu Shuzai-han. *"Kannichi kankei" no sai kento - 40-nen no kiseki* [A Reexamination of "ROK-Japan Relations": the 40-year Record]. Tokyo: Chosen Seinensha, 1985.

Chosen Seisaku no Kaizen o Motomeru Kai. *Teigen: Nihon no Chosen seisaku* [Proposal: Japan's Policy Toward Korea]. Tokyo: Iwanami shoten, 1989.

Chung, Il Young, ed. *Hanguk oegyo pansegi ui chaejomyong* [A Reassessment of the Half Century of ROK Diplomacy]. Seoul: Nanam, 1993.

Colbert, Evelyn. "Japan and the Republic of Korea: Yesterday, Today, and Tomorrow." *Asian Survey* 26, no. 3 (March 1986): 273-91.

Cumings, Bruce. *Korea's Place in the Sun: A Modern History*. New York: W.W.Norton & Co., 1997.

Curtis, Gerald L., ed. *Japan's Foreign Policy after the Cold War: Coping With Change*. Armonk, NY: M.E. Sharpe, 1993.

"Deta: Nishimura Shinso gi'in no teishutsu shita `kita Chosen kosaku soshiki ni yoru Nihonjin yukai rachi ni kansuru shitsumon shuisho'" [Data: "Statement of Questions Regarding the Abduction of Japanese Nationals by North Korean Agents" Submitted by Dietman Nishimura Shinso]. *Gendai koria* [Modern Korea] (Tokyo), no. 369 (March 1997): 51-53.

Doran, Charles F. "The United States, Japan and Korea: The New International Political Economy." *Asian Perspective* (Seoul) 17, no. 1 (Spring/Summer 1993): 53-68.

Drifte, Reinhard. *Japan's Foreign Policy*. London: Royal Institute of International Affairs, 1990.

Eya, Osamu. *Kita Chosen kaitai shinsho* [New Book on the Dissolution of North Korea]. Tokyo: Shogakkan, 1997.

Foreign Press Center Japan. *Statement by Foreign Minister Kono on Japan's Rice Assistance to North Korea*. F.P.C. Press Release No. 0368-09. Tokyo: June 30, 1995.

Fujii, Arata. "Nitcho kankei joseika kosho no keika to tenbo" [The Progress and Prospects of Japan-Democratic People's Republic of Korea Negotiations on Diplomatic Normalization]. *Toa* [East Asia] (Tokyo), no. 334 (April 1995): 15-20.

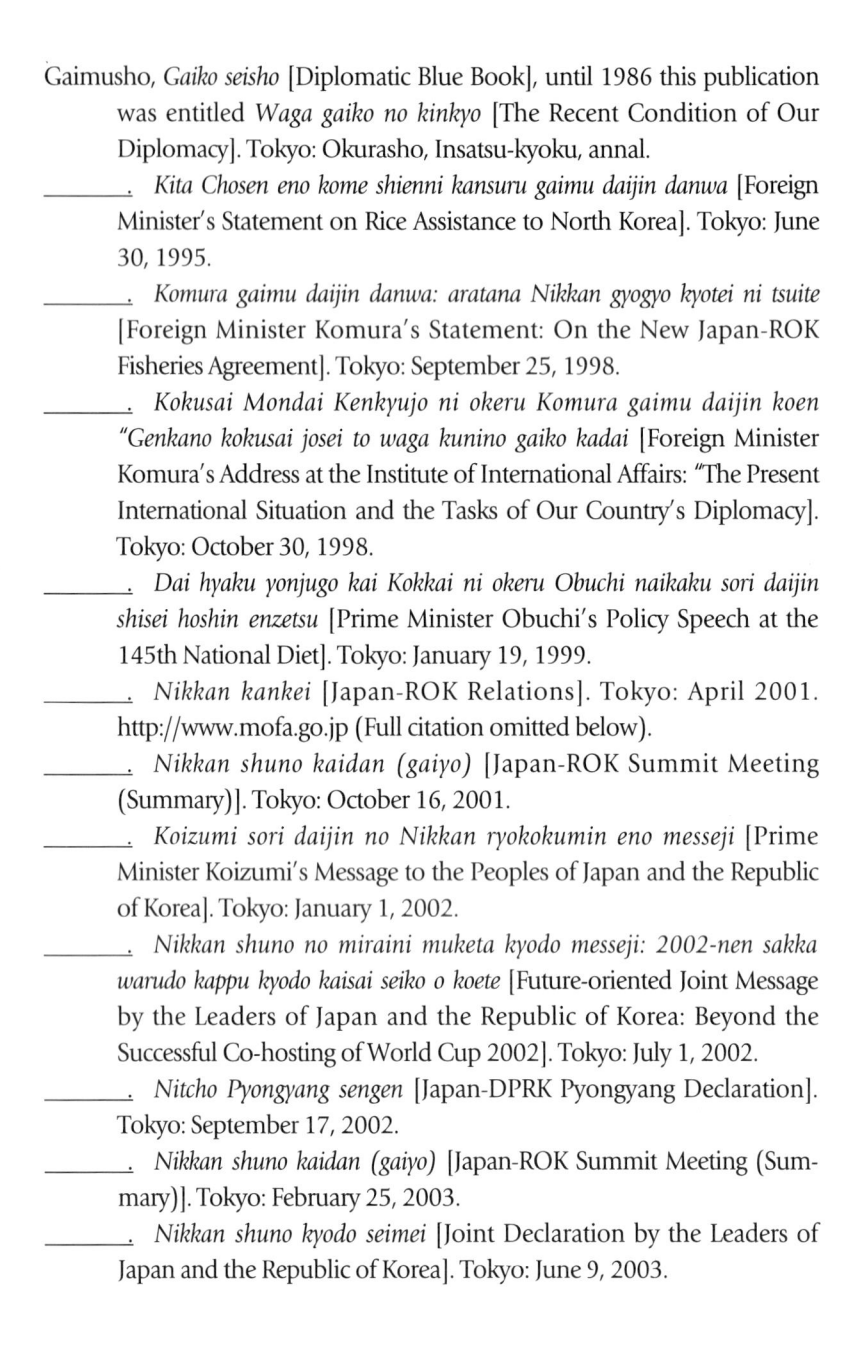

Gaimusho, *Gaiko seisho* [Diplomatic Blue Book], until 1986 this publication was entitled *Waga gaiko no kinkyo* [The Recent Condition of Our Diplomacy]. Tokyo: Okurasho, Insatsu-kyoku, annal.

———. *Kita Chosen eno kome shienni kansuru gaimu daijin danwa* [Foreign Minister's Statement on Rice Assistance to North Korea]. Tokyo: June 30, 1995.

———. *Komura gaimu daijin danwa: aratana Nikkan gyogyo kyotei ni tsuite* [Foreign Minister Komura's Statement: On the New Japan-ROK Fisheries Agreement]. Tokyo: September 25, 1998.

———. *Kokusai Mondai Kenkyujo ni okeru Komura gaimu daijin koen "Genkano kokusai josei to waga kunino gaiko kadai* [Foreign Minister Komura's Address at the Institute of International Affairs: "The Present International Situation and the Tasks of Our Country's Diplomacy]. Tokyo: October 30, 1998.

———. *Dai hyaku yonjugo kai Kokkai ni okeru Obuchi naikaku sori daijin shisei hoshin enzetsu* [Prime Minister Obuchi's Policy Speech at the 145th National Diet]. Tokyo: January 19, 1999.

———. *Nikkan kankei* [Japan-ROK Relations]. Tokyo: April 2001. http://www.mofa.go.jp (Full citation omitted below).

———. *Nikkan shuno kaidan (gaiyo)* [Japan-ROK Summit Meeting (Summary)]. Tokyo: October 16, 2001.

———. *Koizumi sori daijin no Nikkan ryokokumin eno messeji* [Prime Minister Koizumi's Message to the Peoples of Japan and the Republic of Korea]. Tokyo: January 1, 2002.

———. *Nikkan shuno no miraini muketa kyodo messeji: 2002-nen sakka warudo kappu kyodo kaisai seiko o koete* [Future-oriented Joint Message by the Leaders of Japan and the Republic of Korea: Beyond the Successful Co-hosting of World Cup 2002]. Tokyo: July 1, 2002.

———. *Nitcho Pyongyang sengen* [Japan-DPRK Pyongyang Declaration]. Tokyo: September 17, 2002.

———. *Nikkan shuno kaidan (gaiyo)* [Japan-ROK Summit Meeting (Summary)]. Tokyo: February 25, 2003.

———. *Nikkan shuno kyodo seimei* [Joint Declaration by the Leaders of Japan and the Republic of Korea]. Tokyo: June 9, 2003.

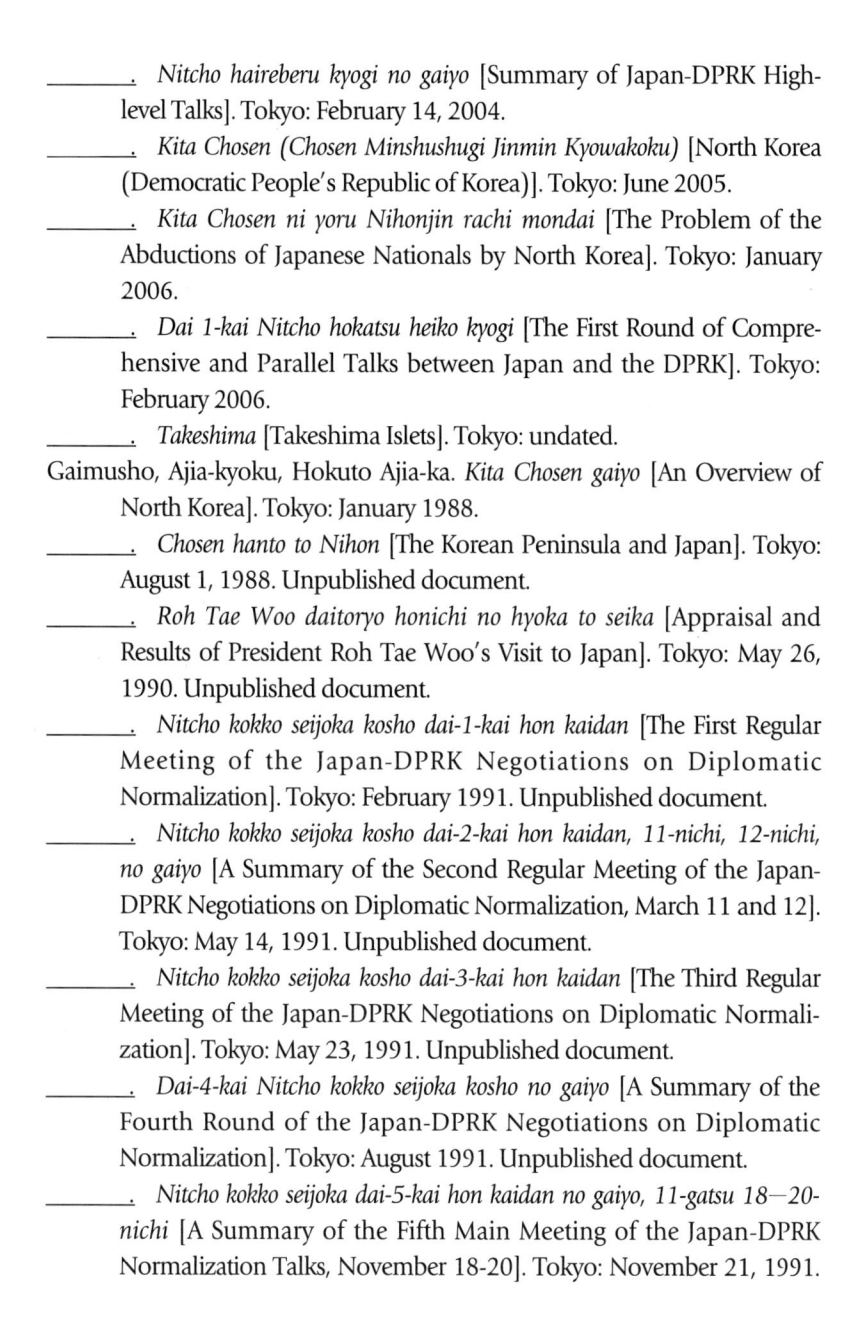

———. *Nitcho haireberu kyogi no gaiyo* [Summary of Japan-DPRK High-level Talks]. Tokyo: February 14, 2004.

———. *Kita Chosen (Chosen Minshushugi Jinmin Kyowakoku)* [North Korea (Democratic People's Republic of Korea)]. Tokyo: June 2005.

———. *Kita Chosen ni yoru Nihonjin rachi mondai* [The Problem of the Abductions of Japanese Nationals by North Korea]. Tokyo: January 2006.

———. *Dai 1-kai Nitcho hokatsu heiko kyogi* [The First Round of Comprehensive and Parallel Talks between Japan and the DPRK]. Tokyo: February 2006.

———. *Takeshima* [Takeshima Islets]. Tokyo: undated.

Gaimusho, Ajia-kyoku, Hokuto Ajia-ka. *Kita Chosen gaiyo* [An Overview of North Korea]. Tokyo: January 1988.

———. *Chosen hanto to Nihon* [The Korean Peninsula and Japan]. Tokyo: August 1, 1988. Unpublished document.

———. *Roh Tae Woo daitoryo honichi no hyoka to seika* [Appraisal and Results of President Roh Tae Woo's Visit to Japan]. Tokyo: May 26, 1990. Unpublished document.

———. *Nitcho kokko seijoka kosho dai-1-kai hon kaidan* [The First Regular Meeting of the Japan-DPRK Negotiations on Diplomatic Normalization]. Tokyo: February 1991. Unpublished document.

———. *Nitcho kokko seijoka kosho dai-2-kai hon kaidan, 11-nichi, 12-nichi, no gaiyo* [A Summary of the Second Regular Meeting of the Japan-DPRK Negotiations on Diplomatic Normalization, March 11 and 12]. Tokyo: May 14, 1991. Unpublished document.

———. *Nitcho kokko seijoka kosho dai-3-kai hon kaidan* [The Third Regular Meeting of the Japan-DPRK Negotiations on Diplomatic Normalization]. Tokyo: May 23, 1991. Unpublished document.

———. *Dai-4-kai Nitcho kokko seijoka kosho no gaiyo* [A Summary of the Fourth Round of the Japan-DPRK Negotiations on Diplomatic Normalization]. Tokyo: August 1991. Unpublished document.

———. *Nitcho kokko seijoka dai-5-kai hon kaidan no gaiyo, 11-gatsu 18—20-nichi* [A Summary of the Fifth Main Meeting of the Japan-DPRK Normalization Talks, November 18-20]. Tokyo: November 21, 1991.

Unpublished document.

———. *Dai-6-kai Nitcho kokko seijoka kosho no gaiyo* [A Summary of the Sixth Round of the Japan-DPRK Negotiations on Diplomatic Normalization]. Tokyo: February 6, 1992. Unpublished document.

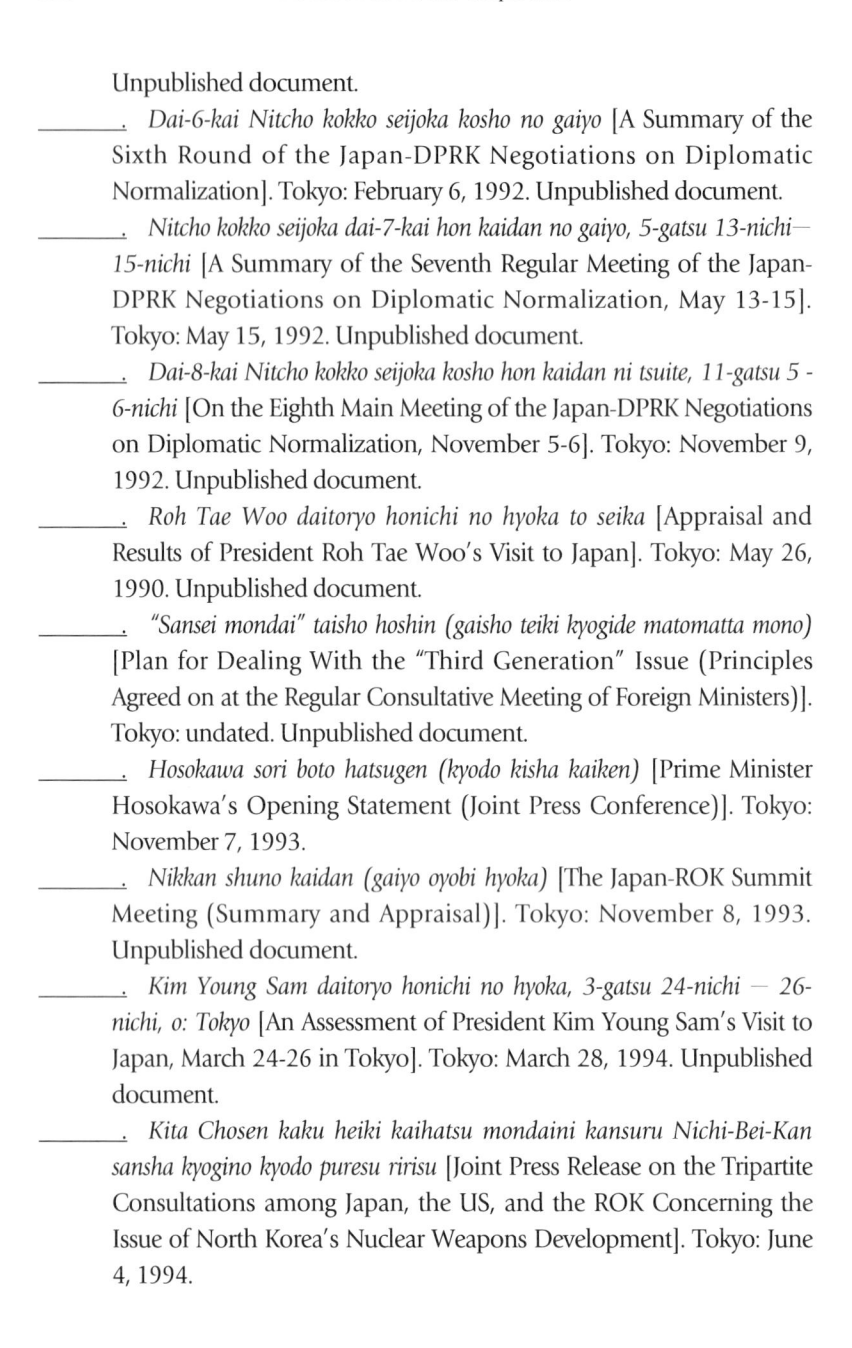

———. *Nitcho kokko seijoka dai-7-kai hon kaidan no gaiyo, 5-gatsu 13-nichi—15-nichi* [A Summary of the Seventh Regular Meeting of the Japan-DPRK Negotiations on Diplomatic Normalization, May 13-15]. Tokyo: May 15, 1992. Unpublished document.

———. *Dai-8-kai Nitcho kokko seijoka kosho hon kaidan ni tsuite, 11-gatsu 5 - 6-nichi* [On the Eighth Main Meeting of the Japan-DPRK Negotiations on Diplomatic Normalization, November 5-6]. Tokyo: November 9, 1992. Unpublished document.

———. *Roh Tae Woo daitoryo honichi no hyoka to seika* [Appraisal and Results of President Roh Tae Woo's Visit to Japan]. Tokyo: May 26, 1990. Unpublished document.

———. *"Sansei mondai" taisho hoshin (gaisho teiki kyogide matomatta mono)* [Plan for Dealing With the "Third Generation" Issue (Principles Agreed on at the Regular Consultative Meeting of Foreign Ministers)]. Tokyo: undated. Unpublished document.

———. *Hosokawa sori boto hatsugen (kyodo kisha kaiken)* [Prime Minister Hosokawa's Opening Statement (Joint Press Conference)]. Tokyo: November 7, 1993.

———. *Nikkan shuno kaidan (gaiyo oyobi hyoka)* [The Japan-ROK Summit Meeting (Summary and Appraisal)]. Tokyo: November 8, 1993. Unpublished document.

———. *Kim Young Sam daitoryo honichi no hyoka, 3-gatsu 24-nichi — 26-nichi, o: Tokyo* [An Assessment of President Kim Young Sam's Visit to Japan, March 24-26 in Tokyo]. Tokyo: March 28, 1994. Unpublished document.

———. *Kita Chosen kaku heiki kaihatsu mondaini kansuru Nichi-Bei-Kan sansha kyogino kyodo puresu ririsu* [Joint Press Release on the Tripartite Consultations among Japan, the US, and the ROK Concerning the Issue of North Korea's Nuclear Weapons Development]. Tokyo: June 4, 1994.

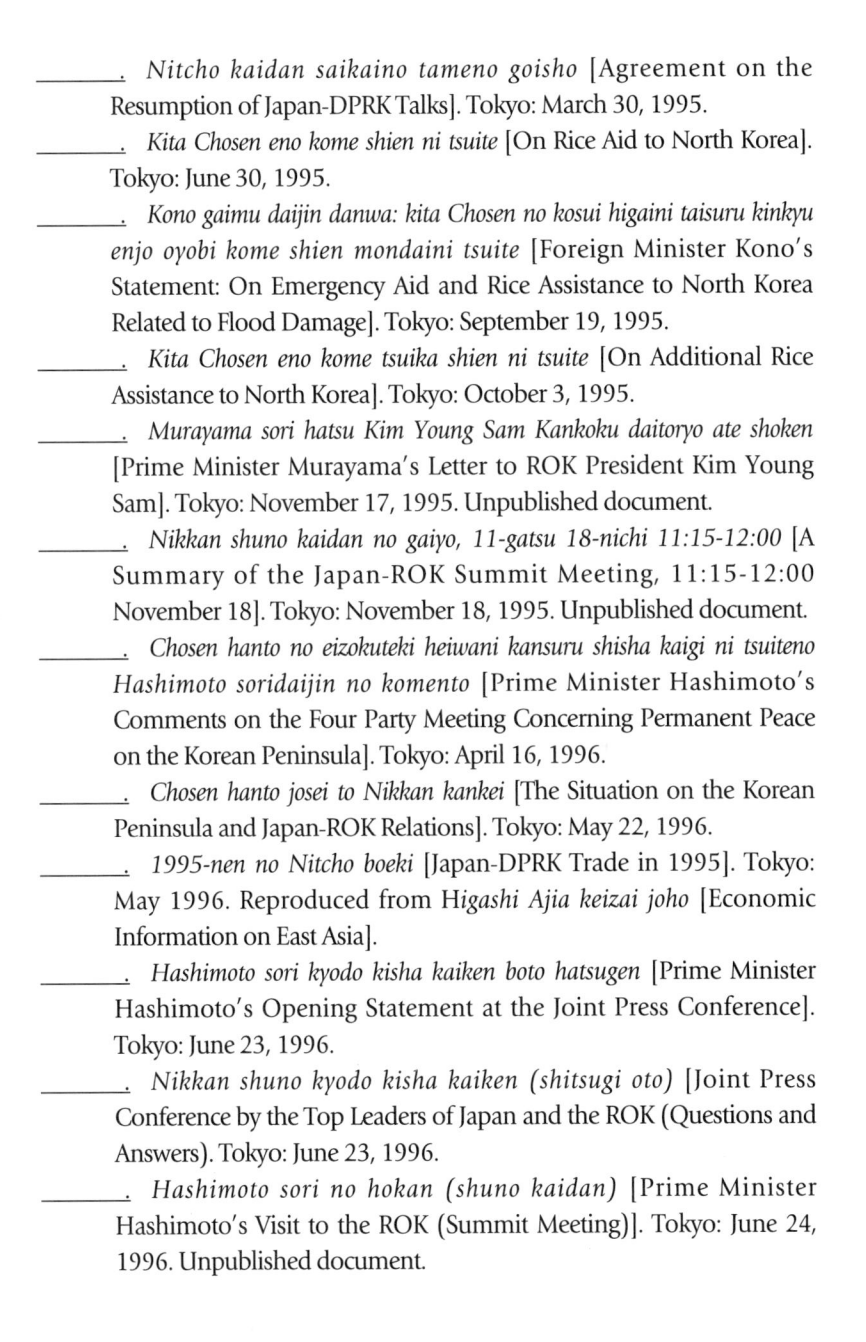

_____. *Nitcho kaidan saikaino tameno goisho* [Agreement on the Resumption of Japan-DPRK Talks]. Tokyo: March 30, 1995.

_____. *Kita Chosen eno kome shien ni tsuite* [On Rice Aid to North Korea]. Tokyo: June 30, 1995.

_____. *Kono gaimu daijin danwa: kita Chosen no kosui higaini taisuru kinkyu enjo oyobi kome shien mondaini tsuite* [Foreign Minister Kono's Statement: On Emergency Aid and Rice Assistance to North Korea Related to Flood Damage]. Tokyo: September 19, 1995.

_____. *Kita Chosen eno kome tsuika shien ni tsuite* [On Additional Rice Assistance to North Korea]. Tokyo: October 3, 1995.

_____. *Murayama sori hatsu Kim Young Sam Kankoku daitoryo ate shoken* [Prime Minister Murayama's Letter to ROK President Kim Young Sam]. Tokyo: November 17, 1995. Unpublished document.

_____. *Nikkan shuno kaidan no gaiyo, 11-gatsu 18-nichi 11:15-12:00* [A Summary of the Japan-ROK Summit Meeting, 11:15-12:00 November 18]. Tokyo: November 18, 1995. Unpublished document.

_____. *Chosen hanto no eizokuteki heiwani kansuru shisha kaigi ni tsuiteno Hashimoto soridaijin no komento* [Prime Minister Hashimoto's Comments on the Four Party Meeting Concerning Permanent Peace on the Korean Peninsula]. Tokyo: April 16, 1996.

_____. *Chosen hanto josei to Nikkan kankei* [The Situation on the Korean Peninsula and Japan-ROK Relations]. Tokyo: May 22, 1996.

_____. *1995-nen no Nitcho boeki* [Japan-DPRK Trade in 1995]. Tokyo: May 1996. Reproduced from *Higashi Ajia keizai joho* [Economic Information on East Asia].

_____. *Hashimoto sori kyodo kisha kaiken boto hatsugen* [Prime Minister Hashimoto's Opening Statement at the Joint Press Conference]. Tokyo: June 23, 1996.

_____. *Nikkan shuno kyodo kisha kaiken (shitsugi oto)* [Joint Press Conference by the Top Leaders of Japan and the ROK (Questions and Answers). Tokyo: June 23, 1996.

_____. *Hashimoto sori no hokan (shuno kaidan)* [Prime Minister Hashimoto's Visit to the ROK (Summit Meeting)]. Tokyo: June 24, 1996. Unpublished document.

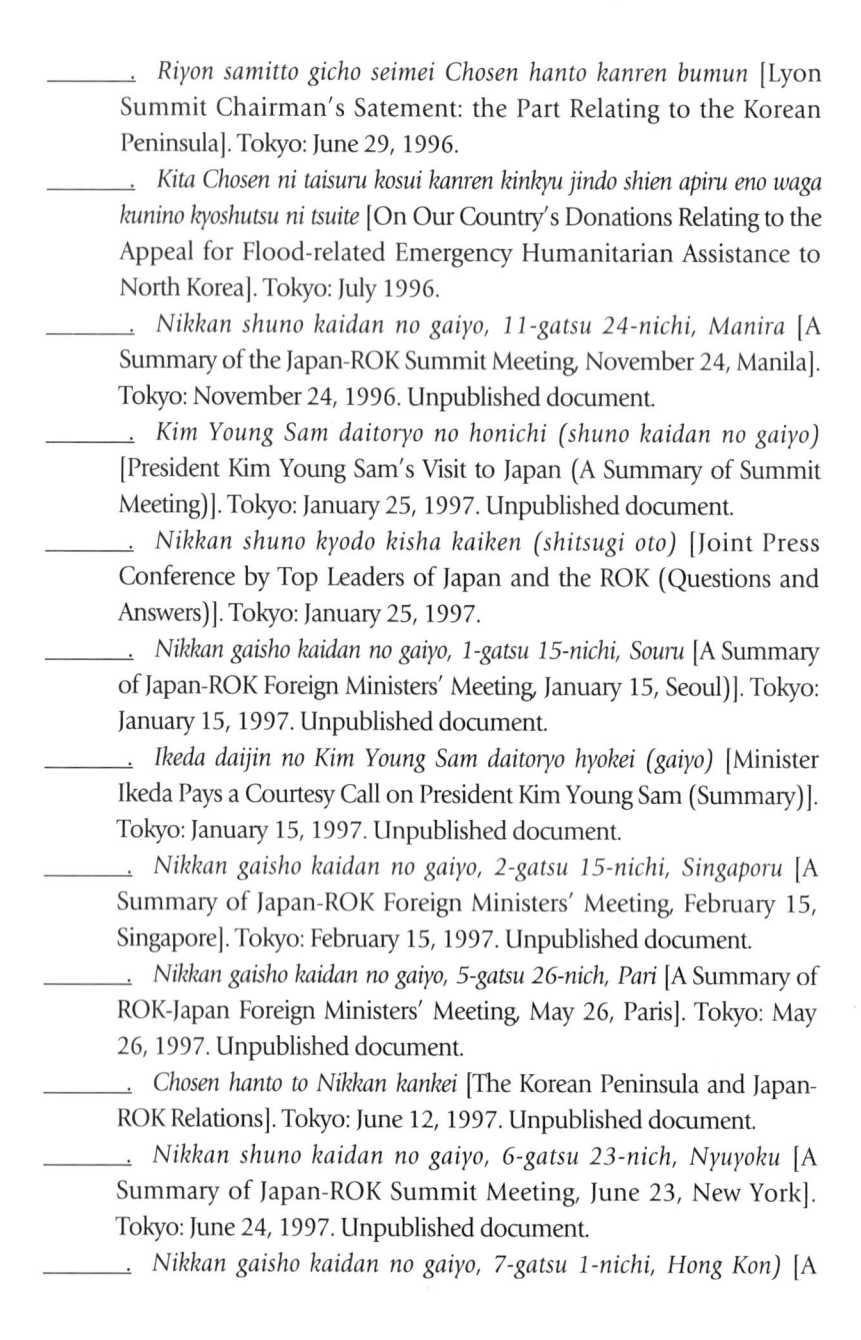

_____. *Riyon samitto gicho seimei Chosen hanto kanren bumun* [Lyon Summit Chairman's Satement: the Part Relating to the Korean Peninsula]. Tokyo: June 29, 1996.

_____. *Kita Chosen ni taisuru kosui kanren kinkyu jindo shien apiru eno waga kunino kyoshutsu ni tsuite* [On Our Country's Donations Relating to the Appeal for Flood-related Emergency Humanitarian Assistance to North Korea]. Tokyo: July 1996.

_____. *Nikkan shuno kaidan no gaiyo, 11-gatsu 24-nichi, Manira* [A Summary of the Japan-ROK Summit Meeting, November 24, Manila]. Tokyo: November 24, 1996. Unpublished document.

_____. *Kim Young Sam daitoryo no honichi (shuno kaidan no gaiyo)* [President Kim Young Sam's Visit to Japan (A Summary of Summit Meeting)]. Tokyo: January 25, 1997. Unpublished document.

_____. *Nikkan shuno kyodo kisha kaiken (shitsugi oto)* [Joint Press Conference by Top Leaders of Japan and the ROK (Questions and Answers)]. Tokyo: January 25, 1997.

_____. *Nikkan gaisho kaidan no gaiyo, 1-gatsu 15-nichi, Souru* [A Summary of Japan-ROK Foreign Ministers' Meeting, January 15, Seoul)]. Tokyo: January 15, 1997. Unpublished document.

_____. *Ikeda daijin no Kim Young Sam daitoryo hyokei (gaiyo)* [Minister Ikeda Pays a Courtesy Call on President Kim Young Sam (Summary)]. Tokyo: January 15, 1997. Unpublished document.

_____. *Nikkan gaisho kaidan no gaiyo, 2-gatsu 15-nichi, Singaporu* [A Summary of Japan-ROK Foreign Ministers' Meeting, February 15, Singapore]. Tokyo: February 15, 1997. Unpublished document.

_____. *Nikkan gaisho kaidan no gaiyo, 5-gatsu 26-nich, Pari* [A Summary of ROK-Japan Foreign Ministers' Meeting, May 26, Paris]. Tokyo: May 26, 1997. Unpublished document.

_____. *Chosen hanto to Nikkan kankei* [The Korean Peninsula and Japan-ROK Relations]. Tokyo: June 12, 1997. Unpublished document.

_____. *Nikkan shuno kaidan no gaiyo, 6-gatsu 23-nich, Nyuyoku* [A Summary of Japan-ROK Summit Meeting, June 23, New York]. Tokyo: June 24, 1997. Unpublished document.

_____. *Nikkan gaisho kaidan no gaiyo, 7-gatsu 1-nichi, Hong Kon)* [A

Summary of Japan-ROK Foreign Ministers' Meeting, July 1, Hong Kong). Tokyo: July 1, 1997. Unpublished document.

———. *Chosen hanto ererugi kaihatsu kiko (KEDO) no kei'i to genjo* [Specifics and Current Situation of the Korean Peninsula Energy Development Organization (KEDO)]. Tokyo: July 1997. Unpublished document.

———. *Nikkan kyodo sengen-21 seikini muketa aratana Nikkan patonashippu* [Japan-Republic of Korea Joint Declaration: A New Japan-ROK Partnership towards the 21st Century]. Tokyo: October 8, 1998.

———. *Obuchi naikaku sori daijin, Kim Dae Jung Kankoku taitoryo kyodo kasha kaiken-roku, Heisei 10-nen 10-gatsu 8-nichi* [Record of Joint Press Conference by Prime Minister Obuchi and ROK President Kim Dae Jung, October 8, 1998]. Tokyo: October 8, 1998.

———. *Kankoku keizai no kenjo to Nikkan keizai kankei* [The Current Condition of the ROK Economy and Japan-ROK Economic Relations]. Tokyo: August 2005.

Gaimusho, Sengo Gaikoshi Kenkyukai, ed. *Nihon gaiko 30-nen: sengo no kiseki to tenbo, 1952-1982* [Thirty Years of Japanese Diplomacy: The Postwar Record, 1952-1982]. Tokyo: Sekaino Ugoki-sha, 1982.

Gekkan Chosen shiryo [Monthly Materials on Korea]. Tokyo: Chosen Mondai Kenkyujo.

Gong, Yooshik. "Hanbando t'ongil kwa Ilbon ui yokhal: Ilbonui tae Hanbando chongch'aek ui pyonhwa wa a'puro ui chonmang" [The Reunification of the Korean Peninsula and the Role of Japan: Change in Japan's Policy Toward the Korean Peninsula and Future Prospects]. A paper presented to the Fall Conference of the Korean Sociological Association. Seoul: December 13-14, 1990.

Gurtov, Melvin. "Prospects for Korea-U.S.-Japan Trilateral Security Relations." *Asian Survey* 17, no. 1 (Spring/Summer 1993): 69-88.

Ha, Young Sun, ed. *Hanguk kwa Ilbon* [The Republic of Korea and Japan]. Seoul: Nanam, 1997.

Habeeb, William Mark. *Power and Tactics in International Negotiation: How Weak Nations Bargain with Strong Nations*. Baltimore: Johns Hopkins University Press, 1988.

Hahn, Bae-ho et al. *Ilbon chongch'aek kyoljong ui haebu* [Autopsy on Policymaking in Japan]. Seoul: Chongum-sa, 1984.

Halloran, Richard. "North Korean Relations with Japan." In *North Korea after Kim Il Sung*, edited by Dae-Sook Suh and Chae-Jin Lee, 211-29. Boulder, CO: Lynne Rienner Publisher, Inc., 1998.

Hanguk Unhaeng. *Kyongje t'onggye yonbo 2005* [Economic Statistics Yearbook, 2005]. Seoul: Hanguk Unhaeng, 2005.

Han, Sung-jo et al. *Tongbuga chongse pyonhwa wa Han'il kwangye* [Change in Northeast Asia's Environment and ROK-Japan Relations]. Seoul: Chimmun-dang, 1995.

Han'il chongsang hoedam kyolgwa tae'oe palp'yomun [Press Release on the Results of the ROK-Japan Summit Meeting]. Kyoto: November 8, 1992. Released by ROK Chief Presidential Press Secretary Kim Hak-joon.

Han'il 21-segi Wiwonhoe. *Han'il kyoryu ui hyonsang kwa kwaje* [The Present Condition and Tasks of ROK-Japan Exchanges]. Seoul: January 7, 1991.

Harada, Takeo. *Kita Chosen gaiko no shinjitsu* [The Truth About North Korean Diplomacy]. Tokyo: K.K. Tsukuba Shobo, 2005.

Harms, Jane. "Distant Countries Coming Closer? Japan-North Korea Relations: Past, Present and Future." B.A. (hons) diss., School of East Asian Studies, University of Sheffield, U.K., March 1992.

Hasegawa, Hiroshi. "Tsuiseki Nihonjin rachi giwaku" [Pursuit: Suspected Kidnaping of Japanese Nationals]. *AERA* (Asahi Shimbun Weekly), no. 27 (July 5, 1997): 21-22.

Hattori, Tamio. "Nikkan keizai kankei no 30-nen" [30 Years of Japan-ROK Economic Relations], Parts I and II. *Gendai Koria*, no. 357 (December 1995): 20-27 and no. 358 (Jan/Feb. 1996): 34-56.

Henkin, Louis et al. *International Law: Cases and Materials*, 3rd ed. St.Paul, MN: West Publishing Co., 1993.

Hermann, Charles F., Charles W. Kegley, and James N. Rosenau, eds. *New Directions in the Study of Foreign Policy*. Boston: Allen & Unwin, 1987.

Homusho. *Nihonjin no shukkoku jokyo* [Japanese Citizens' Departure from the Country]. Tokyo: December 1998.

⸻. *Gaikokujin no nyukoku jokyo* [Foreigners' Entry into the Country]. Tokyo: December 1998.

Homusho, Nyukoku Kanri-kyoku. *Shutsunyukoku kanri* [Control of Exit from and Entry into Japan]. Tokyo: August 31, 2004.

Hyondae Ilbon Hakhoe, ed. *Ishibilsegi Han'il kwangye* [ROK-Japan Relations in the 21st Century]. Seoul: Pommunsa, 1997.

Inoguchi, Takashi. "Japan's Foreign Policy in East Asia." *Current History* (December 1992): 407-12.

International Monetary Fund. *IMF Approves SDR 15.5 Billion Stand-by Credit for Korea*, Press Release No. 97/55. Washington, DC: December 4, 1997.

⸻. *Korea Decides to Make Repurchases Under SRF Totaling US $2.8 Billion*, News Brief No. 98149. Washington, DC: December 9, 1998.

Iriye, Akira. *Shin - Nihon no gaiko: chikyuka jidai no Nihon no sentaku* [New Japan's Diplomacy: Japan's Choice in the Era of Globalization]. Tokyo: Chuo Koronsha, 1991.

Ishibilsegi Munhwa Yonguhoe. *Kyosu 10-in'i p'urobon Hanguk kwa Ilbon pangjongsik* [The Equation Between the ROK and Japan As Solved by Ten Professors]. Seoul: Samsung Kyongje Yonguso, 1996.

Ishii, Hajime. *Chikazuite kita toi kuni* [A Distant Country Getting Closer]. Tokyo: Nihon Seisan Honbu, 1991.

Ishikawa, Sho. "`Nikkan shinjidai' to shinbun hodo" ["The New Era in Japan-ROK Relations" and Newspaper Coverage]. *Sekai* [The World] (Tokyo), no. 468 (November 1984): 112-18.

Ito Naoki. "Zainichi Kankokujin `sansei' mondai" [The Problem of "Third Generation" ROK Residents in Japan]. *Gaiko foramu* [Diplomatic Forum] (Tokyo) (April 1990): 74-75.

Izumi Hajime. "Kita Chosen no kokusai josei ninshiki to waga kuni no sentaku" [North Korea's Perceptions of International Developments and Our Country's Choice]. *Toa* [East Asia] (Tokyo), no. 266 (August 1989): 69-89.

⸻. "Tokyo's Policy toward North Korea and Korean Reunification." In *Korean Peninsula Developments and U.S.-Japan-South Korea Relations*. vol. 1, edited by Gerrit W. Gong, Seizaburo Sato, and Tae Hwan Ok,

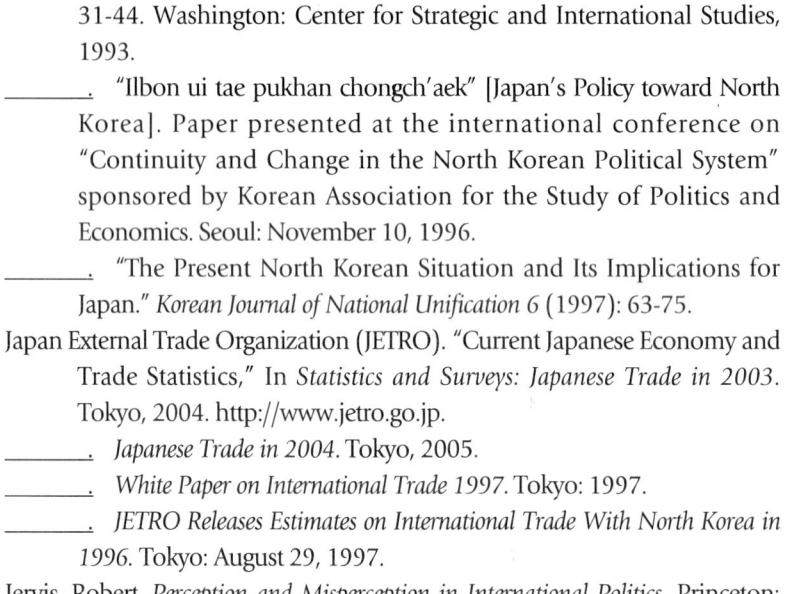

31-44. Washington: Center for Strategic and International Studies, 1993.

_____. "Ilbon ui tae pukhan chongch'aek" [Japan's Policy toward North Korea]. Paper presented at the international conference on "Continuity and Change in the North Korean Political System" sponsored by Korean Association for the Study of Politics and Economics. Seoul: November 10, 1996.

_____. "The Present North Korean Situation and Its Implications for Japan." *Korean Journal of National Unification* 6 (1997): 63-75.

Japan External Trade Organization (JETRO). "Current Japanese Economy and Trade Statistics," In *Statistics and Surveys: Japanese Trade in 2003*. Tokyo, 2004. http://www.jetro.go.jp.

_____. *Japanese Trade in 2004*. Tokyo, 2005.

_____. *White Paper on International Trade 1997*. Tokyo: 1997.

_____. *JETRO Releases Estimates on International Trade With North Korea in 1996*. Tokyo: August 29, 1997.

Jervis, Robert. *Perception and Misperception in International Politics*. Princeton: Princeton University Press, 1976.

Kagoshima Heiwa Kenkyujo, ed. *Nihon gaiko shuyo bunsho, nenpyo, dai-2-ken* [Basic Documents of Japanese Foreign Relations. vol. 2], *1961-1970*. Tokyo: Hara Shobo, 1984.

"Kaikyo o Hedatete", In *Kaikyo o hedatete* [Separating the Strait], edited by Kanko Iinkai. Tokyo: Gendai Shokan, 1985.

Kamiya Fuji and Tanino Sakutaro. "Taidan: mada futomeina Chosen hanto no seiji josei" [Conversation: The Still Opaque Political Situation on the Korean Peninsula]. *Gaiko foramu*, no. 21 (June 1990): 26-40.

Kanemaru Shin and Tanabe Makoto. "Taidan: ima issono hakusha o" [Conversation: Now, More Efforts Than Ever]. *Sekai*, temporary, extra issue (April 1992): 43-52.

Keizai Sangyosho, *Tsusho hakusho, 2000-2005* [Trade Whitepaper, 2000-2005]. Tokyo: K.K. Gyosei, 2000-2005 (The translation of the title is the Ministry of Economy, Trade, and Industry's).

Kim, Dae Jung and Yamahana Sadao. "Sokoku minshuka no tameni tatakau" [Struggling for the Democratization of the Fatherland]. *Gekkan shakaito*, no. 328 (September 1983): 125-31.

Kim, Hong Nack. "Japanese-Korean Relations in the 1980s." *Asian Survey* 27, no. 5 (May 1987): 497-514.

———. "The Normalization of North Korea-Japan Diplomatic Relations: Problems and Prospects." *Korea & World Affairs* (Seoul) 14, no. 4 (Winter 1990): 649-70.

———. "Japan's Relations with North Korea." *Current History* 90 (April 1991): 164-67.

———. "North Korea's Policy toward Japan and the United States." *Journal of East Asian Affairs* (Seoul) 6, no. 2 (1992): 246-58.

———. "North Korea's Policy toward Japan." In *Foreign Relations of North Korea during Kim Il Sung's Last Days*, edited by Kim Douug Joong, 159-92. Seoul: Sejong Institute, 1994.

———. "Japan and North Korea: Normalization Talks between Pyongyang and Tokyo." In *Korea and the World: beyond the Cold War*, edited by Young Whan Kihl, 111-132. Boulder, CO: Westview Press, 1994.

———. "Japan's Policy toward the Two Koreas in the Post-Cold War Era." *International Journal of Korean Studies* (Washington, DC) 1, no. 1 (Spring 1997): 131-58.

Kim, Il Sung. "Hyon chongse wa uri tang ui kwaop" [The Current Situation and the Tasks of Our Party]. In *Kim Il Sung chojak sonjip* [Selected Works of Kim Il sung]. vol. 4, pp. 323-26. Pyongyang: Choson Rodongdang Ch'ulp'ansa, 1968.

———. *Nitcho yuko no tameni* [For DPRK-Japan Friendship]. Translated by Kim Il Sung Shuseki Chosaku Hon'yaku Iinkai. Tokyo: Chuch'e Siso Kokusai Kenkyujo, 1986.

Kim, Samuel S., ed. *North Korean Foreign Relations in the Post-Cold War Era*. New York: Oxford University Press, 1998.

Kim, Tong-jo. *Hoesang 30-nyon Han'il hoedam* [Thirty-year Reminiscences: ROK-Japan Negotiations]. Seoul: Chungang Ilbosa, 1986.

Kim, Yang Ki. *Ima Nihon to Kankoku o kangaeru: dosureba makotono "kyosei" ga dekirunoka* [Thinking about Today's Japan and the ROK: How Can We Achieve True "Symbiosis"?]. Tokyo: Daiwa Shuppan, 1992.

Kim, Young C. "North Korea's Strange Quest for Nuclear Weapons." *Problems of post-Cmmunism*, March-april 2003:3-11.

_____. "North Korea Confronts Japan: Politics of Normalization and Rice." In *North Korea and the World: Explaining Pyongyang's Foreign Policy*, edited by Byung Chul Koh, 133-198. Seoul: kyungnam University press, 2004.

"Kita Chosen Nihonjin tsuma no taibo seigatsu `kusuri mo kaenai'" [Austere Life of Japanese Wives in North Korea: "We Cannnot Even Afford to Buy Medicine"]. *AERA* (April 7, 1997).

Ko, Jun Suk. *Sengo Chonichi kankeishi* [History of Postwar Korea-Japan Relations]. Tokyo: K.K. Tahata Shoten, 1974.

Ko, Pyong-ik et al. *Ilbon ui hyondaehwa wa Han'il kwangye* [The Modernization of Japan and Korea-Japan Relations]. Seoul: Munhak kwa Chisong-sa, 1992.

Ko, Seung Kyun. "Japan and Two Koreas: Japanese Policy toward South Korea's New Nordpolitik." *Korea Observer* (Seoul) 22, no. 2 (Summer 1991): 173-88.

Kobayashi Kenji. "Kanemaru bocho eno michiwa Paride hajimatta" [The Road to Kanemaru's North Korea Visit Began in Paris]. *AERA* (December 11, 1990): 24-28.

Koh, B. C. "South Korea, North Korea, and Japan." *Pacific Community* (Tokyo) 6, no. 2 (January 1975): 205-19.

_____. *The Foreign Policy Systems of North and South Korea*. Berkeley: University of California Press, 1984.

_____. *Japan's Administrative Elite*. Berkeley: University of California Press, 1989.

_____. "Confrontation and Cooperation on the Korean Peninsula: The Politics of Nuclear Nonproliferation." *Korean Journal of Defense Analysis* (Seoul) 6, no. 2 (Winter 1994): 53-83.

_____. "South Korea in 1995: Tremors of Transition." *Asian Survey* 36, no. 1 (January 1996): 53-60.

_____. "South Korea in 1996: Internal Strains and External Challenges." *Asian Survey* 37, no. 1 (January 1997): 1-9.

_____. "North Korea's Approaches to the United States and Japan."

International Journal of Korean Studies 1, no. 1 (Spring 1997): 111-30.

———. "Japan and Korea." In *The Korean Peninsula and Major Powers*, edited by Bae-Ho Hahn and Chae-Jin Lee, 33-68. Seoul: Sejong Institute, 1998.

———. ed. *North Korea and the World: Explaining Pyongyang's Foreign Policy.* Seoul: Kyungnam University Press, 2004.

Komazawa Kazuo et al. "Gaiko rongi no shoten" [Focal Points of Foreign Policy Debate]. *Rippo to chosa* [Legislation and Investigation] (Tokyo), no. 224 (October 1984): 11.

Korean Industry in the World, 1994. Seoul: Korea Development Bank, 1994.

"Korega `Kanemaru hochodan' no budai urada" [This Is What Happened behind the Stage in Connection With the "Kanemaru Delegation Visiting North Korea"]. *Gekkan Asahi* [Asahi Monthly] (Tokyo) (December 1990): 74-81.

"Kuchu bansankai okotoba" [The Emperor's Statement at a Banquet in the Imperial Palace]. In Oemubu, *Taet'ongnyong pangil charyo* [Materials on the President's Visit to Japan]. Seoul: undated and unpaged.

Kukbangbu. *Kukbang paekso* [Defense White Paper]. Seoul: annual.

Lee, Chae-Jin. "U.S. and Japanese Policies toward Korea: Continuity and Change." In *Korean Options in a Changing International Order*, edited by Hong Yung Lee and Chung Chongwook, 33-51. Berkeley: Institute of East Asian Studies, University of California, 1993.

———. and Hideo Sato. *U.S. Policy toward Japan and Korea: A Changing Influence Relationship.* New York: Praeger, 1982.

Lee, Chong-Sik. *The Politics of Korean Nationalism.* Berkeley: University of Califorrna Press, 1965.

———. *Japan and Korea: The Political Dimension.* Stanford, CA: Hoover Institution Press, Stanford University, 1985.

Lee, Jung-Hoon. "Korean-Japanese Relations: The Past, the Present, and Future." *Papers of the British Association for Korean Studies* 3 (1992): 107-124.

Ministry of Internal Affairs and Communication, Statistics Bureau and Statistical Research and Training Institute. *Statistical Handbook of Japan, 2005.* Tokyo: 2005.

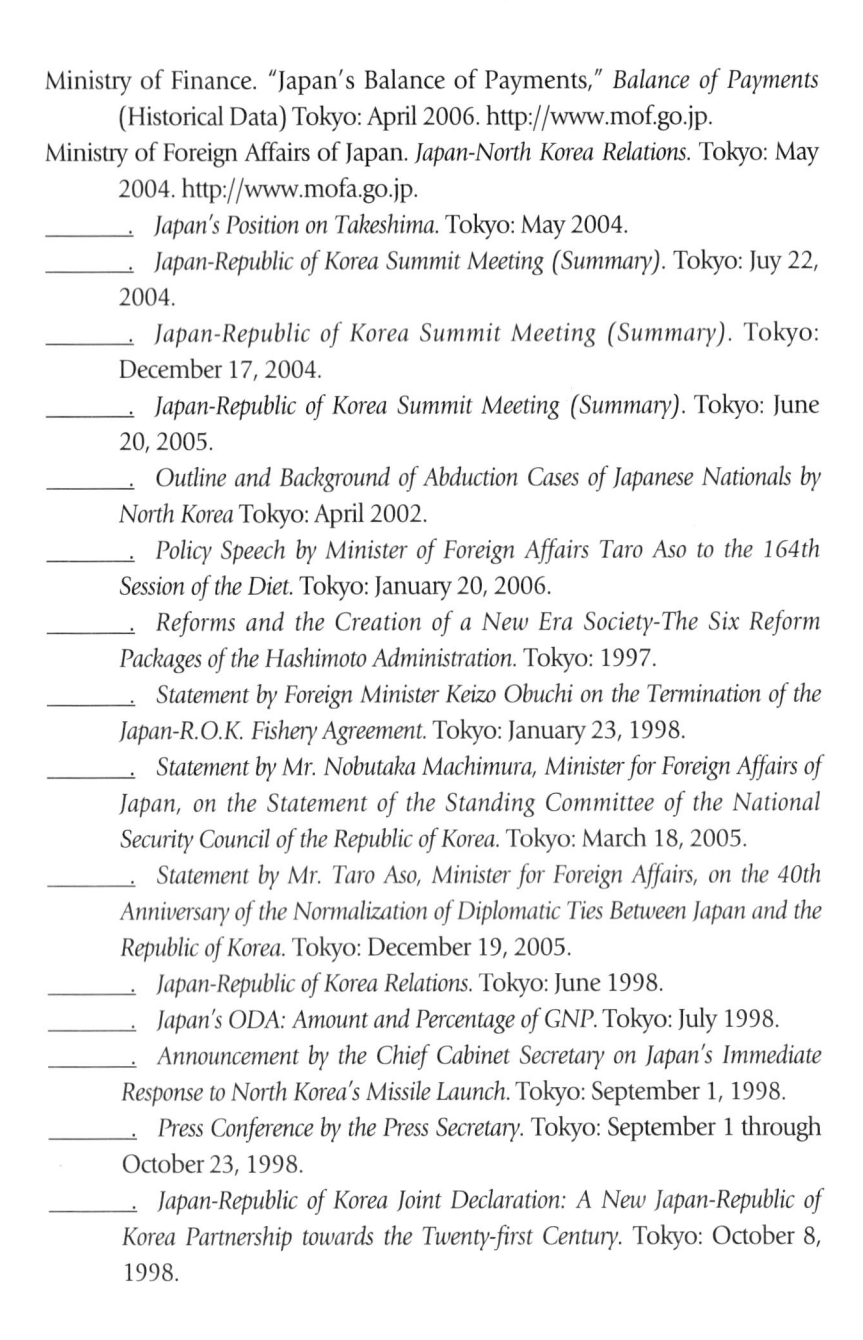

Ministry of Finance. "Japan's Balance of Payments," *Balance of Payments* (Historical Data) Tokyo: April 2006. http://www.mof.go.jp.

Ministry of Foreign Affairs of Japan. *Japan-North Korea Relations*. Tokyo: May 2004. http://www.mofa.go.jp.

_____. *Japan's Position on Takeshima*. Tokyo: May 2004.

_____. *Japan-Republic of Korea Summit Meeting (Summary)*. Tokyo: Juy 22, 2004.

_____. *Japan-Republic of Korea Summit Meeting (Summary)*. Tokyo: December 17, 2004.

_____. *Japan-Republic of Korea Summit Meeting (Summary)*. Tokyo: June 20, 2005.

_____. *Outline and Background of Abduction Cases of Japanese Nationals by North Korea* Tokyo: April 2002.

_____. *Policy Speech by Minister of Foreign Affairs Taro Aso to the 164th Session of the Diet*. Tokyo: January 20, 2006.

_____. *Reforms and the Creation of a New Era Society-The Six Reform Packages of the Hashimoto Administration*. Tokyo: 1997.

_____. *Statement by Foreign Minister Keizo Obuchi on the Termination of the Japan-R.O.K. Fishery Agreement*. Tokyo: January 23, 1998.

_____. *Statement by Mr. Nobutaka Machimura, Minister for Foreign Affairs of Japan, on the Statement of the Standing Committee of the National Security Council of the Republic of Korea*. Tokyo: March 18, 2005.

_____. *Statement by Mr. Taro Aso, Minister for Foreign Affairs, on the 40th Anniversary of the Normalization of Diplomatic Ties Between Japan and the Republic of Korea*. Tokyo: December 19, 2005.

_____. *Japan-Republic of Korea Relations*. Tokyo: June 1998.

_____. *Japan's ODA: Amount and Percentage of GNP*. Tokyo: July 1998.

_____. *Announcement by the Chief Cabinet Secretary on Japan's Immediate Response to North Korea's Missile Launch*. Tokyo: September 1, 1998.

_____. *Press Conference by the Press Secretary*. Tokyo: September 1 through October 23, 1998.

_____. *Japan-Republic of Korea Joint Declaration: A New Japan-Republic of Korea Partnership towards the Twenty-first Century*. Tokyo: October 8, 1998.

_____. *Asian Economic Crisis and Japan's Contribution.* Tokyo: December 1998.

_____. *The Year of Japan-ROK National Exchange in 2002.* Tokyo: October 2001.

Minjok T'ongil Yonguwon. *Ilbon ui tae Hanbando chongch'aek* [Japan's Policy toward the Korean Peninsula]. Seoul: December 1992.

_____. *Han'il kwangye pyonhwa chonmang kwa Hanguk ui tae'ung pangan* [Prospects for Change in ROK-Japan Relations and the ROK's Options]. Seoul: September 1995.

_____. *Han'il anbo hyomnyok pangan yongu* [A Study of Methods of Security Cooperation Between the ROK and Japan]. Seoul: December 1996.

Morita Yoshio. *Suji ga gadaru zainichi Kankoku, Chosenjin no rekishi* [History of ROK and DPRK Residents in Japan As Told by Statistics]. Tokyo: Meiseki Shoten, 1996.

Moon, Chung-in. "South Korea: Recasting Security Paradigms." In *Asian Security Practice,* edited by Muthiah Alagappa, 264-287. Standford, CA: Standford University press, 1988.

_____. "North Korean Foreign Policy in Comparative and Theoretical Perspective." In *North Korea and the World: Explaining Pyongyang's Foreign Policy,* edited by Byung Chul Koh, 327-368. Seoul: kyungnam University press. 2004.

Nabatame Tadao et al. "Gaiko rongi no shoten" [Focal Points in Discussion on Diplomacy]. *Rippo to chosa,* no. 117 (August 1983): 9-10.

Nagamori Yoshitake. "Okotoba de fukamatta Nikkan gyappu" [The Japan-ROK Gap That Has Deepened Due to the Emperor's Statement]. *Gendai koria,* no. 303 (July 1990): 50-55.

Nagano Nobutoshi, ed. *Nihon gaiko handobukku: juyo shiryo, kaisetsu, nenpyo* [A Handbook of Japanese Diplomacy: Selected Documents With Comments and Chronology of Events]. Tokyo: Saimaru Shuppankai, 1981.

Nihon Boeki Shinkokai. *Kita Chosen no keizai to boeki no tenbo* [Prospects for North Korea's Economy and Trade]. Tokyo: JETRO Kaigai Keizai Joho Senta, 1996.

_____. *97-nen no Kita Chosen taigai boeki* [North Korea's External Trade in 1997]. Tokyo: August 18, 1998.

Nikkan Kankei Kenkyukai, ed. *Nikkan kankei no kiso chishiki: deta to bunseki* [Basic Information on Japan-ROK Relations: Data and Analysis]. Tokyo: Tabata Shoten, 1975.

Nishimura Hideki. *Kita Chosen: yami karano seikan: Fujisan Maru supai jiken no shinso* [North Korea: Returning Alive from Darkness: The Truth about the Fujisan Maru Spy Incident]. Tokyo: Kobunsha, 1997.

"Nishimura Shinos gi'in no shitsumon ni taisuru seifu no tobensho" [Government's Response to the Questions Raised by Dietman Nishimura Shinso]. *Gendai koria*, no. 369 (March 1997): 51-53.

Nishioka Tsutomu. *Nikkan gokai no shin'en* [The Gulf of Misunderstanding Between Japan and the Republic of Korea]. Tokyo: Aki Shobo, 1992.

Oberdorfer, Don. *The Two Koreas: A Contemporary History.* Reading, MA: Addison-Wesley, 1997.

Oegyo T'ongsangbu. *Ilbon kaehwang* [The General Condition of Japan]. Seoul: March 1998.

_____. *Han'il kwangye chuyo ilji (2005. 3 wolbun)* [Chronology of Key Events in ROK-Japan Relations, March 2005]. Seoul: April 16, 2005. http://www.mofat.go.kr.

_____. *"Han'il kyongje-in hoeui" kija purip'ing charyo* [Press Briefing Material on "ROK-Japan Economic Personnel Meeting"]. Seoul: April 20, 1998.

_____. *Kim Dae Jung taet'ongnyong Ilbon kongsik pangmun kyolgwa, 1990.10. 7-10* [Results of President Kim Dae Jung's State Visit to Japan, 1990.10. 7-10]. Seoul: October 7-10, 1998.

_____. Kukje Popkyuka. *Han'il oop hyopjong charyo surok* [Collection of Materials on ROK-Japan Fisheries Agreement]. Seoul: October 1998.

Oemubu. *Hanguk oegyo samsimnyon 1948-1978* [Thirty Years of ROK Diplomacy 1948-1978]. Seoul, 1979.

_____. *Oegyo paekso* [Diplomatic White Paper]. Seoul: annual.

_____. *Ilbon kaehwang* [The General Condition of Japan]. Seoul: May 1990.

_____. *Roh Tae Woo taet'ongnyong Ilbon-guk konsik pangmun yonsolmun-jip*

[Collection of Speeches by President Roh Tae Woo During His State Visit to Japan]. Seoul: June 1990.

———. *Kaifu Ilbon susang panghan uiui mit songkwa* [The Significance and Results of Japanese Prime Minister Kaifu's Visit to the ROK]. Seoul: January 10, 1991.

———. *Han'ilgan chuyo hyon'an mit ch'amgo charyo* [Main Issues Between the ROK and Japan and Reference Material]. Seoul: August 1991.

———. *Ilbon kaehwang* [The General Condition of Japan]. Seoul: March 1994.

———. *Ilbon kaehwang.* Seoul: February 1996.

———. *Taehan Minguk oegyo yonp'yo, 1994* [Chronology of ROK Diplomacy, 1994]. Seoul: October 1995.

———. *Tokdo kwallyon ch'amgo charyo* [Reference Material Relating to Tokdo]. Seoul: April 1996.

———. *Han'il kwangye hyonhwang* [The Present Condition of ROK-Japan Relations]. Seoul: June 1996.

———. *Han'il kwangye hyon'an mit Ilbon chongse* [Issues in ROK-Japan Relations and the Situation in Japan]. Seoul: August 1997.

———. "Han'il oemu changgwan hoedam kyolgwa" [The Results of a Meeting between the Foreign Ministers of the ROK and Japan]. *Oegyo charyosil* [Diplomatic Archives] Seoul: August 1997.

Oemubu, Ajuguk. "Taet'ongnyong pangil, pangjung kyolgwa, 1994. 4. 4." [The Results of the President's Visits to Japan and China, April 4, 1994]. *Oegyodan purip'ing charyo* [Briefing Material for the Diplomatic Corps].

Oemubu, Ajuguk, Tongbuga 1-kwa. *Han'il kwangye* [ROK-Japan Relations]. Seoul: July 16, 1997.

———. *Han'il oemujanggwan hoedam kyolgwa* [Results of ROK-Japan Foreign Ministers' Meeting]. Seoul: July 29, 1997.

———. *Ilbon ui Tokdo joban sisol chungongsik hangui e taehan oemubu taebyonin nonp'yong* [Foreign Ministry Spokesman's Comment on Japan's Protest against the Start of Wharf Construction on Tokdo]. Seoul: November 7, 1997.

———. *Oemubu taebyonin songmyong (Ilbon ui Han'il oop hyopjong chongnyo*

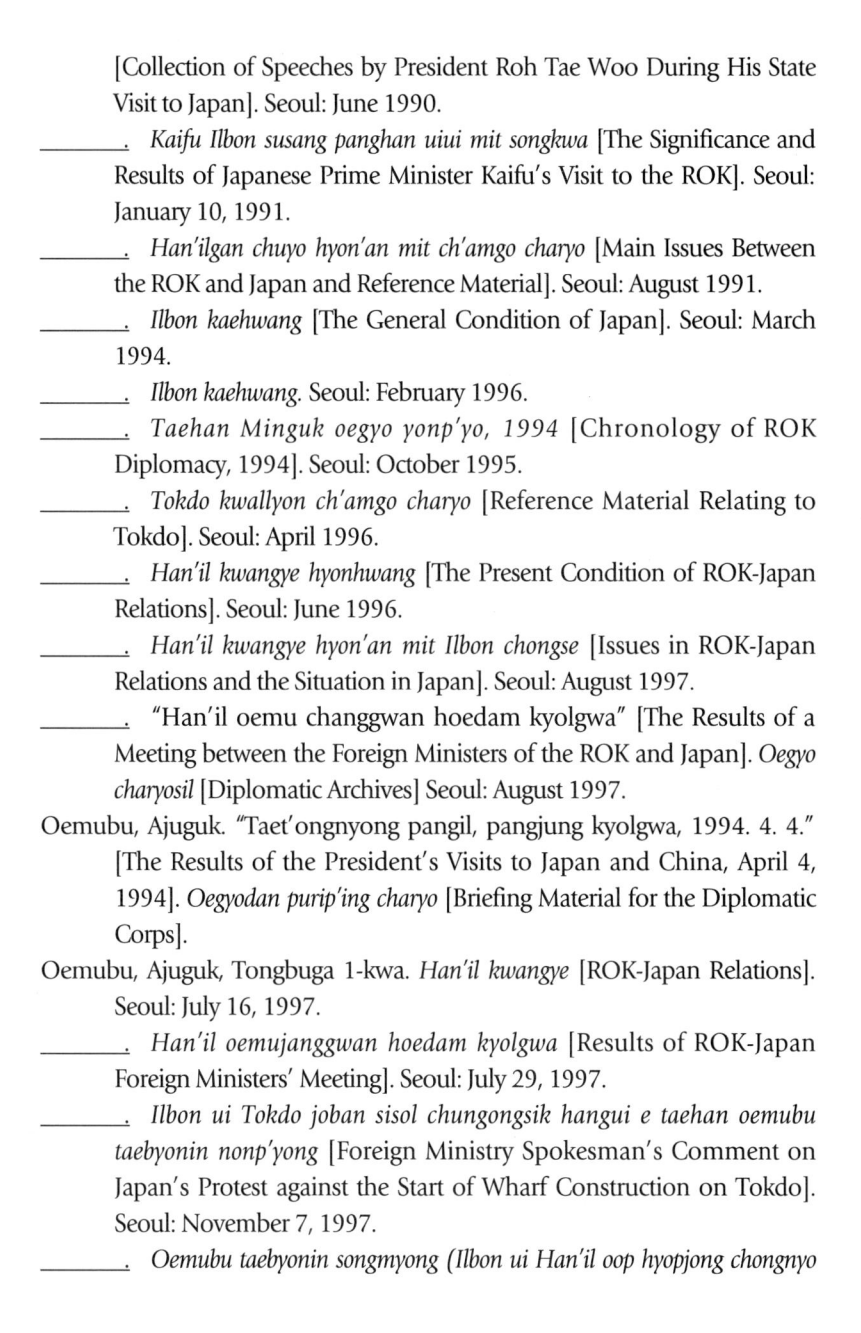

t'ongbo kwallyon [Statement by the Spokesman for the Ministry of Foreign Affairs (Concerning Japan's Notification on the Termination of the ROK-Japan Fisheries Agreement)]. Seoul: January 23, 1998.

Oemubu, Aju T'ongsang-tim. *"Han'il kyongje-in hoeui" kija purip'ing charyo* [Press Briefing Material on "ROK-Japan Economic Leaders' Meeting"]. Seoul: April 20, 1998.

Oemubu, Choyak-guk, Kukje Popkyu-kwa. *Che 3-ch'a Han'il EEZ kyongye hoekjong hoedam kyolgwa* [Results of the Second ROK-Japan Meeting on the Delineation of EEZ Boundaries]. Seoul: November 4, 1997.

Ogawa Shinichi. "The Nuclear Security of Japan and South Korea: A Japanese View." *Korean Journal of Defense Analysis* 9, no. 1 (Summer 1987): 29-50.

Okonogi Masao. "Japan's Policy toward North Korea: Diplomatic Normalization Talks and the Nuclear Issue." In *Foreign Relations of North Korea during Kim Il Sung's Last Days,* edited by Kim Doug Joong, 193-222. Seoul: Sejong Institute, 1994.

_____. "The Political Dynamics of Japan-North Korea Relations." *Korea & World Affairs* 13, no. 2 (Summer 1989): 331-46.

_____. *Nihon to Kita Chosen: korekarano 5-nen* [Japan and North Korea: The Next Five Years]. Tokyo: PHP Kenkyujo, 1991.

_____. ed. *Posuto reisen no Chosen hanto* [The Korean Peninsula after the Cold War]. Tokyo: Nihon Kokusai Mondai Kenkyujo, 1994.

_____. and Suh Dae-Sook, eds. *Shiryo Kita Chosen, I seiji, shiso* [Materials on North Korean Studies, vol. 1: Politics and Ideology]. Tokyo: Keiso Gizuku Daigaku Shuppankai, 1998.

Park, Kyung-Ae. "Explaining North Korea's Negotiated Cooperation with the U.S." *Asian Survey* 37, no. 7 (July 1997): 623-36.

Quester, George H. "America, Korea and Japan: The Crucial Triangle." *Journal of East Asian Affairs* 9, no. 2 (Summer/Fall 1995): 228-51.

Radiopress Inc. *Kuronoroji de miru Kita Chosen* [North Korea Seen through Chronology]. Tokyo: Radiopress, 2004.

"Roh daitoryo honichi wa do uketomeraretaka: Kankokuji futatsuno shasetsu kara" [How Was President Roh's Japan Visit Received? From the Editorials of Two ROK Newspapers]. *Sekai* (July 1990): 118-21.

Roh, Tae Woo and Shiba Ryutaro. "Tokubetsu taidan: warewarewa konnani kotonari konnani chikai zuita" [Special Conversation: We Are Different in These Ways, We Are Getting Closer in These Ways]. *Bungei shunju* (Tokyo) (August 1989): 92-117.

Ryang, Sonia. *North Koreans in Japan: Language, Ideology, and Identity*. Boulder, CO: Westview Press, 1997.

Sakurai Yoshiko. "`Shazai' gaiko ni `ri' nashi" [No "Benefit" in the Diplomacy of "Apology"]. *Voice* (Tokyo) (August 1990): 114-24.

SAPIO, ed. *Nihonjin to Kankokujin: hannichi kenkan 50-nen no hate* [The Japanese and the Koreans: The Consequences of 50 Years of Opposing Japan and Hating Korea]. Tokyo: Shogakkan, 1995.

Scalapino, Robert A, ed. *The Foreign Policy of Modern Japan*. Berkeley: University of California Press, 1977.

———. "North Korean Relations with Japan and the United States." In *North Korea Today: Strategic and Domestic Issues*, edited by Robert A. Scalapinio and Jun-Yop Kim, 331-350. Berkeley: Institute of East Asian Studies, University of California, 1983.

———. and Chong-Sik Lee, *Communism in Korea*, Parts I and II. Berkeley: University of California Press, 1972.

Sekai, rinji zokan: Nitcho kankei: sono rekishi to genzai [The World, temporary, expanded issue: Japan-DPRK Relations: Their History and Current Situation]. Tokyo: Iwanami Shoten, April 1992.

Sengo 50-nen Nikkan Koryu Jigyo Iinkai, ed. *Kokoro wa nami o koete* [With Heart Crossing Over Waves]. Tokyo: Koma Shorin, 1996.

Shigemura Toshimitsu. *Kita Chosen deta bukku* [North Korea Data Book]. Tokyo: Kodansha, 1997.

———. *Pukhan un munojiji annunda* [North Korea Will Not Collapse]. Translated by Sin Chi-ho. Seoul: Chisik Kongjak-so, 1997.

Shin, Jung Hyun. "North Korea's Relations with Japan: The Possibilities for Bilateral Reconciliation." In *North Korea in a Regional and Global Context*, edited by Robert A. Scalapino and Hong Koo Lee, 240-264. Berkeley: Institute of East Asian Studies, 1986.

Sigal, Leon V. *Disarming Strangers: Nuclear Diplomacy with North Korea*. Princeton: Princeton University Press, 1998.

Somusho, *Tokei-kyoku*, ed. *Nihon no tokei, 2005* [Japan's Statistics, 2005]. Tokyo: Kokuritsu Insatsu-kyoku, 2005.

Sorifu, Kohoshitsu, ed. *Gekkan seron chosa* [Public Opinion Survey Monthly]. Issues containing the results of surveys relating to "diplomacy"—e.g., attitudes toward various countries and issues—include: April 1987, April 1988, August 1988, May 1989, April 1990, March 1991, April 1992, April 1993, April 1994, May 1996, and May 1997.

Suh, Dae-Sook. *Korean Communism, 1945-1980: A Reference Guide to the Political System*. Honolulu: University Press of Hawaii, 1981.

———. *Kim Il Sung: The North Korean Leader*. New York: Columbia University Press, 1988.

Sunobe Ryozo. "Nikkan kankei no arubeki sugata o motomete" [In Search of Japan-ROK Relations That Ought to Exist]. *Gaiko foramu*, no. 21 (June 1990): 21-25.

———. "Masatsu to kyoson" [Friction and Coexistence]. *Gendai koria*, no. 304 (August/September 1990): 22-29.

———. and Okonogi Masao. "Taidan: saikin no Nikkan kankei o kangeru" [Conversation: Thinking Recent Japan-ROK Relations]. *Kokusai mondai* [International Issues] (Tokyo), no. 281 (August 1983): 2-15.

Suzuki Masayuki. "Nitcho kankei: Chosen Minshushugi Jinmin Kyowakoku no tainichi seisaku o chushin ni" [Japan-North Korean Relations: With Focus on the DPRK's Policy toward Japan]. 1990. Unpublished paper.

———. *Kita Chosen: shakai shugi to dento no kyomei* [North Korea: Resonance of Socialism and Tradition]. Tokyo: Tokyo Daigaku Shuppankai, 1992.

Suzuki Masayuki, Hiraiwa Shunji, and Kurota Hideya, eds. *Chosen hanto no kokusai seiji* [The International Politics of the Korean Peninsula]. Tokyo: Keio Gijuku Daigaku Shuppankai, 2005.

Suzuki Yuko. *Jugun ianfu, naisen kekkon: sei no shinryaku, sengo sekinin o kangaeru* [Comfort Women, Marriages Between Japanese and Koreans During the Colonial Period: Thinking About Sexual Aggression and Postwar Responsibility]. Tokyo: K.K. Miraisha, 1992.

Takesada Hideshi. *Boeicho kyokan no Kita Chosen shinso bunseki* [Defense Agency Instructor's Indepth Analysis of North Korea]. Tokyo: K.K. Besuto Serazu, 1998.

Tanabe Makoto. "Nitcho kankei no atarashii juritsu" [Newly Establishing Japan-DPRK Relations]. *Gekkan shakaito* (December 1990): 125-36.

Tanino Sakutaro. *Ajia no shoryu: ichi gaikokan no mita yakushin Kankoku* [Asia's Rising Dragon: One Diplomat's View of the Galloping Republic of Korea]. Tokyo: Sekai no Ugoki-sha, 1988.

———. *Nihon no Chosen hanto seisaku* [Japan's Policy toward the Korean Peninsula]. A lecture given at the 8th international symposium on the problems of Korean unification, sponsored by Kan Taiheiyo Kenkyujo, May 17, 1992.

"The 110th Special Issue on Tokdo." Special Issue, *Korea Observer* (Seoul) 28, no.3 (Autumn 1997).

"Tokushu: Atarashii jigen o mukaeta Nikkan kankei" [Special Issue: Japan-ROK Relations That Has Entered a New Phase]. *Gaiko foramu*, no. 21 (June 1990): 21-88.

"Tokushu: Chosen hanto to Nihon" [Special Issue: The Korean Peninsula and Japan]. *Gunshuku mondai shiryo* [Materials on Arms Control Issues] (Tokyo), no. 129 (August 1991).

"Tokushu: Nikkan kankei no genjusho" [Special Issue: The Current Status of Japan-ROK Relations]. *Gendai koria*, no. 357 (December 1995), no. 360 (April 1996), no. 363 (July/August 1996), and no. 368 (January/February 1997).

"Tokushu: towaru Nihon no gaiko shisei" [Special Issue: Japan's Diplomatic Posture under Question]. *Gendai koria*, no. 367 (December 1996).

"Tokushu: zainichi Kankoku Chosenjin no hoteki jokyo" [Special Issue: The Legal Status of ROK and DPRK Nationals in Japan]. *Horitsu jiho* (Law Review) (Tokyo) 62, no. 7 (June 1990).

T'ongilbu. *Wolgan kyoryu hyomnyok tonghyang* [Monthly Trends in Exchanges and Cooperation]. Seoul: monthly.

———. *98 nyondo taebuk chongch'aek p'yongka* [Assessment of Policy Toward the North During 1998]. Seoul: January 4, 1999.

T'onggyech'ong. *Hanguk kyongje chuyo chip'yo, 1997. 3* [Major Statistics of the

Korean Economy, March 1997]. Seoul, 1997.

_____. *Hanguk kyongje chuyo chip'yo, 1998. 9* [Major Statistics of the Korean Economy, September 1998]. Seoul, 1998.

T'ongil-won. *Nambuk taehwa* [South-North Dialogue] (Seoul), no. 54 (1992).

"Tsuiseki Nihonjin rachi giwaku" [Pursuit: Suspected Kidnaping of Japanese Nationals]. *AERA*, no. 27 (July 5, 1997): 19-23.

Tsujimura Akira et al. *Nihon to Kankoku no bunka masatsu: Nikkan komyunikeshon gyappu no kenkyu* [Cultural Friction Between Japan and the ROK: A Study of the Japan-ROK Communication Gap]. Tokyo: Shukko Shoten, 1982.

Tsusho Sangyosho, ed. *Tsusho hakusho, Heisei 10-nenban* [White Paper on Trade and Commerce, 1998]. Tokyo: Okurasho Insatsu-kyoku, 1998.

Unger, Danny and Paul Blackburn, eds. *Japan's Emerging Global Role.* Boulder, CO: Lynne Rienner Publications, Inc., 1993.

U.S. Department of State. *The Record on Korean Unification, 1943-1960: Narrative Summary with Principal Documents.* Washington, DC: Government Printing Office, 1961.

_____. *Daily Press Briefing.* Monday, July 14, 1997.

Usuki Hideo. *"Han'nichi" to "shinnichi" no hazama: Kankoku, Taiwan kara mita Nihon* [The interstice between "Anti-Japan" and "Pro-Japan": Japan As Viewed From the ROK and Taiwan]. Tokyo: Toyo Keizai Shinposha, 1997.

Wada Haruki. "Taikan ninshiki ni miru genjitsu tsuijushugi" [The Propensity to Bow to Reality as Reflected in Perceptions of the ROK]. *Sekai*, no. 437 (April 1982): 204-214.

_____. *Kita Chosen: yugekitai kokka no genzai* [North Korea: The Current Condition of a Guerrilla Unit State]. Tokyo: Iwanami Shoten, 1998.

Wakatsuki Yasuo. *Kankoku, Chosen to Nihonjin* [The ROK, the DPRK, and the Japanese]. Tokyo: Hara Shobo, 1989.

Watanabe Akio. *Sengo Nihon no taigai seisaku* [Postwar Japan's Foreign Policy]. Tokyo: Yuhikaku, 1985.

Watanabe Shoichi and Oh Sunhwa. *Nihon no ogori, Kankoku no takaburi: shin Nikkan kankei no hoto* [Japan's Arrogance, Korea's Haughtiness: Approach to New Japan-ROK Relations]. Tokyo: Tokuma Shoten,

1993.

Wolgan pukhan tonghyang [Monthly Summary of Developments in North Korea]. Seoul: Tongil-won, Chongbo Punsok-sil, monthly.

Yamamoto Taketoshi, ed. *Nikkan shinjidai-Kankokujin no Nihonkan* [The New Era between Japan and the ROK: ROK Citizens' View of Japan]. Tokyo: Dobunkan Shuppan, K.K., 1994.

Yamamoto Tsuyoshi. "Nihon to Kankoku" [Japan and the ROK]. In Yamamoto Susumu et al, *Sengo Nihon gaikoshi, VI: Namboku mondai to Nihon* [History of Japan's Postwar Diplomacy, vol. 6: The North-South Problem and Japan], 158-93. Tokyo: Sanseito, 1984.

——. "Nitcho kankei to Nihon no sentaku" [Japan-DPRK Relations and Japan's Choice]. In Yamamoto Susumu et al. *Sengo Nihon gaikoshi, VII: Nihon gaiko no kadai* [History of Japan's Postwar Diplomacy, vol. 7: The Tasks of Japan's Diplomacy], 180-94. Tokyo: Sanseito, 1985.

——. "Nitcho fuchosei kankeishi" [The History of Abnormal Relations between Japan and North Korea]. *Sekai*, temporary, expanded issue (April 1992): 150-97.

——. Nitcho kokko seijoka kosho no shoten" [Focal Points in Japan-DPRK Negotiations on Diplomatic Normalization]. *Sekai*, temporary, expanded issue (April 1992): 78-86.

Yi Chang-hui, ed. *Han'il kibon choyak ui chaegomt'o wa tongbuga chilso* [A Reexamination of the ROK-Japan Basic Treaty and Northeast Asian Order]. Seoul: Asia Sahoe Kwahak Yongu-won: June 1996.

——. ed. *Han'il-gan ui kukjebopjok hyonan munje* [International Law Issues Between the Republic of Korea and Japan]. Seoul: Asayon, 1998.

Youn Jung Suk. *Ilbon ui taeoe chongch'aek kwa Hanguk* [Japan's Foreign Policy and the ROK]. Seoul: Hyongsong-sa, 1982.

Yun Tok-min. "Ilbon ui tae-pukhan chongch'i kyongje kwangye" [Japan's Political and Economic Relations with North Korea]. In *Hanbando chubyon 4-guk ui tae-pukhan chongch'aek* [The North Korea Policies of the Four Countries Surrounding the Korean Peninsula], edited by Yu Chang-hui, 92-94. Seoul: Tae'oe Kyongju Chongch'aek Yongu-won, 1996.

Zainichi Kankokujin no kyojuken [The Residency Right of ROK Nationals in Japan]. Tokyo: Zainichi Taikanminkoku Seinenkai, 1989.

Zainichi Kankoku Minshu Joseikai. *Chosenjin jugun ianfu* [Korean Comfort Women], 2—vol. Tokyo, 1991 and 1992.

NEWSPAPERS

Asahi shinbun (Tokyo). Internet edition: http://www.asahi.com.
Chosen shinpo (Tokyo). Internet edition: http://www.korea-np.co.jp.
Chosun ilbo (Seoul). Internet edition: http://www.chosun.co.kr.
Daily Yomiuri (Tokyo). Internet edition: http://www.yomiuri.co.jp.
Dong-A Ilbo (Seoul). Internet edition: http://www.donga.com.
Hankook ilbo (Seoul). Internet edition: http://times.hankooki.com.
Hangyore sinmun (Seoul). Internet edition: http://www.hani.co.kr.
Japan Times. Internet edition: http://www.japantimes.co.jp.
JoongAng ilbo (Seoul). Internet edition: http://www.joins.com.
Korea Herald (Seoul). Internet edition: http://www.koreaherald.co.kr.
Kyodo news agency (Tokyo). Internet edition: http://www.kyodo.co.jp.
Mainichi shinbun (Tokyo). Internet edition: http://www.mainichi.co.jp.
New York Times. Internet edition: http://www.nytimes.com.
Nihon keizai shinbun (Tokyo). Internet edition: http://www.nikkei.co.jp.
Rodong sinmun (Pyongyang). Internet edition: http://www.kcna.co.jp.
People's Korea (Tokyo). Internet edition: http://www.korea-np.co.jp.
Pyongyang Times.
T'ongil sinbo (Pyongyang).
Washington Post. Internet edition: http://www.washingtonpost.com.
Yomiuri shinbun (Tokyo). Internet edition: http://www.yomiuri.co.jp.

.Index

A

Abe Shintaro 243, 482, 488, 489
Absolute gains 183
Agency for National Security Plnning (ANSP) 142, 368
Agreed Framework between the DPRK and the US 206
Alagappa, Muthiah 30
Anarchy 16
Annan, Kofi 221
Asia-Europe Meeing (ASEM) 18, 349
Asian Development Bank (ADB) 178, 393
Asia-Pacific Economic Cooperation (APEC) 213, 216, 322, 335, 353, 447
Association of Southeast Asian Nations (ASEAN) 440
ASEAN Regional Forum (ARF) 175, 203, 405-408, 410, 414, 418, 422-426, 430, 431, 438, 440, 443, 448, 504

B

Ban Ki Moon 462, 485
Banco Delta Asia 251
Bridges, Brian 27, 28
Bush, George W. (administration) 191, 199, 209, 211, 259

C

Carter, Jimmy 51
Cha, Victor 28
Chang Myon 269, 271, 275
Chon In-ch'ol 78, 79, 85, 88, 89, 101
Ch'on yong-bok 66, 104
Ch'ongnyon 220, 284, 297
Chosoren (Chosen Soren) 196, 284-286
Chuch'e (sasang) 188, 207, 258
Chun Doo Hwan 52, 287-290, 292, 297, 298, 430
Clinton, Bill 118, 181, 356
Comfort women 98, 316, 318, 320, 328, 330, 356, 500
Complete, verifiable and irreversible dismantlement (CVID) 231
Constructivism 16, 19, 295

D

DPRK-Japan Pyongyang Declaration 223
DPRK-US high-level talks 115, 116

E

East Sea 344, 472
Emperor Akihito 310, 323
Emperor Showa 310
Exclusive Economic Zone (EEZ) 364-366, 378, 380, 484, 490
Export-Import Bank 290, 399

F

Federation of International Foodball Association (FIFA) 350
FIFA World Cup Korea/Japan 2002 441, 444, 497, 508
Ford-Miki joint statement 50
Four-party agreement 130, 131, 133, 187
Free trade agreement (FTA) 408, 442
Fujisan Maru 67, 73, 74, 110
Fukuda Takeo 51

G

Gallucci, Robert L. 118
Game theory 14
Gong Ro-myung 335, 471
Green, Michael J. 31
Grieco, Joseph M. 19

H

Habeeb, Mark 111
Han Sungjoo 358
Hashimoto Ryutaro 135, 149, 330, 348, 349, 355, 367, 376, 394, 433
Hata Tsutomu 327
Heavy fuel oil (HFO) 123, 128, 184, 217
Highly-enriched uranium (HEU) 192, 211
Hiramatsu Kenji 195, 202, 216
Hong Soon Young 155, 377, 381, 386
Hosokawa Morihiro 321, 339

I

Ikeda Yukihiko 347, 360, 367, 369
Imperial Household Agency 291, 309
International Atomic Energy Agency (IAEA) 82, 87, 92, 94, 104, 117, 121, 186, 217, 314, 324
Ishii Hajime 64

J

Japan's Maritime Safety Agency 370, 371
Japan Coast Guard 197
Japanese emperor's *okotoba* 293, 299, 310, 311
Japanese Imperial Army 296, 357
Japanese Society for History Textbook Reform (*Tsukurukai*) 411, 414, 477

Jenkins, Charles 223, 234
Jo Myong Rok 181

K

Kaifu Toshiki 70, 81, 92, 306, 313
Kajiyama Seiroku 361, 432
Kanemaru Shin 63-68
Kang In Duk 386
Kang Sok Ju 118, 120, 210, 224
Kanter, Arnold 97
Kawaguchi Yoriko 203, 448, 457
Kelly, James 210, 222, 259
Keohane, Robert O. 13
Kim Dae Jung 29, 175, 281, 282, 286-288, 293, 296-299, 344, 372-377, 382, 383, 386, 394, 398-402
Kim Hyon-hui 88, 90
Kim Il Sung 44, 46, 48, 60, 67, 105, 171, 327, 501, 502
Kim Jong Il 120, 175, 181, 182, 191, 194, 205, 206, 208, 405, 406, 410, 500, 503
Kim Jong Pil 281, 386
Kim Kye Gwan 226
Kim, Samuel S. 29
Kim Tae Zhee 332, 373
Kim Tong-jo 268, 286
Kim Yong Nam 230
Kim, Young C. 32, 208
Kim Young Sam 124, 133, 140, 188, 293, 321, 324, 325, 328, 334, 337, 339, 348, 349, 352, 354-356, 362, 363, 368, 373, 426
Kimura Toshio 52, 285
Kishi Nobusuke 270, 271
Koizumi Junichiro 205, 208, 213, 215, 414, 417, 423-425, 500
Kono Yohei 52, 175, 334, 335, 358
Korean Peninsula Energy Development Organization (KEDO) 122, 123, 155, 158, 186, 217, 350
Korean wave (*kanryu*) 459
Kubo Wataru 129, 131

L

Lee, Chong-Sik 26, 267, 271, 272
Lee Ki-Joo 360
Level II game 298
Li Gun 222
Light-water reactor (LWR) 119-121, 123

M

Machimura Nobutaka 243, 462, 468
Ministry of Education, Culture, Sports, Science and Technology (MEXT) 411
Ministry of International Trade and Industry (MITI) 40, 60
Minobe Ryokichi 220
Miyazawa Kiichi 50, 98, 316
Moon, Chung-in 31
Mori Yoshiro 148, 405, 406, 409, 410, 449
Mun Se-gwang 283-285, 297, 299
Murayama Tomiichi 132, 168, 327, 398, 340, 477

N

Nakahira Noboru 80, 82, 86, 103
Nakasone Yasuhiro 290, 292, 449
Nam Il 38
Nanjing incident 329, 413
Neoliberalism 18, 258
Neorealism 16, 258
Nuclear Nonproliferation Treaty (NPT) 82, 117, 118, 186, 217

O

Obuchi Keizo 156, 175, 371, 375-377, 383, 398, 399, 406, 426
Ohira Masayoshi 287
Official development assistance (ODA) 275, 290
Okonogi Masayoshi 287

P

Paek Nam Sun 203
Park Chung Hee 271, 273, 283, 287, 290, 296, 298, 430
Permanent residency 306-308
Perry, William 167
Pohang Iron and Steel Company (POSCO) 279
Powell, Colin 449
Putnam, Robert D. 13, 107

Q

Qian Qichen 449

Quasi-alliance 25, 85

R

Ra Jong Yil 485
Reagan, Ronald 395
Red Cross 168, 170, 171, 268
Regime theory 18
Relative gains 18
Rhee Syngman 270, 295, 302, 346
Roh Moo Hyun 448, 451, 458, 460, 471, 490, 496, 505
Roh Tae Woo 38, 60, 305, 319
ROK-USSR normalization 74
Rusk, Dean 273

S

San Francisco Treaty 274, 331
Sasae Kenichiro 243, 244
Sato Eisaku 43, 285, 290, 354
Sea of Japan 344, 472
Seikei bunri 37, 49, 52, 62, 72
Shiina Etsusaburo 285
Sigal, Leon V. 128
Sin Gwang Su 248, 256, 261
Six-party talks 508
Snyder, Scott 105
Soeya Yoshihide 30
Soga Hitomi 231, 234
Song Il Ho 227, 247, 249
State identity 20, 105
Structural realism 16

T

Taehwat'ae 371, 379
Takeshima 280, 344-347, 363, 365, 366, 380, 383, 427, 466, 467, 488
Takeshita Noboru 62, 81
Tanabe Makoto 63, 65
Tanaka Hitoshi 204, 216, 224, 227
Tanaka Kakuei 270, 284
Tanino Sakutaro 71
Three-party declaration 68, 130, 131
Tit for tat 197, 257
Tokdo 280, 347, 363, 365, 366, 380, 383, 427
Two-level game 15, 107, 177, 183, 340

U

UN Commission on Human Rights 240, 359
UN General Assembly Resolution 195 (III) 275
UN Security Council 140, 324, 353
UN Convention on the Law of the Sea 347, 375
Utsunomiya Tokuma 50

V

Vietnam War 272

W

Waltz, Kenneth N. 16
Watanabe Michio 129, 331
Watanabe Tsuneo 486
Weizsacker, Richard von 449
Wendt, Alexander 19
World Trade Organization (WTO) 353, 441, 492

Y

Yabunaka Mitoji 222, 224, 227
Yachi Shotaro 472, 493
Yamahana Sadao 328
Yamasaki Taku 228, 348
Yamashita Shintaro 330, 360
Yamatotai 371, 379
Yasukuni Shrine 416, 418, 424, 425, 434, 456, 466, 482, 496
Yi Sam-no 101, 103
Yi Un-hye 88, 90, 91, 96, 101, 102, 104, 131, 137
Yodo-go 87, 248
Yokota Megumi 136, 210, 237
Yongbyon 107, 119, 121, 127, 324
Yoo Chong Ha 354, 360, 367, 369, 372
Yoshida Shigeru 304
Yu Myung Hwan 493

Z

Zantei suiiki 380
Zero-sum games 258

About the Author

Byung Chul (B.C.) Koh is Professor Emeritus of Political Science at the University of Illinois, Chicago, where he taught comparative politics, international law, and international organization from 1965 to 2002. From 2002 to 2004 he served as director of the Institute for Far Eastern Studies, Kyungnam University, Seoul.

He has also taught at Louisiana State University, Baton Rouge; Temple University Japan, Tokyo; Seoul National University (as a Fulbright grantee); and Yonsei University, Seoul. He was a visiting researcher at the University of Tsukuba, Japan, in 1993 on a fellowship from the Japan-Korea Cultural Foundation.

A native of Seoul, Koh was educated at Seoul National University (LL.B) and Cornell University (M.P.A. and Ph.D). He is author of four books, including *Japan's Administrative Elite* (University of California Press, 1989; paper edition, 1991) and *The Foreign Policy Systems of North and South Korea* (University of California Press, 1984). His edited volumes include *Journey to North Korea: Personal Perceptions* (co-edited with C. I. Eugene Kim; Institute of East Asian Studies, University of California, Berkeley, 1983) and *North Korea and the World: Explaining Pyongyang's Foreign Policy* (editor and contributor; Kyungnam University Press, Seoul, 2004).